The Brief
McGraw-Hill Reader

The Brief McGraw-Hill Reader

Issues across the Disciplines

Gilbert H. Muller

The City University of New York
LaGuardia College

The McGraw·Hill Companies

Connect
Learn
Succeed™

Published by McGraw-Hill, an imprint of The McGraw-Hill Companies, Inc., 1221 Avenue of the Americas, New York, NY 10020. Copyright © 2012. All rights reserved. No part of this publication may be reproduced or distributed in any form or by any means, or stored in a database or retrieval system, without the prior written consent of The McGraw-Hill Companies, Inc., including, but not limited to, in any network or other electronic storage or transmission, or broadcast for distance learning.

This book is printed on acid-free paper.

1 2 3 4 5 6 7 8 9 0 QTN/QTN 9 8 7 6 5 4 3 2 1

ISBN: 978-0-07-340599-5
MHID: 0-07-340599-X

Vice President Editorial: *Michael Ryan*
Publisher: *David Patterson*
Sponsoring Editor: *John Kindler*
Marketing Manager: *Allison Jones*
Developmental Editor: *Anne Stameshkin*
Production Editor: *Holly Paulsen*
Manuscript Editor: *Patricia Ohlenroth*
Design Manager: *Allister Fein*

Text Designer: *Linda Robertson*
Cover Designer: *Allister Fein*
Photo Research Coordinator: *Natalia Peschiera*
Photo Researcher: *Emily Tietz, Editorial Image, LLC*
Buyer II: *Louis Swaim*
Composition: *10/12 Palatino by Aptara®, Inc.*
Printing: *#45 New Era Matte Thin, Quad/Graphics*

Cover: (top) © B. O'Kane/Alamy; (bottom) Stele of Unas (c. 2375–2345 BC) Old Kingdom (stone), Egyptian, 5th Dynasty (c. 2494–2345 BC)/Saqqara, Egypt/Giraudon/The Bridgeman Art Library/Getty Images

Credits: The credits section for this book begins on page 487 and is considered an extension of the copyright page.

Library of Congress Cataloging-in-Publication Data

The brief McGraw-Hill reader : issues across·the disciplines / [edited by] Gilbert H. Muller.
    p. cm.
  Includes index.
  ISBN-13: 978-0-07-340599-5 (pbk. : alk. paper)
  ISBN-10: 0-07-340599-X (pbk. : alk. paper)   1. College readers.   2. Interdisciplinary approach in education—Problems, exercises, etc.   3. English language—Rhetoric—Problems, exercises, etc.
4. Academic writing—Problems, exercises, etc. I. Muller, Gilbert H.
  PE1417.B7128 2011
  808'.0427—dc22

2010049098

The Internet addresses listed in the text were accurate at the time of publication. The inclusion of a Web site does not indicate an endorsement by the authors or McGraw-Hill, and McGraw-Hill does not guarantee the accuracy of the information presented at these sites.

www.mhhe.com

About the Author

GILBERT H. MULLER is professor emeritus of English at the LaGuardia campus of the City University of New York. He has also taught at Stanford University, where he received a PhD in English and American Literature; Vassar College; and several universities overseas. Dr. Muller is the author of the award-winning *Nightmares and Visions: Flannery O'Connor and the Catholic Grotesque; Chester Himes; New Strangers in Paradise: The Immigrant Experience and Contemporary American Fiction; William Cullen Bryant: Author of America*; and other critical studies. His essays and reviews have appeared in *The New York Times, The New Republic, The Nation, The Sewanee Review, The Georgia Review,* and elsewhere. He has written and edited best-selling textbooks in English and composition, including McGraw-Hill's *The Short Prose Reader*, with Harvey Wiener, now in its twelfth edition, and *The McGraw-Hill Reader,* now in its eleventh edition. Among Dr. Muller's awards are fellowships from the National Endowment for the Humanities, the Fulbright Commission, the Ford Foundation, and the Mellon Foundation.

To Parisa and Darius
My favorite readers

Brief Contents

PART 1
AN OVERVIEW OF COLLEGE WRITING

PART 2
ISSUES ACROSS THE DISCIPLINES

Contents

PART 2
ISSUES ACROSS THE DISCIPLINES

Networking Assignments

Preface

ISSUES ACROSS DISCIPLINES, LITERACIES ACROSS MEDIA

The Brief McGraw-Hill Reader is a textbook for twenty-first century composition class-rooms. Like the bestselling comprehensive edition (*The McGraw-Hill Reader*, Eleventh Edition), this new reader engages students with the finest classic and contemporary essays—works that span myriad ages, cultures, and disciplines—and prepares students for an expanded universe of literacies, encouraging fluency with print, audio, visual, digital, electronic, interactive, and hybrid texts. Eudora Welty speaks of reading as "a sweet devouring," and this book invites students to participate in—and enjoy—the vast and varied pleasures of responding to texts in any form.

Organization

Composed of two parts and 11 chapters, *The Brief McGraw-Hill Reader* covers the major modes of writing and many of the disciplines that college students will encounter as undergraduates.

Part 1: An Overview of College Writing Chapter 1 presents an introduction to the ways we read and respond to texts today. Chapter 2 focuses on strategies for critical thinking, reading, and writing, emphasizing multiple 21st-century electronic options, while Chapter 3 provides extensive coverage of argument and persuasion. Finally, Chapter 4 offers up-to-date coverage of 21st-century research writing, including citation and documentation.

Part 2: Issues across the Disciplines Chapters 5–11 explore core liberal arts disciplines, including education, the social sciences, the humanities, and the sciences. Each chapter asks a key question, drawn from the disciplines it represents, designed to elicit constructive class discussion and sound critical writing. Each of these disciplinary chapters offers 5-8 prose models that encourage students to practice skills they will need throughout college—including analysis, criticism, argumentation, and facility with digital texts.

Key Features

Informed by the comments and suggestions of instructors from across the country who reviewed the comprehensive eleventh edition of *The McGraw-Hill Reader* and plans for this concise edition, *The Brief McGraw-Hill Reader* offers the following proven and significant features.

- **A rich selection of readings.** The essays and images in this book address themes of current and enduring interest. Topics like the Obama generation, marriage equality, global climate change, social networking, the legacy of Michael Jackson, the appeal of *Mad Men,* globalization,

torture, and the wars in Iraq and Afghanistan should elicit lively student response and effective writing. The essays have been selected carefully to embrace a rich assortment of authors, to achieve balance among constituencies, to cover major histori-cal periods, and to provide prose mod-els and styles for class analysis,

"Why we Love *Mad Men"* by Lauren M. E. Goodlad

"Our Mutual Joy: The Religious Case for Gay Marriage" by Lisa Miller

discussion, and imitation. The authors in this text—from Frederick Douglass to Susan Sontag, Rachel Carson to Jared Diamond, and Julia Alvarez to David Brooks—all have high visibility as writers and thinkers of value. All of these authors—writing from such vantage points as literature, jour-nalism, anthropology, sociology, art history, biology, and philosophy—start from the perspective that ideas exist in the world, that we should be alert to them, and that we should be able to deal with them in our own discourse.

- **A text that works with a wide variety of levels and approaches.** Because the selections range from very simple essays to more abstract and complex modes of discourse, teachers and students will be able to use *The Brief McGraw-Hill Reader* at virtually all levels of a program. It can be used with any of the major pedagogical perspectives common to the practice of composition today: as a writing-across-the-curricula text, as the basis for a rhetorically focused course, as a the-matic reader, as a multicultural anthology, or as an in-depth reader. Teachers can develop their own sequences of essays that will contribute not only to their stu-dents' reading and writing proficiency but also to their growing intellectual power.

- **Chapter introductions that encourage students to reflect on major issues.** The introduction to each disciplinary chapter gives students a broad perspective on the field at hand by putting major issues and concerns in context. Each introduc-tion ends with a preview section that alerts stu-dents to strategies for reading, discussion, and writing.

- **Integrated and focused treatment of argument.** A focused chapter on persuasive writing is re-inforced throughout the book by "Writing an Argument" essay assignments accompanying each reading. The Album of Advertisements in Chapter 9 prompts students to examine visual arguments about topics like health care reform. *The Brief McGraw-Hill Reader* encourages stu-dents to consider complex, multiple perspec-tives, moving beyond pro-con thinking.

- **Necessary coverage of plagiarism, summary and précis, and the research process.** The chapters in Part 1 provide integrated guidelines on each of these topics. Chapter 4 offers an up-to-date (2010) tour of research, research writing, and MLA/APA documentation in this age of new media.
- **Uniform apparatus that reinforces critical reading and writing.** Each selection in this text is preceded by a brief introduction that offers biographical information about the author. The questions that follow each essay are organized in a consistent format created to reinforce essential reading, writing, and oral communication skills. Arranged in four categories—Comprehension, Rhetoric, Writing, and Networking: Applying 21st-Century Literacies—these questions reflect current compositional theory as they move students from audience analysis to various modes, processes, and media of composition. The integrated design of these questions makes each essay—simple or complex, short or long, old or new—accessible to college students who possess varied reading and writing abilities.
- **"Networking: Applying 21st-Century Literacies" assignments.** Designed to foster digital, multimedia, and real-world literacy skills, these new assignments send students online; to video, audio, or interactive sources; or away from their desks to create visual texts or conduct primary research. These assignments may provide opportunities for collaborative work, enhanced research projects, or composition in different genres or across media. For easy reference, these are listed on pages xix–xx.

NETWORKING
Applying 21st-Century Literacies

Analyzing a Web Page: Use the questions on page 28 to analyze the Web page shown below, particularly its use of images. To see an updated version of the page, or to see it in color, access the site via Chapter 1's Networking page (at *www.mhhe.com/mhreaderbrief1e*). Consider expanding your analysis to the larger site.

The home page of the National Campaign to Prevent Teen and Unplanned Pregnancy (www.thenationalcampaign.org).

- **Enhanced Web-based resources (*www.mhhe.com/mhreaderbrief1e*), with access to Connect Composition 2.0.** This reader's online component features launch pages for Networking assignments; bibliographical, biographical, and cultural links; and additional readings—as well as access to Connect Composition's extensive additional resources: electronic peer review utilities; a database of sample student projects; tutorials on avoiding plagiarism, using document design, and understanding visual rhetoric; over 4,500 exercises with feedback on grammar, punctuation, and usage; and more.
- **"Synthesis: Connections for Critical Thinking" sections.** The topics listed at the end of each chapter help students to gain practice in synthesis and critique, and make comparative assessments of various groups of essays.

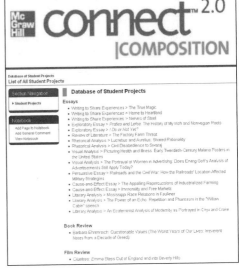

- **Classic and Contemporary Images.** These paired visuals appear at the beginning of each chapter. These photographs, paintings, cartoons, and other visual texts, along with the accompanying "Using a Critical Perspective" questions, serve to interest students in the chapter's central topics and get them thinking and writing.

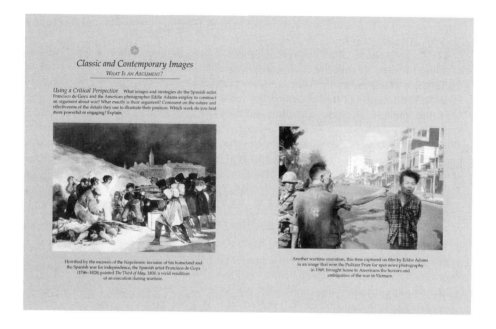

A GUIDE TO THE BRIEF MCGRAW-HILL READER

This instructor's guide—devised by Jim Iddings, Karen Laing-Urbina, and Christian Clark (all of the College of Southern Nevada)—offers well-considered strategies for teaching individual essays, sample rhetorical analyses, answers to questions, additional thought-provoking questions, comparative essay discussion formats, and tips for prewriting and guided writing activities. There is also a bibliography of criticism and research on the teaching of composition. This guide is available for instructors at www.mhhe.com/mhreaderbrief1e.

ACKNOWLEDGMENTS

It is a pleasure to acknowledge the support, assistance, and guidance of numerous individuals who helped create *The Brief McGraw-Hill Reader*. I want to thank the excellent McGraw-Hill family of assistants, editors, and executives who participated enthusiastically in the project from the outset and who encouraged me at every step. My editors, Christopher Bennem and John Kindler, have been loyal, enthusiastic supporters of The *McGraw-Hill Reader* series for many years. Thanks, too, to others on the McGraw-Hill editorial team who have made valuable contributions to this first edition:

Dawn Groundwater, Zachary Norton, and Jesse Hassenger. Cleatta Morris from Louisiana State University in Shreveport has done a first-rate job enhancing the chapter on research writing to reflect 21st-century practices. Thanks to Jim Iddings, Karen Laing-Urbina, and Christian Clark (all from the College of Southern Nevada) for their excellent work on the *Guide to The Brief McGraw-Hill Reader*. I also want to thank Judith Brown and Patricia Ohlenroth, my astute copyeditors, and Holly Paulsen, my superlative production editor. Above all, I offer sincere thanks to Anne Stameshkin, my development editor, who in countless ways helped make this brief edition fresh and exciting.

The final content and design of *The Brief McGraw-Hill Reader* reflects the expertise and advice offered by college instructors across the country who gave generously of their time when asked to review the development of *The McGraw-Hill Reader*, Eleventh Edition, and the creation of this first edition text:

Brenda Hardin Abbott, Bay Path College
Amy Adams, St. Edwards University
Stephen Adkison, Idaho State University
Jacob Agatucci, Central Oregon Community College
Jack Ahrens, College of the Canyons
Gillian F. Anderson, Eastern New Mexico University
Rebecca Babcock, The University of Texas of the Permian Basin
Christine Barkley, Palomar College
Candace Boeck, San Diego State University
Laurel Bollinger, The University of Alabama in Huntsville
Gene Browning, Austin Community College—Eastview
Todd Bunnell, Mississippi University for Women
Mary Elizabeth Cicchetti, College of DuPage
Robert Cox, Southeastern Kentucky Community and Technical
    College—Middlesboro
Linda Cullum, Kutztown University
Jay T. Dolmage, West Virginia University
Lynn Eckersley-Ray, University of Southern Maine
Florence Emch, California State University—Los Angeles
Kevin Ferns, Woodland Community College
Tom Flanigan, Idaho State University
Lawrence Gorman, East-West University
Kimberly Greenfield, Lorain County Community College
M. Katherine Grimes, Ferrum College
Randolph Handel, Santa Fe College
Curtis Harrell, NorthWest Arkansas Community College
Rebecca M. Heintz, Polk Community College
Vicki Hill, Brewton-Parker College
Bev Hogue, Marietta College
Jennifer Kaufman, State University of New York—Ulster
Anna Keah, Austin Community College
Alicia Leopold, Community College of Allegheny County
Walter Lowe, Green River Community College—Auburn
Miles McCrimmon, J. Sargent Reynolds Community College
Mark Meritt, University of San Francisco

A. Modarres, Ventura County Community College—Moorpark
Cleatta Morris, Louisiana State University in Shreveport
Rebecca J. Neagle, Wake Technical Community College
Helen Rapaport, Columbia College
Ron Reed, Hazard Community and Technical College
Jane Rosencrans, J. Sargeant Reynolds Community College
Deborah Ruth, Owensboro Community and Technical College
Murray M. Sellers, Lander University
Janice R. Showler, Holy Family University—Northeast
Carolyn Stevenson, East-West University
Doug Swartz, Indiana University Northwest
Deron Walker, California Baptist University
Ted Whisnant, Francis Marion University
Kathleen G. White, Bellevue College

I am pleased to acknowledge support from the Mellon Foundation, the Graduate Center of The City University of New York, and the United States Department of Education (Title III and Title IV) that enabled me to develop this text.

                                                                    Gilbert H. Muller

part 1

An Overview of College Writing

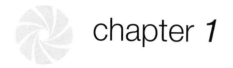

chapter *1*

Reading and Responding to Texts in the 21st Century

This book will help you read and write critically in college and beyond. In academic courses and the workplace, many critical reading and writing skills—such as the ability to analyze, critique, and synthesize information—are seemingly timeless; however, to gain a voice in the 21st-century information age, you must also master multiple literacies and technological skills and learn how to apply these skills in new and developing contexts. College assignments, work challenges, and individual lifestyles are diverse, rapidly changing, technology driven, and increasingly global. Changes in technology and society itself are transforming the way we read and respond to texts.

Today, you are composing more than ever before and in numerous environments in print and online. In all likelihood, you are texting, tweeting, and blogging (or at least reading others' blogs); maintaining Web sites of your own; creating and uploading podcasts; sharing video clips on YouTube or audio files through peer-to-peer programs; and interacting in multiple formats on social networking sites. And of course you are making electronic presentations in the classroom while still using pen and paper to fill out blue books, take at least some of your class notes, or make journal entries. In brief, your literacy environment is far more complex than in previous generations.

According to the National Council of Teachers of English, a literate person in the 21st century must be able to

- develop proficiency with the tools of technology;
- build relationships with others to pose and solve problems collaboratively and cross-culturally;
- design and share information for global communities to meet a variety of purposes;
- manage, analyze, and synthesize multiple streams of simultaneous information;
- create, critique, analyze, and evaluate multimedia texts; and
- attend to the ethical responsibilities required by these complex environments.

Clearly you need a wide range of competencies and abilities to succeed as a reader and writer in this changing and challenging world, and the way you write will often determine your academic, vocational, and personal success. In short, you need a *literate identity*—a voice attuned to the democratic sphere and global society.

Composition in all its forms—from written works to audio and visual projects—is the essence of academic life, which typically involves the reading of and responding to challenging texts. As a 21st-century college student, you will be swimming in an ocean of discourse; and you will need to approach texts with both focus and skills that go beyond casual reading, the type you may do for leisure or escapism. Even in courses in which a preponderance of work involves learning forms of knowledge and new technologies, such as computer science, mathematics, or biochemistry, you are sure to find a healthy amount of reading that will supplement any other work done in the classroom or laboratory. And increasingly the read-write universe that awaits you will necessitate an interactive approach fostered by Web 2.0 (and beyond) culture.

The reading and writing skills you develop during your college years will also help you in your future profession. Think of a lawyer reviewing legal history or preparing a brief, a nurse reviewing current literature on medical innovations or writing a detailed progress report on a patient's recovery, or an environmental researcher reading and writing about issues regarding pollution and global warming. All these activities require the ability to think, read, and write about complex material. Learning the tools of critical reading and writing not only teaches you the "what" of an issue but also helps you think about and respond intelligently to the relative strength of the writer's opinions, ideas, and theories. Critical thinking, reading, and writing enable you to distinguish between informed ideas and pure speculation, rational arguments and emotional ones, and organized essays and structurally deficient ones.

As you hone your critical thinking, reading, and writing skills by tackling the essays in this anthology, you should soon understand how the written word is still the primary medium with which thinkers transmit the intricacies of controversial issues involving the family, society, politics, work, gender, and class. You will encounter complex and varied texts—both in print and online, in formats you can read, see, hear, and even interact with—that require you to extract maximum meaning from them, compare your views with those of the authors you read, and respond to what you read in an informed and coherent manner. The reading selections in this textbook have been chosen specifically to assist you in developing such skills. As you tackle these texts, you will realize that sound reading habits permit you to understand the fine points of logic, reasoning, analysis, argumentation, and evaluation.

READING CRITICALLY AND ACTIVELY

You can find numerous reasons to rationalize a failure to read carefully and critically. You have a headache. You're hungry. The material is boring. The writer puts you to sleep. Your roommates are talking. You have a date. In short, there are many internal and external barriers to critical reading. Fortunately, there are techniques—in a critical reading process—to guide you through this maze of distractions. Consider these five essential strategies:

1. *Develop an attitude of "critical consciousness."* In other words, do not be passive, uncritical, or alienated from the writer or the text. Instead, be active, critical, and engaged with the writer and his or her text.
2. *Read attentively.* Give your full attention to the text in order to understand it. Do not let your mind wander.
3. *Paraphrase.* Periodically restate what you read. Learn to process bits of key information. Keep a running inventory of highlights. Take mental or actual notes on the text's main points. (More information on paraphrasing and summarizing appears in this chapter and in Chapter 4.)
4. *Ask questions.* If for any reason you are uncertain about any aspect of the text, pose a question about it and try to answer it yourself. You might seek help from a friend

or classmate. If you still are unable to answer your question, ask for clarification from the instructor.

5. *Control your biases.* You must both control and correct any prejudices that might interfere with the claim, information, or tone of a text. You might, for example, have misgivings about a liberal or conservative writer, or about a feminist or a creationist, but such strong emotions can erode your ability to keep an open mind and your power to think critically about a subject or issue.

These five strategies will help you begin to overcome the barriers to critical reading.

One way to view critical reading is through the concept of active reading. Active reading suggests that you, as a reader, have an obligation to yourself and the author to bring an alert, critical, and responsive perspective to your encounter with the written word. Active reading means learning to annotate (a strategy discussed later in this chapter), to reflect on what you read, and to develop personal responses in order to prepare yourself for writing assignments that your instructor will present to you during the term. This process—reading critically in order to write critically—is not merely an academic exercise. It is a skill that can enrich you as a person throughout your life and career. It will teach you to respond critically to the admonitions of politicians or to the seductions of advertisements and, if you choose, to participate intelligently in the national conversation, which can lead to a rewarding life and responsible citizenship.

When you read an essay or any other type of text, you create meaning out of the material the author has presented. If the essay is relatively simple, clear, and concise, the meaning that you construct from your reading may be very similar to what the author intended. Nevertheless, the way you interact with even the most comprehensible texts will never be identical to the way another reader interacts.

As your class reads and discusses essays in this book, a majority of you will probably arrive at a broad consensus on the intention, meaning, and methods of each author. However, individual responses to a text will undoubtedly vary within an acceptable range of interpretation. When analyzing and evaluating an essay, several responses might all be appropriate, especially when dealing with a complicated or argumentative text. In other words, your interpretation of an essay will be conditioned by unique personal experience and background; race and ethnicity; age and gender; religious and political attitudes; biases and beliefs, and more. This is not to say that you can engage in farfetched or idiosyncratic responses. But even as your class attempts to construct a common reading for an essay, you have some latitude to craft your own meaning based on an informed and carefully considered response to the text.

RESPONDING TO ESSAYS

Between its print and online components, this textbook contains essays covering a variety of subjects by writers from a wealth of backgrounds and historical periods. You may be familiar with some, unfamiliar with others. All, however, have something to say and a way of saying it that others have found significant. Hence, many have stood the test of time, whether a year, a decade, or centuries. Essays are a recognized genre, or form of literature, and the finest essays have staying power. As Ezra Pound said, "Literature is news that stays news," and the best examples of the essay convey this sense of permanent value.

Therefore, you have an obligation to be an active and critical reader to do justice to the work that was put into these texts. Most were written with care, over extended periods of time, and by people who themselves studied the art of writing and the topics of their discourse. During your first week of class, you may wish to read some of their brief biographies to understand these authors' personal and educational backgrounds, their beliefs and credos, and some of the significant moments of their lives. You will often find that there are logical connections between the stories of their lives and the topics they have written about.

Sharpening your reading skills will be important because you may not be able to personally choose the essays from the text. You may find some topics and essays more interesting than others. But if you are prepared to read critically, you will be able to bring the same set of skills to any selection your instructor assigns. With this principle in mind, we present an overview of the active reading process and an example of using this process on pages 16–18 with an annotated essay titled "The Cult of Ethnicity," by Arthur M. Schlesinger Jr.

When you are given a reading assignment from the textbook, a good strategy in preparing to read is to locate the text as well as possible within its broader context. Read the biographical notes about the author. Focus on the title of the essay. What can you infer from the title? How long is the essay? Although many students delight at the thought of reading shorter texts rather than longer ones, you may find that this variable is not always the deciding one in determining how easily you "get through" the essay. Short essays can be intricate and difficult; long ones can be simpler and more transparent. A long essay on a topic in which you are interested may be more rewarding than a short essay that you find lacking in relevance.

Other basic prereading activities include noting whether there are section breaks in the essay, whether there are subheadings, whether the author has used footnotes, and if so, how extensive they are. Other preliminary questions to answer could be, What is the date of the original publication of the essay? In what medium was it originally published? Is the essay a fully contained work, or is it an excerpt from a larger text? Are there visual or mathematical aids, such as graphs, charts, diagrams, or lists? Because authors often use typographical signals to highlight things or to help organize what they have written, you might ask, Does the author use quotation marks to signal certain words? Is italic type used, and if so, what is its purpose? Are other books and authors cited in the essay? Does the author use organizational tools such as Arabic or Roman numerals? Once you have answered these questions regarding mechanics, you will be prepared to deal more substantively with the essay as a unit of meaning and communication.

Preparing to read also means understanding that you bring your own knowledge, opinions, experiences, and attitudes to the text. You are not an empty glass to be filled with the knowledge and opinions of the authors, but rather a learner who can bring to bear your own reflections on what you read even if you think your knowledge is minimal. Often we do not know just how much ability we have in thinking about a topic until we actively respond to what others confront us with in their writings. By tackling the reading assignments in the text, you will not only learn new information and confront opinions that may challenge your own but also find that reading frees up your ability to express your opinions. For this reason, most English teachers look on reading as a two-way process: an exchange between writer and reader.

Although the credentials and experience of a professional writer may seem impressive, they should not deter you from considering your own critical talents as you read. But first, you must find a way to harness those abilities.

Following is a summary for reading and responding to texts critically.

GUIDELINES FOR READING CRITICALLY

- Who is the author? What do you know about his or her life, credentials, and professional background? (*Headnotes,* or author introductions that appear at the start of the essays in this book, provide some of this information.) If there is more than one author (and 21st-century texts increasingly reflect collaborative writing processes), what is the personal or professional relationship between these writers?

- Where did the selection first appear? What do you know about this publication? Is the text an entire selection, an excerpt, or part of a chapter?

- Did the selection appear in print, online, or both? Is there something specific about its content that this format (or that multiple formats) enhances or works well with? If it is online, how interactive is the selection? What role does the reader play in its purpose and content?

- Who is the author's audience? Is this audience general, specific, or targeted even more narrowly for a highly specialized group? What assumptions does the author make about this audience's education and background and its potential interest in the subject? How does the author adjust the elements of *style*—language, sentence structure, and complexity of thought—to this audience?

- What is significant about the title? Does the title present the author's general subject in a straightforward way, hint at the topic, or create a sense of mystery, irony, or humor?

- What is the author's purpose? Normally authors write to inform, argue, persuade, entertain, express a personal idea or opinion—or a combination of these objectives. Does the author's purpose complement or seem right for the topic?

- What is the author's main point? Does the author state the main point (termed a *thesis* or *claim*) clearly and concisely in the introduction, place it elsewhere in the text, permit it to evolve slowly, or require you to infer it after reading the entire essay?

- What are the main subpoints? How do these subordinate points inform or support the main point? Are there enough subpoints? Is there sufficient information or evidence to support the main point?

- How does the author organize the essay? What constitutes the introductory section, the body or middle of the essay, and conclusion? Are there subdivisions or numbered units, and how are they linked logically? Are there any missing links?

- How does your personal experience affect your response to the author's ideas? Do you detect any authorial biases (or your own potential biases) that influence your response?

Thinking Critically

The following essay, "From Ancient Greece to Iraq, the Power of Words in Wartime," by Robin Tolmach Lakoff, appeared in the *New York Times* on May 18, 2004. Read the essay and respond in writing to each of the questions in the Guidelines for Reading Critically box on the previous page.

From Ancient Greece to Iraq, the Power of Words in Wartime

Robin Tolmach Lakoff

Robin Tolmach Lakoff is a linguistics professor at the University of California at Berkeley and the author of The Language War.

An American soldier refers to an Iraqi prisoner as "it." A general speaks not of 1 "Iraqi fighters" but of "the enemy." A weapons manufacturer doesn't talk about people but about "targets."

Bullets and bombs are not the only tools of war. Words, too, play their part. 2

Human beings are social animals, genetically hard-wired to feel compas- 3 sion toward others. Under normal conditions, most people find it very difficult to kill.

But in war, military recruits must be persuaded that killing other people is 4 not only acceptable but even honorable.

The language of war is intended to bring about that change, and not only for 5 soldiers in the field. In wartime, language must be created to enable combatants and noncombatants alike to see the other side as killable, to overcome the innate queasiness over the taking of human life. Soldiers, and those who remain at home, learn to call their enemies by names that make them seem not quite human—inferior, contemptible and not like "us."

The specific words change from culture to culture and war to war. The 6 names need not be obviously demeaning. Just the fact that we can name them gives us a sense of superiority and control. If, in addition, we give them nicknames, we can see them as smaller, weaker and childlike—not worth taking seriously as fully human.

7   The Greeks and Romans referred to everyone else as "barbarians"—etymologically those who only babble, only go "bar-bar." During the American Revolution, the British called the colonists "Yankees," a term with a history that is still in dispute. While the British intended it disparagingly, the Americans, in perhaps the first historical instance of reclamation, made the word their own and gave it a positive spin, turning the derisive song "Yankee Doodle" into our first, if unofficial, national anthem.

8   In World War I, the British gave the Germans the nickname "Jerries," from the first syllable of German. In World War II, Americans referred to the Japanese as "Japs."

9   The names may refer to real or imagined cultural and physical differences that emphasize the ridiculous or the repugnant. So in various wars, the British called the French "Frogs." Germans have been called "Krauts," a reference to weird and smelly food. The Vietnamese were called "slopes" and "slants." The Koreans were referred to simply as "gooks."

10   The war in Iraq has added new examples. Some American soldiers refer to the Iraqis as "hadjis," used in a derogatory way, apparently unaware that the word, which comes from the Arabic term for a pilgrimage to Mecca, is used as a term of respect for older Muslim men.

11   The Austrian ethnologist Konrad Lorenz suggested that the more clearly we see other members of our own species as individuals, the harder we find it to kill them.

12   So some terms of war are collective nouns, encouraging us to see the enemy as an undifferentiated mass, rather than as individuals capable of suffering. Crusaders called their enemy "the Saracen," and in World War I, the British called Germans "the Hun."

13   American soldiers are trained to call those they are fighting against "the enemy." It is easier to kill an enemy than an Iraqi.

14   The word "enemy" itself provides the facelessness of a collective noun. Its non-specificity also has a fear-inducing connotation; enemy means simply "those we are fighting," without reference to their identity.

15   The terrors and uncertainties of war make learning this kind of language especially compelling for soldiers on the front. But civilians back home also need to believe that what their country is doing is just and necessary, and that the killing they are supporting is in some way different from the killing in civilian life that is rightly punished by the criminal justice system. The use of the language developed for military purposes by civilians reassures them that war is not murder.

16   The linguistic habits that soldiers must absorb in order to fight make atrocities like those at Abu Ghraib virtually inevitable. The same language that creates a psychological chasm between "us" and "them" and enables American troops to kill in battle, makes enemy soldiers fit subjects for torture and humiliation. The reasoning is: They are not really human, so they will not feel the pain.

17   Once language draws that line, all kinds of mistreatment become imaginable, and then justifiable. To make the abuses at Abu Ghraib unthinkable, we would have to abolish war itself.

Engaging with Digital, Hyperlinked Texts: On the Chapter 1 Networking page at *www.mhhe.com/mhreaderbrief1e,* click on the link to read the article "Judging Honesty by Words, Not Fidgets" in the *New York Times*. First, respond in writing to the questions in the Guidelines for Reading Critically box on page 6. Then reread the article, connecting to the hyperlinks within the *Times* and outside it. Also consider the image attached to the article, the two podcasts, the interview with Carey on WNYC, suggestions for related searches, and links to past coverage of the topic. Take notes on your findings, and share your research in class discussion and/or a class online forum or blog.

ENGAGING IN CRITICAL READING

It should be evident to you by now that you are not a mere recipient of information who passively accepts what the writer conveys. Instead, you should feel comfortable about engaging the author as you might a friend in a lively conversation or argument. And just as a talk with a friend involves active listening, rebuttal, and the use of facts and logic, the interaction between yourself and the author needs to be a dynamic one as well.

Active reading is so important in the learning process that a well-known American philosopher and public intellectual, Mortimer Adler, wrote an essay that has become a classic on this topic: "How to Mark a Book."

As with most of the essays included in this text, this one contains a headnote providing information about the author and is followed by questions for response and writing.

How to Mark a Book

Mortimer J. Adler

Mortimer Jerome Adler (1902–2001) was born in New York City and received his PhD from Columbia University in 1928. A staunch advocate for classical philosophy, Adler believed that there are unshakable truths—an idea rejected by most contemporary philosophers. For this reason, Adler has not been taken seriously by the academic establishment. He was a champion of knowledge, believing that philosophy should be a part of everyone's life and that the great ideas in philosophy can be of value to everyone. Many of his over 75 books attempt to edify the general reader by explaining basic philosophical concepts in everyday language. He was also chairman of the editorial board of the Encyclopaedia Britannica. *To make knowledge more accessible to everyone, he also assumed editorship of the Encyclopaedia Britannica's Great Books project, partly sponsored by the University of Chicago. This project, which has put 443 of the world's "classics" into a 54-volume set, graces the bookcases of many dens and studies in American homes. Despite his advancing years, Adler continued to work on many projects to promote his goal of universal education and enlightenment. "How to Mark a Book" is typical of his didactic, pragmatic approach to education.*

1   You know you have to read "between the lines" to get the most out of anything. I want to persuade you to do something equally important in the course of your reading. I want to persuade you to "write between the lines." Unless you do, you are not likely to do the most efficient kind of reading.

2   I contend, quite bluntly, that marking up a book is not an act of mutilation but of love.

3   You shouldn't mark up a book which isn't yours. Librarians (or your friends) who lend you books expect you to keep them clean, and you should. If you decide that I am right about the usefulness of marking books, you will have to buy them. Most of the world's great books are available today, in reprint editions, at less than a dollar.

4   There are two ways in which one can own a book. The first is the property right you establish by paying for it, just as you pay for clothes and furniture. But this act of purchase is only the prelude to possession. Full ownership comes only when you have made it a part of yourself, and the best way to make yourself a part of it is by writing in it. An illustration may make the point clear. You buy a beefsteak and transfer it from the butcher's ice-box to your own. But you do not own the beefsteak in the most important sense until you consume it and get it into your bloodstream. I am arguing that books, too, must be absorbed in your bloodstream to do you any good.

5   Confusion about what it means to own a book leads people to a false reverence for paper, binding, and type—a respect for the physical thing—the craft of the printer rather than the genius of the author. They forget that it is possible for a man to acquire the idea, to possess the beauty, which a great book contains, without staking his claim by pasting his bookplate inside the cover. Having a fine library doesn't prove that its owner has a mind enriched by books; it proves nothing more than that he, his father, or his wife, was rich enough to buy them.

6   There are three kinds of book owners. The first has all the standard sets and best-sellers—unread, untouched. (This deluded individual owns woodpulp and ink, not books.) The second has a great many books—a few of them read through, most of them dipped into, but all of them as clean and shiny as the day they were bought. (This person would probably like to make books his own, but is restrained by a false respect for their physical appearance.) The third has a few books or many—every one of them dog-eared and dilapidated, shaken and loosened by continual use, marked and scribbled in from front to back. (This man owns books.)

7   Is it false respect, you may ask, to preserve intact and unblemished a beautifully printed book, an elegantly bound edition? Of course not. I'd no more scribble all over the first edition of *Paradise Lost* than I'd give my baby a set of crayons and an original Rembrandt! I wouldn't mark up a painting or a statue. Its soul, so to speak, is inseparable from its body. And the beauty of a rare edition or of a richly manufactured volume is like that of a painting or a statue.

But the soul of a book *can* be separated from its body. A book is more like the 8
score of a piece of music than it is like a painting. No great musician confuses a
symphony with the printed sheets of music. Arturo Toscanini reveres Brahms,
but Toscanini's score of the C-minor Symphony is so thoroughly marked up that
no one but the maestro himself can read it. The reason why a great conductor
makes notations on his musical scores—marks them up again and again each
time he returns to study them—is the reason why you should mark up your
books. If your respect for magnificent binding or typography gets in the way,
buy yourself a cheap edition and pay your respects to the author.

Why is marking up a book indispensable to reading it? First, it keeps you 9
awake. (And I don't mean merely conscious; I mean wide awake.) In the second
place, reading, if it is active, is thinking, and thinking tends to express itself in
words, spoken or written. The marked book is usually the thought-through
book. Finally, writing helps you remember the thoughts you had, or the
thoughts the author expressed. Let me develop these three points.

If reading is to accomplish anything more than passing time, it must be active. 10
You can't let your eyes glide across the lines of a book and come up with an understanding of what you have read. Now an ordinary piece of light fiction, like say,
Gone with the Wind, doesn't require the most active kind of reading. The books you
read for pleasure can be read in a state of relaxation, and nothing is lost. But a great
book, rich in ideas and beauty, a book that raises and tries to answer great fundamental questions, demands the most active reading of which you are capable. You
don't absorb the ideas of John Dewey the way you absorb the crooning of Mr. Vallee.
You have to reach for them. That you cannot do while you're asleep.

If, when you've finished reading a book, the pages are filled with your 11
notes, you know that you read actively. The most famous *active* reader of great
books I know is President Hutchins, of the University of Chicago. He also has
the hardest schedule of business activities of any man I know. He invariably
reads with a pencil, and sometimes, when he picks up a book and pencil in the
evening, he finds himself, instead of making intelligent notes, drawing what he
calls "caviar factories" on the margins. When that happens, he puts the book
down. He knows he's too tired to read, and he's just wasting time.

But, you may ask, why is writing necessary? Well, the physical act of 12
writing, with your own hand, brings words and sentences more sharply before your mind and preserves them better in your memory. To set down your
reaction to important words and sentences you have read, and the questions
they have raised in your mind, is to preserve those reactions and sharpen
those questions.

Even if you wrote on a scratch pad, and threw the paper away when you 13
had finished writing, your grasp of the book would be surer. But you don't
have to throw the paper away. The margins (top and bottom, as well as side),
the end-papers, the very space between the lines, are all available. They aren't
sacred. And, best of all, your marks and notes become an integral part of the
book and stay there forever. You can pick up the book the following week or
year, and there are all your points of agreement, disagreement, doubt, and

inquiry. It's like resuming an interrupted conversation with the advantage of being able to pick up where you left off.

14   And that is exactly what reading a book should be: a conversation between you and the author. Presumably he knows more about the subject than you do; naturally, you'll have the proper humility as you approach him. But don't let anybody tell you that a reader is supposed to be solely on the receiving end. Understanding is a two-way operation; learning doesn't consist in being an empty receptacle. The learner has to question himself and question the teacher. He even has to argue with the teacher, once he understands what the teacher is saying. And marking a book is literally an expression of your differences, or agreements of opinion, with the author.

15   There are all kinds of devices for marking a book intelligently and fruitfully. Here's the way I do it:

1. Underlining: Of major points, of important or forceful statements.
2. Vertical lines at the margin: To emphasize a statement already underlined.
3. Star, asterisk, or other doo-dad at the margin: To be used sparingly, to emphasize the ten or twenty most important statements in the book. (You may want to fold the bottom corner of each page on which you use such marks. It won't hurt the sturdy paper on which most modern books are printed, and you will be able to take the book off the shelf at any time and, by opening it at the folded-corner page, refresh your recollection of the book.)
4. Numbers in the margin: To indicate the sequence of points the author makes in developing a single argument.
5. Numbers of other pages in the margin: To indicate where else in the book the author made points relevant to the point marked; to tie up the ideas in a book, which, though they may be separated by many pages, belong together.
6. Circling of key words or phrases.
7. Writing in the margin, or at the top or bottom of the page, for the sake of: Recording questions (and perhaps answers) which a passage raised in your mind; reducing a complicated discussion to a simple statement; recording the sequence of major points right through the book. I use the end-papers at the back of the book to make a personal index of the author's points in the order of their appearance.

16   The front end-papers are, to me, the most important. Some people reserve them for a fancy bookplate. I reserve them for fancy thinking. After I have finished reading the book and making my personal index on the back end-papers, I turn to the front and try to outline the book, not page by page, or point by point (I've already done that at the back), but as an integrated structure, with a basic unity and an order of parts. This outline is, to me, the measure of my understanding of the work.

17   If you're a die-hard and anti-book-marker, you may object that the margins, the space between the lines, and the end-papers don't give you room enough. All right. How about using a scratch pad slightly smaller than the page-size of

the book—so that the edges of the sheets won't protrude? Make your index, outlines, and even your notes on the pad, and then insert these sheets permanently inside the front and back covers of the book.

Or, you may say that this business of marking books is going to slow up your 18 reading. It probably will. That's one of the reasons for doing it. Most of us have been taken in by the notion that speed of reading is a measure of our intelligence. There is no such thing as the right speed for intelligent reading. Some things should be read quickly and effortlessly, and some should be read slowly and even laboriously. The sign of intelligence in reading is the ability to read different things differently according to their worth. In the case of good books, the point is not to see how many of them you can get through, but rather how many can get through you—how many you can make your own. A few friends are better than a thousand acquaintances. If this be your aim, as it should be, you will not be impatient if it takes more time and effort to read a great book than it does a newspaper.

You may have one final objection to marking books. You can't lend them to 19 your friends because nobody else can read them without being distracted by your notes. Furthermore, you won't want to lend them because a marked copy is a kind of intellectual diary, and lending it is almost like giving your mind away.

If your friend wishes to read your *Plutarch's Lives*, "Shakespeare," or *The Feder-* 20 *alist Papers*, tell him gently but firmly, to buy a copy. You will lend him your car or your coat—but your books are as much a part of you as your head or your heart.

COMPREHENSION

1. Summarize what Adler means by "marking up a book."
2. In your own words, explain how you believe Adler would define the word *book*.
3. Adler mentions books throughout the essay. What particular type of book is he referring to?

RHETORIC

1. What is the tone of the essay? What can you infer from this tone about Adler's emotional relationship to books?
2. Paragraph 15 lists devices for marking a book. What is the function of enumerating them in this way? How would the tone of this section have been altered if Adler had summarized these devices in paragraph form?
3. The author makes reference to various intellectual and artistic figures and works in the essay. How does this help determine for whom the essay has been targeted?
4. Study the relationship between paragraph 9 and paragraphs 10–12. What is the rhetorical format of this section? What method of argumentation is Adler employing?
5. Adler uses the analogy that "reading a book should be: a conversation between you and the author." What other analogies can you find in the essay?
6. Adler raises objections to his argument and then refutes the objections. Where does he make use of this rhetorical device? How effective is it in advancing his argument?
7. Adler calls *Gone with the Wind* "light fiction." Is this opinion or fact? Is it a mere observation or a criticism of the book?

WRITING

1. Mark up Adler's essay in the same manner he recommends that you mark up any good piece of writing. Then write an essay using process analysis to summarize the various methods you used.
2. Compare and contrast two books: one that Adler would regard as "light reading" and one that he would regard as worthy of marking up. Indicate the primary differences between these books in terms of their diction, level of discourse, insight, purpose, and scholarship.
3. **Writing an Argument:** Argue for or against the proposition that this essay has lost its relevance owing to the introduction of new forms of educational media.

NETWORKING
Applying 21st-Century Literacies

Marking a Text Electronically: From Chapter 1's Networking page (at *www .mhhe.com/mhreaderbrief1e*), choose an online article or essay. Cut and paste the text into a new document. Then locate "Track Changes" (or a similar editing feature) in your word-processing program, and experiment with using this software to mark the article electronically. As an alternative, use a program like WebNotes (*www.webnotes.net*) or Fleck (*www.fleck.com*) to mark up the online article on the Web itself. For you as a reader, determine whether Track Changes or a program like Fleck is as useful as the more traditional reading practices advocated by Adler. Why or why not? Which method of marking a text appeals more to you, and why? There is no single correct answer to this, but be sure that your response is backed up by specific, detailed reasons.

Even if some technologically advanced tools can enhance the critical reading process, Adler's essay, which focuses on traditional ways to interact with texts, reveals that you don't need anything high-tech to respond to them. Among the essential elements of close reading that have widespread appeal and application are annotating, note taking, and questioning the text.

Annotating

Annotating refers to marking your text (by hand or online) by making content notes, by using symbols such as question marks and exclamation points, and by recording personal reactions. Annotating is not mere underlining or highlighting. These latter two methods often serve little purpose in helping you comprehend a text. Most likely, when you return to passages you've marked with these simple procedures, you will have forgotten why you felt they were important. If you do underline or highlight, be sure to link your marking with a note in the margin. Simply drawing attention to someone else's words does little in the way of expanding your own thoughts on a topic. Learning is best accomplished by restating ideas in your own words.

Taking Notes

Many essays in your anthology will require more than simply jotting down marginal notes in order to comprehend them fully or to respond to them in depth. Just as you might take notes during a classroom lecture, you may find it useful to take notes to supplement your annotations. You may wish, for example, to type quotations so that you can see them together. Or you may wish to summarize the essay by outlining its key points, a reversal of the process you would use to develop your own essay, wherein you begin with an outline and expand it into paragraphs. By collapsing an essay into an outline, you have a handy reference of the author's thesis (main idea) and supporting points, and the methods used to develop them. Another function of note taking is to overcome the simple habit most of us have of thinking we will remember things without jotting them down or typing them, only to find out later that we cannot recall significant information from memory. You will appreciate the benefits of taking notes when you tackle lengthy essays, which may run 15 or 20 pages.

Questioning the Text

Posing key questions about a text and then answering them to the best of your ability is a helpful means of understanding an essay's substance and structure. Certain basic questions, like the ones below, are salient for nearly any text you confront, and answering them for yourself can be a powerful means of enhancing your comprehension. As you read the text, such questions help you spot the significant issues that lie within most essays, regardless of their form or length. It is a good habit to have these questions in mind as you read and then to return to them once you've thought through your responses. They serve as guideposts along the way of your reading experience and assist you in focusing on those issues that are most important to a text. When you become comfortable with them, you will probably find that your mind automatically poses them as you read, making your comprehension of difficult texts easier.

- What is the thesis or main point of the text?
- What methods does the author use to support these points, for instance, illustration, example, description, personal experience, or history? Does he or she cite authorities or studies or statistics?
- What value position, if any, does the author present? In other words, is the author either directly or indirectly presenting her or his moral framework on an issue, or is she or he summarizing or describing an issue?
- Does the author use any special terms or expressions that need to be elucidated to understand the essay? You will find that authors, when addressing innovative or revolutionary ideas within the context of their times, must use vocabulary that often needs to be defined. Take, for example, the term *multiculturalism*. Exactly what might an author mean by that word?
- What is the level of discourse of the essay? Or what is the audience's level of educational attainment the author presumes?
- Who is the implied audience for the essay? Is it written for a specialized profession (such as scientists or educators)? Is it written for individuals with a focus on their particular role in society, for example, as parents or consumers or citizens?

An Example   The following essay, "The Cult of Ethnicity," by the influential historian Arthur M. Schlesinger Jr., has been annotated to demonstrate how a student might respond to it. Schlesinger's essay also will be used to explain aspects of the reading and writing process as we move through this section.

The history of the world has been in great part the history of the mixing of peoples. Modern communication and transport accelerate mass migrations from one continent to another. Ethnic and racial diversity are more than ever a salient fact of the age.

This seems like the thesis. Where are his supports? Or is it the thesis?

But what happens when people of different origins, speaking different languages and professing different religions, inhabit the same locality and live under the same political sovereignty? Ethnic and racial conflict—far more than ideological conflict—is the explosive problem of our times.

Look these up. Demonstrates knowledge on the part of the author.

On every side today ethnicity is breaking up nations. The Soviet Union, India, Yugoslavia, Ethiopia, are all in crisis. Ethnic tensions disturb and divide Sri Lanka, Burma, Indonesia, Iraq, Cyprus, Nigeria, Angola, Lebanon, Guyana, Trinidad—you name it. Even nations as stable and civilized as Britain and France, Belgium and Spain, face growing ethnic troubles. Is there any large multiethnic state that can be made to work?

The answer to that question has been, until recently, the United States. "No other nation," Margaret Thatcher has said, "has so successfully combined people of different races and nations within a single culture." How have Americans succeeded in pulling off this almost unprecedented trick?

Historical figure— who was he?

We have always been a multiethnic country. Hector St. John de Crevecoeur, who came from France in the 18th century, marveled at the astonishing diversity of the settlers—"a mixture of English, Scotch, Irish, French, Dutch, Germans and Swedes . . . this promiscuous breed." He propounded a famous question: "What then is the American, this new man?" And he gave a famous answer: "Here individuals of all nations are melted into a new race of men." *E pluribus unum.*

*Is this a partly American phenomenon? *prevents racial and ethnic conflict*

The United States escaped the divisiveness of a multiethnic society by a brilliant solution: the creation of a brand-new national identity. The point of America was not to preserve old cultures but to *forge a new, American culture. "By an intermixture with our people," President George Washington told Vice President John Adams, immigrants will "get assimilated to our customs, measures and laws: in a word, soon become one people." This was the ideal that a century later Israel Zangwill crystallized in the title of his popular 1908 play *The Melting Pot.* And no institution was more potent in molding Crevecoeur's "promiscuous breed" into Washington's "one people" than the American public school.

Why?-doesn't explain

The new American nationality was inescapably English in language, ideas, and institutions. The pot did not melt everybody, not even all the white immigrants; deeply bred racism put black Americans, yellow Americans, red Americans and brown Americans well outside the pale. Still, the (infusion) of other (stocks,) even of nonwhite stocks, and the experience of the New World reconfigured the British legacy and made the United States, as we all know, a very different country from Britain.

In the 20th century, new immigration laws altered the composition of the American people, and a cult of ethnicity erupted both among non-Anglo whites and among nonwhite minorities. This had many healthy consequences. The American culture at last began to give shamefully overdue recognition to the achievements of groups subordinated and spurned during the high noon of Anglo dominance, and it began to acknowledge the great swirling world beyond Europe. Americans acquired a more complex and invigorating sense of their world—and of themselves.

But, pressed too far, the cult of ethnicity has unhealthy consequences. It gives rise, for example, to the conception of the United States as a nation composed not of individuals making their own choices but of inviolable ethnic and racial groups. It rejects the historic American goals of assimilation and integration.

And, in an excess of (zeal,) well-intentioned people seek to transform our system of education from a means of creating "one people" into a means of promoting, celebrating and perpetuating separate ethnic origins and identities. The balance is shifting from *unum* to *pluribus*.

That is the issue that lies behind the hullabaloo over "multiculturalism" and "political correctness," the attack on the ("Eurocentric") curriculum and the rise of the notion that history and literature should be taught not as disciplines but as therapies whose function is to raise minority self-esteem. Group separatism crystallizes the differences, magnifies tensions, intensifies hostilities. Europe—the unique source of the liberating ideas of democracy, civil liberties and human rights—is portrayed as the root of all evil, and non-European cultures, their own many crimes deleted, are presented as the means of redemption.

I don't want to sound (apocalyptic) about these developments. Education is always in (ferment,) and a good thing too. The situation in our universities, I am confident, will soon right itself. But the impact of separatist pressures on our public schools is more troubling. If a (Kleagle) of the Ku Klux Klan wanted to use the schools to disable and handicap black Americans, he would hardly come up with anything more effective than the "Afrocentric" curriculum. And if separatist tendencies go unchecked, the result can only be the fragmentation, resegregation and tribalization of American life.

I remain optimistic. My impression is that the historic forces driving toward "one people" have not lost their power. The eruption of ethnicity is, I believe, a rather superficial enthusiasm

Note S's use of historical process analysis
Vocab.: infusion stocks zeal Eurocentric apocalyptic ferment Kleagle crucible

Signals a warning— danger

Is this thesis or related to thesis?

Support against multiculturalism

General—where are the specific examples?

Is this an exaggeration? How does he know?

Who are these people?
He doesn't mention
them specifically.

<u>stirred by romantic ideologues on the one hand and by unscrupulous con men on the other: self-appointed spokesmen whose claim to represent their minority groups is carelessly accepted by the media.</u> Most American-born members of minority groups, white or nonwhite, see themselves primarily as Americans rather than primarily as members of one or another ethnic group. <u>A notable indicator today is the rate of intermarriage across ethnic lines, across religious lines, even (increasingly) across racial lines.</u> "We Americans," said Theodore Roosevelt, "are children of the ⬭crucible⬭"

Reality is stronger
than "ideology"? Is
this his "solution"?

A sharp conclusion →
argument?
United States must
be example. This is the
thesis.

The growing diversity of the American population makes the quest for unifying ideals and a common culture all the more urgent. In a world savagely rent by ethnic and racial antagonisms, the United States must continue as an example of how a highly differentiated society holds itself together.

What has this annotating accomplished? It has allowed the reader/annotator to consider and think about what she has read, integrate her ideas with the ideas of the author, challenge those she may disagree with, raise issues for further study, find the seeds of ideas that may become the focus of an essay in response to the writing, review what she has read with more facility, and quickly and efficiently return to those parts of the essay she found the most salient.

The aforementioned strategies will assist you in responding intelligently in the classroom, remembering the main points of what you have read, and internalizing the critical reading skill so that it becomes automatic. However, such activities are not as challenging as the ultimate goal of most of your reading assignments, which will be to respond in formal writing to the works you've read. For this, you will need to enhance your study skills a bit further so that they will prepare you to write.

Formal writing assignments require you to demonstrate that you understood what you have read and are able to respond in an informed and intelligent manner to the material. They also require you to use appropriate form, organization, and exposition. Above all, regardless of what you want to express, you will have to communicate your ideas clearly and concisely. To this end, you will need to acquire skills that you can call on when it comes to writing at length about what you have read. To do so, you will find your ability to paraphrase, summarize, and quote directly from the original material particularly helpful.

When you move to this next phase, however, try to avoid a common practice among readers that causes them to waste time and effort. Many students think they have completed a reading assignment when they read the last word of an essay. They utter a sigh of relief, look inside the refrigerator for something to eat, call up friends, or browse online. However, as a critical reader, you need to spend additional time reinforcing what you have read by thinking about the author's views, considering her or his rhetorical methods, and reviewing or adding to your notes and annotations. For example, one culminating activity at this point can be to either mentally or verbally summarize what you have read. You can summarize verbally by enlisting a classmate and simply stating in your own terms the main points of your reading assignment. This oral summarizing will prevent a common problem many readers experience: the natural tendency to forget most of what they read shortly after reading.

Message-Making: An Interactive Approach

An essayist attempts to communicate a message to his or her audience. This message is the *content*. But "message making" is a process—the exchange of information through a shared system of verbal or visual symbols. Your goal in reading critically is to understand not just the informational content of a text but also how the writer shares meaning and typically tries to influence your beliefs and behavior. A good writer, to paraphrase Plato in *Phaedrus,* tries to "enchant" your mind.

From Plato to the present—including the emergence of Web 2.0 as a pathway for collaborating, sharing information, and interacting with others—theorists have stressed this interactional aspect of reading and writing. Someone constructs a message (for our purposes, a written text) and transmits it, and we have to receive it, decode it, and respond to it. Thus any "piece"of writing, whether designed to inform, persuade, or entertain, is the product of a complex process of actions and interactions by which we perceive, order, and verify (or make sense of) what we read. Whether we have the capacity to grasp the argument of a text, think logically about a thesis, or understand the cultural background of a writer and how it informs a text depends on how well we *perceive* the ways in which the writer creates meaning in the text.

Defined simply, *perception* is the process by which you create meaning for your world. As a process, it deals with the way you interpret the behavior of others as well as yourself. Thus, understanding perception helps to explain how we process information about self, others, and our world. Our senses—seeing, hearing, touching, tasting, smelling—provide us initial contact with the outside world, enabling us to establish our perceptual field of reference. However, we also perceive what we want to perceive, which we call *psychological selectivity.* There is a third form of perception known as *cultural selectivity:* from a cultural perspective, we are conditioned by our culture's code of values and modes of understanding. For example, the phenomenon of *binocular rivalry* demonstrates that people from two different cultures exposed to two pictures at the same time will remember elements compatible with their own culture. With critical reading, you can have diverging interpretations of passages or an entire text because you perceive them from different perspectives.

In addition to differences in perception, you should be mindful of how an author presents information. This can be as important as the information itself. Strategies for writing may include the overall pattern of an essay—for example, is it an argument, an explanation, a definition, an evaluation, a comparison, or a contrast? While you may not think of essays in terms of genre, as you do literature (poetry, short fiction, drama), such forms can help you to understand the motivation behind the writer's work and to seek out significant passages. For example, if the essay is argumentative, you should focus on the supporting points the author has provided, determining whether they offer adequate support for the author's point of view. In an essay arguing for the return to traditional family values, for instance, the use of one anecdote to prove a point would probably not be enough to persuade most readers.

As you read an essay, you should also consider the author's *purpose* for writing. An essay about a personal experience would probably contain physical description; at the same time, the author's purpose would probably be to communicate an element in his or her life that can provide insight into personal development in general. Among the more common purposes are the following: to inform, to persuade, to disprove, to describe, to narrate, to demonstrate, to compare and contrast, to seek a solution to a problem, to explain a process, to classify, to define, to warn, and to summarize. While most essays contain a variety of purposes, one often will stand out among the others.

All of the traditional forms of read-write culture are being transformed by new multimedia practices. We now have to make meaning from multimedia texts that incorporate such new literacy forms and representations as Amazon's Kindle (and other e-reader devices), audio editions of publications that you can listen to on a phone or MP3 player, and streaming video of authors discussing or reading from their work. Digital technologies change the ways you perceive and respond to texts. Visual representations—as a forthcoming section in this chapter reveals—are particularly significant in enhancing content while changing perceptions of the written text. In summary, new media texts alter read-write culture, presenting new opportunities for composition but also demanding new paths of perception.

PARAPHRASING, SUMMARIZING, QUOTING, AND SYNTHESIZING

As you prepare to respond to the writing of others, you need to develop skills so that your own writing will reflect the hard work that went into the reading process. To this end, you can benefit from learning some shortcuts that will assist you in garnering information about what you have read. These skills include paraphrasing, summarizing, quoting directly from, and synthesizing another author's work.

Paraphrasing

Paraphrasing means taking what you have read and putting it in your own words. Students occasionally complain about this process, using the argument that it is a waste of time to paraphrase when the author's own words are the best way to articulate his or her ideas. However, paraphrasing serves two main purposes. The more obvious one is that it prevents you from plagiarizing, even inadvertently, what you have read. In terms of learning, however, it is particularly helpful because it requires that you digest what you have read and then rewrite it. As you do so, you will develop writing patterns that over time will improve your ability to communicate. Paraphrasing forces you to truly think about what you have read and reinforces what you've read, since your mind has now been cognitively stimulated. You may find that paraphrasing often leads you to challenge the text or think more deeply about it simply because the paraphrasing process requires that you fully comprehend what you read.

It is important while paraphrasing to retain all the essential information of the original while not using any of the author's original vocabulary or style. One rule of thumb is to never use three or more words that appeared together in the original. However, you can keep words such as articles (*a, an, the*) and conjunctions (*and, for, but,* and so on).

The following are two examples of paraphrasing that demonstrate unsuccessful and successful application of the technique.

Original

But, pressed too far, the cult of ethnicity has unhealthy consequences. It gives rise, for example, to the conception of the United States as a nation composed not of individuals making their own choices but of inviolable ethnic and racial groups. It rejects the historic American goals of assimilation and integration.

her or his vocabulary simply cannot be changed without injuring the meaning of the original. Review the following quotations taken from the Schlesinger essay, and consider how paraphrasing them would diminish their rhetorical power.

Direct Quotations That Reflect the Conciseness of the Original
"The history of the world has been in great part the history of the mixing of peoples."

"On every side today ethnicity is breaking up nations."

"And if separatist tendencies go unchecked, the result can only be the fragmentation, resegregation and tribalization of American life."

Direct Quotations That Have Particular Stylistic Strength
"The pot did not melt everybody."

"The balance is shifting from *unum* to *pluribus*."

Direct Quotations That Establish the Writer's Authority
"The point of America was not to preserve old cultures but to forge a new, American culture. 'By an intermixture with our people,' President George Washington told Vice President John Adams, immigrants will 'get assimilated to our customs, measures and laws: in a word, soon become one people.'"

"A notable indicator today is the rate of intermarriage across ethnic lines, across religious lines, even (increasingly) across racial lines."

Direct Quotation That Demonstrates Conceptual Power
"The eruption of ethnicity, is, I believe, a rather superficial enthusiasm stirred by romantic ideologues on the one hand and by unscrupulous con men on the other."

Avoiding Plagiarism

When you employ summary, paraphrase, and quotation in an essay or a research paper, you must avoid *plagiarism*—the attempt to pass off the work of others as your own. The temptation to plagiarize is not only one of the oldest "crimes" in academe but also an unfortunate by-product of the computer revolution, for there are numerous opportunities for harried, enterprising, or—let's face it—dishonest students to download bits of information or entire texts and appropriate them without acknowledgment. At the same time, you should be aware that numerous Web sites and software programs allow your instructors to locate even the most inventive forms of plagiarism—right down to words and phrases—and that when writing research papers you may be required to attach all downloaded materials. Be warned: College teachers treat plagiarism as academic treason. If you plagiarize, you can fail a course, be suspended from college, and even be expelled.

We discuss plagiarism again in Chapter 4, which presents information on writing research papers. For now, you can avoid plagiarism by following these basic rules:

- Cite (provide a reference for) all quoted, summarized, or paraphrased information in your paper, unless that information is commonly understood. (For example, you would not have to cite the information that Barack Obama won the 2008 presidential election, because it is common knowledge.)
- Cite all special phrases or unique stylistic expressions that you derive from another writer's work. You might love a phrase by one of the famous writers in this book—say,

E. B. White or Alice Walker—but that writer invented it, and it belongs to him or her. You cannot employ it without acknowledging the source.

- Work hard to summarize and paraphrase material in your own words. Constantly check your language and sentence structure against the language and syntax in the source that you are using. If your words and sentences are too close to the original, change them.

Finally, it is perfectly legitimate to ask your instructor or a tutor in your college's writing center to look at your draft and render a verdict on any information you have summarized, paraphrased, or quoted. Whether this material has been taken intentionally or unintentionally from another source is immaterial. It is your responsibility to present honest written work.

Synthesizing: Drawing Connections from Texts

The ability to summarize, paraphrase, or quote from a single source prepares you for successful academic reading and writing. However, critical reading in college courses typically requires you to think about relationships between and among essays, newspaper articles, sections in textbooks, research findings, interviews, or other types of texts. If, for example, your instructor assigns a block of essays, you probably will need to infer relationships among these texts. We call this process of inferring relationships among various works *synthesis:* drawing connections from two or more written or non-written sources.

If you read online with any regularity, you are probably familiar with clicking on embedded hyperlinks or additional recommended links to materials related to the topic you are reading about. Such links encourage further synthesis by giving you access to other texts that help create a larger context for that topic. They might offer a similar, different, or now outdated perspective on a topic; definitions of certain terms; or more detailed coverage of particular organizations, people, places, theories, or anything else discussed.

You are probably already familiar with synthesis as an academic exercise. The act of reading two or more texts naturally prompts you to consider connections that link types of evidence, various ideas, or competing arguments. When you employ synthesis, you build strength in academic prose, skillfully condensing and connecting information, ideas, and arguments drawn from more than one text.

Any paper drawing on two or more sources requires you to construct relationships among materials that you quote, summarize, or paraphrase. (Remember that reading and writing are intimately connected, overlapping processes.) Suppose you paraphrase two complex passages from two texts. At the first level of critical response, you make the passages more intelligible. Then, at the next level, you convey the *essence* of the relationship between these two sources—whether it relates to the thesis or central argument, the accuracy of the data, or the structuring of materials.

In the process of synthesizing sources, you will often make judgments and arrive at conclusions about the validity of the information or arguments under consideration. In other words, you *critique* the texts—offering formalized, critical readings that express both your understanding of passages and your assessment of their content. With synthesis, what begins as an isolated moment (critically reading a single text) spirals into a series of moments (reading several texts), which demands your powers of comparative analysis and well-developed ability to evaluate relationships among sources.

The Art of Synthesis   With synthesis, you enter into a conversation with two or more writers, attempting to understand their main ideas or arguments, analyze the evidence they provide, and evaluate their conclusions. As with any academic conversation, you must present the writers' ideas with accuracy and respect—but also with an eye to the purpose or aim of your writing. The noted writer and composition specialist Peter Elbow (see his essay in Chapter 2) calls this attempt to present fairly the ideas of other writers "the believing game." In other words, you enter into the minds of other writers in order to appreciate their ideas and critical perspectives, but you do not suspend your beliefs or lose yourself entirely in the believing game. After all, you too have a specific purpose in writing: You merely want to exercise a degree of understanding and fairness as you synthesize the ideas of others.

It is relatively easy to consider two or more sources objectively when you use synthesis to explain the authors' ideas. (*Explanatory synthesis* is one of the two main types of synthesis. The other type, *argumentative synthesis,* will be treated briefly in this chapter and more fully in Chapter 3.) With explanatory synthesis, your purpose is to convey information using the tools of summary, paraphrase, and quotation to emphasize those aspects of certain texts that you find useful in constructing your essay. In a sense, you are detached and objective, an observer of information. Your purpose in using explanatory synthesis is to inform.

With argumentative synthesis, your conversation or dialogue with other writers shifts from objective explanation to the use of source material to bolster your *claim*—a major proposition or conclusion that other readers can agree or disagree with. You still might have to explain what others have said, but now you want to give a fair hearing to their arguments over a shared issue or topic while at the same time staking out your position on the matter. To support your argument, you seek *evidence* (facts and expert opinions) from relevant sources, analyze and evaluate the merits of that evidence, and use it to support your argument.

When you use argumentative synthesis, try to locate expert testimony, reliable sources, and verifiable types of evidence to reinforce your claim. Use this evidence so that it informs and strengthens your viewpoint. At the same time, you should acknowledge alternative viewpoints, for one feature of successful argument is the willingness to present and refute opposing claims. The challenge is to use any evidence that strengthens your text—but not at the risk of misrepresenting another writer's position or engaging in a biased or unfair presentation of the evidence.

Guidelines for Synthesis

1. *Consider your purpose.* Is your purpose to *explain* or to *argue*—or perhaps a combination of both? How will this purpose affect your search for sources?
2. *Select and identify your sources.* Where did the article first appear, and what might this publication tell you about the writer's perspective? Identify the author, noting his or her credentials, publications, and occupation. How does the title or subtitle reveal the writer's purpose? Does the title seem to conform to your purpose? Why or why not?
3. *Read critically and actively.* Follow the steps and procedures outlined on page 6. What is the writer's primary purpose? What is the main idea or argument? What are the minor points? How do the subpoints relate to the central point? What is the structure of the text—the introduction, middle sections, and conclusion? How does the text reinforce a key idea that you may have in mind for an essay?

4. *Take notes and summarize.* Use the techniques of print and/or electronic annotation illustrated on pages 14–18. Identify the writer's main point and rewrite it in one or two sentences.

5. *Establish connections among readings.* What relationships do you detect as you move from text to text? How do major and minor points stressed by the writers in their texts overlap or diverge? What elements of their arguments are similar and dissimilar? (Draw up a list of similar and dissimilar points for handy reference.)

6. *Write your synthesis.* First, write down your *thesis* (main point) or *claim* (argument), and develop it in an introductory paragraph. Next, draft body or middle paragraphs that offer support for the thesis or claim; write topic sentences for all paragraphs; incorporate explanatory or argumentative details drawn from the sources that you synthesize; and document your sources properly in order to avoid any charge of plagiarism. Finally, write a conclusion that grows organically from the preceding paragraphs and reinforces your main idea. And, then, revise your essay. (*Note:* You can find information on the writing process, techniques of argumentation, and strategies for research in the pages and chapters that follow.)

READING AND RESPONDING TO ONLINE TEXTS

As a 21st-century reader and writer, you will be reviewing and experimenting frequently with texts that you locate online. Engaging with materials online, you should apply the same critical thinking and reading skills outlined in this chapter—along with a keen perception of the strengths and weaknesses of texts in the digital universe. For even as the Internet breaks new ground in the flow of (and access to) knowledge, the Web also contains a torrent of information—much of it unreliable. An ability to navigate these less charted waters, to interpret and judge online texts, will be crucial to your success in college and beyond.

Because online texts in all their variety—academic articles, government documents, wikis, blog postings, social networking sites, and more—constitute new models of composing, you need new ways to approach and manage them. Fortunately, college libraries across the nation are in the forefront of the attempt to harness the size, speed, and global interconnectedness of the Internet to benefit students.

According to the UCLA library staff, a good Web site does all of the following:

1. Clearly states the author and/or organizational **source** of the information;

2. Clearly states the **date** the material was written and the date the site was last revised;

3. Provides **accurate** data whose parameters are clearly defined;

4. Provides **type and level** of information you need;

5. Keeps **bias** to a minimum, and clearly indicates point of view;

6. Provides live **links** to related high-quality Web sites;

7. In the case of **commercial** sites, keeps advertising separate from content, and does not let advertisers determine content; and

8. Is clearly **organized and designed** for ease of use.

Each of these guidelines might require you to consider qualifications, compare and contrast information, evaluate depth of coverage, check and review data, look elsewhere, and more. More information on online research appears in Chapter 4.

READING AND ANALYZING VISUAL TEXTS

In this new era of information technology, we seem to be immersed in a visual culture requiring us to contend with and think critically about the constant flow of images we encounter—images that typically are reinforced by verbal elements.

Courses in engineering, social science, computer science, the humanities, fine arts, and elsewhere will require you to analyze and understand visual elements that are embedded in texts. Textbooks increasingly promote visuals as frames of reference that help readers comprehend and appreciate information. Some visual elements—charts, tables, and graphs—are integral to an understanding of verbal texts. Other visuals—comic art, drawings, photographs, paintings, and advertisements—offer contexts and occasions for enjoyment and deeper understanding of the reading, writing, and thinking processes. Visual images convey messages that often are as powerful as well-composed written texts. When they appear together, image and word are like French doors, both opening to reveal a world of heightened perception and understanding.

When visual elements stand alone, as in painting and photography, they often make profound statements about the human experience and frequently reflect certain persuasive purposes that are composed as skillfully as an argumentative essay. Consider, for example, Eddie Adams's potent stills of the execution of a prisoner by the notorious chief of the Saigon national police, General Nguyen Ngoc Loan. In the framed sequence, the chief of police aims his pistol at the head of the prisoner and presses the trigger, and the viewer, in that captured instant, sees the jolt of the prisoner's head and a sudden spurt of blood. Reproduced widely in the American press in February 1968, Adams's prize-winning image (p. 81) did as much as any written editorial to transform the national debate over the Vietnam War.

Although paintings, photographs, advertisements, and other artistic and design forms that rely heavily on visual elements often function as instruments of persuasion, great literary artists from Homer to Norman Mailer have captured the horrors of war as vividly as visual artists. Stephen Crane in *The Red Badge of Courage* illustrates the sordidness of America's Civil War in language as graphic as the images of the war's most noted photographer, Mathew Brady. Consider the visual impact of Crane's depiction of battlefield dead:

> The corpse was dressed in a uniform that once had been blue but was now faded to a melancholy shade of green. The eyes, staring at the youth, had changed to the dull hue to be seen on the side of a dead fish. The mouth was opened. Its red had changed to an appalling yellow. Over the grey skin of the face ran little ants. One was trundling some sort of a bundle along the upper lip.

Ultimately, the best verbal and visual texts construct meaning in vivid and memorable ways. When used in combination, verbal and visual texts can mix words and images to create uniquely powerful theses and arguments.

Just as you analyze or take apart a verbal text during the process of critical reading, you also have to think critically about visual images or elements. If you encounter charts, graphs, and tables in a text, you have to understand the information these visuals present, the implications of the numbers or statistics, the emphases and highlights that are conveyed, and the way the visual element—the picture, so to speak—shapes your understanding of the material and its relationship to the text. Sometimes the material presented in such visuals is technical, requiring you to carefully analyze, say, a bar graph: its structure, the relationship of parts to the whole, the assertions that are advanced, and the validity of the evidence conveyed. In short, critical reading of visual material is as demanding as critical reading of the printed word. Just as you often have to reread a verbal text, you also might have to return to charts, graphs, and tables, perhaps from a fresh perspective, in order to comprehend the content of the visual text.

The following questions can guide your critical analysis of such visual texts as charts, graphs, tables, photographs, maps, and Web pages:

- What is the design, format, and structure of the visual? Is it black and white, or are other colors used? How does the placement of design elements affect the message?
- Is the image abstract or realistic—or both? What is the relationship among the elements making up the image?
- Who is the intended audience? Does the image call for a specific audience response?
- What textual information do you immediately notice? What is the relationship between image and text?
- What is the purpose of the visual? What emotions or attitudes does the image convey?
- What thesis or point of view does the information in the visual suggest?
- What is the nature of the evidence, and how can it be verified?
- What emphases and relationships do you detect among the visual details?

When responding to charts, tables, and graphs, you must develop the confidence to read such visual texts accurately and critically. This means taking nothing for granted and trusting your ability to sift through the evidence and the images with a critical eye in order to understand the strategies the author or graphic artist has employed to convey a specific message.

By and large, informative visuals such as tables and graphs rarely have the striking impact of the sort of graphics found in the best commercial and political advertising or in the illustrations we encounter in slick magazines or cutting-edge comics or graphic novels. The visual elements used by advertisers, for example, take advantage of our innate capacity to be affected by symbols—from McDonald's Golden Arch to the president framed by American flags. Such visual emblems convey unspoken ideas and have enormous power to promote products, personalities, and ideas. For example, the two powerful images on pages 30–31 convey important ideas about the cultures that produced them. Visual symbols achieve even more intense effects when they are reinforced by verbal elements.

When viewing art reproductions, photographs, advertisements, and cartoons from a critical perspective, you often have to detect the explicit and implicit messages being conveyed by certain images and symbols, and the design strategies that condition your response. Because these visuals combine many different elements, you have to consider all critical details: color, light, and shadow; the number and arrangement of objects and the relationships among them; the foregrounding and backgrounding of images within the frame; the impact of typography; the impact of language if it is employed; the medium in which the visual appears; and the inferences and values that you draw from the overall composition. Learn to treat visuals in any medium as texts that need to be "read" critically. Every visual requires its own form of annotation, in which you analyze the selection and ordering of its parts and interpret the emotional effects and significant ideas and messages it presents. Throughout this text, paired "classic and contemporary" images such as the two on pages 30–31 give you opportunities to read visual texts with a critical eye.

NETWORKING
Applying 21st-Century Literacies

Analyzing a Web Page: Use the questions on page 28 to analyze the Web page shown below, particularly its use of images. To see an updated version of the page, or to see it in color, access the site via Chapter 1's Networking page (at *www .mhhe.com/mhreaderbrief1e*). Consider expanding your analysis to the larger site.

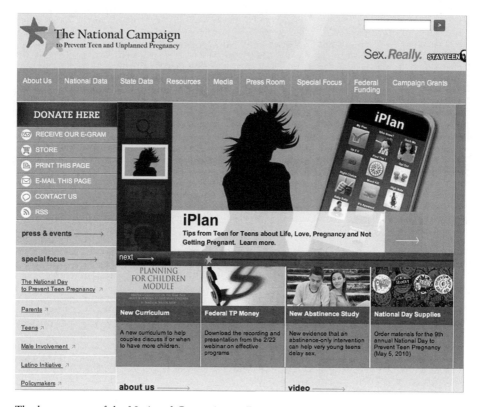

The home page of the National Campaign to Prevent Teen and Unplanned Pregnancy (*www.thenationalcampaign.org*).

Classic and Contemporary Images
HOW DO WE COMMUNICATE?

Using a Critical Perspective   Carefully examine these two illustrations. What is your overall impression of these images? What details and objects in each scene capture your attention? What similarities and differences do you detect? How does each image communicate ideas and values about the culture that has produced it? Does one appeal to you more than the other? Why or why not?

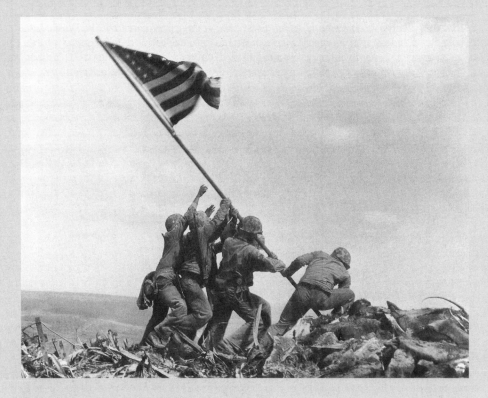

Pulitzer Prize–winning combat photographer Joe Rosenthal captured this scene of U.S. Marines raising the American flag on the Pacific Island of Iwo Jima on February 25, 1945. The campaign to capture the island from Japanese troops cost nearly 7,000 American lives. Rosenthal's photo has been reproduced widely in the media and served as the model for the Marine Corps War Memorial in Washington, D.C.

Photographer Thomas E. Franklin captured a memorable moment
in the wake of the terrorist attack on the World Trade Center in
New York City in September 2001.

- *Learning > Writing to Learn Exercises:* Interactive exercises to develop and strengthen active reading skills
- *Research > Avoiding Plagiarism:* Interactive tutorial
- *Writing > Visual Rhetoric Tutorial:* Roles of images and design in academic writing, with interactive glossary
- *Image Gallery:* Chapter images in color
- *Reading and Responding:* Information on the authors in this chapter
- *Ch. 1 Networking*

chapter *2*

Writing: Process and Communication

COMPOSING IN ANY MEDIUM: PROCESSES FOR WRITING

New methods of communication—notably, various digital technologies and the emergence of Web 2.0 interactions and collaborations—might characterize 21st-century literacies, but regardless of the new media at your disposal, you still have to know how to write. Whether you have been provided an assignment by your instructor or developed your own topic, the various tools for critical reading and analysis covered in the first chapter should equip you with the foundation for embarking on college writing assignments. You might use the Internet to gather information, to chat about the assignment, or to e-mail the instructor with a pressing question about an essay you have read; however, the Web only facilitates or partially informs the many challenges of composition.

Even if your instructor encourages you to put your essay in a digital format, remember that composing an essay in any medium is a dynamic, recursive process. It is especially dynamic today when you can share your writing with other students around the world, submit assignments electronically for review by others, have conversations about drafts and assignments in chat rooms and on message boards, and so forth.

Whether you write for a local or global audience, you usually compose an essay in a three-part process: invention (also called prewriting), drafting, and revising and editing. Of course, in actual practice these stages should not be treated as strictly linear or clear-cut "steps." (Revision, for example, typically occurs at every stage of the writing process, especially when using the many word-processing tools at your disposal.) As your word-processing talents and mastery of other digital options suggest, you often move back and forth within the overall writing process as you generate the raw materials of composition and gradually refine them.

We therefore should acknowledge at the outset that everyone approaches the writing process somewhat differently. Your needs and skills likely differ from the student sitting next to you, as do your specific cultural practices and your possible knowledge of other languages. To illuminate this varied and supple writing process, we will examine strategies employed by several student and professional writers, including one student, Jamie Taylor, as she read and responded to the essay by Schlesinger presented in the first chapter. But first we require an overview of the writing process, starting with the origin and development of a writer's ideas.

Think of the process of writing as a craft involving the planning, transcribing, polishing, and production of a text for an audience. In Old English, the word *craft* signifies strength and power. By treating writing as a craft, you empower yourself to make the most complex compositional tasks manageable. By thinking of the writing process as a habit of mind involving prewriting, writing, and revision, you can create effective essays and documents. In the world of 21st-century literacy, typified by blogs, social networking sites, and more, you also might be interacting with other students and communities, and thus writing collaboratively.

INVENTION

Invention, or prewriting, which you encountered as you negotiated the reading-writing connection in Chapter 1, is the discovery, exploration, and planning stage of the composing process. It is the stage in which you discover a reason to write, select and narrow a subject, consider audience and purpose, perhaps determine the tone or personal voice you wish to employ, and engage in preliminary writing activities designed to generate textual material.

During invention, you are free to let ideas incubate, to let thoughts and writing strategies ripen. You are also free to get in the mood to write. Ernest Hemingway used to sharpen all his pencils as preparation for a day's writing; the French philosopher Voltaire soaked his feet in cold water to get the creative juices flowing. As a digital native, you might want to chat with a classmate via texts or IM, bounce ideas around with others in an online discussion forum, do searches for and read articles about your topic, consult a relevant e-book, or even adopt a virtual identity for yourself in a blog or on Second Life.

Considering Purpose and Audience

Any writing situation requires you to make choices and decisions about purpose, audience, planning, writing, revision, and transmission of your text. Determining your purpose or goal—the reason you are writing—at the outset of the composing process is one of the first steps. It prevents you from expending useless energy on thinking that is ultimately unimportant, misdirected, or unrelated to the problem because it forces you to ask, What do I hope to obtain from this text? With a specific purpose in mind, you start to anticipate the type of composing task ahead of you and to identify the problems that might be inherent in this task.

Traditionally, the main forms of writing—narration, description, exposition, and argumentation—help to guide or mold your purpose.

Form	Purpose	Example
Narration	To relate a sequence of events	To tell about an accident
Description	To provide a picture or produce an impression	To describe a moth
Exposition	To explain, inform, or analyze	To compare two teachers
Argumentation	To convince or persuade	To oppose abortion

Classic and Contemporary Images
How Do We Compose?

Using a Critical Perspective   Consider these two illustrations of authors engaged in the writing process. What is the dominant impression in each photo? What similarities and differences do you see? Which setting seems more conducive to your writing process, and why?

The American novelist Edith Wharton (1862–1937), sitting at her desk, writing.

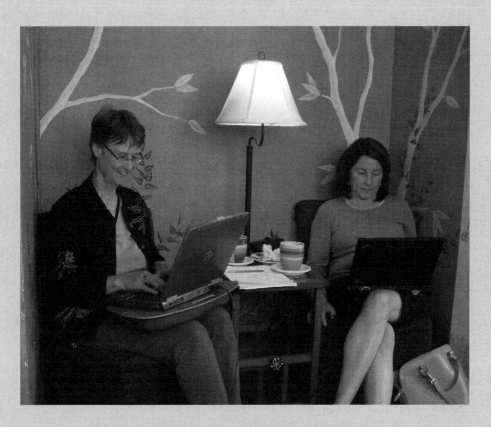

Children's book authors Jennifer Jacobson and Jane Kurtz
writing together at a coffee shop.

Most writing actually combines more than one of these rhetorical modes or forms, but these basic categories help shape your text to a specific purpose.

Even as you determine your purpose, you must also create common ground between yourself and your audience. In fact, to define your audience is to define part of your purpose. Think of your audience as the readers of your text. What do they know about the topic? How do they perceive you—your status, expertise, and credibility? In turn, what do you know about their opinions and backgrounds? Are they likely to agree or disagree with you? (This last question is especially important in argumentative writing, which will be discussed in Chapter 3.) By defining your audience carefully, you can begin to tailor your text. Only by analyzing your readership will you be able to appeal to an audience.

Moreover, you need to know that in the real-world environment of the 21st century, especially the world of work, you often need to identify multiple audiences for a variety of purposes. Even in an academic setting, your primary audience might be your professor, but secondary readers might be classmates you share your work with or a college publication that might be interested in reprinting your essay.

Choosing an Appropriate Tone

Tone is the attitude that you plan to take with your audience. It is the *voice* that your readers will hear when they read your essay. Part of the task of invention is to select a voice that is appropriate to the writing task, the situation, and the audience you address. The intimate or even profane voice that you use when texting a close friend would not be the appropriate tone for an essay you compose for your philosophy professor.

As you think critically about your writing task, it should be clear that your audience has expectations that go beyond the form and content of your essay. Most important, this audience will be listening for the voice that you project. Perhaps, if you are reporting an event factually, you will want to project a balanced, objective, largely dispassionate tone. On the other hand, if you are writing a narrative essay on the death of a family member, your tone might be one of controlled emotion or poignant in effect. Likewise, the tone of an argumentative essay might be logical, insistent, compelling (if you have a persuasive goal), even satirical. Different writing situations demand different tones.

Consider tone as integral to the interactive and social dimension of the writing process. It requires a degree of self-awareness, for tone at all times should inspire trust: you should sound reasonable, well informed about your subject, and fair. Above all, you do not want to sound abrupt, long-winded, sarcastic, or just plain confused. Effective writers know how to move easily among various ranges of tone as they plan their writing task.

Generating Ideas: Freewriting and Brainstorming

When you start a writing project, you need to generate ideas as you search for something to say. Some writers doodle, others create cluster trees of ideas, and still others prefer extensive lists. Two especially useful methods of getting in touch with what you already know or believe are freewriting and brainstorming.

Freewriting is quite simple. Merely select a predetermined amount of time, say, from 5 to 15 minutes, and write or type everything that you can think of regarding the subject at hand. Don't worry about punctuation or grammar. This activity is mainly to get your cognitive wheels rolling. Brainstorming is a variant of freewriting in which you jot down or type ideas and questions, often in numbered form. If you find freewriting and brainstorming helpful, you will probably find the length of time that suits you best. When you have finished, review what you have written. Freewriting and brainstorming can help writers generate ideas and respond to others' ideas. For example, examine the following freewriting and brainstorming exercises by another student, James Moore, which he wrote after reading an excerpt from Schlesinger's "The Cult of Ethnicity."

Freewriting Sample

This essay shows that the author really knows his history because he cites so many historical figures, places, and can quote word for word authorities that back up his argument. He makes a great argument that America's strength is in its diversity and at the same time its unity. I never thought of these two things as being able to complement one another. I always thought of them as being separate. It opens my mind to a whole new way of thinking. One thing that would have strengthened his argument, though, is the fact that although he criticizes people who want to separate themselves into subgroups, he doesn't really mention them by name. He's great when it comes to advancing his own argument but he seems to be a bit too general when he comes to attacking the opposition. I would have liked it if he had mentioned by name people who are undermining America's strengths and listen in their own words.

Brainstorming Sample

1. The author says that ideological conflict isn't such a big problem, but what about the gap between rich and poor? Maybe if there were less of a gap, people wouldn't look for "false idols."

2. Schlesinger seems to be part of the white mainstream. Does this mean he is destined not to understand fully the reasons why people on the margins of society get so tempted to join "cults"?

3. He uses supporting points very well but doesn't exactly explain why "multiculturalism" and "political correctness" are happening now in our society. What is it about today that has opened the door to these ideas?

4. There are so many references to places with ethnic tensions around the world. It would be great to study one of them and see if they have any similarities to the ones that exist in the United States.

5. He seems to be writing for a very educated audience. I wonder really if he can reach the "common person" with this kind of sophisticated writing. I don't know about most of the places he mentions.

6. What's the solution? That could be the start of a topic for my paper. I don't think the author offers any.

Let's consider the benefits these processes can have. First, you can comment on the subject matter of the essay without censoring your thoughts. This prepares you for the second reading by marshaling a more coherent idea of your perspective. Freewriting and brainstorming can be tools that help you understand how you can have something to contribute in the writer-reader "conversation" or help you see a topic in a new way. For example, in the freewriting example, Moore discovered for himself the idea that the strength of American society is a combination of commonality and diversity. Second, during the brainstorming process, you might come up with a potential idea for a response essay, as Moore did in the example.

Now let us return to the prewriting process that Jamie Taylor followed.

Brainstorming Notes

1. Schlesinger seems to be saying that multiculturalism poses a danger because it threatens to create ethnic divisiveness rather than healthy identification.

2. This not only undermines us now, but threatens the very democratic principles upon which the United States was founded.

3. He says America must set an example for the rest of the world, which is torn with racial and ethnic strife.

4. He believes that there is a small group of individuals with a "hidden agenda" who are trying to create this divisiveness. These individuals are self-centered and have their own interests at heart, not the interests of the people they represent.

5. One flaw in the essay was that it seemed vague. He didn't mention any names or give specific examples. Only generalities.

6. He suggests the "battle" will be won by ordinary citizens; for example, he cites the many intermarriages occurring today.

7. Although he sees danger, he is optimistic because he thinks democracy is a strong institution.

8. He writes from a position of authority. He cites many historical figures and seems very well read.

9. The major problem I see in his essay is that he seems to lump everyone together in the same boat. He doesn't give enough credit to the average person to see through the hollowness of false idols. You don't need a Ph.D. to see the silliness of so many ideas floating around out there.

10. So many things to consider, how should I focus my essay??? What should be my theme??

11. Hmmm. Idea!!! Since I agree with his basic points, but find he doesn't provide specifics, and doesn't give the average person enough credit to see through the emptiness of cult rhetoric, why not use my personal observations to write a response paper in which I show just how reasonable we are in distinguishing mere rhetoric from substance?

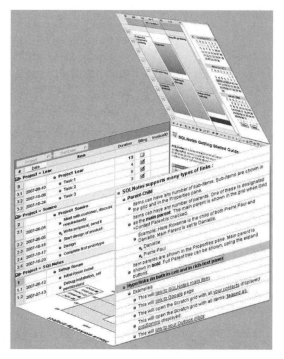

Image from the home page of InfoQube, an "information management system" that can be used for electronic outlining. This visual showcases several of the software's capabilities, including hyperlinked outlines, which you could use to organize ideas during prewriting and research. The most recent version of this software is available as a free download at *www.infoqube.biz*.

Outlining

In addition to this brainstorming, Taylor developed a scratch outline—yet another prewriting strategy—to guide her into the drafting stage of the composing process.

Outline

   I. Introduction: Summarize essay and thesis; provide counterthesis.

  II. University life as a demonstration of "ethnic" democracies.

 III. The emptiness and false promises of self-styled ethnic leaders.

 IV. The rejection of "home-grown" cults.

  V. Conclusion.

Many word-processing programs offer outlining software that you might want to use in lieu of pen and paper. And there are a number of free online outlining (or mind-mapping) programs; some of these, such as SproutLiner (*http://sproutliner.com/*) and InfoQube, offer the convenience of being able to bookmark relevant links within your outline to external sites, or to pages of your own Web-based project. Others, such as FreeMind (*http://freemind.sourceforge.net*), offer the chance to draw connections among complex information groups.

Although Taylor employed brainstorming and a scratch outline to organize her thoughts prior to writing her essay, not everyone uses these prewriting activities. Some students need to go through a series of prewriting activities, while others can dive into a first draft. Nevertheless, the process of discovering the materials and form for an essay includes a search for ideas, a willingness to discard ideas and strategies that don't work, an ability to look at old ideas in a fresh way, and a talent for moving back and forth across a range of composing activities. Rarely does that flash of insight or first draft produce the ideal flow of words resulting in a well-written and well-ordered essay.

DRAFTING

Everyone approaches the composing process differently. There are, however, certain basic principles for this stage; these are discussed in the following section.

Developing the Thesis

Every essay requires a main idea or thesis that holds all your information together. What you seek is not just any idea relevant to the bulk of your topic, but the underlying idea that best expresses your purpose in writing the essay. Your thesis is the controlling idea for the entire essay.

The thesis requires you to take a stand on your topic. It is your reason for wanting to inform or persuade an audience. The noted teacher and scholar Sheridan Baker has expressed nicely this need to take a stand or assume an angle of interpretation: "When you have something to say about *cats*, you have found your underlying idea. You have something to fight about: not just 'Cats,' but 'The cat is really man's best friend.'" Not all thesis statements involve arguments or fights. Nevertheless, you cannot have a thesis unless you have something to demonstrate or prove.

The thesis statement, which normally appears as a single sentence near the beginning of your essay, serves several important functions:

- It introduces the topic to the reader.
- It limits the topic to a single idea.
- It expresses your approach to the topic—the opinion, attitude, or outlook that creates your special angle of interpretation for the topic.
- It may provide the reader with hints about the way the essay will develop.
- It should arouse the reader's interest by revealing your originality and your honest commitment to the topic.

Here is a sample thesis statement by a student:

The automobile—America's metallic monster—takes up important public space,

pollutes the environment, and makes people lazy, rude, and overweight.

In this thesis, the writer has staked out a position, limited the topic, and given the reader some idea of how the essay will develop.

Your thesis cannot always be captured in a single sentence. Indeed, professional writers often offer an implied or unstated thesis or articulate a thesis statement that permeates an entire paragraph. Always ask if a thesis hooks you. Do you find it provocative? Do you know where the author is coming from? Does the author offer a map for the entire essay? These are some of the issues to consider as you compose your own thesis sentences.

Writing Introductory Paragraphs

A good introduction should be like a door that entices readers into the world of your essay, arousing their curiosity about the topic and thesis with carefully chosen material and through a variety of techniques. The introduction, normally a single paragraph composed of a few sentences, serves several important functions:

- It introduces the topic.
- It states the writer's attitude toward the subject, normally in the form of a thesis statement.
- It offers readers a guide to the essay.
- It draws readers into the topic through a variety of techniques.

A solid introduction informs, orients, interests, and engages the audience. "Beginnings," wrote the English novelist George Eliot, "are always troublesome." Getting the introduction just right takes effort, considerable powers of invention, and often several revisions. Fortunately, there are special strategies that make effective introductions possible:

- Use a subject-clarification-thesis format. Present the essay's general subject, clarify and explain the topic briefly, and then present your attitude toward the topic in a thesis statement.
- Offer a brief story or incident that sets the stage for your topic and frames your thesis.
- Start with a shocking, controversial, or intriguing opinion.
- Begin with a comparison or contrast.
- Use a quotation or reference to clarify and illustrate your topic and thesis.
- Ask a question or series of questions directed toward establishing your thesis.
- Offer several relevant examples to support your thesis.
- Begin with a vivid description that supports your main idea.
- Cite a statistic or provide data.
- Correct a false assumption.

All these strategies should introduce your topic and state your thesis. They should be relatively brief and should direct the reader into the body of the essay. Finally, they should reveal your perspective and your tone or voice. In each introductory paragraph, the reader—your audience—should sense that you are prepared to address your topic in an honest and revealing manner.

Writing Body Paragraphs

The body is the middle of the essay. Usually, the body consists of a series of paragraphs whose purpose is to satisfy your readers' expectations about the topic and thesis you presented in the introduction. The body of an essay gives substance, stability, and balance to your thesis. It offers facts, details, explanations, and claims supporting your main idea.

Body paragraphs reflect your ability to think critically, logically, and carefully about your topic. They are self-conscious units of expression whose indentations signal a new main point (or topic sentence) or unified and coherent unit of thought. The contour created by the series of body paragraphs that you design grows organically from the rhetorical or composing strategies that you select. As the English critic Herbert Read states in *English Prose Style*, "As thought takes shape in the mind, it takes *a* shape. . . . There is about good writing a visual actuality. It exactly reproduces what we should metaphorically call the contour of our thought. . . . The paragraph is the perception of this contour or shape." In other words, we see in the shape of an essay the shape of our thoughts. The contour created by the series of body paragraphs proceeds naturally from the material you include and the main point you use to frame this material in each paragraph.

Effective paragraph development depends on your ability to create a unit of thought that is *unified* and *coherent,* and that presents ideas that flesh out the topic sentence or controlling idea for the paragraph, thereby informing or convincing the reader. To achieve a sense of completeness as you develop body paragraphs, be sure to have enough topic sentences and sufficient examples or evidence for each key idea. College writers often have problems writing complete essays with adequately developed body paragraphs. Remember that topic sentences are relatively general ideas. Your primary task is to make readers understand what those ideas mean or why they are important. Your secondary task is to keep readers interested in those central thoughts. The only way to accomplish these two related goals is by explaining the central ideas through various kinds of evidence or support.

Choosing Strategies for Development   Different topics and paragraphs lend themselves to different types of development. These types of rhetorical approaches are essentially special writing and reasoning strategies designed to support your critical evaluation of a topic or hypothesis. Among the major rhetorical approaches are description, narration, illustration, process analysis, comparison and contrast, causal analysis, definition, classification, and argumentation. Each strategy might very well serve as your dominant approach to a topic. Alternatively, your essay might reflect a variety of methods. Remember, however, that any blending of rhetorical strategies should not be a random sampling of approaches but should contribute to your overall point.

Description   Good descriptive writing is often your best tool for explaining your observations about objects, people, scenes, and events. Simply, description is the creation of a picture using words. It is the translation of what the writer sees into what the writer wants the reader to imagine. Description has many applications in academic courses. For example, for a psychology course, you might need to describe the behavior of an autistic child. At an archaeological dig or site, you might need to indicate accurately how a section of the excavated area looks. In a botany course, you might need to describe in detail a particular plant.

Effective description depends on several characteristics:

- It conveys ideas through images that appeal to our various senses: sight, hearing, touch, smell, and taste.
- It selects and organizes details carefully in a clearly identifiable spatial ordering— left to right, top to bottom, near to far, and so forth.
- It creates a dominant impression, a special mood or feeling.
- It is objective or subjective depending on the writer's purpose, the demands of an assignment, or the expectations of an audience.

In the following paragraph from her book *Spanish Harlem,* Patricia Cayo Sexton captures the sights, sounds, and rhythms of life in New York's East Harlem:

Later, when the children return from school, the sidewalks and streets will jump with activity. Clusters of men, sitting on orange crates on the sidewalks, will play checkers or cards. The women will sit on the stoop, arms folded, and watch the young at play; and the young men, flexing their muscles, will look for some adventure. Vendors, ringing their bells, will hawk hot dogs, orange drinks, ice cream; and the caressing but often jarring noise of honking horns, music, children's games, and casual quarrels, whistles, singing, will go on late into the night. When you are in it you don't notice the noise, but when you stand away and listen to a taped conversation, the sound suddenly appears as a background roar. This loud stimulation of the senses may produce some of the emotionalism of the poor.

Narration   Telling stories—or narration—is a basic pattern of organizing your thoughts. You employ narration on a daily basis—to tell what happened at work, in the cafeteria, or on Saturday night. Narration is also essential to many forms of academic writing, ranging from history, to sociology, to science. When planning and writing narration, keep in mind the following guidelines:

1. Present the events of your narration in a logical and coherent order. Make certain that you link events through the use of appropriate transitional words.
2. Select the narrative details carefully in order to suit the purpose of the essay. Narrate only those aspects of the event that serve to illustrate and support your thesis.
3. Choose a point of view and perspective suitable for your topic and audience. Narrative point of view may be either first or third person. A first-person narrative (*I*, *we*) is suitable for stories about yourself. A third-person narrative (*he, she, it, they*) conveys stories about others. The narrative perspective you use depends on your audience and purpose. Obviously, you would use a different perspective and tone in narrating a laboratory experiment than you would narrating a soccer match you participated in.
4. Use dialogue, if appropriate to your topic, to add realism and interest to your narrative.
5. Limit the scope of the event you are narrating, and bring it to a suitable conclusion or climax.

When narration is used for informational or expository purposes, the story makes a point, illustrates a principle, or explains something. In other words, in expository narration, the event tends to serve as evidence in support of your thesis.

Here is a sample student paragraph based on narration:

Like most little girls I thought it would be very grown up to get my hair done in a beauty parlor instead of by my mother or older sister. For more than a month I cried and badgered my family. Finally, after hearing enough of my whining, my mother gave in and made an appointment for me. At the beauty parlor, I sat with my mother and a few older women, naively waiting for my transformation into another Shirley Temple. Finally the hairdresser placed me in a chair and began to chop a mass of hair onto the floor and then subject me to a burning sensation as rollers wound my remaining hair tight. The result was a classic example of the overworked permanent. At home later that day, I tried washing and rewashing my hair to remove the tangled mess. It took a week until I would see anyone without a scarf or hat over my head and a month before I could look at someone without feeling that they were making fun of me the minute I turned my back. In a way I feel that such a fruitless journey to the hairdresser actually helped me along the road to adulthood since it was a perfect example of a disappointment that only time and patience, rather than tantrums and senseless worrying, can overcome.

Narration answers the question, What happened? It can be used to tell real or fictional stories, to relate historical events, to present personal experience, or to support an analysis of events. It has broad utility in college as a critical writing skill.

Illustration   To make your paragraph or essay complete—without padding, repetition, or digression—be sure to have sufficient examples or illustrations to support key ideas. Different topics lend themselves to different types of examples or supporting evidence. Here are some types of illustration that will help you write well-developed paragraphs and essays:

- *Fact:* The Supreme Court ordered the desegregation of public schools in 1964.
- *Statistic:* A majority of schools in San Diego that were once 90 percent black are now almost 45 percent white.
- *Example:* One example of the success of San Diego's integration effort is its magnet schools.
- *Personal experience:* I attended the new computer science magnet school from 1996 to 1998. . . .
- *Quotation:* According to the *Phi Delta Kappan,* "On the first day of Los Angeles's mandatory desegregation program, 17,700 out of the total of 40,000 were not on the bus."
- *Process:* With the magnet concept, a school first creates a special theme and emphasis for its curriculum. Then it . . . .
- *Comparison and contrast:* In contrast, when Los Angeles announced its forced busing plan, an estimated 15.1 percent of the white population moved out of the system into private schools.
- *Case study:* Jamie, an eighth-grader, had seen very few black students at the Math-Science Center prior to the implementation of San Diego's desegregation plan. . . .

Illustrations develop your paragraph beyond the topic sentence. Such illustrations or examples may be short or extended. However, to make sure that your paragraphs are complete and properly developed, watch out for weak or poorly presented illustrations. For every main idea or topic sentence in a paragraph, use specific supporting evidence that sufficiently proves or amplifies your point. If you do not have the right evidence in the proper amount, your paragraph and essay will be underdeveloped, as in the following case:

The concept of choice does seem to appeal to students. On the first day of San Diego's new plan, the only people who were absent from the programs who had volunteered were those who were sick.

This two-sentence paragraph has promise but does not follow through with the main idea adequately. The concept at the heart of the topic sentence is clearer and more complete in the revised version:

The concept of choice does seem to appeal to San Diego's parents and students. On the first day of San Diego's new plan, the only people who were absent from the program who had volunteered were those who were sick. In contrast, on the first day of Los Angeles's mandatory desegregation program, 17,700 out of the total of 40,000 were not on the bus, according to the *Phi Delta Kappan*. Moreover, when Los Angeles announced its busing plan, an estimated 15.1 percent of the white population moved out of the district or into a private school. In San Diego, there was virtually no "white flight."

In the revision, the student chose to use contrasting evidence, highly specific in nature, to provide adequate support for the topic sentence. Other details and illustrative strategies might have been selected. In selecting illustrative material, you should always ask, Are there other examples that are more lively, specific, concrete, revealing, or interesting? It is not enough to just present examples. Illustration should be as effective as possible.

Process Analysis   When you describe how something works, how something is assembled, how something is done, or how something happens, you are explaining or analyzing a process. The complexity of your explanation will depend on how complex the process itself is, how detailed you want your explanation to be, and what you want your audience to be able to do or understand as a result of reading your explanation. Are you providing relatively simple how-to-do-it instructions for a relatively simple task, or are you attempting to explain a complicated laboratory experiment or computer program? The explanation of a process can make demands on your analytical and problem-solving abilities because you have to break down operations into component parts and actions. Process analysis always involves the systematic presentation of step-by-step or stage-by-stage procedures. You must show *how* the steps or parts in a process lead to its completion or resolution.

The explanation of processes is relevant to many college courses. Such topics as the stages of economic growth, Hobbes's view of the evolution of the state, the origins of the city, the development of the English lyric, the phenomenon of photosynthesis, and the history of abstract art could benefit from process analysis. Often process analysis can be combined with other writing strategies or even be subordinated to a more dominant writing strategy like narration, to which it bears a certain resemblance.

As with all other forms of mature and effective writing, you must assess your audience when writing process papers. You must decide whether you primarily want to inform or to give directions. When you give directions, you normally can assume that your audience wants to learn to do what you tell them about. If your primary purpose is to inform, you must assess the degree of interest of general readers and approach your subject from an objective perspective. Remember that there are natural, physical, mechanical, technical, mental, and historical types of processes. Certain topics might cut across these types, yet in each instance, your purpose is to direct the reader in how to do something or to inform the reader about the nature of the process.

Your analysis of a process can occur at the paragraph level, or it can control the development of an entire essay. Note how Laurence J. Peter, author of the book *The Peter Prescription*, uses process to structure the following paragraph:

> If you are inexperienced in relaxation techniques, begin by sitting in a comfortable chair with your feet on the floor and your hands resting easily in your lap. Close your eyes and breathe evenly, deeply, and gently. As you exhale each breath let your body become more relaxed. Starting with one hand direct your attention to one part of your body at a time. Close your fist and tighten the muscles of your forearm. Feel the sensation of tension in your muscles. Relax your hand and let your forearm and hand become completely limp. Direct all your attention to the sensation of relaxation as you continue to let all tension leave your hand and arm. Continue this practice once or several times each day, relaxing your other hand and arm, your legs, back, abdomen, chest, neck, face, and scalp. When you have this mastered and can relax completely, turn your thoughts to scenes of natural tranquility from your past. Stay with your

inner self as long as you wish, whether thinking of nothing or visualizing only the loveliest of images. Often you will become completely unaware of your surroundings. When you open your eyes you will find yourself refreshed in mind and body.

Peter establishes his relationship and his purpose with his audience in the very first sentence, and then offers step-by-step procedures that move readers toward a full understanding of the process. Remember that you are the expert when writing about a process and that you have to think carefully about the degree of knowledge that your audience shares.

To develop a process paper, follow these guidelines:

1. Select an appropriate topic.
2. Decide whether your primary purpose is to direct or explain.
3. Determine the knowledge gap between you and your audience.
4. Explain necessary equipment or define special terms.
5. Organize paragraphs in a complete sequence of steps.
6. Explain each step clearly and completely.
7. State results or outcomes.

Numerous subjects lend themselves to process analysis. You must decide, especially for a particular course, which topic is most appropriate and which topic you know or want to learn about the most.

Comparison and Contrast   Comparison and contrast is an analytical method organizing thought to show similarities and differences between two persons, places, things, or ideas. Comparing and contrasting comes naturally to us. If, for example, you must decide on which candidate to vote for, you might compare the party affiliations, records, and positions on issues of both candidates to find the one who best meets your expectations. Comparison and contrast serves three useful purposes in writing:

- To evaluate the relative worth or performance of two things by comparing them point for point
- To increase understanding of two familiar things by exploring them for significant similarities and differences
- To explain something unfamiliar by comparing it with something familiar

The organization of comparison-and-contrast paragraphs and essays is fairly specialized and somewhat more prescribed than other methods of writing. The following are some basic guidelines for preparing comparison-and-contrast papers.

Most important, limit your comparison to only two subjects (from here on we'll refer to them as A and B). If you attempt to work with more, you may find that your writing becomes confused. In addition, subjects A and B should be from the same category of things. You would do better, for example, to compare two jazz pianists than to compare a jazz pianist and Dixieland jazz as a whole. Moreover, there needs to be a *purpose* for your comparison. Unless you explain your purpose, the comparison, which might otherwise be structurally sound, will ultimately seem meaningless.

The organization of comparison-and-contrast papers generally follows two basic patterns, or methods: the *block method* and the *alternating method*. The block method presents all material on subject A and then all material on subject B. With the block method, each subtopic must be the same for both subjects. The alternating method presents all the material on each subtopic together, analyzing these subtopics in an AB, AB, AB pattern. Although there is no hard-and-fast rule, the alternating method is probably the best choice for most essays in order to avoid the standard pitfalls of the block method. Unless you are an experienced writer, using the block method can lead to an insufficiently developed paper, with some subtopics receiving more attention than others. It can also lead to a paper that seems like two separate essays, with a big chunk about subject A followed by a disconnected chunk about subject B. Whether you are using the block or the alternating method, follow through in an orderly manner, stating clearly the main thesis or reason for establishing the comparison, and providing clear transitions as you move from idea to idea.

Consider the following paragraph, written by a student, John Shin:

The story of Noah and the Great Flood is probably the best known story of a deluge in the Mesopotamian Valley. However, there are several other accounts of a large flood in the valley. Of these, the Akkadian story of Utnapishtim, as told by Gilgamesh, is the most interesting due to its similarities to the biblical story of Noah. Utnapishtim is a king who is forewarned of the coming of a great flood. He is advised to build an ark and does so. After many days the waters recede and Utnapishtim exits the ark and is turned into a god. The stories of Noah and Utnapishtim bear a striking resemblance in several parts: a god or gods cause a flood to punish men and women; arks, of certain dimensions, are built; animals are taken on board; birds are released to find land; and the arks come to rest on mountains. These parallels are so striking that many think the two to be the same tale.

Given the design of this paragraph, we can assume that Shin could develop body paragraphs that deal in detail with each of the key resemblances in the order they are mentioned: the coming of the flood, the building of the ark, the animals taken on board, the release of the birds, and the lodging of both arks on mountains. By employing the alternating method, he constructs a well-organized comparative framework for his analysis of the story of Noah and the story of Utnapishtim.

Causal Analysis   Frequently in college writing, you must explain the causes or effects of some event, situation, or phenomenon. This type of investigation is termed *causal analysis.* When you analyze something, you divide it into its logical parts or processes for the purpose of close examination. Thus phenomena as diverse as divorce in America, the Civil War, carcinogens in asbestos, the death of Martin Luther King Jr., or the 2010 earthquake in Haiti can be analyzed in terms of their causes and effects.

Cause-and-effect relationships are part of everyday thinking and living. Why did you select the college you now attend? Why did you stop dating Freddy or Barbara, and what effect has this decision had on your life? Why did the football team lose five straight games? You need causal analysis to explain why something occurred, to predict what will occur, and to make informed choices based on your perceptions. With causal analysis, you cannot simply tell a story, summarize an event, or describe an object or phenomenon. Instead, you must explain the *why* and *what* of a topic. The analysis of causes seeks to explain why a particular condition occurred. The analysis of effects seeks to explain what the consequences or results were, are, or will be.

Causal reasoning is common to writing in many disciplines: history, economics, politics, sociology, literature, science, education, and business, to list a few. Some essays and reports focus on causes, others on effects, and still others on both causes and effects.

Sometimes even the simplest sort of causal reasoning based on personal experience does not admit to the complete separation of causes and effects but depends instead on the recognition that causes and effects are interdependent. For example, the following paragraph from a student's sociology paper focuses on a cause-and-effect relationship:

My parents came to New York with the dream of saving enough money to return to Puerto Rico and buy a home with some land and fruit trees. Many Puerto Ricans, troubled by the problem of life on the island, find no relief in migration to New York City. They remain poor, stay in the barrio, are unable to cope with American society and way of life, and experience the destruction of their traditionally close family life. My parents were fortunate. After spending most of their lives working hard, they saved enough to return to the island. Today they tend their orange, lemon, banana, and plantain trees in an area of Puerto Rico called "El Paraíso." It took them most of a lifetime to find their paradise—in their own backyard.

Here the writer blends personal experience with a more objective analysis of causes and effects, presenting the main cause-effect relationship in the first sentence, analyzing typical effects, providing an exception to this conventional effect, and describing the result.

Sometimes you will want to focus exclusively on causes or on effects. For example, in a history course, the topic might be to analyze why World War II occurred, as this student sought to do:

It is popularly accepted that Hitler was the major cause of World War II, but the ultimate causes go much deeper than one personality. There were long-standing German grievances against reparations levied on the nation following its defeat in World War I. Moreover, there were severe economic strains that caused resentment among the German people. Compounding these problems was the French and English reluctance to work out a sound disarmament policy and American noninvolvement in the matter. Finally, there was the European fear that Communism was a much greater danger than National Socialism. All these factors contributed to the outbreak of World War II.

Note that in his attempt to explain fully the causes of an event, the writer goes beyond *immediate* causes, that is, the most evident causes that trigger the event being analyzed. He tries to identify the *ultimate* causes, the deep-rooted reasons that completely explain the problem. In order to present a sound analysis of a problem, you need to be able to trace events logically to their underlying origins. Similarly, you have to engage in strategic thinking about immediate and ultimate effects in order to explain fully an event's results.

Writing about cause-and-effect relationships demands sound critical thinking skills with attention to logic and thorough preparation for the demands of the assignment. To write effective and logical essays of causal analysis, follow these guidelines:

1. Be honest, objective, and reasonable when establishing your thesis. As a critical thinker, you have to avoid prejudices and logical fallacies, including unsupportable claims, broad generalizations and overstatements, and false relationships. (For a discussion of logical fallacies, see pages 102–103.)
2. Distinguish between causes and effects, and decide whether you plan to focus on causes, effects, or both. As a prewriting strategy, draw up a list of causes and a corresponding list of effects. You can then organize your paper around the central causes and effects.

3. Distinguish clearly between immediate and ultimate causes and effects. Explore those causes and effects that best serve the purpose of your paper and your audience's expectations.
4. Provide evidence. Do not rely on simple assertions. Statistics and testimony from reliable authorities are especially effective types of evidence to support your analysis.
5. Try to establish links between causes or effects. Seek a logical sequence of related elements, a chain of causality that helps readers understand the totality of your topic.

Ultimately, there are many ways to write about causes and effects, depending on whether you are looking for explanations, reasons, consequences, connections, results, or any combination of these elements.

Definition Concepts or general ideas often require careful definition if readers are to make sense of them or make intelligent decisions. Could you discuss supply and demand in economic theory without knowing the concept of the invisible hand? And isn't it best to know what a politician actually believes in before casting your vote? Concepts form the core of any discipline, line of inquiry, or problem. Because concepts are abstract, they may mean different things to different readers. In order to make ourselves understood, we must be able to specify their meaning in a particular context.

There are three types of definition. The simple *lexical* definition, or dictionary definition, is useful when briefly identifying concrete, commonplace, or uncontroversial terms for the reader. Many places, persons, and things can be defined in this manner. The *extended* definition is an explanation that might involve a paragraph or an entire essay. It is frequently used for abstract, complex, or controversial terms. In the *stipulative* definition, you offer a special definition of a term or set limitations on your use of the term. A solid definition, whether it is lexical, extended, or stipulative, involves describing the essential nature and characteristics of a concept that distinguish it from related ideas.

Consider the following paragraph by a student, Geeta Berrera:

The degree of loneliness that we feel can range from the mild or temporary case to a severe state which may eventually lead to depression or other psychological disorders. Being able to recognize the signs and signals of loneliness may help you to avoid it in the future. Do you find yourself unable to communicate with others? If so, you might be lonely. Do you find it difficult to put your faith in other human beings? If so, then you are setting up a situation that may be conducive to loneliness because you are preventing yourself from becoming too close to another person. Do you find yourself spending great amounts of time alone on a regular basis? Do you find that you are never invited to parties or other social events? Are you unable to love or care for another human being because you are afraid of permanent responsibilities and commitments? These are all signs and signals of either loneliness or situations that may eventually lead to loneliness. Loneliness is the feeling of sadness or grief experienced by a person at the realization that he or she lacks the companionship of other people.

Notice how Berrera introduces and emphasizes the central concept—loneliness—that is defined in this paragraph. She adds to the definition through a series of questions and answers—a strategy that permits her to analyze the qualities or manifestations of the concept. These symptoms serve as examples that reveal what is distinctive or representative about the condition of loneliness.

Definition can be used for several purposes. It may explain a difficult concept like phenomenology or a lesser-known activity like cricket. Definition can be used to identify and illustrate the special nature of a person, object, or abstract idea.

Classification Classification is a mode of critical thinking and writing based on the division of a concept into groups and subgroups, and the examination of important elements within these groups. We have generalized ideas of classes of objects that help us organize and thereby understand the world. Many of these concepts lend themselves to classification. You think and talk frequently about types of college teachers, types of cars, types of boyfriends or girlfriends, and types of movies or music. When registering for courses, you know that English is in the humanities, psychology in the social sciences, and geology in the physical sciences; you select these courses on the basis of consistent classification principles, perhaps distribution requirements or the demands of your major. What you are doing is thinking about concepts within a class, sorting out and organizing information, and often evaluating possible alternatives. Classification, in short, is a basic mode of critical thought.

As a pattern of writing, classification enables you to make sense of large and potentially complex concepts. You divide a concept into groups and subgroups, and you classify elements within categories. Assume, for instance, that your politics professor asks for an analysis of the branches of the U.S. federal government. You divide the federal government into the executive, legislative, and judicial branches, and, depending on your purpose, you subdivide even further into departments, agencies, and so forth. Then, according to some consistent principle or thesis—say, a critical look at the erosion of the division of powers—you develop information for each category reflecting common characteristics. Essentially, if you classify in a rigorous and logical way, you sort out for analysis the parts and ideas within a scheme, progressing from general to specific in your treatment of the topic.

In developing a classification essay, you also have to determine the *system* of classification that works best for the demands of the assignment. The system you select would depend to an extent on your reader's expectations and the nature of the subject. Imagine that you have been asked to write an essay on sports by a physiology teacher, a psychology teacher, or a sociology teacher. Your system might be types of sports injuries for the physiology professor, behavior patterns of tennis players for your psychology professor, or levels of violence and aggression in team sports for your sociology professor. For a broad concept like sports, there are many possible classificatory systems depending on the purpose of your paper.

Although several classification and division strategies might be appropriate for any given concept, the following guidelines should be reviewed and applied for any classification essay:

1. Think about the controlling principle for your classification. *Why* are you classifying the concept? *What* is the significance? Create a thesis statement that gives your reader a clear perspective on your classification scheme.
2. Divide the subject into major categories and subdivide categories consistently. Make certain that you isolate all important categories and that these categories do not overlap excessively.
3. Arrange the classification scheme in an effective, emphatic order—as a chronology, in spatial terms, in order of importance, or from simple to complex.
4. Present and analyze each category in a clear sequence, proceeding through the categories until the classification scheme is complete.

5. Define or explain any difficult concepts within each category, providing relevant details and evidence.
6. Combine classification with other appropriate writing strategies—comparison and contrast, process analysis, definition, and so forth.

Examine the following student paragraph:

To many people, fishing is finding a "fishy-looking" spot, tossing a hooked worm into the water, and hoping that a hungry fish just happens to be nearby. Anyone who has used this haphazard method can attest to the fact that failures usually outnumber successes. The problem with the "bait and wait" method is that it is very limited. The bait has less chance of encountering a fish than it would if it were presented in different areas of water. A more intelligent approach to fishing is to use the knowledge that at any given moment fish can be in three parts of a lake. Assuming that a lake has fish, anglers will find them on the surface, in the middle, or on the bottom of the lake. Fishing each of these areas involves the use of a separate technique. By fishing the surface, fishing the middle, or fishing the bottom, you greatly increase the chances of catching a fish.

This example is the student's introductory paragraph to a classification essay that blends description, process analysis, comparison and contrast, and the use of evidence to excellent effect. From the outset, however, the reader knows that this will be a classification essay.

Argumentation   Argumentation is a form of critical thinking in which you try to convince an audience to accept your position on a topic or persuade members of this audience to act in a certain way. In a sense, everything is an argument, for much of what you read and write, see and hear, is designed to elicit a desired response. Whether reading texts, viewing various media forms, or listening to the spoken word (especially of politicians), you know that just about anything is potentially debatable.

Argumentation in writing, however, goes beyond ordinary disagreements. With an argumentative essay, your purpose is to convince or persuade readers in a logical, reasonable, and appealing way. In other words, with formal argumentation, you must distinguish mere personal opinion from opinions based on reasons derived from solid evidence. An argumentative essay has special features and even step-by-step processes that will be treated in greater detail in Chapter 3. For now, it is worth noting that solid argumentative writing can combine many of the forms and purposes that have been discussed in this chapter. Your understanding of such forms and purposes of discourse as narration, illustration, analysis, and comparison and contrast, and the ways these strategies can combine in powerful ways, will help you compose solid argumentative essays.

Above all, with argumentation, you must develop what Virginia Woolf called "some fierce attachment to an idea." Once you commit yourself to a viewpoint on a topic or issue, you will find it easy to bring an argumentative edge to your writing. Consider the following excerpt from a well-known essay by Caroline Bird that begins with the provocative title "College Is a Waste of Time and Money":

A great majority of our 9 million college students are in school not because they want to be or because they want to learn. They are there because it has become the thing to do or because college is a pleasant place to be; because it's the only way they can get parents or taxpayers to support them without working at a job they don't like; because Mother wanted them to go, or some other reason entirely irrelevant to the course of studies for which college is supposedly organized.

Clearly, Bird's claim has that argumentative edge you encounter in essays designed to convince readers of a particular viewpoint or position on an issue. Do you agree or disagree with Bird's claim? How would you respond to her assertions? What evidence would you provide to support your claim?

Argumentation is a powerful way to tap into the aspirations, values, and conduct of your audience. It makes demands on readers and writers to do something, believe something, or even become somebody different—say, a more tolerant person or a more active citizen. True, argument can provoke conflict, but it can also resolve it. In fact, many experts today emphasize the value of argument in solving problems and defusing or managing conflicts.

At the outset of any argument process, you must recognize that you have a problem to solve and decisions to make. Problem solving often is at the heart of argumentation; it is a process in which situations, issues, and questions are analyzed and debated, and decisions arrived at. The basic steps to problem solving in argumentation are these:

1. Define and analyze the problem. Examine all available information to identify the problem precisely.
2. Interpret the facts and review alternative approaches.
3. Make a claim or a decision—that is, assert the best course of action.
4. Implement the decision in order to persuade or convince your audience that the problem has been addressed and solved.
5. Evaluate the outcome in follow-up documents.

At times, it will be hard to diagnose a problem and find solutions for it. At other times, there is no ideal solution to a problem. Argumentation is not a simple academic exercise but rather an indispensable tool in personal and professional situations. It is indispensable in addressing increasingly complex political, economic, social, and technological trends on both a domestic and a global scale. Moreover, argument can produce ethically constructive and socially responsible results. Argument makes special demands on a writer that will be treated comprehensively in Chapter 3.

Writing End Paragraphs

If an essay does not have a strong, appropriate ending, it may leave the reader feeling confused or dissatisfied, with the sense that the intention and promises built up in earlier parts of the essay have not been fulfilled. In contrast, an effective closing paragraph leaves the reader with the impression that the essay is complete and satisfying.

The techniques that follow permit you to end your essay emphatically and with grace:

- Use a full-circle pattern by echoing or repeating a phrase, idea, or detail that you presented in your introductory paragraph.
- State your conclusions, proofs, or theories based on the facts and supporting ideas of the essay. This strategy works especially well in papers for social science, science, and philosophy courses.

- Show the outcome or effects of the facts and ideas of the essay.
- Suggest a solution as a way to clarify your position on the problem you have discussed.
- Ask a question that sums up the main point of the essay.
- Offer an anecdote, allusion, or lighthearted point that sums up your thesis.
- Use a quotation that supports your main point or illuminates an aspect of the topic.

Other basic ways to end an essay include restating your thesis and main points, calling for action, providing a final summary evaluation, and looking at future consequences based on the essay's analysis or argument. A closing, like your introduction, should be brief. It is your one last attempt at clarity, your one last chance to illuminate your topic.

Student Essay

Here is the essay that Jamie Taylor wrote in response to Schlesinger's "The Cult of Ethnicity." Consider the strategies that she used to make her composing process a success.

Jamie Taylor
Humanities 101, sec. 008
Professor Fred Segal
4 November 2009

Cultist Behavior or Doltish Behavior?

The introductory paragraph presents Schlesinger's main argument, amplifies Schlesinger's inferred claims, and then presents the writer's counterargument.

In Schlesinger's "The Cult of Ethnicity," the author warns that there are forces at work within our nation that undermine our principles of democracy. These forces come in the guise of individuals and groups who claim that they know what's right for the people whom they represent. Although he doesn't mention them all specifically, one can infer he means that certain leaders from the African American community, the Latino community, the Native American community, the Asian community, and so forth are advocating strong identification within groups to keep their identities alive since they claim Eurocentric culture has had a history of stealing and suppressing their own historic roots. But Schlesinger seems to fear that only divisiveness can result. In this regard, he does not give the individual enough credit. Rather than have a paternalistic attitude about what he fears these groups are doing, he should give more credit to the members of these groups to be able to discern which messages regarding ethnicity to accept as being benign and which to reject as being downright silly.

Take, for example, the many clubs in the average college or university. Nearly every ethnic group is represented by one of these organizations. For example, my university has many groups that represent African Americans, Latinos, Asians, Native Americans, even subgroups like the Korean Society, the

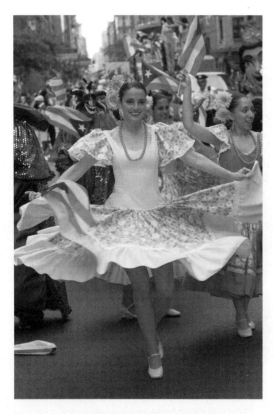

Fig. 1. During the Puerto Rican Parade, participants share some cultural traditions and fashions with the community.

Chinese Student Association, and so on. Belonging to these groups gives students a healthy place to socialize, discuss common areas of interest and concern, and assist with community outreach. For example, many of these clubs sponsor programs to give demonstrations of cultural traditions such as cooking, dance, clothing, and so on to civic and business groups. They also assist the needy in gaining access to social services, particularly for shut-ins and the elderly who may not speak English. Also, there is strength in numbers, and the fact that these clubs are popular attests to the fact that they tolerate a range of ideas so that no one "ideology" is promoted over another. Besides, if that were to happen, it is the right of the organization to vote a person out of office or membership. To say that these clubs promote divisiveness would be like saying that the Newman Society for Catholic students or Hillel House for Jewish students promotes religious intolerance.

Second, self-styled leaders of various racial and ethnic groups—in their efforts to be divisive—actually help people to see through their rhetoric, or at least, to apply only that which is

The first body paragraph presents Taylor's first point supported with evidence and examples.

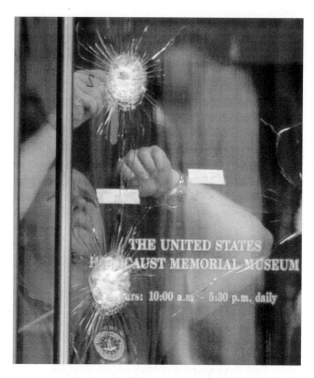

Fig. 2. On June 9, 2009, a security guard at the Holocaust museum in Washington, D.C. was shot and killed by a white supremacist and known Holocaust denier who entered the museum wielding a rifle and began shooting.

The second point offers a unique slant on divisive ethnic and racial leaders and the ability of Americans to reject their claims. Again, specific examples and evidence buttress Taylor's argument.

reasonable and reject that which is intolerable. Because of today's media, such leaders cannot "hide" their views and thus can become their own worst enemies when presenting them in front of a national audience. For example, Louis Farrakhan has not only alienated Jewish individuals owing to his open anti-Semitism, and many among the gay population for his antigay sentiments, but many African Americans as well, particularly women, who often condemn him for his patriarchal views regarding the family and society. A simple proof of his lack of power is the fact that he has been presenting these antidemocratic ideals for decades now, and there is little evidence that anyone is listening to them. Another example is the late Rabbi Meyer Kahane, who advocated the expulsion of all Arabs from Israel. An open opponent of democracy, he was condemned by Jewish leaders in the United States to the point where he was shunned from any discussion regarding religious issues.

The writer's third and final point encompasses a variety of "antidemocratic" groups and rejects their "postures."

Finally, one can feel confident that even within the margins of mainstream white America, cultist groups are their own worst enemy. Take for example, the various groups of survivalists (primarily white Americans), white extremists and separatists, antigay groups, and radical anti-abortionists. The philosophy and tactics of these organizations are condemned by the vast majority of Americans owing to their antidemocratic postures, not to mention their often violent, even murderous activities. They may capture the headlines for a while, but they will never capture the hearts of Americans so long as we stay true to the "measures and laws" that Washington spoke of in his discussion with John Adams.

In conclusion, the open democratic society we have created is just too strong a force to be weakened or undermined by "romantic ideologies" or "unscrupulous con men" as Schlesinger puts it. Mr. Schlesinger has little to worry about. Just look around your school or university cafeteria. There's no white section or Latino section or Asian section: Nowadays, it's just one big American section.

> The conclusion returns to Schlesinger, while recapitulating Taylor's main points.

REVISING

Revising—the rethinking and rewriting of material—takes place during every stage of the composing process. It is integral to the quest for clarity and meaning. "Writing and rewriting are a constant search for what one's saying," declares celebrated American author John Updike. Similarly, the famous essayist E. B. White admits, "I rework a lot to make it clear." If these two great prose stylists revise material in order to seek clarity for their ideas, then you too should adopt the professional attitude that you can improve what you first say or think and what you first put down on paper. In fact, one trait that distinguishes experienced from inexperienced writers is that the experienced writers understand fully the need to revise.

Revision is an art. It is the only way to make your writing match the vision of what you want to accomplish. Whether at word, sentence, paragraph, or essay level, you should develop a repertoire of choices that will permit you to solve writing problems and sharpen your ideas. You might also share your draft with another reader who can let you know what is or is not working and give you suggestions for improvement. To make the process of revision worthwhile, you should ask yourself the following questions during your prewriting and drafting activities (you can also give these questions to your reader):

- Is the essay long enough (or too long) to meet the demands of the assignment?
- Is the topic suitable for the assignment?
- Do you have a clear thesis statement?
- Does your writing make sense? Are you communicating with your reader instead of just with yourself?
- Have you included everything that is important to the development of your thesis or argument?
- Is there anything you should discard?
- Do you offer enough examples or evidence to support your key ideas?
- Have you ordered and developed paragraphs logically?
- Do you have a clear beginning, middle, and end?

Once you have answered these questions, you will be able to judge the extent to which you have to revise your first draft.

Proofreading

Proofreading is part of the revision process. You do not have final copy until you have carefully checked your essay for mistakes and inconsistencies. Proofreading differs from the sort of revision that moves you from an initial draft to subsequent versions of an essay in that it does not offer the opportunity to make major changes in content or organization. It does give you a last chance to correct typos and other minor errors that arise from carelessness, haste, or inaccuracy during the writing process.

When you proofread, do so word by word and line by line. Concentrate on spelling, punctuation, grammar, mechanics, and paragraph form. Read each sentence aloud—from the computer screen or a printed hard copy. If something sounds or looks wrong to you, consult a handbook, dictionary, or other reference work. Then make corrections accordingly.

Here are some basic guidelines for proofreading your essay:

1. Check the title. Are words capitalized properly?
2. Check all words in the essay that should be capitalized.
3. Check the spelling of any word you are uncertain about.
4. Check the meaning of any word you think you might have misused.
5. Check to see if you have unintentionally omitted or repeated any words.
6. Check paragraph form. Have you indented each paragraph?
7. Check to make certain you have smooth, grammatically correct sentences. This is your last chance to eliminate awkward and grammatically incorrect sentences.
8. Check to make sure your paper follows your professor's formatting guidelines, such as appropriate margins, font size, and documentation style (see Chapter 4 for more on documentation).

Responding to Editorial Comments

Even when you submit what you *think* is the final version of your essay, your teacher might not agree that the essay has reached its best possible form. Teachers are experienced in detecting essays' strengths and weaknesses, pinpointing mistakes, and suggesting how material can be improved. Their comments are not attacks; they do want you to pay attention to them, to recognize and correct errors, and possibly to revise your essay once again—most likely for a higher grade. If you receive editorial comment in an objective manner and respond to it constructively, you will become a more effective writer.

When reading your essays, your instructor will use standard correction symbols that appear in English handbooks. He or she will make additional comments in the margins and compose an overall assessment of the paper at the end. Any worthwhile comment on your paper will blend supportive observations with constructive criticism. Often your instructor will offer concrete suggestions for revision. When you receive a graded paper, you typically are expected to make the necessary revisions and either add it to your portfolio or resubmit the essay.

Ultimately, refinement is integral to the entire writing process. From reading materials that you confront at the outset and respond to in various ways, you move through many composing stages to create a finished product. In *The Field of Vision*, the American novelist and critic Wright Morris refers to the important task of refinement that confronts the writer: "By raw material, I mean that comparatively crude ore that has not yet been processed by the imagination—what we refer to as *life*, or as experience, in contrast to art. By technique I mean the way the artist smelts this material down for human consumption." Your best writing is the result of this smelting process, which involves the many strategies covered in this introduction that are designed to help you acquire greater control over the art of critical reading and writing.

Three Brief Essays on Writing and Communication

Freewriting

Peter Elbow

Peter Elbow (b. 1935) was born in New York and received degrees from Williams College, Exeter College, Oxford, and Brandeis University. He has taught at the University of Massachusetts at Amherst, the State University of New York at Stony Brook, the Massachusetts Institute of Technology, Franconia College, and Evergreen State College. He is considered by some writing teachers to have revolutionized the teaching of writing through his popularization of the concept and practice called "freewriting." He is the author or editor of more than 15 books on writing, including Writing without Teachers, Writing with Power, Embracing Contraries, What Is English? *and, most recently,* Everyone Can Write: Essays toward a Hopeful Theory of Writing and Teaching Writing *(2000). In "Freewriting," taken from* Writing without Teachers, *Elbow explains an exercise for writing students that he helped popularize in American colleges, universities, and writing workshops.*

The most effective way I know to improve your writing is to do freewriting 1 exercises regularly. At least three times a week. They are sometimes called "automatic writing," "babbling," or "jabbering" exercises. The idea is simply to write for ten minutes (later on, perhaps fifteen or twenty). Don't stop for anything. Go quickly without rushing. Never stop to look back, to cross something out, to wonder how to spell something, to wonder what word or thought to use, or to think about what you are doing. If you can't think of a

From Peter Elbow, *Writing without Teachers*, 2nd ed., pp. 3–7. Copyright © 1973, 1998 by Oxford University Press, Inc. By permission of Oxford University Press, Inc.

word or a spelling, just use a squiggle or else write, "I can't think of it." Just put down something. The easiest thing is just to put down whatever is in your mind. If you get stuck it's fine to write "I can't think what to say, I can't think what to say" as many times as you want; or repeat the last word you wrote over and over again; or anything else. The only requirement is that you *never* stop.

2   What happens to a freewriting exercise is important. It must be a piece of writing which, even if someone reads it, doesn't send any ripples back to you. It is like writing something and putting it in a bottle in the sea. The teacherless class helps your writing by providing maximum feedback. Freewritings help you by providing no feedback at all. When I assign one, I invite the writer to let me read it. But also tell him to keep it if he prefers. I read it quickly and make no comments at all and I do not speak with him about it. The main thing is that a freewriting must never be evaluated in any way; in fact there must be no discussion or comment at all.

3   Here is an example of a fairly coherent exercise (sometimes they are very incoherent, which is fine):

> I think I'll write what's on my mind, but the only thing on my mind right now is what to write for ten minutes. I've never done this before and I'm not prepared in any way—the sky is cloudy today, how's that? now I'm afraid I won't be able to think of what to write when I get to the end of the sentence—well, here I am at the end of the sentence—here I am again, again, again, again, at least I'm still writing—Now I ask is there some reason to be happy that I'm still writing—ah yes! Here comes the question again—What am I getting out of this? What point is there in it? It's almost obscene to always ask it but I seem to question everything that way and I was gonna say something else pertaining to that but I got so busy writing down the first part that I forgot what I was leading into. This is kind of fun oh don't stop writing—cars and trucks speeding by somewhere out the window, pens clittering across people's papers. The sky is cloudy—is it symbolic that I should be mentioning it? Huh? I dunno. Maybe I should try colors, blue, red, dirty words—wait a minute—no can't do that, orange, yellow, arm tired, green pink violet magenta lavender red brown black green— now that I can't think of any more colors—just about done—relief? maybe.

Freewriting may seem crazy but actually it makes simple sense. Think of the difference between speaking and writing. Writing has the advantage of permitting more editing. But that's its downfall too. Almost everybody interposes a massive and complicated series of editings between the time words start to be born into consciousness and when they finally come off the end of the pencil or typewriter onto the page. This is partly because schooling makes us obsessed with the "mistakes" we make in writing. Many people are constantly thinking about spelling and grammar as they try to write. I am always thinking about the awkwardness, wordiness, and general mushiness of my natural verbal product as I try to write down words.

4   But it's not just "mistakes" or "bad writing" we edit as we write. We also edit unacceptable thoughts and feelings, as we do in speaking. In writing there is more time to do it so the editing is heavier: when speaking, there's someone

right there waiting for a reply and he'll get bored or think we're crazy if we don't come out with *something*. Most of the time in speaking, we settle for the catch-as-catch-can way in which the words tumble out. In writing, however, there's a chance to try to get them right. But the opportunity to get them right is a terrible burden: you can work for two hours trying to get a paragraph "right" and discover it's not right at all. And then give up.

Editing, *in itself,* is not the problem. Editing is usually necessary if we want 5 to end up with something satisfactory. The problem is that editing goes on *at the same time* as producing. The editor is, as it were, constantly looking over the shoulder of the producer and constantly fiddling with what he's doing while he's in the middle of trying to do it. No wonder the producer gets nervous, jumpy, inhibited, and finally can't be coherent. It's an unnecessary burden to try to think of words and also worry at the same time whether they're the right words.

The main thing about freewriting is that it is *nonediting*. It is an exercise in 6 bringing together the process of producing words and putting them down on the page. Practiced regularly, it undoes the ingrained habit of editing at the same time you are trying to produce. It will make writing less blocked because words will come more easily. You will use up more paper, but chew up fewer pencils.

Next time you write, notice how often you stop yourself from writing 7 down something you were going to write down. Or else cross it out after it's written. "Naturally," you say, "it wasn't any good." But think for a moment about the occasions when you spoke well. Seldom was it because you first got the beginning just right. Usually it was a matter of a halting or even garbled beginning, but you kept going and your speech finally became coherent and even powerful. There is a lesson here for writing: trying to get the beginning just right is a formula for failure—and probably a secret tactic to make yourself give up writing. Make some words, whatever they are, and then grab hold of that line and reel in as hard as you can. Afterwards you can throw away lousy beginnings and make new ones. This is the quickest way to get into good writing.

The habit of compulsive, premature editing doesn't just make writing hard. 8 It also makes writing dead. Your voice is damped out by all the interruptions, changes, and hesitations between the consciousness and the page. In your natural way of producing words there is a sound, a texture, a rhythm—a voice— which is the main source of power in your writing. I don't know how it works, but this voice is the force that will make a reader listen to you, the energy that drives the meanings through his thick skull. Maybe you don't *like* your voice; maybe people have made fun of it. But it's the only voice you've got. It's your only source of power. You better get back into it, no matter what you think of it. If you keep writing in it, it may change into something you like better. But if you abandon it, you'll likely never have a voice and never be heard.

Freewritings are vacuums. Gradually you will begin to carry over into your 9 regular writing some of the voice, force, and connectedness that creep into those vacuums.

COMPREHENSION

1. What is the thesis of the essay? Is it implied or stated directly in the text?
2. In paragraph 5, Elbow refers to the "producer" and the "editor." Who are they? Where are they located? How did they develop?
3. In paragraph 8, the author makes a connection between one's personal "voice" and the idea of "power." Why does Elbow focus so strongly on this connection?

RHETORIC

1. Elbow frequently uses the "imperative" (or command) sentence form in the opening paragraph. Why? What would have been the effect had he used the simple declarative form?
2. Writers often use examples to help illustrate their point. Does the example of a freewriting exercise Elbow provides in paragraph 3 help you to understand the method? Why or why not?
3. The author uses colloquial terms such as "squiggle" (paragraph 1), "crazy" and "mushiness" (paragraph 3), and "lousy" (paragraph 7). How does his use of such words affect the tone of the essay?
4. Are there any elements in Elbow's own style that suggest his essay may have started as a freewriting exercise? Consider the reasons he provides for the importance of freewriting—for example, generating ideas, discovering one's own voice, or expressing oneself succinctly and naturally.
5. Elbow is himself a college writing teacher. Based on your assessment of the tone of the essay, whom do you think is his intended audience? Is it broad or narrow? Specialized or general? Or could he have in mind more than one type of audience? Explain your answer.
6. Note the number of times Elbow begins his sentences with coordinating conjunctions ("but," "and," "or"). For example, in paragraph 4, he does it three times. Many writing teachers frown on this method of structuring sentences. Why does Elbow employ it?
7. Compare the essay's introduction to its conclusion. Note how the introduction is rather long and the conclusion is quite short (two sentences, in fact). How do these two elements contribute to the overall "pace" of the essay?

WRITING

1. During one week, complete three freewriting exercises. Wait one week, and then review what you have written. Explore any insights your freewriting gives you into your writer's "voice"— your concerns, interests, style, and "power."
2. Write an expository paper explaining the difficulties you have when writing an essay homework assignment or writing an essay-length response during an exam.
3. Write a comparison and contrast essay wherein you examine the similarities and differences of speaking and writing.
4. **Writing an Argument:** Write an essay in which you support or discourage the act of freewriting.

NETWORKING
Applying 21st-Century Literacies

Paper vs. Screen: When freewriting, do you prefer to do so on paper or on your computer? In a paragraph, discuss what you see as two or three key advantages to your preferred way of freewriting, acknowledging (and rebutting) at least one anticipated counterargument.

The Maker's Eye: Revising Your Own Manuscripts

Donald M. Murray

Donald M. Murray (1917–2006) combined a career as teacher, journalist, fiction writer, poet, and author of several important textbooks on writing. He worked as a teacher, journalist, and editor for Time *magazine. His books include* A Writer Teaches Writing, Write to Learn, Read to Write, *and more recently* Shoptalk: Learning to Write with Writers *(1991),* Crafting a Life in Essay, Story, Poem *(1996), and* The Craft of Revision *(1997). In this essay, originally published in the magazine* The Writer, *Murray argues for the absolute importance of the revision process to the writer. As he presents the stages of the revision process, Murray illustrates their usefulness to any writer—whether beginner or experienced—and offers his personal views and those of other authors.*

When students complete a first draft, they consider the job of writing done— 1 and their teachers too often agree. When professional writers complete a first draft, they usually feel that they are at the start of the writing process. When a draft is completed, the job of writing can begin.

That difference in attitude is the difference between amateur and profes- 2 sional, inexperience and experience, journeyman and craftsman. Peter F. Drucker, the prolific business writer, calls his first draft "the zero draft"—after that he can start counting. Most writers share the feeling that the first draft, and all of those which follow, are opportunities to discover what they have to say and how best they can say it.

To produce a progression of drafts, each of which says more and says it 3 more clearly, the writer has to develop a special kind of reading skill. In school we are taught to decode what appears on the page as finished writing. Writers, however, face a different category of possibility and responsibility when they read their own drafts. To them the words on the page are never finished. Each can be changed and rearranged, can set off a chain reaction of confusion or clarified meaning. This is a different kind of reading, which is possibly more difficult and certainly more exciting.

4   Writers must learn to be their own best enemy. They must accept the criticism of others and be suspicious of it; they must accept the praise of others and be even more suspicious of it. Writers cannot depend on others. They must detach themselves from their own pages so that they can apply both their caring and their craft to their own work.

5   Such detachment is not easy. Science fiction writer Ray Bradbury supposedly puts each manuscript away for a year to the day and then rereads it as a stranger. Not many writers have the discipline or the time to do this. We must read when our judgment may be at its worst, when we are close to the euphoric moment of creation.

6   Then the writer, counsels novelist Nancy Hale, "should be critical of everything that seems to him most delightful in his style. He should excise what he most admires, because he wouldn't thus admire it if he weren't . . . in a sense protecting it from criticism." John Ciardi, the poet, adds, "The last act of the writing must be to become one's own reader. It is, I suppose, a schizophrenic process, to begin passionately and to end critically, to begin hot and to end cold; and, more important, to be passion-hot and critic-cold at the same time."

7   Most people think that the principal problem is that writers are too proud of what they have written. Actually, a greater problem for most professional writers is one shared by the majority of students. They are overly critical, think everything is dreadful, tear up page after page, never complete a draft, see the task as hopeless.

8   The writer must learn to read critically but constructively, to cut what is bad, to reveal what is good. Eleanor Estes, the children's book author, explains: "The writer must survey his work critically, coolly, as though he were a stranger to it. He must be willing to prune, expertly and hard-heartedly. At the end of each revision, a manuscript may look . . . worked over, torn apart, pinned together, added to, deleted from, words changed and words changed back. Yet the book must maintain its original freshness and spontaneity."

9   Most readers underestimate the amount of rewriting it usually takes to produce spontaneous reading. This is a great disadvantage to the student writer, who sees only a finished product and never watches the craftsman who takes the necessary step back, studies the work carefully, returns to the task, steps back, returns, steps back, again and again. Anthony Burgess, one of the most prolific writers in the English-speaking world, admits, "I might revise a page twenty times." Roald Dahl, the popular children's writer, states, "By the time I'm nearing the end of a story, the first part will have been reread and altered and corrected at least 150 times. . . . Good writing is essentially rewriting. I am positive of this."

10   Rewriting isn't virtuous. It isn't something that ought to be done. It is simply something that most writers find they have to do to discover what they have to say and how to say it. It is a condition of the writer's life.

There are, however, a few writers who do little formal rewriting, primarily 11 because they have the capacity and experience to create and review a large number of invisible drafts in their minds before they approach the page. And some writers slowly produce finished pages, performing all the tasks of revision simultaneously, page by page, rather than draft by draft. But it is still possible to see the sequence followed by most writers most of the time in rereading their own work.

Most writers scan their drafts first, reading as quickly as possible to catch 12 the larger problems of subject and form, then move in closer and closer as they read and write, reread and rewrite.

The first thing writers look for in their drafts is *information.* They know that 13 a good piece of writing is built from specific, accurate, and interesting information. The writer must have an abundance of information from which to construct a readable piece of writing.

Next writers look for *meaning* in the information. The specifics must build a 14 pattern of significance. Each piece of specific information must carry the reader toward meaning.

Writers reading their own drafts are aware of *audience.* They put themselves 15 in the reader's situation and make sure that they deliver information which a reader wants to know or needs to know in a manner which is easily digested. Writers try to be sure that they anticipate and answer the questions a critical reader will ask when reading the piece of writing.

Writers make sure that the *form* is appropriate to the subject and the audi- 16 ence. Form, or genre, is the vehicle which carries meaning to the reader, but form cannot be selected until the writer has adequate information to discover its significance and an audience which needs or wants that meaning.

Once writers are sure the form is appropriate, they must then look at the 17 *structure,* the order of what they have written. Good writing is built on a solid framework of logic, argument, narrative, or motivation which runs through the entire piece of writing and holds it together. This is the time when many writers find it most effective to outline as a way of visualizing the hidden spine by which the piece of writing is supported.

The element on which writers may spend a majority of their time is *develop-* 18 *ment.* Each section of a piece of writing must be adequately developed. It must give readers enough information so that they are satisfied. How much information is enough? That's as difficult as asking how much garlic belongs in a salad. It must be done to taste, but most beginning writers underdevelop, underestimating the reader's hunger for information.

As writers solve development problems, they often have to consider ques- 19 tions of *dimension.* There must be a pleasing and effective proportion among all the parts of the piece of writing. There is a continual process of subtracting and adding to keep the piece of writing in balance.

Finally, writers have to listen to their own voices. *Voice* is the force which 20 drives a piece of writing forward. It is an expression of the writer's authority and concern. It is what is between the words on the page, what glues the piece of writing together. A good piece of writing is always marked by a consistent, individual voice.

21   As writers read and reread, write and rewrite, they move closer and closer to the page until they are doing line-by-line editing. Writers read their own pages with infinite care. Each sentence, each line, each clause, each phrase, each word, each mark of punctuation, each section of white space between the type has to contribute to the clarification of meaning.

22   Slowly the writer moves from word to word, looking through language to see the subject. As a word is changed, cut, or added, as a construction is rearranged, all the words used before that moment and all those that follow that moment must be considered and reconsidered.

23   Writers often read aloud at this stage of the editing process, muttering or whispering to themselves, calling on the ear's experience with language. Does this sound right—or that? Writers edit, shifting back and forth from eye to page to ear to page. I find I must do this careful editing in short runs, no more than fifteen or twenty minutes at a stretch, or I become too kind with myself. I begin to see what I hope is on the page, not what actually is on the page.

24   This sounds tedious if you haven't done it, but actually it is fun. Making something right is immensely satisfying, for writers begin to learn what they are writing about by writing. Language leads them to meaning, and there is the joy of discovery, of understanding, of making meaning clear as the writer employs the technical skills of language.

25   Words have double meanings, even triple and quadruple meanings. Each word has its own potential for connotation and denotation. And when writers rub one word against the other, they are often rewarded with a sudden insight, an unexpected clarification.

26   The maker's eye moves back and forth from word to phrase to sentence to paragraph to sentence to phrase to word. The maker's eye sees the need for variety and balance, for a firmer structure, for a more appropriate form. It peers into the interior of the paragraph, looking for coherence, unity, and emphasis, which make meaning clear.

27   I learned something about this process when my first bifocals were prescribed. I had ordered a larger section of the reading portion of the glass because of my work, but even so, I could not contain my eyes within this new limit of vision. And I still find myself taking off my glasses and bending my nose towards the page, for my eyes unconsciously flick back and forth across the page, back to another page, forward to still another, as I try to see each evolving line in relation to every other line.

28   When does this process end? Most writers agree with the great Russian writer Tolstoy, who said, "I scarcely ever reread my published writings, if by chance I come across a page, it always strikes me: all this must be rewritten; this is how I should have written it."

29   The maker's eye is never satisfied, for each word has the potential to ignite new meaning. This article has been twice written all the way through the writing process, and it was published four years ago. Now it is to be republished in

a book. The editors make a few small suggestions, and then I read it with my maker's eye. Now it has been re-edited, re-revised, re-read, re-re-edited, for each piece of writing to the writer is full of potential and alternatives.

A piece of writing is never finished. It is delivered to a deadline, torn out of 30 the typewriter on demand, sent off with a sense of accomplishment and shame and pride and frustration. If only there were a couple more days, time for just another run at it, perhaps then . . .

COMPREHENSION

1. In paragraph 1, what does Murray mean by the statement "When a draft is completed, the job of writing can begin"? Isn't a draft a form of writing?
2. According to Murray, what are the major differences between student and professional writers? Why do the differences help make the "professional" more accomplished at his or her work?
3. What are the differences between the reading styles of novice and experienced writers? How do the differences affect their own writings?

RHETORIC

1. Compare the introduction of this essay to that of Elbow's "Freewriting." How do they differ in tone and structure?
2. Murray begins to classify various aspects of the writer's concern in paragraph 13. Why does he wait so long to begin this analysis? Why are certain key words in paragraphs 13–20 italicized?
3. Murray uses analogy, comparing one thing with another, very different thing, to make the writing process concrete and familiar. Identify some of these analogies. Why are they models of clarity?
4. Murray refers to a writer as "the maker" several times in the essay. What does he imply by this usage? What other professions might be included in this category?
5. What is the purpose of the essay? Is it to inform? To persuade? To serve as a model? Anything else? Explain your response.
6. Murray ends the essay with an ellipses. Why?
7. Notice the sentence in paragraph 29 that has four consecutive words with the prefix "re-." What is the purpose and effect of this rhetorical device?

WRITING

1. Murray focuses on the process, craft, and purpose of the writer, but he does not define "writer." Write an extended definition explaining what he means by this occupation or profession.
2. Write an essay explaining your own writing process. Do not be intimidated if it is not like the one described by Murray. Compare and contrast your method with that of one or more of your classmates.
3. **Writing an Argument:** Murray suggests that revision is actually "fun" (paragraph 24). Do you agree or disagree? Write an essay defending your position.

NETWORKING
Applying 21st-Century Literacies

Redefining *Writer:* After completing question 1 under Writing, write a new definition for *writer* that takes into account the changing technologies and mediums we work in today. Compare and contrast this definition with the one Murray's essay suggests.

Sex, Lies and Conversation: Why Is It So Hard for Men and Women to Talk to Each Other?

Deborah Tannen

Deborah Tannen (b. 1945), born in Brooklyn, New York, holds a PhD in linguistics from the University of California at Berkeley. She is University Professor and Professor of Linguistics at Georgetown University. Tannen published numerous specialized articles and books on language and linguistics before becoming nationally known as a best-selling author. She publishes regularly in such magazines as Vogue *and* New York, *and her book* That's Not What I Meant: How Conversational Style Makes or Breaks Your Relations with Others *(1986) drew national attention to her work on interpersonal communication. Her other popular books on communication include* You Just Don't Understand: Women and Men in Conversation *(1990),* Talking from 9 to 5: How Women's and Men's Conversational Styles Affect Who Gets Heard, Who Gets Credit, and What Gets Done at Work *(1994), and* I Only Say This Because I Love You: How the Way We Talk Can Make or Break Family Relationships Throughout Our Lives *(2001). The following essay was published in the* Washington Post *in 1990.*

1   I was addressing a small gathering in a suburban Virginia living room—a women's group that had invited men to join them. Throughout the evening, one man had been particularly talkative, frequently offering ideas and anecdotes, while his wife sat silently beside him on the couch. Toward the end of the evening, I commented that women frequently complain that their husbands don't talk to them. This man quickly concurred. He gestured toward his wife and said, "She's the talker in our family." The room burst into laughter; the man looked puzzled and hurt. "It's true," he explained. "When I come home from work I have nothing to say. If she didn't keep the conversation going, we'd spend the whole evening in silence."

This episode crystallizes the irony that although American men tend to talk 2
more than women in public situations, they often talk less at home. And this
pattern is wreaking havoc with marriage.

The pattern was observed by political scientist Andrew Hacker in the late 3
'70s. Sociologist Catherine Kohler Riessman reports in her new book *Divorce
Talk* that most of the women she interviewed—but only a few of the men—gave
lack of communication as the reason for their divorces. Given the current divorce rate of nearly 50 percent, that amounts to millions of cases in the United
States every year—a virtual epidemic of failed conversation.

In my own research, complaints from women about their husbands most 4
often focused not on tangible inequities such as having given up the chance for
a career to accompany a husband to his, or doing far more than their share of
daily life-support work like cleaning, cooking, social arrangements and errands. Instead, they focused on communication: "He doesn't listen to me," "He
doesn't talk to me." I found, as Hacker observed years before, that most wives
want their husbands to be, first and foremost, conversational partners, but few
husbands share this expectation of their wives.

In short, the image that best represents the current crisis is the stereotypical 5
cartoon scene of a man sitting at the breakfast table with a newspaper held up
in front of his face, while a woman glares at the back of it, wanting to talk.

Linguistic Battle of the Sexes

How can women and men have such different impressions of communication in 6
marriage? Why the widespread imbalance in their interests and expectations?

In the April [1990] issue of *American Psychologist,* Stanford University's 7
Eleanor Maccoby reports the results of her own and others' research showing
that children's development is most influenced by the social structure of peer
interactions. Boys and girls tend to play with children of their own gender,
and their sex-separate groups have different organizational structures and
interactive norms.

I believe these systematic differences in childhood socialization make talk 8
between women and men like cross-cultural communication, heir to all the attraction and pitfalls of that enticing but difficult enterprise. My research on
men's and women's conversations uncovered patterns similar to those described for children's groups.

For women, as for girls, intimacy is the fabric of relationships, and talk is 9
the thread from which it is woven. Little girls create and maintain friendships
by exchanging secrets; similarly, women regard conversation as the cornerstone
of friendship. So a woman expects her husband to be a new and improved version of a best friend. What is important is not the individual subjects that are
discussed but the sense of closeness, of a life shared, that emerges when people
tell their thoughts, feelings, and impressions.

Bonds between boys can be as intense as girls', but they are based less on 10
talking, more on doing things together. Since they don't assume talk is the

cement that binds a relationship, men don't know what kind of talk women want, and they don't miss it when it isn't there.

11   Boys' groups are larger, more inclusive, and more hierarchical, so boys must struggle to avoid the subordinate position in the group. This may play a role in women's complaints that men don't listen to them. Some men really don't like to listen, because being the listener makes them feel one-down, like a child listening to adults or an employee to a boss.

12   But often when women tell men, "You aren't listening," and the men protest, "I am," the men are right. The impression of not listening results from misalignments in the mechanics of conversation. The misalignment begins as soon as a man and a woman take physical positions. This became clear when I studied videotapes made by psychologist Bruce Dorval of children and adults talking to their same-sex best friends. I found that at every age, the girls and women faced each other directly, their eyes anchored on each other's faces. At every age, the boys and men sat at angles to each other and looked elsewhere in the room, periodically glancing at each other. They were obviously attuned to each other, often mirroring each other's movements. But the tendency of men to face away can give women the impression they aren't listening even when they are. A young woman in college was frustrated: Whenever she told her boyfriend she wanted to talk to him, he would lie down on the floor, close his eyes, and put his arm over his face. This signaled to her, "He's taking a nap." But he insisted he was listening extra hard. Normally, he looks around the room, so he is easily distracted. Lying down and covering his eyes helped him concentrate on what she was saying.

13   Analogous to the physical alignment that women and men take in conversation is their topical alignment. The girls in my study tended to talk at length about one topic, but the boys tended to jump from topic to topic. The second-grade girls exchanged stories about people they knew. The second-grade boys teased, told jokes, noticed things in the room and talked about finding games to play. The sixth-grade girls talked about problems with a mutual friend. The sixth-grade boys talked about 55 different topics, none of which extended over more than a few turns.

Listening to Body Language

14 Switching topics is another habit that gives women the impression men aren't listening, especially if they switch to a topic about themselves. But the evidence of the 10th-grade boys in my study indicates otherwise. The 10th-grade boys sprawled across their chairs with bodies parallel and eyes straight ahead, rarely looking at each other. They looked as if they were riding in a car, staring out the windshield. But they were talking about their feelings. One boy was upset because a girl had told him he had a drinking problem, and the other was feeling alienated from all his friends.

15   Now, when a girl told a friend about a problem, the friend responded by asking probing questions and expressing agreement and understanding. But the boys dismissed each other's problems. Todd assured Richard that his

drinking was "no big problem" because "sometimes you're funny when you're off your butt." And when Todd said he felt left out, Richard responded, "Why should you? You know more people than me."

Women perceived such responses as belittling and unsupportive. But the boys seemed satisfied with them. Whereas women reassure each other by implying, "You shouldn't feel bad because I've had similar experiences," men do so by implying, "You shouldn't feel bad because your problems aren't so bad." 16

There are even simpler reasons for women's impression that men don't listen. Linguist Lynette Hirschman found that women make more listener-noise, such as "mhm," "uhuh," and "yeah," to show "I'm with you." Men, she found, more often give silent attention. Women who expect a stream of listener-noise interpret silent attention as no attention at all. 17

Women's conversational habits are as frustrating to men as men's are to women. Men who expect silent attention interpret a stream of listener-noise as overreaction or impatience. Also, when women talk to each other in a close, comfortable setting, they often overlap, finish each other's sentences and anticipate what the other is about to say. This practice, which I call "participatory listenership," is often perceived by men as interruption, intrusion and lack of attention. 18

A parallel difference caused a man to complain about his wife, "She just wants to talk about her own point of view. If I show her another view, she gets mad at me." When most women talk to each other, they assume a conversationalist's job is to express agreement and support. But many men see their conversational duty as pointing out the other side of an argument. This is heard as disloyalty by women, and refusal to offer the requisite support. It is not that women don't want to see other points of view, but that they prefer them phrased as suggestions and inquiries rather than as direct challenges. 19

In his book *Fighting for Life,* Walter Ong points out that men use "agonistic" or warlike, oppositional formats to do almost anything; thus discussion becomes debate, and conversation a competitive sport. In contrast, women see conversation as a ritual means of establishing rapport. If Jane tells a problem and June says she has a similar one, they walk away feeling closer to each other. But this attempt at establishing rapport can backfire when used with men. Men take too literally women's ritual "troubles talk," just as women mistake men's ritual challenges for real attack. 20

The Sounds of Silence

These differences begin to clarify why women and men have such different expectations about communication in marriage. For women, talk creates intimacy. Marriage is an orgy of closeness: you can tell your feelings and thoughts, and still be loved. Their greatest fear is being pushed away. But men live in a hierarchical world, where talk maintains independence and status. They are on guard to protect themselves from being put down and pushed around. 21

22   This explains the paradox of the talkative man who said of his silent wife, "She's the talker." In the public setting of a guest lecture, he felt challenged to show his intelligence and display his understanding of the lecture. But at home, where he has nothing to prove and no one to defend against, he is free to remain silent. For his wife, being home means she is free from the worry that something she says might offend someone, or spark disagreement, or appear to be showing off; at home she is free to talk.

23   The communication problems that endanger marriage can't be fixed by mechanical engineering. They require a new conceptual framework about the role of talk in human relationships. Many of the psychological explanations that have become second nature may not be helpful, because they tend to blame either women (for not being assertive enough) or men (for not being in touch with their feelings). A sociolinguistic approach by which male-female conversation is seen as cross-cultural communication allows us to understand the problem and forge solutions without blaming either party.

24   Once the problem is understood, improvement comes naturally, as it did to the young woman and her boyfriend who seemed to go to sleep when she wanted to talk. Previously, she had accused him of not listening, and he had refused to change his behavior, since that would be admitting fault. But then she learned about and explained to him the differences in women's and men's habitual ways of aligning themselves in conversation. The next time she told him she wanted to talk, he began, as usual, by lying down and covering his eyes. When the familiar negative reaction bubbled up, she reassured herself that he really was listening. But then he sat up and looked at her. Thrilled she asked why. He said, "You like me to look at you when we talk, so I'll try to do it." Once he saw their differences as cross-cultural rather than right and wrong, he independently altered his behavior.

25   Women who feel abandoned and deprived when their husbands won't listen to or report daily news may be happy to discover their husbands trying to adapt once they understand the place of small talk in women's relationships. But if their husbands don't adapt, the women may still be comforted that for men, this is not a failure of intimacy. Accepting the difference, the wives may look to their friends or family for that kind of talk. And husbands who can't provide it shouldn't feel their wives have made unreasonable demands. Some couples will still decide to divorce, but at least their decisions will be based on realistic expectations.

26   In these times of resurgent ethnic conflicts, the world desperately needs cross-cultural understanding. Like charity, successful cross-cultural communication should begin at home.

COMPREHENSION

1. What is the thesis or claim of this essay? Where does Tannen most clearly articulate it?
2. To advance her argument, the author cites political scientists and sociologists, while she herself is a linguist. What exactly is the nature of these three professions? What

do professionals in the first two fields do? Why does Tannen use their observations in developing her argument?

3. Why does the author employ a question in her title? What other device does she employ in her title to capture the reader's attention?

RHETORIC

1. Tannen begins her essay with an anecdote. Is this an effective way of opening this particular essay? Why or why not?

2. Besides anecdotes, the author uses statistics, social science research, appeals to authority, and definition in advancing her argument. Find at least one example of each device. Explain the effectiveness or lack thereof.

3. Where and how does the author imply that she is an authority on the subject? How does this contribute to or detract from her ability to win the reader's confidence?

4. Tannen divides her essay into four sections: one untitled and three with headings. How does each section relate to the others structurally and thematically?

5. Concerning the lack of proper communication between men and women, Tannen states, "Once the problem is understood, improvement comes naturally" (paragraph 24). Is this statement substantiated or backed up with evidence? Explain.

WRITING

1. Another linguist has written an essay titled "The Communication Panacea," which argues that much of what is blamed on lack of communication actually has economic and political causes. Argue for or against this proposition in the light of the ideas advanced in Tannen's essay.

2. Using some of the observational methods described in the essay, conduct your own ethnographic research by observing a couple communicating. Write a report discussing your findings.

3. **Writing an Argument:** Tannen states, "Once the problem is understood, improvement comes naturally." Argue for or against this proposition.

NETWORKING
Applying 21st-Century Literacies

Exploring Gender and Online Communication: From the Chapter 2 Networking page at *www.mhhreader.com/mhreaderbrief1e,* link to and read the overview of the report "How Women and Men Use the Internet." How might the issues raised in Tannen's article inform the different ways men and women communicate online?

Synthesis: Connections for Critical Thinking

1. Examine the "how-to" aspect of the essays by Elbow and Murray. What general strategies do they use to develop a comprehensive process analysis of an elusive subject—for example, reading or writing? Write an essay in which you compare the tactics these writers employ to demonstrate their processes.

2. Study the tone of Schlesinger's essay "The Cult of Ethnicity" (in Chapter 1). How does he remain "civil" while arguing against a contemporary view he seems to abhor? Next, study Deborah Tannen's "Sex, Lies and Conversation" and examine the tone she uses in addressing the complex subject of language. Make some general observations about how the stylistic elements of an essay contribute to the ability of the author to communicate difficult subjects in a manner that is appealing to the reader.

3. Synthesize the ideas in Elbow's "Freewriting" and those in Murray's "The Maker's Eye: Revising Your Own Manuscripts" so that you can write a coherent essay on writing that takes into account the transition from inspiration to craft.

 CH 2   **www.mhhe.com/mhreaderbrief1e**

- *Writing > Paragraph/Essay Development:* Prewriting strategies
- *Writing > Writing Tutors:* Various patterns and genres
- *Writing > Paragraph/Essay Development > Introductions*
- *Writing > Paragraph Patterns:* Methods of development
- *Writing > Paragraph/Essay Development > Conclusions*
- *Image Gallery:* Chapter images in color
- *Writing:* Information on the authors in this chapter
- *Ch. 2 Networking*

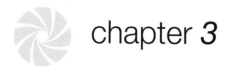

chapter *3*

Reading and Writing Effective Arguments

You encounter various forms of argumentation in everyday situations, in Internet-based discourse and online communities, and of course in many college courses where debate is the essence of class discussion. People argue for many reasons, but one of the most compelling is to sift through opposing or competing viewpoints in order to achieve a mutually satisfying consensus that everyone can live with. In our increasingly globalized world, where diverse peoples and belief systems can converge in a nanosecond, we must find ways to learn more about and consider positions different from our own, and to communicate our beliefs in ways that are thoughtful, considerate, and interesting. You will be better prepared to address consequential issues in a personal, academic, professional, or civic context—whether you are convincing someone to share your position or to take action, and whether you are making a point or refuting one—if you learn more about argumentation as a mode of thinking, reading, and writing.

As a common form of academic writing, *argumentation* seeks to explore differences of opinion and attempts to promote agreement. As such, argument is useful not only in classroom situations but also in the realm of civic life and discourse, for it provides reasons for people to agree with a particular point of view or at least come to an understanding of an individual's or a group's perspective on an issue. Aristotle, who wrote the first major work on argument, thought that the best and most effective argumentative writing blends rational, emotional, and ethical appeals in order to move an audience—whether one person or an entire nation—to some desired action. Aristotle's threefold approach to argument might serve you especially well as you navigate and evaluate the many Web sites, wikis, blogs, social networking sites, and other online publications and venues that offer resources (but also pitfalls) for 21st-century writers.

When you engage in argumentation, you offer reasons to support a position, belief, or conclusion. A typical argumentative essay presents a debatable thesis and defends it in logical fashion. Closely allied with argumentation is *persuasion,* in which the writer appeals to readers' intelligence, emotions, and beliefs in order to influence them to adopt a position or act in a certain way. Logic and persuasive appeal often combine when a writer tries to convince an audience that his or her position is valid and that other perspectives, while understandable perhaps, require reconsideration.

It is important to distinguish between oral arguments and written ones. Admittedly, both spoken and written arguments have a common purpose in their attempt to convince someone to agree with a particular position, make a certain decision, or take a specific action. In both your oral and written arguments, you will usually invoke reasons and attempt to manipulate language skillfully. However, with an oral argument, you rarely have access to the types of specific evidence needed to support your reasons, nor do you have the time or ability to martial reasons and evidence in well-organized and coherent ways. Oral arguments, as you well know, tend to involve excessive emotion; after all, oral arguments often erupt spontaneously and are rarely thoughtfully constructed and presented.

Unlike most oral arguments, effective written arguments are carefully and logically planned, organized, researched, and revised. The writer analyzes the audience and anticipates objections to the assertions being made. As she or he develops the argument, the writer considers and selects various rhetorical strategies—for example, analysis, definition, or comparison and contrast—to shape the presentation. Moreover, the writer has time to choose the appropriate language and style for the argument, exploring the use of striking diction, figurative language, rhythmic sentence patterns, and various tonalities and shades of meaning during the prewriting, drafting, and revision stages. Finally, especially when composing arguments for college courses, writers must attend to logic and the techniques of valid persuasive appeal.

LEARNING THE LANGUAGE OF ARGUMENT

Writers of argument often employ various modes of exposition like definition, comparison and contrast, illustration, and analysis, but they incorporate these modes of critical thinking as the means of justifying, or supporting, a logical position. The study of the special language, logic, and structure of argumentation fills volumes. For college writing, there is a core group of critical terms that you should know before you design an argumentative paper:

- A *claim* is a statement to be justified or upheld. It is the main idea or position that you plan to present in an argument.
- *Thesis, proposition, assertion,* and *premise* are all similar to a claim in that each is a positive statement or declaration to be supported with reasons and evidence. *Premise,* however, should be distinguished from the other terms: It is a statement or assumption that is established before an argument is begun and is important to an understanding of logic and various errors or fallacies in reasoning.
- *Grounds* are the reasons, support, and evidence presented to support your claim.
- A *warrant* is a stated or unstated belief, rule, or principle that underlies an argument. A *backing* is an even broader principle that serves as the foundation for a warrant.
- The *major proposition* is the main point of an argument, which is supported by the minor propositions.
- The *minor propositions* are the reasons you offer in support of the major proposition.
- *Evidence* is that part of the argument that supports the minor propositions. In argumentation, effective evidence is based either on facts, examples, statistics, and other forms of evidence or on accepted opinions. Without adequate evidence, the audience will not accept your major and minor propositions. Evidence in argument must be accurate and true.
- A *fact* is a verifiable statement. A valid *opinion* is a judgment based on the facts and careful deductive or inductive reasoning. *Induction* is a process of reasoning by which you develop evidence in order to reach a useful generalization. *Deduction* is a process of reasoning that proceeds from the general to the particular.

Classic and Contemporary Images
WHAT IS AN ARGUMENT?

Using a Critical Perspective   What images and strategies do the Spanish artist Francisco de Goya and the American photographer Eddie Adams employ to construct an argument about war? What exactly is their argument? Comment on the nature and effectiveness of the details they use to illustrate their position. Which work do you find more powerful or engaging? Explain.

Horrified by the excesses of the Napoleonic invasion of his homeland and the Spanish war for independence, the Spanish artist Francisco de Goya (1746–1828) painted *The Third of May, 1808,* a vivid rendition of an execution during wartime.

Another wartime execution, this time captured on film by Eddie Adams in an image that won the Pulitzer Prize for spot news photography in 1969, brought home to Americans the horrors and ambiguities of the war in Vietnam.

- A valid *conclusion* of an argument derives logically from the major and minor propositions. The logical conclusion is termed the *inference*, in which you arrive at a decision by reasoning from the previous evidence.
- A *fallacy* is a line of incorrect reasoning from premises.
- *Refutation* is the acknowledgment and handling of opposing viewpoints. You must anticipate opposing viewpoints and counter them effectively (what we term *rebuttal*) in order to convince or persuade readers.

Constructing an effective argument depends on the careful arrangement of major and minor propositions, evidence, and refutation. Like a lawyer, you build a position and subject your opponent's position to dissection in an effort to win the case.

USING THE TEST OF JUSTIFICATION

Whatever its components, whether a writer can construct an argument or not essentially hinges on the concept of *justification*—the recognition that a subject lends itself to legitimate difference of opinion. Justification also involves proving or demonstrating that a claim is in accordance with the reasons and evidence offered to support it.

Not all statements require justification. A statement that is a verifiable fact or a commonly accepted assumption or belief—what we term a *warrant*—generally does not need justification. To test the concept of justification, consider the following four statements.

1. President John F. Kennedy was assassinated on November 22, 1963.
2. Children shouldn't smoke.
3. Abortion is the destruction of a human life.
4. African Americans should receive reparations for the damages caused by slavery.

Which of these statements require justification? The first statement about President Kennedy is a verifiable fact, and the second statement strikes any reasonable audience as common sense. Thus, the first two statements do not require justification and consequently could not be the subject of a useful argument, although the second statement could serve as the warrant for a more specific claim about smoking by children. In contrast, the third statement, concerning abortion, makes a critical assumption that would elicit either agreement or disagreement but in either case would demand substantiation. Similarly, the fourth statement, about reparations for slavery, is an issue that is debatable from a variety of positions. Therefore, statements 3 and 4 require justification: They are open to argumentation.

READING AND ANALYZING ARGUMENTS

From the time of Aristotle to the present, numerous critical approaches to the study of argument have been devised. One of the most useful recent approaches to argument appears in *An Introduction to Reasoning* and *The Uses of Argument* by British logician and philosopher Stephen Toulmin. In his studies, Toulmin observes that any argument involves a *claim* supported by *reasons* and *evidence*. Whether writing a memo to your instructor contesting a certain grade, or a letter to the editor of your campus newspaper advocating a change in the cafeteria vendor because the food is terrible, or a petition to provide more parking spaces for commuting students, the argumentative method is the same. Essentially, you make a general assertion—a claim—and then offer the smaller propositions or supporting reasons along with the relevant facts, examples, statistics, and expert testimony to justify all claims. And underlying the nature of claims and evidence is recognition of the importance of *warrants,* those unstated beliefs that lead from evidence to claim.

Here is the way Toulmin presents his model:

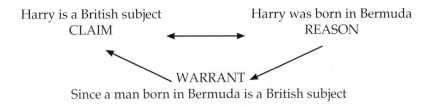

In truth, Toulmin's example is basic and perhaps too simplistic. The claims that you deal with when reading or writing arguments typically are more complex and controversial than Toulmin's diagram suggests, and the need for extensive evidence more demanding. Nevertheless, Toulmin's model offers a useful way to understand the nature of argumentative reasoning.

Understanding Claims and Warrants

When you argue in writing, you make a specific claim, which is an assertion that you plan to prove. You present this claim or proposition as being true, and you support the claim with a series of logically related statements that are true. Think of the claim as the thesis or the main point of the argument that holds all other logically related statements together. The claim is the main idea that you set out to prove, and in a well reasoned argument, everything makes the claim seem inevitable. Any paper you write that fails to state a claim—your position in an argument—will leave readers shaking their heads and wondering if you actually have an argument to present.

Think of a claim as an arguable point, one that you can build a carefully reasoned paper around. By applying the test of justification, you can exclude numerous opinions, nonarguable propositions, and statements of taste and fact that might be common in everyday situations but not legitimate subjects for papers. To say "Turn down that rap music" to your roommate is the sort of command (containing perhaps an implied opinion) that doesn't in itself qualify as a claim but could get you involved in a heated conversation. To transform this command into a legitimate claim or an arguable point, you would have to state a proposition that expresses your main idea about rap.

A complex, extended argument in essay form often reveals several types of claims that the writer advances. A *claim about meaning* (What is rap music?) is a proposition that defines or interprets a subject as it establishes an arguable point. A *claim about value* (Rap music is good or bad) advances an ideally open-minded view of the subject based on a coherent framework of aesthetic or ethical values. A *claim about policy* (Music stations should be forced to regulate the most offensive forms of rap music) advances propositions concerning laws, regulations, and initiatives designed to produce specific outcomes. Finally, *claims about consequences* (Children who listen to rap musicians begin to mimic their vulgar behavior) are rooted in propositions involving various forms of cause-and-effect relationships. Constructing an argument around one or more of these types of claims is essential to gaining an audience's assent.

Many claims, of course, cannot be presented as absolute propositions—certainly not as absolute as Aristotle's major premise in his famous syllogism (see page 87) that "all human beings are mortal." Writers must seek common ground with readers and foster a degree of trust by anticipating that some members of any audience will disagree with their claim, treat it with skepticism, and perhaps even respond with hostility. For this reason, it is important to qualify or clarify the nature of your claim. A *qualifier* restricts the absoluteness of a claim by using such cue words and phrases as *sometimes, probably, usually,* and *in most cases.*

Qualifiers can also explain certain circumstances or conditions under which the claim might not be true. The use of qualifiers enables the writer to anticipate certain audience reactions and handle them in an effective and subtle way.

Even more important than the possible need to qualify a claim is the need to justify it in a new way: by linking the claim with reasons and evidence in such a way that the audience sees the train of thinking that leads from the data to the claim. If you look again at the model that Toulmin provides, you see that the datum "Harry was born in Bermuda" does not completely support the claim "Harry is a British subject." What is required is what Toulmin calls a *warrant,* a form of justification—a general belief, principle, or rule—that links the claim and the data or support. Thus the warrant "Since a man born in Bermuda is a British subject" explains *why* the claim follows from the datum.

Another way of understanding this admittedly challenging concept of warrant is to treat it as the process of thinking that leads writers to hold the opinions they present. Thought of from this perspective, we can see that a weak or unclear warrant will undermine an argument and render it invalid. For example, the claim "Sara graduated from an excellent high school and consequently should do well in college" is based on the warrant or unstated (and untested) belief that all students who graduate from good high schools perform well at the college level. Obviously, this warrant is not satisfactory: To state that college success is based solely on the quality of one's high school education is to base the argument on a warrant that few readers would find acceptable. If, on the other hand, a writer claims that "Sara graduated from an excellent high school with a 3.97 cumulative average, the third highest in her class, and consequently should do well in college," we see that the warrant establishing the link between claim and conclusion becomes more acceptable. In fact, there is a consensus, or general belief, among experts that a person's grade point average in high school is a sound predictor—perhaps sounder than SAT scores—of his or her potential for success in college.

If you disagree with a writer's assumptions, you basically are questioning the warrants underlying the argument. An effective argument should rest on an acceptable warrant and also on the *backing*—some explanation or support—for it. Remember that even if a warrant, stated or unstated, is clear, understood, and backed with support, readers might still disagree with it. For example, one could argue that Sara might have obtained her lofty GPA in high school by taking easy courses and that consequently we cannot readily predict her success in college. Not everyone will accept even the most reasonable of warrants.

Reasoning from Evidence

Evidence is the data, or *grounds,* used to make claims or general assertions clear, concrete, and convincing. In argumentation, the presentation of evidence must be examined from the perspective of logic or sound reasoning. Central to logic is the relationship of evidence to a *generalization,* a statement or conclusion that what is applicable in one situation also applies to similar situations. You cannot think and write clearly unless you test evidence to see that it supports your claims, assumptions, or general statements. Evidence in an argumentative essay creates a common ground of understanding that you and your reader can share.

You know that one of the keenest pleasures in reading mystery fiction or viewing whodunits on television or film is the quest for evidence. The great writers of crime and mystery fiction—Edgar Allan Poe, Sir Arthur Conan Doyle, Agatha Christie—were adept at creating a chain of clues, or evidence, leading with the inevitability of logic to the solution to the crime. Whether it is a letter lying on a desk in Poe's "The Purloined Letter" or a misplaced chair in Christie's *The Murder of Roger Ackroyd,* it is evidence that we seek in order to solve the crime.

In argumentative writing, evidence is used more to prove a point than to solve a mystery. College writers must know what constitutes evidence—examples, facts, statistics, quotations and information from authoritative sources, personal experience, careful reasoning—and how to use it to support certain claims. They must also determine if the evidence and assumptions surrounding the evidence are valid.

Here are some basic questions about evidence to consider when reading and writing argumentative essays:

- *Is the evidence typical and representative?* Examples must fairly represent the condition or situation if your claim is to be valid. If evidence is distorted or unrepresentative, a claim will not be logical or convincing.
- *Is the evidence relevant?* The evidence should speak directly to the claim. It should not utilize peripheral or irrelevant data.
- *Is the evidence specific and detailed?* In reading and writing arguments, do not trust broad, catchall statements presented as "evidence." Valid evidence should involve accurate quotations, paraphrases, and presentations of data from authoritative sources.
- *Is the evidence accurate and reliable?* A claim is only as valid as the data supporting it. Facts should come from reliable sources. (See pages 112 and 116–118 for help with evaluating sources.) Current rather than outdated evidence should predominate in a current argument. Sources should be cited accurately for the convenience of the reader. Although personal observation and personal experience are admissible as types of evidence, such testimony rarely serves as conclusive proof for a claim.
- *Is the evidence sufficient?* There must be enough evidence to support claims and reasons. One extended piece of evidence, no matter how carefully selected, rarely is sufficient to win an argument.

Any argumentative essay should provide a clear, logical link between the writer's claim, assertion, generalization, or conclusion and the evidence. If an argumentative essay reveals false or illogical reasoning—that is, if the step from the evidence to the generalization is wrong, confusing, or deceptive—readers will not accept the truth of the claim or the validity of the evidence.

THINKING CRITICALLY ABOUT ARGUMENTS

Whether you are reading another writer's argument or starting to plan one of your own, you need to consider the purposes of the argument. When you are reading an argument, you should also look for the appeals to reason, emotion, and ethics the writer is using and decide whether those appeals are effective for you, the writer's audience. In your own arguments, you will need to decide the types of appeals that will carry the most weight with *your* audience.

The Purpose of Argumentation

As a college writer, your general aim is to communicate or convey messages in essay form to a literate and knowledgeable audience of teachers and scholars. When thinking about the subject for an essay, you also have to consider a more specialized *purpose*—the special nature or aim—behind your composition. You might have to report the result of an experiment in animal behavior, analyze a poem, compare and contrast Mario Puzo's novel *The Godfather* with its film adaptation, or assert the need for capital punishment. In each instance, your essay requires a key rhetorical strategy or set of strategies. These strategies reflect your purpose—your intention—in developing the essay.

An argumentative essay may serve one or more purposes:

- To present a position, belief, or conclusion in a rational and effective way
- To defend a position against critics or detractors
- To persuade people to agree with a position or take a certain action
- To attack a position without necessarily presenting an alternative or opposing viewpoint

An effective argumentative essay often combines a variety of forms and purposes. For example, an argumentative essay on legalizing marijuana might explain effects, analyze laws, or evaluate experiments, among a broad range of options. When you take time to consider your purpose before you even begin to write, the decisions you make will help you to think more clearly about both the design and intention of your essay.

Appeals to Reason, Emotion, and Ethics

As the definitions of special terms and the discussion of justification presented earlier in the chapter suggest, argumentation places a premium on rational discourse. In fact, the *appeal to reason* is the fundamental purpose of argumentation. However, classical rhetorical theory acknowledges that the *appeal to emotion* and the *appeal to ethics* are also important elements in the construction of argument and the effort to persuade. A mere presentation of reasons is usually not an effective argument. For your argument to be effective, you need to pay attention to the value of strategic emotional and ethical appeals.

Appeals to Reason   The *appeal to reason* or logic is the primary instrument of effective argument. The most common way of developing an argument according to the principles of sound reasoning is *deduction*, which is most readily understood as an ordering of ideas from the general to the particular. With deduction, you move from a general assertion through reasons and support focused on the main assertion. Consider the following student paragraph, which uses the deductive method:

Anti-marijuana laws make people contemptuous of the legal system. This contempt is based in part on the key fact that there are too many contradictions and inconsistencies in criminal penalties for marijuana use. Laws vary radically from state to state. In Texas, you can be sentenced to life imprisonment for first-time use of marijuana. In contrast, in the District of Columbia, the same "crime" would most likely result in a suspended sentence.

Deduction is a convincing way of arranging ideas and information logically. By stating the proposition or generalization first, you present the most important idea. Then, as in the paragraph above, you move to more specific ideas and details. Examined more rigorously, deductive reasoning involves a process of critical thinking known as *syllogism*, in which you move from a major statement or premise, through another minor premise, to a third statement or conclusion. Aristotle's famous syllogism captures this mental process:

Major premise: All human beings are mortal.

Minor premise: Socrates is a human being.

Conclusion: Socrates is mortal.

The soundness of any deductive argument rests on the *truth* of the premises and the *validity* of the syllogism itself. In other words, if you grant the truth of the premises, you must also grant the conclusion. The deductive method can be used effectively in many forms of expository as well as argumentative essays.

Inductive reasoning reverses the process of deduction by moving from particular ideas to general ones. In the paragraph that follows, from an essay by F. M. Esfandiary, "The Mystical West Puzzles the Practical East," the writer presents various ideas and evidence that lead to a major proposition at the end:

Twenty-five hundred years ago, Buddha, like other Eastern philosophers before him, said: "He who sits still, wins." Asia, then immobilized in primitive torpor, had no difficulty responding. It sat still. What it won for sitting still was the perpetuation of famines and terrorizing superstitions, oppression of children, subjugation of women, emasculation of men, fratricidal wars, persecutions, mass killings. The history of Asia, like the history of all mankind, is a horrendous account of human suffering.

By presenting his supporting—and provocative—ideas first, the author is able to interest us before we reach the climactic argument at the end of the paragraph. Of course, whether we accept Esfandiary's argument—his statement of truth—or are prepared to debate his claim depends on the strength of the reasons and evidence he offers.

Many of the argumentative essays you read and much of the argumentative writing you undertake will reflect the mental processes of deduction and induction. The novelist

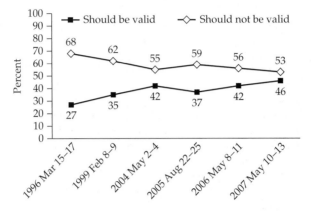

Logical appeal. This graph uses polling data to show the growth of popular support for marriage equality between 1996 and 2007. Quantifiable data usually adds solid support to an argument, and such data can have a powerful (and instant) impact when expressed visually in a graph or chart.
Source: Gallup.com.

Robert M. Pirsig offers his version of these critical thinking strategies in his cult classic, *Zen and the Art of Motorcycle Maintenance:*

> If the cycle goes over a bump and the engine misfires, and then goes over another bump and the engine misfires, and then goes over another bump and the engine misfires, and then goes over a long smooth stretch of road and there is no misfiring, and then goes over a fourth bump and the engine misfires again, one can logically conclude that the misfiring is caused by the bumps. That is induction: reasoning from particular experiences to general truths.
>
> Deductive inferences do the reverse. They start with general knowledge and predict a specific observation. For example if, from reading the hierarchy of facts about the machine the mechanic knows the horn of the cycle is powered exclusively by electricity from the battery, then he can logically infer that if the battery is dead the horn will not work. That is deduction.

Constructing an argument through the use of logical reasoning is a powerful way to convince or persuade a particular audience about the validity of your claims.

Appeals to Emotion   In addition to developing your argument logically using the appeal to reason, you should consider the value of incorporating *appeals to emotion* into an argumentative paper. A letter home asking for more money would in all likelihood require a certain carefully modulated emotional appeal. Martin Luther King Jr.'s famous "I Have a Dream" speech at the 1963 March on Washington, which begins on page 283 in

Emotional appeal. In the context of an argument for marriage equality, this photograph of two brides on their wedding day would appeal to readers' feelings: This is a happy couple. Their dresses might remind people of their own weddings, creating a sense of shared experience and interests. Photographs can make powerful emotional appeals, but in academic arguments, pathos needs to be supported by logos and ethos.

this textbook, is one of the finest contemporary examples of emotional appeal. King's speech ends with this invocation:

> When we let freedom ring, when we let it ring from every village and every hamlet, from every state and every city, we will be able to speed up that day when all of God's children, black men and white men, Jews and Gentiles, Protestants and Catholics, will be able to join hands and sing in the words of the old Negro spiritual, "Free at last! Free at last! Thank God almighty, we are free at last!"

King's skillful application of balanced biblical cadences and connotative and figurative language, and a strong, almost prophetic tone demonstrates the value of carefully crafted emotional appeal in the hands of an accomplished writer of argument.

Of course, in constructing an argument, you should avoid the sort of cynical manipulation of emotion that is common in the world of spoken discourse and the media in general. (For a list of unfair emotional appeals, see page 101.) But honest emotional appeal provides a human context for the rational ideas and evidence you present in an argumentative essay—ideas that might otherwise be uninteresting to your audience. Assuredly, if you want to persuade your audience to undertake a particular course of action, you must draw members of this audience closer to you as a person, and perhaps even inspire them by your feelings about the subject or issue. In truth, you *must* establish rapport with your reader in an argumentative essay. If you fail to engage the reader's feelings, the best-constructed rational appeal could fall flat.

Appeals to Ethics   For an emotional appeal to achieve maximum effectiveness, it must reinforce not only the rational strength of your argument but also the ethical basis of your ideas. When you use *ethical appeal,* you present yourself as a well-informed, fair-minded, honest person. Aristotle acknowledged the importance of *ethos,* or the character of the writer, in the construction of argument, for if you create a sense that you are trustworthy, your readers or listeners will be inspired or persuaded. The "sound" or "voice" of your essay, which you convey to the reader through your style and tone, and which can only be perfected through the process of careful drafting and revision, will help in convincing the audience to share your opinion.

In an appeal to ethics, you try to convince the reader that you are a person of sound character—that you possess good judgment and values. As a person of good-will and good sense, you also demonstrate an ability to empathize with your audience, to understand their viewpoints and perspectives. The psychologist Carl Rogers suggests that a willingness to embrace a potentially adversarial audience, to treat this audience more like an ally in an ethical cause, is a highly effective way to establish goodwill and the credibility of your beliefs. In Rogerian argument, your willingness to understand an opposing viewpoint and actually rephrase it reflectively for mutual understanding enables you to further establish your ethical and personal qualities. As

Ethical appeal. In this photograph, President Obama signs the Matthew Shepard bill into law on October 28, 2009, recognizing crimes motivated by a victim's sexual orientation as hate crimes. A claim could be made that this mobilization of support from the federal government demonstrates a step toward (and argument for) equal rights for the GLBT community. In an essay, you would need to support such an appeal with logic too.

the world grows more and more interconnected, and the pace of globalization acceler-ates, Rogerian argument might offer a form of cross-cultural discourse that bridges divides among people.

You can appreciate the powerful combination of rational, emotional, and ethical appeals in Abraham Lincoln's Gettysburg Address, which follows for analysis and discussion.

The Gettysburg Address

Abraham Lincoln

Abraham Lincoln (1809–1865) was born the son of a pioneer in 1809 in Hodgesville, Kentucky, and moved to Illinois in 1831. After brief experiences as a clerk, postmaster, and county surveyor, he studied law and was elected to the state legislature in 1834. A prominent member of the newly formed Republican Party, Lincoln became president on the eve of the Civil War. In 1862, after the Union victory at Antietam, Lincoln is-sued the Emancipation Proclamation freeing the slaves—the crowning achievement of an illustrious presidency. Although he was an outstanding orator and debater throughout his political career, the Gettysburg Address is one of his greatest speeches—and certainly his most famous one. It was delivered at the dedication of the Gettysburg National Cemetery in 1863. Its form and content reflect the philosophical and moral views of the time as well as the rhetorical skill of its speaker. Lincoln was assassinated by John Wilkes Booth in 1865, shortly after Robert E. Lee's surrender and the end of the Civil War.

Four score and seven years ago our fathers brought forth on this continent, a 1
new nation, conceived in Liberty, and dedicated to the proposition that all men are created equal.

Now we are engaged in a great civil war, testing whether that nation, or 2
any nation so conceived and so dedicated, can long endure. We are met on a great battlefield of that war. We have come to dedicate a portion of that field as a final resting-place for those who here gave their lives that that nation might live. It is altogether fitting and proper that we should do this.

But, in a larger sense, we cannot dedicate—we cannot consecrate—we can- 3
not hallow—this ground. The brave men, living and dead, who struggled here have consecrated it, far above our poor power to add or detract. The world will little note, nor long remember, what we say here, but it can never forget what they did here. It is for us the living, rather, to be dedicated here to the unfin-ished work which they who fought here have thus far so nobly advanced. It is rather for us to be here dedicated to the great task remaining before us—that from these honored dead we take increased devotion to that cause for which

they gave the last full measure of devotion; that we here highly resolve that these dead shall not have died in vain; this nation, under God, shall have a new birth of freedom; and that government of the people, by the people, for the people, shall not perish from the earth.

COMPREHENSION

1. Although this speech was supposed to be a "dedication," Lincoln states that "we cannot dedicate." What does he mean by this?
2. Lincoln uses abstract words such as "liberty," "freedom," and "nation." What does he mean specifically by each of these terms?
3. What exactly happened "four score and seven years ago" in the context of the speech? Why is this reference so significant to the purpose of Lincoln's address?

RHETORIC

1. Note the progression of imagery from that of "death" to that of "birth." How does this structure contribute to the claim and coherence of the speech?
2. How do the syntax, punctuation, and choice of the first-person plural form of address contribute to our understanding that this message was intended to be spoken rather than written?
3. Note how Lincoln refers to the combatants as "brave" and "honored." How does he suggest that their struggle was distinguished from that of "us the living"? How does this comparison and contrast create clear similarities and differences between those who fought and those who are present to carry on the work of the soldiers?
4. The American Civil War was a battle between the North and the South as were the opponents at the Battle of Gettysburg. However, Lincoln does not mention this. What is the reason behind this omission? How does it make the speech focus on more comprehensive issues?
5. Besides being president, Lincoln was by definition a politician. In what ways can we determine that this is a political speech as well as a dedication?
6. Speeches are intended to be heard. What are some elements—for example, vocabulary, syntax, length or brevity of the sentences, and juxtaposition of sentences—that appeal to the sense of sound?
7. Does this speech appeal primarily to the intellect or the emotions, or equally to the two? What are two or three sentences that demonstrate one or both of these appeals? What was the rationale behind your selections? Does Lincoln include any ethical appeals?

WRITING

1. Research the actual historical events that occurred during the Battle of Gettysburg. Write an argumentative essay in which you discuss the significance of this particular speech at this point in the Civil War. Use a minimum of three secondary source materials.

2. Read the speech three times. Then write a paraphrase of it. Examine your paraphrase to discover what elements you recalled. Then reread the speech and write an expository essay focusing on how the structure of the speech contributed to helping you recall the information you did remember.

NETWORKING
Adapting to 21st-Century Literacies

Using Search Phrases: Do an online search for the literary influences on the language and style of Abraham Lincoln. Try a search phrase such as "Lincoln AND reading." Select three authoritative sources and write a research paper titled "Literary Influences on Abraham Lincoln." (See Chapter 4 for information about citing your sources correctly.)

WRITING POWERFUL ARGUMENTS

One of the most common writing assignments in college courses, especially courses in the humanities and social sciences, is the argumentative essay. Unlike narrative and descriptive essays and the major forms of expository writing—comparison and contrast, definition, classification, process, and causal analysis—the argumentative paper requires the writer to take a stand and to support a position as effectively as possible. As mentioned earlier, the rhetorical strategies underlying expository or informative writing often appear in argumentative papers. However, given the purpose of the argumentative essay, you must present your ideas as powerfully as possible in order to advance your point of view and convince your readers to accept your position or take a specific course of action. For this reason, you must construct your argumentative paper carefully and effectively.

Argument, as stated in Chapter 2, is not a mere academic enterprise but rather an integral part of our personal, social, and professional lives. Whether you consider the 2008 presidential debates between John McCain and Barack Obama, recent decisions of the Supreme Court, actions taken by the United States in the Middle East, or tax provisions enacted by Congress argument determines in many ways the nature of life in the United States. More personally, argument—whether in the form of reviews or commercials—influences the films we watch, the music we listen to, the clothes we wear, and the food we eat. And argument—the way you sell yourself in an interview—can get you a job or lose it.

In many other ways, argument impacts your professional life. It is most clearly in evidence in newspaper and television journalism and communications, where argument and persuasion express an institution's deepest convictions. Consider the role of editorials and the op-ed page of any newspaper (including your college newspaper) in the nation. Editorial writing offers carefully crafted debates and informed opinions on a variety of topics and issues. Many newspapers also develop guidelines to promote convincing but open-minded positions on the issues of the day.

A deputy editorial page director for the *Chicago Tribune* offers a series of questions for essays that, with slight modification, provide an excellent guide for writing an argument:

- *To whom are you writing?* Are you writing to authorities? Power elites? Professors? Average readers? Yourself?
- *What is your attitude?* Are you angry? Pleased? Perplexed? What tone will you project?
- *What, exactly, are you trying to accomplish?* An official response? A public change of attitude? An explanation? Entertainment?
- *What are you contributing to the debate?* What's the added value here? Just your opinion? New facts? New arguments, contexts, or dimensions to consider?
- *Do you have something new to say?* Are you advancing the conversation or just rehashing old facts, opinions, and wisdom? Aside from an opinion, do you have a solution?
- *Have you fiercely attacked your own premise?* Will your position survive scrutiny? How would your opponents answer your most compelling arguments? Are you correct or simply wrong?
- *Are you stirring up a "three-bowler"?* This borrowed phrase refers to the reader who is so bored with your writing that her face falls in the cereal bowl not once or twice but three times. You must compose your argument in such a way that the reader is hooked by your writing and persuaded by the force of your argument.

The process for writing powerful arguments that appears in this section is useful, but it is not a formula. Ultimately, you can construct powerful arguments in numerous ways, but you always must consider the relationship between your ideas, your purpose, and your audience. And you should be aware that argument has increasingly broad implications: How you present yourself in argument—your voice or ethical bearing— might have consequences in the public sphere, both on- and offline.

Identify an Issue

Not every subject lends itself to useful or necessary argument. The notion that *"everything is an argument"* probably contains a grain of truth, but in reality some things make for more powerful arguments than others. Certain subjects—for example, stamp collecting—might appeal to you personally and powerfully, but are they worth arguing about? Consequently, your first step in writing an effective argumentative essay is to identify a subject that contains an issue—in other words, a subject that will elicit two or more differing opinions.

Clearly, there are certain subjects that touch on current problems and inspire strong opinions. President Lincoln's Gettysburg Address dealt with a monumental issue central to the very survival of the nation; for virtually everyone in the United States at that time, the issues raised by Lincoln were debatable. Similarly, the issue of the right to bear arms can produce two diametrically opposed and seemingly irreconcilable viewpoints. Whether or not we should have embarked on a war of choice rather than necessity in Iraq continues to influence current discourse. Social and political issues tend to be ripe subjects for debate, fostering pro and con viewpoints. But remember that there are often more than two sides to a complex issue. Such issues, by their very nature, often raise powerful and conflicting systems of belief that place heavy burdens on the writer to provide convincing reasons and evidence to support a claim.

Not all issues in argumentative papers have to be of national or global concern. In fact, issues like capital punishment, gay marriage, or global climate change might not be of special interest to you. However, if an instructor requires an argumentative essay on one of these broad hot-button topics, you will need to prepare to write the paper by first establishing an argumentative perspective on it—in other words, by choosing your side on the issue. Fortunately, you often have opportunities to select issues of more immediate, personal, or local concern: Should fast-food franchises be permitted in the student cafeteria? Should there be a campus policy on hate language? Should sophomores be required to pass standardized tests in reading, writing, and mathematics before advancing to their junior year? Many powerfully constructed arguments can deal with issues close to home and with subjects that are of considerable personal interest. Whether dealing with an issue mandated by the instructor or selecting your own issue for an argumentative paper, ask yourself at the outset of this critical process what your position on the issue is and how it can be developed through logic and evidence.

Take a Stand and Clarify Your Claim

Once you have identified an issue that lends itself to argumentation—an issue that people might reasonably disagree about—you must take a clear stand on this issue. In other words, your claim will advance your viewpoint over all other viewpoints. The aim is not to defeat an opponent but to persuade readers—your audience—to accept your opinion. Consequently, the first step at this stage is to establish as clearly as possible what your claim is going to be. You might want to experiment with one or more of the following strategies:

- Gather and explore information on the issue from debates on radio, television, or the Internet. (For help with critically evaluating online and electronic sources, see page 112.)
- Brainstorm or write informally about the issue, writing up your immediate response to it—how it makes you feel or what you think about it. If the issue provokes an emotional response, what are the causes? What are your more thoughtful or intellectual responses to the issue?
- List some preliminary reasons you respond to the issue in the way you do. By listing reasons, as well as the types of evidence you will need to support those reasons, you will be able to determine at an early stage whether you have enough material for a solid argumentative paper and what forms of research you will have to conduct.
- Keep notes of examples, facts, and ideas that might support your claim.
- Begin to think about possible objections to your position, and list these opposing viewpoints.

There are numerous strategies to think and write critically as you approach an issue during the prewriting stage. Essentially, you want to begin to articulate and pinpoint your claim, and thereby start to limit, control, and clarify the scope of your argument.

Once you have developed a preliminary approach to an issue, you should be prepared to state your claim in the form of a thesis sentence. From your reading of the information on the thesis statement in the second chapter of this textbook (see page 43), you know that you must limit the scope and purpose of your thesis or claim. Too broad a claim will be hard to cover in convincing fashion in a standard argumentative paper. One useful way to limit and clarify your claim is to consider the purpose of your argument. Do you want to argue a position on a particular issue? Do you want to argue that a certain activity, belief, or situation is good or bad, harmful or beneficial, effective or ineffective? Do you want to persuade readers to undertake or avoid a particular course of action? Do you want readers to simply consider an issue in a new light? Do you want readers to endorse your interpretation or evaluation of an artistic or literary work? By sifting through the primary purposes of argument, which involve value judgments, policies, and interpretations, you will arrive at the main point of your argument—your claim.

Analyze Your Audience

All writing can be considered a process of communication, a conversation with an audience of readers. In argumentative writing, it is especially important to establish a common ground of belief with your readers if you expect them to accept your claim or undertake a certain course of action. Of course, you cannot change your ideas and approaches to an issue merely to please a particular audience. However, you do not construct an argumentative paper in order to be misunderstood, disbelieved, or rejected. Within the limits set by who you are, what you believe, and what your purpose is, you can match your argumentative style and approach to audience expectations.

To establish common ground with your audience, it is important to know them well so that you can dispose them favorably to your claim and the reasons and evidence supporting it. Your audience might be a professor, a prospective employer, an admissions or financial aid officer, an editor, or a member of your family. If you determine the nature of your audience *before* you compose the first draft of your argumentative paper, you will be able to tailor style, content, and tone to a specific person or group.

Try to imagine and anticipate audience expectations by asking basic questions about your readers:

- What are the age, gender, professional background, educational level, and political orientation of most of the members of the audience?
- How much does the audience know about the issue? Is it an audience of experts or a general audience with only limited knowledge of the issue?
- What does the audience expect from you in terms of the purpose behind your claim? Does the audience expect you to prove your claim or persuade them to accept it, or both?
- Will the audience be friendly, hostile, or neutral toward your argument? What political, cultural, ethical, or religious factors contribute to the audience's probable position on this issue?
- What else do you know about the audience's opinions, attitudes, and values? How might these factors shape your approach to the argument?

Suppose you are planning to write an argumentative essay on pollution. What common expectations would an English professor, a sociology professor, and a chemistry professor have concerning your argument? What differences in approach and content would be dictated by your decision to write for one of these instructors? Or consider these different audiences for a paper on the topic of pollution: a group of grade school children in your hometown, or the Environmental Protection Agency, or the manager of a landfill operation, or a relative in Missouri whose town has been experiencing chemical pollution. In each instance, the type and nature of the audience will influence your approach to the issue and even your purpose. Remember that through your *purpose* you find the proper context for your argument. Any writer who wants to communicate effectively with his or her audience will adjust the content and tone of an argument so as not to lose, confuse, or mislead the reader.

Establish Your Tone

You recall from Chapter 2 that by *tone* we mean the attitude you take toward your subject. Tone is the personal *voice* that a reader "hears" in your writing. This voice may vary, depending on the situation, your purpose, and your audience. It may be personal or impersonal and range across a spectrum of attitudes: serious or humorous, subjective or objective, straightforward or ironic, formal or casual, and so forth. You adjust your tone to match your purpose in writing.

In argumentation an effective tone will be a true and trustworthy reflection of the writing situation. After all, you are writing an argumentative essay in order to convince and persuade, and consequently, you need to sound like a reasonable, well-organized, and rational individual. When writing for college instructors, that "community of scholars," you must be especially careful to maintain a reasonable and principled tone and attend to ethical responsibilities, including the need to document sources with integrity. You do not have to sound scholarly, legalistic, or overly technical in presenting your argument, but you do have to employ a personal voice that is appropriate to the writing occasion and audience expectations.

To achieve an appropriate tone in argumentative writing, you will often need to be forceful in presenting your ideas. Remember that you are staking out a position, perhaps on a controversial issue, and you must seem willing to defend it. Try to maintain a consistent voice of authority, but do not be overbearing: Do not move from the lecture hall to the locker room, mixing voices in a way that will confuse or alienate your audience. A tone or voice that exceeds the limits of good taste and commonly accepted norms of argumentative style is likely to be ineffectual. A voice that is too emotional, overblown, or irrational will in all likelihood alienate the reader and erode your claim.

Your tone—your voice—is a revelation of yourself. It derives from your claims and supporting ideas, your language and sentence structure. Even if your audience is one person—typically, your professor—you certainly must present yourself to that audience as convincingly as possible. When your tone is adjusted to the issue, the claim, and the supporting evidence, and also to the nature of the opposition, you stand a good chance of writing an effective argumentative essay.

Develop and Organize the Grounds for Your Claim

You establish the validity of your claim by setting out the reasons and evidence—the *grounds*—that support your main point. Whereas the claim presents your general proposition or point of view, as you develop your grounds you organize the argument into minor propositions, evidence, and refutation. By establishing the grounds for your claim, you explain the particular perspective or point of view you take on an issue. The grounds for your claim permit the reader to "see" the strength of your position.

There are numerous ways to state the primary reasons or grounds for holding your position. Think of these primary reasons as minor propositions underlying the basis of your claim—reasons that readers would find it difficult to rebut or reject. Three possible models for organizing claims and grounds in an essay can now be considered:

Model 1
Introduction: statement and clarification of claim

First minor proposition and evidence

Second minor proposition and evidence

Third minor proposition and evidence

Refutation of opposing viewpoints for minor propositions

Conclusion

Model 2
Introduction: statement and clarification of claim

First minor proposition and evidence; refutation

Second minor proposition and evidence; refutation

Third minor proposition and evidence; refutation

Conclusion

Model 3
Statement and clarification of claim

Summary of opposing viewpoints and refutation

First minor proposition and evidence

Second minor proposition and evidence

Third minor proposition and evidence

Conclusion

In practice, arguments rarely adhere slavishly to these models. In fact, you can arrange your argument in numerous ways. However, the models can serve a useful purpose, especially in exams that require argumentative responses to a question, for they provide a handy template for your answer. In argument, to support your claim, you will need substantial reasons, sometimes more than the three minor propositions illustrated in these models. Remember that one reason generally will not provide sufficient grounds to prove an argument. Moreover, you should keep in mind the need to distinguish between your *opinions,* which in the broadest sense are beliefs that you cannot verify logically, and reasons, which are based on logic, evidence, and direct proof.

Gather and Evaluate Your Evidence

Once you have established your claim and your reasons, you can turn your attention to developing evidence for your claim, a subject introduced in the first chapter. Collecting evidence is a bit like the strategies for successful fishing presented by the student in his classification paragraph in the second chapter (see page 54): You want to fish the top, the middle, and the bottom of your subject. Phrased somewhat differently, you want to cast a wide net as you seek evidence designed to support your claim and reasons.

At the outset, a carefully designed online search can yield ample evidence, permitting you to establish links to sites and listservs where you can download or print full or abstracted texts from periodicals, books, documents, and reports. Remember, however, that searching online can be like navigating a minefield: Useless "facts," misinformation, hoaxes, and informational marketing ploys mix with serious research, honest reporting, and critical analysis. To guard against the pitfalls involved in relying exclusively on browser-based searching, you should also make a trip to the college library. Research librarians can help you to evaluate Web sites and direct you to the best sources—both traditional and electronic—for the types of evidence you are seeking. (For more on library and online research, see Chapter 4.) Depending on your subject, you might consider interviewing individuals who can provide expert testimony designed to support your claim and reasons. Finally, your personal experience and the experiences of your friends and acquaintances might provide useful evidence, although such kinds of anecdotal or firsthand support should be treated judiciously and not serve as the entire basis for your paper. For instance, you and your friends might claim that a current horror movie is great, but such personal evidence must be tempered by a willingness to consult established critics for additional support.

If you cast a wide net and fish the whole lake, you will almost always catch more than you require. Yet the very process of searching comprehensively for evidence can produce exciting, unintended consequences. You might, for example, discover that certain evidence suggests a need to revise or qualify your claim. Evidence can also help you to articulate or confirm the warrants that are the foundation of your argument, for experts writing on an issue often state the assumptions, principles, or beliefs that offer connections between a claim and its grounds. The insights gained by considering other evidence might cause you to develop a new reason for your claim that you had not considered initially. You might also discover evidence that helps you to refute the ideas of your anticipated opposition. Having a wealth of evidence at your disposal is an embarrassment of riches that you can exploit skillfully.

After you have collected adequate evidence to bolster your claim and the key reasons supporting that claim, the next necessary step is to evaluate and select the best evidence available to you. Writers who carefully evaluate and select their evidence produce effective arguments. At the outset, the nature of the writing situation—an exam, a term paper, a letter to the editor—will dictate to an extent the type of evidence you need to evaluate. In most instances, however, your evidence should be *credible, comprehensive,* and *current.* Your evidence is credible when your sources are reliable and the evidence itself is representative. Your evidence is comprehensive when you provide a broad range of facts, information, and data designed to cover all aspects of your argument. In presenting evidence comprehensively, you also make certain that there is sufficient support for each of your reasons—not too much evidence for one and too little for another, but an even balance between and among the minor propositions. Finally, always try to locate the most current evidence available to support your claim. Data and statistics often do not age well and tend to lose their relevance. However, in some arguments, older evidence can be compared with newer information. For example, a paper arguing that immigration to the United States is out of control could make skillful use of data from the 1960 Census *and* the 2010 Census.

Evidence is the heart of any argument. Without evidence, readers will not be interested in your claim and supporting reasons. Make certain that the evidence—the facts, examples, and details—you present is accurate and skillfully presented so that readers become interested in your more abstract propositions, identify with your position, and come away convinced of the validity of your argument.

Consider Your Warrants

Even as you clarify your claim and assemble your reasons and evidence, you must also consider the assumptions underlying your argument. Think of the assumption or warrant as the link between a claim and the supporting evidence—the underlying set of beliefs or principles governing your essential perception of the world and the human condition. Warrants answer the question of *how* the data are connected to the claim. Sometimes these warrants are stated, but often they remain unstated. In either instance, they are not necessarily self-evident or universally accepted. They are significant nevertheless, for as generalizations that are far broader than claims and evidence, warrants serve as the bedrock of an argument.

Warrants help to guarantee that a reader will accept your argument, and consequently, it is important to consider them. When you are writing for a friendly or supportive audience, you can usually assume that your readers will accept the warrants supporting your claim, and so you might not even need to state them. For example, if you claim in a report for your biology professor that creationism should not be taught in high school science classrooms, your argument is based on several assumptions or warrants: that the Constitution, for example, requires the separation of church and state, or that there is no scientific basis for creationism. In fact, when making your claim about creationism before a scientist, you also are relying on certain *backings*, which are the principles underlying the warrants themselves—for instance, the idea that a scientist is concerned with scientific objectivity rather than literal interpretations of the Bible, or that scientists deal with the empirical reality and not matters of faith. But what if you were to make your claim in a letter to a local school board, several of whose members want to revise the ninth-grade earth science curriculum to emphasize creationism and evolution equally? In this instance, you would be presenting your argument to a potentially skeptical or hostile audience, so you would have to state your warrants clearly, bolster them with adequate support, and establish solid causal links between your warrants and your backing.

Whether you are writing an argumentative paper or reading an argumentative essay critically, you need to develop the habit of looking for and evaluating the warrants and the backing behind the argument. If you are reading an argumentative essay, and the warrants are stated, it will make this task easier. If the warrants are unstated, you will have to detect and evaluate them. If you are writing an argumentative essay, you should consider whether your audience will probably understand and consent to the warrants that serve as the foundation of your paper. If you have any doubt, then you should include them.

Deal with Opposing Viewpoints

To make your argument as effectively as possible, you need to acknowledge and deal with opposing viewpoints. Any controversial issue is going to have more than one viewpoint, and you must recognize contending claims and handle them fairly. As suggested in the section on audience analysis, you can enhance your credibility by describing these opposing viewpoints fully and accurately, with a respectful rather than hostile tone, even as you demonstrate that your position is the most reasonable and valid.

As a prewriting strategy for refutation, you might try dividing a sheet of paper or your computer screen into three columns, labeling them, from left to right, "Supporting Viewpoints," "Opposing Viewpoints," and "Refutation." Then list the main supporting points for your claim, thinking of possible opposing responses and writing them down as you go. Imagining how the opposition will respond to your supporting reasons will help you to develop refutations, or counterarguments. You can use the resulting chart as a guide to organize sections of your argumentative paper.

The listing technique for refutation forces you to acknowledge opposing viewpoints and also to refute them in a systematic way. It is perfectly appropriate—and even necessary—to demonstrate the weakness or insufficiency of opposing arguments, for refutation strengthens your position. Any complex argument that you present will not be complete unless you skillfully refute all predictable opposing viewpoints, using one of the following techniques:

- Question the opposition's claim: Is it too flimsy or broad, overstated, or improperly grounded in minor propositions?
- Question the evidence: Is it insufficient, outdated, or inaccurate?
- Question the warrants and backing of an opposing argument—those assumptions and beliefs that underpin the opposition's claim.
- Concede some part of the opposition's viewpoint, a subtle but extremely attractive strategy that shows that you are a courteous and unbiased thinker and writer, and that therefore constitutes an appeal to ethics.

Avoid Unfair Emotional Appeals and Errors in Reasoning

When you write and revise an argumentative essay, you need to avoid certain temptations and dangers that are unique to this form of discourse. You always have to make certain that your argumentative strategies are fair and appropriate and that you have avoided oversimplifying your argument. You also need to resist the temptation to include persuasive appeals that distort critical reasoning and to avoid errors in logical reasoning.

Emotional appeals are effective when used appropriately in argumentation, but used unfairly they can distort your logical reasoning. Such loaded arguments are filled with appeals to the reader's emotions, fears, and prejudices. Here are three of the most common fallacies of emotional distortion to avoid:

1. *Transfer* is the association of a proposition with a famous person. Transfer can be either positive ("In the spirit of President Franklin Delano Roosevelt, we should create a jobs program for the nation's unemployed") or negative ("President George W. Bush was the symbol of unbridled capitalism"). Another term for negative transfer is *name calling*. In both the positive and negative types of transfer, however, there is no logical basis for the connection.

2. *Argumentum ad hominem* (to the man) is a strategy that discredits a person in an effort to discredit his or her argument. It attacks the person rather than the position: "Richards is a homosexual and consequently cannot understand the sanctity of heterosexual marriage." In this instance, the individual becomes a false issue.

3. *Argumentum ad populum* (to the people) deliberately arouses an audience's emotions about certain institutions and ideas. Certain words have strong positive or negative connotations. Such words as *patriotism* and *motherhood* are *virtue* words that often prompt the creation of *glittering generalities*. Suggestive words can be used to distort meaning by illogical association and to manipulate an audience to take a stand for or against a proposition: "USC should not take the *totalitarian* step of requiring athletes to maintain a full course load." A related strategy is the *bandwagon* approach, in which the writer generalizes falsely that the crowd or majority is always right: "Everyone is voting for Erikson and you should too."

These unfair emotional appeals are often found in political speech writing, advertising, and propaganda. When you write argumentative essays, you should use persuasive appeal to reinforce rather than distort the logical presentation of your ideas, blending reasonable claims and valid emotional and ethical appeals to convince rather than trick your audience into agreeing with you.

Equally important is the need to avoid errors in reasoning in the construction of an argument. Here are seven types of errors in reasoning, or *logical fallacies,* that are common in argumentative writing:

1. *Hasty generalizations.* A hasty generalization is a conclusion based on insufficient, unrepresentative, or untrue evidence: "The president of the college successfully raised 100 million dollars, so other college presidents should be able to do the same." When you indulge in hasty generalizations, you jump to false conclusions. Hasty generalizations are also at the heart of stereotyping—the uncritical application of an oversimplified generalization to a group or to individual members of the group. Make certain that you have adequate and accurate evidence to support any claim or conclusion.

2. *Broad generalizations.* A broad generalization typically employs words like *all, never,* and *always* to state something absolutely or categorically. It is actually a form of overstatement, as in the sentence "Freud always treated sexuality as the basis of human behavior." Usually, readers can easily find exceptions to such sweeping statements, so it is best to qualify them.

3. *Oversimplification.* Oversimplification reduces alternatives. Several forms of oversimplification can be distinguished:
   a. *Either/or.* Don't assume that there are only two sides to an issue, only two possibilities, only yes or no, only right or wrong: "Either we make English a one-year requirement or college students will not be able to write well."
   b. *No choice.* Don't assume that there is only one possibility: "The United States has no other alternative than to build the Star Wars missile defense system." Parents and politicians are prone to no-other-choice propositions.
   c. *No harm or cost.* Don't assume that a potential benefit will not have significant harms, consequences, or costs: "We should sell North Korea as much wheat as it needs." No-harm generalizations or arguments may overlook dangerous implications. Always consider alternative evidence.
   d. *One solution.* Don't assume that a complicated issue has only one solution: "Embryonic stem cells should not be used for research, for using them in this way will lead to the destruction of human life." Always consider evidence for other solutions or alternative approaches to issues and problems.

4. *Begging the question.* Do not assume in your premises or in your evidence what is to be proved in the conclusion. For example, if you argue that vandalism by teenagers is unavoidable because teenagers are young and irresponsible, you are begging the question because you are not proving your premise. Another form of begging the question is to take a conclusion for granted before it is proved.

5. *False cause-and-effect relationships.* Perhaps the most common error in trying to establish causal relationships is known as the *post hoc, ergo propter hoc* fallacy (after this, therefore because of this). The fact that one event *follows* another is not proof that the first *caused* the second. If you maintain, for instance, that there is an increase in the crime rate every time there is a full moon, you are falsely identifying an unrelated event as a cause. Many superstitions—popular, political, and otherwise—illogically assume that one event somehow causes another.

6. *Disconnected ideas.* Termed *non sequitur* (it does not follow), this fault in reasoning arises when there is no logical connection between two or more ideas. Put differently, an argument's conclusion is not related to its premises: "Barack Obama makes a good president because he works out every morning." Sometimes you think that a connection exists but you fail to state it in writing. For example, you may think that presidents need to stay in shape for several reasons. In other words,

you may see the logical connection between your ideas, but if you don't make it explicit, readers may think there is a non sequitur.

7. *Weak or false analogies.* An *analogy* is a type of comparison that explains a subject by comparing it to the features of another essentially dissimilar subject: "Unless we learn to think critically about the Niagara of information that washes over us every day, we will be lost in a flood of rumors and gossip." Analogies can be used to illustrate a point, although they should always be used carefully and with discretion. More significantly, an analogy can *never* function as evidence or logical proof of a position.

The hallmark of argumentation is sound critical thinking. If you present your claims, grounds, and evidence carefully; are willing to assemble the best and most objective data; treat the opposition with respect; and are flexible in responding to new ideas, you will be well on your way to constructing a solid argumentative essay. A successful argumentative paper reveals a writer who possesses an inquiring mind—who is able to judge opinions on the basis of evidence, reason well, and back up ideas and beliefs in a convincing and valid way.

Argumentative Synthesis

Synthesis, as discussed in Chapter 1, is the process we use to combine information from two or more sources and infer relationships among them. Whereas the primary aim of explanatory synthesis is to convey information, the aim of argumentative synthesis is to convince readers that a claim is correct or valid. Whether we evaluate the relative quality of the readings (in other words, provide a *critique* of the texts) or draw material from readings to support a claim of our own, argumentative synthesis requires us to take a position on the materials at hand.

With explanatory synthesis, as we have seen, we try to accurately identify the key ideas and purposes of various writers, but we do not argue for or against a certain viewpoint. For example, here is the student's thesis based on the readings by Elbow and Murray from Chapter 2:

Both Peter Elbow and Donald Murray stress the importance of process in the craft of composition, but approach the process from different perspectives.

In this instance, the student makes a modest but useful attempt to convey information accurately through explanatory synthesis.

Consider the shift from explanation to argument as the writer now takes sides in presenting the ideas of Elbow and Murray:

Although Peter Elbow's theory of freewriting might be useful to certain students with basic writing problems, Donald Murray in his stress on revision offers far more useful advice for mainstream college students who want to improve their writing.

Observe how the writer moves from explanatory to argumentative synthesis as she critiques the two readings and their authors. She takes sides. She presents a claim (which she will have to support with convincing grounds or evidence). She wants us to agree with her interpretation and assessment.

Critiquing   As you prepare for argumentative synthesis, rely on the strategies for critical reading and writing that were outlined in Chapters 1 and 2 as well as the guidelines for argumentative synthesis presented in this chapter. At the outset, it would also be wise to focus your critical response on *critiquing*—the evaluation of each text's quality or worth based on a clearly defined set of guidelines. With critiquing, you cannot rely on a personal opinion or preference. Critiquing demands clear criteria and objective assessment of the text. It is a necessary aspect of successful argumentative synthesis.

When critiquing texts, you follow either *general academic standards* of evaluation (criteria that apply to many disciplines) or *discipline-specific standards* (for instance, criteria used by scholars in cognitive psychology or specialists in international law). In most cases, you will be working with general standards when critiquing sources in college composition courses. You will consider issues like the style, organization, importance of subject, effectiveness of a writer's claim, and quality of evidence as the evaluative criteria for your critique. Stated differently, you will agree, disagree, or (in certain cases) agree *and* disagree to varying degrees with a writer and his or her text—but do so from the vantage point of informed judgment.

The formal demands of critiquing are neither mysterious, intimidating, nor overwhelming. In everyday situations, we engage in critiquing: arguing over the merits of two recent films, evaluating the skills of various sports stars, praising our favorite musicians, supporting one candidate for political office over all others, or logging into a Web site to check and perhaps comment on the best (or worst) professors on campus. Writing a formal critique is perhaps more of a challenge than situations from everyday life, but if you follow basic steps the process of critiquing becomes manageable.

1. *Carefully read and evaluate each text.* Annotate the selection: Cite the source of the article and the author's intended audience, look for the thesis or claim, identify the author's purpose (to inform, argue, or entertain), highlight the primary and secondary evidence, and consider the style and organization of the piece.
2. *Summarize your findings,* focusing on the author's main points.
3. *Evaluate the reading.* Consider the overall validity of the author's presentation: Has the writer achieved his or her purpose? What is the quality of the supporting evidence? Is the information or evidence convincing and representative? Has the author interpreted material correctly and argued logically?
4. *Write your response.* Establish your claim, focusing on specific aspects of the text that best illuminate your thesis or argument. Explain to what extent you agree or disagree with the author and what standards you are applying. Offer examples to explain your judgments and support your interpretation.
5. *Revise the draft.* Clarify your position in relation to the author's text. Check the accuracy of your information about the text. Make certain that your assessment or interpretation is based on clear criteria. Refine and thoroughly develop your assertions, correcting any fallacies in reasoning and argumentation.

Guidelines for Argumentative Synthesis   As you read and respond to texts using argumentative synthesis, you might find certain essays easy to understand. However, you should be prepared to contend with challenging subjects—for instance, essays about genetic engineering or the constitutional implications of electronic surveillance. In each instance, you will have to make complex topics intelligible for your primary and secondary audiences. Sometimes your instructor will offer clear guidelines for determining the relative strengths and weaknesses of the texts. Or your instructor might ask you to formulate your own argument based on several assigned texts and/or your own research on the subject. Whether the instructor assigns the texts or you locate sources on your own, you must decide on how best to treat these texts fairly and accurately while at the same time positing a claim, organizing evidence and documenting sources (see Chapter 4), and presenting findings in a coherent way.

As you start to formulate a strategy, realize that there is no single solution to effective argumentative synthesis. In reality, argumentative synthesis, like any form of writing, is a recursive, or back-and-forth, process in which the strategies you employ can be drawn from a vast repertoire of rhetorical possibilities. For example, you could use the block method explained in the section in Chapter 2 on comparison and contrast (see pages 49–50) to organize a paper in which you critique essays A and B, which present opposing viewpoints on a recent film. For a different assignment requiring you to defend a position on Wal-Mart, you might have to synthesize material from several sources, relying on the introduction to writing research papers that appears in Chapter 4. Even with the many strategies available to you, it is possible to establish a set of useful guidelines for argumentative synthesis:

1. *Analyze the assignment.* Determine whether your primary purpose will be to critique texts or to argue your position based on several readings. (While it is easy to separate these goals, it should be evident that critiquing sources is relevant to both.)
2. *Select and carefully review the readings.* Perhaps your instructor will assign the readings— which should make your task easier. But if you have to find the readings, whether your purpose is to critique the texts or generate your own argument, you will have to highlight the key claims, warrants, and support in those texts that suit your essential aim.
3. *Take notes and formulate a claim or major proposition.* Critically read and reread passages, identifying key claims and presentation of ideas. Label and define terms that the author introduces. Write brief summaries, preferably in single sentences, of all texts. Formulate your claim, checking it against the texts you are critiquing to make certain it is accurate and conclusive. Decide on an organizational plan: Will you, for instance, rely on comparison and contrast, classification, or some other strategy to structure your claim?
4. *Write the first draft.* Establish your claim at the outset. Introduce the authors, texts, or passages that you will critique. Present the key definition, principle, or standard of evaluation you will apply to analyze and assess these texts. Evaluate the validity of each text, pointing to such elements as logic, evidence, weight or importance of the subject, and overall presentation. Agree or disagree with a text's assumptions and viewpoints. Document your sources. (See Chapter 4.)
5. *Revise your synthesis.* Refine the introduction so that your claim is clearly defined. Improve the organization of the main parts of your synthesis, making certain that support is well ordered, critical observations are compelling, transitions are strong, and information about the texts under consideration is presented in a fair and balanced way. Strengthen the conclusion by stating convincingly the importance of your insights and findings and the validity of your argument.

Argumentative synthesis, like all types of argumentative writing, presents a claim about which reasonable people might agree or disagree. The challenge is to formulate your synthesis in such a way that it convinces or persuades your audience to agree with your assessment and basic viewpoint.

CH 3   **www.mhhe.com/mhreaderbrief1e**

- *Portfolio on Argumentation*
- *Image Gallery:* Chapter images in color
- *Ch. 3 Networking*

chapter *4*

Writing a Research Project in the 21st Century

A research project is a report—often but not always an essay, or paper—in which you synthesize information on your topic, contributing your own analysis and evaluation to the subject. Research writing is a form of problem solving. You identify a problem, form a hypothesis (an unproven thesis, theory, or argument), gather and organize information from various sources, assess and interpret data, evaluate alternatives, reach conclusions, and provide documentation.

Research writing is a skill to be developed rather than a trial to be borne. Online library catalogs, electronic searches, and word processing have taken much of the drudgery out of writing research papers. And effective research writing goes beyond reporting information in a bland and boring recitation of facts.

Research actually means the careful investigation of a subject in order to discover or revise facts, theories, or applications. Your purpose is to demonstrate how other researchers approach a problem, how you synthesize their most useful ideas, and how you treat that problem yourself. A good research paper subtly blends your ideas and synthesizes the attitudes or findings of others. In research writing, you are dealing with ideas that are already in the public domain, but you are also contributing to knowledge.

RESEARCH WRITING: PRECONCEPTIONS AND PRACTICE

When your ideas—rather than the ideas of others—become the center of the research process, writing a research project becomes dynamic instead of static.

Consider the following tasks:

- Evaluating critical responses to a best-selling novel, a book of poetry, an album, or an award-winning film
- Analyzing the impact of voter turnout on presidential politics during a recent decade
- Investigating a literary, political, or scientific scandal of the previous century
- Assessing the effectiveness of urban, suburban, and rural schools, comparing specific measures of student success
- Defining a popular dietary or health-related term, examining how it influences consumer behavior when shopping for food
- Examining how media outlets use social networking Web sites to deliver content to audiences in target demographics

How would a professional researcher view these projects? First, the researcher sees a subject as a *problem* rather than a mere topic. Often this problem is authorized or assigned by a collaborator, an editor, or a supervisor in the researcher's workplace. The researcher has the task of developing or testing a hypothesis stemming from the particular problem—for example, whether a vegetarian diet effectively wards off cancer. *Hypothesis formation* is at the heart of professional research.

Second, the researcher often conducts primary as well as secondary research. *Primary research* relies on analysis and synthesis of texts, letters, manuscripts, and other materials, whether written, visual, or aural. *Secondary research* relies on sources that comment on the primary sources. For example, a critic's commentary on *Citizen Kane* or a historian's analysis of the 2008 presidential election would be secondary sources; the film itself or a speech delivered by Barack Obama in 2008 would be primary sources. Because primary sources are not necessarily more reliable than secondary sources, you must always evaluate the reliability of both types of material. Critics can misinterpret, and experts often disagree, forcing you to weigh evidence and reach your own conclusions.

Third, all researchers face deadlines. The solution to a research problem is required to take action, to reach a decision, to influence policy, or to determine a business plan. Confronted with deadlines, professional researchers learn to *telescope* their efforts in order to obtain information quickly. Common strategies include networking (using personal and professional contacts as well as guides to organizations), browsing or searching online, conducting bibliographical searches, and turning to online databases, annotated bibliographies (listing articles on the topic with commentaries on each item), and specialized indexes (focusing on a particular field or discipline). Other strategies include consulting review articles, which evaluate other resources, and browsing through current journals and periodicals (which may provide useful background as well as the most current thinking about the topic).

Finally, good researchers recognize that knowledge in this era tends increasingly toward interdisciplinary concerns and that they cannot confine their search for evidence to one subject area, such as history or physics. Much professional researching cuts across academic subjects and disciplines. The interdisciplinary nature of many research projects creates special problems for the researcher, especially in the use of bibliographical materials, which tend to be subject-oriented. Such research is not beyond your talents and abilities. Learn not only how to use library and electronic sources selectively and efficiently, but also how to view the world outside your library and computer as a vast laboratory to be used fruitfully in order to solve your research problems.

NAVIGATING THE RESEARCH PROCESS

The research process involves thinking, searching, reading, writing, and rewriting. The final product—the research paper or project—is the result of your discoveries in and contributions to the realm of ideas about your topic. The process of researching and composing moves back and forth over a series of activities, and the actual act of writing remains unique to the individual researcher. Regardless of a writer's experience or individual idiosyncrasies, he or she can benefit from thinking about the research process as a series of several interrelated phases.

Phases in the Research Process

Phase I: Defining Your Objective

1. Choose a *researchable* topic.
2. Identify a *problem* inherent in the topic that gives you the reason for writing about the topic.
3. Examine the *purpose* of or the *benefits* to be gained from conducting research on the topic.
4. Think about the assumptions, interests, and needs of your *audience*.
5. Decide how you are going to *limit* your topic.
6. Establish a working *hypothesis* to guide and control the scope and direction of your research.

Phase 2: Locating Your Sources

1. Decide on your *methodology*—the types or varieties of primary and secondary research you plan to conduct. Determine the method of collecting data.
2. Explore your library's online catalog (a utility that lets you search its holdings and databases to which it subscribes) to *determine the viability of your topic,* including how much secondary research has been done on your topic and whether your hypothesis is likely to stand up.
3. Develop a *tentative working bibliography,* a file listing sources that seem relevant to your topic.
4. Review your bibliography, and *reassess your topic and hypothesis.*

Phase 3: Gathering and Organizing Data

1. *Obtain your sources,* taking notes on all information related directly to your thesis.
2. Analyze and organize your information. Design a *preliminary outline* with a *tentative thesis* if your findings support your hypothesis.
3. *Revise your thesis* if your findings suggest alternative conclusions.

Phase 4: Writing and Submitting the Paper

1. Write a *rough draft* of the paper, concentrating on the flow of thoughts and integrating research findings into the text of the paper.
2. Write a *first revision* to tighten organization, improve style, and check on the placement of data. Prepare citations that identify the sources of your information. Assemble a list of the references you have cited in your paper.
3. *Prepare the manuscript* using the format called for by the course, the discipline, or the person authorizing the research paper.

Phase 1: Defining Your Objective

The first step in research writing is to select a topic that promises an adventure for you in the realm of ideas and that will interest, if not excite, your audience while meeting the expectations and requirements of your assignment.

You can maximize time and effort if you approach the research project as a problem to be investigated and solved, a controversy to take a position on, or a question to be answered. As a basis, you need a strong hypothesis or working thesis (which may be little more than a calculated guess). The point of your investigation is to identify, illustrate, explain, argue, or prove that thesis. Develop a hypothesis before you actually begin to conduct research; otherwise, you will discover that you are simply reading in or about a topic, instead of reading toward the objective of substantiating your thesis or proposition.

Of course, before you can formulate a hypothesis, you need to start with a general idea of what subject you want to explore, what your purpose is going to be, and how you plan to select and limit a topic from your larger subject area.

FORMULATING A HYPOTHESIS

A topic will lead to a researchable hypothesis if it does the following:

- Meets the demands of your assignment
- Strongly interests you
- Engages knowledge you already possess
- Raises questions that will require both primary and secondary research to answer
- Provokes you toward an opinion or argument

To help you find and limit a research topic, try the following strategies:

- *Reflect on the assignment.* If your professor gave you a specific written assignment— even if it doesn't include a specific topic—review the assignment with an eye toward keywords that indicate the purpose of your research work. Highlight or underline key verbs such as *solve, argue, find, discover,* or *present.* Write out questions for your professor, and either ask them in class or arrange for a conference with her or him.
- *Ask questions.* Ask yourself, in writing, a series of specific questions about your subject, combining related questions. Phrase questions in such a way as to pose problems that demand answers. Then try to determine which topic best fits the demands of the assignment.
- *Prewrite and brainstorm.* Idea generation strategies such as prewriting and brainstorming can help you to determine what you already know or believe about an assigned topic. If your assignment is to research gender roles in popular culture, you might begin by brainstorming on how male characters were depicted in the last three movies you saw. For more on prewriting strategies, see pages 35–43.
- *Do some background reading.* Your professor will probably assign a research topic that has something to do with the content of your class. Review the assigned readings for your course as well as your own notes. If your professor has suggested additional readings on the research topic or provided a bibliography, consult a few of those sources as

well. Although the purpose of your background reading is to generate ideas, you should still use the note-taking strategies discussed in the following pages to ensure that you give proper credit later for any ideas you use from this preliminary reading.

Throughout, keep in mind that your purpose is to solve a *specific* problem, shed light on a *specific* topic, state an opinion on a *specific* controversy, or offer *specific* proofs or solutions. Your audience does not want a welter of general information, a bland summary of the known and the obvious, or free associations or meditations on an issue or problem. You know that your audience wants answers; consequently, a way to locate your ideal topic is to ask questions about it.

Phase 2: Locating Your Sources

Begin locating your sources as early as possible for a number of reasons. First, research takes time and patience. Second, you most likely will have to share sources with other students working on similar projects. Many sources are not available online, even through library databases, and some print sources only have one copy or are not in the library. Third, your library may not have access to every source you need; when this is the case, you will have to depend on interlibrary loan services (in which your library borrows the source temporarily or obtains photocopies or scans of it), which can take additional time.

If you have a sufficiently narrowed topic and a working hypothesis, you should know what type of information will be most useful for your report. Not all information on a topic is relevant, of course; with a hypothesis, you can distinguish between useful and irrelevant material.

To use your time efficiently, you have to *streamline* your method for collecting data. Most research writing for college courses relies heavily on secondary research material available in libraries or online. To develop a preliminary list of sources, go directly to general reference works or a list of sources or reserved readings provided by your professor. If you already have some knowledge about the subject, begin with resources that permit you to find a continuing series of articles and books on a single issue—specifically, periodical indexes, newspaper indexes, and online catalogs. Again, you should be moving as rapidly as possible from the general to the specific.

Should You Begin Your Research Online?   The immense capabilities of the Internet make it very tempting to begin your search for information online, via a commercial search engine such as Google. If your research topic demands very contemporary and localized knowledge (a current political campaign, a recent medical breakthrough, a trend in popular culture), beginning your search online can be optimal. This method can also be useful for background reading and idea generating. However, traditional research—both academic and professional—is generally more productive and efficient if begun via a library's online catalog. Commercial search engines usually generate very limited returns when research topics require you to provide deeper contexts and backgrounds, or when primary and secondary sources are restricted to academic journals and databases. Although we begin our discussion of locating sources with guidelines for searching online, only you can determine the most efficient and effective way of beginning your research.

Finding Online Materials   The Internet is composed of millions of Web pages, so knowing where to begin your search might seem like a daunting task. Your library, your college Web site, or your instructor's home page may list useful sites, organized by discipline or interest area. Online clearinghouses and print materials also identify especially useful sites for researchers. Depending on your topic, there are subject-specific online pages that link you to everything you could want, including both primary and secondary sources. *Findlaw* is a good example for law-related content; most of the sciences and many of the liberal arts have useful pages like this. The UC-Berkeley Library suggests also using subject directories (whose subject-specific contents are supplied by humans rather than computer programs), like *lii.org, academicinfo.net,* or *infomine.ucr.edu,* to look for academic resources. Once you have located a URL (universal resource locator) for a site on the Web, you can go directly to that location. The end of the address is one indication of the kind of location you will reach. Some of the most popular domain extensions include:

.org = nonprofit organizations, including professional groups

.edu = colleges, universities, and other educational institutions

.com = businesses and commercial enterprises

.gov = government branches and agencies

.mil = branches of the military

.net = major computer networks

.tv = video content

.museum = museums

.info = informational sites

.store = retail businesses

.web = sites about the World Wide Web

.coop = cooperative organizations

.int = international organizations

.pro = credentialed professionals

Domain extensions can also include the Web site's country of origin (like .au for Australia or .uk for United Kingdom). New domain extensions are created often to accommodate the ever-expanding volume of Web content. Keep in mind, though, that the domain extension is but the initial way to identify the content of a site. For example, some museums use the .museum extension, while others use .org; still others are part of universities and therefore use .edu. Some .com sites offer both commerce and information, just as some .org sites sell products or services. A careful evaluation of the contents and research about the organization responsible for the site's maintenance are called for before you rely on a source to help prove your hypothesis.

If you need to search the Internet for sources, try using a search engine like Google, using keywords. Given the enormous number of Web sites and their component pages, you need to select your search terms carefully so that you locate reasonable numbers of pertinent sources.

A Web page often supplies links to other useful sites, separately or as hyperlinked text. If you click on the link, usually distinguished from plain text by formatting or color, you can go directly to that related site. For example, the site *www.fedworld.gov*, sponsored by the federal government, includes links to federal databases and a keyword search that can lead to particular resources.

Following a chain of links requires critical thinking to assess whether each link seems reliable and current. This kind of research can take a great deal of time, especially if you explore each link and then follow it to the next. As you move from link to link, keep your hypothesis in mind so that you are not distracted from your central purpose.

Look beyond conventional online sources too. Streaming media, like Webcasts (television and radio content) and podcasts (downloadable media files), can be gleaned for information, as can professional blogs (Web-based journals or commentaries written by content experts) and professional bulletin boards (sites where users can post and exchange content-specific information). Before using open source (wikis) and casual networking sites as sources for your paper, however, always ask your instructor for his/her policy. The content from such sites can be problematical because you cannot always verify its accuracy or the authority of the poster, and it is often not cited correctly (if at all).

EVALUATING ONLINE SOURCES

- Is the author identified? Is the site sponsored by a reputable business, agency, or organization? Does the site supply information so that you can contact the author or the sponsor?

- Does the site provide information comparable to that in other reputable sources, including print sources?

- Does the site seem accurate and authoritative or quirky and idiosyncratic?

- Does the site seem unbiased, or is it designed to promote a particular business, industry, organization, political position, or philosophy?

- Does the site supply appropriate, useful links? Do these links seem current and relevant? Do most of them work? Does the site document sources for the information it supplies directly?

- Has the site been updated or revised recently?

- Does the site seem carefully designed? Is it easy and logical to navigate? Are its graphics well integrated and related to the site's overall purpose or topic? Is the text carefully edited?

Using the Library's Online Catalog   The library's catalog lists information by author, title, subject, and keyword. Of the four, the subject listings are the best place to look for sources, but they are not necessarily the place to start your research. Begin by determining what your library offers. For instance, the online catalog may include all library materials or only holdings acquired fairly recently. The catalog also may or may not supply up-to-date information because books may take several years to appear in print and some weeks to be cataloged. Thus you may need to turn to separate indexes of articles, primary documents, and online materials for the most current material. Remember also that when you search by subject, you are searching the subject fields that are assigned by the cataloger. This differs from a keyword search in which the researcher—you, the writer—selects key terms that describe the research situation and enters them into a search engine that will find these terms anywhere within the item record—whether they happen to be in the title, comments, notes, or subject fields.

On the other hand, if your library has a consolidated online system, you may have immediate access to materials available regionally and to extensive online databases. You may be able to use the same terminal to search for books shelved in your own library, materials available locally through the city or county library, and current periodicals listed in specialized databases. Such access can simplify and consolidate your search.

Subject indexing can be useful when you are researching a topic around which a considerable body of information and analysis has already developed. Identify as many keywords or relevant subject classifications as possible. Use these same terms as you continue your search for sources, and add additional terms identified in the entries you find. The example below illustrates a keyword search for materials on gender issues and advertising.

Results of an article search through the Ohio State University library's Web site. This search across subscription databases uses keywords and Boolean logic—"gender AND advertising." In this screen, the topic has been narrowed to EBSCOHost results and further limited to "Magazines, Masculinity." The researcher has also filtered results to include only peer-reviewed and full-text articles.

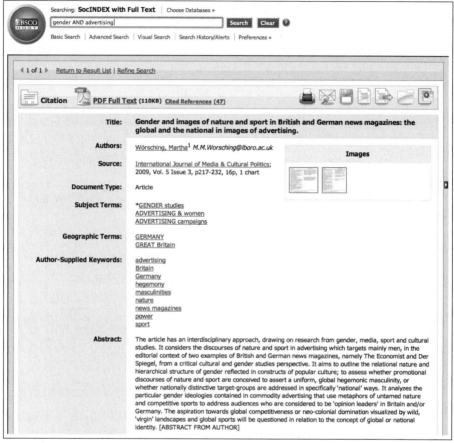

Detailed bibliographic entry in EBSCOHost for a potential source. Among other features, this page includes an abstract and a link to a PDF of the full-text article.

Clicking on the Extended Display option for an item supplies full bibliographic information as well as the location of the book in the library and its availability. On the facing page, you can see the wealth of information shown for the first item listed on the search screen above.

There are two ways to make this search of the keywords *Gender* and *Advertising* more complete. First, think of alternate terms that might come into play; for example, *sex* is a synonym for *gender,* and *advertising* is only one form of the verb *to advertise.* A searcher would probably want to include *advertise* or *advertisement.* Using the truncation symbol (in this case, *, but it varies in different library catalogs) would help to catch these variations. The best course is to review the search tips that nearly always accompany any public catalog. Alternatively, select one of the titles you feel is most closely related to your subject, and pull up that record. For example, "Sex in advertising" and "Sex role in advertising" could yield fruitful links, directing you to other materials that have been assigned the same headings. This is a much more direct search than thumbing through the red Library of Congress Subject Headings volumes to find out what an appropriate subject heading might be, and it will catch those titles you might have missed when selecting your keywords.

Checking General Reference Sources　General reference sources include encyclopedias, dictionaries, handbooks, atlases, biographies, almanacs, yearbooks, abstracts, and annual reviews of scholarship within a field. Many of these sources are available both in print and online. Begin your search for these sources in your library's reference room. General reference sources can be useful for background reading and for an introduction to your topic. The bibliographies they contain (such as those that end articles in an encyclopedia) are generally limited, however, and frequently out-of-date. Professional researchers do not rely exclusively on general reference sources to solve research problems, and neither should you.

Searching Indexes and Databases　Electronic and print indexes and databases include up-to-date articles in journals, magazines, and newspapers. Indexes usually list materials that you will then need to locate. Some databases, however, may include complete texts

---

ELECTRONIC AND PRINT INDEXES AND DATABASES

General Resources

American Statistics Index

Congressional Information Service Index

Expanded Academic Index

FirstSearch Catalog

Magazine Index

National Newspaper Index

New York Times Index

Specialized Resources

Applied Science and Technology Index

Biological and Agricultural Index

Business Periodicals Index

Education Index

ERIC (Educational Resources Information Center)

General Business File

Humanities Index

Index Medicus or Medline

MLA (Modern Language Association) International Bibliography

PsychLit

Public Affairs Information Service (PAIS)

Social Sciences Index

of articles or even books. Ask a reference librarian how to access materials on microfiche, microfilm, CD-ROM, or online. If you need historical information or want to trace a topic back in time, however, you may need to use print indexes as well because electronic sources may date back only a few years or cover only a certain number of years.

The indexes and databases listed here are just a few of the many resources that are widely available. Some are general; others are specialized by discipline or field. Such indexes supply ready access to a wide array of useful materials, including articles, books, newspaper stories, statistics, and government documents. Ask the librarian in the reference area or the catalog area whether these are available in print or online.

Each index or database restricts the sources it lists in specific ways, based on the particular topics covered or the types of sources included. For example, the full title of the *MLA Bibliography* indicates that it lists "Books and Articles on the Modern Languages and Literatures." Besides books and articles, however, it includes essays or chapters collected in a book, conference papers, films, recordings, and other similar sources, but it does not list summaries or encyclopedia articles. Its primary subjects include literary criticism, literary themes and genres, linguistics, and folklore. Thus you can search for an author's name, a title, a literary period, or subjects as varied as hoaxes, metaphysical poetry, and self-knowledge, all in relation to studies in language and literature. This bibliography is available online and is updated regularly during the year.

As your search progresses and your hypothesis evolves, you will find resources even more specifically focused on your interests.

EVALUATING PRINT SOURCES

- Is the author a credible authority? Does the book cover, preface, or byline indicate the author's background, education, or other publications? Do other writers refer to this source and accept it as reliable? Is the publisher or publication reputable?

- Does the source provide information comparable to that in other reputable sources?

- Does the source seem accurate and authoritative, or does it make claims that are not generally accepted?

- Does the source seem unbiased, or does it seem to promote a particular business, industry, organization, political position, or philosophy?

- Does the source supply notes, a bibliography, or other information to document its sources?

- If the source has been published recently, does it include current information? Are its sources current or dated?

- Does the source seem carefully edited and printed?

Using Nonprint Sources   In the library and online, you have access to potentially useful nonprint materials of all kinds—videos, DVDs, CD-ROMs, films, slides, works of art, records of performances, microfiche, microfilm, or other sources that might relate to your topic. When you search for these sources, you may find them in your library's main catalog or in a separate listing. In the catalog entry, be sure to note the location of the source and its access hours, especially if they are limited. If you need a projector or other equipment to use the material, ask the reference librarian where you go to find such equipment.

Developing Field Resources   You may want to *interview* an expert, *survey* the opinions of other students, *observe* an event or situation, or examine it over a long period of time as a *case study*. Ask your instructor's advice as you design questions for an interview or a survey or procedures for a short- or long-term observation. Also be sure to find out whether you need permission to conduct this kind of research on campus or in the community.

The questions you ask will determine the nature and extent of the responses that you receive; as a result, your questions should be developed after you have established clear objectives for your field research. You also need to plan how you will analyze the answers before, not after, you administer the questionnaire or conduct the interview. Once you have drafted interview or survey questions, test them by asking your friends or classmates to respond. Use these preliminary results to revise any ambiguous questions and to test your method of analysis. If you are an observer, establish in advance what you will observe, how you will record your observations, and how you will analyze them. Get permission, if needed, from the site where you will conduct your observation. Your field sources can help you expand your knowledge of the topic, see its applications or discover real-world surprises, or locate more sources, whether print, electronic, or field.

Using Visuals in Your Paper   Some of the nonprint sources you consult in your research might be useful to include, rather than just cite or refer to, in your own final paper. Technology has made it very easy to cut and paste visuals from sources into your own work, as well as to create and incorporate your own visuals. Be sure that when you incorporate other visuals into your paper (or when you create a visual, such as a graph or chart, that draws on data from another source) you correctly and completely cite the source of the visual data. A caption that briefly describes the visual and gives its source information is not always sufficient; be sure to check what your professor or style guide (MLA, APA, etc.) stipulates.

Using Nonprint Sources in Electronic or Online Versions of Your Paper   Working in some formats, you can enhance your paper's content, not only with visuals, but also with other media or resources. If you are submitting your project electronically or posting it online, you could create hyperlinks to electronic versions of primary and secondary sources. Hyperlinks are also useful when you need to link to electronic sources like audio or video files or when you want to make supplemental information on a topic or keyword available to be viewed by readers at their discretion. Occasionally you might also embed a feature like a YouTube clip in your project; however, be careful not to violate any copyright laws—especially if your work will appear on the open (not password-protected) Internet.

In order to gain expert information, you may wish to contact an informed individual directly by e-mail, following up on contact information supplied at a Web site or through other references. If your topic is of long-term interest to you and you have plenty of time to do your research, you may want to join a *listserv* or *e-mail conference*, a group of people interested in a particular topic, whose messages are sent automatically to all participants. Exchanges among those interested in a topic may also be posted on a *bulletin board server* or a *newsgroup*, where you can read both past and ongoing messages and exchanges. The information you receive from others may be very authoritative and reliable, but it may also represent the biased viewpoint of the individual. Assess it carefully by comparing it with information from other sources, print as well as electronic.

CONSIDERATIONS IN USING NONPRINT SOURCES IN YOUR RESEARCH

- Is a nonprint source the most effective and useful way to present data? For example, if your paper is researching the ways in which photojournalists depict presidential candidates, you will probably want to include sample photographs in your paper. If your topic is trends in voter turnout, you might consult charts and graphs in your research but describe in words the evidence from those visuals rather than reproduce them in your paper. The reverse can also be true: If a source contains great quantities of data, arranging it in an appropriate graph or chart can help readers understand a lot of complex information at a glance. Also, carefully constructed charts and graphs can help communicate across language and cultural barriers.

- Can the source be easily reproduced? What kinds of technology will you need to capture an image, import it into your text, and print it legibly (and, if necessary, in color)? What capabilities will your audience need to access a visual? For example, if you are submitting a paper electronically, remember that large visual files can take a long time to download. Also, your audience might need plug-ins, add-ins, or specific programs to view videos or listen to audio files.

- Have you gathered and noted all of the necessary source information, so that you can provide context (and, if necessary, a caption) for the visual as well as accurate bibliographical citation?

Preparing a Working Bibliography   The purpose of compiling a working bibliography is to keep track of possible sources, to determine the nature and extent of the information available, to provide a complete and accurate list of sources to be presented in the paper, and to make preparing the final bibliography much easier. Include in your working bibliography all sources that you have a hunch will be potentially useful. After all, you may not be able to obtain all the items listed, and some material will turn out to be useless, repetitious, or irrelevant to your topic. Such entries can easily be eliminated at a later stage when you prepare your final bibliography.

One way to simplify the task of preparing your final Works Cited or References section is to use a standard form for your working bibliography, whether you use cards or computer entries. The models given later in this chapter are based on two guides, abbreviated as MLA and APA. The *MLA Handbook for Writers of Research Papers* (New York: Modern Language Association of America, 2009; 7th ed.) is generally followed in English, foreign languages, and other fields in the humanities. Instructors in the social sciences, natural sciences, education, and business are likely to favor the style presented

---

INFORMATION FOR A WORKING
BIBLIOGRAPHY

Record the following information for a book:

1. Name(s) of author(s)

2. Title of book, italicized

3. Place of publication

4. Publisher's name

5. Date of publication

6. Call number or location in library

7. URL or DOI and date of access online

Record the following information for an article in a periodical:

1. Name(s) of author(s)

2. Title of article, in quotation marks

3. Title of periodical, italicized

4. Volume number or issue number

5. Date of publication

6. Page numbers on which article appears

7. Call number or location in library

8. URL or DOI and date of access online

---

in the *Publication Manual of the American Psychological Association* (Washington, DC: American Psychological Association, 2010; 6th ed.). Because the preferred form of citation of sources varies considerably from field to field, check with your instructors to determine which of these two formats they prefer or if they recommend another style. Follow any specific directions from an instructor carefully.

As you locate relevant sources, take down complete information on each item on a 3 × 5 note card or start a bibliographic file on your computer. Complete information, properly recorded, will save you the trouble of having to scurry back to the library or back to a Web page for missing data when compiling your final bibliography. Be sure to list the source's call number and location in the library or its URL or DOI (digital object identifier); then you can easily find the material once you are ready to begin reading and relocate it if you need to refer to it again. When preparing bibliography cards for entries listed in annotated bibliographies, citation indexes, and abstracts, you might want to jot down notes from any pertinent summaries that are provided. Complete a separate card or file entry for each item that you think is promising.

Once you begin to build a bibliographic database, you can refer to your listings and supplement them each time you are assigned a paper.

Author	Taranto, Gina
Title of book	*Discourse Adjectives*
Place of publication	New York
Publisher Name	Routledge
Date of publication	2006
Call Number	P273.T372006

Author's first name: Erin
Author's last name: Minear
Title of article: "Music and the Crisis of Meaning in *Othello*"
Title of periodical: *Studies in English Literature 1500–1900*
Volume number: 49
Issue number: 2
Date of publication: Spring 2009
Page numbers of article: 355–70
URL: *Wilson Web*
Date of access online: 15 August 2009

Reassessing Your Topic   Once you have compiled your working bibliography, take the time to reassess the entire project before you get more deeply involved in it. Analyze your bibliography cards or files carefully to determine whether you should proceed to the next stage of information gathering.

Your working bibliography should send out signals that help you shape your thinking about the topic. The dominant signal should indicate that your topic is neither too narrow nor too broad. Generally, a bibliography of 10–15 promising entries for a 1,500-word paper indicates that your topic might be properly limited at this stage. A listing of only 3 or 4 entries signals that you must expand the topic or consider discarding it. Conversely, a listing of 100 entries warns that you might be working yourself into a research swamp.

Another signal from your working bibliography should help you decide whether your hypothesis is on target or could be easily recast to make it more precise. Entry titles, abstracts, and commentaries on articles are excellent sources of confirmation. If established scholarship does not support your hypothesis, it would be best to discard your hypothesis and begin again.

Finally, the working bibliography should provide signals about the categories or parts of your research. Again, titles, abstracts, and commentaries are useful. In other words, as you compile the entries, you can begin to think through the problem and to perceive contours of thought that will dictate the organization of the paper even before you begin to do detailed research. Your working bibliography should be filled with such signals.

Phase 3: Gathering and Organizing Data

If your working bibliography confirms the value, logic, and practicality of your research project, you can move to the next phase of the research process: taking notes and organizing information. Information shapes and refines your thinking; you move from an overview to a more precise understanding, analysis, and interpretation of the topic. By the end of this third phase, you should be able to transform your hypothesis into a thesis and your assembled notes into an outline.

Plagiarism and Intellectual Property   In this phase of the research process, it is especially critical that you maintain a clear distinction between ideas, opinions, information, words from other sources and your interpretation of that information. *Plagiarism,* or the illicit appropriation of content and ideas, can result from sloppy note taking or poor study habits. Taking care to summarize, paraphrase, and quote from sources with scrupulous care—as well as ensuring that you have given yourself enough time to consider your argument and write your paper—will go a long way toward avoiding plagiarism.

The temptation to plagiarize is especially keen in an age when essays can easily be purchased online and when primary and secondary source information can be cut and pasted at the click of a button into your work. Be aware that such behavior in the classroom may result in a failing grade, suspension, or worse. In the professional world, plagiarism can even result in the loss of a job, the destruction of a reputation, and criminal charges. Plagiarism is a kind of theft. What a plagiarist steals is called, in legal terms, *intellectual property*—the ideas, opinions, inventions, and discoveries in which another writer or researcher has invested considerable time and resources.

When you are unsure of whether or how to give credit to another source, *always* assume that you should give credit (and ask your professor or a writing center instructor for help with citation guidelines). If you are tempted to buy or "borrow" another person's work because of extenuating circumstances, remember that it is *always* better to ask for a deadline extension (and for additional help with your paper). Just as there is never any excuse for the theft of property, there is never any excuse for the theft of ideas.

Evaluating Sources   As you move into the third phase, begin by skimming your source material to sort out the valuable sources from the not-so-valuable ones. For a book, check the table of contents and index for information on your topic; then determine whether the information is relevant to your problem. For an article, see if the abstract or topic sentences in the body of the essay confirm your research interests. The guidelines below can help you determine if a source will be useful.

CRITERIA FOR ASSESSING THE VALUE OF A SOURCE FOR YOUR PROJECT

- Is it directly relevant to your topic?
- Does it discuss the topic extensively, uniquely, and authoritatively?
- Does it bear on your hypothesis, supporting, qualifying, or contradicting it?
- Does it present relatively current information, especially for research in the social and natural sciences?
- Does it meet the criteria for credibility discussed in "Evaluating Online Sources" (page 112) and "Evaluating Print Sources" (page 116)?

Taking Notes   Once you have a core of valuable material, you can begin to read these sources closely and take detailed notes. Skillful note taking—be it on your computer or mobile device, in a notebook, or on note cards—requires a subtle blend of critical thinking skills. It is not a matter of recording all the information available or simply copying long quotes. You want to select and summarize the general ideas that will form the outline of your paper, record specific evidence to support your ideas, and copy exact statements you plan to quote for evidence or interest. You also want to add your own ideas and evaluation of the material. All the notes you take must serve the specific purpose of your paper as stated in your hypothesis. It is essential that you record source information for *every* note that you take, whether that note is a summary, a paraphrase, or a direct quotation.

GUIDELINES FOR TAKING NOTES ABOUT YOUR TOPIC

1. Write the author's last name, the title of the source, and the page number at the top of each card or entry. (Complete information on the source should already be recorded on a card or in a file.)

2. Record only one idea or a group of closely related facts on each card or in each entry.

3. List a subtopic at the top of the card or entry. This will permit you to arrange your cards or entries from various sources into groups, and these groups can then serve as the basis of your outline.

4. List three types of information: (*a*) summaries of material, (*b*) paraphrases of material, in which you recast the exact words of the author, and (*c*) direct quotations, accurately transcribed.

5. Add your own ideas at the bottom of the card or following specific notes.

Summarizing, Paraphrasing, and Quoting   When you write a *summary* of a source, you focus on its main points and restate them in your own words. Summary notes can be especially helpful to remind you, as you draft, of sources that you might want to revisit and look at more closely. Summaries can also be introduced into the body of your essay, especially in an argument research paper, to provide additional information and support for your thesis. Here is an example of a primary source text and a student's summary:

Primary Source: Carl Elliott, "Humanity 2.0,"* The Wilson Quarterly, *Autumn 2003
Even technologies that unambiguously provide enhancements will raise issues of social justice not unlike those we currently face with ordinary medical technologies (wealthy Americans, for example, get liver transplants, while children in the developing world die from diarrhea). We live comfortably with such inequities, in part because we have so enthusiastically embraced an individualistic ethic. But to an outsider, a country's expenditure of billions of dollars on liposuction, face-lifts, and Botox injections while many of its children go without basic health care might well seem obscene.

Student Summary

Topic label	"Transhumanism" and bioethics
Author of article	Elliott
Relevant pages/URL	http://wwics.si.edu
Summary	Bioethicist and philosopher Carl Elliott defines "transhumanism" and describes a conference of "transhumanists" that he attended. As a bioethicist, Elliott argues that we need to pay attention to the ethical implications of the medical "enhancements" currently practiced or being developed that might contribute to the "transhumanist" goal of creating perfect human beings. In particular, our society's emphasis on developing medical technologies to make us more beautiful or intelligent at the expense of those less fortunate is especially disturbing.

A *paraphrase* focuses on one specific point or piece of information in an article and restates it in your words. Writing a paraphrase of a source can help you to better understand it. When you paraphrase, follow the original writer's argument but do not mimic the writer's sentence structure or simply replace keywords with synonyms.

Student Paraphrase

Topic label	"Transhumanism" and bioethics
Author of article	Elliott
Relevant pages/URL	http://wwics.si.edu
Unacceptable paraphrase: The sentence structure of the original is imitated, and synonyms replace the original terms (*scandalous* for *obscene*).	Even procedures designed for cosmetic purposes raise controversies over fairness (rich people get transplants while poor children die from basic diseases). Americans are fine with these inequalities because our culture values the individual. To non-Americans, the money we spend on plastic surgery even though many American children lack health insurance probably appears scandalous.
Acceptable paraphrase: Key terms from the original source are directly quoted, and the source argument is rephrased in the student's terms.	Elliott points out that our culture already seems to overlook the injustice of some individuals spending a great deal of money on cosmetic surgery (or "enhancements") while many lack access to basic health care. Elliott describes this as a uniquely American "individualist ethic" but points out that other cultures might see this inequality as "obscene." By extension, the willingness of the transhumanist movement to explore medical "enhancements" that will only benefit a very few wealthy people is also, ethically, "obscene."

As these examples demonstrate, an acceptable paraphrase shows that the researcher is genuinely engaged with the source's *argument*—not just the words—and has thought about how this particular component of the argument supports the original author's thesis. The summary and paraphrase are introduced with signal phrases, which include the name of the source and an action verb (*says, suggest, acknowledge, maintain*, etc.). Signal phrases help your reader discern what comes from you and what comes from a source. They can also signal your tone, or attitude, toward the source.

When the language of source material is essential to understanding its argument, *quotation* is the most effective strategy. When you quote directly from a source, put quotation marks around the material that you are selecting.

Topic label	"Transhumanism" and bioethics
Author of article	Elliott
Relevant pages/URL	http://wwics.si.edu
Quotation	"But to an outsider, a country's expenditure of billions of dollars on liposuction, face-lifts, and Botox injections while many of its children go without basic health care might well seem obscene."

When you have completed all your research, organize your notes under the various subtopics or subheadings that you have established. Now, by reviewing your notes and assessing the data, you should be able to transform the calculated guess that was your hypothesis into a much firmer thesis. Focus on your thesis by stating it at the top of the page where you are working on your outline. If possible or desirable, try to combine some subtopics and eliminate others so that you have three to five major categories for analysis and development. You are now ready to develop an outline for the essay.

Designing an Outline   Because you must organize a lot of material in a clear way, an outline is especially valuable in a research essay. Spend as much time as is reasonable drafting an outline. Begin by creating a rough outline that simply lists your general subheadings and their supporting data. Next, work more systematically through your notes and fill in the rough outline with as much detail as possible, developing each point logically and in detail. If you are required to submit an outline with your research paper, you should begin to develop a full, formal outline at this stage. Such an outline would be structured like this:

I.
   A.
   B.
      1.
      2.
      3.
         a.
         b.
II.

Use roman numerals for your most important points, capital letters for the next most important points, arabic numbers for supporting points, and lowercase letters for pertinent details or minor points. If you are including visuals such as photographs or graphics, include them in the outline as well.

Phase 4: Writing and Submitting the Paper

As you enter the fourth and final phase of the research process, keep in mind that a research paper is a formal essay, not a rag-tag compilation of notes. You should be prepared to take your research effort through several increasingly polished versions, most likely at least a rough draft, a revised draft, and a final manuscript.

Writing the Rough Draft   For your rough draft, concentrate on filling in the gaps in your outline. Take the time to rearrange your notes in the topic order that your outline assumes. In this way, you will be able to integrate notes and writing more efficiently and effectively.

Even as you adhere to your formal outline in beginning the rough draft, you should be open to alternate possibilities and prospects for presenting ideas and information. Although your primary task in writing a first draft is to rough out the shape and content of your paper, the flow of your ideas will often be accompanied by self-adjusting operations of your mind, all aimed at making your research effort even better than you thought it could be at the outline stage.

Whether you incorporate quotations from your notes into the rough draft is a matter of preference. Some writers prefer to transcribe quotations and paraphrases at this point in order to save time at a later stage. Other writers copy and insert these materials directly from entries in a computer file for notes. Still others believe that their thought processes are interrupted by having to write out summarized, quoted, and paraphrased material and to design transitions between their own writing and the transcribed material. They simply write "insert" in the draft with a reference to the appropriate notes. Whatever your strategy, it is essential that you keep track of the sources of summarized, quoted, and paraphrased material so that you can properly cite the sources and avoid plagiarism.

The need to integrate material from several sources will test your reasoning ability during the writing of the rough draft. For any given subtopic in your outline, you will be drawing together information from a variety of sources. To an extent, your outline will tell you how to arrange some of this information. At the same time, you must contribute your own commentary, arrange details in an effective order, and sort out conflicting claims and interpretations. A great deal of thinking as well as writing goes into the design of your first draft. You are not involved in a dull transcription of material when writing the rough draft of a research paper. Instead, you are engaged in a demanding effort to think your way through a problem of considerable magnitude, working in a logical way from the introduction and the statement of your thesis, through the evidence, to the outcome or conclusion that supports everything that has come before.

Revising the Draft   In the rough draft, you thought and wrote your way through the problem. Now you must rethink and rewrite in order to give better form and expression to your ideas. Use the guidelines outlined below to approach your revision. Consider every aspect of your paper, from the most general to the most specific. Look again at the overall organization, key topics, paragraphs, and sentences; read through for clarity of expression and details of grammar, punctuation, and spelling. A comprehensive revision effort will result in a decidedly more polished version of your paper.

CRITERIA FOR REVISING YOUR RESEARCH WRITING

- Does your title illuminate the topic of the essay and capture the reader's interest?

- Have you created the proper tone to meet the expectations of your audience?

- Does your opening paragraph hook the reader? Does it clearly establish and limit the topic? Is your thesis statement clear, limited, and interesting?

- Does the order of body paragraphs follow the order of your thesis? Do all the body paragraphs support your thesis? Is there a single topic and main idea for each paragraph? Do you achieve unity, coherence, and proper development? Is there sufficient evidence in each paragraph to support the main idea?

- Are there clear and effective transitions linking your ideas within and between paragraphs?

- Have you selected the best strategies to meet the demands of the assignment and the expectations of your audience?

- Are your assertions clearly stated, defined, and supported? Do you use sound logic and avoid faulty reasoning? Do you acknowledge other people's ideas properly? Do you use signal phrases to introduce your sources when summarizing, paraphrasing, and quoting? Are all of your summaries, paraphrases, and quotations appropriately cited?

- Is your conclusion strong and effective?

- Are your sentences grammatically correct? Have you avoided errors in the use of verbs, pronouns, adjectives, and prepositions? Have you corrected errors of agreement?

- Are your sentences complete? Have you corrected all fragments, comma splices, and fused sentences?

- Have you varied your sentences effectively? Have you employed clear coordination and subordination? Have you avoided awkward constructions?

- If you include visual information, do you provide adequate context? Is the placement of the visual logical? Is the visual clearly reproduced?

- For an electronic paper, if you include hyperlinks, are they clearly and appropriately placed in the text? Are the hyperlinks active? Do they connect to the correct files or pages?

- Are all words spelled correctly? Do your words mean what you think they mean? Are they specific? Are they concrete? Is your diction appropriate to college writing? Is your language free of clichés, slang, jargon, and euphemism? Do you avoid needless abstractions? Is your usage sound?

- Have you carefully attended to such mechanical matters as apostrophes, capitals, numbers, and word divisions?

- Does your manuscript conform to acceptable guidelines for submitting printed or online work?

Preparing the Final Manuscript   Leave time in your research effort to prepare a neat, clean, attractively designed manuscript. Store all of your files (notes, drafts, and final version) on a backup flash drive or external hard drive, and print a duplicate copy of the paper. Submit a neat, clear version, and keep the copy. Consult your instructor for the desired format, and carefully follow the guidelines for manuscript preparation in your final version. Look also at the sample paper later in this chapter, which illustrates how to present the final version of a paper in accordance with MLA style (see pages 140–160).

DOCUMENTING SOURCES

Documentation is an essential part of any research paper. Documenting your sources throughout the paper and in a Works Cited or References section tells your audience just how well you have conducted your research. It offers readers the opportunity to check on authorities, do further reading, and assess the originality of your contribution to an established body of opinion. Neglect of proper documentation can lead to charges of plagiarism (see page 121).

Quotations, paraphrases, and summaries obviously require credit, for they are the actual words or the theories or interpretations of others. Paraphrases and summaries also frequently offer statistics or data that are not well known, and this type of information requires documentation as well. Facts in a controversy (facts open to dispute or to varying interpretations) also fall within the realm of documentation. Visual information (maps, graphics, and photos) also require documentation, even if they show common knowledge (such as a map of Japan). Video and audio sources (like music files and podcasts), and even conversations, lectures, and e-mails, require documentation.

MATERIALS THAT REQUIRE DOCUMENTATION

- Direct quotations
- Paraphrased material
- Summarized material
- Any key idea or opinion adapted and incorporated into your paper
- Specific data (whether quoted, paraphrased, or tabulated in graphs, charts, lists, or tables)
- Visual media like illustrations, maps, photographs, or screenshots
- Disputed facts

Parenthetical documentation—briefly identifying sources within parentheses in the text—is the most common method of indicating sources. The purpose of a parenthetical citation is to identify a source briefly yet clearly enough that it can be located in the list of references at the end of the paper. In MLA style, the author's last name and the page number in the source are included. APA style uses the author's last name and the year of publication; page numbers are included primarily for direct quotations. Then complete information is listed, alphabetically by author or title (if a source has no specific author), in the Works Cited or References section following the text of the paper. The bibliographic information you have collected should provide you with the details needed for the preparation of both parenthetical documentation and a list of sources.

GENERAL GUIDELINES FOR PARENTHETICAL DOCUMENTATION

1. Give enough information so that the reader can readily identify the source in the Works Cited (MLA) or References (APA) section of your paper.

2. Supply the citation information in parentheses placed where the material occurs in your text.

3. Give the specific information required by the documentation system you are using, especially when dealing with multivolume works, editions, newspapers, and legal documents.

4. Make certain that the sentence containing the parenthetical documentation is readable and grammatically correct.

With your parenthetical documentation prepared, turn your attention next to a final Works Cited or References section. To prepare this list of sources, simply transcribe those bibliography cards or entries that you actually used to write your paper, following the appropriate format.

GENERAL GUIDELINES FOR PREPARING A LIST OF SOURCES

1. Use the title Works Cited (MLA) or References (APA).

2. Include only works actually cited in the research paper unless directed otherwise by your instructor.

3. Arrange all works alphabetically according to author's last name or according to the title of a work if there is no author. Ignore *A, An,* or *The.*

4. Begin each entry at the left margin. Indent everything in an entry that comes after the first line by five spaces or ½ inch (MLA style) or by five to seven spaces (following APA style for students, unless your instructor directs otherwise).

5. Double-space every line, both between and within sources.

6. Punctuate with periods after the three main divisions in most entries—author, title, and publishing information. Do not use a period after a URL, however.

In the following sections, you will find examples of MLA and APA documentation forms. Use these examples to help you cite your sources efficiently and clearly.

MLA (MODERN LANGUAGE ASSOCIATION) DOCUMENTATION

Make it as clear as possible to your reader where a source begins (with a signal phrase) and ends (with a parenthetical citation) in your paper. When you cannot provide specific parenthetical information (such as when a source does not have page numbers), make it as easy as possible for your reader to find the citation on your Works Cited page by including key identification elements like the source's name within the sentence. The following examples illustrate how to cite some of the most common sources in the text and in the list of works cited at the end of a paper.

MLA Parenthetical Documentation

A basic MLA in-text citation includes the author's last name and the page number (for sources that use numbered pages), identifying exactly where the quotation or information is located. This in-text citation leads readers to an entry on the Works Cited page, which provides more complete information about the source.

Book

> In the conclusion, he offers a gruesome description of the dying man's physical and
>
> emotional struggles (Tolstoy 1252–3).

If the author's name is included in the text, it does not need to be repeated in the citation.

> Garcia Marquez uses another particularly appealing passage as the opening of the
>
> story (105).

If citing a quotation longer than four typed lines, set it off from the text of the paper and indented one inch from the left margin. Double-space the quote and move the period before the parenthetical citation. (See the student paper on pages 140–160 for examples.)

Work without an Author   Use the full title of the work if it is brief; if the title is longer, however, use a shortened version, beginning with the word you will use to alphabetize the work on the Works Cited page.

> *Computerworld* has developed a thoughtful editorial on the issue of government and
>
> technology ("Uneasy Silence" 54).

Work in an Anthology   Use the name of the author of the work, not the editor of the anthology.

> The narrator describes it as "a big, squarish frame house that had once been
>
> white, decorated with cupolas and spires and scrolled balconies in the heavily

lightsome style of the seventies, set on what had once been our most select street"

(Faulkner 449).

One Work Quoted in Another

Samuel Johnson praises *She Stoops to Conquer* because Goldsmith's play achieves

"the great end of comedy—making an audience merry" (qtd. in Boswell 171).

More Than One Work in a Single Parenthetical Reference

Multiple studies conducted since 2000 indicate that educating children as young as

six about healthy eating and exercising habits reduces the incidents of childhood

obesity by 30% (Mickelson, par. 5; Waller and Jackson 45).

Common or Classical Literature   If an often-studied literary work exists in multiple editions, readers may need more information than just a page number if they have a different edition than the one you used. Including the chapter number helps them locate your source more easily.

After Billy's violent death, Sonny feels "that he [is] the only person in town"

(McMurtry 277; ch. 26).

Act, Scene, and Line Number(s) for a Play   Use Arabic numbers unless your instructor tells you to do otherwise.

Shakespeare makes use of the classic anagnorisis, or recognition of one's tragic flaw,

in the play when Hamlet tells Horatio he has learned to "Let be" (5.2.209).

Line Number(s) for Poem, or Song Lyrics   For the first quote, use the notation "line" or "lines" and the line number(s); afterward, use only the line number(s).

Owen is particularly adept at using onomatopoeia to reinforce the persona's terror

as he watches a fellow soldier's suffering: "In all my dreams, before my helpless

sight, / He plunges at me, guttering, choking, drowning" (lines 15–16). Even the

phrase "Gas! Gas!" imitates the insidious hissing sound of the mustard gas as it is

released from the shell (9).

Citation for Visual Media (Map, Diagram, Graph, Chart, Photograph, Slide, Graphic, Cartoon, Screen Shot, etc.)   The label *Fig. 1* and caption of the medium should be placed below it, flush with the left margin. Figures should be numbered sequentially, and captions should be used to describe their contents; source information and any notations not discussed in the text should follow the figure.

According to the US Centers for Disease Control and Prevention (CDC), 350–500 million people contract malaria each year ("Malaria Facts"). Figure 1 illustrates the densest geographic distribution of the disease. The CDC reports that tropic and sub-tropic areas see the overwhelming majority of malaria cases, particularly Southern Africa ("Geographic Distribution and Epidemiology").

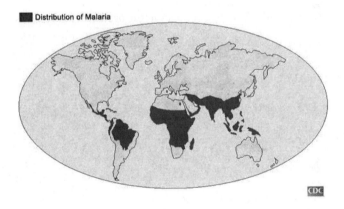

Fig. 1. Geographic Distribution of Malaria, United States, Centers for Disease Control and Prevention; "Malaria: Geographic Distribution." US CDC; 23 April 2004; Web; 1 August 2009.

Online Sources   Sometimes PDF files of articles and online versions of printed journals label the article's pages to correspond to the printed version, so use them if they are provided. Sometimes a source without page numbers will provide numbered screens, paragraphs, sections, chapters, or references, so use them to help your reader locate your sources. MLA parenthetical citation does not use a comma to separate the author's name from the page number (as does APA), but it does use commas to separate the author's name from the paragraph, section, or reference number.

(Markus, par. 15)   (Markus, sec. 3)

Most online sources, however, do not have page numbers for easy parenthetical citation. In that case, use the author's name or the title of the article or Web page.

MLA List of Works Cited

Following your paper, list the references you have cited in alphabetical order on a separate page titled "Works Cited." See the Works Cited page of the sample paper (page 159) for an illustration of how you should prepare this page. Use the following sample entries to help you format your references in MLA style. Pay special attention to abbreviated names of publishers, full names of authors, details of punctuation, and other characteristic features of MLA citations, like noting the medium of access or publication. When publication information is not available, indicate the missing data by using *n.d.* (no date), *n.p.* (no place or no publisher), and the like.

Book   Note the punctuation and use of italics in the basic entry for a book.

Reynolds, David S. *John Brown, Abolitionist.* New York: Knopf, 2005. Print.

Work without an Author

Sir Gawain and the Green Knight. Trans. Bernard O'Donoghue. New York: Penguin,

2006. Print.

Work or Chapter in an Edited Book or Anthology

Sher, Ira. "Nobody's Home." *Paraspheres: Extending beyond the Spheres of Literary and*

Genre Fiction. Eds. Rusty Morrison and Ken Keegan. Richmond: Omindawn,

2006. 303–10. Print.

Work Translated from Another Language   The first entry below emphasizes the work of the original author by placing his name first. The next example shifts emphasis to the work of the translators by identifying them first.

Eco, Umberto. *On Literature.* Trans. Martin McLaughlin. New York: Harcourt, 2004.

Print.

Young, David, trans. *DuFu: A Life In Poetry.* By Du Fu. New York: Knopf-Random,

2008. Print.

Work Appearing as Part of a Series

Oulton, Carolyn W. de la L. *Romantic Friendship in Victorian Literature.* Hampshire:

Ashgate, 2007. Print. The 19th Cen. Ser.

New Edition of an Older Book

Wharton, Edith. *The Custom of the Country.* 1913. Northridge: Aegypan, 2006. Print.

Citation Entries for Online Sources

List the author, the title of the document/specific page (in quotes), and the title of the Web site (in italics), as well as any translator, editor, and entity responsible for the site's upkeep (if not available, use *n.p.*), and the date of the electronic publication or last update (if not available, use *n.d.*). Include the medium (Web) and conclude with the date on which you visited the electronic site where the source is located. MLA's newest guidelines stipulate that researchers should include a URL *only* if readers would have difficulty locating the source through a conventional Web or database search.

Book Accessed via an Electronic Database

Joseph, Jay. *The Missing Gene: Psychiatry, Heredity, and the Fruitless Search for Genes.*

New York: Algora, 2006. *NetLibrary.* Web. 27 Dec. 2008.

Article in a Scholarly Journal   Include the volume number (if available) and issue number (if available), followed by the year and the pages of the entire article.

Robson, Mark. "The Ethics of Anonymity." *Modern Language Review* 103.2 (2008):

350–63. Print.

Journal Article Accessed via an Online Database

Nenon, Thomas J. "Some Differences between Kant's and Husserl's Conceptions of

Transcendental Philosophy." *Continental Philosophy Review* 41.4 (2008): 427–39.

Humanities Full Text. Web. 3 Jan. 2009.

Article in a Magazine   Include the day, month, year, and page numbers. If no author is listed, begin with the article's title. If an article in a magazine or newspaper does not continue on consecutive pages, follow the page number on which it begins with a plus sign.

Orlean, Susan. "The It Bird." *New Yorker* 28 Sept. 2009: 26–31. Print.

Rosen, Jeffrey. "Forced into a Gun Debate." *Time.com.* Time, Inc., 26 Apr. 2007.

     Web. 2 May 2008.

Article in a Daily Newspaper

Skidmore, Sarah. "New Coupons Mean Users Clip Less." *Times* [Shreveport]

     30 Aug. 2009: 11A+. Print.

Magazine or Newspaper Article Accessed through an Online Database

Roberts, Shearon. "Activists See Chance to Cleanse Streams: State Review Spurs

     Campaign." *Washington Post* 3 Aug. 2006, final ed.: T03. *LexisNexis Academic.*

     Web. 14 Oct. 2007.

Interview

Poehler, Amy. Interview by James Lipton. *Inside the Actor's Studio.* Bravo.

     21 Sept. 2009. Television.

Document or Individual Page on a Web Site

Latham, Ernest. "Conducting Research at the National Archives into Art Looting,

     Recovery, and Restitution." *The National Archives Library.* National Archives

     and Records Administration, Sept. 2009. Web. 15 Sept. 2009.

Blog Post

Mehta, Seema. "Two Swine Flu Clinics Open Today for Uninsured and At-Risk L.A.

     County Residents." Blog Entry. *L.A. Now.* Tribune, 23 Oct. 2009. Web.

     28 Oct. 2009.

CD, LP, MP3, or Other Sound Recording   What you want to emphasize determines how you will cite the source (e.g., a performer, a conductor, composer, etc.). Song titles are placed in quotation marks, while the entire compilation (album, in whatever format) is italicized. Remember to identify the format.

> Basie, Count. "Sunday at the Savoy." *88 Basie Street*. Rec. 11–12 May 1983. Pablo
>
> Records, 1984. MP3.

Film, Slide, Videotape, Blu-Ray Disc, or DVD   Start with any actor, producer, director, or other person whose work you wish to emphasize. Otherwise, simply begin with the title of the film itself. Note the form cited—*DVD, Videocassette,* and so forth, or *Film* for the movie itself.

> *The Lovely Bones*. Prod. and dir. Peter Jackson. Perf. Saoirse Ronan, Mark Wahlberg,
>
> and Rachel Weisz. Dreamworks, 2009. Film.

Programs on Radio or Television   You can cite the entire series (title in italics), a specific episode (title in quotation marks), and you can focus on a particular individual's performance or contribution.

> Hamm, John, perf. "Wee Small Hours." Dir. Scott Hornbacher. By Dahvi Waller and
>
> Matthew Weiner. *The Wire*. AMC. 11 Oct. 2009. Television episode.

Webcast or Web-based Video

> "Nobody Knows the Trouble They've Seen: Close Combat in Iraq." By nickwalnut.
>
> *YouTube*. Google, 18 June 2008. Web. 12 Dec. 2008.

PDF, MP3, or Other Digital Files Online / Offline

> Commission on Teaching Credentialing. "California School Paraprofessional
>
> Teacher Training Program." *Commission on Teaching Credentialing*. State of
>
> California, 8 Jan. 2009. Web. 2 June 2009. PDF file.

Files downloaded and stored independent of the Internet should be cited by title of the file, and other pertinent information, including the medium.

> Norman, Kimberley. "Drama during the English Renaissance." 2008. PDF file.

Map or Other Visual Media

"The Origins of Human Beings." Map. *Atlas of African-American History.* By James

Ciment. New York: Facts-Infobase, 2007. 2. Print.

Artwork   Include the title of the work (in italics), the year of completion (*n.d.* if unknown), the medium, and the location of the artwork.

Rodin, *Torso of a Young Woman.* 1910. Bronze. Musée Rodin, Paris.

Advertisement

Golden Double Stuf Oreo. Advertisement. *Entertainment Weekly* 11 Sept. 2009:

14-5. Print.

APA (AMERICAN PSYCHOLOGICAL ASSOCIATION) DOCUMENTATION

The samples below show how to use APA style for citing a source in the text and in the
References section at the end of a paper.

APA Parenthetical Documentation

The basic APA parenthetical citation includes the author's last name and the date of publication, information generally sufficient to identify the source in the reference list. Although
researchers in the social sciences often cite works as a whole, you should add the page
number to identify exactly where a quotation or other specific information is located. If the
source is not paginated (e.g., a Web site), use paragraph numbers or headings to help your
reader find the information. Consider that the danger of not using some sort of citation
(like the author/year or page number) at the end of a paraphrased passage is that your
reader may not be able to separate the outside source from your ideas. If the author's
name (or the year) is included in the text, it does not need to be repeated in the citation.

Direct Quotation with Author Name in Internal Citation

One argues that "for the most part, Justice Scalia's opinion for the majority of the

Supreme Court in *Heller* is a solid presentation of textual arguments and historical

evidence for interpreting the Second Amendment broadly to protect non-military

use of guns" (Rostron, 2009, p. 386).

Direct Quotation with Author Name in Signal Phrase

Rostron (2009) maintained that "for the most part, Justice Scalia's opinion for the majority of the Supreme Court in *Heller* is a solid presentation of textual arguments and historical evidence for interpreting the Second Amendment broadly to protect non-military use of guns" (p. 386).

How to Use a Page or Paragraph Number with a Paraphrase

Clarke (2005) maintained that the lackluster response of FEMA after Hurricane Katrina can be traced in part to the Bush administration's lack of support for the Department of Homeland Security (p. 38).

The city's most current traffic flow analysis (McPherson, 2008) proposed two alternatives (pp. 45–53).

In 2008, Wyatt compared the costs and benefits of both designs (Conclusion section, para. 12).

APA List of References

As you examine the following illustrations, notice how capitalization, italics, punctuation, and other features change with the type of source noted. Note also that authors' names are listed with last names first, followed by initials only. Although the entries in an APA reference list follow very specific patterns, references in your paper—to titles, for instance—should use standard capitalization (that is, only the first word of titles and subtitles). Similarly, the word *and* should be spelled out in your paper even though the ampersand (&) is used with authors' and editors' names in parenthetical citations and References entries. Note that the names of months (in periodical and online citations) are spelled out, not abbreviated. For updated examples and further guidance on APA style, see the American Psychological Association Web site at *www.apastyle.org*.

Book

Wodarski, J. S. (2009). *Behavioral medicine: A social worker's guide*. New York, NY: Routledge.

Work in an Edited Book   Do not put the title of the work/chapter in quotation marks.

Fox, J. J., & Gable, R. A. (2004). Functional behavior assessment. In R. B. Rutherford,

Jr., M. M. Quinn, & S. R. Mathur (Eds.), *Handbook of research in emotional and*

behavioral disorders (pp. 143–62). New York, NY: Guilford Press.

Electronic Version of a Printed Book   The URL takes the place of the publisher information. Do not use a period after a URL.

Cameron, S. (2009). *The economics of hate* [Electronic version]. Retrieved from http://

ezproxy.lsus.edu:2194/Reader/

Article in a Journal with Pagination by Volume   Use initial caps for all important
words in the titles of journals, magazines, and newspapers. Include the volume in italics.

Stansel, D. (2008). Local government investment and long-run economic growth.

Journal of Social, Political and Economic Studies, 34, 244–259.

Article in a Journal with Pagination by Issue   Include both the volume (in italics) and
the issue number (in parentheses).

Boulden, W. T. (2008). Evaluation of the advancing young adult learning project.

Adult Basic Education and Literacy Journal 2(1), 3–12.

Article from an Electronic Journal   Many online scholarly sources now include a digital object identifier (DOI), a series of symbols, letters, and numbers that help the reader
identify and locate the source. When the DOI is available, include it in your citation; it
takes the place of the publisher information or the URL where you accessed the article.
Check out *www.doi.org* for more information or *www.crossref.org* to look up an article's
DOI. When citing an article accessed on a subscription database, do not include the
name of the database in your entry.

Baggio, G. (2008, December). Processing temporal constraints: An ERP study.

Language learning, 58, 35–55. doi:10.1111/j.1467-9922.2008.00460.x

Article in a Magazine   If the publication includes a month, season, or specific date, list
it after the year. Do not abbreviate. For online articles, include the URL of the magazine's
home page, not a direct link to the article.

Searcy, W. A., & Nowicki, S. (2008, March/April). Bird song and the problem of

honest communication. *American Scientist, 96*(2), 114–121.

Underwood, Anne. (2008, April 14). Ten fixes for the planet. *Newsweek, 151*(15),

52–56.

Beinart, P. (2008, June 26). The war over patriotism. *Time*. Retrieved from

http://www.time.com

Article in a Daily Newspaper Use p. or pp. to indicate page numbers. If the article continues to another page that is not consecutive, list all the pages (pp. A24, A27).

Thompson, G. (2009, February 12). Report faults homeland security's efforts on

immigration. *The New York Times*, p. A24.

Miller, C. C. (2009, July 22). Marketing small businesses with Twitter. *The New York*

Times. Retrieved from http://www.nytimes.com

Blog

Siemens, G. (2009, September 18). Re: Untangling the web [Web log post].

Elearnspace.org. Retrieved from http://www.elearnspace.org/blog

Podcast or Webcast

Star talk: Apollo 40th anniversary (2009, July 31) [Audio podcast]. Retrieved from

http://www.discovermagazine.com

Images—Maps, Photographs, Tables, Charts

US Geological Survey (Cartographer). (2009). Maps of recent earthquake activity in

California-Nevada [Seismic activity map]. Retrieved from http://quake.usgs

.gov/recenteqs/latestfault.htm

The following sample student paper shows how one student correctly incorporated appropriate sources into a research paper in order to prove her thesis.

SAMPLE STUDENT PAPER
(MLA STYLE)

Header:
Last name and page
number ½ inch
below top of page

Lee 1

Clara Lee

Heading 1 inch
below top of page

Professor Paul Smith

All lines double-
spaced, including
heading and title

Writing Workshop II

5 September 2009

Title centered
Title defines topic

The Courage of Intimacy:

Movie Masculinity in the 1990s and Early 21st Century

Paragraph indented
½ inch or 5 spaces

Mike Newell's 1997 film *Donnie Brasco* begins and ends

1-inch side margins.

with an extreme close-up of Johnny Depp's eyes. Shot in wide-

screen so that the eyes literally span the entire screen, the im-

age is a black-and-white snapshot that appears during the

Opening interests
reader with detail
from film

opening credits and returns as a full-color close-up at the end

of the movie. Depp's lustrous eyes are large and black and

beautiful, and gazing at them up close gives the viewer a sur-

prisingly intimate sensation (See Fig. 1).

Even within the conventional narrative that makes up the

body of the movie, they become noticeably important; Web-

Quotation from
electronic source

site critic Rob Blackwelder observes that "Depp has [the cen-

tral conflict of the movie] in his eyes in every scene," and Susan

Support from print
source

Wloszczyna of *USA Today* notes, "It's all in the eyes. Depp's

intense orbs focus like surveillance cameras, taking in each

crime and confrontation. He's sucked into the brutal, bullying

lifestyle, and so are we" (28). The close-up image at the begin-

FIG. 1. A close-up of Johnny Depp's eyes from the opening sequence of *Donnie Brasco,* Dir. Mike Newell, Sony, 1997.

ning and end is one of the few instances in which the film draws blatant attention to its own style, but the device calls attention to the film's central focus, its constant probing into the character at the center of the movie.

Somehow, without restricting the film to a first-person narration by Depp's undercover FBI agent, the audience comes to identify with him and understand the many pressures increasing inside his head simply by watching his eyes. They reflect his watchfulness, his uncertainty, his frustration, and his guilt—all without drawing too much attention to himself from his unsuspecting wiseguy companions. He is guarded with his words, causing his closest Mafioso friend to remark, "You never say anything without thinking about it first." His quietness invites viewers to read his looks and expressions, to become intimately

Quotation from film

1-inch margin at top
Heading ½ inch
below top of page
continues last name
and page numbering

acquainted with a character who constantly has to hide part of

himself from the people around him, until they can virtually feel

every twinge of fear or regret that the character feels. Seeing

Thesis stated

this man trapped in situations in which he faces crisis after cri-

sis, unwillingly alienated from his family and eventually his em-

ployers, trying only to protect the people he loves, viewers can

ultimately recognize him as a more sensitive, struggling, and

courageous hero than those celebrated in the past.

Past contrasted
with present

Over the decades, Hollywood has glorified the gruff mas-

culinity of actors from Humphrey Bogart to Sylvester Stallone.

Joan Mellen notes in her 1977 book *Big Bad Wolves:*

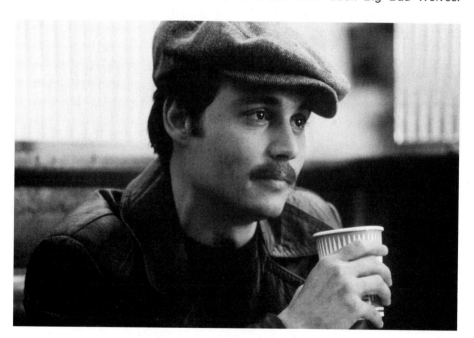

FIG. 2. Johnny Depp in the title role of *Donnie Brasco,* Dir.

Mike Newell, Sony, 1997.

Masculinity in the American Film that in traditional Hollywood films, especially the stoic action films of the 1970s, "physical action unencumbered by effeminate introspection is what characterizes the real man" (5). In the 1990s, it seems that much changed; introspection became a central part of leading-male roles. We can see this clearly in the character-driven films of 1997 alone, which won accolades for such intimate roles as Robert Duvall's tormented evangelical preacher in *The Apostle,* Matt Damon's emotionally needy genius and Robin Williams's mourning therapist in *Good Will Hunting,* and the unemployed guys struggling over issues like impotence and child custody in *The Full Monty.* Thoughtfulness, vulnerability, and the ability to handle relationships became virtual requirements for the male "hero" in the 1990s. The old-fashioned masculinity of characters played by Clint Eastwood or John Wayne in the past has come to be regarded as emotionally repressed and overly macho.

The change is partly cyclical. Mellen cites the 1930s and 1950s as eras in film in which leading men were given greater depth. She says, "Despite the limitations imposed by a repressive society [in the fifties], film recovered for men an individual self with a distinctive identity and a flourishing ego" (191–92). Actors like Marlon Brando and James Dean, in particular, played insecure, emotionally torn rebels who express tenderness in their relationships with women and with other men.

Source identified in text

Quotation from book with page number

Other examples noted

Background tied to thesis

Clarification added in brackets
Quotation with page numbers

FIG. 3. John Wayne, the epitome of mid-20th century masculinity.

Ellipses for words omitted

However, in the sixties, "as the Vietnam War progressed . . . maleness itself appeared under siege and in need of defense," and "traumatic events of the sixties induced the Hollywood hero to tighten up, reveal as little about himself as possible,

Quotations and summary from source

and to find comfort in his own recalcitrance" (248–49). Things scarcely got better when "glorification of the vigilante male [be-came] the dominant masculine myth of the seventies" (295) with films like *Dirty Harry* and *Taxi Driver.* Mellen notes, "In the

Lee 6

seventies film, people are allowed no option: they must meet force with force" (307). Following two decades of grim testosterone, there was a definite reaction in the bubble gum pop culture of the eighties, with flashy cartoon violence starring Sylvester Stallone or Arnold Schwarzenegger presenting highly unrealistic images of masculinity, and lighter portrayals like Marty McFly and Indiana Jones gaining in popularity. By the nineties, American audiences were no longer taking tough guy masculinity seriously, leading to a trend of ironic humor in action films from *True Lies* to *Independence Day*. It is doubtful that Will Smith would have been a favorite action hero before the 1990s.

However, the crucial underlying shift in American culture is the debilitation of the conventional white male hero in a country he once monopolized. Trends in society within the past forty years have led to greater freedom for women, minorities, and homosexuals, and as pride and power among these groups increased, there has been a backlash against the white male. The hero of the 1990s has to prove that he is sensitive and completely respectful of every group mentioned above in order to remain sympathetic, forcing his previous role of unquestioned dominance to change drastically. In addition, now that women are going to work and less is expected of men in terms of being the provider and protector of the family and society, more is expected of them in their personal relationships. As noted in

Transition back
to present day

1996 by Sylvester Stallone, a fitting symbol of the old macho masculinity who tried to change his image to a more sensitive

Quotation from published interview

one, "I think the leading man of the future will be one who is beleaguered by the need to constantly define on film the male-female relationship." He also notes, "People want to nurture the underdog. The day of the strongman is over" (94). The themes of inefficacy in society, sensitivity in relationships, and a reaction to the old strongman ideal show up clearly in *Donnie Brasco.*

Analysis of film

In the movie, FBI agent Joe Pistone, alias Donnie Brasco, goes undercover in the belief that he is on the side of law and order, with the simple goal of booking some major criminals; instead he finds a bunch of endearing but disturbingly violent men who become his closest companions for several years. Particu-

Plot summary and interpretation

larly perplexing is his relationship with Benjamin "Lefty" Ruggiero, the trod-upon hit man whose thirty years of faithful service are rewarded with dirty-work assignments while younger wiseguys are promoted over him. Lefty is the one who notices Donnie and recruits him into the organization, and from the start his faith in Donnie is clear; as Pistone smugly reports to a contact early in

Character analysis

the movie, "I got my hooks in this guy." However, Pistone's smugness wears off as Lefty repeatedly invites him into his home, confides in him with his complaints and his dreams, and says unexpectedly one day waiting in the hospital where his own son is in the E.R. for a drug overdose, "I love you, Donnie."

It is appropriate that the fictional Donnie Brasco is an orphan, because Lefty essentially becomes a surrogate father to him. Pistone, concerned for Lefty's fate, becomes more and more reluctant to "pull out" of his undercover assignment, revealing Donnie Brasco as a spy and leaving the blame (and death sentence) on Lefty. At one point he stops meeting his FBI contacts because they are pressuring him to pull out. Instead, he lets himself take on his mob alter ego more and more, tearing both his professional and personal lives apart.

In a way, the film is an interesting commentary on how ideals have changed, because it is set in the 1970s, the last decade of the full-fledged he-man hero, but made with a 1990s ideology. Because it is based on a book by the real agent Joe Pistone, who is currently living under the Witness Protection Program, one might think the portrayal would be strictly fact-based and would not be affected by the obsession with the sensitive male; but of course, one must never underestimate the power of filmmakers in any era to interpret their material with their own contemporary vision (note the portrayal of the Three Musketeers as aging and vulnerable in the 1998 screen adaptation of *The Man in the Iron Mask;* the seventies version of the same book depicted the Musketeers as brash and irreverent).

There is plenty of traditional macho posturing in the Mafia sequences of *Donnie Brasco,* but director Mike Newell places special emphasis on Pistone's sensitive relationship with Lefty

Ruggiero, his mentor in the mob, and on his imperiled relation-

ship with his wife, turning *Donnie Brasco* into "a relationship

movie . . . about conflict of loyalty" ("Interview"). Newell, a Brit-

ish director most famous for his vastly different romantic com-

edy *Four Weddings and a Funeral,* also boasted about *Donnie*

Brasco's "'absolutely novel point of view about the Mob,'" fo-

cusing on "'the lowest rung, the have-nots'" (Schickel, Booth,

and Harbison), rather than the rich and powerful men at the top

so often depicted in mob movies. The film focuses on the soulful

side of a male protagonist in a genre in which sensitivity is rare.

In fact, *Donnie Brasco* has been recognized as an evolu-

tionary step in the genre of gangster films. *Time* calls it a "neo-

Scorsesian study of lowlife Mob life," and says that it "rises

above the mire of its shopworn genre by showing the cracks in

its characters' armor" (Schickel, Booth, and Harbison). Con-

ventional gangster films usually depict the rise and fall of a

charismatic criminal. The gangster movies of the thirties and

forties featured fast-talking tough guys like James Cagney and

Humphrey Bogart; Francis Ford Coppola's 1972 epic *The God-*

father, which revived the genre, depicted the same glamour,

ruthlessness, and power of the Mafia, on an even greater ro-

manticized scale. But after a spate of stylized mob movies in

the previous thirty years, many reviewers of *Donnie Brasco*

Electronic source
cited by authors'
names only

Lee 10

welcomed a new approach in a genre that was growing old and

stale. Put another way, *Donnie Brasco* is the film that finally

brings its genre into the nineties by replacing its tough, glamor-

ous hero with a real guy who can't live up to the stereotypes.

Contrasts lead back to thesis

Almost in direct response to the ideal of masculinity pre-

sented in the past, Newell shows that although at first Pistone

is doing everything right—fitting perfectly into his undercover

persona, doing top-rate work for the FBI, and sending checks

home regularly to his family—he cannot "be the man in the

f—kin' white hat" that he thought he could be, as he puts it late

in the movie. He knows how impossible it is to fulfill his male

responsibilities in all three of his very different worlds after he

has ditched the FBI, almost lost his marriage, and realized that

his undercover work, once revealed, will be the cause of Lefty's

death. He has failed his own expectations of himself to save the

day and make everything right. The contemporary audience

recognizes the realism of the situation. As Stallone states in his

interview, "The male is [only] the illusion of the protector and

guardian, . . . [b]ecause in this day and age, there is no security

he can offer" (94). By now the audience realizes that a hero

cannot always save the day in a conventional sense. In an odd

way, viewers even appreciate his failure because it has knocked

all of his arrogance out of him and left only an exposed, vulner-

able character.

Analysis of main character

A contemporary audience can especially relate to the issues of family breakdown, recognizing in Donnie's situation the
roots of the culture of estrangement and divorce which is so
widespread today. Violating the conventional lone male gang-

Analysis of
relationships with
other characters

ster/cop figure, Joe Pistone has not only a wife but three small
daughters hidden away in suburbia, and he can't tell them anything about his job without putting them at risk. His visits home
are less and less frequent, sometimes months apart, due to the
consuming nature of his "job." Although viewers can see from
the start the tenderness and love he has for his wife and daughters, his prolonged absences and broken promises (he misses
his daughter's first Communion) lead to intensifying arguments
between him and his wife. As she constantly reminds him, his
job is tearing their home apart, and not knowing what he is doing makes it all the more unbearable. Pistone knows, as his
identification with the Mafia grows deeper and deeper, that his
involvement has serious consequences for his family, and this
mounting pressure becomes impossible to resolve when
weighed against the life of Lefty Ruggiero.

Contrasting example

Regarding the role of women in Mafia movies, Mellen
points out that "well into the seventies the male protagonist of
films from *The Godfather* (I or II) to *Serpico* uses women solely
to discard them" (327). Wives in *The Godfather* are cheated on,
lied to, and in one case, violently beaten. At a pivotal moment

at the end of the movie, the wife of Michael Corleone tearfully
asks him if he has ordered the death of his sister's husband,
and he looks directly into her eyes and lies, saying he did not.
She smiles and believes him. Her character is, in fact, constantly under the thumb of her husband who misleads her,
ignores her, and coaxes her into marrying him after not con-
tacting her for over a year. She and the other women in the
movie are not once consulted or listened to, no matter how
much their husbands' actions affect their lives.

Donnie Brasco could have been made in precisely the
same way. Pistone's wife Maggie is, after all, left at home for
months at a time while her husband is off doing his job for the
FBI. However, Newell makes the relationship between them a
pivotal storyline in the movie. Repeatedly in the course of the
narrative, interrupting the Mafia sequences, the audience sees
Pistone call or visit home, reinforcing his identity as a husband
and father. Viewers also note the progression as his relationship begins to sour. The lowest point comes when Pistone
shows up at his home in the middle of the night to retrieve a
bag containing $3 million in cash and confronts Maggie, who
has found it and hidden it. When she tells him that he has become "like one of them," he strikes her, and both recoil in surprise, less shocked at the blow than at the realization of what
their marriage has become. At this critical moment, he tries to

Contrasting example
related to film

Incident from film
substantiates
interpretation

tell her the truth. He awkwardly explains the situation with Lefty

and his fear of being responsible for his death. He tells her that

Quotation from film   he is not sure of what is right anymore. He tells her, "I'm not like

them. I am them." It is evident that the troubles of Pistone's

marriage hurt himself as much as his wife, and in a sense, deal-

ing with them takes more courage than risking his life as an

undercover agent in the Mafia. The film treats this relationship

delicately, and the woman here is not merely discarded or lied

to, but confronted and confided in, with her concerns pre-

sented as clearly as his own.

What makes Pistone's situation so compelling is that he

starts out believing that he can be one of the traditional "soli-

Source identified   tary heroes who solve all problems for themselves" (Mellen 23)
in citation

and instead comes up against situations that are too difficult to

handle. Joe Pistone slaps his wife, not to exert his male domi-

nance, but because he has lost control. When he tries to make

things right, he doesn't sweep her into his arms (and probably

have his way with her, in the true tradition of male heroes); he is

Detail from film   almost frightened to make a move and instead makes a
supports
interpretation   gesture—kissing the back of her head—to try and reestablish

the emotional (not sexual) intimacy between them. In his early

scenes with Lefty, Pistone is noticeably on his guard and de-

tached from the affection Lefty is developing for him; later,

when he has the opportunity to be promoted within the ranks of the mob and Lefty feels betrayed, Pistone tries to express his devotion by visiting him at the hospital where his son has overdosed. When Lefty orders him to leave, he refuses.

These gestures are some of Pistone's most heroic acts, at least as Newell presents it. Although he is given a medal and a check for $500 at the end of the movie for his undercover work (which is enough to secure scores of convictions), his feelings about it are clearly mixed; his loyalty to the FBI has been disintegrating as he has lost faith in their good guy/bad guy rhetoric, and his primary concern—Lefty's safety—is now uncertain. His success in infiltrating a group of depressed Brooklyn wiseguys is now a cause for guilt. Pistone's ambivalence and impotence are "like a version of *Death of a Salesman* . . . about a man at the end of his tether and at the end of his time, realizing that his whole life [has come] down to the point, really, of a cheap [reward], but set in mob terms" (Newell).

It is at this point at the end of the movie, as Pistone accepts his reward and his wife tells him it's all over, that Newell returns to the extreme close-up of Depp's eyes (see Fig. 1), and the audience sees how troubled they are. Viewers are left with that image, indicating that Newell intended for them to leave the theater asking themselves what it was all for—whether doing his job was really the right thing or not. True to life, there is no easy, happy ending, in which a man can die in battle or save

Return to detail used in first paragraph

the day and thus fulfill his "masculine" duties. What matters, however, as viewers return to that close-up, is that they have seen Joe Pistone/Donnie Brasco's vulnerability and his devotion within his relationships. If he feels confused or uncertain at the end, it is because he has faced these emotional issues, which are far more subtle than the challenges related to his job. The audience has seen him show more courage in his private struggles than John Wayne ever did out on the frontier and can applaud him for that.

Return to thesis

Like many films, *Donnie Brasco* is a cultural reflection of its makers and the audience, who were trying to come to grips with the changing view of the white male's place in society since the 1970s. By 1999, the sensitive, flawed hero was joined by what Chris Holmlund calls the "macho [man] in crisis," who acts out his frustrations in movies like *Fight Club* and *Magnolia* (229). Holmlund echoes the argument of social critic Susan Bordo that things like "cosmetic surgery and androgynous fashion were turning masculinity into a fluid, problematic category" for American men at the cusp of the 21st century (229), and that violence seemed to be a natural antidote to the confusion. She notes, however, that such violence has been used ironically by some filmmakers as an acknowledgment that traditional expressions of masculinity are "mere performance" (229).

Lee 16

Within a few years, however, a version of the straightforward hero of yore came roaring back in reaction to the anger and fear Americans felt after the terrorist attacks on 11 September 2001. In those first few years after 9/11, Susan Faludi observed "a powerful resurgence in traditional sex roles and a glorification of he-man virility as embodied by [John] Wayne, the ur-savior of virtuous but helpless damsels in distress." She points to Steven Spielberg's 2005 film *War of the Worlds* as an example of how American films tried to reshape and reclaim masculinity in the mid-2000s: "'It's some bizarre, weirdly out-of-proportion fixation, . . . an exaltation of American masculinity in an intergalactic crisis'" (qtd. in Cohen). The terror and anger the nation experienced as a result of 9/11 felt nearly that epic to most Americans for years, but with the diminishing sense of panic by the end of the decade, American films have turned an eye toward other kinds of masculinity.

Since 2007, writers and directors seem to have adopted a near-schizophrenic approach to capturing the changing idea of modern American masculinity on film. Romantic comedies have offered up a new kind of hero: the pasty, overweight underachiever; and with ticket sales soaring for such films, the less-than-heroic leading man is suddenly in vogue in virtually every film genre in Hollywood. More than ever, hapless men, incapable of or unwilling to assume the alpha-male stance,

Relates to modern cinema

have come to symbolize masculinity in American films. Christopher Goodwin bemoans this "sorry state of masculinity in American movies today" and points out that even action heroes are "schlub[s] . . . pathetic, if well-meaning, losers [who] inevitably end up with the hottest chicks." He blames the trend, born in films like *Forgetting Sarah Marshall* and *Knocked Up,* in part on "wish fulfillment for most men, who can't imagine scoring so high" and on the acceptance of everyone's inner "nerd" (8). In looking at the proliferation of comedic "schlemiel" protagonists, David Buchbinder also touches on traditional masculinity as "performance" and explores whether the schlemiel is

Paraphrase

popular because he is indicative of men who refuse to live by such artificial constraints (235) or because he makes them feel more capable when measured against him (236).

This Hollywood portrayal of masculinity perhaps signals a paradigm shift in how women see men and, more important, how they see themselves. Guy Garcia says that the American man's identity crisis is thanks to the emergent power of women. He claims that as women make strides in education and the business world, men are struggling with "the very definition of what it means to be a man" (185). Garcia believes that Americans enjoy "shows like *Ice Road Truckers* and *Deadliest Catch,* which glorify men who do dangerous, physically demanding jobs, [and which] have struck a nostalgic chord in the zeitgeist"

(185). Perhaps to rage against this emotional paralysis, some filmmakers are introducing a new level of brutality in dramatic films and shifting the focus from the traditional hero onto a sinister figure, who would normally be identified as the antagonist. Ong Sor Fern cites two examples of films that concentrate on sadistic antiheroes, *There Will Be Blood* and *No Country for Old Men*. Fern muses, "It is tempting, even inevitable, to infer that this current obsession with strong male figures has something to do with the lack of [them] in America today." Buchbinder also sees films that promote traditional masculinity as Hollywood's "nostalgic" attempt to pacify "a certain hysteria, an anxiety on the part of at least some men that a familiar form of masculinity may be fading" (243). In the age of the metrosexual, the popularity of these testosterone-fueled escapades is an attempt to rehabilitate our definition of masculinity and reclaim a portion of the power white men felt during the days of *Dirty Harry*.

Given Mellen's assertion of the cyclical pattern of masculinity in American cinema, though, we can only hope that it won't be long before we see a renaissance of the enlightened hero, at his best when he is true-to-life, flawed so we can identify with him but not so flawed that we spend our time laughing at his ineptitude. We need the occasional stoic cowboy or renegade cop, but sometimes we really want a hero we can admire and emulate because he is able to triumph in the end despite his personal struggles. Such a depiction of masculinity would be a welcome alternative to the two extreme portraits that permeate American films today. Perhaps if we could agree on what masculinity means in 21st-century America, we wouldn't need to turn every good guy into one of Goodwin's "schulbs," nor would we need to bathe in the glorified violence of the antihero who rages against his social and cultural impotence. We could once again celebrate the personal triumphs of our Donnie Brascos, who can be both human and heroic.

Lee 20

Works Cited

Blackwelder, Rob. Rev. of *Donnie Brasco*, dir. Mike Newell,

 perf. Johnny Depp. *SPLICEDwire.com.* SPLICEDwire Film

 Rev. and Feature Content Svcs., n.d. Web. 12 Aug. 2009.

Buchbinder, David. "Enter the Schlemiel: The Emergence of

 Inadequate or Incompetent Masculinities in Recent Film

 and Television." *Canadian Review of American Studies*

 38.2 (2008): 227–45. *Project Muse*. Web. 22 Aug. 2009.

Cohen, Patricia: "Towers Fell, and Attitudes Were Rebuilt: An

 Interview with Susan Faludi." *New York Times*. New York

 Times, 27 Sept. 2007, late ed.: B10. Web. 19 Aug. 2009.

Donnie Brasco. Dir. Mike Newell. Perf. Johnny Depp. Tristar,

 1997. Film.

Fern, Ong Sor. "There Will Be Masculinity: Two Oscar-

 Nominated Films Look at What It Means to Be a Man in the

 Context of American Society." *The Straits Times.com*. Sin-

 gapore Press Holdings, 14 Feb. 2008. Web. 10 Aug. 2009.

Garcia, Guy. "Men: The New Misfits." *Fortune* 13 Oct. 2008:

 185–6. Print.

Goodwin, Christopher. "Enter the Flat Pack: The Sorry State of

 Masculinity in American Movies." *Times Online* [London].

 News International Group, 27 Apr. 2008, Culture sec.: 8.

 Web. 9 Aug. 2009.

Begins new page
Title 1 inch below
top of page and
centered

All lines double-
spaced, including
title and entries

Entries in
alphabetical order

First line at margin

Next lines indented
½ inch or 5 spaces

Article title in
quotation marks

Lee 21

Holmlund, Chris. "1999: Movies and Millennial Masculinity."

American Cinema in the 1990s: Themes and Variations.

Ed. Chris Holmlund. New Brunswick: Rutgers UP, 2008,

225–48. Print.

Book title italicized   Mellen, Joan. Big Bad Wolves: Masculinity in American Film.

New York: Pantheon, 1977. Print.

Movie title italicized   Newell, Mike. "Interview on Donnie Brasco." Interview. YouTube.

Google. 30 June 2007. Web. 16 Aug. 2009.

Schickel, Richard, Cathy Booth, and Georgia Harbison. "Depp

Charge." Time.com. Time, Inc., 3 Mar. 1997. Web. 10 Aug.

2009.

Stallone, Sylvester. "The Masculine Mystique." Interview by

Susan Faludi. Esquire Dec. 1996: 89–96. Print.

Wloszczyna, Susan. "Donnie Brasco: A High Point for Low-

lifes." Rev. of Donnie Brasco, dir. Mike Newell, perf.

Johnny Depp. USA Today 28 Feb. 1997: 1D. Print.

CH 4   **www.mhhe.com/mhreaderbrief1e**

- Research > Source Evaluation Tutor
- Research > Taking Notes
- Writing > Outline Tutor: An interactive tutorial on creating outlines
- Research > Bibliomaker: Software to help you format your citations (MLA and APA)
- Professional Research Papers: An introduction to professional and academic journals across the disciplines
- Image Gallery: Chapter images in color

part *2*

Issues across the Disciplines

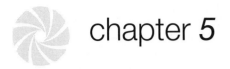

chapter 5

Education and Society
How, What, and Why Do We Learn?

In "Learning to Read and Write," a chapter from his autobiography, Frederick Douglass offers a spirited affirmation of the rights we all should have to pursue an education. For Douglass, who was born into slavery, knowledge began not only with experience but also with the need to articulate that experience through literacy. The ability to read and write should be the possession of all human beings, and Douglass was willing to risk punishment—even death—to gain that ability. Today, all over the globe, as ethnic and political conflicts arise, men and women face the same challenge of expressing themselves. For even with a tool like the Internet, if one does not have the tools to express oneself or if the expression of thought is suppressed, the vehicle for conveying ideas, no matter how powerful, is rendered useless.

Perhaps the struggle for an education always involves a certain amount of effort and risk, but the struggle also conveys excitement and the deep, abiding satisfaction that derives from achieving knowledge of oneself and of the world. Time and again in the essays in this chapter, we discover that there is always a price to be paid for acquiring knowledge, developing intellectual skills, and attaining wisdom. However, numerous task forces and national commissions tell us that students today are not willing to pay this price and that, as a consequence, we have become academically mediocre. Is it true that we no longer delight in educating ourselves through reading, as Richard Rodriguez recounts in "The Lonely, Good Company of Books"? Is it true that we take libraries for granted—we expect them to be available but never visit them? A democratic society requires an educated citizenry, people who refuse to commit intellectual suicide or self-neglect. The writers in this chapter, who take many pathways to understanding, remind us that we cannot afford to be passive or compliant when our right to an education is challenged.

Today we are in an era of dynamic change in attitudes toward education. Such issues as sex education, multiculturalism, racism, sexism, and immigration suggest the liveliness of the educational debate on campus. Any debate over contemporary education touches on the themes of politics, economics, religion, or the social agenda, forcing us to recognize that configurations of power are at the heart of virtually all educational issues in society today.

Without education, many of our ideas and opinions can be stereotyped or prejudiced, bearing no relationship to the truth. It is easy to understand how such views can arise if we are merely passive vessels for others' uninformed opinions rather than active learners who seek true knowledge. If we judge the tenor of the essayists in this section, we discover that many of them are subversives, waging war against both ignorance *and* received dogma. These writers treat education as the key to upsetting the status quo and effecting change. Operating from diverse backgrounds, they challenge many assumptions about our educational system and invite us to think critically about its purpose.

PREVIEWING THE CHAPTER

As you read the essays in this chapter and respond to them in discussion and writing, consider the following questions:

- What is the main educational issue that the author deals with?
- What tone does the author establish in treating the subject? Does the author take a positive or a negative position?
- Does the author define *education?* If so, how? If not, does the author suggest what he or she means by it?
- What is the impact of society at large on how education is perceived?
- What forms of evidence do the authors use to support their views on education?
- How do the rhetorical features of the essays that focus on personal experience differ from those of the essays that examine education from a more global perspective?
- What have you learned about the value of education from reading these selections?
- Which essays persuaded you the most? Which the least? Why?

Classic and Contemporary Images

DOES EDUCATION CHANGE OVER TIME?

Using a Critical Perspective   Consider these two photographs of students in science laboratories, the first from the 19th century and the second from the present. What is the setting of each laboratory like? Who are the people? What does each photographer frame and leave out of the scene? Which educational setting seems more conducive to scientific or educational inquiry? Why?

Founded in 1833, Oberlin College in Ohio was the first U.S. college
to grant undergraduate degrees to women. The photograph reprinted
here shows both male and female students in a zoology lab
at Oberlin sometime during the 1890s.

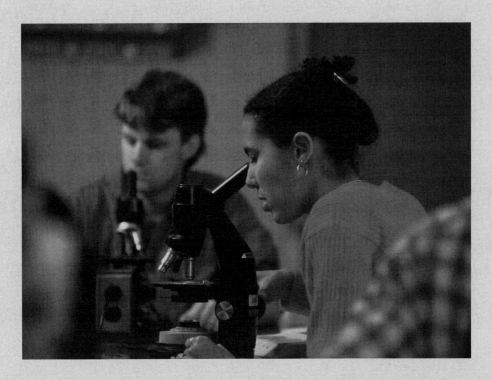

At the beginning of the 21st century, most colleges and universities in the United States are coeducational, and it is no longer unusual to see both male and female students in a laboratory setting, as shown in this contemporary photo of a biology lab at the University of Maine.

Classic and Contemporary Essays
WHAT IS THE VALUE OF EDUCATION?

A famous adage proclaims that "the pen is mightier than the sword." In Frederick Douglass's narrative and the excerpt from the work of Richard Rodriguez, we get two portraits that demonstrate the truth of the adage. Douglass's efforts at becoming fully literate freed him from what would have been a life of slavery. No weapon could have done that for him. It is obvious that Douglass learned his lesson well, for his prose is stately, clear, direct, and precise. His story speaks of a determined youth and man who had a powerful motivation in learning to read and write. Would he have done so without this motivation? Perhaps, because he seems to be a very self-directed individual, as is evident from the anecdotes he relates. Rodriguez, too, has a strong motivation to master, and even to excel at, reading and writing. Writing nearly 150 years after Douglass, and at a time when he needn't fear slavery looming over him, Rodriguez nevertheless perceived that by emulating his teachers, who promoted book reading, his own reading would make him a better person. He, like Douglass, sensed that there was something about acquiring knowledge and about expanding one's view of the world by learning how others viewed it that would provide him with a certain amount of independence. As you read the following two essays, you may wish to consider whether the quiet, modest tone each author projects may have something to do with the subject matter. For reading, although active and mind-opening, is still a private and "lonely" activity.

Learning to Read and Write

Frederick Douglass

Frederick Douglass (1817–1895) was an American abolitionist, orator, and journalist. Born of the union between a slave and a white man, Douglass later escaped to Massachusetts. An impassioned antislavery speech brought him recognition as a powerful orator; thereafter he was much in demand for speaking engagements. He described his experience as a black man in America in Narrative of the Life of Frederick Douglass *(1845). After managing to buy his freedom, Douglass founded the* North Star, *a newspaper he published for the next 17 years. In the following excerpt from his stirring autobiography, Douglass recounts the tremendous obstacles he overcame in his efforts to become literate.*

1 I lived in Master Hugh's family about seven years. During this time, I succeeded in learning to read and write. In accomplishing this, I was compelled to resort to

various stratagems. I had no regular teacher. My mistress, who had kindly commenced to instruct me, had, in compliance with the advice and direction of her husband, not only ceased to instruct, but had set her face against my being instructed by any one else. It is due, however, to my mistress to say of her, that she did not adopt this course of treatment immediately. She at first lacked the depravity indispensable to shutting me up in mental darkness. It was at least necessary for her to have some training in the exercise of irresponsible power, to make her equal to the task of treating me as though I were a brute.

My mistress was, as I have said, a kind and tender-hearted woman; and in 2 the simplicity of her soul she commenced, when I first went to live with her, to treat me as she supposed one human being ought to treat another. In entering upon the duties of a slaveholder, she did not seem to perceive that I sustained to her the relation of a mere chattel, and that for her to treat me as a human being was not only wrong, but dangerously so. Slavery proved as injurious to her as it did to me. When I went there, she was a pious, warm, and tender-hearted woman. There was no sorrow or suffering for which she had not a tear. She had bread for the hungry, clothes for the naked, and comfort for every mourner that came within her reach. Slavery soon proved its ability to divest her of these heavenly qualities. Under its influence, the tender heart became stone, and the lamb-like disposition gave way to one of tiger-like fierceness. The first step in her downward course was in her ceasing to instruct me. She now commenced to practise her husband's precepts. She finally became even more violent in her opposition than her husband himself. She was not satisfied with simply doing as well as he had commanded; she seemed anxious to do better. Nothing seemed to make her more angry than to see me with a newspaper. She seemed to think that here lay the danger. I have had her rush at me with a face made all up of fury, and snatch from me a newspaper, in a manner that fully revealed her apprehension. She was an apt woman; and a little experience soon demonstrated, to her satisfaction, that education and slavery were incompatible with each other.

From this time I was most narrowly watched. If I was in a separate room 3 any considerable length of time, I was sure to be suspected of having a book, and was at once called to give an account of myself. All this, however, was too late. The first step had been taken. Mistress, in teaching me the alphabet, had given me the *inch,* and no precaution could prevent me from taking the *ell.*

The plan which I adopted, and the one by which I was most successful, 4 was that of making friends of all the little white boys whom I met in the street. As many of these as I could, I converted into teachers. With their kindly aid, obtained at different times and in different places, I finally succeeded in learning to read. When I was sent on errands, I always took my book with me, and by doing one part of my errand quickly, I found time to get a lesson before my return. I used also to carry bread with me, enough of which was always in the house, and to which I was always welcome; for I was much better off in this regard than many of the poor white children in our neighborhood. This bread I used to bestow upon the hungry little urchins, who, in return, would give me that more valuable bread of knowledge. I am strongly tempted to give the names of two or three of those little boys, a testimonial of the gratitude and affection I bear them; but prudence forbids— not that it would injure me, but it might embarrass them; for it is almost an unpardonable offence to teach slaves to read in this Christian country. It is enough to say of the dear little fellows, that they lived on Philpot Street, very near Durgin and Bailey's shipyard. I used to talk this matter of slavery over with them. I would sometimes say to them, I wished I could be as free as they would be when they got to be men. "You will be free as soon as you are twenty-one, *but I am a slave for life!* Have not I as good a right to be free as you have?" These words used to trouble them; they would express for me the liveliest sympathy, and console me with the hope that something would occur by which I might be free.

5   I was now about twelve years old, and the thought of being a *slave for life* began to bear heavily upon my heart. Just about this time, I got hold of a book entitled "The Colombian Orator." Every opportunity I got, I used to read this book. Among much of other interesting matter, I found in it a dialogue between a master and his slave. The slave was represented as having run away from his master three times. The dialogue represented the conversation which took place between them, when the slave was retaken the third time. In this dialogue, the whole argument in behalf of slavery was brought forward by the master, all of which was disposed of by the slave. The slave was made to say some very smart as well as impressive things in reply to his master—things which had the desired though unexpected effect; for the conversation resulted in the voluntary emancipation of the slave on the part of the master.

6   In the same book, I met with one of Sheridan's mighty speeches on and in behalf of Catholic emancipation. These were choice documents to me. I read them over and over again with unabated interest. They gave tongue to interesting thoughts of my own soul, which had frequently flashed through my mind, and died away for want of utterance. The moral which I gained from the dialogue was the power of truth over the conscience of even a slaveholder. What I got from Sheridan was a bold denunciation of slavery, and a powerful vindication of human rights. The reading of these documents enabled me to utter my thoughts, and to meet the arguments brought forward to sustain slavery; but while they relieved me of one difficulty, they brought on another even more painful than the one of which I was relieved. The more I read, the more I was led to abhor and detest my enslavers. I could regard them in no other light than a band of successful robbers, who had left their homes, and gone to Africa, and stolen us from our homes, and in a strange land reduced us to slavery. I loathed them as being the meanest as well as the most wicked of men. As I read and contemplated the subject, behold! that very discontentment which Master Hugh had predicted would follow my learning to read had already come, to torment and sting my soul to unutterable anguish. As I writhed under it, I would at times feel that learning to read had been a curse rather than a blessing. It had given me a view of my wretched condition,

without the remedy. It opened my eyes to the horrible pit, but to no ladder upon which to get out. In moments of agony, I envied my fellow-slaves for their stupidity. I have often wished myself a beast. I preferred the condition of the meanest reptile to my own. Any thing, no matter what, to get rid of thinking! It was this everlasting thinking of my condition that tormented me. There was no getting rid of it. It was pressed upon me by every object within sight or hearing, animate or inanimate. The silver trump of freedom had roused my soul to eternal wakefulness. Freedom now appeared, to disappear no more forever. It was heard in every sound, and seen in every thing. It was ever present to torment me with a sense of my wretched condition. I saw nothing without seeing it, I heard nothing without hearing it, and felt nothing without feeling it. It looked from every star, it smiled in every calm, breathed in every wind, and moved in every storm.

I often found myself regretting my own existence, and wishing myself 7 dead; and but for the hope of being free, I have no doubt but that I should have killed myself, or done something for which I should have been killed. While in this state of mind, I was eager to hear anyone speak of slavery. I was a ready listener. Every little while, I could hear something about the abolitionists. It was some time before I found what the word meant. It was always used in such connections as to make it an interesting word to me. If a slave ran away and succeeded in getting clear, or if a slave killed his master, set fire to a barn, or did any thing very wrong in the mind of a slaveholder, it was spoken of as the fruit of *abolition*. Hearing the word in this connection very often, I set about learning what it meant. The dictionary afforded me little or no help. I found it was "the act of abolishing"; but then I did not know what was to be abolished. Here I was perplexed. I did not dare to ask any one about its meaning, for I was satisfied that it was something they wanted me to know very little about. After a patient waiting, I got one of our city papers, containing an account of the number of petitions from the north, praying for the abolition of slavery in the District of Columbia, and of the slave trade between the States. From this time I understood the words *abolition* and *abolitionist,* and always drew near when that word was spoken, expecting to hear something of importance to myself and fellow-slaves. The light broke in upon me by degrees. I went one day down on the wharf of Mr. Waters; and seeing two Irishmen unloading a scow of stone, I went, unasked, and helped them. When we had finished, one of them came to me and asked me if I were a slave. I told him I was. He asked, "Are ye a slave for life?" I told him that I was. The good Irishman seemed to be deeply affected by the statement. He said to the other that it was a pity so fine a little fellow as myself should be a slave for life. He said it was a shame to hold me. They both advised me to run away to the north; that I should find friends there, and that I should be free. I pretended not to be interested in what they said, and treated them as if I did not understand them; for I feared they might be treacherous. White men have been known to encourage slaves to escape, and then, to get the reward, catch them and return them to their masters. I was afraid that these seemingly good men might use me so; but I nevertheless remembered their advice, and from that time I resolved to run away. I looked forward to a time at which it would be safe for me to escape. I was too young to think of doing so immediately; besides, I wished to learn how to write, as I might have occasion to write my own pass. I consoled myself with the hope that I should one day find a good chance. Meanwhile, I would learn to write.

8   The idea as to how I might learn to write was suggested to me by being in Durgin and Bailey's ship-yard, and frequently seeing the ship carpenters, after hewing, and getting a piece of timber ready for use, write on the timber the name of that part of the ship for which it was intended. When a piece of timber was intended for the larboard side, it would be marked thus—"L." When a piece was for the starboard side, it would be marked thus—"S." A piece for the larboard side forward, would be marked thus—"L. F." When a piece was for starboard side forward, it would be marked thus—"S. F." For larboard aft, it would be marked thus—"L. A." For starboard aft, it would be marked thus— "S. A." I soon learned the names of these letters, and for what they were intended when placed upon a piece of timber in the ship-yard. I immediately commenced copying them, and in a short time was able to make the four letters named. After that, when I met with any boy who I knew could write, I would tell him I could write as well as he. The next word would be, "I don't believe you. Let me see you try it." I would then make the letters which I had been so fortunate as to learn, and ask him to beat that. In this way I got a good many lessons in writing, which it is quite possible I should never have gotten in any other way. During this time, my copy-book was the board fence, brick wall, and pavement; my pen and ink was a lump of chalk. With these, I learned mainly how to write. I then commenced and continued copying the Italics in Webster's Spelling Book, until I could make them all without looking on the book. By this time, my little Master Thomas had gone to school, and learned how to write, and had written over a number of copy-books. These had been brought home, and shown to some of our near neighbors, and then laid aside. My mistress used to go to class meeting at the Wilk Street meetinghouse every Monday afternoon, and leave me to take care of the house. When left thus, I used to spend the time in writing in the spaces left in Master Thomas's copy-book, copying what he had written. I continued to do this until I could write a hand very similar to that of Master Thomas. Thus, after a long, tedious effort for years, I finally succeeded in learning how to write.

COMPREHENSION

1. What strategies does Douglass use to continue his education after his mistress's abandonment?
2. Why did the author's mistress find his reading newspapers particularly threatening?
3. Why does Douglass call learning to read "a curse rather than a blessing" (paragraph 6)?

RHETORIC

1. What is the thesis of Douglass's narration? How well is it supported and developed by the body paragraphs? Explain.
2. The first couple of sentences in the story, though simple, are very powerful. How do they serve to set up the mood of the piece and the reader's expectations?
3. Cite examples of Douglass's use of metaphors, and discuss why they work in those paragraphs.
4. How would you describe Douglass's writing style and level of language? Does it reveal anything about his character? Justify your response.
5. Explain the way in which the author uses comparison and contrast.
6. What is Douglass's definition of *abolition,* and how does he help the reader define it? How does this method contribute to the reader's understanding of the learning process?

WRITING

1. What does Douglass mean when he writes that "education and slavery were incompatible with each other" (paragraph 2)? Write an essay in which you consider the relationship between the two.
2. Both Douglass and his mistress were in inferior positions to Master Hugh. Write an essay in which you compare and contrast their positions in society at the time.
3. Illiteracy is still a major problem in the United States. Write an account of what your day-to-day life would be like if you couldn't write or read. What impact would this deficiency have on your life? Use concrete examples to illustrate your narrative.
4. **Writing an Argument:** Write an essay in which you argue for or against the proposition that American education continues to discriminate against minority groups.

NETWORKING
Applying 21st-Century Literacies

Analyzing a News Report on 21st-Century Illiteracy: On the Chapter 5 Networking page at *www.mhhe.com/mhreaderbrief1e*, link to and watch this 2009 CBS report on adult illiteracy in the United States. What challenges has John Jones faced because of his illiteracy? Why do you think the report chose to focus not only on larger statistics, such as results from the Board of Education's report, but also on illiteracy's effects on an individual? How does John Jones's story contribute to the report's purpose and argument? How does the report make use of its medium (television) to convey its message?

The Lonely, Good Company
of Books

Richard Rodriguez

Richard Rodriguez (b. 1944) was born in San Francisco and received degrees from Stanford University and Columbia University. He also did graduate study at the University of California, Berkeley, and at the Warburg Institute, London. Rodriguez became a nationally known writer with the publication of his autobiography, Hunger of Memory: The Education of Richard Rodriguez *(1982). In it, he describes the struggles of growing up biculturally—feeling alienated from his Spanish-speaking parents yet not wholly comfortable in the dominant culture of the United States. He opposes bilingualism and affirmative action as they are now practiced in the United States, and his stance has caused much controversy in educational and intellectual circles. Rodriguez continues to write about social issues such as acculturation, education, and language in* Days of Obligation: An Argument with My Mexican Father *(1992) and* Brown: The Last Discovery of America *(2002). In the following essay, Rodriguez records his childhood passion for reading.*

1   From an early age I knew that my mother and father could read and write both Spanish and English. I had observed my father making his way through what, I now suppose, must have been income tax forms. On other occasions I waited apprehensively while my mother read onion-paper letters air-mailed from Mexico with news of a relative's illness or death. For both my parents, however, reading was something done out of necessity and as quickly as possible. Never did I see either of them read an entire book. Nor did I see them read for pleasure. Their reading consisted of work manuals, prayer books, newspapers, recipes. . . .

2   In our house each school year would begin with my mother's careful instruction: "Don't write in your books so we can sell them at the end of the year." The remark was echoed in public by my teachers, but only in part: "Boys and girls, don't write in your books. You must learn to treat them with great care and respect."

3   OPEN THE DOORS OF YOUR MIND WITH BOOKS, read the red and white poster over the nun's desk in early September. It soon was apparent to me that reading was the classroom's central activity. Each course had its own book. And the information gathered from a book was unquestioned. READ TO LEARN, the sign on the wall advised in December. I privately wondered: What was the connection between reading and learning? Did one learn something only by reading it? Was an idea only an idea if it could be written down? In June, CONSIDER BOOKS YOUR BEST FRIENDS. Friends? Reading was, at best, only a chore. I needed to look up whole paragraphs of words in a dictionary. Lines of type were dizzying, the eye having

to move slowly across the page, then down, and across. . . . The sentences of the first books I read were coolly impersonal. Toned hard. What most bothered me, however, was the isolation reading required. To console myself for the loneliness I'd feel when I read, I tried reading in a very soft voice. Until: "Who is doing all that talking to his neighbor?" Shortly after, remedial reading classes were arranged for me with a very old nun.

At the end of each school day, for nearly six months, I would meet with her 4 in the tiny room that served as the school's library but was actually only a storeroom for used textbooks and a vast collection of *National Geographics.* Everything about our sessions pleased me: the smallness of the room; the noise of the janitor's broom hitting the edge of the long hallway outside the door; the green of the sun, lighting the wall; and the old woman's face blurred white with a beard. Most of the time we took turns. I began with my elementary text. Sentences of astonishing simplicity seemed to me lifeless and drab: "The boys ran from the rain. . . . She wanted to sing. . . . The kite rose in the blue." Then the old nun would read from her favorite books, usually biographies of early American presidents. Playfully she ran through complex sentences, calling the words alive with her voice, making it seem that the author somehow was speaking directly to me. I smiled just to listen to her. I sat there and sensed for the very first time some possibility of fellowship between a reader and a writer, a communication, never *intimate* like that I heard spoken words at home convey, but one nonetheless *personal.*

One day the nun concluded a session by asking me why I was so reluctant 5 to read by myself. I tried to explain; said something about the way written words made me feel all alone—almost, I wanted to add but didn't, as when I spoke to myself in a room just emptied of furniture. She studied my face as I spoke; she seemed to be watching more than listening. In an uneventful voice she replied that I had nothing to fear. Didn't I realize that reading would open up whole new worlds? A book could open doors for me. It could introduce me to people and show me places I never imagined existed. She gestured toward the bookshelves. (Bare-breasted African women danced, and the shiny hubcaps of automobiles on the back covers of the *Geographic* gleamed in my mind.) I listened with respect. But her words were not very influential. I was thinking then of another consequence of literacy, one I was too shy to admit but nonetheless trusted. Books were going to make me "educated." *That* confidence enabled me, several months later, to overcome my fear of the silence.

In fourth grade I embarked upon a grandiose reading program. "Give me 6 the names of important books," I would say to startled teachers. They soon found out that I had in mind "adult books." I ignored their suggestion of anything I suspected was written for children. (Not until I was in college, as a result, did I read *Huckleberry Finn* or *Alice's Adventures in Wonderland.*) Instead, I read *The Scarlet Letter* and Franklin's *Autobiography.* And whatever I read I read for extra credit. Each time I finished a book, I reported the achievement to a teacher and basked in the praise my effort earned. Despite my best efforts, however, there seemed to be more and more books I needed to read. At the library I would literally tremble as I came upon whole shelves of books I hadn't read. So I read and I read and I read: *Great Expectations;* all the short stories of Kipling; *The Babe Ruth Story;* the entire first volume of the *Encyclopaedia Britannica* (A–ANSTEY); the *Iliad; Moby Dick; Gone with the Wind; The Good Earth; Ramona; Forever Amber; The Lives of the Saints; Crime and Punishment; The Pearl.* . . . Librarians who initially frowned when I checked out the maximum ten books at a time started saving books they thought I might like. Teachers would say to the rest of the class, "I only wish the rest of you took reading as seriously as Richard obviously does."

7   But at home I would hear my mother wondering, "What do you see in your books?" (Was reading a hobby like her knitting? Was so much reading even healthy for a boy? Was it the sign of "brains"? Or was it just a convenient excuse for not helping around the house on Saturday mornings?) Always, "What do you see . . . ?"

8   What *did* I see in my books? I had the idea that they were crucial for my academic success, though I couldn't have said exactly how or why. In the sixth grade I simply concluded that what gave a book its value was some major idea or theme it contained. If that core essence could be mined and memorized, I would become learned like my teachers. I decided to record in a notebook the themes of the books that I read. After reading *Robinson Crusoe,* I wrote that its theme was "the value of learning to live by oneself." When I completed *Wuthering Heights,* I noted the danger of "letting emotions get out of control." Rereading these brief moralistic appraisals usually left me disheartened. I couldn't believe that they were really the source of reading's value. But for many years, they constituted the only means I had of describing to myself the educational value of books.

9   In spite of my earnestness, I found reading a pleasurable activity. I came to enjoy the lonely, good company of books. Early on weekday mornings, I'd read in my bed. I'd feel a mysterious comfort then, reading in the dawn quiet—the blue-gray silence interrupted by the occasional churning of the refrigerator motor a few rooms away or the more distant sounds of a city bus beginning its run. On weekends I'd go to the public library to read, surrounded by old men and women. Or, if the weather was fine, I would take my books to the park and read in the shade of a tree. Neighbors would leave for vacation and I would water their lawns. I would sit through the twilight on the front porches or in backyards, reading to the cool, whirling sounds of the sprinklers.

10   I also had favorite writers. But often those writers I enjoyed most I was least able to value. When I read William Saroyan's *The Human Comedy,* I was immediately pleased by the narrator's warmth and the charm of his story. But as quickly I became suspicious. A book so enjoyable to read couldn't be very "important." Another summer I determined to read all the novels of Dickens. Reading his fat novels, I loved the feeling I got—after the first hundred pages—of being at home in a fictional world where I knew the names of the characters and cared about what was going to happen to them. And it bothered me that I was forced away at the conclusion, when the fiction closed tight, like a fortune-teller's fist—the futures of all the major characters neatly resolved. I never knew how to take such feelings seriously, however. Nor did I suspect that these experiences could be part

of a novel's meaning. Still, there were pleasures to sustain me after I'd finish my books. Carrying a volume back to the library, I would be pleased by its weight. I'd run my fingers along the edge of the pages and marvel at the breadth of my achievement. Around my room, growing stacks of paperback books reinforced my assurance.

I entered high school having read hundreds of books. My habit of reading 11 made me a confident speaker and writer of English. Reading also enabled me to sense something of the shape, the major concerns, of Western thought. (I was able to say something about Dante and Descartes and Engels and James Baldwin in my high school term papers.) In these various ways, books brought me academic success as I hoped that they would. But I was not a good reader. Merely bookish, I lacked a point of view when I read. Rather, I read in order to acquire a point of view. I vacuumed books for epigrams, scraps of information, ideas, themes—anything to fill the hollow within me and make me feel educated. When one of my teachers suggested to his drowsy tenth-grade English class that a person could not have a "complicated idea" until he had read at least two thousand books, I heard the remark without detecting either its irony or its very complicated truth. I merely determined to compile a list of all the books I had ever read. Harsh with myself, I included only once a title I might have read several times. (How, after all, could one read a book more than once?) And I included only those books over a hundred pages in length. (Could anything shorter be a book?)

There was yet another high school list I compiled. One day I came across a 12 newspaper article about the retirement of an English professor at a nearby state college. The article was accompanied by a list of the "hundred most important books of Western Civilization." "More than anything else in my life," the professor told the reporter with finality, "these books have made me all that I am." That was the kind of remark I couldn't ignore. I clipped out the list and kept it for the several months it took me to read all of the titles. Most books, of course, I barely understood. While reading Plato's *Republic,* for instance, I needed to keep looking at the book jacket comments to remind myself what the text was about. Nevertheless, with the special patience and superstition of a scholarship boy, I looked at every word of the text. And by the time I reached the last word, relieved, I convinced myself that I had read *The Republic.* In a ceremony of great pride, I solemnly crossed Plato off my list.

COMPREHENSION

1. What was Rodriguez's parents' attitude toward reading? Did it influence his attitude? Cite examples from the essay that support your opinion.
2. What does Rodriguez mean by the "fellowship between a reader and a writer" (paragraph 4)? Why does he differentiate between "intimate" and "personal" forms of communication?
3. Rodriguez hoped that reading would fill "the hollow" inside him. What was the cause of his emptiness? Did he succeed in filling the void? Why did he find reading a lonely experience? Did reading fulfill any of his expectations?

RHETORIC

1. What is the thesis of Rodriguez's essay? Is it stated or implied? Explain.
2. How does the author's use of narrative advance his views on reading and education?
3. What is the writer's tone? How effective is it in conveying his point of view?
4. Rodriguez uses uppercase letters (small capitals) when referring to signs advocating reading. Why does he use this device? How does it support his point of view?
5. The essay ends with an ironic anecdote. Why did Rodriguez choose to conclude this way? Does it satisfactorily illustrate his attitude?
6. What words or phrases imply that there is an ethnic component in Rodriguez's conflict? Is the subtlety effective? Justify your response.

WRITING

1. Rodriguez's parents had a pragmatic attitude toward reading. What was the attitude in your home as you were growing up? Did your parents encourage your interest in reading? Did they read themselves? What is the first book you remember reading by yourself? Write an essay in which you describe your reading history.
2. Is reading still a significant source of information and entertainment, or has it been usurped by television? Is it important (or necessary) to be a reader today?
3. **Writing an Argument:** Rodriguez believed reading would make him "educated." Do you agree or disagree? Is reading vital to a person's education? How do you define *education*? Can it be acquired only through reading, or are there other contributing factors? Write an argumentative essay on this topic.

NETWORKING
Applying 21st-Century Literacies

Considering the Impact of e-Books: From the Chapter 5 Networking page at *www.mhhe.com/mhreaderbrief1e*, link to and read "How the e-Book Will Change the Way We Read and Write" from the *Wall Street Journal*. In this article, Steven Johnson argues that the advent of e-readers and online books means that soon reading will no longer be something people do in isolation. "As you read," Johnson predicts, "you will know that at any given moment, a conversation is available about the paragraph or even *sentence* you are reading. Nobody will read alone anymore. Reading books will go from being a fundamentally private activity—a direct exchange between author and reader—to a community event, with every isolated paragraph the launching pad for a conversation with strangers around the world."

If Richard Rodriguez had embarked on reading in a world like the one Johnson describes, how might his experience with books have been different? In what ways do you think it would have been less, or more, rewarding? What do you see as some advantages of reading offline, alone, and what are some advantages of reading online, in a network?

Hillary, left, and Julie Goodridge, lead plaintiffs in the landmark Massachusetts gay marriage lawsuit, receive their wedding rings from their daughter, Annie, 8, as Unitarian Reverend William Sinkford presides over their marriage ceremony in Boston during the first day of state-sanctioned gay marriage in the United States on May 17, 2004.

Classic and Contemporary Essays
HOW MUCH DO FAMILIES MATTER?

E. B. White and Barbara Kingsolver represent two generations, each raised with different values regarding the function, structure, and role of the family. Both authors are master stylists, but each reflects a style of writing, an intellectual universe, and an external world that views the healthy family differently. White writes in clear, concise, elegiac prose. It marches on in a quiet, evenly patterned rhythm. Perhaps it is a metaphor of his view of life in general and family life in particular. Tradition is to be treasured; continuity is to be celebrated. He attends to the details of a nature outing and suggests that the sights, sounds, and smells that imbue the events he and his son experience are the same as those he experienced years before with his own father. For White, it seems, pleasure is derived from connectivity and permanence.

Kingsolver is passionate about her perspective on what constitutes a healthy family structure, but it is a family transformed, reconfigured, and rearranged by contemporary events and values. Kingsolver's notion of family is various while White's view is archetypal. Kingsolver seems to believe that change in families creates security, particularly if one is moving from a dysfunctional environment to a more coherent one. Is White conservative in his views? Is Kingsolver a liberal? Perhaps a better way to get a sense of their differences is to inquire whether our amorphous contemporary world requires us to be more flexible and critical. And, of course, we must consider that Kingsolver adds a woman's voice to the conversation about family, a voice that was not as frequently heard by the members of White's generation.

Once More to the Lake

E. B. White

E(lwyn) B(rooks) White (1899–1985), perhaps the finest American essayist of the 20th century, was at his most distinctive in his treatments of people and nature. A recipient of the National Medal for Literature, and associated for years with the New Yorker, *White is the author of* One Man's Meat *(1942),* Here Is New York *(1949), and* The Second Tree from the Corner *(1954), among numerous other works. He was also one of the most talented writers of literature for children, the author of* Stuart Little *(1945),* Charlotte's Web *(1952), and* The Trumpet of the Swan *(1970). In this essay, White combines narration and description to make a poignant and vivid statement about past and present, youth and age, life and death.*

One summer, along about 1904, my father rented a camp on a lake in Maine and   1
took us all there for the month of August. We all got ringworm from some kit-
tens and had to rub Pond's Extract on our arms and legs night and morning, and
my father rolled over in a canoe with all his clothes on; but outside of that the
vacation was a success and from then on none of us ever thought there was any
place in the world like that lake in Maine. We returned summer after summer—
always on August 1st for one month. I have since become a saltwater man, but
sometimes in summer there are days when the restlessness of the tides and the
fearful cold of the sea water and the incessant wind which blows across the afternoon and into the evening make me wish for the placidity of a lake in the woods.
A few weeks ago this feeling got so strong I bought myself a couple of bass
hooks and a spinner and returned to the lake where we used to go, for a week's
fishing and to revisit old haunts.

    I took along my son, who had never had any fresh water up his nose and   2
who had seen lily pads only from train windows. On the journey over to the lake
I began to wonder what it would be like. I wondered how time would have
marred this unique, this holy spot—the coves and streams, the hills that the sun
set behind, the camps and the paths behind the camps. I was sure the tarred road
would have found it out and I wondered in what other ways it would be deso-
lated. It is strange how much you can remember about places like that once you
allow your mind to return into the grooves which lead back. You remember one
thing, and that suddenly reminds you of another thing. I guess I remembered
clearest of all the early mornings, when the lake was cool and motionless, remembered how the bedroom smelled of the lumber it was made of and of the wet
woods whose scent entered through the screen. The partitions in the camp were
thin and did not extend clear to the top of the rooms, and as I was always the first
up I would dress softly so as not to wake the others, and sneak out into the sweet
outdoors and start out in the canoe, keeping close along the shore in the long
shadows of the pines. I remembered being very careful never to rub my paddle
against the gunwale for fear of disturbing the stillness of the cathedral.

    The lake had never been what you would call a wild lake. There were cot-   3
tages sprinkled around the shores, and it was in farming country although the
shores of the lake were quite heavily wooded. Some of the cottages were owned
by nearby farmers, and you would live at the shore and eat your meals at the
farmhouse. That's what our family did. But although it wasn't wild, it was a
fairly large and undisturbed lake and there were places in it which, to a child at
least, seemed infinitely remote and primeval.

    I was right about the tar: It led to within half a mile of the shore. But when I   4
got back there, with my boy, and we settled into a camp near a farmhouse and
into the kind of summertime I had known, I could tell that it was going to be
pretty much the same as it had been before—I knew it, lying in bed the first
morning, smelling the bedroom, and hearing the boy sneak quietly out and go
off along the shore in a boat. I began to sustain the illusion that he was I, and
therefore, by simple transposition, that I was my father. This sensation persisted,

kept cropping up all the time we were there. It was not an entirely new feeling, but in this setting it grew much stronger. I seemed to be living a dual existence. I would be in the middle of some simple act, I would be picking up a bait box or laying down a table fork, or I would be saying something, and suddenly it would be not I but my father who was saying the words or making the gesture. It gave me a creepy sensation.

5   We went fishing the first morning. I felt the same damp moss covering the worms in the bait can, and saw the dragonfly alight on the tip of my rod as it hovered a few inches from the surface of the water. It was the arrival of this fly that convinced me beyond any doubt that everything was as it always had been, that the years were a mirage and there had been no years. The small waves were the same, chucking the rowboat under the chin as we fished at anchor, and the boat was the same boat, the same color green and the ribs broken in the same place, and under the floor-boards the same fresh-water leavings and débris—the dead hellgrammite, the wisps of moss, the rusty discarded fishhook, the dried blood from yesterday's catch. We stared silently at the tips of our rods, at the dragonflies that came and went. I lowered the tip of mine into the water, tentatively, pensively dislodging the fly, which darted two feet away, poised, darted two feet back, and came to rest again a little farther up the rod. There had been no years between the ducking of this dragonfly and the other one—the one that was part of memory. I looked at the boy, who was silently watching his fly, and it was my hands that held his rod, my eyes watching. I felt dizzy and didn't know which rod I was at the end of.

6   We caught two bass, hauling them in briskly as though they were mackerel, pulling them over the side of the boat in a businesslike manner without any landing net, and stunning them with a blow on the back of the head. When we got back for a swim before lunch, the lake was exactly where we had left it, the same number of inches from the dock, and there was only the merest suggestion of a breeze. This seemed an utterly enchanted sea, this lake you could leave to its own devices for a few hours and come back to, and find that it had not stirred, this constant and trustworthy body of water. In the shallows, the dark, water-soaked sticks and twigs, smooth and old, were undulating in clusters on the bottom against the clean ribbed sand, and the track of the mussel was plain. A school of minnows swam by, each minnow with its small individual shadow, doubling the attendance, so clear and sharp in the sunlight. Some of the other campers were in swimming, along the shore, one of them with a cake of soap, and the water felt thin and clear and unsubstantial. Over the years there had been this person with the cake of soap, this cultist, and here he was. There had been no years.

7   Up to the farmhouse to dinner through the teeming, dusty field, the road under our sneakers was only a two-track road. The middle track was missing, the one with the marks of the hooves and the splotches of dried, flaky manure. There had always been three tracks to choose from in choosing which track to walk in; now the choice was narrowed down to two. For a moment I missed terribly the middle alternative. But the way led past the tennis court, and something about the way it lay there in the sun reassured me; the tape had loosened

along the backline, the alleys were green with plantains and other weeds, and the net (installed in June and removed in September) sagged in the dry noon, and the whole place steamed with midday heat and hunger and emptiness. There was a choice of pie for dessert, and one was blueberry and one was apple, and the waitresses were the same country girls, there having been no passage of time, only the illusion of it as in a dropped curtain—the waitresses were still fifteen; their hair had been washed, that was the only difference—they had been to the movies and seen the pretty girls with the clean hair.

Summertime, oh summertime, pattern of life indelible, the fade-proof lake, 8 the woods unshatterable, the pasture with the sweetfern and the juniper forever and ever, summer without end; this was the background, and the life along the shore was the design, the cottagers with their innocent and tranquil design, their tiny docks with the flagpole and the American flag floating against the white clouds in the blue sky, the little paths over the roots of the trees leading from camp to camp and the paths leading back to the outhouses and the can of lime for sprinkling, and at the souvenir counters at the store the miniature birch-bark canoes and the post cards that showed things looking a little better than they looked. This was the American family at play, escaping the city heat, wondering whether the newcomers in the camp at the head of the cove were "common" or "nice," wondering whether it was true that the people who drove up for Sunday dinner at the farmhouse were turned away because there wasn't enough chicken.

It seemed to me, as I kept remembering all this, that those times and those 9 summers had been infinitely precious and worth saving. There had been jollity and peace and goodness. The arriving (at the beginning of August) had been so big a business in itself, at the railway station the farm wagon drawn up, the first smell of the pine-laden air, the first glimpse of the smiling farmer, and the great importance of the trunks and your father's enormous authority in such matters, and the feel of the wagon under you for the long ten-mile haul, and at the top of the last long hill catching the first view of the lake after eleven months of not seeing this cherished body of water. The shouts and cries of the other campers when they saw you, and the trunks to be unpacked, to give up their rich burden. (Arriving was less exciting nowadays, when you sneaked up in your car and parked it under a tree near the camp and took out the bags and in five minutes it was all over, no fuss, no loud wonderful fuss about trunks.)

Peace and goodness and jollity. The only thing that was wrong now, really, 10 was the sound of the place, an unfamiliar nervous sound of the outboard motors. This was the note that jarred, the one thing that would sometimes break the illusion and set the years moving. In those other summertimes all motors were inboard; and when they were at a little distance, the noise they made was a sedative, an ingredient of summer sleep. They were one-cylinder and two-cylinder engines, and some were make-and-break and some were jump-spark, but they all made a sleepy sound across the lake. The one-lungers throbbed and fluttered, and the twin-cylinder ones purred and purred, and that was a quiet sound too. But now the campers all had outboards. In the daytime, in the hot mornings, these motors made a petulant, irritable sound; at night, in the still evening when the afterglow lit the water, they whined about one's ears like mosquitoes. My boy loved our rented outboard, and his great desire was to achieve singlehanded mastery over it, and authority, and he soon learned the trick of choking it a little (but not too much), and the adjustment of the needle valve. Watching him I would remember the things you could do with the old one-cylinder engine with the heavy flywheel, how you could have it eating out of your hand if you got really close to it spiritually. Motor boats in those days didn't have clutches, and you would make a landing by shutting off the motor at the proper time and coasting in with a dead rudder. But there was a way of reversing them, if you learned the trick, by cutting the switch and putting it on again exactly on the final dying revolution of the flywheel, so that it would kick back against compression and begin reversing. Approaching a dock in a strong following breeze, it was difficult to slow up sufficiently by the ordinary coasting method, and if a boy felt he had complete mastery over his motor, he was tempted to keep it running beyond its time and then reverse it a few feet from the dock. It took a cool nerve, because if you threw the switch a twentieth of a second too soon you would catch the flywheel when it still had speed enough to go up past center, and the boat would leap ahead, charging bull-fashion at the dock.

11   We had a good week at the camp. The bass were biting well and the sun shone endlessly, day after day. We would be tired at night and lie down in the accumulated heat of the little bedrooms after the long hot day and the breeze would stir almost imperceptibly outside and the smell of the swamp drift in through the rusty screens. Sleep would come easily and in the morning the red squirrel would be on the roof, tapping out his gay routine. I kept remembering everything, lying in bed in the mornings—the small steamboat that had a long rounded stern like the lip of a Ubangi, and how quietly she ran on the moonlight sails, when the older boys played their mandolins and the girls sang and we ate doughnuts dipped in sugar, and how sweet the music was on the water in the shining night, and what it had felt like to think about girls then. After breakfast we would go up to the store and the things were in the same place— minnows in a bottle, the plugs and spinners disarranged and pawed over by the youngsters from the boys' camp, the fig newtons and the Beeman's gum. Outside, the road was tarred and cars stood in front of the store. Inside, all was just as it had always been, except there was more Coca-Cola and not so much Moxie and root beer and birch beer and sarsaparilla. We would walk out with a bottle of pop apiece and sometimes the pop would backfire up our noses and hurt. We explored the streams, quietly, where the turtles slid off the sunny logs and dug their way into the soft bottom, and we lay on the town wharf and fed worms to the tame bass. Everywhere we went I had trouble making out which was I, the one walking at my side, the one walking in my pants.

12   One afternoon while we were there at that lake a thunderstorm came up. It was like the revival of an old melodrama that I had seen long ago with childish awe. The second-act climax of the drama of the electrical disturbance over a lake in America had not changed in any important respect. This was the big scene, still the big scene. The whole thing was so familiar, the first feeling of oppression

and heat and a general air around camp of not wanting to go very far away. In midafternoon (it was all the same) a curious darkening of the sky, and a lull in everything that had made life tick; and then the way the boats suddenly swung the other way at their moorings with the coming of a breeze out of the new quarter, and the premonitory rumble. Then the kettle drum, then the snare, then the bass drum and cymbals, then crackling light against the dark, and the gods grinning and licking their chops in the hills. Afterward the calm, the rain steadily rustling in the calm lake, the return of light and hope and spirits, and the campers running out in joy and relief to go swimming in the rain, their bright cries perpetuating the deathless joke about how they were getting simply drenched, and the children screaming with delight at the new sensation of bathing in the rain, and the joke about getting drenched linking the generations in a strong indestructible chain. And the comedian who waded in carrying an umbrella.

When the others went swimming my son said he was going in too. He 13 pulled his dripping trunks from the line where they had hung all through the shower, and wrung them out. Languidly, and with no thought of going in, I watched him, his hard little body, skinny and bare, saw him wince slightly as he pulled up around his vitals the small, soggy, icy garment. As he buckled the swollen belt suddenly my groin felt the chill of death.

COMPREHENSION

1. At what point in the essay do you begin to sense White's main purpose? What is his purpose? What type of reader might his purpose appeal to?
2. What motivates White to return to the lake in Maine? Explain the "simple transposition" that he mentions in paragraph 4. List the illustrations that he gives of this phenomenon. What change does he detect in the lake?
3. Explain the significance of White's last sentence. Where are there foreshadowings of this statement?

RHETORIC

1. Describe White's use of figurative language in paragraphs 2, 10, and 12.
2. Identify those words and phrases that White invokes to establish the sense of mystery about the lake. Why are these words and their connotations important to the nature of the illusion that he describes?
3. Explain the organization of the essay in terms of the following paragraph units: 1–4, 5–7, 8–10, and 11–13. Explain the function of paragraphs 8 and 12.
4. There are many vivid and unusual descriptive details in this essay—for example, the dragonfly in paragraph 5 and the two-track road in paragraph 7. How does White create symbolic overtones for these descriptive details and others? Why is the lake itself a complex symbol? Explain with reference to paragraph 6.
5. Describe the persona that White creates for himself in the essay. How does this persona function?
6. What is the relation between the introductory and concluding paragraphs, specifically in terms of irony of statement?

WRITING

1. Explore in an essay the theme of nostalgia in "Once More to the Lake." What are the beauties and the dangers of nostalgia? Can the past ever be recaptured or relived? Justify your answer.
2. Referring to revisiting a site on the lake that he had visited years before with his father, White remarks in paragraph 4, "I could tell that it was going to be pretty much the same as it had been before." How does this observation reflect the general sentiment White has about the role and function of the family? Respond to the question in an analytical essay.
3. **Writing an Argument:** Argue for or against the proposition that nostalgia can obscure the true nature of family relationships and even suppress painful memories that should be confronted.

NETWORKING
Applying 21st-Century Literacies

Alluding to Print on the Web: Do a Google Images search for *once more to the lake.* Explore how various people around the world used this caption or description with their own photographs, blog entries, or professional articles. Choose three or four examples and discuss how they use this allusion to the E. B. White essay. Do they mention the piece itself, or only its title? What power of nostalgia might this essay possess in and of itself, for readers who have known it for years? What books, poems, stories, or songs make you nostalgic—for family, friends, a particular time in your life? How does thinking about these specific examples influence your response to question 3 under Writing?

Stone Soup

Barbara Kingsolver

Barbara Kingsolver (b. 1955) was born in Annapolis, Maryland; grew up in rural Kentucky, and was educated at DePauw University and the University of Arizona. Her fiction includes The Bean Trees *(1988);* Homeland *(1990);* Animal Dreams *(1991), for which she won a PEN fiction prize and an Edward Abbey Ecofiction Award;* Pigs in Heaven *(1993), which won a Los Angeles Times Book Award for Fiction; and* The Poisonwood Bible *(1998). Kingsolver's nonfiction includes* High Tide in Tusson: Essays from Now or Never *(1995),* Last Stand: America's Virgin Lands *(2002), and* Animal, Vegetable, Miracle: A Year of Food Life *(2007). She has also worked as a biologist, is active in the field of human rights, and plays keyboard with an amateur rock 'n' roll band. The following essay, first published in the January 1995 issue of* Parenting, *eschews the idea of the nuclear family as the standard by which the healthy family should be judged.*

In the catalog of family values, where do we rank an occasion like this? A curly-haired boy who wanted to run before he walked, age seven now, a soccer player scoring a winning goal. He turns to the bleachers with his fists in the air and a smile wide as a gap-toothed galaxy. His own cheering section of grown-ups and kids all leap to their feet and hug each other, delirious with love for this boy. He's Andy, my best friend's son. The cheering section includes his mother and her friends, his brother, his father and stepmother, a stepbrother and stepsister, and a grandparent. Lucky is the child with this many relatives on hand to hail a proud accomplishment. I'm there too, witnessing a family fortune. But in spite of myself, defensive words take shape in my head. I am thinking: I dare *anybody* to call this a broken home. 1

Families change, and remain the same. Why are our names for home so slow to catch up to the truth of where we live? 2

When I was a child, I had two parents who loved me without cease. One of them attended every excuse for attention I ever contrived, and the other made it to the ones with higher production values, like piano recitals and appendicitis. So I was a lucky child too. I played with a set of paper dolls called "The Family of Dolls," four in number, who came with the factory-assigned names of Dad, Mom, Sis, and Junior. I think you know what they looked like, at least before I loved them to death and their heads fell off. 3

Now I've replaced the dolls with a life. I knit my days around my daughter's survival and happiness, and am proud to say her head is still on. But we aren't the Family of Dolls. Maybe you're not, either. And if not, even though you are statistically no oddity, it's probably been suggested to you in a hundred ways that yours isn't exactly a real family, but an impostor family, a harbinger of cultural ruin, a slapdash substitute—something like counterfeit money. Here at the tail end of our century, most of us are up to our ears in the noisy business of trying to support and love a thing called family. But there's a current in the air with ferocious moral force that finds its way even into political campaigns, claiming there is only one right way to do it, the Way It Has Always Been. 4

In the face of a thriving, particolored world, this narrow view is so pickled and absurd I'm astonished that it gets airplay. And I'm astonished that it still stings. 5

Every parent has endured the arrogance of a child-unfriendly grump sitting in judgment, explaining what those kids of ours really need (for example, "a good licking"). If we're polite, we move our crew to another bench in the park. If we're forthright (as I am in my mind, only, for the rest of the day), we fix them with a sweet imperious stare and say, "Come back and let's talk about it after you've changed a thousand diapers." 6

But it's harder somehow to shrug off the Family-of-Dolls Family Values crew when they judge (from their safe distance) that divorced people, blended families, gay families, and single parents are failures. That our children are at 7 risk, and the whole arrangement is messy and embarrassing. A marriage that ends is not called "finished," it's called *failed*. The children of this family may have been born to a happy union, but now they are called *the children of divorce*.

8   I had no idea how thoroughly these assumptions overlaid my culture until I went through divorce myself. I wrote to a friend: "This might be worse than being widowed. Overnight I've suffered the same losses—companionship, financial and practical support, my identity as a wife and partner, the future I'd taken for granted. I am lonely, grieving, and hard-pressed to take care of my household alone. But instead of bringing casseroles, people are acting like I had a fit and broke up the family china."

9   Once upon a time I held these beliefs about divorce: that everyone who does it could have chosen not to do it. That it's a lazy way out of marital problems. That it selfishly puts personal happiness ahead of family integrity. Now I tremble for my ignorance. It's easy, in fortunate times, to forget about the ambush that could leave your head reeling: serious mental or physical illness, death in the family, abandonment, financial calamity, humiliation, violence, despair.

10   I started out like any child, intent on being the Family of Dolls. I set upon young womanhood believing in most of the doctrines of my generation: I wore my skirts four inches above the knee. I had that Barbie with her zebra-striped swimsuit and a figure unlike anything found in nature. And I understood the Prince Charming Theory of Marriage, a quest for Mr. Right that ends smack dab where you find him. I did not completely understand that another whole story *begins* there, and no fairy tale prepared me for the combination of bad luck and persistent hope that would interrupt my dream and lead me to other arrangements. Like a cancer diagnosis, a dying marriage is a thing to fight, to deny, and finally, when there's no choice left, to dig in and survive. Casseroles would help. Likewise, I imagine it must be a painful reckoning in adolescence (or later on) to realize one's own true love will never look like the soft-focus fragrance ads because Prince Charming (surprise!) is a princess. Or vice versa. Or has skin the color your parents didn't want you messing with, except in the Crayola box.

11   It's awfully easy to hold in contempt the straw broken home, and that mythical category of persons who toss away nuclear family for the sheer fun of it. Even the legal terms we use have a suggestion of caprice. I resent the phrase "irreconcilable differences," which suggests a stubborn refusal to accept a spouse's little quirks. This is specious. Every happily married couple I know has loads of irreconcilable differences. Negotiating where to set the thermostat is not the point. A nonfunctioning marriage is a slow asphyxiation. It is waking up despised each morning, listening to the pulse of your own loneliness before the radio begins to blare its raucous gospel that you're nothing if you aren't loved. It is sharing your airless house with the threat of suicide or other kinds of violence, while the ghost that whispers, "Leave here and destroy your children," has passed over every door and nailed it shut. Disassembling a marriage in these circumstances is as much *fun* as amputating your own gangrenous leg. You do it, if you can, to save a life—or two, or more.

I know of no one who really went looking to hoe the harder row, especially 12
the daunting one of single parenthood. Yet it seems to be the most American of
customs to blame the burdened for their destiny. We'd like so desperately to
believe in freedom and justice for all, we can hardly name that rogue bad luck,
even when he's a close enough snake to bite us. In the wake of my divorce,
some friends (even a few close ones) chose to vanish, rather than linger within
striking distance of misfortune.

But most stuck around, bless their hearts, and if I'm any the wiser for my 13
trials, it's from having learned the worth of steadfast friendship. And also, what
not to say. The least helpful question is: "Did you want the divorce, or didn't
you?" Did I want to keep that gangrenous leg, or not? How to explain, in a culture that venerates choice: two terrifying options are much worse than none at
all. Give me any day the quick hand of cruel fate that will leave me scarred but
blameless. As it was, I kept thinking of that wicked third-grade joke in which
some boy comes up behind you and grabs your ear, starts in with a prolonged
tug, and asks, "Do you want this ear any longer?"

Still, the friend who holds your hand and says the wrong thing is made of 14
dearer stuff than the one who stays away. And generally, through all of it, you
live. My favorite fictional character, Kate Vaiden (in the novel by Reynolds
Price), advises: "Strength just comes in one brand—you stand up at sunrise and
meet what they send you and keep your hair combed."

Once you've weathered the straits, you get to cross the tricky juncture from 15
casualty to survivor. If you're on your feet at the end of a year or two, and have
begun putting together a happy new existence, those friends who were kind
enough to feel sorry for you when you needed it must now accept you back to
the ranks of the living. If you're truly blessed, they will dance at your second
wedding. Everybody else, for heavens sake, should stop throwing stones.

Arguing about whether nontraditional families deserve pity or tolerance is a 16
little like the medieval debate about left-handedness as a mark of the devil. Divorce, remarriage, single parenthood, gay parents, and blended families simply
are. They're facts of our time. Some of the reasons listed by sociologists for these
family reconstructions are: the idea of marriage as a romantic partnership rather
than a pragmatic one; a shift in women's expectations, from servility to self-
respect and independence; and longevity (prior to antibiotics no marriage was
expected to last many decades—in Colonial days the average couple lived to be
married less than twelve years). Add to all this, our growing sense of entitlement to happiness and safety from abuse. Most would agree these are all good
things. Yet their result—a culture in which serial monogamy and the conse-
quent reshaping of families are the norm—gets diagnosed as "failing."

For many of us, once we have put ourselves Humpty-Dumpty–wise back 17
together again, the main problem with our reorganized family is that other people think we have a problem. My daughter tells me the only time she's uncomfortable about being the child of divorced parents is when her friends say they
feel sorry for her. It's a bizarre sympathy, given that half the kids in her school
and nation are in the same boat, pursuing childish happiness with the same

energy as their married-parent peers. When anyone asks how she feels about it, she spontaneously lists the benefits: our house is in the country and we have a dog, but she can go to her dad's neighborhood for the urban thrills of a pool and sidewalks for roller-skating. What's more, she has three sets of grandparents!

18   Why is it surprising that a child would revel in a widened family and the right to feel at home in more than one house? Isn't it the opposite that should worry us—a child with no home at all, or too few resources to feel safe? The child at risk is the one whose parents are too immature themselves to guide wisely; too diminished by poverty to nurture; too far from opportunity to offer hope. The number of children in the U.S. living in poverty at this moment is almost unfathomably large: twenty percent. There are families among us that need help all right, and by no means are they new on the landscape. The rate at which teenage girls had babies in 1957 (ninety-six per thousand) was twice what it is now. That remarkable statistic is ignored by the religious right—probably because the teen birth rate was cut in half mainly by legalized abortion. In fact, the policy gatekeepers who coined the phrase "family values" have steadfastly ignored the desperation of too-small families, and since 1979 have steadily reduced the amount of financial support available to a single parent. But, this camp's most outspoken attacks seem aimed at the notion of families getting too complex, with add-ons and extras such as a gay parent's partner, or a remarried mother's new husband and his children.

19   To judge a family's value by its tidy symmetry is to purchase a book for its cover. There's no moral authority there. The famous family comprised by Dad, Mom, Sis, and Junior living as an isolated economic unit is not built on historical bedrock. In *The Way We Never Were*, Stephanie Coontz writes, "Whenever people propose that we go back to the traditional family, I always suggest that they pick a ballpark date for the family they have in mind." Colonial families were tidily disciplined, but their members (meaning everyone but infants) labored incessantly and died young. Then the Victorian family adopted a new division of labor, in which women's role was domestic and children were allowed time for study and play, but this was an upper-class construct supported by myriad slaves. Coontz writes, "For every nineteenth-century middle-class family that protected its wife and child within the family circle, there was an Irish or German girl scrubbing floors . . . a Welsh boy mining coal to keep the home-baked goodies warm, a black girl doing the family laundry, a black mother and child picking cotton to be made into clothes for the family, and a Jewish or an Italian daughter in a sweatshop making 'ladies' dresses or artificial flowers for the family to purchase."

20   The abolition of slavery brought slightly more democratic arrangements, in which extended families were harnessed together in cottage industries; at the turn of the century came a steep rise in child labor in mines and sweat-shops. Twenty percent of American children lived in orphanages at the time; their parents were not necessarily dead, but couldn't afford to keep them.

21   During the Depression and up to the end of World War II, many millions of U.S. households were more multigenerational than nuclear. Women my

grandmother's age were likely to live with a fluid assortment of elderly relatives, in-laws, siblings, and children. In many cases they spent virtually every waking hour working in the company of other women—a companionable scenario in which it would be easier, I imagine, to tolerate an estranged or difficult spouse. I'm reluctant to idealize a life of so much hard work and so little spousal intimacy, but its advantage may have been resilience. A family so large and varied would not easily be brought down by a single blow: It could absorb a death, long-illness, an abandonment here or there, and any number of irreconcilable differences.

The Family of Dolls came along midcentury as a great American experiment. A booming economy required a mobile labor force and demanded that women surrender jobs to returning soldiers. Families came to be defined by a single breadwinner. They struck out for single-family homes at an earlier age than ever before, and in unprecedented numbers they raised children in suburban isolation. The nuclear family was launched to sink or swim. 22

More than a few sank. Social historians corroborate that the suburban family of the postwar economic boom, which we have recently selected as our definition of "traditional," was no panacea. Twenty-five percent of Americans were poor in the mid-1950s, and as yet there were no food stamps. Sixty percent of the elderly lived on less than $1,000 a year, and most had no medical insurance. In the sequestered suburbs, alcoholism and sexual abuse of children were far more widespread than anyone imagined. 23

Expectations soared, and the economy sagged. It's hard to depend on one other adult for everything, come what may. In the last three decades, that amorphous, adaptable structure we call "family" has been reshaped once more by economic tides. Compared with fifties families, mothers are far more likely now to be employed. We are statistically more likely to divorce, and to live in blended families or other extranuclear arrangements. We are also more likely to plan and space our children, and to rate our marriages as "happy." We are less likely to suffer abuse without recourse, or to stare out at our lives through a glaze of prescription tranquilizers. Our aged parents are less likely to be destitute, and we're half as likely to have a teenage daughter turn up a mother herself. All in all, I would say that if "intact" in modern family-values jargon means living quietly desperate in the bell jar, then hip-hip-hooray for "broken." A neat family model constructed to service the Baby Boom economy seems to be returning gradually to a grand, lumpy shape that human families apparently have tended toward since they first took root in the Olduvai Gorge. We're social animals, deeply fond of companionship, and children love best to run in packs. If there is a *normal* for humans, at all, I expect it looks like two or three Families of Dolls, connected variously by kinship and passion, shuffled like cards and strewn over several shoeboxes. 24

The sooner we can let go the fairy tale of families functioning perfectly in isolation, the better we might embrace the relief of community. Even the admirable parents who've stayed married through thick and thin are very likely, at present, to incorporate other adults into their families—household help and 25 baby-sitters if they can afford them or neighbors and grandparents if they can't. For single parents, this support is the rock-bottom definition of family. And most parents who have split apart, however painfully, still manage to maintain family continuity for their children, creating in many cases a boisterous phenomenon that Constance Ahrons in her book *The Good Divorce* calls the "binuclear family." Call it what you will—when ex-spouses beat swords into plowshares and jump up and down at a soccer game together, it makes for happy kids.

26   Cinderella, look, who needs her? All those evil stepsisters? That story always seemed like too much cotton-picking fuss over clothes. A childhood tale that fascinated me more was the one called "Stone Soup," and the gist of it is this: Once upon a time, a pair of beleaguered soldiers straggled home to a village empty-handed, in a land ruined by war. They were famished, but the villagers had so little they shouted evil words and slammed their doors. So the soldiers dragged out a big kettle, filled it with water, and put it on a fire to boil. They rolled a clean round stone into the pot, while the villagers peered through their curtains in amazement.

27   "What kind of soup is that?" they hooted.

28   "Stone soup," the soldiers replied. "Everybody can have some when it's done."

29   "Well, thanks," one matron grumbled, coming out with a shriveled carrot. "But it'd be better if you threw this in."

30   And so on, of course, a vegetable at a time, until the whole suspicious village managed to feed itself grandly.

31   Any family is a big empty pot, save for what gets thrown in. Each stew turns out different. Generosity, a resolve to turn bad luck into good, and respect for variety—these things will nourish a nation of children. Name-calling and suspicion will not. My soup contains a rock or two of hard times, and maybe yours does too. I expect it's a heck of a bouillabaisse.

COMPREHENSION

1. What is the essay's thesis?
2. According to Kingsolver, why is our society so apt to condemn divorce?
3. What is the author's view of family symmetry (paragraph 19)?

RHETORIC

1. What rhetorical function does the opening anecdote serve in introducing the essay's subject matter?
2. What is Kingsolver's purpose in capitalizing, italicizing, and placing quotation marks around certain phrases—for example, the Way It Has Always Been (paragraph 4), *failed* and *the children of divorce* (paragraph 7), and "family values" (paragraph 18)?
3. What is the author's purpose in creating a gap between paragraphs 15 and 16? What is the focus of her argument after this break?

4. Compare the introductory paragraph with the concluding one. How do they differ? How are they similar? How do they help set the boundaries of the essay?
5. This essay contains personal observations, personal experiences, historical data, and anecdotes. How would you describe the author's overall method to a person who has not read the essay?
6. Unlike the titles of most essays, the title "Stone Soup" gives no hint at the essay's content. What is the rhetorical purpose in keeping the meaning of the title a mystery until the very end?
7. In paragraph 2, Kingsolver asks the question, "Why are our names for home so slow to catch up to the truth of where we live?" Does the author suggest an answer to this question either implicitly or explicitly during the course of the essay? If so, where?

WRITING

1. Interview two individuals at least 25 years apart in age. Compare and contrast their views on divorce.
2. Describe the dynamics of a blended family with which you are familiar. It may be your own or a friend's.
3. **Writing an Argument:** Write an essay arguing that some negative outcomes could occur in the type of family the author celebrates.

NETWORKING
Applying 21st-Century Literacies

Using Keyword Searches to Find Articles: Do a keyword search in your library's online databases for popular or scholarly articles about *Family Values*. Write an extended analysis about the results of this initial search. Which databases did you search? What kinds of sources did they (and these keywords) lead you to? If the term *Family Values* is defined in any of the abstracts you encountered, compile a few of these definitions and compare them.

Synthesis: Classic and Contemporary Questions for Comparison

1. Compare and contrast the tone of each writer. How does tone affect purpose? How does it affect mood? Select at least three passages from White and three from Kingsolver that demonstrate how their tones differ. Do they offer any hints as to the "voice" or personality of the writers? Why or why not?
2. What contemporary issues does Kingsolver address that White either ignores or is unaware of? Consider that White was born 58 years before Kingsolver, so his world was quite a different one. Are there other variables that might help us distinguish their concerns and outlooks—for example, gender, class, and environment?
3. What central values does each author have regarding the family? How are they similar? How do they differ? How do their values reflect their times?

An American Childhood

Annie Dillard

Annie Dillard (b. 1945 in Pittsburgh) received her BA and MA degrees from Hollins College. Her first book, Pilgrim at Tinker Creek *(1975), won the Pulitzer Prize for general nonfiction. Her other published works of nonfiction include* Teaching a Stone to Talk *(1982) and* An American Childhood *(1987). Dillard expanded her range of writing with the publication of her first novel,* The Living *(1992), and her latest novel,* The Maytrees *(2007). She has received awards from the National Endowment for the Arts and the Guggenheim Foundation as well as many other sources. As an essayist, poet, memoirist, and literary critic, she focuses her themes on the relationships among the self, nature, religion, and faith. Her writing is recognizable by its observations of the minutiae of life and its search for meaning in unlikely places, such as a stone or an insect. In this passage from* An American Childhood, *the author gives us a portrait of her mother by focusing on her small idiosyncrasies of speech, gesture, and attitude.*

1   One Sunday afternoon Mother wandered through our kitchen, where Father was making a sandwich and listening to the ball game. The Pirates were playing the New York Giants at Forbes Field. In those days, the Giants had a utility infielder named Wayne Terwilliger. Just as Mother passed through, the radio announcer cried—with undue drama—"Terwilliger bunts one!"

2   "Terwilliger bunts one?" Mother cried back, stopped short. She turned. "Is that English?"

3   "The player's name is Terwilliger," Father said. "He bunted."

4   "That's marvelous," Mother said. "'Terwilliger bunts one.' No wonder you listen to baseball. 'Terwilliger bunts one.'"

5   For the next seven or eight years, Mother made this surprising string of syllables her own. Testing a microphone, she repeated, "Terwilliger bunts one"; testing a pen or a typewriter, she wrote it. If, as happened surprisingly often in the course of various improvised gags, she pretended to whisper something else in my ear, she actually whispered, "Terwilliger bunts one." Whenever someone used a French phrase, or a Latin one, she answered solemnly, "Terwilliger bunts one." If Mother had had, like Andrew Carnegie, the opportunity to cook up a motto for a coat of arms, hers would have read simply and tellingly, "Terwilliger bunts one." (Carnegie's was "Death to Privilege.")

6   She served us with other words and phrases. On a Florida trip, she repeated tremulously, "That . . . is a royal poinciana." I don't remember the tree; I remember the thrill in her voice. She pronounced it carefully, and spelled it. She also liked to say "portulaca."

7   The drama of the words "Tamiami Trail" stirred her, we learned on the same Florida trip. People built Tampa on one coast, and they built Miami on

another. Then—the height of visionary ambition and folly—they piled a slow, tremendous road through the terrible Everglades to connect them. To build the road, men stood sunk in muck to their armpits. They fought off cottonmouth moccasins and six-foot alligators. They slept in boats, wet. They blasted muck with dynamite, cut jungle with machetes; they laid logs, dragged drilling machines, hauled dredges, heaped limestone. The road took fourteen years to build up by the shovelful, a Panama Canal in reverse, and cost hundreds of lives from tropical, mosquito-carried diseases. Then, capping it all, some genius thought of the word Tamiami: they called the road from Tampa to Miami, this very road under our spinning wheels, the Tamiami Trail. Some called it Alligator Alley. Anyone could drive over this road without a thought.

Hearing this, moved, I thought all the suffering of road building was worth 8 it (it wasn't my suffering), now that we had this new thing to hang these new words on—Alligator Alley for those who liked things cute, and, for connoisseurs like Mother, for lovers of the human drama in all its boldness and terror, the Tamiami Trail.

Back home, Mother cut clips from reels of talk, as it were, and played them 9 back at leisure. She noticed that many Pittsburghers confuse "leave" and "let." One kind relative brightened our morning by mentioning why she'd brought her son to visit: "He wanted to come with me, so I left him." Mother filled in Amy and me on locutions we missed. "I can't do it on Friday," her pretty sister told a crowded dinner party, "because Friday's the day I lay in the stores."

(All unconsciously, though, we ourselves used some pure Pittsburghisms. 10 We said "tele pole," pronounced "telly pole," for that splintery sidewalk post I loved to climb. We said "slippy"—the sidewalks are "slippy." We said, "That's all the farther I could go." And we said, as Pittsburghers do say, "This glass needs washed," or "The dog needs walked"—a usage our father eschewed; he knew it was not standard English, nor even comprehensible English, but he never let on.)

"Spell 'poinsettia,'" Mother would throw out at me, smiling with pleasure. 11 "Spell 'sherbet.'" The idea was not to make us whizzes, but, quite the contrary, to remind us—and I, especially, needed reminding—that we didn't know it all just yet.

"There's a deer standing in the front hall," she told me one quiet evening in 12 the country.

"Really?"   13

"No. I just wanted to tell you something once without your saying, 'I know.'" 14

Supermarkets in the middle 1950s began luring, or bothering, customers by 15 giving out Top Value Stamps or Green Stamps. When, shopping with Mother, we got to the head of the checkout line, the checker, always a young man, asked, "Save stamps?"

"No," Mother replied genially, week after week, "I build model airplanes." I 16 believe she originated this line. It took me years to determine where the joke lay.

Anyone who met her verbal challenges she adored. She had surgery on one 17 of her eyes. On the operating table, just before she conked out, she appealed feelingly to the surgeon, saying, as she had been planning to say for weeks, "Will I be able to play the piano?" "Not on me," the surgeon said. "You won't pull that old one on me."

18   It was, indeed, an old one. The surgeon was supposed to answer, "Yes, my dear, brave woman, you will be able to play the piano after this operation," to which Mother intended to reply, "Oh, good, I've always wanted to play the piano." This pat scenario bored her; she loved having it interrupted. It must have galled her that usually her acquaintances were so predictably unalert; it must have galled her that, for the length of her life, she could surprise everyone so continually, so easily, when she had been the same all along. At any rate, she loved anyone who, as she put it, saw it coming, and called her on it.

19   She regarded the instructions on bureaucratic forms as straight lines. "Do you advocate the overthrow of the United States government by force or violence?" After some thought she wrote, "Force." She regarded children, even babies, as straight men. When Molly learned to crawl, Mother delighted in buying her gowns with drawstrings at the bottom, like Swee'pea's, because, as she explained energetically, you could easily step on the drawstring without the baby's noticing, so that she crawled and crawled and crawled and never got anywhere except into a small ball at the gown's top.

20 When we children were young, she mothered us tenderly and dependably; as we got older, she resumed her career of anarchism. She collared us into her gags. If she answered the phone on a wrong number, she told the caller, "Just a minute," and dragged the receiver to Amy or me, saying, "Here, take this, your name is Cecile," or, worse, just, "It's for you." You had to think on your feet. But did you want to perform well as Cecile, or did you want to take pity on the wretched caller?

21   During a family trip to the Highland Park Zoo, Mother and I were alone for a minute. She approached a young couple holding hands on a bench by the seals, and addressed the young man in dripping tones: "Where have you been? Still got those baby-blue eyes; always did slay me. And this"—a swift nod at the dumbstruck young woman, who had removed her hand from the man's— "must be the one you were telling me about. She's not so bad, really, as you used to make out. But listen, you know how I miss you, you know where to reach me, same old place. And there's Ann over there—see how she's grown? See the blue eyes?"

22   And off she sashayed, taking me firmly by the hand, and leading us around briskly past the monkey house and away. She cocked an ear back, and both of us heard the desperate man begin, in a high-pitched wail, "I swear, I never saw her before in my life . . ."

23 On a long, sloping beach by the ocean, she lay stretched out sunning with Father and friends, until the conversation gradually grew tedious, when without forethought she gave a little push with her heel and rolled away. People were stunned. She rolled deadpan and apparently effortlessly, arms and legs

extended and tidy, down the beach to the distant water's edge, where she lay at ease just as she had been, but half in the surf, and well out of earshot.

She dearly loved to fluster people by throwing out a game's rules at a 24 whim—when she was getting bored, losing in a dull sort of way, and when everybody else was taking it too seriously. If you turned your back, she moved the checkers around on the board. When you got them all straightened out, she denied she'd touched them; the next time you turned your back, she lined them up on the rug or hid them under your chair. In a betting rummy game called Michigan, she routinely played out of turn, or called out a card she didn't hold, or counted backward, simply to amuse herself by causing an uproar and watching the rest of us do double-takes and have fits. (Much later, when serious suitors came to call, Mother subjected them to this fast card game as a trial by ordeal; she used it as an intelligence test and a measure of spirit. If the poor man could stay a round without breaking down or running out, he got to marry one of us, if he still wanted to.)

She excelled at bridge, playing fast and boldly, but when the stakes were 25 low and the hands dull, she bid slams for the devilment of it, or raised her opponents' suit to bug them, or showed her hand, or tossed her cards in a handful behind her back in a characteristic swift motion accompanied by a vibrantly innocent look. It drove our stolid father crazy. The hand was over before it began, and the guests were appalled. How do you score it, who deals now, what do you do with a crazy person who is having so much fun? Or they were down seven, and the guests were appalled. "Pam!" "Dammit, Pam!" He groaned. What ails such people? What on earth possesses them? He rubbed his face.

She was an unstoppable force; she never let go. When we moved across 26 town, she persuaded the U.S. Post Office to let her keep her old address— forever—because she'd had stationery printed. I don't know how she did it. Every new post office worker, over decades, needed to learn that although the Doaks' mail is addressed to here, it is delivered to there.

Mother's energy and intelligence suited her for a greater role in a larger 27 arena—mayor of New York, say—than the one she had. She followed American politics closely; she had been known to vote for Democrats. She saw how things should be run, but she had nothing to run but our household. Even there, small minds bugged her; she was smarter than the people who designed the things she had to use all day for the length of her life.

"Look," she said. "Whoever designed this corkscrew never used one. Why 28 would anyone sell it without trying it out?" So she invented a better one. She showed me a drawing of it. The spirit of American enterprise never faded in Mother. If capitalizing and tooling up had been as interesting as theorizing and thinking up, she would have fired up a new factory every week, and chaired several hundred corporations.

"It grieves me," she would say, "it grieves my heart," that the company that 29 made one superior product packaged it poorly, or took the wrong tack in its advertising. She knew, as she held the thing mournfully in her two hands, that she'd never find another. She was right. We children wholly sympathized, and so did Father; what could she do, what could anyone do, about it? She was Samson in chains. She paced.

30   She didn't like the taste of stamps so she didn't lick stamps; she licked the corner of the envelope instead. She glued sandpaper to the sides of kitchen drawers, and under kitchen cabinets, so she always had a handy place to strike a match. She designed, and hounded workmen to build against all norms, doubly wide kitchen counters and elevated bathroom sinks. To splint a finger, she stuck it in a lightweight cigar tube. Conversely, to protect a pack of cigarettes, she carried it in a Band-Aid box. She drew plans for an over-the-finger toothbrush for babies, an oven rack that slid up and down, and—the family favorite—Lendalarm. Lendalarm was a beeper you attached to books (or tools) you loaned friends. After ten days, the beeper sounded. Only the rightful owner could silence it.

31   She repeatedly reminded us of P. T. Barnum's dictum: You could sell anything to anybody if you marketed it right. The adman who thought of making Americans believe they needed underarm deodorant was a visionary. So, too, was the hero who made a success of a new product, Ivory soap. The executives were horrified, Mother told me, that a cake of this stuff floated. Soap wasn't supposed to float. Anyone would be able to tell it was mostly whipped-up air. Then some inspired adman made a leap: Advertise that it floats. Flaunt it. The rest is history.

32   She respected the rare few who broke through to new ways. "Look," she'd say, "here's an intelligent apron." She called upon us to admire intelligent control knobs and intelligent pan handles, intelligent andirons and picture frames and knife sharpeners. She questioned everything, every pair of scissors, every knitting needle, gardening glove, tape dispenser. Hers was a restless mental vigor that just about ignited the dumb household objects with its force.

33   Torpid conformity was a kind of sin; it was stupidity itself, the mighty stream against which Mother would never cease to struggle. If you held no minority opinions, or if you failed to risk total ostracism for them daily, the world would be a better place without you.

34   Always I heard Mother's emotional voice asking Amy and me the same few questions: "Is that your own idea? Or somebody else's?" "*Giant* is a good movie," I pronounced to the family at dinner. "Oh, really?" Mother warmed to these occasions. She all but rolled up her sleeves. She knew I hadn't seen it. "Is that your considered opinion?"

35   She herself held many unpopular, even fantastic, positions. She was scathingly sarcastic about the McCarthy hearings while they took place, right on our living-room television; she frantically opposed Father's wait-and-see calm. "We don't know enough about it," he said. "I do," she said. "I know all I need to know."

36   She asserted, against all opposition, that people who lived in trailer parks were not bad but simply poor, and had as much right to settle on beautiful land, such as rural Ligonier, Pennsylvania, as did the oldest of families in the

finest of hidden houses. Therefore, the people who owned trailer parks, and sought zoning changes to permit trailer parks, needed our help. Her profound belief that the country-club pool sweeper was a person, and that the department-store saleslady, the bus driver, telephone operator, and house-painter were people, and even in groups the steelworkers who carried pickets and the Christmas shoppers who clogged intersections were people—this was a conviction common enough in democratic Pittsburgh, but not altogether common among our friends' parents, or even, perhaps, among our parents' friends.

Opposition emboldened Mother, and she would take on anybody on any issue—the chairman of the board, at a cocktail party, on the current strike; she would fly at him in a flurry of passion, as a songbird selflessly attacks a big hawk. 37

"Eisenhower's going to win," I announced after school. She lowered her magazine and looked me in the eyes: "How do you know?" I was doomed. It was fatal to say, "Everyone says so." We all knew well what happened. "Do you consult this Everyone before you make your decisions? What if Everyone decided to round up all the Jews?" Mother knew there was no danger of cowing me. She simply tried to keep us all awake. And in fact it was always clear to Amy and me, and to Molly when she grew old enough to listen, that if our classmates came to cruelty, just as much as if the neighborhood or the nation came to madness, we were expected to take, and would be each separately capable of taking, a stand. 38

COMPREHENSION

1. Dillard creates a picture of her mother's personality through a number of anecdotes and explanations. How would you sum up the mother's personality?
2. Dillard's mother appears to have a special appreciation for words and language. To what purpose does she apply this appreciation? What effect does it have on her family and acquaintances?
3. What values does the mother hold? What behaviors and attitudes does she abhor and discourage?

RHETORIC

1. In paragraph 7, Dillard explains that the highway from Tampa to Miami is referred to either as "Tamiami Trail" or "Alligator Alley." What is the connotation of each of these terms? Why does her mother prefer to call it "Tamiami Trail"?
2. The author herself seems to have inherited a special fascination for language. Study her use of dashes and semicolons in paragraphs 26 and 27. How do they help contribute to energetic writing?
3. What are the functions of the spaces between paragraphs 19 and 20, 22 and 23, and 32 and 33? How do these divisions contribute to the structure of the essay as a whole?
4. How does Dillard use her writing talents to create paragraph 8 out of one long sentence? What other examples can you provide of long sentences in the essay? How do they contribute to the overall style of the writing?

5. What is the overall emotional "tone" of the writer toward her subject—admiring, or loving, or cautionary? What adjectives does she use in describing her mother that provides the reader with clues to the tone?
6. Dillard quotes her mother directly on several occasions. Can we assume that she is quoting precisely, given that the essay was written years after the incidents described? Does it matter?
7. The final paragraph not only provides closure to the essay but transmits a lesson the mother wants her family to learn. How do the style and structure of this paragraph contribute to the ultimate message of the essay? In other words, how does the form help convey the meaning?

WRITING

1. Write a descriptive essay about someone you know very well, using at least five anecdotes from that person's life, so that by the end of the essay, we have a mental picture of your subject's personality, values, and attitudes. This could be someone in your biological family, or someone else you are or were very close to.
2. Describe an incident in your life when the unexpected taught you an important lesson.
3. **Writing an Argument:** Argue for or against the proposition that an effective parent should have—at least—a touch of unconventionality.

NETWORKING
Applying 21st-Century Literacies

Creating a Playlist Narrative: Enhance your response to question 1 under Writing by creating a playlist of five songs that contribute to your description of that person you are or were close to. For each song, write a short paragraph about what it says about either this person or your relationship with him or her. The specific song might have a story behind it—if so, tell it—or it might describe (literally or figuratively) some aspect or quality of that person's character, appearance, beliefs, experiences, interests, location, talents, regrets, or hopes. What is the music capable of describing about this person that words couldn't?

Love, Internet Style

David Brooks

David Brooks (b. 1961) is a columnist for the op-ed page of the New York Times. *Prior to joining the* Times, *he was a senior editor at the* Weekly Standard, *an op-ed page editor at the* Wall Street Journal, *and a contributing editor to* Newsweek. *He is also a weekly guest on the* PBS NewsHour. *A graduate of the University of Chicago,*

*Brooks writes on a wide range of topics, often from a conservative perspective; he has
edited* Backward and Upward: The New Conservative Writing. *Brooks's recent
books* Bobos in Paradise: The New Upper Class and How They Got There *(2000)
and* On Paradise Drive *(2004), which explores the lives of people living in the suburbs, offer fascinating and often amusing insights into contemporary American culture. In this essay, which appeared in the* New York Times *in 2003, Brooks examines
the ways in which the Internet facilitates personal relationships.*

The Internet slows things down.   1

If you're dating in the Age of the Hook-Up, sex is this looming possibility 2
from the first moment you meet a prospective partner. But couples who meet
through online dating services tend to exchange e-mail for weeks or months.
Then they'll progress to phone conversations for a few more weeks. Only then
will there be a face-to-face meeting, almost always at some public place early in
the evening, and the first date will often be tentative and Dutch.

Online dating puts structure back into courtship. For generations Americans 3
had certain courtship rituals. The boy would call the girl and ask her to the movies. He might come in and meet the father. After a few dates he might ask her to
go steady. Sex would progress gradually from kissing to petting and beyond.

But over the past few decades that structure dissolved. And human beings, 4
who are really good at adapting, found that the Internet, of all places, imposes
the restraints they need to let relationships develop gradually. So now 40 million Americans look at online dating sites each month, and we are seeing a
revolution in the way people meet and court one another.

The new restraints are not like the old restraints. The online dating scene is 5
like a real estate market where people go to fulfill their most sensitive needs. It
is at once ruthlessly transactional and strangely tender.

It begins with sorting. Online daters can scan through millions of possible 6
partners in an evening and select for age, education, height, politics, religion and
ethnic background. JDate is a popular site for Jews. EHarmony insists that members fill out a long, introspective questionnaire, and thus is one of the few sites
where most members are women. Vanity Date is for the South Beach crowd. "At
Vanity Date," the Web site declares, "we have a vision of creating the largest
database of the world's most good-looking, rich and superficial people."

Most of the sites have programs that link you up with people like yourself. 7
One of the side effects of online dating is that it is bound to accelerate social
stratification, as highly educated people become more efficient at finding and
marrying one another.

Each member at a dating site creates his or her own Web page. The most 8
important feature on the page is the photo; studies show that looks are twice as
powerful as income in attracting mates.

9   But there are also autobiographical essays. If you judge by these essays, skinny-dipping with intellectuals is the most popular activity in America. All the writers try to show they are sensual yet smart.

10   The women on these sites are, or project themselves as being, incredibly self-confident. "I am a vivacious, intelligent, warm-hearted, attractive, cool chick, with a sharp, witty, and effervescent personality," writes one on Match .com. Another says: "I am a slender, radiantly beautiful woman on fire with passion and enthusiasm for life. I am articulate, intelligent and routinely given the accolade of being brilliant."

11   Still, men almost always make the first contact. Prospective partners begin a long series of e-mail interviews. Internet exchanges encourage both extreme honesty (the strangers-on-a-train phenomenon) and extreme dishonesty, as people lie about their ages, their jobs, whether they have kids and, most often, whether they are married. (About a fifth of online daters are married men.)

12   Whatever else has changed, men are more likely to be predators looking for sex, while women try to hold back. Men will ask women for more photos "from different angles." A woman, wanting to be reassured that this guy is not some rapist, will shut off anyone who calls her "hottie" or who mentions sex first. Women generally control the pace of the relationship.

13   But despite all the crass competition, all the marketing, all the shopping around, people connect. Studies by Katelyn McKenna at N.Y.U. and others indicate that Internet relationships are at least as powerful as relationships that begin face to face. Many people are better at revealing their true selves through the keyboard than through conversation. And couples who slow down and prolong the e-mail phase have a better chance of seeing their relationships last than people who get together more quickly.

14   The online dating world is superficially cynical. The word "love" will almost never appear on a member's page, because it is so heavy and intimidating. But love is what this is all about. And the heart, even in this commercial age, finds a way.

COMPREHENSION

1. How does Brooks describe Internet "love"? What does he mean by his opening sentence, "The Internet slows things down"?
2. What features of Internet culture does the writer identify as facilitating human relationships?
3. According to Brooks, how do men and women differ in their approach to online relationships?

RHETORIC

1. What is Brooks's purpose in beginning his essay with a single-sentence paragraph? Is this sentence the thesis? Why or why not?
2. How would you describe the writer's stance? What is his attitude toward his subject? Offer examples to support your answer.

3. What are Brooks's main reasons in support of his thesis or claim? What forms of evidence does he offer to support his claim?
4. How does the writer develop an extended definition of Internet "love"?
5. Brooks frequently structures his essay by means of comparison and contrast. Why do you think he uses this strategy? Do you find the method effective? Why or why not?
6. Does the final paragraph provide a solid conclusion? Justify your answer.

WRITING

1. Write a definition essay on "Internet love." Be certain to provide examples and utilize other rhetorical strategies like comparison and contrast to develop this extended definition.
2. **Writing an Argument:** Write a persuasive essay arguing that online dating is either dangerous or harmless. Provide at least three minor propositions and sufficient evidence to support your position.

NETWORKING
Applying 21st-Century Literacies

Reflecting on Online Relationships: Narrate and describe your own experience with Internet-based relationships or online dating. Explain why the Internet has helped or hindered your relationships.

Once Upon a Quinceañera

Julia Alvarez

Julia Alvarez (b. 1950), a novelist, poet, and nonfiction writer, was born in New York City but raised until age 10 in the Dominican Republic. She was forced to flee with her family after her father, a physician, was implicated in a plot to overthrow the dictator Rafael Trujillo, an event alluded to in her semiautobiographical novel, How the Garcia Girls Lost Their Accents *(1991). (A second novel,* Yo!, *which continues the Garcia/Alvarez family saga, appeared in 1997.) Alvarez attended Middlebury College (BA, 1971) and Syracuse University (MFA, 1975), and she is currently on the English and American Literatures faculty at Middlebury. In addition to her fiction, Alvarez has published several volumes of poetry, books for children, a collection of essays, and numerous articles for major magazines. One of her latest books is* Saving the World *(2006), in which Alvarez examines the global attempt to eradicate smallpox. In this selection from* Once Upon a Quinceañera *(2007), Alvarez provides readers with insight into one of the most common and compelling rituals that frame the lives of young Latinas.*

1   I'm sitting in my room at the Pan American Hotel feeling pretty much like Cinderella before her fairy godmother shows up. I drove down from Vermont early this morning, a five-hour drive that had taken me six hours since I'm not used to finding my way through the urban labyrinths of parkways and expressways with exits popping up out of nowhere to this multicultural, multilingual, multimulti area of Queens where forty years ago my own immigrant adolescence was spent.

2   I've driven down here to attend Monica Ramos's quinceañera. The plan was that I would phone the Ramoses as soon as I arrived and they would come and get me so I could follow the quinceañera in the last few hours of her preparations. But I've been calling the family home number and Monica's father's cell number for the last half hour and nobody answers. Maybe it's the busy floral pattern of the hotel bedspread or the scented air freshener recently sprayed in the room, but I'm beginning to feel lightheaded with misgivings. Did I come this far just to spend a night in my overpriced room at the Pan American, only to have to turn around tomorrow morning and drive back to Vermont without even a glimpse of this Queens quinceañera?

3   Like many USA-born Latinas, Monica, whose parents were both born in the Dominican Republic, is actually celebrating her quinceañera on her sixteenth birthday. This is just one more adaptation of the old-country tradition which has now survived more than four decades on American soil. But with a persistence unique to this immigrant group that seems to retain at least some of its Spanish and its feeling that "home" is still south of the Rio Grande even into a second and third generation, Monica calls her sweet sixteen a "quinceañera sort of."

4   Monica's quinceañera had sounded great over the phone. It was going to be so special, she told me during several long-distance conversations. Open, friendly, easy to talk to, Monica was one of the most verbal and forthcoming quinceañeras I interviewed. She didn't want a party at first, but she was finally won over by two things: the chance to dress up in a beautiful princess gown and the opportunity to give a speech in front of her whole family and all her friends. Monica's party will include the lighting of seventeen candles, each one dedicated to a special person with a little speech about why this person is so special to her.

5   "There's always an added candle, dedicated to someone absent," Monica explains about the extra candle. "Mine's going to be dedicated to God for giving me such a special life."

6   Monica has told me that she is a devoted Catholic. I have to bite my tongue so as not to point out that a candle meant for someone absent is perhaps not the best category for a God who I'm sure Monica believes is everywhere. But it's hard enough to get these young ladies to confide in a virtual stranger without

peppering them with prickly questions. As one young lady told me when I pursued a line of questioning about how exactly she thought she was going to go from being a girl to being a woman by having a quinceañera, "This is becoming annoying."

Instead I asked Monica if her quinceañera was going to have a theme. 7 Themes are popular: The quinceañera is a butterfly, emerging from a flower. The quinceañera is a princess, sitting on a throne. The quinceañera is a cowgirl, with a court of boys sporting lassos. The quinceañera, like a magician's trick, rises up out of a trapdoor in a puff of smoke.

"Mine is all based on Disney characters," Monica announced excitedly. The 8 girlfriends in her court were going to be Sleeping Beauty, Snow White, Jasmine, Belle . . . "We're going to do like a little play where my prince is going to find my heels on the dance floor and bring them to my dad to put on my feet," Monica gushed on.

Before hanging up, I asked Monica what her quinceañera meant to her. Al- 9 though she had been quite garrulous about the party details, Monica seemed stumped by the question. Every quinceañera I've asked has given me the same pat answer. Claudia in Lawrence, Massachusetts, a short, stocky girl in sweat pants, pressured by her mami to have a quince party; Ashley in San Antonio, a popular, petite girl with a string of girlfriends who had celebrated or were in line to celebrate their quinces; Leticia in East L.A., who ran off with her chambelán seven months later—all of them echoed Monica as if reciting the mantra of quinceañeras: "I'm going from being a girl to being a woman." When I pressed Monica about what this meant, she answered vaguely: "It's like part of my culture."

"So, did your mother have a quinceañera back in the D.R.?" I wondered.   10

Monica wasn't sure. "Mami!" she called out from her end of the phone. 11 "Did you have a quinceañera?" The answer came back, "A quinceañera, no, mi'ja."

I found out about Monica's quinceañera only four days ago in that word-of- 12 mouth way so reminiscent of our home cultures. A Dominican student's Colombian friend has a mother who owns a flower shop in Queens that does a lot of quinceañeras, and she (the mother) was doing Monica's flowers and also providing some of the props, and she told the Ramoses about me. By the time I got word back that the Ramoses would be happy to have me attend Monica's party and, phone number in hand, I called them, they were into that forty-eight-hour countdown usually associated with weddings in which everyone is racing around, hyperventilating, arguing, bursting into tears, and the bride is threatening to call the whole thing off. In fact, Monica's party is taking place soon after the headline story about the runaway bride, Jennifer Wilbanks, who disappeared days before her wedding in Duluth, Georgia. As I sit in my hotel room, waiting to get through to the Ramoses, I wonder if no one is answering because Monica has run off. Perhaps she will be the first runaway quinceañera to get national media attention.

On the phone, a very generous Mr. Ramos ("José, por favor!") had offered 13 to pick me up at the airport should I come by plane. "I wouldn't think of it with as much as you have to do," I declined. In part, I thought it wise to have a way to get from the church, where a Mass or blessing would precede the party, to the Dance Club, where the ceremony, supper, and dance would take place, and back to the hotel at a reasonable hour, as these parties tend to go on past the Cinderella stroke of midnight. Bringing my own wheels will turn out to be an inspired decision in more ways than I would ever have anticipated. But at the moment, I am wondering if the long drive has been in vain as none of the messages I've left on Mr. Ramos's cell phone or home phone have been returned. Foolishly, I have no address, no other way to contact the family. I look out the grimy picture window of the Pan American past the back parking lot toward street after street of fenced-in row houses, and I know, with a sinking heart, that this is not the kind of neighborhood where everyone knows everybody else.

14   An hour goes by. It's Friday, so back in Vermont, my husband is still at work. I had suggested we both fly down, wimpy city driver that I am, and make a weekend of it, but before I could finish outlining the fun of two nights at the Pan American Hotel, my husband was shaking his head. He'd had enough of quinceañeras, thank you. "You've only been to a few," I argued, feeling vaguely wounded at his obvious disenchantment with one of *my* cultural traditions. "I've been to four and that's three too many," he countered. I don't know if it's his thrifty German-Lutheran roots, but from the beginning he has looked askance at these over the top celebrations, many of them costing much more than working-class families can afford.

15   His skepticism about this tradition is also my own. The incredible expense; a girl encouraged in the dubious fantasy of being a princess as if news of feminism had never reached her mami; the marketing of a young lady as attractive, marriageable goods. Why not save the money for education? I've snuck in that question in all of my interviews. Why not have coming-of-age celebrations for boys as well as girls? But still, every time the young lady makes an entrance through her archway, or curtains part and there she is, sitting on her swing or a throne or a carousel horse, while the whole familia and roomful of friends applaud her, my eyes tear up and my throat catches. The tradition, whatever its trappings, is homing in on a need to acknowledge and celebrate these new arrivals in the field of time. From my spot in the crowd I am torn between optimism for this tender, young being emerging from the cocoon of her childhood and a sense of dread that the world she is entering, unlike the fantasy she is enjoying this one night, will not allow for such winged flight.

COMPREHENSION

1. Why does Alvarez inject herself into this story? What is her purpose?
2. Why, according to Alvarez, is quinceañera so important in Latino/Hispanic culture? Do you think she makes a convincing case for its importance? Why or why not?
3. What, ultimately, is Alvarez's attitude toward quinceañera? How do you know? Why doesn't Alvarez's husband want to accompany her as she attends the Ramos's quinceañera?

RHETORIC

1. Although she writes in various literary modes, Alvarez is best known as a novelist. What elements of fiction do you detect in this essay? Identify specific passages to support your analysis. How effective are these strategies, and why?
2. How would you describe Alvarez's audience for this essay? How successful is she in tailoring the tone and content of the selection to this audience? Does she present herself as an authority on the subject or an investigator, and what is the importance of this stance?
3. Does Alvarez establish a thesis or claim about quinceañeras? Why or why not?
4. Alvarez gradually establishes an extended or working definition of quinceañera. Locate passages where the reader receives information about this custom or ritual.
5. How does Alvarez link her introductory and concluding paragraphs? How do these two paragraphs serve as a framing device for the body of the selection?

WRITING

1. Write a narrative essay in which you tell about a ritual, custom, or celebration that is important to your family or culture.
2. Compose a comparative essay on quinceañeras and sweet sixteen celebrations, bar/bat mitzvahs, or other coming-of-age celebrations.
3. **Writing an Argument:** Argue for or against the proposition that coming-of-age celebrations have become too expensive and ostentatious in contemporary American culture.

NETWORKING
Applying 21st-Century Literacies

Shooting a Video Essay or Documentary: Approach question 1 under Writing as a video essay/documentary. If you don't own camera equipment borrow some from the school. Shoot and narrate a video documenting a ritual, custom, holiday, or other type of celebration important to your family or culture. To make your video especially engaging, before you begin the actual shooting, think of questions to ask participants, and write yourself at least the outline of a script. You can also edit sound in later for the main narration. You might focus on something specific, like the preparation of a particular type of dish, or show a broader overview of the events that make up the tradition.

Our Mutual Joy: The Religious Case for Gay Marriage

Lisa Miller

Lisa Miller is a senior writer and religion editor at Newsweek. *She writes the magazine's Belief Watch column and also prepares longer articles on spirituality and belief. After graduating from Oberlin College (BA, 1984), Miller began her career at the* Harvard Business Review; *she also held positions at the* New Yorker *and the* Wall Street Journal *before joining* Newsweek *as the magazine's society editor in 2000. Miller's essay on gay marriage and Scripture, which appeared in* Newsweek's *December 15, 2008, issue, provoked thousands of responses, some supportive but others taking issue with her argument.*

1   Let's try for a minute to take the religious conservatives at their word and define marriage as the Bible does. Shall we look to Abraham, the great patriarch, who slept with his servant when he discovered his beloved wife Sarah was infertile? Or to Jacob, who fathered children with four different women (two sisters and their servants)? Abraham, Jacob, David, Solomon and the kings of Judah and Israel—all these fathers and heroes were polygamists. The New Testament model of marriage is hardly better. Jesus himself was single and preached an indifference to earthly attachments—especially family. The apostle Paul (also single) regarded marriage as an act of last resort for those unable to contain their animal lust. "It is better to marry than to burn with passion," says the apostle, in one of the most lukewarm endorsements of a treasured institution ever uttered. Would any contemporary heterosexual married couple—who likely woke up on their wedding day harboring some optimistic and newfangled ideas about gender equality and romantic love—turn to the Bible as a how-to script?

2   Of course not, yet the religious opponents of gay marriage would have it be so.

3   The battle over gay marriage has been waged for more than a decade, but within the last six months—since California legalized gay marriage and then, with a ballot initiative in November, amended its Constitution to prohibit it—the debate has grown into a full-scale war, with religious-rhetoric slinging to match. Not since 1860, when the country's pulpits were full of preachers pronouncing on slavery, pro and con, has one of our basic social (and economic) institutions

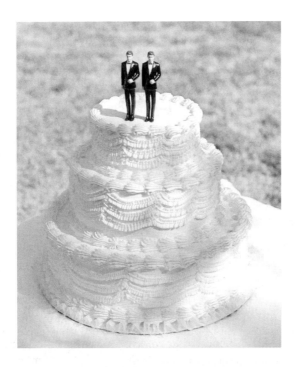

been so subject to biblical scrutiny. But whereas in the Civil War the traditional-ists had their James Henley Thornwell—and the advocates for change, their Henry Ward Beecher—this time the sides are unevenly matched. All the reli-gious rhetoric, it seems, has been on the side of the gay-marriage opponents, who use Scripture as the foundation for their objections.

The argument goes something like this statement, which the Rev. Richard 4 A. Hunter, a United Methodist minister, gave to the Atlanta *Journal-Constitution* in June: "The Bible and Jesus define marriage as between one man and one woman. The church cannot condone or bless same-sex marriages because this stands in opposition to Scripture and our tradition."

To which there are two obvious responses: First, while the Bible and Jesus 5 say many important things about love and family, neither explicitly defines mar-riage as between one man and one woman. And second, as the examples above illustrate, no sensible modern person wants marriage—theirs or anyone else's—to look in its particulars anything like what the Bible describes. "Marriage" in America refers to two separate things, a religious institution and a civil one, though it is most often enacted as a messy conflation of the two. As a civil institu-tion, marriage offers practical benefits to both partners: contractual rights having to do with taxes; insurance; the care and custody of children; visitation rights; and inheritance. As a religious institution; marriage offers something else: a com-mitment of both partners before God to love, honor and cherish each other—in sickness and in health, for richer and poorer—in accordance with God's will. In a religious marriage, two people promise to take care of each other, profoundly, the way they believe God cares for them. Biblical literalists will disagree, but the Bible is a living document, powerful for more than 2,000 years because its truths speak to us even as we change through history. In that light, Scripture gives us no good reason why gays and lesbians should not be (civilly and religiously) married—and a number of excellent reasons why they should.

6   In the Old Testament, the concept of family is fundamental, but examples of what social conservatives would call "the traditional family" are scarcely to be found. Marriage was critical to the passing along of tradition and history, as well as to maintaining the Jews' precious and fragile monotheism. But as the Barnard University Bible scholar Alan Segal puts it, the arrangement was between "one man and as many women as he could pay for." Social conservatives point to Adam and Eve as evidence for their one man, one woman argument—in particular, this verse from Genesis: "Therefore shall a man leave his mother and father, and shall cleave unto his wife, and they shall be one flesh." But as Segal says, if you believe that the Bible was written by men and not handed down in its leather bindings by God, then that verse was written by people for whom polygamy was the way of the world. (The fact that homosexual couples cannot procreate has also been raised as a biblical objection, for didn't God say, "Be fruitful and multiply"? But the Bible authors could never have imagined the brave new world of international adoption and assisted reproductive technology—and besides, heterosexuals who are infertile or past the age of reproducing get married all the time.)

7   Ozzie and Harriet are nowhere in the New Testament either. The biblical Jesus was—in spite of recent efforts of novelists to paint him otherwise—emphatically unmarried. He preached a radical kind of family, a caring community of believers, whose bond in God superseded all blood ties. Leave your families and follow me, Jesus says in the gospels. There will be no marriage in heaven, he says in Matthew. Jesus never mentions homosexuality, but he roundly condemns divorce (leaving a loophole in some cases for the husbands of unfaithful women).

8   The apostle Paul echoed the Christian Lord's lack of interest in matters of the flesh. For him, celibacy was the Christian ideal, but family stability was the best alternative. Marry if you must, he told his audiences, but do not get divorced. "To the married I give this command (not I, but the Lord); a wife must not separate from her husband." It probably goes without saying that the phrase "gay marriage" does not appear in the Bible at all.

9 If the Bible doesn't give abundant examples of traditional marriage, then what are the gay-marriage opponents really exercised about? Well, homosexuality, of course—specifically sex between men. Sex between women has never, even in biblical times, raised as much ire. In its entry on "Homosexual Practices," the Anchor Bible Dictionary notes that nowhere in the Bible do its authors refer to sex between women, "possibly because it did not result in true physical 'union' (by male entry)." The Bible does condemn gay male sex in a handful of passages. Twice Leviticus refers to sex between men as "an abomination" (King

James version), but these are throwaway lines in a peculiar text given over to codes for living in the ancient Jewish world, a text that devotes verse after verse to treatments for leprosy, cleanliness rituals for menstruating women and the correct way to sacrifice a goat—or a lamb or a turtle dove. Most of us no longer heed Leviticus on haircuts or blood sacrifices; our modern understanding of the world has surpassed its prescriptions. Why would we regard its condemnation of homosexuality with more seriousness than we regard its advice, which is far lengthier, on the best price to pay for a slave?

Paul was tough on homosexuality, though recently progressive scholars 10 have argued that his condemnation of men who "were inflamed with lust for one another" (which he calls "a perversion") is really a critique of the worst kind of wickedness: self-delusion, violence, promiscuity and debauchery. In his book "The Arrogance of Nations," the scholar Neil Elliott argues that Paul is referring in this famous passage to the depravity of the Roman emperors, the craven habits of Nero and Caligula, a reference his audience would have grasped instantly. "Paul is not talking about what we call homosexuality at all," Elliott says. "He's talking about a certain group of people who have done everything in this list. We're not dealing with anything like gay love or gay marriage. We're talking about really, really violent people who meet their end and are judged by God." In any case, one might add, Paul argued more strenuously against divorce—and at least half of the Christians in America disregard that teaching.

Religious objections to gay marriage are rooted not in the Bible at all, 11 then, but in custom and tradition (and, to talk turkey for a minute, a personal discomfort with gay sex that transcends theological argument). Common prayers and rituals reflect our common practice: The Episcopal Book of Common Prayer describes the participants in a marriage as "the man and the woman." But common practice changes—and for the better; as the Rev. Martin Luther King Jr. said, "The arc of history is long, but it bends toward justice." The Bible endorses slavery, a practice that Americans now universally consider shameful and barbaric. It recommends the death penalty for adulterers (and in Leviticus, for men who have sex with men, for that matter). It provides conceptual shelter for anti-Semites. A mature view of scriptural authority requires us, as we have in the past, to move beyond literalism. The Bible was written for a world so unlike our own, it's impossible to apply its rules, at face value, to ours.

12   Marriage, specifically, has evolved so as to be unrecognizable to the wives of Abraham and Jacob. Monogamy became the norm in the Christian world in the sixth century; husbands' frequent enjoyment of mistresses and prostitutes became taboo by the beginning of the 20th. (In the *Newsweek* Poll, 55 percent of respondents said that married heterosexuals who have sex with someone other than their spouses are more morally objectionable than a gay couple in a committed sexual relationship.) By the mid-19th century, U.S. courts were siding with wives who were the victims of domestic violence, and by the 1970s most states had gotten rid of their "head and master" laws, which gave husbands the right to decide where a family would live and whether a wife would be able to take a job. Today's vision of marriage as a union of equal partners, joined in a relationship both romantic and pragmatic, is, by very recent standards, radical, says Stephanie Coontz, author of "Marriage, a History."

13   Religious wedding ceremonies have already changed to reflect new conceptions of marriage. Remember when we used to say "man and wife" instead of "husband and wife"? Remember when we stopped using the word "obey"? Even Miss Manners, the voice of tradition and reason, approved in 1997 of that change. "It seems," she wrote, "that dropping 'obey' was a sensible editing of a service that made assumptions about marriage that the society no longer holds."

14   We cannot look to the Bible as a marriage manual, but we can read it for universal truths as we struggle toward a more just future. The Bible offers inspiration and warning on the subjects of love, marriage, family and community. It speaks eloquently of the crucial role of families in a fair society and the risks we incur to ourselves and our children should we cease trying to bind ourselves together in loving pairs. Gay men like to point to the story of passionate King David and his friend Jonathan, with whom he was "one spirit" and whom he "loved as he loved himself." Conservatives say this is a story about a platonic friendship, but it is also a story about two men who stand up for each other in turbulent times, through violent war and the disapproval of a powerful parent. David rends his clothes at Jonathan's death and, in grieving, writes a song:

> I grieve for you, Jonathan my brother;
> You were very dear to me.
> Your love for me was wonderful,
> More wonderful than that of women.

Here, the Bible praises enduring love between men. What Jonathan and   15
David did or did not do in privacy is perhaps best left to history and our own
imaginations.

In addition to its praise of friendship and its condemnation of divorce, the   16
Bible gives many examples of marriages that defy convention yet benefit the
greater community. The Torah discouraged the ancient Hebrews from marrying
outside the tribe, yet Moses himself is married to a foreigner, Zipporah. Queen
Esther is married to a non-Jew and, according to legend, saves the Jewish people. Rabbi Arthur Waskow, of the Shalom Center in Philadelphia, believes that
Judaism thrives through diversity and inclusion. "I don't think Judaism should
or ought to want to leave any portion of the human population outside the religious process," he says. "We should not want to leave [homosexuals] outside
the sacred tent." The marriage of Joseph and Mary is also unorthodox (to say
the least), a case of an unconventional arrangement accepted by society for the
common good. The boy needed two human parents, after all.

In the Christian story, the message of acceptance for all is codified. Jesus   17
reaches out to everyone, especially those on the margins, and brings the whole
Christian community into his embrace. The Rev. James Martin, a Jesuit priest and
author, cites the story of Jesus revealing himself to the woman at the well—no matter that she had five former husbands and a current boyfriend—as evidence of
Christ's all-encompassing love. The great Bible scholar Walter Brueggemann, emeritus professor at Columbia Theological Seminary, quotes the apostle Paul when he
looks for biblical support of gay marriage: "There is neither Greek nor Jew, slave
nor free, male nor female, for you are all one in Jesus Christ." The religious argument for gay marriage, he adds, "is not generally made with reference to particular
texts, but with the general conviction that the Bible is bent toward inclusiveness."

The practice of inclusion, even in defiance of social convention, the reaching out   18
to outcasts, the emphasis on togetherness and community over and against
chaos, depravity, indifference—all these biblical values argue for gay marriage.
If one is for racial equality and the common nature of humanity, then the values
of stability, monogamy and family necessarily follow. Terry Davis is the pastor of
First Presbyterian Church in Hartford, Conn., and has been presiding over "holy
unions" since 1992. "I'm against promiscuity—love ought to be expressed in
committed relationships, not through casual sex, and I think the church should
recognize the validity of committed same-sex relationships," he says.

Still, very few Jewish or Christian denominations do officially endorse gay   19
marriage, even in the states where it is legal. The practice varies by region, by
church or synagogue, even by cleric. More progressive denominations—the
United Church of Christ, for example—have agreed to support gay marriage.
Other denominations and dioceses will do "holy union" or "blessing" ceremonies, but shy away from the word "marriage" because it is politically explosive.
So the frustrating, semantic question remains: Should gay people be married in
the same, sacramental sense that straight people are? I would argue that they
should. If we are all God's children, made in his likeness and image, then to deny

access to any sacrament based on sexuality is exactly the same thing as denying it based on skin color—and no serious (or even semiserious) person would argue that. People get married "for their mutual joy," explains the Rev. Chloe Breyer, executive director of the Interfaith Center in New York, quoting the Episcopal marriage ceremony. That's what religious people do: care for each other in spite of difficulty, she adds. In marriage, couples grow closer to God: "Being with one another in community is how you love God. That's what marriage is about."

20   More basic than theology, though, is human need. We want, as Abraham did, to grow old surrounded by friends and family and to be buried at last peacefully among them. We want, as Jesus taught, to love one another for our own good— and, not to be too grandiose about it, for the good of the world. We want our children to grow up in stable homes. What happens in the bedroom, really, has nothing to do with any of this. My friend the priest James Martin says his favorite Scripture relating to the question of homosexuality is Psalm 139, a song that praises the beauty and imperfection in all of us and that glorifies God's knowledge of our most secret selves: "I praise you because I am fearfully and wonderfully made." And then he adds that in his heart he believes that if Jesus were alive today, he would reach out especially to the gays and lesbians among us, for "Jesus does not want people to be lonely and sad." Let the priest's prayer be our own.

COMPREHENSION

1. What is important about the main title of Miller's essay, "Our Mutual Joy"? According to Miller, what does the Bible say about the traditional family, heterosexual love, and gay marriage?
2. What does Miller mean when she writes, "Ozzie and Harriet are nowhere in the New Testament . . ." (paragraph 7)?
3. What is Miller's purpose in relating the story of King David and his friend Jonathan? What other biblical tales does she recount, and why?

RHETORIC

1. How would you describe Miller's voice in paragraph 1? Does she sustain this voice and tone throughout the essay? Is her writing style subjective or objective? Justify your response.
2. What is Miller's claim, and where does she state it most clearly? What constitutes her primary and secondary support? What types of evidence does she present? How does she contend with opposing viewpoints?
3. What connections do you perceive among the three major parts of this essay? How do the beginning and ending paragraphs relate to each other? How does Miller's organizational strategy support the essay's content?
4. In what way might this essay be considered an extended comparative analysis? What is being compared or contrasted, and how is the comparison structured?
5. Miller is fond of recurring motifs. Identify some of these motifs, and explain how these repeated references help to support her claim.

WRITING

1. Write an essay in which you elaborate on Miller's statement, "Religious wedding ceremonies have already changed to reflect new conceptions of marriage."
2. Write a comparative essay explaining the two diverging ways in which the Bible—or another religious text with which you are familiar—can be used to support or reject gay marriage.
3. **Writing an Argument:** Using your own religious background as a foundation, argue for or against gay marriage.

NETWORKING
Applying 21st-Century Literacies

1. **Exploring Extra Features of an Online Article:** Through the Chapter 6 Networking page at *www.mhhe.com/mhreaderbrief1e,* visit *xtra.Newsweek.com* to read about the future of the gay rights movement and watch the magazine's video series on political/ideological divisions among lesbians of various ages and gay men. Write a synthesis of the videos and articles, including Miller's, discussing any larger conclusions they suggest, tensions they reveal, and further questions they raise.
2. **Using Visuals as Appeals:** How do the photographs support Miller's position? What type of appeal do they make, how effective are they in doing so, and why?

Synthesis: Connections for Critical Thinking

1. Both Annie Dillard's "An American Childhood" and E. B. White's "Once More to the Lake" explore the experience of childhood from a different perspective. Do they share a common voice or mood? What is distinctive about each essay? Which essay do you prefer, and why? Consider the style and emotional impact of the writing.
2. Both Barbara Kingsolver's "Stone Soup" and Lisa Miller's "Our Mutual Joy: The Religious Case for Gay Marriage" attempt to alter stereotypes commonly held about contemporary families. What type of family does each author address? How do the authors differ in their rhetorical strategies and their use of supporting points to buttress their arguments? Who is the implied audience for each of the essays? How did you reach your conclusion?
3. Argue for or against the claim that Alvarez's portrayal of a quinceañera and Brooks's take on online dating are biased.
4. Argue for or against the idea that the presentation of relatively new types of relationships like those described in the essays by Kingsolver and Brooks seem more highly romanticized than the "traditional" relationships described by White and Alvarez.

5. Argue for or against the view that changes in society and its norms—specifically, increased geographical mobility, an evolving workplace, ideas about economic class, individual liberties, and sexual preference—have resulted in new forms of identity. Use examples from the work of Brooks, Miller, and others.

6. Write a classification essay analyzing the types of women presented in the essays by Kingsolver, Dillard, Alvarez, and Miller.

NETWORKING
Applying 21st-Century Literacies

1. Join several newsgroups or chat rooms that focus on online dating. Compare and contrast the ideological focus of the conversations among members.

2. Create your own blog, and post a selected quote regarding "the family" taken from one of your essays. Enable comments so fellow students can respond. At the end of the semester, write a report and summary of the responses.

CH 6   **www.mhhe.com/mhreaderbrief1e**

- *Image Gallery:* Chapter images in color
- *Family and Gender:* Information on the authors in this chapter
- *Ch. 6 Networking*

chapter *7*

History, Culture, and Civilization
Are We Citizens of the World?

In the 21st century, the paroxysms caused by conflicts among peoples, nations, ethnic groups, and cultures continue to shake continents. The United States might have emerged from the cold war as the dominant superpower, but numerous local and global challenges remain. We seem to be at a crossroads in history, culture, and civilization, but does the future hold great promise or equally great danger—or both?

The future assuredly holds significant peril as well as promise. History tells us that while there has never been complete absence of barbarism and nonrational behavior in human affairs, there have been societies, cultures, and nations committed to harmonious, or civil, conduct within various social realms. While it is clear that we have not attained an ideal state of cultural or world development, at the same time, we have advanced beyond the point in primitive civilization at which someone chipped at a stone in order to make a better tool.

As we consider the course of contemporary civilization, we must contend with our own personal histories and cultures as well as with the interplay of contradictory global forces. We have become increasingly concerned with finding a purpose beyond the parameters of our very limiting personal and nationalistic identities, something that the Czech writer and statesman Václav Havel calls the "divine revolution." Indeed, we have entered an era of renewed ethnic strife, in which a preoccupation with cultural difference seems stronger than the desire for universal civilization. The writers assembled here grapple with these contradictions; they search for those constituents of history and culture that might hasten the advent of a civilized world.

The idea of civilization suggests a pluralistic ethos whereby people of diverse histories and backgrounds can maintain cultural identities but also coexist with other cultural representatives in a spirit of tolerance and mutual respect. The wars, upheavals, and catastrophes of the 20th century were spawned by a narrow consciousness. Hopefully, in this century, all of us can advance the goal of a universal civilization based on the best that we have been able to create for humankind.

PREVIEWING THE CHAPTER

As you read the essays in this chapter and respond to them in discussion and writing, consider the following questions:

- How does the author define *culture, history,* or *civilization?* Is this definition stated or implied? Is it broad or narrow? Explain.
- Is the writer hopeful or pessimistic about the state of culture and history?
- What values does the author seem to think are necessary to advance the idea of history and culture?
- Is the author's tone objective or subjective? What is his or her purpose? Does the author have a personal motive in addressing the topic in the way he or she does?
- Which areas of knowledge—for example, history, philosophy, and political science—does the author bring to bear on the subject?
- Do you agree or disagree with the author's view of the contemporary state of civilization?
- What cultural problems and historical conflicts are raised by the author in his or her treatment of the subject?
- Does the author have a narrow or a broad focus on the relationship of history and culture to the larger society?
- How does the medium the author writes in contribute to his or her perspective on culture, history, or civilization?
- Which authors altered your perspective on a topic, and why?
- Based on your reading of these essays, how would you define *civilization?* Are you hopeful about the current state of civilization?

Classic and Contemporary Images
How Do We Become Americans?

Using a Critical Perspective   Compare the scene of early-20th-century immigrants at New York City's Ellis Island with the March 1999 X-ray photo taken by Mexican authorities of human forms and cargo in a truck. What mood is conveyed by each representation? Does each photograph have a thesis or argument? Explain. Which photo do you find more engaging and provocative, and why?

From the time of the first European settlers, the North American continent has experienced wave after wave of immigration from every part of the world. One period of heavy immigration occurred in the late 19th and early 20th centuries, when millions of people from eastern and southern Europe entered the United States through Ellis Island in New York City, as shown in this classic photograph.

More recently, immigrants continue to come from all over the world, often entering the country illegally. The X-ray photo shows a wide shot and a close-up image of people being smuggled across Mexico's border with Guatemala.

Classic and Contemporary Essays
ARE WE MOVING TOWARD A WORLD CULTURE?

Both of these essays address the issues of national and global identification. As you read them, consider not only the differing styles and strategies of discourse of their authors, but also their common themes and claims. In addition, consider that J. B. Priestley writes from a classically British experience of the nation-state, while Ishmael Reed is writing as a representative of a racial and (to his mind) cultural minority. Both, however, write within the context of the modern democratic state. And both are forthright and direct in their arguments, offering cultural analysis, appeals to authority, and historical evidence. As keen observers of the modern political scene, Priestley and Reed examine the very contours of civilization. But Priestley, a more traditional or classical writer than Reed, operates from a uniquely English perspective rooted in a clear sense of region. On the other hand, Reed, whose style is more informal, operates from an African American perspective rooted in an understanding that much of Western civilization draws its roots from a multiplicity of sources, not just European. We might be examining the reflections of two different personalities, but consider also the ways in which their agendas overlap.

Wrong Ism

J. B. Priestley

John Boynton Priestley (1894–1984), best-selling English novelist and popular dramatist, was also a prolific writer of essays, many of them involving social and political criticism. His work includes The English Novel *(1927),* The Good Companions *(1929),* Time and the Conways *(1937),* An Inspector Calls *(1946), and* The English *(1973). This selection from* Essays of Five Decades *(1968) offers an astute analysis of contemporary political habits.*

1   There are three isms that we ought to consider very carefully—regionalism, nationalism, internationalism. Of these three the one there is most fuss about, the one that starts men shouting and marching and shooting, the one that seems to have all the depth and thrust and fire, is of course nationalism. Nine people out of ten, I fancy, would say that of this trio it is the one that really counts, the big boss. Regionalism and internationalism, they would add, are comparatively small, shadowy, rather cranky. And I believe all this to be quite wrong. Like

many another big boss, nationalism is largely bogus. It is like a bunch of flowers made of plastics.

The real flowers belong to regionalism. The mass of people everywhere   2
may never have used the term. They are probably regionalists without knowing it. Because they have been brought up in a certain part of the world, they have formed perhaps quite unconsciously a deep attachment to its landscape and speech, its traditional customs, its food and drink, its songs and jokes. (There are of course always the rebels, often intellectuals and writers, but they are not the mass of people.) They are rooted in their region. Indeed, without this attachment a man can have no roots.

So much of people's lives, from earliest childhood onwards, is deeply inter-   3
twined with the common life of the region, they cannot help feeling strongly about it. A threat to it is a knife pointing at the heart. How can life ever be the same if bullying strangers come to change everything? The form and colour, the very taste and smell of dear familiar things will be different, alien, life-destroying. It would be better to die fighting. And it is precisely this, the nourishing life of the region, for which common men have so often fought and died.

This attachment to the region exists on a level far deeper than that of any   4
political hocus-pocus. When a man says "my country" with real feeling, he is thinking about his region, all that has made up his life, and not about that political entity, the nation. There can be some confusion here simply because some countries are so small—and ours is one of them—and so old, again like ours, that much of what is national is also regional. Down the centuries, the nation, itself, so comparatively small, has been able to attach to itself the feeling really created by the region. (Even so there is something left over, as most people in Yorkshire or Devon, for example, would tell you.) This probably explains the fervent patriotism developed early in small countries. The English were announcing that they were English in the Middle Ages, before nationalism had arrived elsewhere.

If we deduct from nationalism all that it has borrowed or stolen from re-   5
gionalism, what remains is mostly rubbish. The nation, as distinct from the region, is largely the creation of power-men and political manipulators. Almost all nationalist movements are led by ambitious frustrated men determined to hold office. I am not blaming them. I would do the same if I were in their place and wanted power so badly. But nearly always they make use of the rich warm regional feeling, the emotional dynamo of the movement, while being almost untouched by it themselves. This is because they are not as a rule deeply loyal to any region themselves. Ambition and a love of power can eat like acid into the tissues of regional loyalty. It is hard, if not impossible, to retain a natural piety and yet be for ever playing both ends against the middle.

Being itself a power structure, devised by men of power, the nation tends to   6
think and act in terms of power. What would benefit the real life of the region, where men, women and children actually live, is soon sacrificed for the power and prestige of the nation. (And the personal vanity of presidents and ministers themselves, which historians too often disregard.) Among the new nations of

our time innumerable peasants and labourers must have found themselves being cut down from five square meals a week to three in order to provide unnecessary airlines, military forces that can only be used against them and nobody
else, great conference halls and official yachts and the rest. The last traces of
imperialism and colonialism may have to be removed from Asia and Africa,
where men can no longer endure being condemned to a permanent inferiority
by the colour of their skins; but even so, the modern world, the real world of
our time, does not want and would be far better without more and more nations, busy creating for themselves the very paraphernalia that western Europe
is now trying to abolish. You are compelled to answer more questions when
trying to spend half a day in Cambodia than you are now travelling from the
Hook of Holland to Syracuse.

7   This brings me to internationalism. I dislike this term, which I used only to
complete the isms. It suggests financiers and dubious promoters living nowhere but in luxury hotels; a shallow world of entrepreneurs and impresarios.
(Was it Sacha Guitry who said that impresarios were men who spoke many
languages but all with a foreign accent?) The internationalism I have in mind
here is best described as world civilisation. It is life considered on a global scale.
Most of our communications and transport already exist on this high wide
level. So do many other things from medicine to meteorology. Our astronomers
and physicists (except where they have allowed themselves to be hush-hushed)
work here. The UN special agencies, about which we hear far too little, have
contributed more and more to this world civilisation. All the arts, when they are
arts and not chunks of nationalist propaganda, naturally take their place in it.
And it grows, widens, deepens, in spite of the fact that for every dollar, ruble,
pound or franc spent in explaining and praising it, a thousand are spent by the
nations explaining and praising themselves.

8   This world civilisation and regionalism can get along together, especially if
we keep ourselves sharply aware of their quite different but equally important
values and rewards. A man can make his contribution to world civilisation and
yet remain strongly regional in feeling: I know several men of this sort. There is of
course the danger—it is with us now—of the global style flattening out the regional, taking local form, colour, flavour, away for ever, disinheriting future generations, threatening them with sensuous poverty and a huge boredom. But to
understand and appreciate regionalism is to be on guard against this danger. And
we must therefore make a clear distinction between regionalism and nationalism.

9   It is nationalism that tries to check the growth of world civilisation. And
nationalism, when taken on a global scale, is more aggressive and demanding
now than it has ever been before. This in the giant powers is largely disguised
by the endless fuss in public about rival ideologies, now a largely unreal quar-
rel. What is intensely real is the glaring nationalism. Even the desire to police
the world is nationalistic in origin. (Only the world can police the world.) Moreover, the nation-states of today are for the most part far narrower in their outlook, far more inclined to allow prejudice against the foreigner to impoverish
their own style of living, than the old imperial states were. It should be part of

world civilisation that men with particular skills, perhaps the product of the very regionalism they are rebelling against, should be able to move easily from country to country, to exercise those skills, in anything from teaching the violin to running a new type of factory to managing an old hotel. But nationalism, especially of the newer sort, would rather see everything done badly than allow a few non-nationals to get to work. And people face a barrage of passports, visas, immigration controls, labour permits; and in this respect are worse off than they were in 1900. But even so, in spite of all that nationalism can do—so long as it keeps its nuclear bombs to itself—the internationalism I have in mind, slowly creating a world civilisation, cannot be checked.

Nevertheless, we are still backing the wrong ism. Almost all our money 10 goes on the middle one, nationalism, the rotten meat between the two healthy slices of bread. We need regionalism to give us roots and that very depth of feeling which nationalism unjustly and greedily claims for itself. We need internationalism to save the world and to broaden and heighten our civilisation. While regional man enriches the lives that international man is already working to keep secure and healthy, national man, drunk with power, demands our loyalty, money and applause, and poisons the very air with his dangerous nonsense.

COMPREHENSION

1. What thesis does Priestley present? State the thesis in your own words.
2. Define *regionalism, nationalism,* and *internationalism* as Priestley presents these terms.
3. Explain Priestley's objections to nationalism. Where does he state these objections in the essay? What alternative does he propose?

RHETORIC

1. What striking metaphor does the author develop to capture the essence of nationalism? What is its sensory impact? Analyze another example of metaphorical language in the essay.
2. How does the suffix *-ism* function stylistically in the essay?
3. What is Priestley's principle of classification in this essay? How does he maintain proportion in the presentation of categories?
4. Analyze the relationship between definition and classification in the essay.
5. Examine Priestley's use of comparison and contrast.
6. Explain the connection between the introductory and concluding paragraphs.

WRITING

1. Priestley makes many assumptions about regionalism, nationalism, and internationalism. Which assumptions do you accept? Which assumptions do you reject? Explain in an essay.

2. Write a classification essay on at least three related isms: capitalism, socialism, and communism; Protestantism, Catholicism, and Judaism; or regionalism, nationalism, and internationalism.

3. **Writing an Argument:** Take issue with Priestley's assertion that the "real flowers belong to regionalism," and argue that regionalism today is a destructive force in world affairs.

NETWORKING
Applying 21st-Century Literacies

Considering the Isms of Online Communities: Write an essay arguing that a particular online community—such as a social networking site (Facebook, Twitter, Meetup, Craigslist), a virtual community like Second Life, a gaming site or subscription (such as X-Box Live), or similar—contributes primarily to a sense of internationalism, nationalism, regionalism, and/or isolationism. Use specific evidence to support your argument.

America: The Multinational Society

Ishmael Reed

Ishmael Reed (b. 1938), an American novelist, poet, and essayist, founded and edited (along with Al Young) Quilt *magazine, begun in 1981. In his writing, Reed uses a combination of standard English, black dialect, and slang to interrogate American society. He believes that African Americans must move away from identification with Europe in order to rediscover their African qualities. Reed's books include* Flight to Canada *(1976),* The Terrible Twos *(1982),* The Terrible Threes *(1989),* Japanese by Spring *(1993), and* The Reed Reader *(2000). In addition, he has written volumes of verse, including* A Secretary to the Spirits *(1975), and has published collections of his essays, including* Airing Dirty Laundry *(1993). In the following essay from* Writin' Is Fightin' *(1990), Reed seeks to debunk the myth of the European ideal and argues for a universal definition of culture.*

At the annual Lower East Side Jewish Festival yesterday, a Chinese woman ate a pizza slice in front of Ty Thuan Duc's Vietnamese grocery store. Beside her a Spanish-speaking family patronized a cart with two signs: "Italian Ices" and "Kosher by Rabbi Alper." And after the pastrami ran out, everybody ate knishes.

—New York Times, *June 23, 1983*

1   On the day before Memorial Day, 1983, a poet called me to describe a city he had just visited. He said that one section included mosques, built by the Islamic

people who dwelled there. Attending his reading, he said, were large numbers of Hispanic people, forty thousand of whom lived in the same city. He was not talking about a fabled city located in some mysterious region of the world. The city he'd visited was Detroit.

A few months before, as I was leaving Houston, Texas, I heard it announced 2 on the radio that Texas's largest minority was Mexican American, and though a foundation recently issued a report critical of bilingual education, the taped voice used to guide the passengers on the air trams connecting terminals in Dallas Airport is in both Spanish and English. If the trend continues, a day will come when it will be difficult to travel through some sections of the country without hearing commands in both English and Spanish; after all, for some western states, Spanish was the first written language and the Spanish style lives on in the western way of life.

Shortly after my Texas trip, I sat in an auditorium located on the campus of 3 the University of Wisconsin at Milwaukee as a Yale professor—whose original work on the influence of African cultures upon those of the Americas has led to his ostracism from some monocultural intellectual circles—walked up and down the aisle, like an old-time southern evangelist, dancing and drumming the top of the lectern, illustrating his points before some serious Afro-American intellectuals and artists who cheered and applauded his performance and his mastery of information. The professor was "white." After his lecture, he joined a group of Milwaukeeans in a conversation. All of the participants spoke Yoruban, though only the professor had ever traveled to Africa.

One of the artists told me that his paintings, which included African and 4 Afro-American mythological symbols and imagery, were hanging in the local McDonald's restaurant. The next day I went to McDonald's and snapped pictures of smiling youngsters eating hamburgers below paintings that could grace the walls of any of the country's leading museums. The manager of the local McDonald's said, "I don't know what you boys are doing, but I like it," as he commissioned the local painters to exhibit in his restaurant.

Such blurring of cultural styles occurs in everyday life in the United States 5 to a greater extent than anyone can imagine and is probably more prevalent than the sensational conflict between people of different backgrounds that is played up and often encouraged by the media. The result is what the Yale professor, Robert Thompson, referred to as a cultural bouillabaisse, yet members of the nation's present educational and cultural Elect still cling to the notion that the United States belongs to some vaguely defined entity they refer to as "Western civilization," by which they mean, presumably, a civilization created by the people of Europe, as if Europe can be viewed in monolithic terms. Is Beethoven's Ninth Symphony, which includes Turkish marches, a part of Western civilization, or the late nineteenth- and twentieth-century French paintings, whose creators were influenced by Japanese art? And what of the cubists, through whom the influence of African art changed modern painting, or the surrealists, who were so impressed with the art of the Pacific Northwest Indians that, in their map of North America, Alaska dwarfs the lower forty-eight in size?

6   Are the Russians, who are often criticized for their adoption of "Western" ways by Tsarist dissidents in exile, members of Western civilization? And what of the millions of Europeans who have black African and Asian ancestry, black Africans having occupied several countries for hundreds of years? Are these "Europeans" members of Western civilization, or the Hungarians, who originated across the Urals in a place called Greater Hungary, or the Irish, who came from the Iberian Peninsula?

7   Even the notion that North America is part of Western civilization because our "system of government" is derived from Europe is being challenged by Native American historians who say that the founding fathers, Benjamin Franklin especially, were actually influenced by the system of government that had been adopted by the Iroquois hundreds of years prior to the arrival of large numbers of Europeans.

8   Western civilization, then, becomes another confusing category like Third World, or Judeo-Christian culture, as man attempts to impose his small-screen view of political and cultural reality upon a complex world. Our most publicized novelist recently said that Western civilization was the greatest achievement of mankind, an attitude that flourishes on the street level as scribbles in public restrooms: "White Power," "Niggers and Spics Suck," or "Hitler was a prophet," the latter being the most telling, for wasn't Adolph [sic] Hitler the archetypal monoculturalist who, in his pigheaded arrogance, believed that one way and one blood was so pure that it had to be protected from alien strains at all costs? Where did such an attitude, which has caused so much misery and depression in our national life, which has tainted even our noblest achievements, begin? An attitude that caused the incarceration of Japanese-American citizens during World War II, the persecution of Chicanos and Chinese Americans, the near-extermination of the Indians, and the murder and lynchings of thousands of Afro-Americans.

9   Virtuous, hardworking, pious, even though they occasionally would wander off after some fancy clothes, or rendezvous in the woods with the town prostitute, the Puritans are idealized in our schoolbooks as "a hardy band" of no-nonsense patriarchs whose discipline razed the forest and brought order to the New World (a term that annoys Native American historians). Industrious, responsible, it was their "Yankee ingenuity" and practicality that created the work ethic. They were simple folk who produced a number of good poets, and they set the tone for the American writing style, of lean and spare lines, long before Hemingway. They worshiped in churches whose colors blended in with the New England snow, churches with simple structures and ornate lecterns.

10   The Puritans were a daring lot, but they had a mean streak. They hated the theater and banned Christmas. They punished people in a cruel and inhuman manner. They killed children who disobeyed their parents. When they came in contact with those whom they considered heathens or aliens, they behaved in such a bizarre and irrational manner that this chapter in the American history comes down to us as a late-movie horror film. They exterminated the Indians,

who taught them how to survive in a world unknown to them, and their encounter with the calypso culture of Barbados resulted in what the tourist guide in Salem's Witches' House refers to as the Witchcraft Hysteria.

The Puritan legacy of hard work and meticulous accounting led to the   11
establishment of a great industrial society; it is no wonder that the American industrial revolution began in Lowell, Massachusetts, but there was the other side, the strange and paranoid attitudes toward those different from the Elect.

The cultural attitudes of that early Elect continue to be voiced in everyday   12
life in the United States: the president of a distinguished university, writing a letter to the *Times*, belittling the study of African civilizations; the television network that promoted its show on the Vatican art with the boast that this art represented "the finest achievements of the human spirit." A modern up-tempo state of complex rhythms that depends upon contacts with an international community can no longer behave as if it dwelled in a "Zion Wilderness" surrounded by beasts and pagans.

When I heard a schoolteacher warn the other night about the invasion of   13
the American educational system by foreign curriculums, I wanted to yell at the television set, "Lady, they're already here." It has already begun because the world is here. The world has been arriving at these shores for at least ten thousand years from Europe, Africa, and Asia. In the late nineteenth and early twentieth centuries, large numbers of Europeans arrived, adding their cultures to those of the European, African, and Asian settlers who were already here, and recently millions have been entering the country from South America and the Caribbean, making Yale Professor Bob Thompson's bouillabaisse richer and thicker.

One of our most visionary politicians said that he envisioned a time when   14
the United States could become the brain of the world, by which he meant the repository of all of the latest advanced information systems. I thought of that remark when an enterprising poet friend of mine called to say that he had just sold a poem to a computer magazine and that the editors were delighted to get it because they didn't carry fiction or poetry. Is that the kind of world we desire? A humdrum homogeneous world of all brains but no heart, no fiction, no poetry; a world of robots with human attendants bereft of imagination, of culture? Or does North America deserve a more exciting destiny? To become a place where the cultures of the world crisscross. This is possible because the United States is unique in the world: The world is here.

COMPREHENSION

1. Why does Reed believe that the conventional notion of Western or European civilization is misleading when applied to the American experience?
2. According to Reed, what are the origins of our monoculturalist view?
3. What are the dangers of such a narrow view? What historical examples does Reed allude to?

RHETORIC

1. How do paragraphs 1–4 help set the stage for Reed's discourse? Does this section contain his thesis?
2. Does the computer analogy in Reed's conclusion work? Do his rhetorical questions underscore the thesis?
3. Comment on the author's extensive use of details and examples. How do they serve to support his point? Which examples are especially illuminating, and why?
4. What kind of humor does Reed use in his essay? Does its use contribute to the force of his essay? Why or why not?
5. Is Reed's reasoning inductive or deductive? Justify your answer.
6. How does Reed employ definitions to structure his essay?

WRITING

1. How does America's insistence that it "belongs to . . . 'Western Civilization'" affect its dealings with other nations? How does it influence the way it treats its own citizens? Explore these questions in a causal-analysis essay, using support from Reed.
2. Write an essay in which you consider how a multinational United States affects you on a day-to-day basis. How does it enrich your life or the life of the country? Use specific examples and details to support your opinion.
3. **Writing an Argument:** Write an essay arguing that a multinational society is often riddled with complex problems. What are some of the drawbacks or disadvantages of such a society? What causes these conflicts? Explore these issues in your writing.

NETWORKING
Applying 21st-Century Literacies

Comparing Style across Media: On the Chapter 7 Networking page at *www .mhhe.com/mhreaderbrief1e*, click on the link to watch Ishmael Reed discuss the concept of being an "ethnic gate-crasher," an advocate of transnationalism. How does this brief video influence your reading of "America: The Multinational Society"? What does Reed convey through his physical presence and voice? Discuss the advantages and disadvantages of this conversational style of conveying ideas, as opposed to the formal but text-only presentation of a polished essay.

Synthesis: Classic and Contemporary Questions for Comparison

1. How do the respective tones of Priestley's and Reed's essays differ? What clues are contained in the texts that make this difference evident? Use examples from both.
2. In his essay, Priestley argues against nationalism and professes to be a proponent of regionalism and internationalism. Compare Priestley's view with Reed's argument that to be an "American" means to accept the variety of influences that have converged into a "multinational society." How do these arguments differ? How are they similar?

3. Discuss both Priestley's and Reed's essays in terms of formality of voice. Does one author speak with more authority than the other? Or are they equally authoritative, but employing the stylistic modes of their times? Use examples from both essays.

The Myth of the Latin Woman: I Just Met a Girl Named María

Judith Ortiz Cofer

Judith Ortiz Cofer (b. 1952) was born in Puerto Rico and immigrated to the United States in 1956. Once a bilingual teacher in Florida public schools, Cofer has written several books of poetry; plays; a novel, The Line of the Sun *(1989); an award-winning collection of essays and poems,* Silent Dancing: A Partial Remembrance of a Puerto Rican Childhood *(1990); and a collection of short stories,* An Island Like You: Stories of the Barrio *(1995). Her more recent books include* Woman in Front of the Sun: On Becoming a Writer *(2000),* The Meaning of Consuelo *(2003), and* A Love Story Beginning in Spanish *(2005). She is a professor of English and creative writing at the University of Georgia. In the following essay, she offers both personal insight and philosophical reflection on the theme of ethnic stereotyping.*

On a bus trip to London from Oxford University where I was earning some 1
graduate credits one summer, a young man, obviously fresh from a pub, spotted me and as if struck by inspiration went down on his knees in the aisle. With both hands over his heart he broke into an Irish tenor's rendition of "María" from *West Side Story*. My politely amused fellow passengers gave his lovely voice the round of gentle applause it deserved. Though I was not quite as amused, I managed my version of an English smile: no show of teeth, no extreme contortions of the facial muscles—I was at this time of my life practicing reserve and cool. Oh, that British control, how I coveted it. But "María" had followed me to London, reminding me of a prime fact of my life: You can leave the island, master the English language, and travel as far as you can, but if you are a Latina, especially one like me who so obviously belongs to Rita Moreno's gene pool, the island travels with you.

   This is sometimes a very good thing. It may win you that extra minute of 2
someone's attention. But with some people, the same things can make *you* an island—not a tropical paradise but an Alcatraz, a place nobody wants to visit.

As a Puerto Rican girl living in the United States and wanting like most children to "belong," I resented the stereotype that my Hispanic appearance called forth from many people I met.

3   Growing up in a large urban center in New Jersey during the 1960s, I suffered from what I think of as "cultural schizophrenia." Our life was designed by my parents as a microcosm of their *casas* on the island. We spoke in Spanish, ate Puerto Rican food bought at the *bodega,* and practiced strict Catholicism at a church that allotted us a one-hour slot each week for mass, performed in Spanish by a Chinese priest trained as a missionary for Latin America.

4   As a girl I was kept under strict surveillance by my parents, since my virtue and modesty were, by their cultural equation, the same as their honor. As a teenager I was lectured constantly on how to behave as a proper *senorita*. But it was a conflicting message I received, since the Puerto Rican mothers also encouraged their daughters to look and act like women and to dress in clothes our Anglo friends and their mothers found too "mature" and flashy. The difference was, and is, cultural; yet I often felt humiliated when I appeared at an American friend's party wearing a dress more suitable to a semiformal than to a playroom birthday celebration. At Puerto Rican festivities, neither the music nor the colors we wore could be too loud.

5   I remember Career Day in our high school, when teachers told us to come dressed as if for a job interview. It quickly became obvious that to the Puerto Rican girls "dressing up" meant wearing their mother's ornate jewelry and clothing, more appropriate (by mainstream standards) for the company Christmas party than as daily office attire. That morning I had agonized in front of my closet, trying to figure out what a "career girl" would wear. I knew how to dress for school (at the Catholic school I attended, we all wore uniforms), I knew how to dress for Sunday mass, and I knew what dresses to wear for parties at my relatives' homes. Though I do not recall the precise details of my Career Day outfit, it must have been a composite of these choices. But I remember a comment my friend (an Italian American) made in later years that coalesced my impressions of that day. She said that at the business school she was attending, the Puerto Rican girls always stood out for wearing "everything at once." She meant, of course, too much jewelry, too many accessories. On that day at school we were simply made the negative models by the nuns, who were themselves not credible fashion experts to any of us. But it was painfully obvious to me that to the others, in their tailored skirts and silk blouses, we must have seemed "hopeless" and "vulgar." Though I now know that most adolescents feel out of step much of the time, I also know that for the Puerto Rican girls of my generation that sense was intensified. The way our teachers and classmates looked at us that day in school was just a taste of the cultural clash that awaited us in the real world, where prospective employers and men on the street would often misinterpret our tight skirts and jingling bracelets as a "come-on."

6   Mixed cultural signals have perpetuated certain stereotypes—for example, that of the Hispanic woman as the "hot tamale" or sexual firebrand. It is a one-dimensional view that the media have found easy to promote. In their special

vocabulary, advertisers have designated "sizzling" and "smoldering" as the adjectives of choice for describing not only the foods but also the women of Latin America. From conversations in my house I recall hearing about the harassment that Puerto Rican women endured in factories where the "boss-men" talked to them as if sexual innuendo was all they understood, and worse, often gave them the choice of submitting to their advances or being fired.

It is custom, however, not chromosomes, that leads us to choose scarlet 7 over pale pink. As young girls it was our mothers who influenced our decisions about clothes and colors—mothers who had grown up on a tropical island where the natural environment was a riot of primary colors, where showing your skin was one way to keep cool as well as to look sexy. Most important of all, on the island, women perhaps felt freer to dress and move more provocatively since, in most cases, they were protected by the traditions, mores, and laws of a Spanish/Catholic system of morality and machismo whose main rule was: *You may look at my sister, but if you touch her I will kill you.* The extended family and church structure could provide a young woman with a circle of safety in her small pueblo on the island; if a man "wronged" a girl, everyone would close in to save her family honor.

My mother has told me about dressing in her best party clothes on Saturday 8 nights and going to the town's plaza to promenade with her girlfriends in front of the boys they liked. The males were thus given an opportunity to admire the women and to express their admiration in the form of *piropos:* erotically charged street poems they composed on the spot. (I have myself been subjected to a few *piropos* while visiting the island, and they can be outrageous, although custom dictates that they must never cross into obscenity.) This ritual, as I understand it, also entails a show of studied indifference on the woman's part; if she is "decent," she must not acknowledge the man's impassioned words. So I do understand how things can be lost in translation. When a Puerto Rican girl dressed in her idea of what is attractive meets a man from the mainstream culture who has been trained to react to certain types of clothing as a sexual signal, a clash is likely to take place. I remember the boy who took me to my first formal dance leaning over to plant a sloppy, overeager kiss painfully on my mouth; when I didn't respond with sufficient passion, he remarked resentfully: "I thought you Latin girls were supposed to mature early," as if I were expected to *ripen* like a fruit or vegetable, not just grow into womanhood like other girls.

It is surprising to my professional friends that even today some people, 9 including those who should know better, still put others "in their place." It happened to me most recently during a stay at a classy metropolitan hotel favored by young professional couples for weddings. Late one evening after the theater, as I walked toward my room with a colleague (a woman with whom I was coordinating an arts program), a middle-aged man in a tuxedo, with a young girl in satin and lace on his arm, stepped directly into our path. With his champagne glass extended toward me, he exclaimed "Evita!"

Our way blocked, my companion and I listened as the man half-recited, 10 half-bellowed "Don't Cry for Me, Argentina." When he finished, the young girl said: "How about a round of applause for my daddy?" We complied, hoping this would bring the silly spectacle to a close. I was becoming aware that our little group was attracting the attention of the other guests. "Daddy" must have perceived this too, and he once more barred the way as we tried to walk past him. He began to shout-sing a ditty to the tune of "La Bamba"—except the lyrics were about a girl named María whose exploits rhymed with her name and gonorrhea. The girl kept saying "Oh, Daddy" and looking at me with pleading eyes. She wanted me to laugh along with the others. My companion and I stood silently waiting for the man to end his offensive song. When he finished, I looked not at him but at his daughter. I advised her calmly never to ask her father what he had done in the army. Then I walked between them and to my room. My friend complimented me on my cool handling of the situation, but I confessed that I had really wanted to push the jerk into the swimming pool. This same man—probably a corporate executive, well-educated, even worldly by most standards—would not have been likely to regale an Anglo woman with a dirty song in public. He might have checked his impulse by assuming that she could be somebody's wife or mother, or at least *somebody* who might take offense. But, to him, I was just an Evita or a María: merely a character in his cartoon-populated universe.

11   Another facet of the myth of the Latin woman in the United States is the menial, the domestic—María the housemaid or countergirl. It's true that work as domestics, as waitresses, and in factories is all that's available to women with little English and few skills. But the myth of the Hispanic menial—the funny maid, mispronouncing words and cooking up a spicy storm in a shiny California kitchen—has been perpetuated by the media in the same way that "Mammy" from *Gone with the Wind* became America's idea of the black woman for generations. Since I do not wear my diplomas around my neck for all to see, I have on occasion been sent to that "kitchen" where some think I obviously belong.

12   One incident has stayed with me, though I recognize it as a minor offense. My first public poetry reading took place in Miami, at a restaurant where a luncheon was being held before the event. I was nervous and excited as I walked in with notebook in hand. An older woman motioned me to her table, and thinking (foolish me) that she wanted me to autograph a copy of my newly published slender volume of verse, I went over. She ordered a cup of coffee from me, assuming that I was the waitress. (Easy enough to mistake my poems for menus, I suppose.) I know it wasn't an intentional act of cruelty. Yet of all the good things that happened later, I remember that scene most clearly, because it reminded me of what I had to overcome before anyone would take me seriously. In retrospect I understand that my anger gave my reading fire. In fact, I have almost always taken any doubt in my abilities as a challenge, the result most often being the satisfaction of winning a convert, of seeing the cold, appraising eyes warm to my words, the body language change, the smile that indicates I have opened some avenue for communication. So that day as I read, I looked directly at that woman. Her lowered eyes told me she was embarrassed

at her faux pas, and when I willed her to look up at me, she graciously allowed me to punish her with my full attention. We shook hands at the end of the reading and I never saw her again. She has probably forgotten the entire incident, but maybe not.

Yet I am one of the lucky ones. There are thousands of Latinas without the privilege of an education or the entrees into society that I have. For them life is a constant struggle against the misconceptions perpetuated by the myth of the Latina. My goal is to try to replace the old stereotypes with a much more interesting set of realities. Every time I give a reading, I hope the stories I tell, the dreams and fears I examine in my work, can achieve some universal truth that will get my audience past the particulars of my skin color, my accent, or my clothes. 13

I once wrote a poem in which I called all Latinas "God's brown daughters." This poem is really a prayer of sorts, offered upward, but also, through the human-to-human channel of art, outward. It is a prayer for communication and for respect. In it, Latin women pray "in Spanish to an Anglo God/with a Jewish heritage," and they are "fervently hoping/that if not omnipotent,/at least He be bilingual." 14

COMPREHENSION

1. What is the thesis of the essay?
2. What does Cofer mean by the expression "cultural schizophrenia" (paragraph 3)?
3. Define the following words: *coveted* (paragraph 1), *Anglo* (paragraph 4), *coalesced* (paragraph 5), *machismo* (paragraph 7), and *entrees* (paragraph 13).

RHETORIC

1. Cofer uses many anecdotes in her discussion of stereotyping. How does this affect the tone of the essay?
2. Who is the implied audience for this essay? What aspects of the writing led you to your conclusion?
3. This essay is written in the first person, which tends to reveal a lot about the writer's personality. What adjectives come to mind when you think of the writer's singular voice?
4. Although this essay has a sociological theme, Cofer demonstrates that she has a poet's sensitivity toward language. What in the following sentence from paragraph 7 demonstrates this poetic style: "It is custom, however, not chromosomes, that leads us to choose scarlet over pale pink"? Select two other sentences from the essay that demonstrate Cofer's stylistic talent, and explain why they, too, are poetic.
5. In paragraph 8, Cofer contrasts cultural perceptions related to Hispanic and Anglo behavior. How is the paragraph structured so that this difference is demonstrated dramatically?
6. Cofer uses quotation marks to emphasize the connotation of certain words. Explain the significance of the following words: *mature* (paragraph 4), *hopeless* (paragraph 5), *hot tamale* (paragraph 6), *wronged* (paragraph 7), and *decent* (paragraph 8).

WRITING

1. Write a problem-solution essay in which you discuss the reasons behind cultural stereotyping and provide suggestions on how to overcome stereotyped thinking.
2. **Writing an Argument:** In an essay, argue for or against the proposition that stereotyping is excusable because it often is based on learned assumptions about which an individual cannot be expected to have knowledge.

NETWORKING
Applying 21st-Century Literacies

Examining Stereotypes in Television Shows and Commercials: Select an ethnic, racial, or cultural group, and explain how group members undergo stereotyping through their depiction in the media, particularly television shows or commercials. Use specific examples from specific programs or commercials to support your claims.

Globalization: The Super-Story

Thomas L. Friedman

Thomas L. Friedman (b. 1953) was born in Minneapolis, Minnesota. He majored in Mediterranean studies at Brandeis University (BA 1975) and received an MA in modern Middle Eastern studies from Oxford University in 1978. As journalist, author, television commentator, and op-ed contributor to the New York Times, *Friedman tries to provide unbiased viewpoints on cultural, political, and economic issues. From 1979 to 1984 he was the* Times *correspondent in Beirut, Lebanon, and subsequently until 1988 served as bureau chief in Jerusalem. His book recounting his 10 years in the Middle East,* From Beirut to Jerusalem *(1983), received the National Book Award for nonfiction. Friedman also has published* The Lexus and the Olive Tree: Understanding Globalization *(2000),* The World Is Flat: A Brief History of the Twenty-First Century *(2005),* Hot, Flat, and Crowded: Why We Need a Green Revolution—And How It Can Renew America *(2008), and a collection of essays,* Longitudes and Attitudes: Explaining the World after September 11 *(2002), which contains the following selection.*

1   I am a big believer in the idea of the super-story, the notion that we all carry around with us a big lens, a big framework, through which we look at the world, order events, and decide what is important and what is not. The events of 9/11 did not happen in a vacuum. They happened in the context of a new international system—a system that cannot explain everything but *can* explain

and connect more things in more places on more days than anything else. That new international system is called globalization. It came together in the late 1980s and replaced the previous international system, the cold war system, which had reigned since the end of World War II. This new system is the lens, the super-story, through which I viewed the events of 9/11.

I define globalization as the inexorable integration of markets, transportation systems, and communication systems to a degree never witnessed before—in a way that is enabling corporations, countries, and individuals to reach around the world farther, faster, deeper, and cheaper than ever before, and in a way that is enabling the world to reach into corporations, countries, and individuals farther, faster, deeper, and cheaper than ever before.

Several important features of this globalization system differ from those of the cold war system in ways that are quite relevant for understanding the events of 9/11. I examined them in detail in my previous book, *The Lexus and the Olive Tree*, and want to simply highlight them here.

The cold war system was characterized by one overarching feature—and that was *division*. That world was a divided-up, chopped-up place, and whether you were a country or a company, your threats and opportunities in the cold war system tended to grow out of who you were divided from. Appropriately, this cold war system was symbolized by a single word—*wall*, the Berlin Wall.

The globalization system is different. It also has one overarching feature—and that is *integration*. The world has become an increasingly interwoven place, and today, whether you are a company or a country, your threats and opportunities increasingly derive from who you are connected to. This globalization system is also characterized by a single word—*web*, the World Wide Web. So in the broadest sense we have gone from an international system built around division and walls to a system increasingly built around integration and webs. In the cold war we reached for the hotline, which was a symbol that we were divided but at least two people were in charge—the leaders of the United States and the Soviet Union. In the globalization system we reach for the Internet, which is a symbol that we are all connected and nobody is quite in charge.

Everyone in the world is directly or indirectly affected by this new system, but not everyone benefits from it, not by a long shot, which is why the more it becomes diffused, the more it also produces a backlash by people who feel overwhelmed by it, homogenized by it, or unable to keep pace with its demands.

The other key difference between the cold war system and the globalization system is how power is structured within them. The cold war system was built primarily around nation-states. You acted on the world in that system through your state. The cold war was a drama of states confronting states, balancing states, and aligning with states. And, as a system, the cold war was balanced at the center by two superstates, two superpowers: the United States and the Soviet Union.

The globalization system, by contrast, is built around three balances, which overlap and affect one another. The first is the traditional balance of power between nation-states. In the globalization system, the United States is now the sole and dominant superpower and all other nations are subordinate to it to one degree or another. The shifting balance of power between the United States and other states, or simply between other states, still very much matters for the stability of this system. And it can still explain a lot of the news you read on the front page of the paper, whether it is the news of China balancing Russia, Iran balancing Iraq, or India confronting Pakistan.

9   The second important power balance in the globalization system is between nation-states and global markets. These global markets are made up of millions of investors moving money around the world with the click of a mouse. I call them the Electronic Herd, and this herd gathers in key global financial centers—such as Wall Street, Hong Kong, London, and Frankfurt—which I call the Supermarkets. The attitudes and actions of the Electronic Herd and the Supermarkets can have a huge impact on nation-states today, even to the point of triggering the downfall of governments. Who ousted Suharto in Indonesia in 1998? It wasn't another state, it was the Supermarkets, by withdrawing their support for, and confidence in, the Indonesian economy. You also will not understand the front page of the newspaper today unless you bring the Supermarkets into your analysis. Because the United States can destroy you by dropping bombs, but the Supermarkets can destroy you by downgrading your bonds. In other words, the United States is the dominant player in maintaining the globalization game board, but it is hardly alone in influencing the moves on that game board.

10   The third balance that you have to pay attention to—the one that is really the newest of all and the most relevant to the events of 9/11—is the balance between individuals and nation-states. Because globalization has brought down many of the walls that limited the movement and reach of people, and because it has simultaneously wired the world into networks, it gives more power to *individuals* to influence both markets and nation-states than at any other time in history. Whether by enabling people to use the Internet to communicate instantly at almost no cost over vast distances, or by enabling them to use the Web to transfer money or obtain weapons designs that normally would have been controlled by states, or by enabling them to go into a hardware store now and buy a five-hundred-dollar global positioning device, connected to a satellite, that can direct a hijacked airplane—globalization can be an incredible force-multiplier for individuals. Individuals can increasingly act on the world stage directly, unmediated by a state.

11   So you have today not only a superpower, not only Supermarkets, but also what I call "super-empowered individuals." Some of these super-empowered individuals are quite angry, some of them quite wonderful—but all of them are now able to act much more directly and much more powerfully on the world stage.

12   Osama bin Laden declared war on the United States in the late 1990s. After he organized the bombing of two American embassies in Africa, the U.S. Air Force retaliated with a cruise missile attack on his bases in Afghanistan as though he were another nation-state. Think about that: on one day in 1998, the United States fired 75 cruise missiles at bin Laden. The United States fired 75

cruise missiles, at $1 million apiece, at a person! That was the first battle in history between a superpower and a super-empowered angry man. September 11 was just the second such battle.

Jody Williams won the Nobel Peace Prize in 1997 for helping to build 13 an international coalition to bring about a treaty outlawing land mines. Although nearly 120 governments endorsed the treaty, it was opposed by Russia, China, and the United States. When Jody Williams was asked, "How did you do that? How did you organize one thousand different citizens' groups and nongovernmental organizations on five continents to forge a treaty that was opposed by the major powers?" she had a very brief answer: "E-mail." Jody Williams used e-mail and the networked world to super-empower herself.

Nation-states, and the American superpower in particular, are still hugely 14 important today, but so too now are Supermarkets and super-empowered individuals. You will never understand the globalization system, or the front page of the morning paper—or 9/11—unless you see each as a complex interaction between all three of these actors: states bumping up against states, states bumping up against Supermarkets, and Supermarkets and states bumping up against super-empowered individuals—many of whom, unfortunately, are super-empowered angry men.

COMPREHENSION

1. What is Friedman's "super-story"? How does he define it?
2. What are the main features of globalization? How does globalization differ from the system characterized by the cold war? Explain the "three balances" (paragraphs 8–10) that Friedman writes about.
3. What does Friedman mean by "super-empowered" individuals (paragraph 11)?

RHETORIC

1. What is Friedman's thesis or claim in this essay? Where does it appear?
2. How and why does Friedman create a personal voice as well as a colloquial style in this selection? What is the effect?
3. What definitions does Friedman establish? Are the definitions too abstract, or does he provide sufficient explanations and evidence? Explain.
4. Locate instances of classification and of comparison and contrast. Why does Friedman use these rhetorical strategies? How do the two methods complement each other?
5. Friedman uses several metaphors in this essay. What are they, and how do they function to enhance meaning?
6. Why does the writer discuss 9/11 in the final three paragraphs? What is the effect on the overall message and purpose of the essay?

WRITING

1. In groups of three or four, use Friedman's essay to brainstorm about globalization. Construct a list of ideas and attributes. Using this list, write a definition essay exploring the subject of globalization. Include comparison and contrast or classification, or both, to help organize the essay.
2. Write a personal essay on how you think globalization is affecting your life.
3. **Writing an Argument:** Write a letter to Friedman, either agreeing or disagreeing with his opinions concerning globalization, supporting or refuting his ideas, or offering alternative views.

NETWORKING
Applying 21st-Century Literacies

Crafting a Comment: Like letters to the editors of newspapers, comments on online articles and blog posts offer readers a chance to question or otherwise engage with published texts. Approach question 3 under Writing from a more concise angle: Imagine as you craft your response that it will be a comment posted after the article, a comment visible, potentially, to anyone from around the world. Include one or two link(s) to credible articles, data, or Web sites that support your response.

A World Not Neatly Divided

Amartya Sen

Amartya Sen (b. 1933), born in Santiniketan, India, was awarded the Nobel Prize in Economics in 1988 for his groundbreaking work on welfare economics. Educated at Presidency College in Calcutta and Cambridge University (PhD, 1959), Sen has taught at Harvard University, the London School of Economics, and Oxford University; currently, he is a professor at Trinity College, Cambridge University. His major works, all of which investigate the role of poverty and inequality in the world, include Collective Choice and Social Welfare *(1970),* On Economic Inequality *(1973),* Poverty and Famines: An Essay on Entitlement and Deprivation *(1981),* Commodities and Capabilities *(1985),* Development as Freedom *(1999), and* Identity and Violence: The Illusion of Destiny *(2006). In the following essay, which appeared in* the New York Times *in 2001, Sen suggests that generalizations about "civilization" tend to blur the realities of complex cultures.*

When people talk about clashing civilizations, as so many politicians and aca- 1
demics do now, they can sometimes miss the central issue. The inadequacy of
this thesis begins well before we get to the question of whether civilizations
must clash. The basic weakness of the theory lies in its program of categorizing
people of the world according to a unique, allegedly commanding system of
classification. This is problematic because civilizational categories are crude
and inconsistent and also because there are other ways of seeing people (linked
to politics, language, literature, class, occupation, or other affiliations).

The befuddling influence of a singular classification also traps those who 2
dispute the thesis of a clash: To talk about "the Islamic world" or "the Western
world" is already to adopt an impoverished vision of humanity as unalterably
divided. In fact, civilizations are hard to partition in this way, given the diversi-
ties within each society as well as the linkages among different countries and
cultures. For example, describing India as a "Hindu civilization" misses the
fact that India has more Muslims than any other country except Indonesia and
possibly Pakistan. It is futile to try to understand Indian art, literature, music,
food, or politics without seeing the extensive interactions across barriers of
religious communities. These include Hindus and Muslims, Buddhists, Jains,
Sikhs, Parsees, Christians (who have been in India since at least the fourth century, well before England's conversion to Christianity), Jews (present since the
fall of Jerusalem), and even atheists and agnostics. Sanskrit has a larger atheistic
literature than exists in any other classical language. Speaking of India as a
Hindu civilization may be comforting to the Hindu fundamentalist, but it is an
odd reading of India.

A similar coarseness can be seen in the other categories invoked, like "the 3
Islamic world." Consider Akbar and Aurangzeb, two Muslim emperors of the
Mogul dynasty in India. Aurangzeb tried hard to convert Hindus into Muslims
and instituted various policies in that direction, of which taxing the non-Muslims
was only one example. In contrast, Akbar reveled in his multiethnic court and
pluralist laws, and issued official proclamations insisting that no one "should
be interfered with on account of religion" and that "anyone is to be allowed to
go over to a religion that pleases him."

If a homogeneous view of Islam were to be taken, then only one of these 4
emperors could count as a true Muslim. The Islamic fundamentalist would
have no time for Akbar; Prime Minister Tony Blair, given his insistence that
tolerance is a defining characteristic of Islam, would have to consider excom-
municating Aurangzeb. I expect both Akbar and Aurangzeb would protest, and
so would I. A similar crudity is present in the characterization of what is called
"Western civilization." Tolerance and individual freedom have certainly been
present in European history. But there is no dearth of diversity here, either.
When Akbar was making his pronouncements on religious tolerance in Agra, in
the 1590s, the Inquisitions were still going on; in 1600, Giordano Bruno was
burned at the stake, for heresy, in Campo dei Fiori in Rome.

Dividing the world into discrete civilizations is not just crude. It propels us 5
into the absurd belief that this partitioning is natural and necessary and must

overwhelm all other ways of identifying people. That imperious view goes not only against the sentiment that "we human beings are all much the same," but also against the more plausible understanding that we are diversely different. For example, Bangladesh's split from Pakistan was not connected with religion, but with language and politics.

6   Each of us has many features in our self-conception. Our religion, important as it may be, cannot be an all-engulfing identity. Even a shared poverty can be a source of solidarity across the borders. The kind of division highlighted by, say, the so-called "antiglobalization" protesters—whose movement is, incidentally, one of the most globalized in the world—tries to unite the underdogs of the world economy and goes firmly against religious, national, or "civilizational" lines of division.

7   The main hope of harmony lies not in any imagined uniformity, but in the plurality of our identities, which cut across each other and work against sharp divisions into impenetrable civilizational camps. Political leaders who think and act in terms of sectioning off humanity into various "worlds" stand to make the world more flammable—even when their intentions are very different. They also end up, in the case of civilizations defined by religion, lending authority to religious leaders seen as spokesmen for their "worlds." In the process, other voices are muffled and other concerns silenced. The robbing of our plural identities not only reduces us; it impoverishes the world.

COMPREHENSION

1. According to Sen, what is the "basic weakness" underlying the idea that the world is composed of "clashing civilizations" (paragraph 1)?
2. What does the writer mean by "singular classification" (paragraph 2)? Why is classifying people in terms of their civilization "crude and inconsistent"? Why is applying singular classification to religions and other features of society wrong?
3. What, according to Sen, is "the main hope of harmony" (paragraph 7) in the world?

RHETORIC

1. What argumentative strategy does Sen employ in the introductory paragraph? What point of view is he arguing against?
2. While arguing against a certain type of classification, Sen actually uses classification as a rhetorical strategy. How, precisely, does he employ classification to organize his argument?
3. What examples does Sen use to support his argument? Why does he use them? Why does he decide not to provide illustrations near the end of the selection?
4. What transitional devices serve to unify the essay?
5. How effective is Sen's concluding paragraph? Does it serve to confirm his claim? Why or why not?

WRITING

1. Write an essay about the problems you see in your community or on campus. Explain how singular classification might explain some of these problems.
2. In an analytical essay, explain how singular classification might help explain the events of September 11, 2001.
3. **Writing an Argument:** Write an essay in which you demonstrate that singular classification actually can be helpful in framing public discourse about groups, nations, or civilizations.

NETWORKING
Applying 21st-Century Literacies

Scripting a Presentation: Use PowerPoint or a similar storyboarding program to create an oral presentation responding to question 1 under Writing. Use animation, images, and text together to effectively illustrate your point about singular classification's role in a specific problem or problems on your campus.

The Arab World

Edward T. Hall

Edward T. Hall (b. 1914) was born in Missouri and earned a master's degree at the University of Arkansas and a PhD in anthropology at Columbia University. He was a professor of anthropology at the Illinois Institute of Technology and at Northwestern University. Hall is also the author of many books on anthropology and culture, among the most famous of which are The Silent Language *(1959),* The Hidden Dimension *(1966),* The Dance of Life *(1983),* Hidden Differences: Doing Business with the Japanese *(1987), and* Understanding Cultural Differences: Germans, French and Americans *(1990). In this selection from* The Hidden Dimension, *Hall demonstrates how such basic concepts as public and private space are perceived far differently depending on one's culture of origin.*

In spite of over two thousand years of contact, Westerners and Arabs still do 1 not understand each other. Proxemic research reveals some insights into this difficulty. Americans in the Middle East are immediately struck by two conflicting sensations. In public they are compressed and overwhelmed by smells, crowding, and high noise levels; in Arab homes Americans are apt to rattle around, feeling exposed and often somewhat inadequate because of too much space! (The Arab houses and apartments of the middle and upper classes which

Americans stationed abroad commonly occupy are much larger than the dwell-
ings such Americans usually inhabit.) Both the high sensory stimulation which
is experienced in public places and the basic insecurity which comes from being
in a dwelling that is too large provide Americans with an introduction to the
sensory world of the Arab.

Behavior in Public

2   Pushing and shoving in public places is characteristic of Middle Eastern culture.
Yet it is not entirely what Americans think it is (being pushy and rude) but stems
from a different set of assumptions concerning not only the relations between
people but how one experiences the body as well. Paradoxically, Arabs consider
northern Europeans and Americans pushy, too. This was very puzzling to me
when I started investigating these two views. How could Americans who stand
aside and avoid touching be considered pushy? I used to ask Arabs to explain
this paradox. None of my subjects was able to tell me specifically what particulars of American behavior were responsible, yet they all agreed that the impression was widespread among Arabs. After repeated unsuccessful attempts to
gain insight into the cognitive world of the Arab on this particular point, I filed
it away as a question that only time would answer. When the answer came, it
was because of a seemingly inconsequential annoyance.

3   While waiting for a friend in a Washington, D.C., hotel lobby and wanting
to be both visible and alone, I had seated myself in a solitary chair outside the
normal stream of traffic. In such a setting most Americans follow a rule, which
is all the more binding because we seldom think about it, that can be stated as
follows: As soon as a person stops or is seated in a public place, there balloons
around him a small sphere of privacy which is considered inviolate. The size of
the sphere varies with the degree of crowding, the age, sex, and the importance
of the person, as well as the general surroundings. Anyone who enters this zone
and stays there is intruding. In fact, a stranger who intrudes, even for a specific
purpose, acknowledges the fact that he has intruded by beginning his request
with "Pardon me, but can you tell me . . . ?"

4   To continue, as I waited in the deserted lobby, a stranger walked up to
where I was sitting and stood close enough so that not only could I easily touch
him but I could even hear him breathing. In addition, the dark mass of his body
filled the peripheral field of vision on my left side. If the lobby had been
crowded with people, I would have understood his behavior, but in an empty
lobby his presence made me exceedingly uncomfortable. Feeling annoyed by
this intrusion, I moved my body in such a way as to communicate annoyance.
Strangely enough, instead of moving away, my actions seemed only to encourage him, because he moved even closer. In spite of the temptation to escape the
annoyance, I put aside thoughts of abandoning my post, thinking, "To hell with
it. Why should I move? I was here first and I'm not going to let this fellow drive
me out even if he is a boor." Fortunately, a group of people soon arrived whom
my tormentor immediately joined. Their mannerisms explained his behavior,

for I knew from both speech and gestures that they were Arabs. I had not been able to make this crucial identification by looking at my subject when he was alone because he wasn't talking and he was wearing American clothes.

In describing the scene later to an Arab colleague, two contrasting patterns 5 emerged. My concept and my feelings about my own circle of privacy in a "public" place immediately struck my Arab friend as strange and puzzling. He said, "After all, it's a public place, isn't it?" Pursuing this line of inquiry, I found that in Arab thought I had no rights whatsoever by virtue of occupying a given spot; neither my place nor my body was inviolate! For the Arab, there is no such thing as an intrusion in public. Public means public. With this insight, a great range of Arab behavior that had been puzzling, annoying, and sometimes even frightening began to make sense. I learned, for example, that if *A* is standing on a street corner and *B* wants his spot, *B* is within his rights if he does what he can to make *A* uncomfortable enough to move. In Beirut only the hardy sit in the last row in a movie theater, because there are usually standees who want seats and who push and shove and make such a nuisance that most people give up and leave. Seen in this light, the Arab who "intruded" on my space in the hotel lobby had apparently selected it for the very reason I had: It was a good place to watch two doors and the elevator. My show of annoyance, instead of driving him away, had only encouraged him. He thought he was about to get me to move.

Another silent source of friction between Americans and Arabs is in an area 6 that Americans treat very informally—the manners and rights of the road. In general, in the United States we tend to defer to the vehicle that is bigger, more powerful, faster, and heavily laden. While a pedestrian walking along a road may feel annoyed he will not think it unusual to step aside for a fast-moving automobile. He knows that because he is moving he does not have the right to the space around him that he has when he is standing still (as I was in the hotel lobby). It appears that the reverse is true with the Arabs who apparently *take on rights to space as they move.* For someone else to move into a space an Arab is also moving into is a violation of his rights. It is infuriating to an Arab to have someone else cut in front of him on the highway. It is the American's cavalier treatment of moving space that makes the Arab call him aggressive and pushy.

Concepts of Privacy

The experience described above and many others suggested to me that Arabs 7 might actually have a wholly contrasting set of assumptions concerning the body and the rights associated with it. Certainly the Arab tendency to shove and push each other in public and to feel and pinch women in public conveyances would not be tolerated by Westerners. It appeared to me that they must not have any concept of a private zone outside the body. This proved to be precisely the case.

In the Western world, the person is synonymous with an individual inside 8 a skin. And in northern Europe generally, the skin and even the clothes may be inviolate. You need permission to touch either if you are a stranger. This rule applies in some parts of France, where the mere touching of another person during an argument used to be legally defined as assault. For the Arab the location of the person in relation to the body is quite different. The person exists somewhere down inside the body. The ego is not completely hidden, however, because it can be reached very easily with an insult. It is protected from touch but not from words. The dissociation of the body and the ego may explain why the public amputation of a thief's hand is tolerated as standard punishment in Saudi Arabia. It also sheds light on why an Arab employer living in a modern apartment can provide his servant with a room that is a boxlike cubicle approximately 5 by 10 by 4 feet in size that is not only hung from the ceiling to conserve floor space but has an opening so that the servant can be spied on.

9   As one might suspect, deep orientations toward the self such as the one just described are also reflected in the language. This was brought to my attention one afternoon when an Arab colleague who is the author of an Arab-English dictionary arrived in my office and threw himself into a chair in a state of obvious exhaustion. When I asked him what had been going on, he said: "I have spent the entire afternoon trying to find the Arab equivalent of the English word 'rape.' There is no such word in Arabic. All my sources, both written and spoken, can come up with no more than an approximation, such as 'He took her against her will.' There is nothing in Arabic approaching your meaning as it is expressed in that one word."

10   Differing concepts of the placement of the ego in relation to the body are not easily grasped. Once an idea like this is accepted, however, it is possible to understand many other facets of Arab life that would otherwise be difficult to explain. One of these is the high population density of Arab cities like Cairo, Beirut, and Damascus. According to the animal studies described in the earlier chapters [of *The Hidden Dimension*], the Arabs should be living in a perpetual behavioral sink. While it is probable that Arabs are suffering from population pressures, it is also just as possible that continued pressure from the desert has resulted in a cultural adaptation to high density which takes the form described above. Tucking the ego down inside the body shell not only would permit higher population densities but would explain why it is that Arab communications are stepped up as much as they are when compared to northern European communication patterns. Not only is the sheer noise level much higher, but the piercing look of the eyes, the touch of the hands, and the mutual bathing in the warm moist breath during conversation represent stepped up sensory inputs to a level which many Europeans find unbearably intense.

11   The Arab dream is for lots of space in the home, which unfortunately many Arabs cannot afford. Yet when he has space, it is very different from what one finds in most American homes. Arab spaces inside their upper middle-class homes are tremendous by our standards. They avoid partitions because Arabs *do not like to be alone.* The form of the home is such as to hold the family together inside a single protective shell, because Arabs are deeply involved with each other. Their personalities are intermingled and take nourishment from each other like the roots and soil. If one is not with people and actively involved in

some way, one is deprived of life. An old Arab saying reflects this value: "Paradise without people should not be entered because it is Hell." Therefore, Arabs in the United States often feel socially and sensorially deprived and long to be back where there is human warmth and contact.

Since there is no physical privacy as we know it in the Arab family, not even a 12 word for privacy, one could expect that the Arabs might use some other means to be alone. Their way to be alone is to stop talking. Like the English, an Arab who shuts himself off in this way is not indicating that anything is wrong or that he is withdrawing, only that he wants to be alone with his own thoughts or does not want to be intruded upon. One subject said that her father would come and go for days at a time without saying a word, and no one in the family thought anything of it. Yet for this very reason, an Arab exchange student visiting a Kansas farm failed to pick up the cue that his American hosts were mad at him when they gave him the "silent treatment." He only discovered something was wrong when they took him to town and tried forcibly to put him on a bus to Washington, D.C., the headquarters of the exchange program responsible for his presence in the U.S.

Arab Personal Distances

Like everyone else in the world, Arabs are unable to formulate specific rules for 13 their informal behavior patterns. In fact, they often deny that there are any rules, and they are made anxious by suggestions that such is the case. Therefore, in order to determine how the Arab sets distances, I investigated the use of each sense separately. Gradually, definite and distinctive behavioral patterns began to emerge.

Olfaction occupies a prominent place in the Arab life. Not only is it one of 14 the distance-setting mechanisms, but it is a vital part of a complex system of behavior. Arabs consistently breathe on people when they talk. However, this habit is more than a matter of different manners. To the Arab good smells are pleasing and a way of being involved with each other. To smell one's friend is not only nice but desirable, for to deny him your breath is to act ashamed. Americans, on the other hand, trained as they are not to breathe in people's faces, automatically communicate shame in trying to be polite. Who would expect that when our highest diplomats are putting on their best manners they are also communicating shame? Yet this is what occurs constantly, because diplomacy is not only "eyeball to eyeball" but breath to breath.

By stressing olfaction, Arabs do not try to eliminate all the body's odors, 15 only to enhance them and use them in building human relationships. Nor are they self-conscious about telling others when they don't like the way they smell. A man leaving his house in the morning may be told by his uncle, "Habib, your stomach is sour and your breath doesn't smell too good. Better not talk too close to people today." Smell is even considered in the choice of a mate. When couples are being matched for marriage, the man's go-between will sometimes ask to smell the girl, who may be turned down if she doesn't "smell nice." Arabs recognize that smell and disposition may be linked.

16   In a word, the olfactory boundary performs two roles in Arab life. It enfolds those who want to relate and separates those who don't. The Arab finds it essential to stay inside the olfactory zone as a means of keeping tab on changes in emotion. What is more, he may feel crowded as soon as he smells something unpleasant. While not much is known about "olfactory crowding," this may prove to be as significant as any other variable in the crowding complex because it is tied directly to the body chemistry and hence to the state of health and emotions. . . . It is not surprising, therefore, that the olfactory boundary constitutes for the Arabs an informal distance-setting mechanism in contrast to the visual mechanisms of the Westerner.

Facing and Not Facing

17 One of my earliest discoveries in the field of intercultural communication was that the position of the bodies of people in conversation varies with the culture. Even so, it used to puzzle me that a special Arab friend seemed unable to walk and talk at the same time. After years in the United States, he could not bring himself to stroll along, facing forward while talking. Our progress would be arrested while he edged ahead, cutting slightly in front of me and turning sideways so we could see each other. Once in this position, he would stop. His behavior was explained when I learned that for the Arabs to view the other person peripherally is regarded as impolite, and to sit or stand back-to-back is considered very rude. You must be involved when interacting with Arabs who are friends.

18   One mistaken American notion is that Arabs conduct all conversations at close distances. This is not the case at all. On social occasions, they may sit on opposite sides of the room and talk across the room to each other. They are, however, apt to take offense when Americans use what are to them ambiguous distances, such as the four- to seven-foot social-consultative distance. They frequently complain that Americans are cold or aloof or "don't care." This was what an elderly Arab diplomat in an American hospital thought when the American nurses used "professional" distance. He had the feeling that he was being ignored, that they might not take good care of him. Another Arab subject remarked, referring to American behavior, "What's the matter? Do I smell bad? Or are they afraid of me?"

19   Arabs who interact with Americans report experiencing a certain flatness traceable in part to a very different use of the eyes in private and in public as well as between friends and strangers. Even though it is rude for a guest to walk around the Arab home eyeing things, Arabs look at each other in ways which seem hostile or challenging to the American. One Arab informant said that he was in constant hot water with Americans because of the way he looked at them without the slightest intention of offending. In fact, he had on several occasions barely avoided fights with American men who apparently thought their masculinity was being challenged because of the way he was looking at them. As noted earlier, Arabs look each other in the eye when talking with an intensity that makes most Americans highly uncomfortable.

Involvement

As the reader must gather by now, Arabs are involved with each other on many [20] different levels simultaneously. Privacy in a public place is foreign to them. Business transactions in the bazaar, for example, are not just between buyer and seller, but are participated in by everyone. Anyone who is standing around may join in. If a grownup sees a boy breaking a window, he must stop him even if he doesn't know him. Involvement and participation are expressed in other ways as well. If two men are fighting, the crowd must intervene. On the political level, *to fail to intervene* when trouble is brewing is to take sides, which is what our State Department always seems to be doing. Given the fact that few people in the world today are even remotely aware of the cultural mold that forms their thoughts, it is normal for Arabs to view *our* behavior as though it stemmed from *their* own hidden set of assumptions.

Feelings about Enclosed Spaces

In the course of my interviews with Arabs the term "tomb" kept cropping up in [21] conjunction with enclosed space. In a word, Arabs don't mind being crowded by people but hate to be hemmed in by walls. They show a much greater overt sensitivity to architectural crowding than we do. Enclosed space must meet at least three requirements that I know of if it is to satisfy the Arabs: There must be plenty of unobstructed space in which to move around (possibly as much as a thousand square feet); very high ceilings—so high in fact that they do not normally impinge on the visual field; and, in addition, there must be an unobstructed view. It was spaces such as these in which the Americans referred to earlier felt so uncomfortable. One sees the Arab's need for a view expressed in many ways, even negatively, for to cut off a neighbor's view is one of the most effective ways of spiting him. In Beirut one can see what is known locally as the "spite house." It is nothing more than a thick, four-story wall, built at the end of a long fight between neighbors, on a narrow strip of land for the express purpose of denying a view of the Mediterranean to any house built on the land behind. According to one of my informants, there is also a house on a small plot of land between Beirut and Damascus which is completely surrounded by a neighbor's wall built high enough to cut off the view from all windows!

Boundaries

Proxemic patterns tell us other things about Arab culture. For example, the [22] whole concept of the boundary as an abstraction is almost impossible to pin down. In one sense, there are no boundaries. "Edges" of towns, yes, but permanent boundaries out in the country (hidden lines), no. In the course of my work with Arab subjects I had a difficult time translating our concept of a boundary into terms which could be equated with theirs. In order to clarify the distinctions between the two very different definitions, I thought it might be helpful to pinpoint acts which constituted trespass. To date, I have been unable to discover anything even remotely resembling our own legal concept of trespass.

23   Arab behavior in regard to their own real estate is apparently an extension of, and therefore consistent with, their approach to the body. My subjects simply failed to respond whenever trespass was mentioned. They didn't seem to understand what I meant by this term. This may be explained by the fact that they organize relationships with each other according to closed social systems rather than spatially. For thousands of years Moslems, Marinites, Druses, and Jews have lived in their own villages, each with strong kin affiliations. Their hierarchy of loyalties is: first to one's self, then to kinsman, townsman, or tribesman, co-religionist and/or countryman. Anyone not in these categories is a stranger. Strangers and enemies are very closely linked, if not synonymous, in Arab thought. Trespass in this context is a matter of who you are, rather than a piece of land or a space with a boundary that can be denied to anyone and everyone, friend and foe alike.

24   In summary, proxemic patterns differ. By examining them it is possible to reveal hidden cultural frames that determine the structure of a given people's perceptual world. Perceiving the world differently leads to differential definitions of what constitutes crowded living, different interpersonal relations, and a different approach to both local and international politics.

COMPREHENSION

1. This excerpt is from Hall's book *The Hidden Dimension*. What is the hidden dimension, according to the author?
2. In paragraph 10, Hall explains that "differing concepts of the placement of the ego in relation to the body are not easily grasped." What does he mean by this statement? How is it relevant to the theme of his essay?
3. The title of this essay is "The Arab World." What does the term *world* mean within the context of the essay?
4. Define the following words: *proxemic* (paragraph 1), *paradox* (paragraph 2), *inviolate* (paragraph 3), *defer* (paragraph 6), *olfaction* (paragraph 14), and *peripherally* (paragraph 17).

RHETORIC

1. Anthropology is often thought of as an intellectual pursuit. How would you characterize Hall's voice, considering his style of language and method of analysis?
2. How does Hall develop his comparison and contrast of the American versus the Arab perception of manners and driving?
3. People often favor their own perspective of life over a foreign perspective. Is Hall's comparison value-free, or does he seem to prefer one cultural system to another? Explain by making reference to his tone.

4. Who is the implied audience for this essay? Explain your view.
5. Hall makes use of personal anecdote in explaining his theme. What other forms of support does he offer? Cite at least two others and provide an example of each.
6. Writers often have various purposes in writing—for example, to entertain, to inform, to effect change, to advise, or to persuade. What is Hall's purpose or purposes in writing this essay? Explain your view.

WRITING

1. Write an expository essay in which you explain the use and interpretation of personal space by observing students in social situations at your college or university.
2. Write a personal anecdote about a time in your life when cultural perception caused a conflict between yourself and another person.
3. **Writing an Argument:** In a persuasive essay, argue for or against the proposition that some cultures are better than others.

NETWORKING
Applying 21st-Century Literacies

Creating a Poster Series: Design a series of posters that explore the use and interpretation of personal space on your campus—and that, collectively, make a point about it. As in question 1 under Writing, observe students in social contexts on campus: Then either take photographs, create illustrations or creative figures (such as graphs), or use images from other sources to depict what you observed. Use these images as a prominent component of your posters, and use minimal, effective text (a tagline, a series of parallel words or phrases) to clarify or cleverly suggest your purpose or point. (*Note:* If you take your own photos, whether they are staged shots or cameos, be sure to ask your subjects for permission to feature them in your poster series.)

S y n t h e s i s :   C o n n e c t i o n s   f o r   C r i t i c a l   T h i n k i n g

1. Cofer writes about Latino culture and Reed about African American culture in their respective essays. What connections do they make between their subjects and cultural affiliation and alienation? How do they present their ideas? How are their tones similar? How are they different?
2. Write an essay exploring the topic of culture and civilization in the essays by Hall, Sen, and Friedman.
3. Consider the current position of women in our culture. Refer to any three essays in this chapter to support your main observations.
4. How does one's experience of being an outsider or stranger to a culture affect one's understanding of that culture? Use essays from this chapter to support your key points.

5. Write an essay exploring the shape of contemporary civilization as it is reflected in the essays in this chapter. Cite specific support from at least three of the selections you have read.

6. How does a nation maintain a strong sense of self and still remain open to outside influences? Is a national identity crucial to a nation's survival? Use the opinions of representative authors in this chapter to address the question.

7. Is there such a thing as ethnic character, something that distinguishes African Americans from Latinos or from Asian Americans? What factors contribute to identification with culture and with nation? Cite at least three essays in this chapter.

8. Argue for or against the proposition that Americans are ignorant of both the contributions and the values of non-Western cultures in our country. Refer specifically to Reed, Hall, and Friedman.

NETWORKING
Applying 21st-Century Literacies

1. Set up a chat room or blog with five class members, and discuss the differences in cultural perspectives among the writers in this chapter. Use hyperlinks to drive the discussion to additional sources.

2. Conduct an online search for reliable information on Judith Ortiz Cofer and Ishmael Reed. Keeping track of your sources, and using sources from at least three different media, write a brief research paper on these writers' perceptions of ethnicity and the American experience.

CH 7   www.mhhe.com/**mhreaderbrief1e**

■ *Image Gallery:* Chapter images in color

■ *History, Culture, and Civilization:* Information on the authors in this chapter

■ *Ch. 7 Networking*

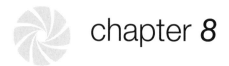

chapter **8**

Government, Politics, and Social Justice
How Do We Decide What Is Fair?

Recent studies indicate that American students have an extremely limited understanding of government and politics. In fact, one-third of all high school juniors cannot identify the main purpose of the Declaration of Independence or say in which century it was signed. This document is one of the selections in this chapter. If we are ignorant of such a basic instrument in the making of our history and society, what might that say about our concepts of citizenship? Do we now see ourselves purely as economic units—that is, in terms of our ability or potential to make money—or as consumers—that is, in terms of the roles we play in spending it? Other notable essays on government, politics, and social justice in this chapter will help us understand our cultural legacies and what has traditionally been thought of as the impetus in developing America as a country.

Skilled writers can bring politics and issues of social justice to life, enabling us to develop a sense of the various processes that have influenced the development of cultures over time. By studying the course of history and politics, we develop causal notions of how events are interrelated and how traditions have evolved. The study of history and politics can be an antidote to the continuous "present tense" of the media, which often have the power to make us believe we live from moment to moment, discouraging reflection on serious issues such as why we live the way we do and how we came to be the people we are. Essays, speeches, documents, biographies, narratives, and many other literary forms capture events and illuminate the past while holding up a mirror to the present. On the one hand, our political story can be brought to life out of the plain but painfully eloquent artifacts of oral culture. On the other, Thomas Jefferson employs classical rhetorical structures—notably argumentation—in outlining democratic vistas in the Declaration of Independence.

Even the briefest reflection will remind us of how important political processes and institutions are. Put simply, a knowledge of government and politics, and of our quest for social justice, validates our memory, a remembrance of how important the past is to our current existence. When, for example, Martin Luther King Jr. approaches the subject of oppression from a theological perspective, we are reminded of how important the concept of freedom is to our heritage and the various ways it can be addressed. Indeed, had we been more familiar with chapters in human history, we might have avoided some of the commensurate responses to the crises in our own era. The essays in this chapter help remind us—as the philosopher Santayana warned—that "those who forget the lessons of history are doomed to repeat them."

Only with a knowledge of government and politics can we make informed choices. Through a study of government and politics, we learn about challenges and opportunities, conflicts and their resolutions, and the use and abuse of power across time in numerous cultures and civilizations. It is through the study of historical processes and political institutions that we seek to define ourselves and to learn how we have evolved.

PREVIEWING THE CHAPTER

As you read the selections in this chapter and respond to them in discussion and writing, consider the following questions:

- On what specific events does the author concentrate? What is the time frame?
- What larger historical and political issues concern the author?
- From what perspective does the author treat the subject—from that of participant, observer, commentator, or some other role?
- What is the author's purpose in treating events and personalities—to explain, to instruct, to amuse, to criticize, or to celebrate?
- What does the author learn about history and politics from his or her inquiry into events?
- What sorts of conflicts—historical, political, economic, social, religious—emerge in the essay?
- Are there any correspondences among the essays? What analogies do the authors themselves draw?
- What is the relationship of people and personalities to the events under consideration?
- Which biases and ideological positions do you detect in the authors' works?
- How has your understanding of history and politics been challenged by the essays in this chapter?

Classic and Contemporary Images

HAVE WE MADE ADVANCES IN CIVIL RIGHTS?

Using a Critical Perspective   Are you optimistic or skeptical about the lofty words in the Declaration of Independence announcing that everyone is created equal? How do these two visual texts, one advertising a slave auction and the other presenting a campaign poster for President Barack Obama, affect your response? What aspects of these visual texts stand out? What is your emotional and ethical response to the images? What do the two illustrations tell us about the evolution of equal rights and justice in the United States?

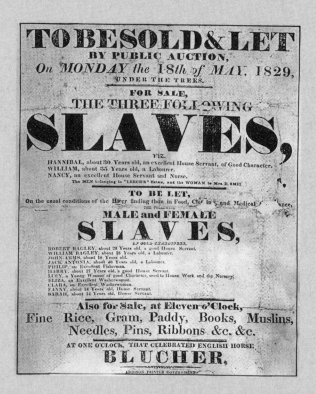

Advertisement of slaves for sale by the company Hewlett & Bright,
May 13, 1835.

Hope, by Shepard Fairey. Street artist and illustrator Shepard Fairey created this iconic poster, based on an Associated Press photograph, for the 2008 Obama presidential campaign.

Classic and Contemporary Essays
WHAT IS THE AMERICAN DREAM?

Both Thomas Jefferson and Martin Luther King Jr. are now safely ensconced within the pantheon of American historical figures. The following two writing samples help indicate why. Both are concerned with perhaps the most significant issue that concerns contemporary humankind: freedom. Jefferson creates a doctrine that is powerful owing to his use of concise and powerful language, which he employs both to enumerate British offenses and to call on his fellow Americans to revolt if need be. While his list of grievances may seem unquestionably correct to the contemporary mind, one must consider that Jefferson was a product of the Enlightenment, when philosophers had finally turned their attention to the primacy of individual rights after millennia of living under monarchic rule. King also provides us with the powerful theme of freedom in his famous speech; while his reflections address the peculiarly American racial divide, his style contains many biblical references, and his rhetoric is that of the sermon. You should consider why these two documents, regardless of their historical context, seem to be milestones in our nation's history.

The Declaration of Independence
In Congress, July 4, 1776

Thomas Jefferson

Thomas Jefferson (1743–1826) was governor of Virginia during the American Revolution, America's first secretary of state, and the third president of the United States. He had a varied and monumental career as politician, public servant, scientist, architect, educator (he founded the University of Virginia), and man of letters. Jefferson attended the Continental Congress in 1775, where he wrote the rough draft of the Declaration of Independence. Other hands made contributions to the document that was signed on July 4, 1776, but the wording, style, structure, and spirit of the final version are distinctly Jefferson's. Like Thomas Paine, Benjamin Franklin, James Madison, and other major figures of the Revolutionary era, Jefferson was notable for his use of prose as an instrument for social and political change. In the Declaration of Independence, we see the direct, precise, logical, and persuasive statement of revolutionary principles that makes the document one of the best-known and best-written texts in world history. Jefferson died in his home at Monticello on July 4, 50 years to the day from the signing of the Declaration of Independence.

When in the Course of human events it becomes necessary for one people to 1 dissolve the political bands which have connected them with another, and to assume among the powers of the earth, the separate and equal station to which the Laws of Nature and of Nature's God entitle them, a decent respect to the opinions of mankind requires that they should declare the causes which impel them to the separation.

We hold these truths to be self-evident, that all men are created equal, that 2 they are endowed by their Creator with certain unalienable Rights, that among these are Life, Liberty and the pursuit of Happiness.—That to secure these rights, Governments are instituted among Men, deriving their just powers from the consent of the governed.—That whenever any Form of Government becomes destructive of these ends, it is the Right of the People to alter or to abolish it, and to institute new Government, laying its foundation on such principles and organizing its powers in such form, as to them shall seem most likely to effect their Safety and Happiness. Prudence, indeed, will dictate that Governments long established should not be changed for light and transient causes; and accordingly all experience hath shewn that mankind are more disposed to suffer, while evils are sufferable, than to right themselves by abolishing the forms to which they are accustomed. But when a long train of abuses and usurpations, pursuing invariably the same Object evinces a design to reduce them under absolute Despotism, it is their right, it is their duty, to throw off such Government, and to provide new Guards for their future security.—Such has been the patient sufferance of these Colonies; and such is now the necessity which constrains them to alter their former Systems of Government. The history of the present King of Great Britain is a history of repeated injuries and usurpations, all having in direct object the establishment of an absolute Tyranny over these States. To prove this, let Facts be submitted to a candid world.

He has refused his Assent to Laws, the most wholesome and necessary for 3 the public good.

He has forbidden his Governors to pass Laws of immediate and pressing 4 importance, unless suspended in their operation till his Assent should be obtained; and when so suspended, he has utterly neglected to attend to them.

He has refused to pass other Laws for the accommodation of large districts 5 of people, unless those people would relinquish the right of Representation in the Legislature, a right inestimable to them and formidable to tyrants only.

He has called together legislative bodies at places unusual, uncomfortable, 6 and distant from the depository of their public Records, for the sole purpose of fatiguing them into compliance with his measures.

He has dissolved Representative Houses repeatedly, for opposing with 7 manly firmness his invasions on the rights of the people.

He has refused for a long time, after such dissolutions, to cause others to be 8 elected; whereby the Legislative powers, incapable of Annihilation, have returned to the People at large for their exercise; the State remaining in the mean time exposed to all the dangers of invasion from without, and convulsions within.

9   He has endeavored to prevent the population of these States; for that purpose obstructing the Laws for Naturalization of Foreigners; refusing to pass others to encourage their migrations hither, and raising the conditions of new Appropriations of Lands.

10   He has obstructed the Administration of Justice, by refusing his Assent to Laws for establishing Judiciary powers.

11   He has made Judges dependent on his Will alone, for the tenure of their offices, and the amount and payment of their salaries.

12   He has erected a multitude of New Offices, and sent hither swarms of Officers to harass our people, and eat out their substance.

13   He has kept among us, in times of peace, Standing Armies without the Consent of our legislatures.

14   He has affected to render the Military independent of and superior to the Civil power.

15   He has combined with others to subject us to a jurisdiction foreign to our constitution, and unacknowledged by our laws; giving his Assent to their Acts of pretended Legislation:

> For quartering large bodies of armed troops among us:

> For protecting them, by a mock Trial, from punishment for any Murders which they should commit on the Inhabitants of these States:

> For cutting off our Trade with all parts of the world:

> For imposing Taxes on us without our Consent:

> For depriving us in many cases, of the benefits of Trial by jury:

> For transporting us beyond Seas to be tried for pretended offences:

> For abolishing the free System of English Laws in a neighboring Province, establishing therein an Arbitrary government, and enlarging its Boundaries so as to render it at once an example and fit instrument for introducing the same absolute rule into these Colonies:

> For taking away our Charters, abolishing our most valuable Laws and altering fundamentally the Forms of our Governments:

> For suspending our own Legislatures, and declaring themselves invested with power to legislate for us in all cases whatsoever.

16   He has abdicated Government here, by declaring us out of his Protection and waging War against us.

17   He has plundered our seas, ravaged our Coasts, burnt our towns, and destroyed the lives of our people.

18   He is at this time transporting large Armies of foreign Mercenaries to complete the works of death, desolation and tyranny, already begun with

circumstances of Cruelty & Perfidy scarcely paralleled in the most barbarous ages, and totally unworthy the Head of a civilized nation.

He has constrained our fellow Citizens taken Captive on the high Seas to 19 bear Arms against their Country, to become the executioners of their friends and Brethren, or to fall themselves by their Hands.

He has excited domestic insurrections amongst us, and has endeavored to 20 bring on the inhabitants of our frontiers, the merciless Indian Savages, whose known rule of warfare, is an undistinguished destruction of all ages, sexes and conditions.

In every stage of these Oppressions We have Petitioned for Redress in the 21 most humble terms: Our repeated Petitions have been answered only by repeated injury. A Prince, whose character is thus marked by every act which may define a Tyrant, is unfit to be the ruler of a free people.

Nor have We been wanting in attentions to our British brethren. We have 22 warned them from time to time of attempts by their legislature to extend an unwarrantable jurisdiction over us. We have reminded them of the circumstances of our emigration and settlement here. We have appealed to their native justice and magnanimity, and we have conjured them by the ties of our common kindred to disavow these usurpations, which would inevitably interrupt our connections and correspondence. They too have been deaf to the voice of justice and of consanguinity. We must, therefore, acquiesce in the necessity, which denounces our Separation, and hold them, as we hold the rest of mankind, Enemies in War, in Peace Friends.

We, therefore, the Representatives of the United States of America, in 23 General Congress, Assembled, appealing to the Supreme Judge of the world for the rectitude of our intentions, do, in the Name, and by Authority of the good People of these Colonies, solemnly publish and declare, That these United Colonies are, and of Right ought to be Free and Independent States; that they are Absolved from all Allegiance to the British Crown, and that all political connection between them and the State of Great Britain, is and ought to be totally dissolved; and that as Free and Independent States, they have full Power to levy War, conclude Peace, contract Alliances, establish Commerce, and to do all other Acts and Things which Independent States may of right do. And for the support of this Declaration, with a firm reliance on the protection of divine Providence, we mutually pledge to each other our Lives, our Fortunes and our sacred Honor.

COMPREHENSION

1. Explain Jefferson's main and subordinate purposes in this document.
2. What is Jefferson's key assertion or argument? Mention several reasons that he gives to support his argument.
3. Summarize Jefferson's definition of human nature and government.

RHETORIC

1. There are many striking words and phrases in the Declaration of Independence, notably in the beginning. Locate three such examples, and explain their connotative power and effectiveness.
2. Jefferson and his colleagues had to draft a document designed for several audiences. What audiences did they have in mind? How do their language and style reflect their awareness of multiple audiences?
3. The Declaration of Independence is a classic model of syllogistic reasoning and deductive argument. What is its major premise, and where is this premise stated? The minor premise? The conclusion?
4. What sort of inductive evidence does Jefferson offer?
5. Why is the middle portion, or body, of the Declaration of Independence considerably longer than the introduction or conclusion? What holds the body together?
6. Explain the function and effect of parallel structure in this document.

WRITING

1. Discuss the relevance of the Declaration of Independence to politics today.
2. Explain in an essay why the Declaration of Independence is a model of effective prose.
3. Write your own declaration of independence—from family, employer, required courses, or the like. Develop this declaration as an op-ed piece for a newspaper.
4. **Writing an Argument:** Do you believe that "all men are created equal"? Justify your answer in an argumentative essay.

NETWORKING
Applying 21st-Century Literacies

Reading and Responding to a Web Site: At the Chapter 8 Networking page (*www.mhhe.com/mhreaderbrief1e*), link to *ushistory.org*'s Web site about the Declaration of Independence. In the menu on the left side of the page, choose several sections to explore: under "Document," you can see images of actual drafts of the text and read transcripts of it in several incarnations, including its final form. The "Related Information" page links to information about people, events, and other laws that influenced the document. Among other resources are two timelines (one chronicling the events of the Revolutionary War) and Jefferson's personal account of writing the Declaration of Independence. After spending some time with the site and the texts and links on it, write a reader response essay arguing that this site's contextual information either enhances or distracts from the content of the document itself. Explain how and why this was your reading experience; support your position with specific examples.

I Have a Dream

Martin Luther King Jr.

Martin Luther King Jr. (1929–1968) was born in Atlanta, Georgia, and received degrees from Morehouse College, Crozer Theological Seminary, Boston University, and Chicago Theological Seminary. As Baptist clergyman, civil rights leader, founder and president of the Southern Christian Leadership Conference, and 1964 Nobel Peace Prize winner, King was a celebrated advocate of nonviolent resistance to achieve equality and racial integration in the world. King was a gifted orator and a highly persuasive writer. His books include Stride toward Freedom *(1958),* Letter from Birmingham City Jail *(1963),* Strength to Love *(1963),* Why We Can't Wait *(1964), and* Where Do We Go from Here: Chaos or Community? *(1967), a book published shortly before he was assassinated on April 4, 1968, in Memphis, Tennessee. This selection, a milestone of American oratory, was the keynote address at the March on Washington, August 28, 1963.*

I am happy to join with you today in what will go down in history as the great- 1
est demonstration for freedom in the history of our nation.

Fivescore years ago, a great American, in whose symbolic shadow we stand 2
today, signed the Emancipation Proclamation. This momentous decree came as
a great beacon light of hope to millions of Negro slaves who had been seared in
the flames of withering injustice. It came as a joyous daybreak to end the long
night of their captivity.

But one hundred years later, the Negro still is not free; one hundred years 3
later, the life of the Negro is still sadly crippled by the manacles of segregation
and the chains of discrimination; one hundred years later, the Negro lives on a
lonely island of poverty in the midst of a vast ocean of material prosperity; one
hundred years later, the Negro is still languishing in the corners of American
society and finds himself in exile in his own land.

So we've come here today to dramatize a shameful condition. In a sense 4
we've come to our nation's capital to cash a check. When the architects of our
republic wrote the magnificent words of the Constitution and the Declaration
of Independence, they were signing a promissory note to which every American was to fall heir. This note was the promise that all men, yes, black men
as well as white men, would be guaranteed the unalienable rights of life, liberty,
and the pursuit of happiness.

It is obvious today that America has defaulted on this promissory note in so 5
far as her citizens of color are concerned. Instead of honoring this sacred obligation, America has given the Negro people a bad check; a check which has come
back marked "insufficient funds." We refuse to believe that there are insufficient funds in the great vaults of opportunity of this nation. And so we've come

to cash this check, a check that will give us upon demand the riches of freedom and the security of justice.

6   We have also come to this hallowed spot to remind America of the fierce urgency of now. This is no time to engage in the luxury of cooling off or to take the tranquilizing drug of gradualism. Now is the time to make real the promises of democracy; now is the time to rise from the dark and desolate valley of segregation to the sunlit path of racial justice; now is the time to lift our nation from the quicksands of racial injustice to the solid rock of brotherhood; now is the time to make justice a reality for all God's children. It would be fatal for the nation to overlook the urgency of the moment. This sweltering summer of the Negro's legitimate discontent will not pass until there is an invigorating autumn of freedom and equality.

7   Nineteen sixty-three is not an end, but a beginning. And those who hope that the Negro needed to blow off steam and will now be content, will have a rude awakening if the nation returns to business as usual.

8   There will be neither rest nor tranquility in America until the Negro is granted his citizenship rights. The whirlwinds of revolt will continue to shake the foundations of our nation until the bright day of justice emerges.

9   But there is something that I must say to my people who stand on the warm threshold which leads into the palace of justice. In the process of gaining our rightful place we must not be guilty of wrongful deeds.

10   Let us not seek to satisfy our thirst for freedom by drinking from the cup of bitterness and hatred. We must forever conduct our struggle on the high plane of dignity and discipline. We must not allow our creative protest to degenerate into physical violence. Again and again we must rise to the majestic heights of meeting physical force with soul force.

11   The marvelous new militancy which has engulfed the Negro community must not lead us to a distrust of all white people, for many of our white brothers, as evidenced by their presence here today, have come to realize that their destiny is tied up with our destiny and they have come to realize that their freedom is inextricably bound to our freedom. This offense we share mounted to storm the battlements of injustice must be carried forth by a biracial army. We cannot walk alone.

12   And as we walk, we must make the pledge that we shall always march ahead. We cannot turn back. There are those who are asking the devotees of civil rights, "When will you be satisfied?" We can never be satisfied as long as the Negro is the victim of the unspeakable horrors of police brutality.

13   We can never be satisfied as long as our bodies, heavy with fatigue of travel, cannot gain lodging in the motels of the highways and the hotels of the cities. We cannot be satisfied as long as the Negro's basic mobility is from a smaller ghetto to a larger one.

14   We can never be satisfied as long as our children are stripped of their selfhood and robbed of their dignity by signs stating "for whites only." We cannot be satisfied as long as a Negro in Mississippi cannot vote and a Negro in New York believes he has nothing for which to vote. No, we are not satisfied, and we

will not be satisfied until justice rolls down like waters and righteousness like a mighty stream.

I am not unmindful that some of you have come here out of excessive trials 15 and tribulation. Some of you have come fresh from narrow jail cells. Some of you have come from areas where your quest for freedom left you battered by the storms of persecution and staggered by the winds of police brutality. You have been the veterans of creative suffering. Continue to work with the faith that unearned suffering is redemptive.

Go back to Mississippi; go back to Alabama; go back to South Carolina; go 16 back to Georgia; go back to Louisiana; go back to the slums and ghettos of the northern cities, knowing that somehow this situation can, and will be changed. Let us not wallow in the valley of despair.

So I say to you, my friends, that even though we must face the difficulties of 17 today and tomorrow, I still have a dream. It is a dream deeply rooted in the American dream that one day this nation will rise up and live out the true meaning of its creed—we hold these truths to be self-evident, that all men are created equal.

I have a dream that one day on the red hills of Georgia, sons of former 18 slaves and sons of former slave-owners will be able to sit down together at the table of brotherhood.

I have a dream that one day, even the state of Mississippi, a state sweltering 19 with the heat of injustice, sweltering with the heat of oppression, will be transformed into an oasis of freedom and justice.

I have a dream my four little children will one day live in a nation where 20 they will not be judged by the color of their skin but by the content of their character. I have a dream today!

I have a dream that one day, down in Alabama, with its vicious racists, with 21 its governor having his lips dripping with the words of interposition and nullification, that one day, right there in Alabama, little black boys and black girls will be able to join hands with little white boys and white girls as sisters and brothers. I have a dream today!

I have a dream that one day every valley shall be exalted, every hill and 22 mountain shall be made low, the rough places shall be made plain, and the crooked places shall be made straight and the glory of the Lord will be revealed and all flesh shall see it together.

This is our hope. This is the faith that I go back to the South with. 23

With this faith we will be able to hear out of the mountain of despair a stone 24 of hope. With this faith we will be able to transform the jangling discords of our nation into a beautiful symphony of brotherhood.

With this faith we will be able to work together, to pray together, to struggle 25 together, to go to jail together, to stand up for freedom together, knowing that we will be free one day. This will be the day when all of God's children will be able to sing with new meaning—"my country 'tis of thee; sweet land of liberty; of thee I sing; land where my fathers died, land of the pilgrims' pride; from every mountain side, let freedom ring"—and if America is to be a great nation, this must become true.

26   So let freedom ring from the prodigious hilltops of New Hampshire.
27   Let freedom ring from the mighty mountains of New York.
28   Let freedom ring from the heightening Alleghenies of Pennsylvania.
29   Let freedom ring from the snow-capped Rockies of Colorado.
30   Let freedom ring from the curvaceous slopes of California.
31   But not only that.
32   Let freedom ring from Stone Mountain of Georgia.
33   Let freedom ring from Lookout Mountain of Tennessee.
34   Let freedom ring from every hill and molehill of Mississippi, from every mountainside, let freedom ring.
35   And when we allow freedom to ring, when we let it ring from every village and hamlet, from every state and city, we will be able to speed up that day when all of God's children—black men and white men, Jews and Gentiles, Catholics and Protestants—will be able to join hands and to sing in the words of the old Negro spiritual, "Free at last, free at last; thank God Almighty, we are free at last."

COMPREHENSION

1. What is the main purpose of this speech? Where does King state this purpose most clearly?
2. Why does King make use of "fivescore years ago" (paragraph 2)? How is this more appropriate than simply saying "a hundred years ago"?
3. Who is King's audience? Where does he acknowledge the special historical circumstances influencing his speech?

RHETORIC

1. From what sources does King adapt phrases to give his work allusive richness?
2. What do the terms *interposition* and *nullification* (paragraph 21) mean? What is their historical significance?
3. Why does King make use of repetition? Does this technique work well in print? Explain.
4. What is the purpose of the extended metaphor in paragraphs 4 and 5? Which point in paragraph 3 does it refer to?
5. In which paragraphs does King address the problems of African Americans?
6. Why is this selection titled "I Have a Dream"? How do dreams serve as a motif for this speech?

WRITING

1. "I Have a Dream" is considered by many people to be among the greatest speeches delivered by an American. Do you think it deserves to be? Explain in an essay.
2. Write a comparative essay analyzing King's assessment of black Americans' condition in 1963 and their condition today. What do you think King would say if he knew of contemporary conditions?

3. Write your own "I Have a Dream" essay, basing it on your vision of America or of a special people.
4. **Writing an Argument:** Prepare a newspaper editorial advocating a solution to one aspect of racial, ethnic, or sexual injustice.

NETWORKING
Applying 21st-Century Literacies

Seeing vs. Reading the Text of a Speech: At the Chapter 8 Networking page (*www.mhhe.com/mhreaderbrief1e*), link to the video of Martin Luther King giving his famous "I Have a Dream" speech. How is the experience of watching and listening to this speech different from reading it? Compare and contrast these two types of experiencing a text, using "I Have a Dream" as an example. Consider what, beyond the words themselves, is *happening* in this video.

Synthesis: Classic and Contemporary Questions for Comparison

1. Compare the Declaration of Independence with King's speech in terms of language, style, and content. Are they equally powerful and resonant? Cite specific passages from the essays to illustrate your response.
2. Rewrite the Declaration of Independence in modern English as you believe Dr. King might have written it, reflecting his concerns about the African American and other minorities in this country. Include a list of grievances similar to the ones concerning British rule.
3. Write a research paper about the lives and times of King and Jefferson. Compare and contrast any significant events or pertinent biographical data in their backgrounds.

Is Texas America?

Molly Ivins

Molly Ivins (1944–2007), a humorous and typically irreverent newspaper commentator whose syndicated column appeared in about 350 newspapers, was born in California but grew up in Texas. The Lone Star State—and especially the Bush family—animated Ivins's writing and prompted her satirical assessment of Texas; its people, politics, and culture. She called Texas the Great State, "reactionary, cantankerous, and hilarious." Growing up in an affluent family, she learned to confront her conservative Republican father, arguing with him over civil rights and the Vietnam War. Ivins attended Smith

*College and the Institute for Political Science in Paris before earning a master's degree
at the Columbia Graduate School of Journalism. She worked for several newspapers,
including the* New York Times *and the monthly* Texas Observer, *and published six
books, among them* Molly Ivins Can't Say That, Can She? *(1991) and two books
on George Bush,* Shrub: The Short but Happy Life of George Bush *(2000) and*
Bushwacked *(2003). "There are two kinds of humor," Ivins once observed; one "makes
us chuckle about our foibles and shared humanity. The other kind holds people up to
public contempt and ridicule. That's what I do." In fact, the following essay, published
in the* Nation *in 2003, indicates that Ivins is adept at both kinds of humor.*

1   Well, sheesh. I don't know whether to warn you that because George Dubya
Bush is President the whole damn country is about to be turned into Texas (a
singularly horrible fate: as the country song has it: "Lubbock on Everythang")
or if I should try to stand up for us and convince the rest of the country we're
not all that insane.

2   Truth is, I've spent much of my life trying, unsuccessfully, to explode the
myths about Texas. One attempts to explain—with all good will, historical evidence, nasty statistics and just a bow of recognition to our racism—that Texas is
not *The Alamo* starring John Wayne. We're not *Giant*, we ain't a John Ford western. The first real Texan I ever saw on TV was *King of the Hill*'s Boomhauer, the
guy who's always drinking beer and you can't understand a word he says.

3   So, how come trying to explode myths about Texas always winds up reinforcing them? After all these years, I do not think it is my fault. The fact is, it's a
damned peculiar place. Given all the horseshit, there's bound to be a pony in
here somewhere. Just by trying to be honest about it, one accidentally under-
lines its sheer strangeness.

4   Here's the deal on Texas. It's big. So big there's about five distinct and different places here, separated from one another geologically, topographically,
botanically, ethnically, culturally and climatically. Hence our boring habit of
specifying East, West and South Texas, plus the Panhandle and the Hill Country. The majority of the state's blacks live in East Texas, making it more like
the Old South than the Old South is anymore. West Texas is, more or less, like
Giant, except, like every place else in the state, it has an incurable tendency toward the tacky and all the cowboys are brown. South Texas is 80 percent
Hispanic and a weird amalgam of cultures. You get names now like Shannon
Rodriguez, Hannah Gonzalez and Tiffany Ruiz. Even the Anglos speak English
with a Spanish accent. The Panhandle, which sticks up to damn near Kansas, is
High Plains, like one of those square states, Nebraska or the Dakotas, except
more brown folks. The Hill Country, smack dab in the middle, resembles nothing else in the state.

5   Plus, plopped on top of all this, we have three huge cities, all among the
ten largest in the country. Houston is Los Angeles with the climate of Calcutta, Dallas is Dutch (clean, orderly and conformist), while San Antonio is
Monterrey North. Many years ago I wrote of this state: "The reason the sky
is bigger here is because there aren't any trees. The reason folks here eat

grits is because they ain't got no taste. Cowboys mostly stink and it's hot, oh God, is it hot. . . . Texas is a mosaic of cultures, which overlap in several parts of the state, with the darker layers on the bottom. The cultures are black, Chicano, Southern, freak, suburban and shitkicker. (Shitkicker is dominant.) They are all rotten for women." All that's changed in thirty years is that suburban is now dominant, shitkicker isn't so ugly as it once was and the freaks are now Goths or something. So it could be argued we're becoming more civilized.

In fact, it was always easy to argue that: Texas has symphony orchestras 6 and great universities and perfect jewels of art museums (mostly in Fort Worth, of all places). It has lots of people who birdwatch, write PhD theses on esoteric subjects and speak French, for chrissake. But what still makes Texas Texas is that it's ignorant, cantankerous and ridiculously friendly. Texas is still resistant to Howard Johnsons, Interstate highways and some forms of phoniness. It is the place least likely to become a replica of everyplace else. It's authentically awful, comic and weirdly charming, all at the same time.

Culturally, Texans rather resemble both Alaskans (hunt, fish, hate gov- 7 ernment) and Australians (drink beer, hate snobs). The food is quite good— Mexican, barbecue, chili, shrimp and chicken-fried steak, an acquired taste. The music is country, blues, folk, mariachi, rockabilly and everything else you can think of. Mexican music—norteño, ranchero—is poised to cross over, as black music did in the 1950s.

If you want to understand George W. Bush—unlike his daddy, an unfortu- 8 nate example of a truly Texas-identified citizen—you have to stretch your imagination around a weird Texas amalgam: religion, anti-intellectualism and machismo. All big, deep strains here, but still an odd combination. Then add that Bush is just another li'l upper-class white boy out trying to prove he's tough.

9 The politics are probably the weirdest thing about Texas. The state has gone from one-party Democrat to one-party Republican in thirty years. Lyndon said when he signed the Civil Rights Act in 1964 that it would take two generations and cost the Democrats the South. Right on both counts. We like to think we're "past race" in Texas, but of course East Texas remains an ugly, glaring exception. After James Byrd Jr. was dragged to death near Jasper, only one prominent white politician attended his funeral—US Senator Kay Bailey Hutchison. Dubya, then governor, put the kibosh on the anti–hate crimes bill named in Byrd's memory. (The deal-breaker for Bush was including gays and lesbians. At a meeting last year of the Texas Civil Liberties Union board, vicious hate crimes against gays in both Dallas and Houston were discussed. I asked the board member from Midland if they'd been having any trouble with gay-bashing out there. "Hell, honey," she said, with that disastrous frankness one can grow so fond of, "there's not a gay in Midland would come out of the closet for fear people would think they're a Democrat.")

10 Among the various strains of Texas right-wingism (it is factually incorrect to call it conservatism) is some leftover loony John Birchism, now morphed into militias; country-club economic conservatism, à la George Bush *père*; and the usual batty antigovernment strain. Of course Texas grew on the tender mercies of the federal government—rural electrification, dams, generations of master pork-barrel politicians and vast subsidies to the oil and gas industry. But that has never interfered with Texans' touching but entirely erroneous belief that this is the Frontier, and that in the Old West every man pulled his own weight and depended on no one else. The myth of rugged individualism continues to afflict a generation raised entirely in suburbs with names like "Flowering Forest Hills of Lubbock."

11 The Populist movement was born in the Texas Hill Country, as genuinely democratic an uprising as this country has ever known. It produced legendary politicians for generations, including Ralph Yarborough, Sam Rayburn, Lyndon and even into the 1990s, with Agriculture Commissioner Jim Hightower. I think it is not gone, but only sleeping.

12 Texans retain an exaggerated sense of state identification, routinely identifying themselves when abroad as Texans, rather than Americans or from the United States. That aggravated provincialism has three sources. First, the state is so big (though not so big as Alaska, as they are sure to remind us) that it can take a couple of days hard travel just to get out of it. Second, we reinforce the sense of difference by requiring kids to study Texas history, including roughly ten years as an independent country. In state colleges, the course in Texas government is mandatory. Third, even national advertising campaigns pitch brands with a Texas accent here and certain products, like the pickup truck, are almost invariably sold with a Texas pitch. (Makes sense: Texas leads the nation with more than four million registered pickups.)

13 The founding myth is the Alamo. I was raised on the Revised Standard Version, which holds that while it was stupid of Travis and the gang to be there at all (Sam Houston told them to get the hell out), it was still an amazing last

stand. Stephen Harrigan in *The Gates of the Alamo* is closer to reality, but even he admits in the end there was something romantic and even noble about the episode, like having served in the Abraham Lincoln Brigade during the Spanish Civil War.

According to the demographers at Texas A&M (itself a source of much 14 Texas lore), Texas will become "majority minority" in 2008. Unfortunately, we won't see it in the voting patterns for at least a generation, and by then the Republicans will have the state so tied up by redistricting (recently the subject of a massive standoff, now over, in the legislature), it's unlikely to shift for another generation beyond that. The Christian right is heavily dominant in the Texas Republican Party. It was the genius of Karl Rove/George W. Bush to straddle the divide between the Christian right and the country club conservatives, which is actually a significant class split. The politics of resentment plays a large role on the Christian right: Fundamentalists are perfectly aware that they are held in contempt by "the intellectuals." (William Brann of Waco once observed, "The trouble with our Texas Baptists is that we do not hold them under water long enough." He was shot to death by an irate Baptist.) In Texas, "intellectual" is often used as a synonym for "snob." George W. Bush perfectly exemplifies that attitude.

Here in the National Laboratory for Bad Government, we have an anti- 15 quated and regressive tax structure—high property, high sales, no income tax. We consistently rank near the bottom by every measure of social service, education and quality of life (leading to one of our state mottoes, "Thank God for Mississippi"). Yet the state is incredibly rich in more than natural resources. The economy is now fully diversified, so plunges in the oil market can no longer throw the state into the bust cycle.

It is widely believed in Texas that the highest purpose of government is to 16 create "a healthy bidness climate." The legislature is so dominated by special interests that the gallery where the lobbyists sit is called "the owners' box." The consequences of unregulated capitalism, of special interests being able to buy government through campaign contributions, are more evident here because Texas is "first and worst" in this area. That Enron was a Texas company is no accident: Texas was also Ground Zero in the savings-and-loan scandals, is continually the site of major ripoffs by the insurance industry and has a rich history of gigantic chicanery going way back. Leland Beatty, an agricultural consultant, calls Enron "Billie Sol Estes Goes to College." Economists call it "control fraud" when a corporation is rotten from the head down. I sometimes think Texas government is a case of control fraud too.

We are currently saddled with a right-wing ideologue sugar daddy, James 17 Leininger out of San Antonio, who gives immense campaign contributions and wants school vouchers, abstinence education and the like in return. The result is a crew of breathtakingly right-wing legislators. This session, Representative Debbie Riddle of Houston said during a hearing, "Where did this idea come from that everybody deserves free education, free medical care, free whatever? It comes from Moscow, from Russia. It comes straight out of the pit of hell."

18   Texans for Lawsuit Reform, *aka* the bidness lobby, is a major player and has effectively eviscerated the judiciary with a two-pronged attack. While round after round of "tort reform" was shoved through the legislature, closing off access to the courts and protecting corporations from liability for their misdeeds, Karl Rove was busy electing all nine state Supreme Court justices. So even if you should somehow manage to get into court, you are faced with a bench noted for its canine fidelity to corporate special interests.

19   Here's how we make progress in Texas. Two summers ago, Governor Goodhair Perry (the man has a head of hair every Texan can be proud of, regardless of party) appointed an Enron executive to the Public Utilities Commission. The next day, Governor Goodhair got a $25,000 check from Ken Lay. Some thought there might be a connection. The guv was forced to hold a press conference, at which he explained that the whole thing was "totally coincidental." So that was a big relief.

20   We don't have a sunshine law in Texas; it's more like a partly cloudy law. But even here a major state appointee has to fill out a bunch of forms that are then public record. When the governor's office put out the forms on the Enron guy, members of the press, that alert guardian watchdog of democracy, noticed that the question about any unfortunate involvement with law enforcement looked funny. The governor's office had whited out the answers. A sophisticated cover-up. The alert guardian watchdogs were on the trail. We soon uncovered a couple of minor traffic violations and the following item: While out hunting a few years earlier, the Enron guy accidentally shot a whooping crane. As a result he had to pay a $15,000 fine under what is known in Texas as the In Danger Species Act. We print this. A state full of sympathetic hunters reacted with, "Hell, anybody could accidentally shoot a whooper." But the press stayed on the story and was able to report that the guy shot the whooper while on a goose hunt. Now the whooper is a large bird—runs up to five feet tall. The goose—short. Now we have a state full of hunters saying, "Hell, if this boy is too dumb to tell a whooper from a goose, maybe he shouldn't be regulatin' public utilities." He was forced to resign.

21   As Willie Nelson sings, if we couldn't laugh, we would all go insane. This is our redeeming social value and perhaps our one gift to progressives outside our borders. We do laugh. We have no choice. We have to have fun while trying to stave off the forces of darkness because we hardly ever win, so it's the only fun we get to have. We find beer and imagination helpful. The Billion Bubba March, the Spam-o-rama, the time we mooned the Klan, being embedded with the troops at the Holiday Inn in Ardmore, Oklahoma, singing "I'm Just an Asshole from El Paso" with Kinky Friedman and the Texas Jewboys, and "Up Against the Wall, Redneck Mother" with Ray Wylie Hubbard laughing at the loonies in the lege—does it get better than this? The late Bill Kugle of Athens is buried in the Texas State Cemetery. On the front of his stone are listed his service in the Marines in World War II, his years in the legislature, other titles and honors. On the back of the stone is, "He never voted for a Republican and never had much to do with them either."

We have lost some great freedom fighters in Texas during the past year. Billie 22
Carr, the great Houston political organizer (you'd've loved her: She got invited
to the White House during the middle of the Monica mess, sashayed through
the receiving line, looked Bill Clinton in the eye and said, "You dumb son of a
bitch"), always said she wanted her funeral to be like her whole life in politics:
It should start half an hour late, she wanted a balanced delegation of pallbearers—
one black, one brown, two women—and she wanted an open casket and a
name tag stuck over her left tit that said, "Hi there! My name is Billie Carr." We
did it all for her.

At the funeral of Malcolm McGregor, the beloved legislator and bibliophile 23
from El Paso, we heard "The Eyes of Texas" and the Aggie War Hymn played
on the bagpipes. At the service for Maury Maverick Jr. of San Antonio, and at
his request, J. Frank Dobie's poem "The Mustangs" was read by the poet Naomi
Shihab Nye. The last stanza is:

So sometimes yet, in the realities of silence and solitude,
For a few people unhampered a while by things,
The mustangs walk out with dawn, stand high, then
Sweep away, wild with sheer life, and free, free, free—
Free of all confines of time and flesh.

COMPREHENSION

1. How does Ivins answer the question posed by her title? In other words, what does
   Texas have that the United States in general possesses? What, according to Ivins, is
   unique about Texas?
2. In paragraph 9, Ivins writes, "The politics are probably the weirdest thing about
   Texas." What examples does she give to support her statement?
3. Ivins seems to warn us about the excesses of Texas life and politics, but clearly she
   is also fascinated by her home state. Does she reconcile these conflicting perspectives? Why or why not?

RHETORIC

1. What is Ivins's claim or main proposition? What are her minor propositions? Do
   you think that her argument is sound or valid? Justify your response.
2. How does Ivins establish herself as an authority on Texas? Would you accuse her of
   bias? Why or why not? Why might her opinions be congenial to an audience reading the *Nation*?
3. Ivins uses phrases like "Well, sheesh" (paragraph 1), "plopped on top"(paragraph 5),
   and "for crissake" (paragraph 6) in the essay. What is the effect of this colloquial
   style and tone? What is her purpose?
4. Locate varieties of humor in the essay. Do you think that Ivins employs humor
   effectively to advance her argument? Explain your response.
5. The essay contains four main sections. What is the core topic of each section? How
   do these topics overlap? What transitions serve to link the parts?

6. Throughout the essay, Ivins alludes to many aspects of Texas life, culture, people, and politics that we might not be familiar with. Do these allusions detract from the essay or make it too topical? Why, for instance, would Ivins want to end her essay with reference to the deaths of two Texans and an allusion to a poem by J. Frank Dobie?

WRITING

1. Write a humorous essay on the state in which you grew up. Decide in advance what varieties of humor and what tone you want to use.
2. Go online or to a library and find out more about a Texan (for instance, George W. Bush), a Texas trait (like *machismo*), or a Texas institution (for example, the state legislature), and then write an essay that seeks to either confirm or refute Ivins's presentation of the subject.
3. **Writing an Argument:** In an essay, argue for or against the proposition that Ivins is too biased and cruel in her exposé of Texas. Defend or refute her argument on a point-by-point basis.

NETWORKING
Applying 21st-Century Literacies

Reading a Visual in Context: In a two- or three-page response, summarize, analyze, and interpret the illustration that accompanies this essay (see page 289). In your response, consider how it works with this piece and what each text lends to the other.

Cyberspace: If You Don't Love It, Leave It

Esther Dyson

Esther Dyson (b. 1951) was born in Zurich, Switzerland; grew up in Princeton, New Jersey; and received a BA in economics from Harvard University. She is the daughter of Freeman Dyson, a physicist prominent in arms control. She was the editor and publisher of the widely respected computer newsletter Release 1.0. *She has also served as chairperson of the Electronic Frontier Foundation and on the boards of the Santa Fe Institute, the Global Business Network, and the Institute for East/West Studies. She served as a reporter for* Forbes *magazine for four years. The following essay appeared in the* New York Times Magazine *in July 1995. In it, Dyson defends the free-market approach to cyberspace content, arguing that regulation of the Internet is simply impossible and counterproductive.*

Something in the American psyche loves new frontiers. We hanker after wide-open spaces; we like to explore; we like to make rules instead of follow them. But in this age of political correctness and other intrusions on our national cult of independence, it's hard to find a place where you can go and be yourself without worrying about the neighbors.

There is such a place: cyberspace. Lost in the furor over porn on the Net is the exhilarating sense of freedom that this new frontier once promised—and still does in some quarters. Formerly a playground for computer nerds and techies, cyberspace now embraces every conceivable constituency: schoolchildren, flirtatious singles, Hungarian-Americans, accountants—along with pederasts and porn fans. Can they all get along? Or will our fear of kids surfing for cyberporn behind their bedroom doors provoke a crackdown?

The first order of business is to grasp what cyberspace *is*. It might help to leave behind metaphors of highways and frontiers and to think instead of real estate. Real estate, remember, is an intellectual, legal, artificial environment constructed *on top of* land. Real estate recognizes the difference between parkland and shopping mall, between red-light zone and school district, between church, state and drugstore.

In the same way, you could think of cyberspace as a giant and unbounded world of virtual real estate. Some property is privately owned and rented out; other property is common land; some places are suitable for children, and others are best avoided by all but the kinkiest citizens. Unfortunately, it's those places that are now capturing the popular imagination: places that offer bomb-making instructions, pornography, advice on how to procure stolen credit cards. They make cyberspace sound like a nasty place. Good citizens jump to a conclusion: Better regulate it.

The most recent manifestation of this impulse is the Exon-Coats Amendment, a well-meaning but misguided bill drafted by Senators Jim Exon, Democrat of Nebraska, and Daniel R. Coats, Republican of Indiana, to make cyberspace "safer" for children. Part of the telecommunications reform bill passed by the Senate and awaiting consideration by the House, the amendment would outlaw making "indecent communication" available to anyone under 18.[1] Then there's the Amateur Action bulletin board case, in which the owners of a porn service in Milpitas, Calif., were convicted in a Tennessee court of violating "community standards" after a local postal inspector requested that the material be transmitted to him.

Regardless of how many laws or lawsuits are launched, regulation won't work.

Aside from being unconstitutional, using censorship to counter indecency and other troubling "speech" fundamentally misinterprets the nature of cyberspace. Cyberspace isn't a frontier where wicked people can grab unsuspecting children, nor is it a giant television system that can beam offensive messages at unwilling viewers. In this kind of real estate, users have to *choose* where they

---

[1]The Communication Decency Act (CDA) was passed by Congress, but the Supreme Court ruled that it was unconstitutional in 1996.

visit, what they see, what they do. It's optional, and it's much easier to bypass a place on the Net than it is to avoid walking past an unsavory block of stores on the way to your local 7-Eleven.

8   Put plainly, cyberspace is a voluntary destination—in reality, many destinations. You don't just get "onto the net"; you have to go someplace in particular. That means that people can choose where to go and what to see. Yes, community standards should be enforced, but those standards should be set by cyberspace communities themselves, not by the courts or by politicians in Washington. What we need isn't Government control over all these electronic communities: We need self-rule.

9 What makes cyberspace so alluring is precisely the way in which it's *different* from shopping malls, television, highways and other terrestrial jurisdictions. But let's define the territory:

10   First, there are private e-mail conversations, akin to the conversations you have over the telephone or voice mail. These are private and consensual and require no regulation at all.

11   Second, there are information and entertainment services, where people can download anything from legal texts and lists of "great new restaurants" to game software or dirty pictures. These places are like bookstores, malls and movie houses—places where you go to buy something. The customer needs to request an item or sign up for a subscription; stuff (especially pornography) is not sent out to people who don't ask for it. Some of these services are free or included as part of a broader service like Compuserve or America Online; others charge and may bill their customers directly.

12   Third, there are "real" communities—groups of people who communicate among themselves. In real-estate terms, they're like bars or restaurants or bathhouses. Each active participant contributes to a general conversation, generally through posted messages. Other participants may simply listen or watch. Some are supervised by a moderator; others are more like bulletin boards—anyone is free to post anything. Many of these services started out unmoderated but are now imposing rules to keep out unwanted advertising, extraneous discussions or increasingly rude participants. Without a moderator, the decibel level often gets too high.

13   Ultimately, it's the rules that determine the success of such places. Some of the rules are determined by the supplier of content; some of the rules concern prices and membership fees. The rules may be simple: "Only high-quality content about oil-industry liability and pollution legislation: $120 an hour." Or: "This forum is unmoderated, and restricted to information about copyright issues. People who insist on posting advertising or unrelated material will be asked to desist (and may eventually be barred)." Or: "Only children 8 to 12, on school-related topics and only clean words. The moderator will decide what's acceptable."

14   Cyberspace communities evolve just the way terrestrial communities do: People with like-minded interests band together. Every cyberspace community

has its own character. Overall, the communities on Compuserve tend to be more techy or professional; those on America Online, affluent young singles; Prodigy, family oriented. Then there are independents like Echo, a hip, downtown New York service, or Women's Wire, targeted to women who want to avoid the male culture prevalent elsewhere on the Net. There's SurfWatch, a new program allowing access only to locations deemed suitable for children. On the Internet itself, there are lots of passionate noncommercial discussion groups on topics ranging from Hungarian politics (Hungary-Online) to copyright law.

And yes, there are also porn-oriented services, where people share dirty 15
pictures and communicate with one another about all kinds of practices, often anonymously. Whether these services encourage the fantasies they depict is subject to debate—the same debate that has raged about pornography in other media. But the point is that no one is forcing this stuff on anybody.

What's unique about cyberspace is that it liberates us from the tyranny of 16
government, where everyone lives by the rule of the majority. In a democracy, minority groups and minority preferences tend to get squeezed out, whether they are minorities of race and culture or minorities of individual taste. Cyberspace allows communities of any size and kind to flourish; in cyberspace, communities are chosen by the users, not forced on them by accidents of geography. This freedom gives the rules that preside in cyberspace a moral authority that rules in terrestrial environments don't have. Most people are stuck in the country of their birth, but if you don't like the rules of a cyberspace community, you can just sign off. Love it or leave it. Likewise, if parents don't like the rules of a given cyberspace community, they can restrict their children's access to it.

What's likely to happen in cyberspace is the formation of new communi- 17
ties, free of the constraints that cause conflict on earth. Instead of a global village, which is a nice dream but impossible to manage, we'll have invented another world of self-contained communities that cater to their own members' inclinations without interfering with anyone else's. The possibility of a real market-style evolution of governance is at hand. In cyberspace, we'll be able to test and evolve rules governing what needs to be governed—intellectual property, content and access control, rules about privacy and free speech. Some communities will allow anyone in; others will restrict access to members who qualify on one basis or another. Those communities that prove self-sustaining will prosper (and perhaps grow and split into subsets with ever-more-particular interests and identities). Those that can't survive—either because people lose interest or get scared off—will simply wither away.

In the near future, explorers in cyberspace will need to get better at defining 18
and identifying their communities. They will need to put in place—and accept—their own local governments, just as the owners of expensive real estate often prefer to have their own security guards rather than call in the police. But they will rarely need help from any terrestrial government.

Of course, terrestrial governments may not agree. What to do, for instance, 19
about pornography? The answer is labeling—not banning—questionable

material. In order to avoid censorship and lower the political temperature, it makes sense for cyberspace participants themselves to agree on a scheme for questionable items, so that people or automatic filters can avoid them. In other words, posting pornography in "alt.sex.bestiality" would be OK; it's easy enough for software manufacturers to build an automatic filter that would prevent you—or your child—from ever seeing that item on a menu. (It's as if all the items were wrapped with labels on the wrapper.) Someone who posted the same material under the title "Kid-Fun" could be sued for mislabeling.

20   Without a lot of fanfare, private enterprises and local groups are already producing a variety of labeling and ranking services, along with kid-oriented sites like Kidlink, EdWeb and Kids' Space. People differ in their tastes and values and can find services or reviewers on the Net that suit them in the same way they select books and magazines. Or they can wander freely if they prefer, making up their own itinerary.

21   In the end, our society needs to grow up. Growing up means understanding that there are no perfect answers, no all-purpose solutions, no government-sanctioned safe havens. We haven't created a perfect society on earth and we won't have one in cyberspace either. But at least we can have individual choice—and individual responsibility.

COMPREHENSION

1. The title of the essay is a variation of a phrase popularized in the 1960s. What is the original expression, and what was its significance? What is its relevance to this essay?
2. What is Dyson's thesis? Is it stated explicitly? If so, where in the essay does it occur? If it is merely suggested, how is it suggested, and where?
3. There are many forms of new media that are not considered communities. Why does Dyson refer to cyberspace as a community?
4. According to Dyson, what distinguishes cyberspace from physical space?
5. What does Dyson mean when she states that cyberspace needs "self-rule" (paragraph 8)?

RHETORIC

1. How does Dyson use her introduction to foreshadow her main concerns about censorship in cyberspace?
2. How does Dyson use metaphor in paragraphs 10–12 to help us understand the structure of cyberspace? Why is metaphor a particularly useful literary device when explaining a new concept?
3. Key to Dyson's views on cyberspace is that it is a "voluntary destination" (paragraph 8). What evidence does Dyson present that it is voluntary? What argument can be made that it is not always "voluntary"?
4. Who is the implied audience for this essay? What level of education does one need to have and how sophisticated about the world of cyberspace does one need to be in order to comprehend and process the author's views? Explain your answer.

5. Dyson refers to laws, rules, and regulations as strategies that various interest groups may use to determine access to content in cyberspace. How does Dyson distinguish these three related tactics? What significance does differentiating these methods have in her presentation of her argument?
6. Dyson concludes her essay with an analogy between human society and cyberspace culture. Why does she save this final support for last? How does it extend her argument rather than merely restate it?

WRITING

1. In paragraph 17, Dyson refers to the "global village," a term coined by the media critic Marshall McLuhan. For a research project, study McLuhan's views on the nature of the global village, and compare and contrast them to Dyson's views of the nature of cyberspace.
2. **Writing an Argument:** Dyson argues that technology can create filters, labeling and ranking services to prevent children from viewing inappropriate material. In an essay, argue for or against the proposition that there can be a nontechnological solution to this issue—for example, instilling values in children or developing a society that does not create a mystique about taboo subject matter.

NETWORKING
Applying 21st-Century Literacies

Exploring Virtual Communities: In a comparison-and-contrast essay, select three cyberspace communities and describe each one's character (refer to Dyson's reference to cyberspace communities in paragraph 14).

Obama vs. Marx

Alan Wolfe

Alan Wolfe (b. 1942) is an American educator and journalist. He was born in Phila-delphia, and attended Temple University (BS, 1963) and the University of Pennsylvania (PhD, 1967), where he majored in sociology and political science. Currently a professor at Boston College, Wolfe straddles the academic and journalistic worlds. He writes, "I am trying to keep alive a tradition of informed commentary on public affairs in the face of sterile academic research and a journalistic tradition that refuses to go into historical and political background." Among Wolfe's many books are The Seamy Side of Democracy *(1973, 1978),* One Nation, After All *(1998),* Moral Freedom *(2001),* Return to Greatness *(2005), and* The Future of Liberalism *(2009). In this essay, published in the* New Republic *in 2009, Wolfe offers insights into liberalism, conservatism, and socialism—and where Barack Obama fits within these political traditions.*

1   The word "liberal" was first used in its modern political sense in 1812, when Spaniards wrote a new constitution liberating themselves from monarchical rule. As it happens, the word "socialism" originated in roughly the same period; it came into existence to describe the utopian ideas of the British reformer Robert Owen. Such timing suggests two possibilities: Either the fates of liberalism and socialism are so interlinked that one is all but synonymous with the other—or the two are actually competitors developed to meet similar conditions, in which case victory for one marks the defeat of the other.

2   These days, one could be forgiven for believing that the former conclusion is correct. It was not so long ago that conservatives were equating liberalism with fascism; today, they have executed a 180-degree swing in order to argue that liberalism is actually synonymous with socialism. "Americans," proclaimed Republican Senator Jim DeMint at the recent meeting of the Conservative Political Action Conference, "have gotten a glimpse of the big-government plans of Obama and the Democrats and are ready to stand up, speak out, and, yes, even to take to the streets to stop America's slide into socialism." But it isn't just the right that has worked itself into a frenzy; on the question of whether we are approaching a new age of socialism, there seems to be remarkable political consensus. In recent weeks, the covers of *National Review* ("Our Socialist Future"), the *Nation* ("Reinventing Capitalism, Reimagining Socialism"), and *Newsweek* ("We Are All Socialists Now") have—respectively—lamented, heralded, and observed the coming rise of socialism.

3   But all these commentators—right, left, and middle—may want to take a deep breath. We aren't headed for an era of socialism at all, since socialism is not a natural outgrowth of liberalism. Liberalism is a political philosophy that seeks to extend personal autonomy to as many people as possible, if necessary through positive government action; socialism, by contrast, seeks as much equality as possible, even if doing so curtails individual liberty. These are differences of kind, not degree—differences that have historically placed the two philosophies in direct competition. Today, socialism is on the decline, in large part because liberalism has lately been on the rise. And, if Barack Obama's version of liberalism succeeds, socialism will be even less popular than it already is.

4   Socialism was born in political conditions that no longer exist. In its most radical form, the one associated with Marx and Engels, it had far more in common with European romanticism than with the moderate reformism of a John Stuart Mill or a Thomas Hill Green, two of Great Britain's most important liberal thinkers. Socialism seemed possible when anything seemed possible. It was an ideology of progress when progress was an unquestioned good. Even its less revolutionary adherents, those more likely to call themselves social democrats rather than socialists, believed in economic planning and social transformation

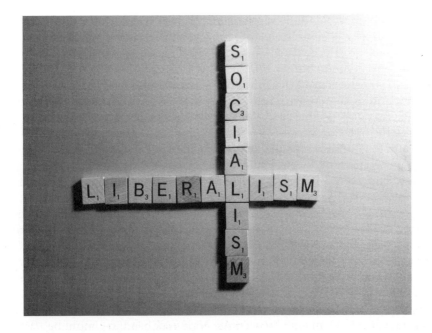

in ways that seem embarrassing now. Once it appeared possible for government to control the major means of production. Now it seems impossible to build a high-speed rail between Boston and Washington.

The story of socialism's decline is essentially a European story. Socialism 5 has never had much appeal in the United States, but that was not always the case on the other side of the Atlantic. The temptation toward socialism was not just on display in Eastern Europe; in the western half of the continent, too, left-wing governments and parties quite openly embraced socialist programs for much of the twentieth century. Those days, however, are largely over. In Britain, the Labour Party no longer pays much homage to its socialist roots. Tony Blair revived the party only after leading a campaign to alter its notorious Clause IV, which had explicitly endorsed the "common ownership of the means of production." The revised version proclaimed Labour a "democratic socialist" party, but the wording was so vague, and Blair so consistently ignored it, that its purposes were symbolic only. On this crucial point, Gordon Brown has not backtracked in the least.

Elsewhere in Europe, the same movement against socialism dominates the 6 political landscape. Socialism in the form of social democracy was long the governing ideology of Scandinavia, but Swedes never much liked the idea of nationalizing industries, and the Danes have for some time been governed by conservatives—called, in European parlance, liberals. Angela Merkel is anything but a socialist; the same is true for Nicolas Sarkozy. "Americanization" was once a dirty word in France. Now it fairly well describes Sarkozy's domestic program. There is talk of reforming the country's Napoleonic legal system with something more resembling our insistence upon rights. Public bureaucracies, including France's complex system of higher education, are to be reformed along more "modern"—read American—lines. Spain, meanwhile, does have a socialist government; but its leftism is a reaction to the extreme conservatism that governed the country for much of the twentieth century. For their part, the Eastern European countries now outdo each other in their love for the free market.

7   It is true that European societies are committed to an active role for government and that a number of their public policies, such as national health insurance, owe something to the socialist tradition. But the roots of the European welfare state are much more complex than is commonly acknowledged. European ideas about government have Christian as well as socialist origins. Two great papal encyclicals—*Rerum Novarum* (1891) and *Quadragesimo Anno* (1931)—spurred Catholic countries to adopt the idea that government should protect the rights of workers and that society has an obligation to help all. One of Great Britain's most eloquent defenders of equality, the Fabian socialist R. H. Tawney, was a devout Protestant. After World War II, Christian parties siphoned off votes that might have gone to more radical politicians by emphasizing traditions of solidarity and community. If Obama is really leading us down the road to Europeanization, an equally accurate *Newsweek* headline might be, "We Are All Christian Democrats Now."

8   And the origins of big government in Europe run deeper than either Marx or Christian politics. It is not exactly socialism that has stifled so much of French economic life with cumbersome regulations but a blunderbuss government that dates back to the *ancien régime*. Socialist politicians in France did not invent the idea of big government. They instead relied on traditions of *étatism* that had long preceded them. Given all this, it's no wonder that liberalism is experiencing a comeback in Europe. The revival of liberal sentiment is as much a reaction against both Christianity and feudalism as anything else.

9 As for Obama, it is absurd to view his program as a step toward socialism. First of all, while he is planning to raise taxes, they will still be lower than what is common in other Western countries. And, according to Brian Reidl of the Heritage Foundation, Obama's budget would increase government spending from 20 percent of GDP to 22 percent. Is it really possible that a society is capitalist when government spending represents 20 percent of GDP—but socialist at 22 percent?

10   Next, consider Obama's stances on the defining issues of our time. At most, his administration might nationalize banks temporarily; a socialist would nationalize them for good. He proposes to fix free trade, not abolish it. He does not favor a single-payer health care system, and any proposal he eventually puts forward is going to involve competition in some form. (It is worth noting that arguably the biggest beneficiaries of health care reform will be businesses, many of which struggle to pay their employees' health care costs.) To address global warming, Obama favors cap and trade, a market-oriented solution to our gravest environmental problem. That's right: This alleged socialist has so much

faith in capitalism, he is willing to put the future of our planet more or less in the hands of a market.

What these ideas have in common is, first, an attachment to economic 11 freedom that no self-respecting socialist would countenance. In fact, most of Obama's measures are designed to save, not destroy, the instruments of capitalism—businesses and the markets in which they compete. Should Obama get everything he wants, liberals will have once again—as has happened so often in the United States—gone a long way toward rescuing capitalism from its worst excesses.

Moreover, it has for some time now been established that the moderate use 12 of government to improve the lives of large numbers of citizens, while producing minor advances in equality, is primarily about giving citizens more liberty. People who, with the help of government, need not postpone medical care or can avoid going into lifetime debt to pay for it are freer people. Progressive taxation, especially the way Obama talks about it, is not about confiscating the wealth of the rich but about giving those at the bottom of the ladder more opportunity. Modest enhancements of what has been called "positive liberty" do not come anywhere close to socialism; they instead make liberalism's benefits more widespread.

Conservatives seem to think that any increase in the size of government 13 means a step toward socialism. But, if this is the case, then George W. Bush ought to come out of the closet as a socialist. It is not just that Bush spent uncountable sums on his Iraqi adventure. Nor is it that he put Keynes to shame by spending money he did not have. Bush, at least at the start of his presidency, wanted to be known for his compassion and sponsored reforms of both Medicare and education that, had a Democrat proposed them, would have been widely denounced by conservatives as socialism run rampant. Socialism, in the Republican imagination, is only something Democrats do, never something they themselves do.

In the United States, liberalism is the alternative to which we turn when 14 conservatism fails, just as in Europe it is what people look to when socialism sputters, Christianity no longer appeals, and the old feudal statism appears moribund. Liberalism has always been more comfortable finding its place between the extremes than mimicking either one of them. Americans tend to be most familiar with the ways in which liberalism distinguishes itself from conservatism. But liberalism has gone to great lengths to distinguish itself from the left as well—from the gulag, the Soviet occupation of Eastern European countries against the will of their people, and all the various forms of socialism from Baathism to Castroism associated with Third World tyrants. These distinctions have reaffirmed the liberal dedication to human rights—and this at a time when conservatives like Bush and Cheney were prepared to dispense with them. Conservatives may denounce Obama for his socialism, but it is he, and not they, who is returning the United States to such liberal commitments as the separation of powers, habeas corpus, and transparency in government.

15   If Barack Obama is a socialist, he sure is good at fooling people. Americans seem to like his quiet demeanor, his sense of caution, his efforts at inclusion. With its emphasis on intellectual modesty and pragmatism, liberalism is a temperament as well as a set of ideas; and Obama's disposition is quintessentially liberal.

16   We cannot at this point know what his legacy will be. But we do know what it will not be. Eight years of Obama, and the United States has its best chance in decades to return to the liberalism that has long defined its heritage. There would be no greater blow to socialism—in America, in Europe, or anywhere else—than for this venture to succeed.

COMPREHENSION

1. How does Wolfe define liberalism and socialism?
2. According to Wolfe, is Barack Obama a liberal, socialist, or conservative? Justify your response by referring to the text.
3. What explanation does Wolfe give for the decline of socialism in Europe? What role has the Christian Church played in this process?

RHETORIC

1. Wolfe's essay appeared in the *New Republic,* a magazine devoted to politics. What aspects of diction, tone, syntax, and paragraph development suggest that he is writing for a highly educated audience—and a readership interested in political discourse?
2. Where does Wolfe state most concisely the thesis or claim that governs his essay?
3. Wolfe divides his essay into three parts. What topic dominates each part? How are the parts interrelated? Comment on whether or not you think the essay is unified.
4. How does Wolfe use comparison and contrast, extended definition, and causal analysis to develop his essay? Identify specific passages that illustrate these rhetorical strategies.
5. Based on your analysis of Wolfe's argument, in what ways would you agree or disagree with the writer's understanding of Barack Obama's politics? Refer to the text to explain your answer. Be as specific as possible.

WRITING

1. Explain your political beliefs in a brief essay.
2. Write an extended definition of liberalism, conservatism, or socialism. Use the comparative method to distinguish your choice from the other two ideologies.
3. **Writing an Argument:** Given your understanding of President Barack Obama's policies, argue for or against the proposition that he is a socialist.

NETWORKING
Applying 21st-Century Literacies

Comparing and Contrasting Visuals: What purpose and point does the photograph (page 301) that accompanies this essay serve? Write an essay comparing and contrasting its relationship with this article, to the relationship of the illustration (page 289) in Molly Ivins's "Is Texas America?" with that essay.

Nickel and Dimed

Barbara Ehrenreich

Barbara Ehrenreich (b. 1941) was born in Butte, Montana. The daughter of working-class parents, she attended Reed College (BA 1963) and Rockefeller University, where she received a PhD in biology in 1968. After deciding not to pursue a career in science, Ehrenreich turned to political causes, using her scientific training to investigate a broad range of social issues. A prolific writer, Ehrenreich has contributed to Time, *the* New Republic, *the* Progressive, *and other magazines. She also has written several books, including* The American Health Empire *(1970),* Complaints and Disorders: The Sexual Politics of Sickness *(1978),* Nickel and Dimed: On (Not) Getting By in America *(2001),* Dancing in the Streets *(2007), and a collection of essays,* This Land Is Their Land: Reports from a Divided Nation *(2008). In the following excerpt from* Nickel and Dimed, *Ehrenreich recounts her experience working for a large cleaning agency.*

I am rested and ready for anything when I arrive at The Maids' office suite 1
Monday at 7:30 A.M. I know nothing about cleaning services like this one, which, according to the brochure I am given, has over three hundred franchises nationwide, and most of what I know about domestics in general comes from nineteenth-century British novels and *Upstairs, Downstairs.* Prophetically enough, I caught a rerun of that very show on PBS over the weekend and was struck by how terribly correct the servants looked in their black-and-white uniforms and how much wiser they were than their callow, egotistical masters. We too have uniforms, though they are more oafish than dignified—ill-fitting and in an overloud combination of kelly-green pants and a blinding sunflower-yellow polo shirt. And, as is explained in writing and over the next day and a half of training, we too have a special code of decorum. No smoking anywhere, or at least not within fifteen minutes of arrival at a house. No drinking, eating, or gum chewing in a house. No cursing in a house, even if the owner is not present, and—perhaps to keep us in practice—no obscenities even in the office.

So this is Downstairs, is my chirpy first thought. But I have no idea, of course, just how far down these stairs will take me.

2   Forty minutes go by before anyone acknowledges my presence with more than a harried nod. During this time the other employees arrive, about twenty of them, already glowing in their uniforms, and breakfast on the free coffee, bagels, and doughnuts The Maids kindly provides for us. All but one of the others are female, with an average age I would guess in the late twenties, though the range seems to go from prom-fresh to well into the Medicare years. There is a pleasant sort of bustle as people get their breakfasts and fill plastic buckets with rags and bottles of cleaning fluids, but surprisingly little conversation outside of a few references to what people ate (pizza) and drank (Jell-O shots are mentioned) over the weekend. Since the room in which we gather contains only two folding chairs, both of them occupied, the other new girl and I sit cross-legged on the floor, silent and alert, while the regulars get sorted into teams of three or four and dispatched to the day's list of houses. One of the women explains to me that teams do not necessarily return to the same houses week after week, nor do you have any guarantee of being on the same team from one day to the next. This, I suppose, is one of the advantages of a corporate cleaning service to its customers: There are no sticky and possibly guilt-ridden relationships involved, because the customers communicate almost entirely with Tammy, the office manager, or with Ted, the franchise owner and our boss. The advantage to the cleaning person is harder to determine, since the pay compares so poorly to what an independent cleaner is likely to earn—up to $15 an hour, I've heard. While I wait in the inner room, where the phone is and Tammy has her desk, to be issued a uniform, I hear her tell a potential customer on the phone that The Maids charges $25 per person-hour. The company gets $25 and we get $6.65 for each hour we work? I think I must have misheard, but a few minutes later I hear her say the same thing to another inquirer. So the only advantage of working here as opposed to freelancing is that you don't need a clientele or even a car. You can arrive straight from welfare or, in my case, the bus station—fresh off the boat.

3   At last, after all the other employees have sped off in the company's eye-catching green-and-yellow cars, I am led into a tiny closet-sized room off the inner office to learn my trade via videotape. The manager at another maid service where I'd applied had told me she didn't like to hire people who had done cleaning before because they were resistant to learning the company's system, so I prepare to empty my mind of all prior house-cleaning experience. There are four tapes—dusting, bathrooms, kitchen, and vacuuming—each starring an attractive, possibly Hispanic young woman who moves about serenely in obedience to the male voiceover: For vacuuming, begin in the master bedroom; when dusting, begin with the room directly off the kitchen. When you enter a room, mentally divide it into sections no wider than your reach. Begin in the section to your left and, within each section, move from left to right and top to bottom. This way nothing is ever overlooked.

I like *Dusting* best, for its undeniable logic and a certain kind of austere 4
beauty. When you enter a house, you spray a white rag with Windex and place
it in the left pocket of your green apron. Another rag, sprayed with disinfectant,
goes in the middle pocket, and a yellow rag bearing wood polish in the right-
hand pocket. A dry rag, for buffing surfaces, occupies the right-hand pocket of
your slacks. Shiny surfaces get Windexed, wood gets wood polish, and everything else is wiped dust-free with disinfectant. Every now and then Ted pops in
to watch with me, pausing the video to underscore a particularly dramatic moment: "See how she's working around the vase? That's an accident waiting to
happen." If Ted himself were in a video, it would have to be a cartoon, because
the only features sketched onto his pudgy face are brown buttonlike eyes and a
tiny pug nose; his belly, encased in a polo shirt, overhangs the waistline of his
shorts. "You know, all this was figured out with a stopwatch," he tells me with
something like pride. When the video warns against oversoaking our rags with
cleaning fluids, he pauses it to tell me there's a danger in undersoaking too,
especially if it's going to slow me down. "Cleaning fluids are less expensive
than your time." It's good to know that *something* is cheaper than my time, or
that in the hierarchy of the company's values I rank above Windex.

Vacuuming is the most disturbing video, actually a double feature begin- 5
ning with an introduction to the special backpack vacuum we are to use. Yes,
the vacuum cleaner actually straps onto your back, a chubby fellow who introduces himself as its inventor explains. He suits up, pulling the straps tight
across and under his chest and then says proudly into the camera: "See, I *am* the
vacuum cleaner." It weighs only ten pounds, he claims, although, as I soon find
out, with the attachments dangling from the strap around your waist, the total
is probably more like fourteen. What about my petulant and much-pampered
lower back? The inventor returns to the theme of human/machine merger:
When properly strapped in, we too will be vacuum cleaners, constrained only
by the cord that attaches us to an electrical outlet, and vacuum cleaners don't
have backaches. Somehow all this information exhausts me, and I watch the
second video, which explains the actual procedures for vacuuming, with the
detached interest of a cineast. Could the model maid be an actual maid and
the model home someone's actual dwelling? And who are these people whose
idea of decorating is matched pictures of mallard ducks in flight and whose
house is perfectly characterless and pristine even before the model maid sets
to work?

At first I find the videos on kitchens and bathrooms baffling, and it takes me 6
several minutes to realize why: There is no *water*, or almost no water, involved. I
was taught to clean by my mother, a compulsive housekeeper who employed
water so hot you needed rubber gloves to get into it and in such Niagara-like
quantities that most microbes were probably crushed by the force of it before
the soap suds had a chance to rupture their cell walls. But germs are never mentioned in the videos provided by The Maids. Our antagonists exist entirely in
the visible world—soap scum, dust, counter crud, dog hair, stains, and smears—
and are to be attacked by damp rag or, in hard-core cases, by Dobie (the brand

of plastic scouring pad we use). We scrub only to remove impurities that might be detectable to a customer by hand or by eye; otherwise our only job is to wipe. Nothing is said about the possibility of transporting bacteria, by rag or by hand, from bathroom to kitchen or even from one house to the next. It is the "cosmetic touches" that the videos emphasize and that Ted, when he wanders back into the room, continually directs my eye to. Fluff up all throw pillows and arrange them symmetrically. Brighten up stainless steel sinks with baby oil. Leave all spice jars, shampoos, etc., with their labels facing outward. Comb out the fringes of Persian carpets with a pick. Use the vacuum cleaner to create a special, fernlike pattern in the carpets. The loose ends of toilet paper and paper towel rolls have to be given a special fold (the same one you'll find in hotel bathrooms). "Messes" of loose paper, clothing, or toys are to be stacked into "neat messes." Finally, the house is to be sprayed with the cleaning service's signature floral-scented air freshener, which will signal to the owners, the moment they return home, that, yes, their house has been "cleaned."

7   After a day's training, I am judged fit to go out with a team, where I soon discover that life is nothing like the movies, at least not if the movie is *Dusting*. For one thing, compared with our actual pace, the training videos were all in slow motion. We do not walk to the cars with our buckets full of cleaning fluids and utensils in the morning, we run, and when we pull up to a house, we run with our buckets to the door. Liza, a good-natured woman in her thirties who is my first team leader, explains that we are given only so many minutes per house, ranging from under sixty for a 1½-bathroom apartment to two hundred or more for a multibathroom "first timer." I'd like to know why anybody worries about Ted's time limits if we're being paid by the hour but hesitate to display anything that might be interpreted as attitude. As we get to each house, Liza assigns our tasks, and I cross my fingers to ward off bathrooms and vacuuming. Even dusting, though, gets aerobic under pressure, and after about an hour of it—reaching to get door tops, crawling along floors to wipe baseboards, standing on my bucket to attack the higher shelves—I wouldn't mind sitting down with a tall glass of water. But as soon as you complete your assigned task, you report to the team leader to be assigned to help someone else. Once or twice, when the normal process of evaporation is deemed too slow, I am assigned to dry a scrubbed floor by putting rags under my feet and skating around on it. Usually, by the time I get out to the car and am dumping the dirty water used on floors and wringing out rags, the rest of the team is already in the car with the motor running. Liza assures me that they've never left anyone behind at a house, not even, presumably, a very new person whom nobody knows.

8   In my interview, I had been promised a thirty-minute lunch break, but this turns out to be a five-minute pit stop at a convenience store, if that. I bring my own sandwich—the same turkey breast and cheese every day—as do a couple of the others; the rest eat convenience store fare, a bagel or doughnut salvaged from our free breakfast, or nothing at all. The two older married women I'm teamed up with eat best—sandwiches and fruit. Among the younger women,

lunch consists of a slice of pizza, a "pizza pocket" (a roll of dough surrounding some pizza sauce), or a small bag of chips. Bear in mind we are not office workers, sitting around idling at the basal metabolic rate. A poster on the wall in the office cheerily displays the number of calories burned per minute at our various tasks, ranging from about 3.5 for dusting to 7 for vacuuming. If you assume an average of 5 calories per minute in a seven-hour day (eight hours minus time for travel between houses), you need to be taking in 2,100 calories in addition to the resting minimum of, say, 900 or so. I get pushy with Rosalie, who is new like me and fresh from high school in a rural northern part of the state, about the meagerness of her lunches, which consist solely of Doritos—a half-bag from the day before or a freshly purchased small-sized bag. She just didn't have anything in the house, she says (though she lives with her boyfriend and his mother), and she certainly doesn't have any money to buy lunch, as I find out when I offer to fetch her a soda from a Quik Mart and she has to admit she doesn't have eighty-nine cents. I treat her to the soda, wishing I could force her, mommylike, to take milk instead. So how does she hold up for an eight- or even nine-hour day? "Well," she concedes, "I get dizzy sometimes."

How poor are they, my coworkers? The fact that anyone is working this job 9 at all can be taken as prima facie evidence of some kind of desperation or at least a history of mistakes and disappointments, but it's not for me to ask. In the prison movies that provide me with a mental guide to comportment, the new guy doesn't go around shaking hands and asking, "Hi there, what are you in for?" So I listen, in the cars and when we're assembled in the office, and learn, first, that no one seems to be homeless. Almost everyone is embedded in extended families or families artificially extended with housemates. People talk about visiting grandparents in the hospital or sending birthday cards to a niece's husband; single mothers live with their own mothers or share apartments with a coworker or boyfriend. Pauline, the oldest of us, owns her own home, but she sleeps on the living room sofa, while her four grown children and three grandchildren fill up the bedrooms.

But although no one, apparently, is sleeping in a car, there are signs, even at 10 the beginning, of real difficulty if not actual misery. Half-smoked cigarettes are returned to the pack. There are discussions about who will come up with fifty cents for a toll and whether Ted can be counted on for prompt reimbursement. One of my teammates gets frantic about a painfully impacted wisdom tooth and keeps making calls from our houses to try to locate a source of free dental care. When my—or, I should say, Liza's—team discovers there is not a single Dobie in our buckets, I suggest that we stop at a convenience store and buy one rather than drive all the way back to the office. But it turns out I haven't brought any money with me and we cannot put together $2 between the four of us.

The Friday of my first week at The Maids is unnaturally hot for Maine in 11 early September—95 degrees, according to the digital time-and-temperature displays offered by banks that we pass. I'm teamed up with the sad-faced Rosalie and our leader, Maddy, whose sullenness, under the circumstances, is almost a relief after Liza's relentless good cheer. Liza, I've learned, is the highest-ranking cleaner, a sort of supervisor really, and said to be something of a snitch, but Maddy, a single mom of maybe twenty-seven or so, has worked for only three months and broods about her child care problems. Her boyfriend's sister, she tells me on the drive to our first house, watches her eighteen-month-old for $50 a week, which is a stretch on The Maids' pay, plus she doesn't entirely trust the sister, but a real day care center could be as much as $90 a week. After polishing off the first house, no problem, we grab "lunch"—Doritos for Rosalie and a bag of Pepperidge Farm Goldfish for Maddy—and head out into the exurbs for what our instruction sheet warns is a five-bathroom spread and a first-timer to boot. Still, the size of the place makes us pause for a moment, buckets in hand, before searching out an appropriately humble entrance. It sits there like a beached ocean liner, the prow cutting through swells of green turf, windows without number. "Well, well," Maddy says, reading the owner's name from our instruction sheet. "Mrs. W. and her big-ass house. I hope she's going to give us lunch."

12   Mrs. W. is not in fact happy to see us, grimacing with exasperation when the black nanny ushers us into the family room or sunroom or den or whatever kind of specialized space she is sitting in. After all, she already has the nanny, a cooklike person, and a crew of men doing some sort of finishing touches on the construction to supervise. No, she doesn't want to take us around the house, because she already explained everything to the office on the phone, but Maddy stands there, with Rosalie and me behind her, until she relents. We are to move everything on all surfaces, she instructs during the tour, and get underneath and be sure to do every bit of the several miles, I calculate, of baseboards. And be mindful of the baby, who's napping and can't have cleaning fluids of any kind near her.

13   Then I am let loose to dust. In a situation like this, where I don't even know how to name the various kinds of rooms, The Maids' special system turns out to be a lifesaver. All I have to do is keep moving from left to right, within rooms and between rooms, trying to identify landmarks so I don't accidentally do a room or a hallway twice. Dusters get the most complete biographical overview, due to the necessity of lifting each object and tchotchke individually, and I learn that Mrs. W. is an alumna of an important women's college, now occupying herself by monitoring her investments and the baby's bowel movements. I find special charts for this latter purpose, with spaces for time of day, most recent fluid intake, consistency, and color. In the master bedroom, I dust a whole shelf of books on pregnancy, breastfeeding, the first six months, the first year, the first two years—and I wonder what the child care–deprived Maddy makes of all this. Maybe there's been some secret division of the world's women into breeders and drones, and those at the maid level are no longer supposed to be reproducing at all. Maybe this is why our office manager, Tammy, who was once a maid herself, wears inch-long fake nails and tarty little outfits—to show she's advanced to the breeder caste and can't be sent out to clean anymore.

14   It is hotter inside than out, un-air-conditioned for the benefit of the baby, I suppose, but I do all right until I encounter the banks of glass doors that line the side and back of the ground floor. Each one has to be Windexed, wiped, and

buffed—inside and out, top to bottom, left to right, until it's as streakless and invisible as a material substance can be. Outside, I can see the construction guys knocking back Gatorade, but the rule is that no fluid or food item can touch a maid's lips when she's inside a house. Now, sweat, even in unseemly quantities, is nothing new to me. I live in a subtropical area where even the inactive can expect to be moist nine months out of the year. I work out, too, in my normal life and take a certain macho pride in the Vs of sweat that form on my T-shirt after ten minutes or more on the StairMaster. But in normal life fluids lost are immediately replaced. Everyone in yuppie-land—airports, for example—looks like a nursing baby these days, inseparable from their plastic bottles of water. Here, however, I sweat without replacement or pause, not in individual drops but in continuous sheets of fluid soaking through my polo shirt, pouring down the backs of my legs. The eyeliner I put on in the morning—vain twit that I am—has long since streaked down onto my cheeks, and I could wring my braid out if I wanted to. Working my way through the living room(s), I wonder if Mrs. W. will ever have occasion to realize that every single doodad and *objet* through which she expresses her unique, individual self is, from another vantage point, only an obstacle between some thirsty person and a glass of water.

When I can find no more surfaces to wipe and have finally exhausted the 15 supply of rooms, Maddy assigns me to do the kitchen floor. OK, except that Mrs. W. is *in* the kitchen, so I have to go down on my hands and knees practically at her feet. No, we don't have sponge mops like the one I use in my own house; the hands-and-knees approach is a definite selling point for corporate cleaning services like The Maids. "We clean floors the old-fashioned way—*on our hands and knees*" (emphasis added), the brochure for a competing firm boasts. In fact, whatever advantages there may be to the hands-and-knees approach—you're closer to your work, of course, and less likely to miss a grimy patch—are undermined by the artificial drought imposed by The Maids' cleaning system. We are instructed to use less than half a small bucket of lukewarm water for a kitchen and all adjacent scrubbable floors (breakfast nooks and other dining areas), meaning that within a few minutes we are doing nothing more than redistributing the dirt evenly around the floor. There are occasional customer complaints about the cleanliness of our floors—for example, from a man who wiped up a spill on his freshly "cleaned" floor only to find the paper towel he employed for this purpose had turned gray. A mop and a full bucket of hot soapy water would not only get a floor cleaner but would be a lot more dignified for the person who does the cleaning. But it is this primal posture of submission—and of what is ultimately anal accessibility—that seems to gratify the consumers of maid services.

I don't know, but Mrs. W.'s floor is hard—stone, I think, or at least a stone- 16 like substance—and we have no knee pads with us today. I had thought in my middle-class innocence that knee pads were one of Monica Lewinsky's prurient fantasies, but no, they actually exist, and they're usually a standard part of our equipment. So here I am on my knees, working my way around the room like some fanatical penitent crawling through the stations of the cross, when I realize that Mrs. W. is staring at me fixedly—so fixedly that I am gripped for a moment by the wild possibility that I may have once given a lecture at her alma mater and she's trying to figure out where she's seen me before. If I were recognized, would I be fired? Would she at least be inspired to offer me a drink of water? Because I have decided that if water is actually offered, I'm taking it, rules or no rules, and if word of this infraction gets back to Ted, I'll just say I thought it would be rude to refuse. Not to worry, though. She's just watching that I don't leave out some stray square inch, and when I rise painfully to my feet again, blinking through the sweat, she says, "Could you just scrub the floor in the entryway while you're at it?"

17   I rush home to the Blue Haven at the end of the day, pull down the blinds for privacy, strip off my uniform in the kitchen—the bathroom being too small for both a person and her discarded clothes—and stand in the shower for a good ten minutes, thinking all this water is *mine.* I have paid for it, in fact, I have earned it. I have gotten through a week at The Maids without mishap, injury, or insurrection. My back feels fine, meaning I'm not feeling it at all; even my wrists, damaged by carpal tunnel syndrome years ago, are issuing no complaints. Coworkers warned me that the first time they donned the backpack vacuum they felt faint, but not me. I am strong and I am, more than that, good. Did I toss my bucket of filthy water onto Mrs. W.'s casual white summer outfit? No. Did I take the wand of my vacuum cleaner and smash someone's Chinese porcelain statues or Hummel figurines? Not once. I was at all times cheerful, energetic, helpful, and as competent as a new hire can be expected to be. If I can do one week, I can do another, and might as well, since there's never been a moment for job-hunting. The 3:30 quitting time turns out to be a myth; often we don't return to the office until 4:30 or 5:00. And what did I think? That I was going to go out to interviews in my soaked and stinky postwork condition? I decide to reward myself with a sunset walk on Old Orchard Beach.

18   On account of the heat, there are still a few actual bathers on the beach, but I am content to sit in shorts and T-shirt and watch the ocean pummel the sand. When the sun goes down I walk back into the town to find my car and am amazed to hear a sound I associate with cities like New York and Berlin. There's a couple of Peruvian musicians playing in the little grassy island in the street near the pier, and maybe fifty people—locals and vacationers—have gathered around, offering their bland end-of-summer faces to the sound. I edge my way through the crowd and find a seat where I can see the musicians up close—the beautiful young guitarist and the taller man playing the flute. What are they doing in this rinky-dink blue-collar resort, and what does the audience make of this surprise visit from the dark-skinned South? The melody the flute lays out over the percussion is both utterly strange and completely familiar, as if it had been imprinted in the minds of my own peasant ancestors centuries ago and forgotten until this very moment. Everyone else seems to be as transfixed as I am. The musicians wink and smile at each other as they play, and I see then that they are the secret emissaries of a worldwide lower-class conspiracy to snatch joy out of degradation and filth. When the song ends, I give them a dollar, the equivalent of about ten minutes of sweat.

COMPREHENSION

1. Why do women work for The Maids when they could earn more money as independent cleaners? How does Ehrenreich distinguish her cleaning practices from her coworkers'? Why do the maids emphasize "cosmetic touches" (paragraph 6)?
2. Describe the plight of Ehrenreich's coworkers. What "signs . . . of real difficulty if not actual misery" (paragraph 10) does she detect? What, if anything, does she do to help them?
3. Who is Mrs. W? What is her lifestyle like, and what does she expect of the maids? How does she treat Ehrenreich?

RHETORIC

1. How does Ehrenreich structure her narrative? How much time elapses? What elements of conflict develop? What transitional devices does she employ to unify the action?
2. Where does the writer employ description, and for what purpose? What descriptive details seem most striking to you? How, for example, does Ehrenreich bring her coworkers and Mrs. W. to life?
3. Identify those instances where the writer uses process analysis and comparison and contrast to organize her essay. Why does she select these strategies?
4. Explain the tone of this selection. What elements of irony and sarcasm do you detect?
5. Do you think this essay provides a straightforward account of Ehrenreich's experience working for The Maids, or does she have an argumentative point? Justify your response.
6. How does the writer conclude this selection? What elements in the last paragraph capture the main purpose behind her account?

WRITING

1. Write a narrative and descriptive essay of a job you have held that involved menial labor. Establish a time frame. Describe any colleagues who worked with you. Have a thesis or an argument that you either state explicitly or permit to emerge from the account.
2. Compare and contrast a bad job that you have held and a job that provided you with a degree of satisfaction.
3. **Writing an Argument:** In *Nickel and Dimed*, Ehrenreich set out to find minimum-wage jobs in several parts of the United States, including a Wal-Mart in Minnesota and a restaurant in Florida. However, she knew at the outset that these jobs were temporary and that she had the luxury of going back to her comfortable life and her career as a writer and activist. Argue for or against the proposition that Ehrenreich was being unethical and exploitative in her behavior. Refer to this selection to support your position.

NETWORKING

Applying 21st-Century Literacies

Examining Comments on a Blog: From the Chapter 8 Networking page (at *www .mhhe.com/mhreaderbrief1e*), link to the 2009 entry "Rich Get Poorer, Poor Disappear" on Barbara Ehrenreich's blog. After reading the entry itself at least twice, go through the comments. How many, and which commenters, make valuable contributions to the conversation? How many, and which do not? Based on your findings, what makes a good blog comment? Do you think blog comments should be moderated by the blog's author? Why or why not?

Stranger in the Village

James Baldwin

James Baldwin (1924–1988), a major American essayist, novelist, short-story writer, and playwright, was born and grew up in Harlem. He won a Eugene Saxon Fellowship and lived in Europe from 1948 to 1956. Always an activist in civil rights causes, Baldwin focused in his essays and fiction on the black search for identity in modern America and on the myth of white superiority. Among his principal works are Go Tell It on the Mountain *(1953),* Notes of a Native Son *(1955),* Giovanni's Room *(1956),* Nobody Knows My Name *(1961),* Another Country *(1962), and* If Beale Street Could Talk *(1974). One of the finest contemporary essayists, Baldwin had a rare talent for portraying the deepest concerns about civilization in an intensely personal style, as the following essay indicates.*

1   From all available evidence no black man had ever set foot in this tiny Swiss village before I came. I was told before arriving that I would probably be a "sight" for the village; I took this to mean that people of my complexion were rarely seen in Switzerland, and also that city people are always something of a "sight" outside of the city. It did not occur to me—possibly because I am an American—that there could be people anywhere who had never seen a Negro.

2   It is a fact that cannot be explained on the basis of the inaccessibility of the village. The village is very high, but it is only four hours from Milan and three hours from Lausanne. It is true that it is virtually unknown. Few people making plans for a holiday would elect to come here. On the other hand, the villagers are able, presumably, to come and go as they please—which they do: to another town at the foot of the mountain, with a population of approximately five thousand, the nearest place to see a movie or go to the bank. In the village there is no movie house, no bank, no library, no theater; very few radios, one jeep, one

station wagon; and, at the moment, one typewriter, mine, an invention which the woman next door to me here had never seen. There are about six hundred people living here, all Catholic—I conclude this from the fact that the Catholic church is open all year round, whereas the Protestant chapel, set off on a hill a little removed from the village, is open only in the summertime when the tourists arrive. There are four or five hotels, all closed now, and four or five *bistros*, of which, however, only two do any business during the winter. These two do not do a great deal, for life in the village seems to end around nine or ten o'clock. There are a few stores, butcher, baker, *épicerie*, a hardware store, and a money-changer—who cannot change travelers' checks, but must send them down to the bank, an operation which takes two or three days. There is something called the *Ballet Haus*, closed in the winter and used for God knows what, certainly not ballet, during the summer. There seems to be only one schoolhouse in the village, and this for the quite young children; I suppose this to mean that their older brothers and sisters at some point descend from these mountains in order to complete their education—possibly, again, to the town just below. The landscape is absolutely forbidding, mountains towering on all four sides, ice and snow as far as the eye can reach. In this white wilderness, men and women and children move all day, carrying washing, wood, buckets of milk or water, sometimes skiing on Sunday afternoons. All week long boys and young men are to be seen shoveling snow off the rooftops, or dragging wood down from the forest in sleds.

The village's only real attraction, which explains the tourist season, is the hot spring water. A disquietingly high proportion of these tourists are cripples, or semi-cripples, who come year after year—from other parts of Switzerland, usually—to take the waters. This lends the village, at the height of the season, a rather terrifying air of sanctity, as though it were a lesser Lourdes. There is often something beautiful, there is always something awful, in the spectacle of a person who has lost one of his faculties, a faculty he never questioned until it was gone, and who struggles to recover it. Yet people remain people, on crutches or indeed on deathbeds; and wherever I passed, the first summer I was here, among the native villagers or among the lame, a wind passed with me—of astonishment, curiosity, amusement, and outrage. The first summer I stayed two weeks and never intended to return. But I did return in the winter, to work; the village offers, obviously, no distractions whatever and has the further advantage of being extremely cheap. Now it is winter again, a year later, and I am here again. Everyone in the village knows my name, though they scarcely ever use it, knows that I come from America—though this, apparently, they will never really believe: black men come from Africa—and everyone knows that I am the friend of the son of a woman who was born here, and that I am staying in their chalet. But I remain as much a stranger today as I was the first day I arrived, and the children shout *Neger! Neger!* as I walk along the streets.

It must be admitted that in the beginning I was far too shocked to have any real reaction. In so far as I reacted at all, I reacted by trying to be pleasant—it being a great part of the American Negro's education (long before he goes to school) that he must make people "like" him. This smile-and-the-world-smiles-with-you routine worked about as well in this situation as it had in the situation for which it was designed, which is to say that it did not work at all. No one, after all, can be liked whose human weight and complexity cannot be, or has not been, admitted. My smile was simply another unheard-of phenomenon which allowed them to see my teeth—they did not, really, see my smile and I began to think that, should I take to snarling, no one would notice any difference. All of the physical characteristics of the Negro which had caused me, in America, a very different and almost forgotten pain were nothing less than miraculous—or infernal—in the eyes of the village people. Some thought my hair was the color of tar, that it had the texture of wire, or the texture of cotton. It was jocularly suggested that I might let it all grow long and make myself a winter coat. If I sat in the sun for more than five minutes some daring creature was certain to come along and gingerly put his fingers on my hair, as though he were afraid of an electric shock, or put his hand on my hand, astonished that the color did not rub off. In all of this, in which it must be conceded there was the charm of genuine wonder and in which there was certainly no element of intentional unkindness, there was yet no suggestion that I was human: I was simply a living wonder.

5　　I knew that they did not mean to be unkind, and I know it now; it is necessary, nevertheless, for me to repeat this to myself each time I walk out of the chalet. The children who shout *Neger!* have no way of knowing the echoes this sound raises in me. They are brimming with good humor and the more daring swell with pride when I stop to speak with them. Just the same, there are days when I cannot pause and smile, when I have no heart to play with them; when, indeed, I mutter sourly to myself, exactly as I muttered on the streets of a city these children have never seen, when I was no bigger than these children are now: *Your* mother *was a nigger.* Joyce is right about history being a nightmare—but it may be the nightmare from which no one can awaken. People are trapped in history and history is trapped in them.

6　　There is a custom in the village—I am told it is repeated in many villages—of "buying" African natives for the purpose of converting them to Christianity. There stands in the church all year round a small box with a slot for money, decorated with a black figurine, and into this box the villagers drop their francs. During the *carnaval* which precedes Lent, two village children have their faces blackened—out of which bloodless darkness their blue eyes shine like ice—and fantastic horsehair wigs are placed on their blond heads; thus disguised, they solicit among the villagers for money for the missionaries in Africa. Between the box in the church and the blackened children, the village "bought" last year six or eight African natives. This was reported to me with pride by the wife of one of the *bistro* owners and I was careful to express astonishment and pleasure at the solicitude shown by the village for the souls of black folk. The *bistro* owner's wife beamed with a pleasure far more genuine than my own and seemed to feel that I might now breathe more easily concerning the souls of at least six of my kinsmen.

I tried not to think of these so lately baptized kinsmen, of the price paid for 7
them, or the peculiar price they themselves would pay, and said nothing about
my father, who having taken his own conversion too literally never, at bottom,
forgave the white world (which he described as heathen) for having saddled
him with a Christ in whom, to judge at least from their treatment of him, they
themselves no longer believed. I thought of white men arriving for the first
time in an African village, strangers there, as I am a stranger here, and tried to
imagine the astounded populace touching their hair and marveling at the color
of their skin. But there is a great difference between being the first white man to
be seen by Africans and being the first black man to be seen by whites. The
white man takes the astonishment as tribute, for he arrives to conquer and to
convert the natives, whose inferiority in relation to himself is not even to be
questioned; whereas I, without a thought of conquest, find myself among a
people whose culture controls me, has even, in a sense, created me, people who
have cost me more in anguish and rage than they will ever know, who yet do
not even know of my existence. The astonishment with which I might have
greeted them, should they have stumbled into my African village a few hundred years ago, might have rejoiced their hearts. But the astonishment with
which they greet me today can only poison mine.

And this is so despite everything I may do to feel differently, despite my 8
friendly conversations with the *bistro* owner's wife, despite their three-year-old
son who has at last become my friend, despite the *saluts* and *bonsoirs* which I
exchange with people as I walk, despite the fact that I know that no individual
can be taken to task for what history is doing, or has done. I say that the culture
of these people controls me—but they can scarcely be held responsible for European culture. America comes out of Europe, but these people have never seen
America nor have most of them seen more of Europe than the hamlet at the foot
of their mountain. Yet they move with an authority which I shall never have;
and they regard me, quite rightly, not only as a stranger in their village but as a
suspect latecomer, bearing no credentials, to everything they have—however
unconsciously—inherited.

For this village, even were it incomparably more remote and incredibly 9
more primitive, is the West, the West onto which I have been so strangely
grafted. These people cannot be, from the point of view of power, strangers
anywhere in the world; they have made the modern world, in effect, even if
they do not know it. The most illiterate among them is related, in a way that I
am not, to Dante, Shakespeare, Michelangelo, Aeschylus, da Vinci, Rembrandt,
and Racine; the cathedral at Chartres says something to them which it cannot
say to me, as indeed would New York's Empire State Building, should anyone
here ever see it. Out of their hymns and dances come Beethoven and Bach. Go
back a few centuries and they are in their full glory—but I am in Africa, watching the conquerors arrive.

The rage of the disesteemed is personally fruitless, but it is also absolutely 10
inevitable; this rage, so generally discounted, so little understood even among the
people whose daily bread it is, is one of the things that makes history. Rage can

only with difficulty, and never entirely, be brought under the domination of the intelligence and is therefore not susceptible to any arguments whatever. This is a fact which ordinary representatives of the *Herrenvolk*, having never felt this rage and being unable to imagine it, quite fail to understand. Also, rage cannot be hidden, it can only be dissembled. This dissembling deludes the thoughtless, and strengthens rage and adds, to rage, contempt. There are, no doubt, as many ways of coping with the resulting complex of tensions as there are black men in the world, but no black man can hope ever to be entirely liberated from this internal warfare—rage, dissembling, and contempt having inevitably accompanied his first realization of the power of white men. What is crucial here is that, since white men represent in the black man's world so heavy a weight, white men have for black men a reality which is far from being reciprocal; and hence all black men have toward all white men an attitude which is designed, really, either to rob the white man of the jewel of his naïveté, or else to make it cost him dear.

11   The black man insists, by whatever means he finds at his disposal, that the white man cease to regard him as an exotic rarity and recognize him as a human being. This is a very charged and difficult moment, for there is a great deal of will power involved in the white man's naïveté. Most people are not naturally reflective any more than they are naturally malicious, and the white man prefers to keep the black man at a certain human remove because it is easier for him thus to preserve his simplicity and avoid being called to account for crimes committed by his forefathers, or his neighbors. He is inescapably aware, nevertheless, that he is in a better position in the world than black men are, nor can he quite put to death the suspicion that he is hated by black men therefore. He does not wish to be hated, neither does he wish to change places, and at this point in his uneasiness he can scarcely avoid having recourse to those legends which white men have created about black men, the most usual effect of which is that the white man finds himself enmeshed, so to speak, in his own language which describes hell, as well as the attributes which lead one to hell, as being as black as night.

12   Every legend, moreover, contains its residuum of truth, and the root function of language is to control the universe by describing it. It is of quite considerable significance that black men remain, in the imagination, and in overwhelming numbers in fact, beyond the disciplines of salvation; and this despite the fact the West has been "buying" African natives for centuries. There is, I should hazard, an instantaneous necessity to be divorced from this so visibly unsaved stranger, in whose heart, moreover, one cannot guess what dreams of vengeance are being nourished; and, at the same time, there are few things on earth more attractive than the idea of the unspeakable liberty which is allowed the unredeemed. When, beneath the black mask, a human being begins to make himself felt one cannot escape a certain awful wonder as to what kind of human being it is. What one's imagination makes of other people is dictated, of course, by the laws of one's own personality and it is one of the ironies of black-white relations that, by means of what the white man imagines the black man to be, the black man is enabled to know who the white man is.

I have said, for example, that I am as much a stranger in this village today   13
as I was the first summer I arrived, but this is not quite true. The villagers wonder less about the texture of my hair than they did then, and wonder rather
more about me. And the fact that their wonder now exists on another level is
reflected in their attitudes and in their eyes. There are the children who make
those delightful, hilarious, sometimes astonishingly grave overtures of friendship in the unpredictable fashion of children; other children, having been taught
that the devil is a black man, scream in genuine anguish as I approach. Some of
the older women never pass without a friendly greeting, never pass, indeed, if
it seems that they will be able to engage me in conversation; other women look
down or look away or rather contemptuously smirk. Some of the men drink
with me and suggest that I learn how to ski—partly, I gather, because they cannot imagine what I would look like on skis—and want to know if I am married,
and ask questions about my *métier*. But some of the men have accused *le sale
nègre*—behind my back—of stealing wood and there is already in the eyes of
some of them that peculiar, intent, paranoiac malevolence which one sometimes surprises in the eyes of American white men when, out walking with
their Sunday girl, they see a Negro male approach.

There is a dreadful abyss between the streets of this village and the streets of   14
the city in which I was born, between the children who shout *Neger!* today and
those who shouted *Nigger!* yesterday—the abyss is experience, the American
experience. The syllable hurled behind me today expresses, above all, wonder: I
am a stranger here. But I am not a stranger in America and the same syllable
riding on the American air expresses the war my presence has occasioned in the
American soul.

For this village brings home to me this fact: that there was a day, and not   15
really a very distant day, when Americans were scarcely Americans at all but
discontented Europeans, facing a great unconquered continent and strolling,
say, into a marketplace and seeing black men for the first time. The shock this
spectacle afforded is suggested, surely, by the promptness with which they decided that these black men were not really men but cattle. It is true that the necessity on the part of the settlers of the New World of reconciling their moral
assumptions with the fact—and the necessity—of slavery enhanced immensely
the charm of this idea, and it is also true that this idea expresses, with a truly
American bluntness, the attitude which to varying extents all masters have had
toward all slaves.

But between all former slaves and slave owners and the drama which be-   16
gins for Americans over three hundred years ago at Jamestown, there are at
least two differences to be observed. The American Negro slave could not suppose, for one thing, as slaves in past epochs had supposed and often done, that
he would ever be able to wrest the power from his master's hands. This was a
supposition which the modern era, which was to bring about such vast changes
in the aims and dimensions of power, put to death; it only begins, in unprecedented fashion, and with dreadful implications, to be resurrected today. But
even had this supposition persisted with undiminished force, the American

Negro slave could not have used it to lend his condition dignity, for the reason that this supposition rests on another: that the slave in exile yet remains related to his past, has some means—if only in memory—of revering and sustaining the forms of his former life, is able, in short, to maintain his identity.

17   This was not the case with the American Negro slave. He is unique among the black men of the world in that his past was taken from him, almost literally, at one blow. One wonders what on earth the first slave found to say to the first dark child he bore. I am told that there are Haitians able to trace their ancestry back to African kings, but any American Negro wishing to go back so far will find his journey through time abruptly arrested by the signature on the bill of sale which served as the entrance paper for his ancestor. At the time—to say nothing of the circumstances—of the enslavement of the captive black man who was to become the American Negro, there was not the remotest possibility that he would ever take power from his master's hands. There was no reason to suppose that his situation would ever change, nor was there, shortly, anything to indicate that his situation had ever been different. It was his necessity, in the words of E. Franklin Frazier, to find a "motive for living under American culture or die." The identity of the American Negro comes out of this extreme situation, and the evolution of this identity was a source of the most intolerable anxiety in the minds and the lives of his masters.

18   For the history of the American Negro is unique also in this: that the question of his humanity, and of his rights therefore as a human being, became a burning one for several generations of Americans, so burning a question that it ultimately became one of those used to divide the nation. It is out of this argument that the venom of the epithet *Nigger!* is derived. It is an argument which Europe has never had, and hence Europe quite sincerely fails to understand how or why the argument arose in the first place, why its effects are so frequently disastrous and always so unpredictable, why it refuses until today to be entirely settled. Europe's black possessions remained—and do remain—in Europe's colonies, at which remove they represented no threat whatever to European identity. If they posed any problem at all for the European conscience, it was a problem which remained comfortingly abstract: in effect, the black man, *as a man,* did not exist for Europe. But in America, even as a slave, he was an inescapable part of the general social fabric and no American could escape having an attitude toward him. Americans attempt until today to make an abstraction of the Negro, but the very nature of these abstractions reveals the tremendous effects the presence of the Negro has had on the American character.

19   When one considers the history of the Negro in America it is of the greatest importance to recognize that the moral beliefs of a person, or a people, are never really as tenuous as life—which is not moral—very often causes them to appear; these create for them a frame of reference and a necessary hope, the hope being that when life has done its worst they will be enabled to rise above themselves and to triumph over life. Life would scarcely be bearable if this

hope did not exist. Again, even when the worst has been said, to betray a belief is not by any means to have put oneself beyond its power; the betrayal of a belief is not the same thing as ceasing to believe. If this were not so there would be no moral standards in the world at all. Yet one must also recognize that morality is based on ideas and that all ideas are dangerous—dangerous because ideas can only lead to action and where the action leads no man can say. And dangerous in this respect: that confronted with the impossibility of becoming free of them, one can be driven to the most inhuman excesses. The ideas on which American beliefs are based are not, though Americans often seem to think so, ideas which originated in America. They came out of Europe. And the establishment of democracy on the American continent was scarcely as radical a break with the past as was the necessity, which Americans faced, of broadening this concept to include black men.

This was, literally, a hard necessity. It was impossible, for one thing, for 20 Americans to abandon their beliefs, not only because these beliefs alone seemed able to justify the sacrifices they had endured and the blood that they had spilled, but also because these beliefs afforded them their only bulwark against a moral chaos as absolute as the physical chaos of the continent it was their destiny to conquer. But in the situation in which Americans found themselves, these beliefs threatened an idea which, whether or not one likes to think so, is the very warp and woof of the heritage of the West, the idea of white supremacy.

Americans have made themselves notorious by the shrillness and the bru- 21 tality with which they have insisted on this idea, but they did not invent it; and it has escaped the world's notice that those very excesses of which Americans have been guilty imply a certain, unprecedented uneasiness over the idea's life and power, if not, indeed, the idea's validity. The idea of white supremacy rests simply on the fact that white men are the creators of civilization (the present civilization, which is the only one that matters; all previous civilizations are simply "contributions" to our own) and are therefore civilization's guardians and defenders. Thus it was impossible for Americans to accept the black man as one of themselves, for to do so was to jeopardize their status as white men. But not so to accept him was to deny his human reality, his human weight and complexity, and the strain of denying the overwhelmingly undeniable forced Americans into rationalizations so fantastic that they approached the pathological.

At the root of the American Negro problem is the necessity of the American 22 white man to find a way of living with the Negro in order to be able to live with himself. And the history of this problem can be reduced to the means used by Americans—lynch law and law, segregation and legal acceptance, terrorization and concession—either to come to terms with this necessity, or to find a way around it, or (most usually) to find a way of doing both these things at once. The resulting spectacle, at once foolish and dreadful, led someone to make the quite accurate observation that "the Negro-in-America is a form of insanity which overtakes white men."

23   In this long battle, a battle by no means finished, the unforeseeable effects of which will be felt by many future generations, the white man's motive was the protection of his identity; the black man was motivated by the need to establish an identity. And despite the terrorization which the Negro in America endured and endures sporadically until today, despite the cruel and totally inescapable ambivalence of his status in his country, the battle for his identity has long ago been won. He is not a visitor to the West, but a citizen there, an American; as American as the Americans who despise him, the Americans who fear him, the Americans who love him—the Americans who became less than themselves, or rose to be greater than themselves by virtue of the fact that the challenge he represented was inescapable. He is perhaps the only black man in the world whose relationship to white men is more terrible, more subtle, and more meaningful than the relationship of bitter possessed to uncertain possessor. His survival depended, and his development depends, on his ability to turn his peculiar status in the Western world to his own advantage and, it may be, to the very great advantage of that world. It remains for him to fashion out of his experience that which will give him sustenance, and a voice.

24   The cathedral at Chartres, I have said, says something to the people of this village which it cannot say to me; but it is important to understand that this cathedral says something to me which it cannot say to them. Perhaps they are struck by the power of the spires, the glory of the windows; but they have known God, after all, longer than I have known him, and in a different way, and I am terrified by the slippery bottomless well to be found in the crypt, down which heretics were hurled to death, and by the obscene, inescapable gargoyles jutting out of the stone and seeming to say that God and the devil can never be divorced. I doubt that the villagers think of the devil when they face a cathedral because they have never been identified with the devil. But I must accept the status which myth, if nothing else, gives me in the West before I can hope to change the myth.

25   Yet, if the American Negro has arrived at his identity by virtue of the absoluteness of his estrangement from his past, American white men still nourish the illusion that there is some means of recovering the European innocence, of returning to a state in which black men do not exist. This is one of the greatest errors Americans can make. The identity they fought so hard to protect has, by virtue of that battle, undergone a change: Americans are as unlike any other white people in the world as it is possible to be. I do not think, for example, that it is too much to suggest that the American vision of the world—which allows so little reality, generally speaking, for any of the darker forces in human life, which tends until today to paint moral issues in glaring black and white—owes a great deal to the battle waged by Americans to maintain between themselves and black men a human separation which could not be bridged. It is only now beginning to be borne in on us—very faintly, it must be admitted, very slowly, and very much against our will—that this vision of the world is dangerously inaccurate, and perfectly useless. For it protects our moral high-mindedness at

the terrible expense of weakening our grasp of reality. People who shut their eyes to reality simply invite their own destruction, and anyone who insists on remaining in a state of innocence long after that innocence is dead turns himself into a monster.

The time has come to realize that the interracial drama acted out on the 26 American continent has not only created a new black man, it has created a new white man, too. No road whatever will lead Americans back to the simplicity of this European village where white men still have the luxury of looking on me as a stranger. I am not, really, a stranger any longer for any American alive. One of the things that distinguishes Americans from other people is that no other people has ever been so deeply involved in the lives of black men, and vice versa. This fact faced, with all its implications, it can be seen that the history of the American Negro problem is not merely shameful, it is also something of an achievement. For even when the worst has been said, it must also be added that the perpetual challenge posed by this problem was always, somehow, perpetually met. It is precisely this black-white experience which may prove of indispensable value to us in the world we face today. This world is white no longer, and it will never be white again.

COMPREHENSION

1. According to Baldwin, what distinguishes Americans from other people? What is his purpose in highlighting these differences?
2. What connections between Europe, Africa, and America emerge from this essay? What is the relevance of the Swiss village to this frame of reference?
3. In the context of the essay, explain what Baldwin means by his statement "People are trapped in history and history is trapped in them" (paragraph 5).

RHETORIC

1. Analyze the effect of Baldwin's repetition of "there is" and "there are" constructions in paragraph 2. What does the parallelism at the start of paragraph 8 accomplish? Locate other examples of parallelism in the essay.
2. Analyze the image of winter in paragraph 2 and its relation to the rest of the essay.
3. Where in the essay is Baldwin's complex thesis condensed for the reader? What does this placement of thesis reveal about the logical method of development in the essay?
4. How does Baldwin create his introduction? What is the focus? What key motifs does he present that will inform the rest of the essay? What is the relationship of paragraph 5 to paragraph 6?
5. What paragraphs constitute the second section of the essay? What example serves to unify this section? What major shift in emphasis occurs in the third part of the essay? Explain the cathedral of Chartres as a controlling motif between these two sections.
6. What comparisons and contrasts help structure and unify the essay?

WRITING

1. Examine the paradox implicit in Baldwin's statement in the final paragraph that the history of the American Negro problem is "something of an achievement."
2. Describe a time when you felt yourself a "stranger" in a certain culture.
3. **Writing an Argument:** Write an argumentative essay on civilization based on the last sentence in Baldwin's essay: "This world is white no longer, and it will never be white again."

NETWORKING
Applying 21st-Century Literacies

Analyzing a Debate: On the Chapter 8 Networking page (at *www.mhhe.com/ mhreaderbrief1e*), follow the link to a video of a Cambridge University debate between James Baldwin and William F. Buckley Jr. What is the central disagreement between these two men? How are the issues raised in "Stranger in the Village" also addressed in this argument? Who do you see as "winning" this debate, and why?

Synthesis: Connections for Critical Thinking

1. Explore the theme of "otherness" in the essays by Baldwin, Ivins, and Ehrenreich.
2. Compare and contrast the diction, level of discourse, style, and vocabulary of Ivins, Ehrenreich, and Wolfe.
3. Both Thomas Jefferson and Martin Luther King Jr. made powerful appeals to the government in power on behalf of their people. Write a comparison-and-contrast essay that examines the language, style, and content of both essays.
4. Select the three essays you find the most and the least appealing or compelling in this chapter. Discuss why you selected them, and explore the way you developed your viewpoint.
5. Esther Dyson writes: "Something in the American psyche loves new frontiers." Apply this idea to at least three essays in this chapter.
6. Interview five parents who have children under age 10, and ask them if and how they control the online content their children view. Report your findings to your class.

NETWORKING
Applying 21st-Century Literacies

1. On Facebook or in a chat room, discuss with classmates Dyson's views on cyberspace regulation. Write a summary of your discussion.
2. Conduct online research on Ivins and Baldwin. Write an analysis of how their senses of place influence their ideas.

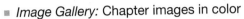

CH 8   **www.mhhe.com/mhreaderbrief1e**

- *Image Gallery:* Chapter images in color
- *Government, Politics, and Social Justice:* Information on the authors in this chapter
- *Ch. 8 Networking*

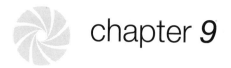

chapter 9

Media and Popular Culture
What Is the Message?

We are surrounded today as never before by images, sounds, and texts—by what Todd Gitlin, who has an essay in this chapter, terms a "media torrent." Radio and television programs, newspapers and Internet sites, MTV and video games, iPods and cell phone gadgetry increasingly mold our place in culture and society. Indeed, the power of media in our waking and subliminal lives might very well condition our understanding (or misunderstanding) of reality. Today, we can download "reality."

Today's media universe, fueled by new technology, is transforming our sense of the world. Consider the ways in which computers permit us to enter the media stream, making us willing, even compulsive, participants in and consumers of popular culture. Video games, streaming advertisements, wraparound music, newsgroups, chat rooms, and more—all provide data and sensation at warp computer speed. Some slow down the torrent: Bloggers (a word that didn't exist until recently) interrogate their lives and the "facts," even holding newspapers and television news channels accountable for information. But if, as Marshall McLuhan declared, the medium is the message, then any medium, whether old or new, has the power to reflect or construct versions of reality.

Perhaps Americans have moved from a print-based culture to an aural/visual one, preferring electronic media for information, distraction, and entertainment. For centuries books were the molders of popular taste and culture. Tocqueville in *Democracy in America* was amazed by the fact that in the rudest pioneer's hut there was a copy of Shakespeare—and probably, we might add, a copy of the best seller of all time, the Bible. Today's typical household might have more media for DVD players, MP3 players, and gaming consoles than books in a library. Of course, print media—say, a book on the ways in which major political parties manipulate the media—offer us the opportunity to scrutinize facts and sources in ways that shock jocks on radio, or talk show hosts on television, or participants in chat rooms cannot. The *medium* or *source* from which we receive sounds, images, and text—the place from which we enter the media torrent— determines the version of reality we carry with us. We can even drown in this torrent, as people who have been captured in virtual reality can attest.

The writers in this chapter invite us to enter the media torrent from a variety of places. They ask broad cultural questions about how we conduct our everyday lives and what choices we make. These questions have both local and worldwide implications, because media and their technological helpmates have created a global village permitting the instant transmission of ideas and images, as well as a subtle transfer of culture— typically American—to the remotest parts of the planet. Whether we navigate the torrent intelligently or succumb passively to the images and sounds washing over us, it is clear that the media in this century will have an increasingly significant impact on human experience.

PREVIEWING THE CHAPTER

As you read the essays in this chapter and respond to them in discussion and writing, consider the following questions:

- What is the main media form and issue on which the author focuses?
- What tone or attitude does the author take toward the subject?
- How does the author fit his or her analysis into the context of popular culture? What social, economic, psychological, or political problems or controversies are treated?
- Which areas of expertise does the author bring to bear on the subject?
- What form of rhetoric—narration and description, exposition, argument—does the writer use? If argument, what is the author's claim? What evidence does she or he provide to support this claim?
- Which essays are similar in subject, thesis, style, purpose, or method, and why?
- What have you learned about the media and popular culture from reading these essays?
- Which essays did you find the most compelling or persuasive? The least? Why?

Classic and Contemporary Images
What Do Gangster Films Reveal about Us?

Using a Critical Perspective   The best gangster films—like *Little Caesar*, *The Godfather*, and the *Sopranos* series—challenge viewers to form ethical opinions about and interpretations of the tale of crime that unfolds. Even if you haven't seen either the film or TV show depicted here, what do you think is happening in each frame? What details do you focus on? Do the two characters capture the essence of the gangster life, and why? What aspects of film art—framing, the use of close-up or distance shots, the handling of light, shadow, and color—convey an ethical statement? More broadly, in what ways can film art serve as a commentary on American life?

During the 1930s, the first decade of sound films, actors such as
Edward G. Robinson, James Cagney, and Paul Muni created the
classic portrait of the gangster as a tough-talking, violent outlaw
in films such as *Little Caesar* (1930), *The Public Enemy* (1931),
and *Scarface* (1932).

HBO's award-winning series *The Sopranos* provided a more nuanced
portrait of the gangster as a member of a corrupt, and corrupting,
organization with shifting loyalties. For example, Tony Soprano, the
character played by James Gandolfini, is a family man
beset by so many problems that he must seek psychiatric help.

Classic and Contemporary Essays
WHY ARE WE FASCINATED BY BAD MEN
IN POPULAR CULTURE?

Both Robert Warshow and Lauren Goodlad examine the portrayal of "bad" men in popular culture, and specifically our fascination with this type in television and film. Warshow in his highly allusive essay argues that the gangster in American film is a type of urban tragic hero. On the other hand, Goodlad, whose essay is also filled with references to other works, argues from a feminist perspective that Don Draper, the protagonist in the wildly popular AMC series *Mad Men,* is an "icon of masculinity-in-crisis." Essentially, both writers suggest that bad, mad men—gangsters, rogues, outlaws, even some businessmen—exert a powerful hold on our imagination because they represent a flawed mythology of American success. These bad men are ill-fated from the start because they are compelled to operate in an unforgiving cultural and economic universe. They are doomed to anxiety and failure because their key point of cultural reference—the American Dream—is intrinsically corrupt. Ultimately both writers urge us to go beyond our fascination with media types of tragic men to examine the ethical dimensions of the world they inhabit.

The Gangster as Tragic Hero

Robert Warshow

Robert Warshow (1917–1955) attended the University of Michigan and worked for the U.S. Army Security Agency from 1942 to 1946. After the war, he served as an editor of Commentary, *writing film criticism for this magazine and also for* Partisan Review. *Before his untimely death from a heart attack, Warshow had written several brilliant essays on film and on popular culture. Writing of Warshow, Lionel Trilling observed, "I believe that certain of his pieces establish themselves in the line of Hazlitt, a tradition in which I would place only one other writer of our time, George Orwell." One of these brilliant essays, focusing on the interrelation of film and society, is "The Gangster as Tragic Hero," which appeared in* The Immediate Experience: Movies, Games, Theatre and Other Aspects of Popular Culture *(1962).*

1   America, as a social and political organization, is committed to a cheerful view of life. It could not be otherwise. The sense of tragedy is a luxury of aristocratic societies, where the fate of the individual is not conceived of as having a direct

and legitimate political importance, being determined by a fixed and supra-political—that is, non-controversial—moral order or fate. Modern equalitarian societies, however, whether democratic or authoritarian in their political forms, always base themselves on the claim that they are making life happier; the avowed function of the modern state, at least in its ultimate terms, is not only to regulate social relations, but also to determine the quality and possibilities of human life in general. Happiness thus becomes the chief political issue—in a sense, the only political issue—and for that reason it can never be treated as an issue at all. If an American or a Russian is unhappy, it implies a certain reprobation of his society, and therefore, by a logic of which we can all recognize the necessity, it becomes an obligation of citizenship to be cheerful; if the authorities find it necessary, the citizen may even be compelled to make a public display of his cheerfulness on important occasions, just as he may be conscripted into the army in time of war.

Naturally, this civic responsibility rests most strongly upon the organs of mass culture. The individual citizen may still be permitted his private unhappiness so long as it does not take on political significance, the extent of this tolerance being determined by how large an area of private life the society can accommodate. But every production of mass culture is a public act and must conform with accepted notions of the public good. Nobody seriously questions the principle that it is the function of mass culture to maintain public morale, and certainly nobody in the mass audience objects to having his morale maintained.[1] At a time when the normal condition of the citizen is a state of anxiety, euphoria spreads over our culture like the broad smile of an idiot. In terms of attitudes towards life, there is very little difference between a "happy" movie like *Good News*, which ignores death and suffering, and a "sad" movie like *A Tree Grows in Brooklyn*, which uses death and suffering as incidents in the service of a higher optimism.

But, whatever its effectiveness as a source of consolation and a means of pressure for maintaining "positive" social attitudes, this optimism is fundamentally satisfying to no one, not even to those who would be most disoriented without its support. Even within the area of mass culture, there always exists a current of opposition, seeking to express by whatever means are available to it that sense of desperation and inevitable failure which optimism itself helps to create. Most often, this opposition is confined to rudimentary or semi-literate forms: in mob politics and journalism, for example, or in certain kinds of religious enthusiasm. When it does enter the field of art, it is likely to be disguised or attenuated: in an unspecific form of expression like jazz, in the basically harmless nihilism of the Marx Brothers, in the continually reasserted strain of hopelessness that often seems to be the real meaning of the soap opera. The

---

[1] In her testimony before the House Committee on Un-American Activities, Mrs. Leila Rogers said that the movie *None But the Lonely Heart* was un-American because it was gloomy. Like so much else that was said during the unhappy investigation of Hollywood, this statement was at once stupid and illuminating. One knew immediately what Mrs. Rogers was talking about; she had simply been insensitive enough to carry her philistinism to its conclusion.

gangster film is remarkable in that it fills the need for disguise (though not sufficiently to avoid arousing uneasiness) without requiring any serious distortion. From its beginnings, it has been a consistent and astonishingly complete presentation of the modern sense of tragedy.[2]

4   In its initial character, the gangster film is simply one example of the movies' constant tendency to create fixed dramatic patterns that can be repeated indefinitely with a reasonable expectation of profit. One gangster film follows another as one musical or one Western follows another. But this rigidity is not necessarily opposed to the requirements of art. There have been very successful types of art in the past which developed such specific and detailed conventions as almost to make individual examples of the type interchangeable. This is true, for example, of Elizabethan revenge tragedy and Restoration comedy.

5   For such a type to be successful means that its conventions have imposed themselves upon the general consciousness and become the accepted vehicles of a particular set of attitudes and a particular aesthetic effect. One goes to any individual example of the type with very definite expectations, and originality is to be welcomed only in the degree that it intensifies the expected experience without fundamentally altering it. Moreover, the relationship between the conventions which go to make up such a type and the real experience of its audience or the real facts of whatever situation it pretends to describe is of only secondary importance and does not determine its aesthetic force. It is only in an ultimate sense that the type appeals to its audience's experience of reality; much more immediately, it appeals to previous experience of the type itself: It creates its own field of reference.

6   Thus the importance of the gangster film, and the nature and intensity of its emotional and aesthetic impact, cannot be measured in terms of the place of the gangster himself or the importance of the problem of crime in American life. Those European moviegoers who think there is a gangster on every corner in New York are certainly deceived, but defenders of the "positive" side of American culture are equally deceived if they think it relevant to point out that most Americans have never seen a gangster. What matters is that the experience of the gangster *as an experience of art* is universal to Americans. There is almost nothing we understand better or react to more readily or with quicker intelligence. The Western film, though it seems never to diminish in popularity, is for most of us no more than the folklore of the past, familiar and understandable only because it has been repeated so often. The gangster film comes much closer. In ways that we do not easily or willingly define, the gangster speaks for us, expressing that part of the American psyche which rejects the qualities and the demands of modern life, which rejects "Americanism" itself.

7   The gangster is the man of the city, with the city's language and knowledge, with its queer and dishonest skills and its terrible daring, carrying his life in his

---

[2]Efforts have been made from time to time to bring the gangster film into line with the prevailing optimism and social constructiveness of our culture; *Kiss of Death* is a recent example. These efforts are usually unsuccessful; the reasons for their lack of success are interesting in themselves, but I shall not be able to discuss them here.

hands like a placard, like a club. For everyone else, there is at least the theoretical possibility of another world—in that happier American culture which the gangster denies, the city does not really exist; it is only a more crowded and more brightly lit country—but for the gangster there is only the city; he must inhabit it in order to personify it: not the real city, but that dangerous and sad city of the imagination which is so much more important, which is the modern world. And the gangster—though there are real gangsters—is also, and primarily, a creature of the imagination. The real city, one might say, produces only criminals; the imaginary city produces the gangster: He is what we want to be and what we are afraid we may become.

Thrown into the crowd without background or advantages, with only those 8 ambiguous skills which the rest of us—the real people of the real city—can only pretend to have, the gangster is required to make his way, to make his life and impose it on others. Usually, when we come upon him, he has already made his choice or the choice has already been made for him, it doesn't matter which: We are not permitted to ask whether at some point he could have chosen to be something else than what he is.

The gangster's activity is actually a form of rational enterprise, involving 9 fairly definite goals and various techniques for achieving them. But thus rationality is usually no more than a vague background; we know, perhaps, that the gangster sells liquor or that he operates a numbers racket; often we are not given even that much information. So his activity becomes a kind of pure criminality: He hurts people. Certainly our response to the gangster film is most consistently and most universally a response to sadism; we gain the double satisfaction of participating vicariously in the gangster's sadism and then seeing it turned against the gangster himself.

But on another level the quality of irrational brutality and the quality of ra- 10 tional enterprise become one. Since we do not see the rational and routine aspects of the gangster's behavior, the practice of brutality—the quality of unmixed criminality—becomes the totality of his career. At the same time, we are always conscious that the whole meaning of this career is a drive for success: the typical gangster film presents a steady upward progress followed by a very precipitate fall. Thus brutality itself becomes at once the means to success and the content of success—a success that is defined in its most general terms, not as accomplishment or specific gain, but simply as the unlimited possibility of aggression. (In the same way, film presentations of businessmen tend to make it appear that they achieve their success by talking on the telephone and holding conferences and that success *is* talking on the telephone and holding conferences.)

From this point of view, the initial contact between the film and its audi- 11 ence is an agreed conception of human life: that man is a being with the possibilities of success or failure. This principle, too, belongs to the city; one must emerge from the crowd or else one is nothing. On that basis the necessity of the action is established, and it progresses, by inalterable paths to the point where the gangster lies dead and the principle has been modified: There is really only one possibility—failure. The final meaning of the city is anonymity and death.

12   In the opening scene of *Scarface,* we are shown a successful man; we know he is successful because he has just given a party of opulent proportions and because he is called Big Louie. Through some monstrous lack of caution, he permits himself to be alone for a few moments. We understand from this immediately that he is about to be killed. No convention of the gangster film is more strongly established than this: It is dangerous to be alone. And yet the very conditions of success make it impossible not to be alone, for success is always the establishment of an *individual* pre-eminence that must be imposed on others, in whom it automatically arouses hatred; the successful man is an outlaw. The gangster's whole life is an effort to assert himself as an individual, to draw himself out of the crowd, and he always dies *because* he is an individual; the final bullet thrusts him back, makes him, after all, a failure. "Mother of God," says the dying Little Caesar, "is this the end of Rico?"—speaking of himself thus in the third person because what has been brought low is not the undifferentiated *man,* but the individual with a name, the gangster, the success; even to himself he is a creature of the imagination. (T. S. Eliot has pointed out that a number of Shakespeare's tragic heroes have this trick of looking at themselves dramatically; their true identity, the thing that is destroyed when they die, is something outside themselves—not a man, but a style of life, a kind of meaning.)

13   At bottom, the gangster is doomed because he is under the obligation to succeed, not because the means he employs are unlawful. In the deeper layers of the modern consciousness, *all* means are unlawful, every attempt to succeed is an act of aggression, leaving one alone and guilty and defenseless among enemies: One is *punished* for success. This is our intolerable dilemma: that failure is a kind of death and success is evil and dangerous, is—ultimately—impossible. The effect of the gangster film is to embody this dilemma in the person of the gangster and resolve it by his death. The dilemma is resolved because it is *his* death, not ours. We are safe; for the moment, we can acquiesce in our failure, we can choose to fail.

COMPREHENSION

1. What are the "organs of mass culture" (paragraph 2)? What properties do they all have in common?
2. Define the term *tragic hero* as Warshow uses it in his title.
3. Compare and contrast Warshow's concepts of the "real city" with those of the "imaginary city" as they relate to modern life and mass culture.

RHETORIC

1. Although the ultimate focus of the essay is on the "gangster," the subject is not referred to until paragraph 4. Why does Warshow need so much exposition before focusing on his main topic?

2. What do terms such as *supra-political* (paragraph 1), *harmless nihilism* (paragraph 3), and *general consciousness* (paragraph 5) suggest about the tone of the essay? What do they imply concerning the target audience for the essay?

3. Study the topic sentence of each paragraph. Are the topic sentences successful in setting up the material that follows? How does this strategy enhance or detract from the coherence of the author's argument?

4. Essayists usually provide their thesis at the beginning of their essays. Where does Warshow provide the thesis in his essay? What is the purpose and effect of placing it where he does?

5. The author explains the nature of the gangster film genre—its function, characters, themes, plots, meanings, and so on—*before* he cites specific films. Is this a rhetorical weakness in the essay, or does it give the essay particular potency? Explain.

6. Does the conclusion summarize the main points of the essay, bolster them, or provide new insights into them? Or does it do a combination of these things? Explain.

7. Study the introductory paragraph and the conclusion. What themes are reiterated or complemented? How do these two paragraphs serve to provide both thematic and structural coherence?

WRITING

1. Select a genre of television show or movie. Analyze its conventions and the degree to which these conventions transgress the implicit values of our society.

2. **Writing an Argument:** Argue for or against the proposition that genre movies are a form of escapism that distorts the individual's concept of the actual society he or she lives in and its citizens.

NETWORKING
Applying 21st-Century Literacies

Analyzing a Film: Select a contemporary gangster movie. Using Warshow's criteria, demonstrate—via reference to its characters, plot, and theme—how your selection reinforces the author's thesis.

Why We Love "Mad Men"

Lauren M. E. Goodlad

Lauren M. E. Goodlad has degrees from Cornell University (BS), New York University (MA), and Columbia University (PhD). She is an associate professor of English at the University of Illinois at Urbana-Champaign, where she teaches Victorian literature and directs the Unit for Criticism and Interpretative Theory. Goodlad has published

Victorian Literature and the Victorian State *(2003) and most recently is a co-editor of* Goth: Undead Subculture *(2007). She worked in the 1980s as a cosmetics and fragrance copywriter in New York City. In the following essay, which was published in the* Chronicle of Higher Education *in 2009, Goodlad combines her personal response to* Mad Men *with unique feminist critical inquiry.*

1   Like most women who call themselves feminists, I've spent my life avoiding men like Don Draper, the incorrigible ladies' man at the center of *Mad Men*, a show about a Madison Avenue advertising agency in the early 1960s. I took a pass on the show during its first season, catching up with it on DVD when the mounting enthusiasm of friends and co-workers piqued my curiosity.

2   By the time the season-three premier was promoted this month, my friends (men and women in their 30s and 40s) had taken to posting Madmenized avatars of themselves on their Facebook pages. And I was one of them, styling myself on madmenyourself.com in a chic red dress, gloves, and cat's-eye glasses. What had happened to make these politically progressive adults in the last days of their youth identify with characters from their parents' generation?

3   I have been intrigued by the mysteries of culture before. In the 1990s, I was writing on gothic subculture and the phenomenon of "men who feel and cry"— men like Anne Rice's vampires, Tim Burton's Edward Scissorhands, and Nine Inch Nails' Trent Reznor, all of whom beckoned young men to dramatize emotion in ways that previous generations had scorned as unmasculine. Alongside those men in black were harsher specimens of masculinity in crisis: men like Tyler Durden, the split personality who launches an underground subculture called Fight Club.

4   While superficially different, both kinds of men were desperate to feel, through catharsis or brutal violence. Yet most of these tales focused on men's relationships with one another, like Tyler's two halves, or Lestat and Louis in Rice's *Interview with the Vampire*. They were men searching for their feelings in the company of other men.

5   And now comes Don Draper, icon of masculinity-in-crisis for the 21st century. Don is in pain, yes, and hurting himself, too (for all his spectacular emotional reserve). But he is also different. No tears or blood on that impeccably pressed suit. No close ties to other men. What is it that makes this odd blend of Jay Gatsby, American Gigolo, and the Man in the Gray Flannel Suit so captivating a figure for today?

6   When I asked a sample of folks close to hand what they thought of the show, strangely enough, the first three said virtually the same thing—all references to Don: *"The guy is hot."* (OK, my mother, a veteran of the *Mad Men* era, said "very handsome," not "hot".) To be sure, the show need not be experienced as the story of a "hot" guy in crisis. A close female colleague, indifferent to Don's eros, tunes in mostly for the Peggy Olson narrative. And there is my husband, who enjoys the show for its complexity and period detail, but hates Don Draper for his selfishness and lies. Like Don, my husband is a

Jon Hamm as Don Draper in the AMC series *Mad Men*.

hard-working professional father of two in his late 30s. Unlike Don . . . well, you could call him the anti-Don.

Although Don Draper is the show's center of gravity, a constellation of in- 7 triguing personalities surrounds him. Several of those characters suggest series that might have been: *Mad Women*, in which Joan Holloway and Peggy Olson take different paths in the struggle for integrity in a man's world; *Mad Closet*, the story of Salvatore Romano's slow-motion sexual awakening; *Bad Men*, a close study of Pete Campbell's toxic cocktail of ambition and insecurity; *Race Men*, in which Paul Kinsey strives to be a hero in the civil-rights movement without exposing himself as an insufferable honkie; *Sad Men*, a nighttime soap in which Roger Sterling deludes himself about his impending mortality; and of course *Mod Men*, a show about style.

And then there is Don's beautiful wife, Betty, who, though clearly his better 8 half, is not his patsy. A kind of Donna Reed on steroids, she is much, much more than the first woman on television to have a passionate affair with a household appliance. Her vigorous horsemanship, her facility with a shotgun: These are the signs that though raised to follow the grooves, Betty cannot be underestimated.

Witness the end of the first season when, opening the phone bill, she learns that Don has been checking up on her with her psychoanalyst. We think she is in the dark about Don's infidelity; but then, as she lies on the couch, we learn that she has known all along. Betty's decision to tell the good doctor wasn't Freud's talking cure but a savvy move on the chess board that is the Draper marriage. She knows that the shrink will tell Don, so that Don will learn, with a minimum of confrontation, that his fooling around isn't fooling anyone.

9   Conventional wisdom says that women are irresistibly attracted to power. And yet, professionally speaking, Don's position is precarious. Less Gordon Gekko in *Wall Street* than Montgomery Clift's character in *A Place in the Sun*, he is vulnerable to corporate management, professional rivals, and the whims of clients. With no family connections to buttress him, Don has nothing to sell but himself. If he is powerful, it's because the particular commodity he has to offer is selling itself: the trick of making selling seem magical in a consumer society. That is why Don's "hotness" is not the garden-variety sort—not the televised equivalent of an Abercrombie & Fitch ad—but the aspect of his character that connects his existential crisis to ours.

10   Don's sexual tensions bespeak his brilliance as an ad man. His genius for spinning fantasies works in boardroom and bedroom alike. Though superficially a "man's man," he does not long for intimacy with other men. Women are his métier; their desire is the complement to the seductive powers his clients pay him to wield. This is not to say that "sex sells"—a crude logic that Don despises. It is to say that in a consumer society, the fine art of selling is a lot like sex.

11   While his milieu is fundamentally misogynistic, Don himself is far less so. At home he is a possessive, philandering husband, but at work he is the least sexist of the lot, respecting the feelings of middle-age women and promoting his talented secretary.

12   If Betty is stuck playing Don's Madonna—the angelic mother he never had—the other women in his life are more like female variations on Don. There is Midge, the independent bohemian who doesn't make breakfast; Bobbie Barrett, the shrewd businesswoman whose frank sexual hunger ignites Don's kinky side; and Rachel, also a businesswoman, but memorable as the one who got away. Her Jewishness stands for a kind of depth that might cut through Don's mad world if only his desire to connect could trump his need to seduce. In one of many grace notes, Don, in need of a pseudonym, calls himself Tilden Katz—the man Rachel marries after she ends their affair. It is Don imagining himself as an anti-Don.

13   In the title poem of *Meditations in an Emergency,* a collection by Frank O'Hara that Don reads, the speaker writes, "no one trusts me" because "I am always looking away." As we eventually learn, Don sends this book to the widow of the man whose identity he stole. But Don's past is really window dressing for a more systemic crisis. There are lots of men with Don's issues who aren't orphans and didn't change their names. If there is anyone who trusts Don it is Peggy, a woman whose loyalty he values too much to throw away—perhaps because he knows that she is like him: Her talent for selling will take her places.

For some viewers, the secret of *Mad Men*'s success is the pleasure of watch- 14
ing characters who don't know, as we do, that "change is gonna come." If that's
true, we have more reason to be anxious voyeurs than smug ones. We may know
more than Don, Roger, and Betty about the dangers of booze and cigarettes—but
we still die as they do (and die increasingly of cancer). And while we have
made real gains in sexual and racial equality, the price we have paid is the reactionary anger that haunts every aspect of our social being.

The open secret of our time is that we are less secure than were our pre- 15
cursors in the *Mad Men* era. If we know them to be in the grips of a cold war
that finally came to an end, we know ourselves to be losing wars of our own
making—a boundless "war on terror" and the destruction of our own environment. We do not watch *Mad Men* because we imagine ourselves as free of vice
and illusions; we watch it because we know that our lives, too, are one long
meditation in an emergency.

In the dwindling prosperity that is capitalism in the 21st century, every one 16
of us knows that we must sell ourselves, make our pitch, compete for our place
in the sun. Though Don has a nice house and car, like most of us, he will never
join the big leagues. Among us today, he would not be a Wall Street banker or
CEO, for he is not cut from that cloth. His golden parachute is the dream of
another life in a California that, if it ever existed, exists no more.

"The guy is hot." If we feast our eyes on Don, wanting him and wanting to 17
be like him, it is perhaps because we, too, want to make it look that good. As
Frank O'Hara wrote, "It is easy to be beautiful; it is difficult to appear so." Don
gratifies the illusion that a life lived as a commodity can somehow be meaningful; that if we close our eyes, the art of selling will be like the best sex we
ever had.

COMPREHENSION

1. Why does Goodlad identify herself as a feminist and why would a self-styled
   feminist defend a character like Don Draper? How does this defense of Don work
   in Goodlad's feminist interpretation of *Mad Men*? Provide examples from the essay
   to support your response.
2. According to Goodlad, the main character in *Mad Men*, Don Draper, is an "icon of
   masculinity-in-crisis" (paragraph 5). What does she mean by this phrase? Where in
   the essay does she explore this idea?
3. What observations does Goodlad make about American culture in this essay?

RHETORIC

1. Goodlad summarizes various plotlines and introduces primary characters in *Mad
   Men*. Why does she devote so much space to this overview? What assumptions is
   she making about her primary audience, who typically would be college teachers

and administrators? (Recall that this essay appeared in the *Chronicle of Higher Education*.) What information does she convey that the average viewer might not know or find interesting?

2. What is Goodlad's thesis? Does she state or imply her main idea? Explain.

3. Identify the allusions that Goodlad uses in this essay. What is her purpose in referring to other characters and works, ranging from Anne Rice's vampires to Frank O'Hara? (Who *was* Frank O'Hara?)

4. Goodlad makes a number of assertions regarding the cultural significance of *Mad Men*. What are they, and do they effectively support her thesis? Are these assertions facts or opinions? Explain your viewpoint.

5. Which paragraphs constitute what we might consider to be Goodlad's conclusion? Is this conclusion effective? Why or why not?

WRITING

1. Watch one episode of *Mad Men*, and then write your own critical response to it.

2. **Writing an Argument:** It could be argued that television series like *Mad Men*, *The Sopranos*, and *Breaking Bad* engage in negative stereotyping. Which side of the debate do you take? Write an argumentative essay on this topic. State your claim, offer evidence, and structure the argument carefully in a series of key reasons in support of your claim.

NETWORKING
Applying 21st-Century Literacies

Critically Interpreting a Television Series: Write a feminist interpretation of a television series that you watch regularly or are familiar with.

Synthesis: Classic and Contemporary Questions for Comparison

1. Warshow critiques the function and role of the gangster in popular media, whereas Goodlad focuses on an analysis of one television series in which the life of an ad man is articulated. How do these different focuses determine the thesis of each essay? What are the positive and negative consequences of addressing a broad issue in "The Gangster as Tragic Hero" without using one extended example, as opposed to the detailed analysis of one TV series in "Why We Love 'Mad Men'"?

2. Goodlad writes an admittedly feminist critique of *Mad Men*. How would you categorize Warshow's critical approach? Is he interested in theory? Why or why not?

3. Compare and contrast Warshow's and Goodlad's observations about American culture in their respective essays. In which of these essays do you find these cultural insights to be most convincing, and why?

Wonder Woman

Gloria Steinem

Gloria Steinem (b. 1934) was born and raised in Toledo, Ohio; she attended Smith College, receiving a BA in government in 1956. A noted feminist and political activist, Steinem in 1968 helped to found New York *magazine; in 1971 she cofounded* Ms. *magazine and served as its editor. Whether campaigning for Robert Kennedy, defending raising money for the United Farm Workers, or championing women's reproductive rights, Steinem has been on the cutting edge of American politics and social activism for almost five decades. Her books include* The Thousand Indias *(1957),* Outrageous Acts and Everyday Rebellions *(1983),* Marilyn: Norma Jean *(1986),* Revolution from Within *(1992),* Moving beyond Words *(1994), and* Doing Sixty and Seventy *(2006). In the following essay, Steinem explains why the comic book heroine Wonder Woman (who was on the first cover of* Ms.*) was such a formative influence during her childhood.*

Wonder Woman is the only female super-hero to be published continuously since 1 comic books began—indeed, she is one of the few to have existed at all or to be anything other than part of a male super-hero group—but this may strike many readers as a difference without much distinction. After all, haven't comic books always been a little disreputable? Something that would never have been assigned in school? The answer to those questions is yes, which is exactly why they are important. Comic books have power—including over the child who still lives within each of us—because they are *not* part of the "serious" grown-up world.

I remember hundreds of nights reading comic books under the covers with 2 a flashlight; dozens of car trips while my parents told me I was ruining my eyes and perhaps my mind ("brain-deadeners" was what my mother called them); and countless hours spent hiding in a tree or some other inaccessible spot where I could pore over their pages in sweet freedom. Because my family's traveling meant I didn't go to school regularly until I was about twelve, comic books joined cereal boxes and ketchup labels as the primers that taught me how to read. They were even cheap enough to be the first things I bought on my own— a customer who couldn't see over the countertop but whose dignity was greatly enhanced by making a choice, counting out carefully hoarded coins, and completing a grown-up exchange.

I've always wondered if this seemingly innate drive toward independence in 3 children isn't more than just "a movement toward mastery," as psychologists say. After all, each of us is the result of millennia of environment and heredity, a unique combination that could never happen before—or again. Like a seed that contains a plant, a child is already a unique person; an ancient spirit born into a body too small to express itself, or even cope with the world. I remember feeling the greatest love for my parents whenever they allowed me to express my own will, whether that meant wearing an inappropriate hat for days on end, or eating dessert before I had finished dinner.

4   Perhaps it's our memories of past competence and dreams for the future that create the need for super-heroes in the first place. Leaping skyscrapers in a single bound, seeing through walls, and forcing people to tell the truth by encircling them in a magic lasso—all would be satisfying fantasies at any age, but they may be psychological necessities when we have trouble tying our shoes, escaping a worldview composed mainly of belts and knees, and getting grown-ups to *pay attention*.

5   The problem is that the super-heroes who perform magical feats—indeed, even mortal heroes who are merely competent—are almost always men. A female child is left to believe that, even when her body is as big as her spirit, she will still be helping with minor tasks, appreciating the accomplishments of others, and waiting to be rescued. Of course, pleasure is to be found in all these experiences of helping, appreciating, and being rescued; pleasure that should be open to boys, too. Even in comic books, heroes sometimes work in groups or are called upon to protect their own kind, not just helpless females. But the truth is that a male super-hero is more likely to be vulnerable, if only to create suspense, than a female character is to be powerful or independent. For little girls, the only alternative is suppressing a crucial part of ourselves by transplanting our consciousness into a male character—which usually means a white one, thus penalizing girls of color doubly, and boys of color, too. Otherwise, choices remain limited: in the case of girls, to an "ideal" life of sitting around like a Technicolor clotheshorse, getting into jams with villains, and saying things like, "Oh, Superman! I'll always be grateful to you"; in the case of boys of color, to identifying with villains who may be the only ethnic characters with any power; and in the case of girls of color, to making an impossible choice between parts of their identity. It hardly seems worth learning to tie our shoes.

6   I'm happy to say that I was rescued from this dependent fate at the age of seven or so; rescued (Great Hera!) by a woman. Not only did she have the wisdom of Athena and Aphrodite's power to inspire love, she was also faster than Mercury and stronger than Hercules. In her all-woman home on Paradise Island, a refuge of ancient Amazon culture protected from nosy travelers by magnetic thought-fields that created an area known to the world as the Bermuda Triangle, she had come to her many and amazing powers naturally. Together with her Amazon sisters, she had been trained in them from infancy and perfected them in Greek-style contests of dexterity, strength, and speed. The lesson was that each of us might have unknown powers within us, if we only believed and practiced them. (To me, it always seemed boring that Superman had bullet-proof skin, X-ray vision, and the ability to fly. Where was the contest?) Though definitely white, as were all her Amazon sisters, she was tall and strong, with dark hair and eyes—a relief from the weak, bosomy, blonde heroines of the 1940s.

Of course, this Amazon did need a few fantastic gadgets to help her once 7
she entered a modern world governed by Ares, God of War, not Aphrodite,
Goddess of Love: a magic golden lasso that compelled all within its coils to
obey her command, silver bracelets that repelled bullets, and an invisible plane
that carried her through time as well as space. But she still had to learn how to
throw the lasso with accuracy, be agile enough to deflect bullets from her silver-
encased wrists, and navigate an invisible plane.

Charles Moulton, whose name appeared on each episode as Wonder Wom- 8
an's writer and creator, had seen straight into my heart and understood the fears
of violence and humiliation hidden there. No longer did I have to pretend to like
the "POW!" and "SPLAT!" of boys' comic books, from Captain Marvel to the Green
Hornet. No longer did I have nightmares after looking at ghoulish images of
torture and murder, bloody scenes made all the more realistic by steel-booted
Nazis and fang-toothed Japanese who were caricatures of World War II enemies
then marching in every newsreel. (Eventually, the sadism of boys' comic books
was so extreme that it inspired Congressional hearings, and publishers were
asked to limit the number of severed heads and dripping entrails—a reminder
that television wasn't the first popular medium selling sadism to boys.) Best of
all, I could stop pretending to enjoy the ridicule, bossing-around, and constant
endangering of female characters. In these Amazon adventures, only the villains
bought the idea that "masculine" meant aggression and "feminine" meant submission. Only the occasional female accomplice said things like "Girls want
superior men to boss them around," and even they were usually converted to
the joys of self-respect by the story's end.

This was an Amazon super-hero who never killed her enemies. Instead, she 9
converted them to a belief in equality and peace, to self-reliance, and respect for
the rights of others. If villains destroyed themselves, it was through their own
actions or some unbloody accident. Otherwise, they might be conquered by
force, but it was a force tempered by love and justice.

In short, she was wise, beautiful, brave, and explicitly out to change "a 10
world torn by the hatreds and wars of men."

She was Wonder Woman.   11

Only much later, when I was in my thirties and modern feminism had be- 12
gun to explain the political roots of women's status—instead of accepting some
"natural" inferiority decreed by biology, God, or Freud—did I realize how hard
Charles Moulton had tried to get an egalitarian worldview into comic book
form. From Wonder Woman's birth myth as Princess Diana of Paradise Island,
"that enlightened land," to her adventures in America disguised as Diana
Prince, a be-spectacled army nurse and intelligence officer (a clear steal from
Superman's Clark Kent), this female super-hero was devoted to democracy,
peace, justice, and "liberty and freedom for all womankind."

One typical story centers on Prudence, a young pioneer in the days of the 13
American Frontier, where Wonder Woman has been transported by the invisi-
ble plane that doubles as a time machine. After being rescued from a Perils of
Pauline life, Prudence finally realizes her own worth, and also the worth of all

women. "From now on," she says proudly to Wonder Woman, "I'll rely on myself, not on a man." Another story ends with Wonder Woman explaining her own long-running romance with Captain Steve Trevor, the American pilot whose crash-landing on Paradise Island was Aphrodite's signal that the strongest and wisest of all the Amazons must answer the call of a war-torn world. As Wonder Woman says of this colleague whom she so often rescues: "I can never love a dominant man."

14   The most consistent villain is Ares, God of War, a kind of metavillain who considers women "the natural spoils of war" and insists they stay home as the slaves of men. Otherwise, he fears women will spread their antiwar sentiments, create democracy in the world, and leave him dishonored and unemployed. That's why he keeps trying to trick Queen Hippolyte, Princess Diana's mother, into giving up her powers as Queen of the Amazons, thus allowing him to conquer Paradise Island and destroy the last refuge of ancient feminism. It is in memory of a past time when the Amazons did give in to the soldiers of Ares, and were enslaved by them, that Aphrodite requires each Amazon to wear a pair of cufflike bracelets. If captured and bound by them (as Wonder Woman sometimes is in particularly harrowing episodes), an Amazon loses all her power. Wearing them is a reminder of the fragility of female freedom.

15   In America, however, villains are marked not only by their violence, but by their prejudice and lust for money. Thomas Tighe, woman-hating industrialist, is typical. After being rescued by Wonder Woman from accidental imprisonment in his own bank vault, he refuses to give her the promised reward of a million dollars. Though the money is needed to support Holliday College, the home of the band of college girls who aid Wonder Woman, Tighe insists that its students must first complete impossible tests of strength and daring. Only after Wonder Woman's powers allow them to meet every challenge does Tighe finally admit: "You win, Wonder Woman! . . . I am no longer a woman hater." She replies: "Then you're the real winner, Mr. Tighe! Because when one ceases to hate, he becomes stronger!"

16   Other villains are not so easily converted. Chief among them is Dr. Psycho, perhaps a parody of Sigmund Freud. An "evil genius" who "abhors women," the mad doctor's intentions are summed up in this scene-setting preface to an episode called "Battle for Womanhood": "With weird cunning and dark, forbidden knowledge of the occult, Dr. Psycho prepares to change the independent status of modern American women back to the days of the sultans and slave markets, clanking chains and abject captivity. But sly and subtle Psycho reckons without Wonder Woman!"

17   When I looked into the origins of my proto-feminist super-hero, I discovered that her pseudonymous creator had been a very non-Freudian psychologist named William Moulton Marston. Also a lawyer, businessman, prison reformer, and inventor of the lie-detector test (no doubt the inspiration for Wonder Woman's magic lasso), he had invented Wonder Woman as a heroine for little girls, and also as a conscious alternative to the violence of comic books for boys. In fact, Wonder Woman did attract some boys as readers, but the

integrated world of comic book trading revealed her true status: at least three Wonder Woman comic books were necessary to trade for one of Superman. Among the many male super-heroes, only Superman and Batman were to be as long-lived as Wonder Woman, yet she was still a second-class citizen.

Of course, it's also true that Marston's message wasn't as feminist as it might have been. Instead of portraying the goal of full humanity for women and men, which is what feminism has in mind, he often got stuck in the subject/object, winner/loser paradigm of "masculine" versus "feminine," and came up with female superiority instead. As he wrote: "Women represent love; men represent force. Man's use of force without love brings evil and unhappiness. Wonder Woman proves that women are superior to men because they have love in addition to force." No wonder I was inspired but confused by the isolationism of Paradise Island: Did women have to live separately in order to be happy and courageous? No wonder even boys who could accept equality might have felt less than good about themselves in some of these stories: Were there *any* men who could escape the cultural instruction to be violent? [18]

Wonder Woman herself sometimes got trapped in this either/or choice. As she muses to herself: "Some girls love to have a man stronger than they are to make them do things. Do I like it? I don't know, it's sort of thrilling. But isn't it more fun to make a man obey?" Even female villains weren't capable of being evil on their own. Instead, they were hyperfeminine followers of men's commands. Consider Priscilla Rich, the upper-class antagonist who metamorphoses into the Cheetah, a dangerous she-animal. "Women have been submissive to men," wrote Marston, "and taken men's psychology [force without love] as their own." [19]

In those wartime years, stories could verge on a jingoistic, even racist patriotism. Wonder Woman sometimes forgot her initial shock at America's unjust patriarchal system and confined herself to defeating a sinister foreign threat by proving that women could be just as loyal and brave as men in service of their country. Her costume was a version of the Stars and Stripes. Some of her adversaries were suspiciously short, ugly, fat, or ethnic as a symbol of "un-American" status. In spite of her preaching against violence and for democracy, the good guys were often in uniform, and no country but the United States was seen as a bastion of freedom. [20]

But Marston didn't succumb to stereotypes as often as most comic book writers of the 1940s. Though Prudence, his frontier heroine, is threatened by monosyllabic Indians, Prudence's father turns out to be the true villain, who has been cheating the Indians. And the irrepressible Etta Candy, one of Wonder Woman's band of college girls, is surely one of the few fat-girl heroines in comics. [21]

There are other unusual rewards. Queen Hippolyte, for instance, is a rare example of a mother who is good, powerful, and a mentor to her daughter. She founds nations, fights to protect Paradise Island, and is a source of strength to Wonder Woman as she battles the forces of evil and inequality. Mother and daughter stay in touch through a sort of telepathic TV set, and the result is a team of equals who are separated only by experience. In the flashback episode in which Queen Hippolyte succumbs to Hercules, she is even seen as a sexual [22] being. How many girl children grew to adulthood with no such example of a strong, sensual mother—except for these slender stories? How many mothers preferred sons, or believed the patriarchal myth that competition is "natural" between mothers and daughters, or tamed their daughters instead of encouraging their wildness and strength? We are just beginning to realize the sense of anger and loss in girls whose mothers had no power to protect them, or forced them to conform out of fear for their safety, or left them to identify only with their fathers if they had any ambition at all.

23   Finally, there is Wonder Woman's ability to unleash the power of self-respect within the women around her; to help them work together and support each other. This may not seem revolutionary to male readers accustomed to stories that depict men working together, but for females who are usually seen as competing for the favors of men—especially little girls who may just be getting to the age when girlfriends betray each other for the approval of boys—this discovery of sisterhood can be exhilarating indeed. Women get a rare message of independence, of depending on themselves, not even on Wonder Woman. "You saved yourselves," as she says in one of her inevitable morals at story's end. "I only showed you that you could."

24 Whatever the shortcomings of William Marston, his virtues became clear after his death in 1947. Looking back at the post-Marston stories I had missed the first time around—for at twelve or thirteen, I thought I had outgrown Wonder Woman and had abandoned her—I could see how little her later writers understood her spirit. She became sexier-looking and more submissive, violent episodes increased, more of her adversaries were female, and Wonder Woman herself required more help from men in order to triumph. Like so many of her real-life sisters in the postwar era of conservatism and "togetherness" of the 1950s, she had fallen on very hard times.

25   By the 1960s, Wonder Woman had given up her magic lasso, her bullet-deflecting bracelets, her invisible plane, and all her Amazonian powers. Though she still had adventures and even practiced karate, any attractive man could disarm her. She had become a kind of female James Bond, though much more boring because she was denied his sexual freedom. She was Diana Prince, a mortal who walked about in boutique, car-hop clothes and took the advice of a male mastermind named "I Ching."

26   It was in this sad state that I first rediscovered my Amazon super-hero in 1972. *Ms.* magazine had just begun, and we were looking for a cover story for its first regular issue to appear in July. Since Joanne Edgar and other of its founding editors had also been rescued by Wonder Woman in their childhoods, we decided to rescue Wonder Woman in return. Though it wasn't easy to persuade her publishers to let us put her original image on the cover of a new and unknown feminist magazine, or to reprint her 1940s Golden Age episodes inside, we finally succeeded. Wonder Woman appeared on newsstands again in all her original glory, striding through city streets like a colossus, stopping planes and bombs with one hand and rescuing buildings with the other.

Clearly, there were many nostalgic grown-ups and heroine-starved readers 27
of all ages. The consensus of response seemed to be that if we had all read more
about Wonder Woman and less about Dick and Jane, we might have been a lot
better off. As for her publishers, they, too, were impressed. Under the direction
of Dorothy Woolfolk, the first woman editor of Wonder Woman in all her long
history, she was returned to her original Amazon status—golden lasso, bracelets, and all.

One day some months after her rebirth, I got a phone call from one of Won- 28
der Woman's tougher male writers. "Okay," he said, "she's got all her Amazon
powers back. She talks to the Amazons on Paradise Island. She even has a Black
Amazon sister named Nubia. Now will you leave me alone?"

I said we would.   29

In the 1970s, Wonder Woman became the star of a television series. As played 30
by Lynda Carter, she was a little blue of eye and large of breast, but she still retained her Amazon powers, her ability to convert instead of kill, and her appeal
for many young female viewers. There were some who refused to leave their
TV sets on Wonder Woman night. A few young boys even began to dress up as
Wonder Woman on Halloween—a true revolution.

In the 1980s, Wonder Woman's story line was revamped by DC Comics, which 31
reinvented its male super-heroes Superman and Batman at about the same time.
Steve Trevor became a veteran of Vietnam; he remained a friend, but was romanti-
cally involved with Etta Candy. Wonder Woman acquired a Katharine Hepburn–
Spencer Tracy relationship with a street-smart Boston detective named Ed
Indelicato, whose tough-guy attitude played off Wonder Woman's idealism. She
also gained a friend and surrogate mother in Julia Kapatelis, a leading archaeolo-
gist and professor of Greek culture at Harvard University who can understand the
ancient Greek that is Wonder Woman's native tongue, and be a model of a smart,
caring, single mother for girl readers. Julia's teenage daughter, Vanessa, is the age
of many readers and goes through all of their uncertainties, trials, and tribulations,
but has the joy of having a powerful older sister in Wonder Woman. There is even
Myndi Mayer, a slick Hollywood public relations agent who turns Wonder
Woman into America's hero, and is also in constant danger of betraying Diana's
idealistic spirit. In other words, there are many of the currents of society today,
from single mothers to the worries of teenage daughters and a commercial culture,
instead of the simpler plots of America's dangers in World War II.

You will see whether Wonder Woman carries her true Amazon spirit into 32
the present. If not, let her publishers know. She belongs to you.

Since Wonder Woman's beginnings more than a half century ago, however, a 33
strange thing has happened: The Amazon myth has been rethought as archaeological relics have come to light. Though Amazons had been considered figments
of the imagination, perhaps the mythological evidence of man's fear of woman,
there is a tentative but growing body of evidence to support the theory that
some Amazon-like societies did exist. In Europe, graves once thought to contain

male skeletons—because they were buried with weapons or were killed by battle wounds—have turned out to hold skeletons of females after all. In the jungles
of Brazil, scientists have found caves of what appears to have been an all-female
society. The caves are strikingly devoid of the usual phallic design and theme;
they feature, instead, the triangular female symbol, and the only cave that does
bear male designs is believed to have been the copulatorium, where Amazons
mated with males from surrounding tribes, kept only the female children, and
returned male infants to the tribe. Such archaeological finds have turned up not
only along the Amazon River in Brazil, but at the foot of the Atlas Mountains in
northwestern Africa, and on the European and Asiatic sides of the Black Sea.

34   There is still far more controversy than agreement, but a shared supposition
of these myths is this: Imposing patriarchy on the gynocracy of pre-history took
many centuries and great cruelty. Rather than give up freedom and worship
only male gods, some bands of women resisted. They formed all-woman cultures that survived by capturing men from local tribes, mating with them, and
raising their girl children to have great skills of body and mind. These bands
became warriors and healers who were sometimes employed for their skills by
patriarchal cultures around them. As a backlash culture, they were doomed, but
they may also have lasted for centuries.

35   Perhaps that's the appeal of Wonder Woman, Paradise Island, and this comic
book message. It's not only a child's need for a lost independence, but an adult's
need for a lost balance between women and men, between humans and nature. As
the new Wonder Woman says to Vanessa, "Remember your *power*, little sister."

36   However simplified, that is Wonder Woman's message: Remember Our
Power.

COMPREHENSION

1. According to Steinem, why are children drawn to comic books and superheroes?
2. Why did Wonder Woman appeal especially to Steinem? What distinctions does she
   draw between the ways boys and girls view action heroes?
3. The writer traces the development of Wonder Woman from her inception during
   the 1940s to the 1980s. How did Wonder Woman change over the years? How did
   she remain true to her creator's (William Marston) conception of her? What does
   Steinem think about these changes?

RHETORIC

1. What is this essay's persuasive thesis?
2. At whom is this essay aimed—lovers of comic books, or women, or a general audience? On what do you base your conclusion?
3. In part, this is a personal essay. How does Steinem create her persona or self-image?
   Does the personal element enhance or detract from the analysis? Explain your response.
4. Sort out the complex cause-and-effect relationships in this essay. How does the
   comparative method reinforce the writer's analysis?

5. What types of evidence does the writer provide? Is it sufficient to convince readers? Where, if anywhere, would more detail be helpful?
6. Steinem divides the essay into five sections. What is her purpose? How successful is she in maintaining the essay's unity by employing this method?
7. What paragraphs form the writer's conclusion? How do they recapitulate and add to the substance of the overall essay?

WRITING

1. Compare and contrast the ways in which females and males approach action heroes. Refer to specific icons like Batman, Spiderman, Ellen Ripley, or Buffy the Vampire Slayer to support your assessment.
2. **Writing an Argument:** Think about the numerous action or superheroes that young children and adolescents encounter today in various media forms. Write an essay in which you contend that exposure to such superheroes either does or does not encourage violent behavior in young people.

NETWORKING
Applying 21st-Century Literacies

Reading Action Heroes in Different Media: Write a personal essay about your favorite action hero or heroine—drawn from comics, television shows, or computer games. Explain why this figure appeals to you and what this appeal reveals about the broader culture. In your exploration, include a discussion of how this particular medium/genre was ideal for this character.

The Globalization of Eating Disorders

Susan Bordo

Susan Bordo (b. 1947) was born in Newark, New Jersey, and was educated at Carleton University (BA, 1972) and the State University of New York at Stony Brook (PhD, 1982). She is the Singletary Chair in the Humanities and a professor of English and gender and women's studies at the University of Kentucky. A feminist philosopher and interdisciplinary scholar who focuses on Western culture's attitudes toward gender and the body, Bordo has written The Flight to Objectivity: Essays on Cartesianism and Culture *(1987),* Unbearable Weight: Feminism, Western Culture, and

the Body *(1993, 2004)*, Twilight Zones: The Hidden Life of Cultural Images
from Plato to O.J. *(1997), and* The Male Body: A New Look at Men in Public and
in Private *(1999). In this selection, Bordo offers an overview of a new kind of epidemic,
fueled by Western media images, that is affecting cultures around the world.*

1   The young girl stands in front of the mirror. Never fat to begin with, she's been
on a no-fat diet for a couple of weeks and has reached her goal weight: 115 lb.,
at 5′4″—exactly what she should weigh, according to her doctor's chart. But in
her eyes she still looks dumpy. She can't shake her mind free of the "Lady
Marmelade" video from Moulin Rouge. Christina Aguilera, Pink, L'il Kim, and
Mya, each one perfect in her own way: every curve smooth and sleek, lean-
sexy, nothing to spare. Self-hatred and shame start to burn in the girl, and envy
tears at her stomach, enough to make her sick. She'll never look like them, no
matter how much weight she loses. Look at that stomach of hers, see how it
sticks out? Those thighs—they actually jiggle. Her butt is monstrous. She's fat,
gross, a dough girl.

2   As you read the imaginary scenario above, whom did you picture standing
in front of the mirror? If your images of girls with eating and body image problems have been shaped by *People* magazine and Lifetime movies, she's probably
white, North American, and economically secure. A child whose parents have
never had to worry about putting food on the family table. A girl with money to
spare for fashion magazines and trendy clothing, probably college-bound. If
you're familiar with the classic psychological literature on eating disorders, you
may also have read that she's an extreme "perfectionist" with a hyper-demanding
mother, and that she suffers from "body-image distortion syndrome" and other
severe perceptual and cognitive problems that "normal" girls don't share. You
probably don't picture her as Black, Asian, or Latina.

3   Read the description again, but this time imagine twenty-something Tenisha
Williamson standing in front of the mirror. Tenisha is black, suffers from anorexia,
and feels like a traitor to her race. "From an African-American standpoint,"
she writes, "we as a people are encouraged to embrace our big, voluptuous
bodies. This makes me feel terrible because I don't want a big, voluptuous
body! I don't ever want to be fat—ever, and I don't ever want to gain weight. I
would rather die from starvation than gain a single pound."[1] Tenisha is no
longer an anomaly. Eating and body image problems are now not only crossing racial and class lines, but gender lines. They have also become a global
phenomenon.

4   Fiji is a striking example. Because of their remote location, the Fiji islands did
not have access to television until 1995, when a single station was introduced. It
broadcasts programs from the United States, Great Britain, and Australia. Until
that time, Fiji had no reported cases of eating disorders, and a study conducted
by anthropologist Anne Becker showed that most Fijian girls and women, no

[1]From the Colours of Ana website (http://coloursofana.com//ss8.asp).

matter how large, were comfortable with their bodies. In 1998, just three years after the station began broadcasting, 11 percent of girls reported vomiting to control weight, and 62 percent of the girls surveyed reported dieting during the previous months.[2]

Becker was surprised by the change; she had thought that Fijian cultural traditions, which celebrate eating and favor voluptuous bodies, would "withstand" the influence of media images. Becker hadn't yet understood that we live in an empire of images, and that there are no protective borders.

In Central Africa, for example, traditional cultures still celebrate voluptuous women. In some regions, brides are sent to fattening farms, to be plumped and massaged into shape for their wedding night. In a country plagued by AIDS, the skinny body has meant—as it used to among Italian Jewish, and Black Americans—poverty, sickness, death. "An African girl must have hips," says dress designer Frank Osodi, "We have hips. We have bums. We like flesh in Africa." For years, Nigeria sent its local version of beautiful to the Miss World Competition. The contestants did very poorly. Then a savvy entrepreneur went against local ideals and entered Agbani Darego, a light-skinned, hyper-skinny beauty. (He got his inspiration from M-Net, the South African network seen across Africa on satellite television, which broadcasts mostly American movies and television shows.) Agbani Darego won the Miss World Pageant, the first Black African to do so. Now, Nigerian teenagers fast and exercise, trying to become "lepa"—a popular slang phrase for the thin "it" girls that are all the rage. Said one: "People have realized that slim is beautiful."[3]

How can mere images be so powerful? For one thing, they are never "just pictures," as the fashion magazines continually maintain (disingenuously) in their own defense. They speak to young people not just about how to be beautiful but also about how to become what the dominant culture admires, values, rewards. They tell them how to be cool, "get it together," overcome their shame. To girls who have been abused they may offer a fantasy of control and invulnerability, immunity from pain and hurt. For racial and ethnic groups whose bodies have been deemed "foreign," earthy, and primitive, and considered unattractive by Anglo-Saxon norms, they may cast the lure of being accepted as "normal" by the dominant culture.

In today's world, it is through images—much more than parents, teachers, or clergy—that we are taught how to be. And it is images, too, that teach us how to see, that educate our vision in what's a defect and what is normal, that give us the models against which our own bodies and the bodies of others are measured. Perceptual pedagogy: "How To Interpret Your Body 101." It's become a global requirement.

I was intrigued, for example, when my articles on eating disorders began to be translated, over the past few years, into Japanese and Chinese. Among

---

[2]Reported in Nancy Snyderman, *The Girl in the Mirror* (New York: Hyperion, 2002), p. 84.
[3]Norimistsu Onishi, "Globalization of Beauty Makes Slimness Trendy," *The New York Times,* Oct. 3, 2002.

the members of audiences at my talks, Asian women had been among the most insistent that eating and body image weren't problems for their people, and indeed, my initial research showed that eating disorders were virtually unknown in Asia. But when, this year, a Korean translation of *Unbearable Weight* was published, I felt I needed to revisit the situation. I discovered multiple reports on dramatic increases in eating disorders in China, South Korea, and Japan. "As many Asian countries become Westernized and infused with the Western aesthetic of a tall, thin, lean body, a virtual tsunami of eating disorders has swamped Asian countries," writes Eunice Park in *Asian Week* magazine. Older people can still remember when it was very different. In China, for example, where revolutionary ideals once condemned any focus on appearance and there have been several disastrous famines, "little fatty" was a term of endearment for children. Now, with fast food on every corner, childhood obesity is on the rise, and the cultural meaning of fat and thin has changed. "When I was young," says Li Xiaojing, who manages a fitness center in Beijing, "people admired and were even jealous of fat people since they thought they had a better life. . . . But now, most of us see a fat person and think 'He looks awful.'"[4]

10   Clearly, body insecurity can be exported, imported, and marketed—just like any other profitable commodity. In this respect, what's happened with men and boys is illustrative. Ten years ago men tended, if anything, to see themselves as better looking than they (perhaps) actually were. And then (as I chronicle in detail in my book *The Male Body*) the menswear manufacturers, the diet industries, and the plastic surgeons "discovered" the male body. And now, young guys are looking in their mirrors, finding themselves soft and ill defined, no matter how muscular they are. Now they are developing the eating and body image disorders that we once thought only girls had. Now they are abusing steroids, measuring their own muscularity against the oiled and perfected images of professional athletes, body-builders, and *Men's Health* models. Now the industries in body-enhancement—cosmetic surgeons, manufacturers of anti-aging creams, spas and salons—are making huge bucks off men, too.

11   What is to be done? I have no easy answers. But I do know that we need to acknowledge, finally and decisively, that we are dealing here with a cultural problem. If eating disorders were biochemical, as some claim, how can we account for their gradual "spread" across race, gender, and nationality? And with mass media culture increasingly providing the dominant "public education" in our children's lives—and those of children around the globe—how can we blame families? Families matter, of course, and so do racial and ethnic traditions. But families exist in cultural time and space—and so do racial groups. In the empire of images, no one lives in a bubble of

---

[4]Reported in Elizabeth Rosenthal, "Beijing Journal: China's Chic Waistline: Convex to Concave," *The New York Times,* Dec. 9, 1999.

self-generated "dysfunction" or permanent immunity. The sooner we recognize that—and start paying attention to the culture around us and what it is teaching our children—the sooner we can begin developing some strategies for change.

COMPREHENSION

1. How does Bordo define the "body-image distortion syndrome" (paragraph 2)?
2. Why have body image and weight problems become a global phenomenon? What is the main cause of this phenomenon?
3. How, according to the author, should we deal with the globalization of eating disorders?

RHETORIC

1. How does the author establish herself as an authority on her subject? Do you think that she succeeds? Why or why not?
2. What is the writer's claim? Where does she place it, and why?
3. Bordo begins with an imaginary situation. Does this strategy enhance or detract from the validity of her argument? Justify your response.
4. How does Bordo develop this selection as a problem-solution essay? Where does the solution appear, and how effective is its placement within the essay?

WRITING

1. Write a causal essay analyzing young Americans' fascination with body image and the consequences of this preoccupation.
2. Why are women in the United States and around the world more susceptible to eating disorders than men? Answer this question in an analytical essay.
3. **Writing an Argument:** Write an essay titled "Body Images, Eating Disorders, and Cultural Imperialism." In this essay, argue for or against the proposition that American media are exporting potentially unhealthy images of the human body.

NETWORKING
Applying 21st-Century Literacies

Critiquing a Web Site about Eating Disorders: On the Chapter 9 Networking page (at *www.mhhe.com/mhreaderbrief1e*), choose one of the listed Web sites and write a careful critique of both its purpose and its effectiveness at achieving that purpose.

Supersaturation, or, The Media Torrent and Disposable Feeling

Todd Gitlin

Todd Gitlin (b. 1943) was born and grew up in New York City. He received a PhD in sociology from the University of California at Berkeley and was president of Students for a Democratic Society (SDS) in the 1960s. Gitlin is a professor of journalism and sociology at Columbia University and has held the chair in American civilization at the École des hautes études en sciences sociales in Paris. Gitlin has also lectured at home and abroad on contemporary culture and history. Among his notable books are Inside Prime Time *(1983),* The Twilight of Common Dreams: Why America Is Wracked by Culture Wars *(1995),* Media Unlimited: How the Torrent of Images and Sounds Overwhelms Our Lives *(2001), and* The Bulldozer and the Big Tent: Blind Republicans *(2008). In the selection from* Media Unlimited *that follows, Gitlin offers an overview of the ways in which the media influence our contemporary lives.*

1   On my bedroom wall hangs a print of Vermeer's *The Concert,* painted around 1660. A young woman is playing a spinet. A second woman, probably her maid, holds a letter. A cavalier stands between them, his back to us. A landscape is painted on the raised lid of the spinet, and on the wall hang two paintings, a landscape and *The Procuress,* a work by Baburen, another Dutch artist, depicting a man and two women in a brothel. As in many seventeenth-century Dutch paintings, the domestic space is decorated by paintings. In wealthy Holland, many homes, and not only bourgeois ones, featured such renderings of the outer world. These pictures were pleasing, but more: They were proofs of taste and prosperity, amusements and news at once.

2   Vermeer froze instants, but instants that spoke of the relative constancy of the world in which his subjects lived. If he had painted the same room in the same house an hour, a day, or a month later, the letter in the maid's hand would have been different, and the woman might have been playing a different selection, but the paintings on the far wall would likely have been the same. There might have been other paintings, etchings, and prints elsewhere in the house, but they would not have changed much from month to month, year to year.

3   In what was then the richest country in the world, "everyone strives to embellish his house with precious pieces, especially the room toward the street," as one English visitor to Amsterdam wrote in 1640, noting that he had observed paintings in bakeries, butcher's shops, and the workshops of blacksmiths and cobblers.[1] Of course, the number of paintings, etchings, and prints in homes

---

[1]Peter Mundy, quoted by Geert Mak, *Amsterdam,* trans. Philipp Blom (Cambridge, Mass.: Harvard University Press, 2000), p. 109.

varied considerably. One tailor owned five paintings, for example, while at the high end, a 1665 inventory of a lavish patrician's house in Amsterdam held two maps and thirteen paintings in one grand room, twelve paintings in his widow's bedroom, and seven in the maid's room. Still, compared with today's domestic imagery, the grandest Dutch inventories of that prosperous era were tiny.[2] Even in the better-off households depicted by Vermeer, the visual field inhabited by his figures was relatively scanty and fixed.[3]

Today, Vermeer's equivalent, if he were painting domestic scenes, or shooting a spread for *Vanity Fair,* or directing commercials or movies, would also display his figures against a background of images; and if his work appeared on-screen, there is a good chance that he would mix in a soundtrack as well. Most of the images would be portraits of individuals who have never walked in the door—not in the flesh—and yet are recognized and welcomed, though not like actual persons. They would rapidly segue into others—either because they had been edited into a video montage, or because they appear on pages meant to be leafed through. Today's Vermeer would discover that the private space of the home offers up vastly more impressions of the larger world than was possible in 1660. In seventeenth-century Delft, painters did not knock on the door day and night offering fresh images for sale. Today, though living space has been set apart from working space, as would have been the case only for the wealthier burghers of Vermeer's time, the outside world has entered the home with a vengeance—in the profusion of media.

The flow of images and sounds through the households of the rich world, and the richer parts of the poor world, seems unremarkable today. Only a visitor from an earlier century or an impoverished country could be startled by the fact that life is now played out against a shimmering multitude of images and sounds, emanating from television, videotapes, videodiscs, video games, VCRs, computer screens, digital displays of all sorts, always in flux, chosen partly at will, partly by whim, supplemented by words, numbers, symbols, phrases, fragments, all passing through screens that in a single minute can display more pictures than a prosperous seventeenth-century Dutch household contained over several lifetimes, portraying in one day more individuals than the Dutch burgher would have beheld in the course of years, and in one week more bits of what we have come to call "information" than all the books in all the households in Vermeer's Delft. And this is not yet to speak of our sonic surroundings: the music, voices, and sound effects from radios, CD players, and turntables. Nor is it to speak of newspapers, magazines,

---

[2]Simon Schama, *The Embarrassment of Riches: An Interpretation of Dutch Culture in the Golden Age* (New York: Knopf, 1987), pp. 313–19. Schama notes that research in the relevant archives is "still in its early days" (p. 315).

[3]Many bourgeois Dutch houses also featured a camera lucida, a mounted magnifying lens trained on objects in the vicinity. Because the lens was movable, motion could be simulated—distant objects being brought nearer and sent farther away. But because the apparatus was mounted in a fixed location, the range of objects in motion was limited to those actually visible from the window. (Svetlana Alpers, personal communication, October 8, 1999.)

newsletters, and books. Most of the faces we shall ever behold, we shall behold in the form of images.

6   Because they arrive with sound, at home, in the car, the elevator, or the waiting room, today's images are capable of attracting our attention during much of the day. We may ignore most of them most of the time, take issue with them or shrug them off (or think we are shrugging them off), but we must do the work of dispelling them—and even then, we know we can usher them into our presence whenever we like. Iconic plenitude is the contemporary condition, and it is taken for granted. To grow up in this culture is to grow into an expectation that images and sounds will be there for us on command, and that the stories they compose will be succeeded by still other stories, all bidding for our attention, all striving to make sense, all, in some sense, *ours*. Raymond Williams, the first analyst to pay attention to the fact that television is not just pictures but flow, and not just flow but drama upon drama, pointed out more than a quarter century ago, long before hundred-channel cable TV and VCRs, that

> we have never as a society acted so much or watched so many others acting. . . .
> [W]hat is really new . . . is that drama . . . is built into the rhythms of everyday
> life. In earlier periods drama was important at a festival, in a season, or as a
> conscious journey to a theater; from honouring Dionysus or Christ to taking in a
> show. What we have now is drama as habitual experience: more in a week, in
> many cases, than most human beings would previously have seen in a lifetime.[4]

7   Around the time Vermeer painted *The Concert*, Blaise Pascal, who worried about the seductive power of distraction among the French royalty, wrote that "near the persons of kings there never fail to be a great number of people who see to it that amusement follows business, and who watch all the time of their leisure to supply them with delights and games, so that there is no blank in it."[5] In this one respect, today almost everyone—even the poor—in the rich countries resembles a king, attended by the courtiers of the media offering a divine right of choice.

Measures of Magnitude

8 Statistics begin—but barely—to convey the sheer magnitude of this in-touchness, access, exposure, plenitude, glut, however we want to think of it.

9   In 1999, a television set was on in the average American household more than seven hours a day, a figure that has remained fairly steady since 1983. According to the measurements of the A. C. Nielsen Company, the standard used by advertisers and the television business itself, the average individual watched television about four hours a day, not counting the time when the set

[4]"Drama in a Dramatised Society," in Alan O'Connor, ed., *Raymond Williams on Television* (Toronto: Between the Lines, 1989 [1974]), pp. 3–5. *Flow* comes up in Williams's *Television: Technology and Cultural Form* (New York: Schocken, 1975), p. 86 ff.
[5]*Pensées*, trans. W. F. Trotter (www.eserver.org/philosophy/pascal-pensees.txt), sec. 2, par. 142.

was on but the individual in question was not watching. When Americans were asked to keep diaries of how they spend their time, the time spent actually watching dropped to a still striking three hours a day—probably an undercount. In 1995, of those who watched, the percentage who watched "whatever's on," as opposed to any specific program, was 43 percent, up from 29 percent in 1979.[6] Though cross-national comparisons are elusive because of differences in measurement systems, the numbers in other industrialized nations seem to be comparable—France, for example, averaging three and a half hours per person.[7] One survey of forty-three nations showed the United States ranking third in viewing hours, after Japan and Mexico. None of this counts time spent discussing programs, reading about their stars, or thinking about either.[8]

Overall, wrote one major researcher in 1990, "watching TV is the domi-   10 nant leisure activity of Americans, consuming 40 percent of the average person's free time as a primary activity [when people give television their undivided attention]. Television takes up more than half of our free time if you count . . . watching TV while doing something else like eating or reading . . . [or] when you have the set on but you aren't paying attention to it."[9] Sex, race, income, age, and marital status make surprisingly little difference in time spent.[10] Neither, at this writing, has the Internet diminished total media use, even if you don't count the Web as part of the media. While Internet users do watch 28 percent less television, they spend more time than nonusers playing video games and listening to the radio and recorded music— obviously a younger crowd. Long-term users (four or more years) say they go on-line for more than two hours a day, and boys and girls alike spend the bulk of their Internet time entertaining themselves with games, hobbies, and the like.[11] In other words, the Internet redistributes the flow of unlimited media but does not dry it up. When one considers the overlapping and additional hours of exposure to radio, magazines, newspapers, compact discs, movies (available via a range of technologies as well as in theaters), and comic books, as well as the accompanying articles, books, and chats about what's on or was on or is coming up via all these means, it is clear that the

[6]Robert D. Putnam, *Bowling Alone: The Collapse and Revival of American Community* (New York: Simon and Schuster, 2000), p. 222, citing John P. Robinson and Geoffrey Godbey, *Time for Life: The Surprising Ways Americans Use Their Time*, 2nd ed. (University Park: Pennsylvania State University Press, 1999), pp. 136–53, 340–41, 222.
[7]This April 2001 figure for individuals fifteen and older comes from Mediamat (Mediametrie www.mediametria.fr/television/mediamat_mensuel/2001/avril.html).
[8]Putnam, *Bowling Alone*, p. 480, citing Eurodata TV (*One Television Year in the World: Audience Report*, April 1999).
[9]John P. Robinson, "I Love My TV," *American Demographics*, September 1990, p. 24.
[10]Robert Kubey and Mihaly Csikszentmihalyi, *Television and the Quality of Life: How Viewing Shapes Everyday Experience* (Hillsdale, N.J.: Lawrence Erlbaum Associates, 1990), pp. 71–73.
[11]UCLA Center for Communication Policy, *The UCLA Internet Report: Surveying the Digital Future*, November 2000, pp. 10, 17, 18, 14 (www.ccp.ucla.edu).

media flow into the home—not to mention outside—has swelled into a torrent of immense force and constancy, an accompaniment to life that has become a central experience *of* life.

11 The place of media in the lives of children is worth special attention—not simply because children are uniquely impressionable but because their experience shapes everyone's future; if we today take a media-soaked environment for granted, surely one reason is that we grew up in it and can no longer see how remarkable it is. Here are some findings from a national survey of media conditions among American children aged two through eighteen. The average American child lives in a household with 2.9 televisions, 1.8 VCRs, 3.1 radios, 2.6 tape players, 2.1 CD players, 1.4 video game players, and 1 computer. Ninety-nine percent of these children live in homes with one or more TVs, 97 percent with a VCR, 97 percent with a radio, 94 percent with a tape player, 90 percent with a CD player, 70 percent with a video game player, 69 percent with a computer. Eighty-eight percent live in homes with two or more TVs, 60 percent in homes with three or more. Of the 99 percent with a TV, 74 percent have cable or satellite service.[12] And so on, and on, and on.

12 The uniformity of this picture is no less astounding. A great deal about the lives of children depends on their race, sex, and social class, but access to major media does not. For TV, VCR, and radio ownership, rates do not vary significantly among white, black, and Hispanic children, or between girls and boys. For television and radio, rates do not vary significantly according to the income of the community.[13]

13 How accessible, then, is the media cavalcade at home? Of children eight to eighteen, 65 percent have a TV in their bedrooms, 86 percent a radio, 81 percent a tape player, 75 percent a CD player. Boys and girls are not significantly different in possessing this bounty, though the relative usages do vary by medium. Researchers also asked children whether the television was "on in their homes even if no one is watching 'most of the time,' 'some of the time,' 'a little of the time,' or 'never.'" Homes in which television is on "most of the time" are termed *constant television households*. By this measure, 42 percent of all American households with children are constant television households. Blacks are more likely than whites or Hispanics to experience TV in their lives: 56 percent of black children live in constant television households (and 69 percent have a TV in

---

[12]Donald F. Roberts, *Kids and Media @ the New Millennium* (Menlo Park, Calif.: Henry J. Kaiser Family Foundation, 1999), p. 9, table 1. There were 3,155 children in the sample, including over-samples of black and Hispanic children, to ensure that results in these minority populations would also be statistically significant. As best as a reader can discern, this was a reliable study, with a margin of error of no more than plus-or-minus five percentage points. Since the results for younger children, ages two to seven, come from parents' reports, they may well be conservative, since parents may be uninformed of the extent of their children's viewing or may be underplaying it in order not to feel ashamed before interviewers.

[13]Ibid., p. 11, tables 3-A, 3-B, 3-C.

their bedrooms, compared to 48 percent of whites). The lower the family education and the median income of the community, the greater the chance that a household is a constant television household.[14]

As for time, the average child spent six hours and thirty-two minutes per day exposed to media of all kinds, of which the time spent reading books and magazines—not counting schoolwork—averaged about forty-five minutes. For ages two to seven, the average for total media was four hours and seventeen minutes; for ages eight to thirteen, eight hours and eight minutes, falling to seven hours and thirty-five minutes for ages fourteen to eighteen.[15] Here, race and social class do count. Black children are most exposed, followed by Hispanics, then whites. At all age levels, the amount of exposure to all media varies inversely with class, from six hours and fifty-nine minutes a day for children in households where the median income for the zip code is under $25,000 to six hours and two minutes for children whose zip code median income is over $40,000. The discrepancy for TV exposure is especially pronounced, ranging from three hours and six minutes a day for children whose zip code incomes are under $25,000 to two hours and twenty-nine minutes for children whose zip code incomes are over $40,000.[16] Still, these differences are not vast. Given everything that divides the rich from the poor, the professional from the working class—differences in physical and mental health, infant mortality, longevity, safety, vulnerability to crime, prospects for stable employment, and so on—the class differences in media access and use are surprisingly slender. So are the differences between American and western European children, the latter averaging six hours a day total, though in Europe only two and a quarter of those hours are spent with TV.[17]

[14]Ibid., pp. 13–15, tables 4, 5-A, 5-B, 6. In general, fewer western European or Israeli children than Americans have TVs in their bedrooms, but 70 percent in Great Britain do. Next highest in Europe is 64 percent in Denmark. The lows are 31 percent in Holland and 24 percent in Switzerland. Leen d'Haenens, "Old and New Media: Access and Ownership in the Home," in Sonia Livingstone and Moira Bovill, eds., *Children and Their Changing Media Environment: A European Comparative Study* (London: Lawrence Erlbaum Associates, 2001), p. 57.

[15]Roberts, *Kids and Media*, pp. 21–23, tables 8-C, 8-D.

[16]The same point applies to differences in media use throughout the prosperous world. As the economist Adair Turner writes: "European Internet penetration lags the US by 18 to 24 months. When cars or television sets were first introduced, the lag was more like 15 years. . . . The shortness of the lag also suggests that social concern about a 'digital divide,' whether within or between nations, is largely misplaced. . . . Time lags between different income groups in the penetration of personal computers, Internet connections or mobile phones are much shorter, once again because all these products are cheap. . . . At the global level the same scepticism about a digital divide should prevail. Africa may lag 15 years or so behind US levels of PC and Internet penetration, but it lags more like a century behind in basic literacy and health care." Adair Turner, "Not the e-conomy," *Prospect* (London), April 2001 (www.prospect-magazine.co.uk/highlights/essay_turner_april01).

[17]Johannes W. J. Beentjes et al., "Children's Use of Different Media: For How Long and Why?" in Livingstone and Bovill, eds., *Children and Their Changing Media Environment*, p. 96.

15   All such statistics are crude, of course. Most of them register the time that people *say* they spend. They are—thankfully—not checked by total surveillance. Moreover, the meaning of *exposure* is hard to assess, since the concept encompasses rapt attention, vague awareness, oblivious coexistence, and all possible shadings in between. As the images glide by and the voices come and go, how can we assess what goes on in people's heads? Still, the figures do convey some sense of the media saturation with which we live—and so far we have counted only what can be counted at home. These numbers don't take into account the billboards, the TVs at bars and on planes, the Muzak in restaurants and shops, the magazines in the doctor's waiting room, the digital displays at the gas pump and over the urinal, the ads, insignias, and logos whizzing by on the sides of buses and taxis, climbing the walls of buildings, making announcements from caps, bags, T-shirts, and sneakers. To vary our experience, we can pay to watch stories about individuals unfold across larger-than-life-size movie screens, or visit theme parks and troop from image to image, display to display. Whenever we like, on foot or in vehicles, we can convert ourselves into movable nodes of communication, thanks to car radios, tape, CD, and game players, cell phones, beepers, Walkmen, and the latest in "personal communication systems"—and even if we ourselves refrain, we find ourselves drawn willy-nilly into the soundscape that others broadcast around us.

16   Crucially, who we are is how we live our time—or *spend* it, to use the term that registers its intrinsic scarcity. What we believe, or say we believe, is less important. We vote for a way of life with our time. And increasingly, when we are not at work or asleep, we are in the media torrent. (Sometimes at work, we are also there, listening to the radio or checking out sports scores, pin-ups, or headlines on the Internet.) Steadily more inhabitants of the wealthy part of the world have the means, incentives, and opportunities to seek private electronic companionship. The more money we have to spend, the more personal space each household member gets. With personal space comes solitude, but this solitude is instantly crowded with images and soundtracks. To a degree that was unthinkable in the seventeenth century, life experience has become an experience in the presence of media.

COMPREHENSION

1. What does Gitlin's title mean? How are the concepts of "supersaturation" and "disposable feeling" reflected in the essay?
2. Summarize Gitlin's treatment of Vermeer. Who was Vermeer? How, according to the writer, would Vermeer's art be produced today?
3. List some of the facts and statistics that the writer presents to support his idea that we are caught in a "media torrent."

RHETORIC

1. What is Gitlin's argument? Where does he state his claim most clearly? What appeals to logic, ethics, and emotion does he make? Does he rely on his own opinions? Justify your answer.
2. How does the writer maintain unity between the two parts of this essay? Why, for example, does he open his essay with the story of Vermeer? How does Vermeer serve as a unifying element? What other unifying motifs can you find?
3. What varieties of evidence does the writer provide to bolster his argument? Does he rely on anecdotal or actual evidence? How do you know?
4. The writer employs a range of rhetorical strategies in this essay. Point to places where he uses description, comparison and contrast, classification, definition, and causal analysis.
5. Is the author's style personal, informal, or formal? How does this style explain Gitlin's relationship to his audience and the expectations he holds of his readers?
6. What strategy does the writer use in his conclusion? Is this strategy effective? Why or why not?
7. What do Gitlin's footnotes add to the essay? Why are they important?

WRITING

1. Write an essay in which you explain how one medium—television or the Internet, for example—has affected or changed your life. Make sure that you provide adequate detail or evidence.
2. **Writing an Argument:** Write an essay in which you either agree or disagree with Gitlin's claim that increasingly "we are in a media torrent." Use appeals to logic, ethics, and emotion to advance your claim. Make certain that you have adequate evidence to support your major and minor propositions.

NETWORKING
Applying 21st-Century Literacies

Comparing New and Old Media: Write a comparative essay in which you analyze the similarities and differences between an "old" and a "new" component of the media—actual books and e-books or audio books, or telephones and cell phones, for example. Use visuals to enhance and support your comparisons.

Escape from Wonderland: Disney and the Female Imagination

Deborah Ross

Deborah Ross is professor of English at Hawai'i Pacific University, where she teaches writing, literature, and humanities. She specializes in popular culture, especially from the perspective of gender. In the following research paper, published in a 2004 issue of Marvels & Tales: Journal of Fairy-Tale Studies, *Ross analyzes a series of Disney films, all based on children's books and fairy tales; she evaluates the Disney ideology as it affects the imaginative and actual lives of girls.*

1   In 1989, Disney's little mermaid first asked the musical question, "When's it my turn?" She asked it again in 1996, when her movie was re-released in theaters, and she continues to ask it, frequently, in many of our living rooms. Never has a protagonist had so many turns to demand a turn: Yet, seemingly, she remains unsatisfied. If even the heroine in a Disney "girls' movie" does not enjoy being a girl, how must the girls watching her feel about it?

2   Behind this gender question lurks a larger political one. If Ariel's feminist rhetoric is undercut by more conservative elements in her movie, so is the environmentalism of *The Lion King,* the multiculturalism of *Pocahontas,* the valuing of difference in *The Hunchback of Notre Dame*—in short, all the quasi-liberal sentiments that focus groups have no doubt caused to grace the surface of the last decade's Disney features. Ideology in Disney is a much vexed question, and I will not attempt here to untangle a knot which began forming for critics when Walt first denied having any politics back in the thirties, and which has only grown in mass and complexity since his death, as his corporation's management style has evolved to cope with a burgeoning staff of artists and technicians, changing public tastes, and changing perceptions of those tastes.

3   One generalization I do suggest, however, is that Disney the man and the corporation are known for a belief in control. The top-down management style Disney epitomizes—Auschwitz (Giroux 55), or Mouschwitz (Lewis 88), is a frequent analogy—thrives on homogeneity and rigid adherence to rules. These are features often decried in Disney production and product, both by critics of capitalism, such as Benjamin and Adorno,[1] and by far less radical proponents of individualism and open debate, from early Disney biographer Richard Schickel to educator Henry Giroux. Yet imagination, the company's major commodity,

---

[1]Miriam Hansen discusses Benjamin's and Adorno's objections to Disney in some detail. Jack Zipes's critique of Disney also occurs within a larger argument about the "freezing" of fairy tales into myths to perpetuate bourgeois, patriarchal values (see his Introduction and Chapter 3).

does not easily lend itself to a program of control. To encourage imagination in artists, and arouse it in viewers, is to invite unique self-expression rather than homogeneity, and spontaneity rather than predictability. Link imagination to the animated cartoon, an art form with roots in dada, surrealism, and radical politics, and matters could well get out of hand.[2]

I believe that this conflict between control and imaginative freedom is visible in the animated features that have come out of the Disney studios, from *Snow White and the Seven Dwarfs* to *Lilo and Stitch*. Of course, ambiguity is rarely viewed now as either a moral or an aesthetic flaw, and the presence of elements that contradict each other may well be preferable to consistent, monologic disapproval of imagination. Neither, however, do conflict and contradiction in themselves necessarily create a space for viewers to question values and exercise judgment. Much depends on how the elements relate to each other, or how an audience is likely to relate them. An audience even partially looking for guides to behavior along with entertainment will have to resolve apparent ambiguities into one suggested course of action. Giroux's attack on Disney rests on the contention that for children, these movies, however apparently bland, do have a didactic effect (18). For them, ambiguity at its best ultimately resolves into a connected but complex world view that embraces difference and spontaneity; at its worst, it can produce confusion and anxiety.

I wish to explore the overall impressions these films may give children about the value of their own imaginations, and thus about their own value as unique individuals able to envision, and eventually to enact, change. In particular, to get back to Ariel, I am concerned about what girls may learn about this potentially explosive aspect of their characters that could so easily burst the bounds of traditional femininity. To help answer this question, I have chosen to examine the way various elements of image, story, and dialogue interact to influence the valuation of imagination in three of Disney's girls' movies: *Alice in Wonderland* (1951), *The Little Mermaid* (1989), and *Beauty and the Beast* (1991, re-released 2001).

I have chosen these three because, although one might be called "prefeminist" and the other two "post-," all specifically concern young women who fantasize about a life more vivid and exciting than their reality. I will suggest that some of these films' discomfort with female imagination has roots far back in didactic narrative for girls by looking at Charlotte Lennox's 1759 novel, *The Female Quixote*, which concerns the fortunes of a young woman who might be considered the great-grandmother, or prototype, of the Disney heroine. Then, comparing the three Disney movies with their written fairy-tale sources, I will show how much more confusing a many-tongued message can become when it is told in pictures as well as words.

---

[2]Janet Wasko notes that Disney deliberately avoided the more "anarchistic and inventive" styles of animation employed at other studios (115). My own belief, on which my approach to Disney is based, is that where there is animation, anarchy can never be wholly suppressed. For discussion of the roots of animation in surrealism and dada, see Inez Hedges.

7 Girls have been learning from stories where to draw the line between fantasy and reality probably since the first story was told, but one sees this didactic purpose especially clearly beginning in the seventeenth century, when romances and literary fairy tales were first written specifically for, about, and even by women. Samuel Johnson was greatly concerned about the effects of fiction on "the young, the ignorant, and the idle," and Paul Hunter has shown that there was indeed a class of new readers early in the eighteenth century who were socially displaced and looking to novels for moral and social guidance as well as entertainment (Hunter 271–72). From that time till the present, conservative authors have used romances and novels to teach girls that their dreams are dangerous and of little relevance to their daily lives. Progressive or feminist authors, on the other hand, have encouraged young women readers' belief in fantasy to help them visualize what they want, perhaps as a first step toward going after it. For example, it can be argued (as I have done elsewhere) that European women's experience with romantic fiction gradually gained them the right, first, to refuse to cooperate in arranged marriages, and eventually, to choose husbands for themselves.[3]

8 Charlotte Lennox's *The Female Quixote* illustrates both these conservative and progressive plot patterns, for it both draws upon and criticizes earlier romances, which themselves often both celebrated and punished female imagination and expressiveness.[4] Therefore, like Disney's movies today, which also use material from the romance and fairy-tale tradition, Lennox's novel can be more muddling than enlightening to young people seeking instruction on the conduct of real life. As the title suggests, the premise is that a young girl is at least as likely to have her head turned by reading romances as Cervantes's knight-errant had been over a century before. Appropriately, the romances devoured by this quixote, Arabella, are the largely female-centered French romances of d'Urfé and Scudéry, which focus more on love than on questing, and in which males are present mainly either to carry off or rescue heroines. A reader who takes too literally stories in which women wield such power, albeit of a limited kind, will not adjust well to woman's lot: being ignored, submitting always to others' convenience, like Jane Austen in her letters, perpetually waiting to be "fetched" by a male relative (Austen 9–10). Thus Arabella's reading sets her up to make many ridiculous mistakes, and ultimately to be humbled, or humiliated, when she learns her own real unimportance.

9 The novel shows its author's ambivalence about Arabella's fantasy in several ways. Overtly, she presents it as an adolescent error the heroine must grow out of in order to find happiness. Yet her very frank satire of the world to which Arabella's cure forces her to conform leaves readers wondering, along with the heroine, whether the world of romance might not be preferable. Romances also receive

---

[3]I develop this argument in *The Excellence of Falsehood*. Marina Warner (169, 277–78) and Jack Zipes (21–23, 28) discuss the seventeenth-century *précieuses'* preoccupation with the issue of forced marriage.

[4]Warner discusses ambivalence about the old woman or "Mother Goose" figure who narrates fairy tales throughout the first half of *From the Beast to the Blonde,* and more specifically the power of the female voice in her discussion of "The Little Mermaid" (394).

implicit support from the central "real" narrative's resemblance to romance: beautiful heroine, beloved by the perfect man, whom after trials and separations she marries, presumably to live happily ever after. If the novel presents a romantic story under the guise of realism, then perhaps Arabella is not so quixotic after all.

The Female Quixote thus presents contradictory impressions about the worthiness of the heroine's desires, the degree to which those desires are ultimately fulfilled or frustrated, and the amount of satisfaction with the outcome the tone directs the reader to feel. Critics of our own time naturally enjoy this ambivalence (the novel has had a comeback of sorts in the last decades and is available in paperback), which particularly lends itself to feminist approaches of the *Madwoman in the Attic*, conformist text–radical subtext variety. Yet the fact that this novel might well make a madwoman out of any young female reader looking for a framework for understanding life should also be part of our critical awareness. Critics may find it a useful model for highlighting similar constellations of ideological paradox in other stories about women's imagination, stories which also leave their audiences struggling to integrate contradictory messages.

Disney's female quixotes are at least as sorely beset by ambiguity as Arabella. The heroines' fantasies reveal desires for many things, including novelty, excitement, power, sex, and knowledge. Some of these desires are ridiculed, others respected; some are fulfilled, others surrendered. And the paradoxes in the plots are further complicated by words and images that seem at times to be telling stories of their own.

The presence of conservative elements in Disney's *Alice in Wonderland* is not surprising, considering that it was released in 1951, when "Hollywood's dark prince" was still very much alive, fighting unions, castigating the League of Women Voters, and exerting strong control over the studio's output.[5] One would perhaps not expect, though, to find an American movie of the mid-twentieth century so much more stereotypically Victorian than its nineteenth-century British source.

Of course, Lewis Carroll's *Alice's Adventures in Wonderland* and *Through the Looking Glass* are not typical of Victorian children's literature. In particular, most girls' stories of this era promoted humility, devotion, punctuality, and tidiness, implying that adventure (as a countess once told Lennox's Arabella) is something a nice girl would be wise to avoid (Lennox 365). The Alice stories, on the other hand, present adventure as positive: Whether wondrous or frightening, it leads the heroine in the direction of personal growth and control over her surroundings. Alice learns how to manage her size, how to talk back to a queen, and, finally, how to wear the crown of adulthood. Carroll celebrates childhood as a brief, fleeting time in which even girls may follow talking rabbits before being overtaken by the "dull reality" (115) of womanhood.

---

[5]I refer here to the title of Marc Eliot's Disney biography. Holly Allen and Michael Denning discuss politics at the Disney studio during the 1940s. For a full discussion of Disney's rather complex politics, see Steven Watts.

14   The Disney movie begins with the same positive message about girls' fantasies. In her opening conversation, Disney's Alice, like Carroll's, expresses the usual quixotic desires: to escape boredom (with lessons), to satisfy curiosity (about the white rabbit), and above all, to exert power. Things would be different "in my world," she notes, though her sister ridicules her ambition. Books, for one thing, would all have pictures—a remark given to Alice by Carroll in a way that almost invites someone to make an Alice movie. The first few minutes of the movie do seem to deliver what Alice wants by introducing such pictorial wonders as singing flowers and surrealistic insects.

15   Soon, however, the plot darkens, signaled by small but significant cuts and alterations in the original dialogue. Speaking with the Cheshire Cat, who tells her everyone in the neighborhood is mad, Alice speaks Carroll's line, "But I don't want to go among mad people" (63). The cat responds that everyone in Wonderland is mad, but he does not go on to say that Alice too is mad, so that already Disney's Alice is presented as out of her element, the lone sane and rational creature among lunatics.

16   After the mad tea party, in a section of plot invented for the movie, Disney's Alice has had enough craziness and wants to go home. Overjoyed to find what looks like a path—symbolic of her now acknowledged need for order and direction—she is reduced to helpless tears when it is erased by a fanciful broom creature. She then passively sits down to wait to be rescued, all the while lecturing herself about the importance of reason and patience, and berating herself for the curiosity that once again has led her into trouble. The movie takes a line from early in the story, "She generally gave herself very good advice (though she very seldom followed it)" (23), puts it in the first person, and makes it the center of a self-lacerating musical lament in which Alice abandons for good her fantasy of excitement and power to dwindle into a tiny, forlorn figure in the center of a large, dark frame. In the end of the movie, the defiance and assertiveness of the line, "You're only a pack of cards," are lost, as she utters it while fleeing for her life from the menacing gang of wonders she has created. She is saved, not by facing them down with dawning maturity and confidence, like the "real" Alice, but by waking up.[6]

17   British reviewers at the time of the movie's release, when the militantly innocuous Enid Blyton held sway over English children's imaginations, objected to Disney's "anarchic" alteration of what they saw as a serene and placid children's tale (Allan 137). But Carroll's story is in fact far more tolerant of anarchy, in the sense of irrationality, than the Disney version. The images used to tell the story further support this rationalist message. Despite Disney artist Claude Coats's comment that the staff had "let [them]selves go with some wild designs" (Allan 138), the visuals in fact are rather staid and restrained, mainly literal, representational renderings of the story done in the highly finished, realistic style for which the studio was famous. The fall down the rabbit hole,

---

[6]Donald Britton comments that in the Disney cartoon universe, "children don't become adults; rather, adults kill children" (120).

for example, which marks Alice's entry into the dream state, might have lent itself to surrealistic treatment like that of *Dumbo*'s "Pink Elephants on Parade" sequence, but instead it is simply a serial listing in images of the objects Carroll mentions that Alice sees on her way down.

Surrealism does appear, briefly, in the visual puns formed by the caterpil- 18 lar's smoke (as he asks "why [k]not"), and in the wild proliferation of crockery at the tea party, the cups and saucers truly "animated" and seeming to breed like, well, rabbits. Yet the story-line ensures that just as this style reaches its climax, Alice is reaching the limits of her fear of imagination. What might have been delightful Daliesque creatures—telephone-ducks, drum-frogs—function rather to frighten the heroine at a point in the plot when she has rejected all this "nonsense" and is anxious to get home to write a book about it.[7] Writing a story, she has decided, is much safer than living one.

Thus all elements combine to entrap the unwary viewer: to entice her to 19 fantasize—even to pay money for the privilege—and then to make her feel, like Alice, guilty and ashamed.

Contrasting Alice's defeated whining with Ariel's anthem of independence in 20 *The Little Mermaid*, one is apt to feel girls have come a long way. Here, as Laura Sells and Marina Warner observe, the tale on which the movie is based is ostensibly more conservative than Disney's retelling (Sells 176, 177, 181; Warner 397, 403).[8] Hans Christian Andersen's story is a tragic celebration of feminine self-sacrifice. His mermaid fantasizes about becoming human partly because, like Alice, she is curious about a world she has only glimpsed (here, from below rather than from above). But that world interests her mainly because in it dwells a man who resembles a handsome statue she already adores. Her love is partly sexual, of course, since she needs to be human from the waist down to win the hero. But her ultimate desire is spiritual, for only by marrying a human can a mermaid, who normally lives three hundred years and then turns into sea foam, gain a soul and eternal life.

In pursuit of this desire Andersen's mermaid is willing to spend all she has: 21 her voice, her health, and eventually her life. She buys her new legs, from which blood oozes with every agonizing step, by letting the sea witch cut out her tongue. The permanent loss of her voice means playing dumb in more ways than one, as she can only listen demurely as the prince lectures her about her own world, the sea (166).[9] Failing to bring the prince to a proposal, she could save her own life by killing him, but she chooses instead to die. Her many acts of self-torture earn her a slight reprieve as she is turned into a spirit of the air, instead of sea-foam, and given a chance to gain a soul by performing more selfless deeds. Andersen gives her this reward, not for having a dream, but for

---

[7]Dali had been at the studio in 1946, and Robin Allan believes his influence was still apparent in Alice (137).

[8]See also Wasko 134.

[9]See Warner's discussion on the significance of this silence, and of the blood which in Andersen's tale connects pain with the dawning of female sexuality (387–408).

desiring martyrdom. No real authorial punishment is needed for a female quixote so intent on punishing herself.

22   Naturally in the Disney version the mutilation and blood would have to go. But much more would have to be altered to make this tragic story look and sound so convincingly like a triumph of adolescent self-will and entitlement, as befit the close of the "me decade." (Warner comments on how often, while she can speak, Ariel utters the verb "want" [403].) For example, instead of making the mermaid love the human world because she loves a human, the movie has Ariel love a human mainly because she is already curious enough about his world to have collected a cave full of human souvenirs (in Andersen's story this collection belongs to a mermaid sister). Like Alice before her initiation, Ariel imagines this other world as in a sense more her own than her actual world. She believes it to be a utopia of free movement: She dreams of legs first for "jumping" and "dancing" and "strolling," and only secondarily for marrying.

23   There is nothing masochistic about this mermaid's fantasy; nor is she willing to sacrifice herself to fulfill it, though she is willing to gamble. Her voice, for example, is not permanently lost but poured into a shell, ready to be returned to her if she succeeds, and she has every intention of succeeding. Eighties heroine that she is, she means to have it all: voice, soul, legs, and husband.

24   For the most part, the movie seems to present this female quixote's fantasy positively and reward her with her desire, as the older generation, in the person of her father, learns to abandon prejudice and let teenagers live their own lives. But there are undercurrents here, so to speak, that work against the theme of imaginative freedom. The odd thing about Ariel's quixotism—what makes the audience recognize it *as* quixotism—is that the exotic world of her fantasy is, to us, boring and commonplace. Even a two-year-old viewer knows, as the heroine does not, that forks are not used to comb hair, and that human fathers do indeed "reprimand their daughters," just like old King Triton. Thus we laugh at Ariel's naïve reveries, as Andersen's listeners must have laughed at his mermaid's amazed reaction to birds (150). In the end, it seems ludicrous that Ariel should put so much rebellious energy into becoming the girl next door.

25   The visual style of the movie makes Andersen's painful story seem oddly encouraging by comparison. Andersen shifts points of view back and forth between the mermaids, who see our world as exotic, and his own audience, who glamorize the unknown world below. He provides lavish descriptions of the shore as well as the sea in order to reawaken his listeners' sense of wonder at their own city lights, sunsets, forests, and hills (151–52). An outsider's desire to live here thus becomes quite understandable. The movie contains no such balance, for beauty and splendor are mainly found "Under the Sea," the title of the dizzying production number in which Sebastian the crab tries to convince Ariel that there's no place like home. Here creatures and objects are surrealistically combined and transformed into an underwater orchestra. Here in abundance are the magical bubbles that have signaled fun with physics in Disney movies from *Snow White* to *Dumbo* to *Cinderella*. The world of humans, in contrast, though picturesque, is static and finite. When Ariel takes a bath at Eric's palace,

while mundane, gossiping laundresses wash her clothes, one is forced to notice that bubbles here just don't *do* anything. Similarly, Grimsby's pipe, which Ariel mistakes for a musical instrument, produces more soot than smoke—nothing approaching the punning puffs from the caterpillar's hookah in *Alice,* or even the smoky ink that billows about in the sea witch's cave. Clearly, Sebastian is right: It is "better down where it's wetter."

The images the movie uses to tell the story thus give its trendy feminism a 26 reverse spin. Whatever Ariel might *say,* or sing, what we see her *do* is flee a world of infinite possibility to settle in the land of the banal. Her fantasy is a sort of anti-fantasy. Yes, she gets her legs, she makes her stand, she marches—but only down the aisle, to marry some guy named Eric.

Many fairy tales, and many more movies, end with a wedding, and for this reason 27 they often draw censure from critics, such as Janet Wasko (116) and Elizabeth Bell (114, 155), who would like to see our daughters presented with other options. Without question there ought to be more than one girls' story out there, relentlessly repeated with minor variations. I would also argue, however, that just as in life there are marriages and marriages, so in fiction living happily ever after is not always a euphemism for dying. When the marriage seems to grant the heroine true personal fulfillment and possibilities for further growth, the ending may actually seem like the beginning of a new life. Such is the case with *Beauty and the Beast,* a tale endowed by ancient archetypes with a feminine power that resists the attempts of individual authors, such as Madame Leprince de Beaumont in 1757, to tie its heroine down to mediocrity. With *The Little Mermaid* behind us, we might expect Disney's version to dole out a similarly dull and didactic message, clothed in mock-progressive nineties clichés of gender equality. But in Disney's *Beauty and the Beast,* thanks in part to the screenplay by Linda Woolverton (the first woman writer of a Disney animated feature), imagination flows freely in the words and the images, allowing the tale to work its magic.[10]

One problem with the plot that ends in marriage, of course, is its reduction 28 of the heroine to an object of desire, and therefore a heroine actually named Beauty would not, on the face of it, seem like a good role model. In this tale, however, with its roots penetrating beyond the Cupid and Psyche tale from Apuleius's *The Golden Ass* to very old stories about beast bridegrooms (Warner 275; Zipes 24–25), the heroine is more subject than object because her quest for a desirable mate drives the plot. (Apuleius intensifies the female point of view by having the tale narrated by an old woman [Warner 275].) Of course, the whole question of the story's sexual politics hinges on whether the heroine's desire can be consciously controlled, by herself or by others; whether, as is often said in Christian wedding ceremonies, love is an act of will rather than a feeling; whether, therefore, she can make herself love the one she "ought." Conservative versions of *Beauty and the Beast* do tend to assume such schooling of the

---

[10]See Bell 114; Murphy 133–34; Warner 313.

will is possible, as Jack Zipes emphasizes (29–40). Nevertheless, an important feature even in such versions is that the beast, though he may be dutifully or even cheerfully endured, cannot become a handsome prince until the heroine actively wants him, truly chooses him for reasons of her own. The young female audience is thus reassured that sex in conjunction with love is pleasant rather than frightening (Bettelheim 306; Warner 312–13); in other words, the beast of one's choice is not a beast at all.

29   At about the same time Charlotte Lennox was composing *The Female Quixote,* Madame Leprince de Beaumont, with similar concerns about young women's imaginations, was dressing this ancient tale in anti-romance, turning to her own purpose a Scudérian vocabulary of love that, to her readers, would be all too familiar. Beauty feels "esteem" for the Beast because of his "great service" to her, and eventually she comes to feel "tenderness" for him as she wants to care for him and ease his distress (Beaumont 37). Out of this tenderness comes a desire to marry him—including, one supposes, some sexual feeling. The romance code word for active sexual desire—"inclination"—never appears.[11] By telling her young readers that esteem and tenderness are the best basis for marriage, Beaumont warns them not to wait for the handsome, witty lover of their fantasies; in the closing words of the rewarding fairy: "You have preferred virtue before either wit or beauty, and you deserve to find one in whom all these are united" (47). In this way, the author joins the tradition of conservative writers who urge girls to face reality and, to the very limited extent they will be permitted to choose, to choose wisely.[12] Still, while schooling the reader in what she ought to desire, Beaumont cannot avoid conveying the importance of the heroine's will, for until Beauty desires the Beast, a beast he will remain.

30   The Disney movie reaches past Beaumont to draw upon older strains of the story. For example, here, as in some older versions, including that of Beaumont's immediate predecessor, Madame de Villeneuve (Warner 290–91), it is the Beast rather than Beauty who is supposed to learn self-control. The heroine is therefore permitted—even encouraged—to fantasize to her heart's content. Where Beaumont only noted that Beauty liked to read, Disney enlarges on Belle's taste in books, which turns out to be just like Arabella's: fairy tales and romances about swordfights, magic, a prince in disguise, and above all, a "she" at the center of the action. Nor is she content just to read about "adventure in the great wide somewhere." Given the chance to tour the Beast's library— ordinarily for Belle the greatest of temptations—she chooses instead to explore the forbidden west wing of his castle, as if somehow aware that she will find there the escape from "provincial life" she has been longing and singing for. For all her quixotism, however, Belle, unlike Arabella, is seen as "rather odd" only by her neighbors, not by her audience.

31   Certainly, as several commentators observe, the movie has its share of politically correct modern touches to underscore the heroine's self-determination

[11]See the Map of Tender in Scudéry's *Clelia* (1:42).
[12]See Warner 292–94.

(Warner 316–17; Zipes 46). Interestingly, however, each apparent innovation in fact draws on the French romance tradition that Belle and Arabella revere. Most notably, the movie makes contemporary-sounding statements about gender stereotypes by introducing a new character as foil to the Beast, the hypermasculine Gaston, who boasts in a Sigmund Romberg-ish aria, "I'm especially good at expectorating," "I use antlers in all of my decorating," and "every last inch of me's covered with hair." He is the real beast, of course, an animal who sneers at the Beast for being so openly in touch with his feminine side, "the Male Chauvinist Pig [. . .] that would turn the women of any primetime talkshow audience into beasts themselves" (Jeffords 170). But Gaston is not really new. He dates back, beyond the Cocteau movie often cited as his source, to the French romance villain who loves the heroine selfishly, determined to possess her by force: by winning her in a duel, carrying her off, or scheming to get her parents to give her to him. Gaston arranges to have Belle's eccentric father locked in a madhouse unless she agrees to marry him. Then he nearly kills the Beast under the illusion that the winner gets Belle as prize. The Beast, in contrast, is the romance hero who fights the villain to win the heroine's freedom, not her hand, which he will accept only as her gift. In fact, he would rather die than oppress her. By choosing the Beast over Gaston, Belle helps this ancient story confirm the value of a woman's equal right to a will of her own.

Gaston also helps this movie make another observation mistakenly thought 32 of as modern: that men and women aren't nearly as different as some men would like them to be. This idea is found in women's romantic writing from the seventeenth century on,[13] and it reverberates in Belle's opening song as she wishes for someone who understands her and shares her interests. Naturally she chooses to marry the gentleman who gives her the key to his extensive library, not the "positively primeval" clod who throws her book in the mud with a warning about what happens to society when women are taught to read. And in the end, when the spell is broken and the Beast resumes his original shape, he markedly resembles Belle, unruly bangs and all. By marrying a man who can help her get what she wants, and who wants the same things, symbolically she is marrying an aspect of herself.[14]

The Beast's oddly familiar new face is not the only image in the movie that 33 makes one feel the heroine's fantasy is a worthy one. Much creativity was lavished on the look of the castle that provides the atmosphere of old romance. Although for most of the movie it resembles a Gothic ruin, and Belle comes here at first as a prisoner, it is really a house of magic in which every object is alive, or "animated"—most famously the dinnerware that dances and sings "Be Our Guest." And the enchantment does not quite end with the breaking of the spell, but is rather replaced with a different kind of magic as the castle comes into its original

---

[13]See for example the pastoral lyrics of Aphra Behn.
[14]See Clarissa Pinkola Estes for an interpretation of the Beast as an aspect of the heroine's own personality (272–73). Warner also discusses how the beast in modern versions of the tale, including Disney's, functions to help the heroine get in touch with her own inner beast, or sexuality (307–13).

baroque splendor with a seeming infinity of detail, something new around every corner, and always a new corner, for the eye to explore. As Belle waltzes with her Prince around that gorgeous marble hall, the title tune welling up around them, one may see as well as feel that she's getting not just a husband, but more books than she can read in a lifetime, and a home as big and beautiful as her imagination.

34 Neither age, divorce, nor parenthood has yet made me cynical enough to see the ending of this movie without a sob of satisfaction. But then Disney did begin training me to react in just that way from a very early age (the first movie I ever saw, at the age of five, was *Sleeping Beauty*). Critics have been warning the public for decades about the Disney program to bring about the complete "invasion and control of children's imaginations" (Schickel 18), as well as the silencing of fairy tales' originally female voice (Warner 416–17); no doubt I am a cipher in the company's success. How much more complete the Disney conquest will become for our children and grandchildren, with the constant replay made possible by video and DVD, is definitely cause for concern.

35 The market forces that drive Disney today are dangerous, to be sure, as is the ideology of the market-place the movies promote, as Giroux and others warn. Fortunately, however, because the overriding goal is self-promotion—because Disney will absorb and use whatever works, or whatever sells the product—the movies lack the philosophical consistency of propaganda.[15] Thus films like *Beauty and the Beast*, which pays more than lip-service to the liberating potential of fantasy, can sometimes appear.

36 Nevertheless, the fact that many Disney movies implant seeds of guilt and fear to spring up along with children's developing imaginations is a serious problem. The mixed messages noticeable in *Alice* are present in earlier movies such as *Dumbo* and "The Sorcerer's Apprentice" in *Fantasia*. They continue in more recent examples such as *Hercules* and *The Hunchback of Notre Dame*, in which only evil and terrifying characters wield the transformative power that is, in essence, the animator's art; thus these movies almost identify themselves as products of black magic.[16] Some recent films seem almost to reject the notion of animation altogether, striking the eye most forcibly with stills such as the battlefield in *Mulan*, or the cathedral of Notre Dame—breathtaking, to be sure, but unlike the Beast's castle, completely static. Clearly the reluctance to embrace imagination with both arms is still present among the many and shifting ideas that make up the Disney ethos.

37 The inconsistencies found in these movies do not lighten either the parent's burden of guiding the young in their adventures with the media, or the critic's task of understanding the various manifestations of culture. On the contrary, they oblige us to do more than count the number of profane words or violent

---

[15]Giroux notes inconsistent values among elements in the films (5, 91). Wasko emphasizes consistent elements that make "classic Disney" a recognizable "brand" (3, 152), but does not explore tensions among the elements she lists as consistent, such as "work ethic" vs. "escape fantasy" (114).

[16]A notable exception is *The Emperor's New Groove*, in which magic transformative potions intended as evil by the villain turn positive and bring about both the narrative and visual climax of the movie.

acts or exposed body parts; and also to do more than catalogue plots, count the numbers of males and females, and quantify relative levels of aggression. Instead, we must watch carefully the interplay of elements within the films and notice how many stories are going on at one time. Watching the faces of our children as they watch, we will often find that imagination, in these movies, is like Alice's garden—just beyond a little locked door, the key to which is tantalizingly, frustratingly out of reach.

Works Cited*

Alice in Wonderland. Dir. Clyde Geronimi, Hamilton Luske, and Wilfred Jackson. Walt Disney Company, 1951.

Allan, Robin. "Alice in Disneyland." *Sight and Sound* 54 (Spring 1985): 136–38.

Allen, Holly, and Michael Denning. "The Cartoonists' Front." *South Atlantic Quarterly* 92.1 (1993): 89–117.

Andersen, Hans Christian. "The Little Mermaid." *Hans Christian Andersen: His Classic Fairy Tales.* Trans. Erik Haugaard. Garden City, NY: Doubleday, 1978. 149–70.

Apuleius. *Transformations of Lucius Otherwise Known as the Golden Ass.* Trans. Robert Graves. New York: Noonday, 1998.

Austen, Jane. *Selected Letters.* Oxford: Oxford UP, 1985.

Beaumont, Madame Leprince de. *Beauty and the Beast.* Trans. P. H. Muir. New York: Knopf, 1968.

Beauty and the Beast. Dir. Gary Trousdale and Kirk Wise. Walt Disney Company, 1991.

Behn, Aphra. *The Works of Aphra Behn: Poetry.* Ed. Janet Todd. Columbus: Ohio UP, 1992.

Bell, Elizabeth. "Somatexts at the Disney Shop." Bell, Haas, and Sells 107–24.

Bell, Elizabeth, Lynda Haas, and Laura Sells, eds. *From Mouse to Mermaid: The Politics of Film, Gender, and Culture.* Bloomington: Indiana UP, 1995.

Bettelheim, Bruno. *The Uses of Enchantment.* New York: Vintage, 1977.

Britton, Donald. "The Dark Side of Disneyland." *Mythomania: Fantasies, Fables, and Sheer Lies in Contemporary American Popular Art.* By Bernard Welt. Los Angeles: Art Issues, 1996. 113–26.

Carroll, Lewis. *Alice's Adventures in Wonderland and Through the Looking-Glass.* New York: New American Library, 1960.

Cinderella. Dir. Hamilton Luske and Wilfred Jackson. Walt Disney Company, 1950.

Dumbo. Dir. Ben Sharpsteen. Walt Disney Company, 1941.

Eliot, Marc. *Walt Disney: Hollywood's Dark Prince.* New York: Birch Lane, 1993.

The Emperor's New Groove. Dir. Mark Dindal. Walt Disney Company, 2000.

Estes, Clarissa Pinkola. *Women Who Run with the Wolves.* New York: Ballantine, 1992.

---

*As noted in the Networking question that follows, this Works Cited section does not follow the latest MLA style. The spacing has also been condensed.

Fantasia. Dir. Ford Beebe and Bill Roberts. Walt Disney Company, 1942.

Gilbert, Sandra, and Susan Gubar. *The Madwoman in the Attic.* New Haven: Yale UP, 1979.

Giroux, Henry. *The Mouse That Roared: Disney and the End of Innocence.* Lanham, MD: Rowman, 1999.

Hansen, Miriam. "Of Mice and Ducks: Benjamin and Adorno on Disney." *South Atlantic Quarterly* 92.1 (1993): 27–61.

Hedges, Inez. *Languages of Revolt: Dada and Surrealist Literature and Film.* Durham: Duke UP, 1983.

Hercules. Dir. Ron Clements and John Musker. Walt Disney Company, 1997.

The Hunchback of Notre Dame. Dir. Gary Trousdale and Kirk Wise. Walt Disney Company, 1996.

Hunter, J. Paul. "'The Young, the Ignorant, and the Idle': Some Notes on Readers and the Beginnings of the English Novel." *Anticipations of the Enlightenment in England, France, and Germany.* Ed. Alan Charles Kors and Paul J. Korshin. Philadelphia: U of Pennsylvania P, 1987. 259–82.

Jeffords, Susan. "The Curse of Masculinity." Bell, Haas, and Sells 161–72.

Johnson, Samuel. *The Rambler.* Ed. W. J. Bate and Albrecht B. Strauss. New Haven: Yale UP, 1969.

Lennox, Charlotte. *The Female Quixote,* 1759. Boston: Pandora, 1986.

Lewis, Jon. "Disney after Disney." *Disney Discourse: Producing the Magic Kingdom.* Ed. Eric Smoodin. New York: Routledge, 1994.

Lilo and Stitch. Dir. Dean DeBlois and Chris Sanders (III). Walt Disney Company, 2002.

The Lion King. Dir. Rob Minkoff and Roger Allers. Walt Disney Company, 1994.

The Little Mermaid. Dir. John Musker and Ron Clements. Walt Disney Company, 1989.

Mulan. Dir. Tony Bancroft and Barry Cook. Walt Disney Company, 1998.

Murphy, Patrick D. "'The Whole Wide World Was Scrubbed Clean': The Androcentric Animation of Denatured Disney." Bell, Haas, and Sells 125–36.

Pocahontas. Dir. Mike Gabriel and Eric Goldberg. Walt Disney Company, 1995.

Ross, Deborah. *The Excellence of Falsehood.* Lexington: UP of Kentucky, 1991.

Schickel, Richard. *The Disney Version.* New York: Simon, 1968.

Scudéry, Madeleine de. *Clelia.* Trans. John Davies. London: Herringman, 1678.

Sells, Laura. "'Where Do the Mermaids Stand?' Voice and Body in *The Little Mermaid.*" Bell, Haas, and Sells 175–92.

The Sleeping Beauty. Dir. Clyde Geronimi. Walt Disney Company, 1959.

Snow White and the Seven Dwarfs. Dir. David Hand. Walt Disney Company, 1938.

Warner, Marina. *From the Beast to the Blonde: On Fairy Tales and Their Tellers.* New York: Noonday, 1994.

Wasko, Janet. *Understanding Disney.* Cambridge, UK: Polity, 2001.

Watts, Steven. "Walt Disney: Art and Politics in the American Century." *Journal of American History* 82.1 (June 1995): 84–110.

Zipes, Jack. *Fairy Tale as Myth/Myth as Fairy Tale.* Lexington: UP of Kentucky, 1994.

COMPREHENSION

1. How does Ross define the ideology inherent in Disney's films for girls?
2. Summarize the content of the three films that Ross discusses. What similarities and differences does Ross see among them?
3. According to the writer, what is a "female Quixote"? Where does she treat this concept directly and indirectly?

RHETORIC

1. This essay appeared in a specialized scholarly journal. What "scholarly" elements appear in the paper? How does Ross adjust her style to this specialized audience? What strategies does she use to make the essay accessible to a wider audience?
2. Where does Ross state her claim most clearly? Analyze the varieties of evidence that she uses to support her claim and the minor propositions.
3. How does the writer organize her essay? What are the main divisions, and how do they cohere?
4. Why does Ross cite other scholars and writers? How does this strategy affect the power of her argument?
5. Ross elaborates a definition of the Disney "program" or ideology. What rhetorical strategies does she use to create this extended definition?
6. How effective do you find the concluding paragraph? Justify your response.

WRITING

1. Select one Disney movie and write an analysis of its "program"—its ethical message or ideology.
2. In an expository essay, explain why children's stories or fairy tales have such a hold on young people's imaginations.
3. **Writing an Argument:** Write a persuasive essay on the benefits of children's literature and film—even the films that Walt Disney produced. Present at least three extended examples to support your claim.

NETWORKING
Applying 21st-Century Literacies

Updating Citations to Reflect Current MLA Style: Since this essay was published, the MLA has made some changes to their guidelines for documenting sources; one change includes noting the medium of each source. Refer to Chapter 4 to help update Ross's Works Cited page; beyond this book's coverage, consult the MLA's Web site (see the Chapter 9 Networking page at *www.mhhe. com/mhreaderbrief1e*), or the seventh edition of the *MLA Handbook* (2009).

Synthesis: Connections for Critical Thinking

1. Examine the role of the media in society and the responsibilities or duties to humanity of individuals associated with the media. Use at least three essays from this chapter to illustrate or support your thesis.
2. Define *popular culture,* using the essays of Ross and Steinem as reference points, along with any additional essays that you consider relevant.
3. Use the essays of Warshow, Goodlad, Ross, and Gitlin to explore the connections of media representations to American cultural experience. What strategies do these writers use? Are their goals similar?
4. Using at least three recent films or television episodes that you have seen, write an essay in which you agree or disagree with Bordo's claim that the media are causing "eating and body image problems" for girls and women.
5. After reading the essays of Warshow, Goodlad, and Steinem, research the issue of the difference between popular entertainment and art. On the basis of your research, discuss whether there are legitimate criteria that distinguish the two forms. Apply these criteria to gangster films, television dramas, and comics.

NETWORKING
Applying 21st-Century Literacies

Select several images of real "gangsters" or other "bad" men from magazines, or print out images of them from the Internet. Compare and contrast them with advertisements depicting gangsters from contemporary crime movies such as *Pulp Fiction.* What are the similarities and differences in the subjects' dress, demeanor, facial expression, and so on? What can you conclude from your comparisons?

 CH 9   www.mhhe.com/**mhreaderbrief1e**

- *Image Gallery:* Chapter images in color
- *Media and Popular Culture:* Information on the authors in this chapter
- *Ch 9 Networking*

An Album of Advertisements: Images of Culture

The advertisements that appear in this album reflect various ideas in the popular culture—what we value and what we desire. Advertising clearly is a powerful force in molding popular culture and taste. Consider what the advertisements in this album say about popular culture and how they embody forms of argument and persuasion that promote a product, person, or idea.

Mobile Outdoor Advertising: NotinLA.com

CONSIDERING THE ADVERTISEMENT

1. What seems to be the purpose behind this mobile ad? What evidence can you cite to support your response? Why would it be helpful to go to the Web site to decipher the ad's message?
2. In an argumentative essay, explain why you think this NotinLA.com ad is or is not successful.

Classic Advertisement: An early 1960s magazine advertisement for a refrigerator, featuring an attractive model in a stylish dress

CONSIDERING THE ADVERTISEMENTS

1. Analyze the use of fashion, fantasy, and story to "sell" products—from a refrigerator (in the magazine ad) to a television show and clothing (in the window display). Who is the intended audience for each ad, and what techniques are being used to appeal to that audience? What cultural assumptions and ideals does each ad build on? Using these classic and contemporary ads as a reference point, write an essay arguing for or against the proposition that the methods and goals of advertising have not changed or improved over time, even though the culture may have changed.

Contemporary Advertisement: A cross-promotional Banana
Republic/*Mad Men* window display (top); a scene from
Mad Men, featuring the ad men's stylish suits (bottom)

2. Imagine that you work for either Banana Republic or *Mad Men*'s network,
AMC. Write a proposal for a cross-promotional ad campaign exactly like, or
similar to, the one featured in this window display. Describe what the ads
would look like, what forms they would take, where they would be featured,
and who their target audience would be. Throughout, provide persuasive
reasons for why this venture would be beneficial to both the store and the
show. As part of your research, watch at least two episodes of *Mad Men* and
visit a Banana Republic store (on foot or online). As an alternative, propose
a similar ad campaign for another television show and store.

International Advertising: Budweiser in China

CONSIDERING THE ADVERTISEMENT

1. Explain the way in which these photographs capture the power of advertising to promote an American product overseas. What details hold your
   attention? Why is the poster advertising Budweiser so large?
2. In an essay, argue for or against the idea that advertising American products like Budweiser, Starbucks, or McDonald's overseas is a form of "cultural
   imperialism" that harms the societies of other countries.

International Branding: Starbucks in the Near East and China

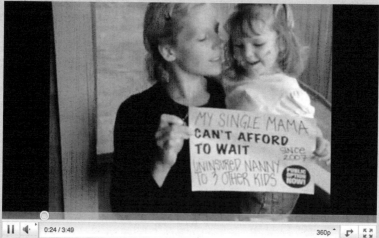

Issue Advertising: Health care reform videos (MoveOn.org)

CONSIDERING THE ADVERTISEMENTS

1. Via the Chapter 9 Networking page (at *www.mhhe.com/mhreaderbrief1e*), watch "Protect Insurance Companies PSA" and "We Can't Afford to Wait" (both sponsored by MoveOn.org). Compare the videos' central claims, as well as their purposes, audiences, contents, and tones. How does each video make logical, ethical, and/or emotional appeals?
2. "Protect Insurance Companies" parodies a commercial sponsored by a group opposing health care reform. Make an argument for or against the effectiveness of parody as argument, using an analysis of this video as support for your point.

Issue Advertising: Health care reform flyer (USCCB.org)

3. Explain the various details and visual elements that create the "message" in this flyer from USCCB.org, a Web site advocating universal health care—with stipulations. Then, via the Chapter 9 Networking page, explore the USCCB Web site. In an essay, analyze the argumentative techniques underlying the verbal and nonverbal elements on the site's home page and other relevant pages. Link to or integrate images you discuss into your essay. Alternately, apply this assignment to another Web site and issue of your choosing.

4. Explore what advantages a short video or Web site has over print, audio, or static visual texts as a medium for persuasion. What opportunities might an online location afford? What are some limitations of this genre or location?

Anti-Advertising: God billboard

CONSIDERING THE ADVERTISEMENT

1. What is your response to this billboard ad? Are you surprised, shocked, or amused, and why? Who might have paid for the billboard ad? What is the ad's purpose? Why might some viewers find the ad controversial? Why might the ad be considered a humorous form of anti-advertising?
2. Write an essay in which you contend that various expressions of faith should or should not be used in advertising, or that God should or should not be used to promote a product, person, or idea.

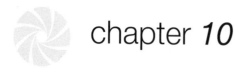

chapter *10*

Literature and the Arts
Why Do They Matter?

Imagine a world without fiction, poetry, or drama, without music, art, or other fine arts. We are so accustomed to taking the arts in their totality for granted that it is hard for us to conceive of contemporary culture without them. Our fondness for stories or paintings or any other creative form might help us understand our culture or might even move us to action. Yet the value of various artistic forms doesn't derive exclusively from their ability to tell us something about life. The arts can also take us into an imaginative realm offering perhaps more intense experiences than anything we encounter in the "real" world.

Think of literature and the arts as an exercise in imaginative freedom. You are free to select the books you read, the music that appeals to you, the exhibitions and concerts you attend, and the entertainment software with which you interact. Some of your decisions might be serious and consequential to your education. Other decisions, perhaps to watch a few soap operas on a rainy afternoon or to buy the latest potboiler, are less important. The way you view the arts—whether as a way to learn something about the temper of civilization or as a temporary escape from conventional reality—is entirely a matter of taste. Regardless of your purpose or intent, you approach literature and the arts initially for the sheer exhilaration and pleasure they provide. Art, as Plato observed, is a dream for awakened minds.

The arts awaken you to the power and intensity of the creative spirit. At the same time, you make judgments and evaluations of the nature of your creative encounter. When you assert that you like this painting or dislike that poem, you are assessing the work and the value of the artistic experience. Clearly, you develop taste and become more equipped to discern the more subtle elements of art the more you are exposed to it. Perhaps you prefer to keep your experience of literature and the other arts a pleasurable pastime or an escape from reality. Or you may wish to participate in them as a creative writer, musician, painter, or photographer. Ultimately, you may come to view literature and the arts as a transformational experience, a voyage of discovery in which you encounter diverse peoples and cultures, learn to see the world in creative terms, and begin to perceive your own creative potential in a new light.

PREVIEWING THE CHAPTER

As you read the essays in this chapter and respond to them in discussion and writing, consider the following questions:

- According to the author, what is the value of the art or literary form under discussion?
- What function does literature or art serve?
- Is the writer's perspective subjective or objective, and why?
- How does the author define his or her subject—whether it is poetry, fiction, art, or photography?
- Is the writer's experience of literature or art similar to or different from your own?
- In what ways do gender and race influence the writer's perspective on the subject?
- What is the main idea that the author wants to present about literature or the arts? Do you agree or disagree with this key concept?
- What have you learned about the importance of literature and the arts from reading these essays?

Classic and Contemporary Images
HOW DO WE EVALUATE A WORK OF ART?

Using a Critical Perspective   Although "greatness" in art and literature might be in the mind of the beholder, it could be argued that you need certain standards of excellence or judgment to determine the quality of any work. The artist's or writer's control of the medium, the projection of a unique vision, the evidence of a superlative style—all enter into the evaluation process. As you consider these sculptures by Auguste Rodin and Jeff Koons, try to evaluate their relative worth. Which work reflects greater artistic control? What makes the sculpture appealing, and why? Which work strikes you as "new" or original, or modern? Explain your response and criteria for evaluation.

Auguste Rodin (1840–1917), a French sculptor famous for his bronze and marble figures, is thought by some critics to be one of the greatest portraitists in the history of sculpture. Yet he was also criticized in his time for the excessive realism and sensuousness of his figures. *Walking Man* hints at some of the objections critics lodged against Rodin's work.

Jeff Koons (b. 1955) is an American artist who, like Rodin, has had his admirers and detractors. Koons studied at the Art Institute of Chicago and elsewhere before becoming a commodities trader in New York City, which helped fund the materials for his art. *Rabbit* reflects Koons's fondness for popular culture and the way in which he takes consumer goods and repositions them as art objects.

Classic and Contemporary Essays
WHAT IS THE VALUE OF LITERATURE?

Although Eudora Welty was born at the beginning of the 20th century in a small Mississippi town and Sherman Alexie half a century later on a tribal reservation in the state of
Washington, half a continent away, these writers share a reverence for the importance of
literature in their childhood. Of course, there are understandable differences in the types
of literature that formed their young minds. Welty, you will discover, grew up in a loving,
middle-class household where virtually every room contained books—a treasury of English and European novels, classic fairy tales, and famous works of literature in the
Western tradition. Alexie, on the other hand, from a family that was "middle-class by
reservation standards" but in actuality poor, had a father who was addicted to alcohol but
also to pulp fiction—westerns, detective stories, spy thrillers, comic books featuring action
heroes. And despite their disparate backgrounds, lives, and reading tastes, Welty and
Alexie grew up to be writers. They might represent different regional, ethnic, and cultural
backgrounds, and they speak as a woman and man of different forms of knowledge and
experience, but both attest to the value of literature. As they recount their childhood,
Welty and Alexie struggle to establish an identity that will last a lifetime. They succeed in
convincing us that whether one child reads Dickens and the other Superman comic books,
their ideas and insights into the world derive from the active reading of texts.

One Writer's Beginnings

Eudora Welty

*Eudora Welty (1909–2001), a celebrated American writer, was born and died in Jack-
son, Mississippi. Raised in a close-knit bookish family, Welty attended the Mississippi
State College for Women for two years and then the University of Wisconsin (BA,
1929). In the 1930s she returned to Mississippi and worked for the Works Progress
Administration as a reporter and photographer, traveling the state and recording the
lives of its citizens during the Depression years. She also began a career as a short-story
writer and novelist. Welty's superb short fiction collections include* A Curtain of
Green *(1941),* The Wide Net *(1943), and* Collected Stories *(1980), which received
an American Book Award. She received the Pulitzer Prize for her novel* The Opti-
mist's Daughter *(1972). The recipient of the President's Medal of Freedom and numerous other major awards, Welty spent virtually her entire life writing about the South
but in ways that transcend her region, radiating outward to embrace universal truths.*

In the selection that follows, one of three lectures delivered at Harvard University in 1983 and published in her memoir One Writer's Beginnings *(1984), Welty speaks of the value of literature and the arts in her life.*

I learned from the age of two or three that any room in our house, at any time of day, was there to read in, or to be read to. My mother read to me. She'd read to me in the big bedroom in the mornings, when we were in her rocker together, which ticked in rhythm as we rocked, as though we had a cricket accompanying the story. She'd read to me in the diningroom on winter afternoons in front of the coal fire, with our cuckoo clock ending the story with "Cuckoo," and at night when I'd got in my own bed. I must have given her no peace. Sometimes she read to me in the kitchen while she sat churning, and the churning sobbed along with *any* story. It was my ambition to have her read to me while *I* churned; once she granted my wish, but she read off my story before I brought her butter. She was an expressive reader. When she was reading "Puss in Boots," for instance, it was impossible not to know that she distrusted *all* cats.

It had been startling and disappointing to me to find out that story books had been written by *people,* that books were not natural wonders, coming up of themselves like grass. Yet regardless of where they came from, I cannot remember a time when I was not in love with them—with the books themselves, cover and binding and the paper they were printed on, with their smell and their weight and with their possession in my arms, captured and carried off to myself. Still illiterate, I was ready for them, committed to all the reading I could give them.

Neither of my parents had come from homes that could afford to buy many books, but though it must have been something of a strain on his salary, as the youngest officer in a young insurance company, my father was all the while carefully selecting and ordering away for what he and Mother thought we children should grow up with. They bought first for the future.

Besides the bookcase in the livingroom, which was always called "the library," there were the encyclopedia tables and dictionary stand under windows in our diningroom. Here to help us grow up arguing around the diningroom table were the Unabridged Webster, the Columbia Encyclopedia, Compton's Pictured Encyclopedia, the Lincoln Library of Information, and later the Book of Knowledge. And the year we moved into our new house, there was room to celebrate it with the new 1925 edition of the Britannica, which my father, his face always deliberately turned toward the future, was of course disposed to think better than any previous edition.

In "the library," inside the mission-style bookcase with its three diamond-latticed glass doors, with my father's Morris chair and the glass-shaded lamp on its table beside it, were books I could soon begin on—and I did, reading them all alike and as they came, straight down their rows, top shelf to bottom. There was the set of Stoddard's Lectures, in all its late nineteenth-century vocabulary and vignettes of peasant life and quaint beliefs and customs, with matching halftone illustrations: Vesuvius erupting, Venice by moonlight, gypsies

glimpsed by their campfires. I didn't know then the clue they were to my father's longing to see the rest of the world. I read straight through his other love-
from-afar: the Victrola Book of the Opera, with opera after opera in synopsis,
with portraits in costume of Melba, Caruso, Galli-Curci, and Geraldine Farrar,
some of whose voices we could listen to on our Red Seal records.

6   My mother read secondarily for information; she sank as a hedonist into
novels. She read Dickens in the spirit in which she would have eloped with
him. The novels of her girlhood that had stayed on in her imagination, besides those of Dickens and Scott and Robert Louis Stevenson, were *Jane Eyre,
Trilby, The Woman in White, Green Mansions, King Solomon's Mines.* Marie
Corelli's name would crop up but I understood she had gone out of favor
with my mother, who had only kept *Ardath* out of loyalty. In time she absorbed herself in Galsworthy, Edith Wharton, above all in Thomas Mann of
the *Joseph* volumes.

7   *St. Elmo* was not in our house; I saw it often in other houses. This wildly
popular Southern novel is where all the Edna Earles in our population started
coming from. They're all named for the heroine, who succeeded in bringing a
dissolute, sinning roué and atheist of a lover (St. Elmo) to his knees. My mother
was able to forgo it. But she remembered the classic advice given to rose grow-
ers on how to water their bushes long enough: "Take a chair and *St. Elmo.*"

8   To both my parents I owe my early acquaintance with a beloved Mark
Twain. There was a full set of Mark Twain and a short set of Ring Lardner in our
bookcase, and those were the volumes that in time united us all, parents and
children.

9   Reading everything that stood before me was how I came upon a worn
old book without a back that had belonged to my father as a child. It was
called *Sanford and Merton.* Is there anyone left who recognizes it, I wonder? It
is the famous moral tale written by Thomas Day in the 1780s, but of him no
mention is made on the title page of *this* book; here it is *Sanford and Merton in
Words of One Syllable* by Mary Godolphin. Here are the rich boy and the poor
boy and Mr. Barlow, their teacher and interlocutor, in long discourses alternating with dramatic scenes—danger and rescue allotted to the rich and the
poor respectively. It may have only words of one syllable, but one of them is
"quoth." It ends with not one but two morals, both engraved on rings: "Do
what you ought, come what may," and "If we would be great, we must first
learn to be good."

10   This book was lacking its front cover, the back held on by strips of pasted
paper, now turned golden, in several layers, and the pages stained, flecked, and
tattered around the edges; its garish illustrations had come unattached but
were preserved, laid in. I had the feeling even in my heedless childhood that
this was the only book my father as a little boy had of his own. He had held
onto it, and might have gone to sleep on its coverless face: He had lost his
mother when he was seven. My father had never made any mention to his own
children of the book, but he had brought it along with him from Ohio to our
house and shelved it in our bookcase.

My mother had brought from West Virginia that set of Dickens; those books 11
looked sad, too—they had been through fire and water before I was born, she
told me, and there they were, lined up—as I later realized, waiting for *me*.

I was presented, from as early as I can remember, with books of my own, 12
which appeared on my birthday and Christmas morning. Indeed, my parents
could not give me books enough. They must have sacrificed to give me on my
sixth or seventh birthday—it was after I became a reader for myself—the ten-
volume set of Our Wonder World. These were beautifully made, heavy books I
would lie down with on the floor in front of the diningroom hearth, and more
often than the rest volume 5, *Every Child's Story Book,* was under my eyes. There
were the fairy tales—Grimm, Andersen, the English, the French, "Ali Baba and
the Forty Thieves"; and there was Aesop and Reynard the Fox; there were the
myths and legends, Robin Hood, King Arthur, and St. George and the Dragon,
even the history of Joan of Arc; a whack of *Pilgrim's Progress* and a long piece of
Gulliver. They all carried their classic illustrations. I located myself in these
pages and could go straight to the stories and pictures I loved; very often "The
Yellow Dwarf" was first choice, with Walter Crane's Yellow Dwarf in full color
making his terrifying appearance flanked by turkeys. Now that volume is as
worn and backless and hanging apart as my father's poor *Sanford and Merton.*
The precious page with Edward Lear's "Jumblies" on it has been in danger of
slipping out for all these years. One measure of my love for Our Wonder World
was that for a long time I wondered if I would go through fire and water for it
as my mother had done for Charles Dickens; and the only comfort was to think
I could ask my mother to do it for me.

I believe I'm the only child I know of who grew up with this treasure in the 13
house. I used to ask others, "Did you have Our Wonder World?" I'd have to tell
them The Book of Knowledge could not hold a candle to it.

I live in gratitude to my parents for initiating me—and as early as I begged 14
for it, without keeping me waiting—into knowledge of the word, into reading
and spelling, by way of the alphabet. They taught it to me at home in time for me
to begin to read before starting to school. I believe the alphabet is no longer considered an essential piece of equipment for traveling through life. In my day it
was the keystone to knowledge. You learned the alphabet as you learned to count
to ten, as you learned "Now I lay me" and the Lord's Prayer and your father's
and mother's name and address and telephone number, all in case you were lost.

My love for the alphabet, which endures, grew out of reciting it but, before 15
that, out of seeing the letters on the page. In my own story books, before I could
read them for myself, I fell in love with various winding, enchanting-looking
initials drawn by Walter Crane at the heads of fairy tales. In "Once upon a
time," an "O" had a rabbit running it as a treadmill, his feet upon flowers.
When the day came, years later, for me to see the Book of Kells, all the wizardry
of letter, initial, and word swept over me a thousand times over, and the illumi-
nation, the gold, seemed a part of the word's beauty and holiness that had been
there from the start.

. . .

16   Learning stamps you with its moments. Childhood's learning is made up of moments. It isn't steady. It's a pulse.

17   In a children's art class, we sat in a ring on kindergarten chairs and drew three daffodils that had just been picked out of the yard; and while I was drawing, my sharpened pencil and the cup of the yellow daffodil gave off whiffs just alike. That the pencil doing the drawing should give off the same smell as the flower it drew seemed a part of the art lesson—as shouldn't it be? Children, like animals, use all their senses to discover the world. Then artists come along and discover it the same way, all over again. Here and there, it's the same world. Or now and then we'll hear from an artist who's never lost it.

18   In my sensory education I include my physical awareness of the *word*. Of a certain word, that is; the connection it has with what it stands for. At around age six, perhaps, I was standing by myself in our front yard waiting for supper, just at that hour in a late summer day when the sun is already below the horizon and the risen full moon in the visible sky stops being chalky and begins to take on light. There comes the moment, and I saw it then, when the moon goes from flat to round. For the first time it met my eyes as a globe. The word "moon" came into my mouth as though fed to me out of a silver spoon. Held in my mouth the moon became a word. It had the roundness of a Concord grape Grandpa took off his vine and gave me to suck out of its skin and swallow whole, in Ohio.

19   This love did not prevent me from living for years in foolish error about the moon. The new moon just appearing in the west was the rising moon to me. The new should be rising. And in early childhood the sun and moon, those opposite reigning powers, I just as easily assumed rose in east and west respectively in their opposite sides of the sky, and like partners in a reel they advanced, sun from the east, moon from the west, crossed over (when I wasn't looking) and went down on the other side. My father couldn't have known I believed that when, bending behind me and guiding my shoulder, he positioned me at our telescope in the front yard and, with careful adjustment of the focus, brought the moon close to me.

20   The night sky over my childhood Jackson was velvety black. I could see the full constellations in it and call their names; when I could read, I knew their myths. Though I was always waked for eclipses, and indeed carried to the window as an infant in arms and shown Halley's Comet in my sleep, and though I'd been taught at our diningroom table about the solar system and knew the earth revolved around the sun, and our moon around us, I never found out the moon didn't come up in the west until I was a writer and Herschel Brickell, the literary critic, told me after I misplaced it in a story. He said valuable words to me about my new profession: "Always be sure you get your moon in the right part of the sky."

. . .

21   My mother always sang to her children. Her voice came out just a little bit in the minor key. "Wee Willie Winkie's" song was wonderfully sad when she sang the lullabies.

22   "Oh, but now there's a record. She could have her own record to listen to," my father would have said. For there came a Victrola record of "Bobby Shafftoe"

and "Rock-a-Bye Baby," all of Mother's lullabies, which could be played to take her place. Soon I was able to play her my own lullabies all day long.

Our Victrola stood in the diningroom. I was allowed to climb onto the seat of   23 a diningroom chair to wind it, start the record turning, and set the needle playing. In a second I'd jumped to the floor, to spin or march around the table as the music called for—now there were all the other records I could play too. I skinned back onto the chair just in time to lift the needle at the end, stop the record and turn it over, then change the needle. That brass receptacle with a hole in the lid gave off a metallic smell like human sweat, from all the hot needles that were fed it. Winding up, dancing, being cocked to start and stop the record, was of course all in one the act of *listening*—to "Overture to *Daughter of the Regiment*," "Selections from *The Fortune Teller*," "Kiss Me Again," "Gypsy Dance from *Carmen*," "Stars and Stripes Forever," "When the Midnight Choo-Choo Leaves for Alabam," or whatever came next. Movement must be at the very heart of listening.

Ever since I was first read to, then started reading to myself, there has never   24 been a line read that I didn't *hear*. As my eyes followed the sentence, a voice was saying it silently to me. It isn't my mother's voice, or the voice of any person I can identify, certainly not my own. It is human, but inward, and it is inwardly that I listen to it. It is to me the voice of the story or the poem itself. The cadence, whatever it is that asks you to believe, the feeling that resides in the printed word, reaches me through the reader-voice. I have supposed, but never found out, that this is the case with all readers—to read as listeners—and with all writers, to write as listeners. It may be part of the desire to write. The sound of what falls on the page begins the process of testing it for truth, for me. Whether I am right to trust so far I don't know. By now I don't know whether I could do either one, reading or writing, without the other.

My own words, when I am at work on a story, I hear too as they go, in the same   25 voice that I hear when I read in books. When I write and the sound of it comes back to my ears, then I act to make my changes. I have always trusted this voice.

COMPREHENSION

1. What is the significance of the essay's title? Does Welty write about one continuous "beginning" or a series of beginnings? Explain.
2. What does Welty mean when she says that her mother was a "hedonist" (paragraph 6)? Does Welty also become a hedonist? Why or why not?
3. Explain the nature of Welty's "sensory" education.

RHETORIC

1. Welty alludes to dozens of works of literature. What does she assume about her audience's knowledge of these works? Can you appreciate the essay even if you are not familiar with most of this literature? Justify your response.
2. What is Welty's thesis, and how does she develop it?

3. What determines the order in which Welty organizes her essay, which she divides into three parts?
4. Welty includes several descriptive passages in this essay. Where are these passages, and what do they contribute to the overall meaning of the selection?
5. How do the last two paragraphs of the essay echo the first two paragraphs?

WRITING

1. Write a description of a scene or series of events from your childhood in which you were reading (or being read to), engaged in an art project, or listening to music. In your essay, explain the impact of this memory or activity on your current life.
2. Write an essay explaining the importance of providing children with sensory stimuli involving reading, artwork, and music.
3. **Writing an Argument:** Argue for or against the proposition that children today read less than those of previous generations—and suffer the consequences.

NETWORKING
Applying 21st-Century Literacies

Can e-Readers Save Reading? It's looking likely that children will soon be reading most texts—from textbooks to novels to comics—electronically. How might an electronic format make reading *more* engaging for today's kids? How might this new form enhance, rather than detract from, reading as a sensory experience?

Superman and Me

Sherman Alexie

Sherman Alexie (b. 1966) is a writer, poet, and performer, and a member of the Spokane/ Coeur d'Alene tribe. He grew up on the Spokane Indian Reservation in Wellpinit, Washington, and contended with a life-threatening illness when he was young. Alexie attended Gonzaga University before transferring to Washington State University (BA, 1991). Alexie writes and creates in many modes, and is also a performer. As many of the titles of his works suggest, the Native American experience informs his short stories, novels, poetry, songs, and films. Alexie's fiction includes Reservation Blues *(1995),* Ten Little Indians: Stories *(2003), and* Flight, A Novel *(2007); his poetry has been collected in* First Indian on the Moon *(1993),* The Man Who Loves Salmon *(1998),* The Absolutely True Diary of a Part-Time Indian *(2007), and other volumes. In the following essay, Alexie attests to the importance of literature—all kinds of literature—in his life.*

I learned to read with a Superman comic book. Simple enough, I suppose. I can- 1
not recall which particular Superman comic book I read, nor can I remember
which villain he fought in that issue. I cannot remember the plot, nor the means
by which I obtained the comic book. What I can remember is this: I was 3 years
old, a Spokane Indian boy living with his family on the Spokane Indian Reservation in eastern Washington state. We were poor by most standards, but one of
my parents usually managed to find some minimum-wage job or another,
which made us middle-class by reservation standards. I had a brother and three
sisters. We lived on a combination of irregular paychecks, hope, fear, and government surplus food.

My father, who is one of the few Indians who went to Catholic school on 2
purpose, was an avid reader of westerns, spy thrillers, murder mysteries, gangster epics, basketball player biographies, and anything else he could find. He
bought his books by the pound at Dutch's Pawn Shop, Goodwill, Salvation
Army, and Value Village. When he had extra money, he bought new novels at
supermarkets, convenience stores, and hospital gift shops. Our house was filled
with books. They were stacked in crazy piles in the bathroom, bedrooms, and
living room. In a fit of unemployment-inspired creative energy, my father built
a set of bookshelves and soon filled them with a random assortment of books
about the Kennedy assassination, Watergate, the Vietnam War, and the entire
23-book series of the Apache westerns. My father loved books, and since I loved
my father with an aching devotion, I decided to love books as well.

I can remember picking up my father's books before I could read. The words 3
themselves were mostly foreign, but I still remember the exact moment when I
first understood, with a sudden clarity, the purpose of a paragraph. I didn't have
the vocabulary to say "paragraph," but I realized that a paragraph was a fence
that held words. The words inside a paragraph worked together for a common
purpose. They had some specific reason for being inside the same fence. This
knowledge delighted me. I began to think of everything in terms of paragraphs.
Our reservation was a small paragraph within the United States. My family's
house was a paragraph, distinct from the other paragraphs of the LeBrets to the
north, the Fords to our south, and the Tribal School to the west. Inside our house,
each family member existed as a separate paragraph but still had genetics and
common experiences to link us. Now, using this logic, I can see my changed family as an essay of seven paragraphs: mother, father, older brother, the deceased
sister, my younger twin sisters, and our adopted little brother.

At the same time I was seeing the world in paragraphs, I also picked up 4
that Superman comic book. Each panel, complete with picture, dialogue, and
narrative was a three-dimensional paragraph. In one panel, Superman breaks
through a door. His suit is red, blue, and yellow. The brown door shatters into
many pieces. I look at the narrative above the picture. I cannot read the words,
but I assume it tells me that "Superman is breaking down the door." Aloud, I
pretend to read the words and say, "Superman is breaking down the door."
Words, dialogue, also float out of Superman's mouth. Because he is breaking
down the door, I assume he says, "I am breaking down the door." Once again,

I pretend to read the words and say aloud, "I am breaking down the door." In this way, I learned to read.

5   This might be an interesting story all by itself. A little Indian boy teaches himself to read at an early age and advances quickly. He reads "Grapes of Wrath" in kindergarten when other children are struggling through "Dick and Jane." If he'd been anything but an Indian boy living on the reservation, he might have been called a prodigy. But he is an Indian boy living on the reservation and is simply an oddity. He grows into a man who often speaks of his childhood in the third person, as if it will somehow dull the pain and make him sound more modest about his talents.

6 A smart Indian is a dangerous person, widely feared and ridiculed by Indians and non-Indians alike. I fought with my classmates on a daily basis. They wanted me to stay quiet when the non-Indian teacher asked for answers, for volunteers, for help. We were Indian children who were expected to be stupid. Most lived up to those expectations inside the classroom but subverted them on the outside. They struggled with basic reading in school but could remember how to sing a few dozen powwow songs. They were monosyllabic in front of their non-Indian teachers but could tell complicated stories and jokes at the dinner table. They submissively ducked their heads when confronted by a non-Indian adult but would slug it out with the Indian bully who was 10 years older. As Indian children, we were expected to fail in the non-Indian world. Those who failed were ceremonially accepted by other Indians and appropriately pitied by non-Indians.

7   I refused to fail. I was smart. I was arrogant. I was lucky. I read books late into the night, until I could barely keep my eyes open. I read books at recess, then during lunch, and in the few minutes left after I had finished my classroom assignments. I read books in the car when my family traveled to powwows or basketball games. In shopping malls, I ran to the bookstores and read bits and pieces of as many books as I could. I read the books my father brought home from the pawnshops and secondhand. I read the books I borrowed from the library. I read the backs of cereal boxes. I read the newspaper. I read the bulletins posted on the walls of the school, the clinic, the tribal offices, the post office. I read junk mail. I read auto-repair manuals. I read magazines. I read anything that had words and paragraphs. I read with equal parts joy and desperation. I loved those books, but I also knew that love had only one purpose. I was trying to save my life.

8   Despite all the books I read, I am still surprised I became a writer. I was going to be a pediatrician. These days, I write novels, short stories, and poems. I visit schools and teach creative writing to Indian kids. In all my years in the reservation school system, I was never taught how to write poetry, short stories, or novels. I was certainly never taught that Indians wrote poetry, short stories, and novels. Writing was something beyond Indians. I cannot recall a single time that a guest teacher visited the reservation. There must have been visiting teachers. Who were they? Where are they now? Do they exist? I visit the schools as often as possible. The Indian kids crowd the classroom. Many are writing their own poems, short stories, and novels. They have read my books. They

have read many other books. They look at me with bright eyes and arrogant wonder. They are trying to save their lives. Then there are the sullen and already defeated Indian kids who sit in the back rows and ignore me with theatrical precision. The pages of their notebooks are empty. They carry neither pencil nor pen. They stare out the window. They refuse and resist. "Books," I say to them. "Books," I say. I throw my weight against their locked doors. The door holds. I am smart. I am arrogant. I am lucky. I am trying to save our lives.

COMPREHENSION

1. Do you find it paradoxical that Alexie learned to read with a Superman comic book? Why or why not? What does Alexie learn from reading the Superman comic?
2. What connections do you see between Alexie and his father?
3. What does Alexie mean when he writes, "A smart Indian is a dangerous person . . . " (paragraph 6)?

RHETORIC

1. Does Alexie state or imply his thesis? State his thesis in your own words.
2. What is Alexie's purpose in writing this essay?
3. Why does Alexie divide his essay into two parts? Do you find this organizational scheme effective? Why or why not?
4. Explain the importance of comparison and contrast in this essay.
5. Alexie's concluding paragraph is quite long. Does it serve as an effective ending? Why or why not?

WRITING

1. Write a personal essay about the types of popular literature that you liked to read as a child.
2. **Writing an Argument:** Do you agree or disagree with Alexie's claim that a literate person—especially a member of any group that has experienced discrimination—is necessarily a dangerous individual? Write an argumentative essay in response to this question.

NETWORKING
Applying 21st-Century Literacies

Comparing Reading and Viewing Habits: Write a comparative essay in which you discuss the reading and viewing habits of your parents and your own tastes. Which media do each of you prefer for popular entertainment, and which do you prefer to get the news? Do you tend to *learn* more from watching a program, reading a print text, or reading an online hyperlinked text? Explore why.

Synthesis: Classic and Contemporary Essays for Comparison

1. Summarize and critique these two writers' agendas, explaining where their ideas overlap and where they diverge.
2. According to both writers, reading in childhood is important. How do Welty and Alexie support this claim? What types of evidence do they present?
3. Compare and contrast the style of each essay. Which essay seems more accessible to you, and why?
4. Imagine what Alexie might say about Welty's essay. What would he see in it that might inform his own writing?

NETWORKING
Applying 21st-Century Literacies

Exploring the Importance of Place: Go online and find out more about these two writers. Focus on Welty's life in Jackson, Mississippi, and Alexie's life on the Spokane Indian Reservation. Then write a brief essay summarizing the importance of place in their writing.

Moving Along

John Updike

John Updike (1932–2009), a major American novelist, short-story writer, poet, and critic, was born in Shillington, Pennsylvania. He graduated from Harvard University (AB, 1954) and attended the Ruskin School of Drawing and Fine Art at Oxford University. Associated for decades with the New Yorker, *where his short fiction, poetry, reviews, and criticism frequently appeared, Updike carved for himself a rare reputation as a master of several literary genres. He published more than 40 books during his career. Focusing in his fiction on suburban middle-class life, Updike received two Pulitzer prizes and many other major awards, including a National Book Award for his novel* The Centaur *(1963). His fiction includes the much-admired "Rabbit" quintet, five novels that track one central character, first introduced in* Rabbit, Run *(1960), through the passages in his life. Updike's poetry collections include* The Carpentered Hen and Other Tame Creatures *(1958) and* Americana: And Other Poems *(2001). Updike included the following essay in* Just Looking *(1981), a collection of his art criticism.*

1   In dreams, one is frequently travelling, and the more hallucinatory moments of our waking life, many of them, are spent in cars, trains, and airplanes. For millennia, Man has walked or run to where he wanted to go; the first naked ape

Artist unknown, *Baz Bahadur and Rupmati Riding by Moonlight,* c. 1780. Pahari miniature in Kangra style, 8¾ × 6¼". The British Museum, Department of Oriental Antiquities, London.

who had the mad idea of mounting a horse (or was it a *Camelops?*) launched a series of subtle internal dislocations of which jet lag is a vivid modern form. When men come to fly through space at near the speed of light, they will return to earth a century later but only a few years older. Now, driving (say) from Boston to Pittsburgh in a day, we arrive feeling greatly aged by the engine's innumerable explosive heartbeats, by the monotony of the highway surface and the constant windy press of unnatural speed. Beside the highway, a clamorous parasitic life signals for attention and halt; localities where generations have lived, bred, labored, and died are flung through the windshield and out through the rearview mirror. Men on the move brutalize themselves and render the world they arrow through phantasmal.

Our two artists, separated by two centuries, capture well the eeriness of travel. ₂ In the Punjab Hills painting, Baz Bahadur, prince of Malwa, has eloped with the lovely Rupmati; in order to keep him faithful to her, the legend goes, she takes him riding by moonlight. The moon appears to exist not only in the sky but behind a grove of trees. Deer almost blend into the mauve-gray hills. A little citadel basks in

Roy de Forest, *Canoe of Fate*, 1974. Polymer on canvas, 66¾ × 90¼". Philadelphia Museum of Art, The Adele Haas Turner and Beatrice Pastorius Turner Fund.

starlight on a hilltop. In this soft night, nothing is brighter than the scarlet pasterns of the horses. Baz Bahadur's steed bears on his hide a paler version of the starry sky, and in his violet genitals carries a hint of this nocturnal ride's sexual undercurrent. To judge from the delicacy of their gestures and glances, the riders are being borne along as smoothly as on a merry-go-round. Though these lovers and their panoply are formalized to static perfection, if we cover them, a surprising depth appears in the top third of the painting, and carries the eye away.

3   The riders in Roy de Forest's contemporary painting move through a forest as crowded, garish, and menacing as the neon-lit main drag of a city. A throng of sinister bystanders, one built of brick and another with eyes that are paste gems, witness the passage of this *Canoe of Fate,* which with the coarseness of its stitching and the bulk of its passengers would make slow headway even on a less crowded canvas. Beyond the mountains, heavenly medallions and balloons of stippled color pre-empt space. Only the gesture of the black brave, echoing that of George Washington in another fabulous American crossing, gives a sense of direction and promises to open a path. Two exotic birds, a slavering wolf, and what may be a fair captive (gazing backward toward settlements where other red-haired bluefaces mourn her) freight the canoe with a suggestion of allegory, of myths to which we have lost the key. The personnel of the

aboriginal New World, at any rate, are here deep-dyed but not extinguished by the glitter and jazz of an urban-feeling wilderness.

In both representations, the movement is from right to left, like that of writ- ₄ ing in the Semitic languages, like the motion of a mother when she instinctively shifts her baby to her left arm, to hold it closer to her heart. It feels natural, this direction, and slightly uphill. We gaze at these dreamlike tapestries of travel confident that no progress will be made—we will awaken in our beds.

COMPREHENSION

1. According to Updike, why does the idea of travel have such a hold on the collective imagination? What is the relationship of the travel motif to art?
2. Describe the two paintings that Updike analyzes in this essay. What other famous painting does he allude to in paragraph 3?
3. Why does Updike emphasize the "eeriness" of the two paintings? What is he saying about the human psyche?

RHETORIC

1. How does Updike design his introductory paragraph? What is his purpose?
2. What is Updike's thesis? Does he state or imply it? Explain.
3. Identify specific passages that highlight Updike's descriptive style. What types of figurative language does he employ?
4. Explain Updike's comparative method. What do the reproductions of the two paintings contribute to the overall comparative effect? Would this brief essay be as effective without these images? Why or why not?
5. Why is Updike's concluding paragraph relatively brief when compared with the preceding paragraphs? Is this end paragraph effective? Justify your response.

WRITING

1. Consider the two paintings that Updike reproduces, and write your own comparative essay based on them.
2. **Writing an Argument:** Argue for or against the proposition that when viewing a work of art, it is not necessary to relate it—as Updike does—to human behavior.

NETWORKING
Applying 21st-Century Literacies

Analyzing Themes in Fine Art: Select two paintings that reflect what you consider to be a common theme, and write a comparative essay about them. Provide images of these paintings in your essay. Recommended sites for viewing paintings are linked to on the Chapter 10 Networking page (at *www.mhhe.com/mhreaderbrief1e*).

Finding Neverland

David Gates

David Gates (b. 1947) is an American journalist and fiction writer. Gates attended Bard College and the University of Connecticut in the mid-1960s, subsequently work- ing as a cab driver and in other capacities while refining his literary craft. His first novel, Jernigan *(1991), was nominated for a Pulitzer prize. Both his second novel,* Preston Falls *(1998), and the collection* The Wonders of the Invisible World: Sto- ries *(1999), were finalists for the National Book Critics Circle Award. Gates is a senior editor and writer at* Newsweek, *covering books and popular music. He also teaches in the graduate writing programs at Bennington College and New School University. In this essay from the July 13, 2009, issue of* Newsweek, *Gates surveys the life, death, and career of music legend Michael Jackson.*

1 True, for a while he was the king of pop—a term apparently originated by his friend Elizabeth Taylor—and he's the last we're ever likely to have. Before Michael Jackson came Frank Sinatra, Elvis Presley, and the Beatles; after him has come absolutely no one, however brilliant or however popular, who couldn't be ignored by vast segments of an ever-more-fragmented audience. Not Kurt Cobain, not Puffy, not Mariah Carey, not Céline Dion, not Beyoncé, not Radiohead—not even Madonna, his closest competitor. When the news of his death broke, the traffic on Twitter caused the site to crash, even though he hadn't had a hit song for years. But starting long before and continuing long after he lorded over the world of entertainment in the 1980s—his 1982 *Thriller* remains the bestselling album of all time—Jackson was the Prince of Artifice. As the prepubescent frontboy of the Jackson 5, he sang in a cherubic mezzo-soprano of sexual longing he could not yet have fully felt. As a young man, however ac- complished and even impassioned his singing was, he never had the sexual credibility of a James Brown or a Wilson Pickett, in part because of his still- high-pitched voice, in part because he seemed never to fully inhabit himself— whoever that self was. In middle age, he consciously took on the role of Peter Pan, with his Neverland Ranch and its amusement-park rides, with his lost-boy "friends" and with what he seemed to believe was an ageless, androgynous physical appearance—let's hope he believed it—thanks to straightened hair and plastic surgery. (No one—least of all Jackson himself—would have wanted to see the Dorian Gray portrait in his attic.) He did his best to construct an alter- nate reality on top of what must have been an initially miserable life: Imagine

Gypsy with—as Jackson claimed in interviews—a physically abusive father in place of Mama Rose, set among Jehovah's Witnesses. Which was the more imaginative creation: his music or his persona?

In retrospect, so much of what Jackson achieved seems baldly symbolic. 2 This was the black kid from Gary, Ind., who ended up marrying Elvis's daughter, setting up Neverland in place of Graceland, and buying the Beatles' song catalog—bold acts of appropriation and mastery, if not outright aggression. (Of course, Elvis and the Beatles had come out of obscurity, too, but that was a long, long time ago, in a galaxy far away.) He made trademarks of the very emblems of his remoteness: his moonwalk dance and his jeweled glove—*noli me tangere,* and vice versa. He morphed relentlessly from the most adorable of kiddie performers (his 1972 movie-soundtrack hit, "Ben," was a love song to a pet rat) to the most sinister of superstars: not by adopting a campy persona, like those of his older contemporaries Alice Cooper or Ozzy Osbourne, but in real life, dodging accusations of child molestation, one of which led to a trial and acquittal in 2005. (One shrink concluded at the time that he was not a pedophile, but merely a case of arrested development.) The 2002 episode in which he briefly dangled his son Prince Michael II (a.k.a. Blanket) over a balcony in Berlin, above horrified, fascinated fans, seemed like a ritualized attempt to dispose of his own younger self. And eventually his several facial surgeries, a skin ailment, serious weight loss, and God knows what else made him look like both a vampire and a mummy—Peter Pan's undead evil twins. That is, like the skeletal, pale-faced zombies he danced with in Jon Landis's 14-minute "Thriller" video. When you watch it today, it appears to be a whole stage full of Michael Jacksons, the real one now the least familiar-looking, the most unreal of all.

3   But whatever strictly personal traumas Jackson may have reenacted and transcended—and then re-reenacted—he performed his dance of death as a central figure in America's long racial horror show. He was, quintessentially, one of those "pure products of America," who, as William Carlos Williams wrote in 1923, "go crazy." To take the uplifting view, enunciated after his death by the likes of the Rev. Al Sharpton, he was a transracial icon, a black person whom white Americans took to their hearts and whose blackness came to seem incidental. In this he resembles such figures as Nat (King) Cole, Sammy Davis Jr., Sidney Poitier, Harry Belafonte, Sam Cooke, Jimi Hendrix, Arthur Ashe, Michael Jordan, Oprah Winfrey, Tiger Woods, and, inevitably, Barack Obama. As a singer-dancer, he clearly belongs not just in the tradition of Jackie Wilson, James Brown, and the Temptations—who seem to have been among his immediate inspirations—but also in the tradition of such dancing entertainers as Fred Astaire and Gene Kelly, who, in turn, drew from such black performers as Bill (Bojangles) Robinson. In the 1978 film version of *The Wiz*, Jackson even seemed to appropriate and reinvent Ray Bolger's role as the Scarecrow in *The Wizard of Oz*. And as a messianic global superstar, he resembles no one so much as his father-in-law, Elvis Presley (who died long before Jackson married his daughter), a transracial figure from the other side of the color line. When Presley's first records were played on the radio in Memphis, DJs made a point of noting that he graduated from the city's all-white Humes High School, lest listeners mistake him for black. Given the ubiquity of television, nobody mistook the wispy-voiced young Michael Jackson for white, but it seemed, superficially, not to matter.

4   Yet Jackson, always the artificer, surely knew that part of his own appeal to white audiences—who contributed substantially to the $50 million to $75 million a year he earned in his prime—lay initially in his precocious cuteness, and when he was a grown man, in his apparent lack of adult sexuality. He was energetic, charismatic, and supremely gifted, but sexually unassertive—unlike swaggeringly heterosexual black male performers from Big Joe Turner ("Shake, Rattle, and Roll") to Jay-Z ("Big Pimpin'"). He neutered himself racially, too: his hair went from kinky to straight, his lips from full to thin, his nose from broad to pinched, his skin from dark to a ghastly pallor. You can't miss the connection between these forms of neutering if you know the history of white America's atavistic dread of black male sexuality; the 1955 murder of 14-year-old Emmett Till, for supposedly flirting with a white woman, is just one *locus classicus*. That happened only three years before Jackson was born; when he was 13, he was singing "Ben." No wonder Jackson chose—with whatever degree of calculation—to remake himself as an American Dream of innocence and belovedness.

No wonder, either, that the artifice eventually turned scary, and the face of the icon came to look more and more corpselike. Readers of Toni Morrison's latest novel, *A Mercy,* might recall the passage in which an African woman tells about her first sight of white slavers: "There we see men we believe are ill or dead. We soon learn they are neither. Their skin is confusing." That's the middle-aged Michael Jackson to a T. Jackson arguably looked his "blackest" on the original cover of 1979's *Off the Wall;* by *Thriller,* the transformation had begun. *Off the Wall* was his declaration of manhood: It came out the year he turned 21, and you could make the case that it was his greatest purely musical moment. Why did he feel so deeply uncomfortable with himself? The hopeless task of sculpting and bleaching yourself into a simulacrum of a white man suggests a profound loathing of blackness. If Michael Jackson couldn't be denounced as a race traitor, who could? Somehow, though, black America overlooked it, and continued to buy his records, perhaps because some African-Americans, with their hair relaxers and skin-lightening creams, understood why Jackson was remaking himself, even if they couldn't condone it.

As with Ernest Hemingway—another case of deeply confused identity and (who knew?) androgynous sexuality—we need to look past the deliberate creation of an image and a persona to appreciate the artistry. A more masterly entertainer never took the stage. In 1988, the *New York Times* dance critic Anna Kisselgoff called him "a virtuoso . . . who uses movement for its own sake. Yes, Michael Jackson is an avant-garde dancer, and his dances could be called abstract. Like Merce Cunningham, he shows us that movement has a value of its own." Better yet, Astaire himself once called Jackson to offer his compliments. As a singer, Jackson was too much of a chameleon—from the tenderness of "I'll Be There" to the rawness of "The Way You Make Me Feel" to the silken sorrow of "She's Out of My Life"—to stamp every song with his distinct personality, as Sinatra did, or Ray Charles, or Hank Williams. But these are demigods—Jackson was merely a giant. (And how'd you like *their* dancing?) As a musical conceptualizer, probably only James Brown has had a comparable influence: Jackson and his visionary producer, Quincy Jones, fused disco, soul, and pop in a manner that can still be heard every hour of every day on every top-40 radio station— only not as well. Tommy Mottola, former head of Sony Music, called Jackson "the corner-stone to the entire music business." The best recordings by Jackson and Jones—"Don't Stop 'Til You Get Enough," "Billie Jean"—belong identifiably to their time, as do Sinatra's 1950s recordings with the arranger Nelson Riddle. Yet like Sinatra's "I've Got the World on a String" or "In the Wee Small Hours of the Morning," they're so perfect of their kind that they'll never sound dated.

The night before he died, Jackson was rehearsing at the Staples Center in Los Angeles for an epic comeback—a series of 50 concerts, beginning in July, at London's O2 Arena. If that sounds impossibly grandiose, consider that all 50 shows had already sold out. People around him had been wondering if he was really up to it, and the opening had already been put off by a week. He was 50 years old, after all: long in the tooth for a *puer aeternus*—eight years older than Elvis when he left the building, and a quarter century past his peak.

Jackson had had health problems for years. Drug problems, too, apparently: In 2007, according to the Associated Press, an L.A. pharmacy sued him, claiming he owed $100,000 for two years' worth of prescription meds. And money problems: In 2008, the ranch nearly went into foreclosure—he defaulted on a $24.5 million debt—and even the $50 million he stood to realize from his potentially grueling London concerts might not have helped that much. And of course, just problems: His very existence—as a son, as a black man—was problematic. In his last days, did the prospect of a comeback, of remythologizing himself one more time, excite him as much as it excited his fans? Did his magical moments in performance have an incandescent density that outweighed what must often have been burdensome hours and days? Ask him sometime, if you see him. Whatever his life felt like from inside, from outside it was manifestly a work of genius, whether you want to call it a triumph or a freak show—those are just words. We'd never seen anyone like this before, either in his artistic inventiveness or his equally artistic self-invention, and we won't forget him—until the big Neverland swallows us all.

COMPREHENSION

1. Summarize Gates's perception of Michael Jackson. How do you interpret the title? Why does Gates call Jackson an "artificer"? What does Gates mean by Jackson's "androgynous sexuality"?
2. Gates alludes to many stars from the world of music, dance, literature, and the arts. Which celebrities can you identify? What is Gates's purpose in listing so many of them?
3. What, in Gates's opinion, is Michael Jackson's legacy?

RHETORIC

1. Does this essay have an explicitly stated thesis? If so, where is it? If the thesis is implied, paraphrase it.
2. The first paragraph of this essay is quite long. What is Gates's strategy and purpose here? Does this lengthy opening paragraph weaken or strengthen the body of the essay? Explain.
3. Identify and comment on Gates's use of figurative language in this essay. How does figurative language—and Gates's overall style—influence the essay's tone?
4. What comparative points does Gates make about Jackson and other artists? How does the comparative method serve to organize the essay?
5. Explain the effect of the last paragraph, which resembles the introductory paragraph in length. Do you think this resemblance was intentional? Why or why not?

WRITING

1. Write your own evaluation of Michael Jackson or another celebrity from the world of music, explaining why you think this artist's achievement is important.

2. Write a comparative essay in which you discuss two artists from the world of music, film, or television.
3. **Writing an Argument:** Argue for or against the proposition that the media make too much of the deaths of prominent celebrities.

NETWORKING
Applying 21st-Century Literacies

Creating a Photo Biography: Strengthen your position in question 1 under Writing by adding a photo biography of Michael Jackson (or another musician-celebrity whose career you've chosen to evaluate). This biography would consist of 12 to 15 images that help tell the story of the celebrity's career; use succinct but compelling captions to supply narration that informs your evaluation.

Regarding the Torture of Others

Susan Sontag

Susan Sontag (1933–2004), one of the most influential critics of her generation, was born in New York City and grew up in Tucson, Arizona, and Los Angeles. After graduating from high school at the age of 15, she started studies at the University of California at Berkeley; subsequently, she received degrees from the University of Chicago and Harvard University. As an art critic as well as a political and cultural commentator, Sontag brought intellectual rigor to her subjects. The main body of her work in prose consists of two collections of essays, Against Interpretation *(1966) and* Where the Stress Falls *(2001), as well as* Trip to Hanoi *(1968),* Illness as Metaphor *(1978), and* AIDS and Its Metaphors *(1988). In addition, Sontag wrote fiction, including* Volcano Lover *(1992) and* In America: A Novel *(2001), and several films and plays. In this essay, published in the* New York Times Magazine *in 2004, Sontag offers a meditation on the photographs of torture taken by American troops at Abu Ghraib prison in Baghdad.*

I.

For a long time—at least six decades—photographs have laid down the tracks   1
of how important conflicts are judged and remembered. The Western memory museum is now mostly a visual one. Photographs have an insuperable power to determine what we recall of events, and it now seems probable that the defining association of people everywhere with the war that the United States launched pre-emptively in Iraq last year will be photographs of the torture of Iraqi prisoners by Americans in the most infamous of Saddam Hussein's prisons, Abu Ghraib.

An Iraqi detainee at Abu Ghraib: The horror of what is shown in the photographs cannot be separated from the horror that the photographs were taken.

2   The Bush administration and its defenders have chiefly sought to limit a public-relations disaster—the dissemination of the photographs—rather than deal with the complex crimes of leadership and of policy revealed by the pictures. There was, first of all, the displacement of the reality onto the photographs themselves. The administration's initial response was to say that the president was shocked and disgusted by the photographs—as if the fault or horror lay in the images, not in what they depict. There was also the avoidance of the word "torture." The prisoners had possibly been the objects of "abuse," eventually of "humiliation"—that was the most to be admitted. "My impression is that what has been charged thus far is abuse, which I believe technically is different from torture," Secretary of Defense Donald Rumsfeld said at a press conference. "And therefore I'm not going to address the 'torture' word."

3   Words alter, words add, words subtract. It was the strenuous avoidance of the word "genocide" while some 800,000 Tutsis in Rwanda were being slaughtered, over a few weeks' time, by their Hutu neighbors 10 years ago that indicated the American government had no intention of doing anything. To refuse to call what took place in Abu Ghraib—and what has taken place elsewhere in Iraq and in Afghanistan and at Guantánamo Bay—by its true name, torture, is as outrageous as the refusal to call the Rwandan genocide a genocide. Here is one of the definitions of torture contained in a convention to which the United States is a signatory: *"any act by which severe pain or suffering, whether physical or mental, is intentionally inflicted on a person for such purposes as obtaining from him or a third person information or a confession."* (The definition comes from the 1984 Convention Against Torture and Other Cruel, Inhuman or Degrading Treatment or Punishment. Similar definitions have existed for some time in customary law and in treaties, starting with Article 3—common to the four Geneva conventions of 1949—and many recent human rights conventions.) The 1984 convention declares, *"No exceptional circumstances whatsoever, whether a state of war or a threat of war, internal political instability or any other public emergency may be invoked as a justification of torture."* And all covenants on torture specify that it

includes treatment intended to humiliate the victim, like leaving prisoners naked in cells and corridors.

Whatever actions this administration undertakes to limit the damage of the 4 widening revelations of the torture of prisoners in Abu Ghraib and elsewhere— trials, courts-martial, dishonorable discharges, resignation of senior military figures and responsible administration officials and substantial compensation to the victims—it is probable that the "torture" word will continue to be banned. To acknowledge that Americans torture their prisoners would contradict everything this administration has invited the public to believe about the virtue of American intentions and America's right, flowing from that virtue, to undertake unilateral action on the world stage.

Even when the president was finally compelled, as the damage to America's 5 reputation everywhere in the world widened and deepened, to use the "sorry" word, the focus of regret still seemed the damage to America's claim to moral superiority. Yes, President Bush said in Washington on May 6, standing alongside King Abdullah II of Jordan, he was "sorry for the humiliation suffered by the Iraqi prisoners and the humiliation suffered by their families." But, he went on, he was "equally sorry that people seeing these pictures didn't understand the true nature and heart of America."

To have the American effort in Iraq summed up by these images must seem, 6 to those who saw some justification in a war that did overthrow one of the monster tyrants of modern times, "unfair." A war, an occupation, is inevitably a huge tapestry of actions. What makes some actions representative and others not? The issue is not whether the torture was done by individuals (i.e., "not by everybody")—but whether it was systematic. Authorized. Condoned. All acts are done by individuals. The issue is not whether a majority or a minority of Americans performs such acts but whether the nature of the policies prosecuted by this administration and the hierarchies deployed to carry them out makes such acts likely.

II.

Considered in this light, the photographs are us. That is, they are representative 7 of the fundamental corruptions of any foreign occupation together with the Bush adminstration's distinctive policies. The Belgians in the Congo, the French in Algeria, practiced torture and sexual humiliation on despised recalcitrant natives. Add to this generic corruption the mystifying, near-total unpreparedness of the American rulers of Iraq to deal with the complex realities of the country after its "liberation." And add to that the overarching, distinctive doctrines of the Bush administration, namely that the United States has embarked on an endless war and that those detained in this war are, if the president so decides, "unlawful combatants"—a policy enunciated by Donald Rumsfeld for Taliban and Qaeda prisoners as early as January 2002—and thus, as Rumsfeld said, "technically" they "do not have any rights under the Geneva Convention," and you have a perfect recipe for the cruelties and crimes committed against the thousands incarcerated without charges or access to lawyers in American-run prisons that have been set up since the attacks of Sept. 11, 2001.

8   So, then, is the real issue not the photographs themselves but what the photographs reveal to have happened to "suspects" in American custody? No: the horror of what is shown in the photographs cannot be separated from the horror that the photographs were taken—with the perpetrators posing, gloating, over their helpless captives. German soldiers in the Second World War took photographs of the atrocities they were committing in Poland and Russia, but snapshots in which the executioners placed themselves among their victims are exceedingly rare, as may be seen in a book just published, "Photographing the Holocaust," by Janina Struk. If there is something comparable to what these pictures show it would be some of the photographs of black victims of lynching taken between the 1880's and 1930's, which show Americans grinning beneath the naked mutilated body of a black man or woman hanging behind them from a tree. The lynching photographs were souvenirs of a collective action whose participants felt perfectly justified in what they had done. So are the pictures from Abu Ghraib.

9   The lynching pictures were in the nature of photographs as trophies—taken by a photographer in order to be collected, stored in albums, displayed. The pictures taken by American soldiers in Abu Ghraib, however, reflect a shift in the use made of pictures—less objects to be saved than messages to be disseminated, circulated. A digital camera is a common possession among soldiers. Where once photographing war was the province of photojournalists, now the soldiers themselves are all photographers—recording their war, their fun, their observations of what they find picturesque, their atrocities—and swapping images among themselves and e-mailing them around the globe.

10   There is more and more recording of what people do, by themselves. At least or especially in America, Andy Warhol's ideal of filming real events in real time—life isn't edited, why should its record be edited?—has become a norm for countless Webcasts, in which people record their day, each in his or her own reality show. Here I am—waking and yawning and stretching, brushing my teeth, making breakfast, getting the kids off to school. People record all aspects of their lives, store them in computer files and send the files around. Family life goes with the recording of family life—even when, or especially when, the family is in the throes of crisis and disgrace. Surely the dedicated, incessant home-videoing of one another, in conversation and monologue, over many years was the most astonishing material in "Capturing the Friedmans," the recent documentary by Andrew Jarecki about a Long Island family embroiled in pedophilia charges.

11   An erotic life is, for more and more people, that which can be captured in digital photographs and on video. And perhaps the torture is more attractive, as something to record, when it has a sexual component. It is surely revealing, as more Abu Ghraib photographs enter public view, that torture photographs are interleaved with pornographic images of American soldiers having sex with one another. In fact, most of the torture photographs have a sexual theme, as in those showing the coercing of prisoners to perform, or simulate, sexual acts

Most of the pictures, like this one of a young woman with a naked man on a leash, seem to depict part of a larger confluence of torture and pornography.

among themselves. One exception, already canonical, is the photograph of the man made to stand on a box, hooded and sprouting wires, reportedly told he would be electrocuted if he fell off. Yet pictures of prisoners bound in painful positions, or made to stand with outstretched arms, are infrequent. That they count as torture cannot be doubted. You have only to look at the terror on the victim's face, although such "stress" fell within the Pentagon's limits of the acceptable. But most of the pictures seem part of a larger confluence of torture and pornography: A young woman leading a naked man around on a leash is classic dominatrix imagery. And you wonder how much of the sexual tortures inflicted on the inmates of Abu Ghraib was inspired by the vast repertory of pornographic imagery available on the Internet—and which ordinary people, by sending out Webcasts of themselves, try to emulate.

III.

To live is to be photographed, to have a record of one's life, and therefore to go   12
on with one's life oblivious, or claiming to be oblivious, to the camera's nonstop attentions. But to live is also to pose. To act is to share in the community of actions recorded as images. The expression of satisfaction at the acts of torture being inflicted on helpless, trussed, naked victims is only part of the story. There is the deep satisfaction of being photographed, to which one is now more inclined to respond not with a stiff, direct gaze (as in former times) but with glee. The events are in part designed to be photographed. The grin is a grin for the camera. There would be something missing if, after stacking the naked men, you couldn't take a picture of them.

Looking at these photographs, you ask yourself, How can someone grin at   13
the sufferings and humiliation of another human being? Set guard dogs at the

genitals and legs of cowering naked prisoners? Force shackled, hooded prisoners to masturbate or simulate oral sex with one another? And you feel naïve for asking, since the answer is, self-evidently, People do these things to other people. Rape and pain inflicted on the genitals are among the most common forms of torture. Not just in Nazi concentration camps and in Abu Ghraib when it was run by Saddam Hussein. Americans, too, have done and do them when they are told, or made to feel, that those over whom they have absolute power deserve to be humiliated, tormented. They do them when they are led to believe that the people they are torturing belong to an inferior race or religion. For the meaning of these pictures is not just that these acts were performed, but that their perpetrators apparently had no sense that there was anything wrong in what the pictures show.

14   Even more appalling, since the pictures were meant to be circulated and seen by many people: it was all fun. And this idea of fun is, alas, more and more—contrary to what President Bush is telling the world—part of "the true nature and heart of America." It is hard to measure the increasing acceptance of brutality in American life, but its evidence is everywhere, starting with the video games of killing that are a principal entertainment of boys—can the video game "Interrogating the Terrorists" really be far behind?—and on to the violence that has become endemic in the group rites of youth on an exuberant kick. Violent crime is down, yet the easy delight taken in violence seems to have grown. From the harsh torments inflicted on incoming students in many American suburban high schools—depicted in Richard Linklater's 1993 film, "Dazed and Confused"—to the hazing rituals of physical brutality and sexual humiliation in college fraternities and on sports teams, America has become a country in which the fantasies and the practice of violence are seen as good entertainment, fun.

15   What formerly was segregated as pornography, as the exercise of extreme sadomasochistic longings—as in Pier Paolo Pasolini's last, near-unwatchable film, "Salò" (1975), depicting orgies of torture in the Fascist redoubt in northern Italy at the end of the Mussolini era—is now being normalized, by some, as high-spirited play or venting. To "stack naked men" is like a college fraternity prank, said a caller to Rush Limbaugh and the many millions of Americans who listen to his radio show. Had the caller, one wonders, seen the photographs? No matter. The observation—or is it the fantasy?—was on the mark. What may still be capable of shocking some Americans was Limbaugh's response: "Exactly!" he exclaimed. "Exactly my point. This is no different than what happens at the Skull and Bones initiation, and we're going to ruin people's lives over it, and we're going to hamper our military effort, and then we are going to really hammer them because they had a good time." "They" are the American soldiers, the torturers. And Limbaugh went on: "You know, these people are being fired at every day. I'm talking about people having a good time, these people. You ever heard of emotional release?"

16   Shock and awe were what our military promised the Iraqis. And shock and the awful are what these photographs announce to the world that the Americans

What formerly was segregated as pornography, as the exercise of extreme sadomasochistic longings, is being normalized, by some, as high-spirited play or venting.

have delivered: a pattern of criminal behavior in open contempt of international humanitarian conventions. Soldiers now pose, thumbs up, before the atrocities they commit, and send off the pictures to their buddies. Secrets of private life that, formerly, you would have given nearly anything to conceal, you now clamor to be invited on a television show to reveal. What is illustrated by these photographs is as much the culture of shamelessness as the reigning admiration for unapologetic brutality.

IV.

The notion that apologies or professions of "disgust" by the president and the secretary of defense are a sufficient response is an insult to one's historical and moral sense. The torture of prisoners is not an aberration. It is a direct consequence of the with-us-or-against-us doctrines of world struggle with which the Bush administration has sought to change, change radically, the international stance of the United States and to recast many domestic institutions and prerogatives. The Bush administration has committed the country to a pseudo-religious doctrine of war, endless war—for "the war on terror" is nothing less than that. Endless war is taken to justify endless incarcerations. Those held in the extralegal American penal empire are "detainees"; "prisoners," a newly obsolete word, might suggest that they have the rights accorded by international law and the laws of all civilized countries. This endless "global war on terrorism"— into which both the quite justified invasion of Afghanistan and the unwinnable folly in Iraq have been folded by Pentagon decree—inevitably leads to the demonizing and dehumanizing of anyone declared by the Bush administration to be a possible terrorist: a definition that is not up for debate and is, in fact, usually made in secret.

18   The charges against most of the people detained in the prisons in Iraq and
Afghanistan being nonexistent—the Red Cross reports that 70 to 90 percent of
those being held seem to have committed no crime other than simply being in
the wrong place at the wrong time, caught up in some sweep of "suspects"—
the principal justification for holding them is "interrogation." Interrogation
about what? About anything. Whatever the detainee might know. If interrogation is the point of detaining prisoners indefinitely, then physical coercion, humiliation and torture become inevitable.

19   Remember: We are not talking about that rarest of cases, the "ticking time
bomb" situation, which is sometimes used as a limiting case that justifies torture of prisoners who have knowledge of an imminent attack. This is general
or nonspecific information-gathering, authorized by American military and
civilian administrators to learn more of a shadowy empire of evildoers about
whom Americans know virtually nothing, in countries about which they are
singularly ignorant: In principle, any information at all might be useful. An
interrogation that produced no information (whatever information might consist of) would count as a failure. All the more justification for preparing prisoners to talk. Softening them up, stressing them out—these are the euphemisms
for the bestial practices in American prisons where suspected terrorists are being held. Unfortunately, as Staff Sgt. Ivan (Chip) Frederick noted in his diary, a
prisoner can get too stressed out and die. The picture of a man in a body bag
with ice on his chest may well be of the man Frederick was describing.

20   The pictures will not go away. That is the nature of the digital world in
which we live. Indeed, it seems they were necessary to get our leaders to acknowledge that they had a problem on their hands. After all, the conclusions of
reports compiled by the International Committee of the Red Cross, and other
reports by journalists and protests by humanitarian organizations about the
atrocious punishments inflicted on "detainees" and "suspected terrorists" in
prisons run by the American military, first in Afghanistan and later in Iraq,
have been circulating for more than a year. It seems doubtful that such reports
were read by President Bush or Vice President Dick Cheney or Condoleezza
Rice or Rumsfeld. Apparently it took the photographs to get their attention,
when it became clear they could not be suppressed; it was the photographs
that made all this "real" to Bush and his associates. Up to then, there had
been only words, which are easier to cover up in our age of infinite digital
self-reproduction and self-dissemination, and so much easier to forget.

21   So now the pictures will continue to "assault" us—as many Americans are
bound to feel. Will people get used to them? Some Americans are already saying they have seen enough. Not, however, the rest of the world. Endless war:
endless stream of photographs. Will editors now debate whether showing more
of them, or showing them uncropped (which, with some of the best-known images, like that of a hooded man on a box, gives a different and in some instances
more appalling view), would be in "bad taste" or too implicitly political? By
"political," read: critical of the Bush administration's imperial project. For there
can be no doubt that the photographs damage, as Rumsfeld testified, "the

reputation of the honorable men and women of the armed forces who are courageously and responsibly and professionally defending our freedom across the globe." This damage—to our reputation, our image, our success as the lone superpower—is what the Bush administration principally deplores. How the protection of "our freedom"—the freedom of 5 percent of humanity—came to require having American soldiers "across the globe" is hardly debated by our elected officials.

Already the backlash has begun. Americans are being warned against indulging in an orgy of self-condemnation. The continuing publication of the pictures is being taken by many Americans as suggesting that we do not have the right to defend ourselves: After all, they (the terrorists) started it. They—Osama bin Laden? Saddam Hussein? what's the difference?—attacked us first. Senator James Inhofe of Oklahoma, a Republican member of the Senate Armed Services Committee, before which Secretary Rumsfeld testified, avowed that he was sure he was not the only member of the committee "more outraged by the outrage" over the photographs than by what the photographs show. "These prisoners," Senator Inhofe explained, "you know they're not there for traffic violations. If they're in Cellblock 1-A or 1-B, these prisoners, they're murderers, they're terrorists, they're insurgents. Many of them probably have American blood on their hands, and here we're so concerned about the treatment of those individuals." It's the fault of "the media" which are provoking, and will continue to provoke, further violence against Americans around the world. More Americans will die. Because of these photos.

There is an answer to this charge, of course. Americans are dying not because of the photographs but because of what the photographs reveal to be happening, happening with the complicity of a chain of command—so Maj. Gen. Antonio Taguba implied, and Pfc. Lynndie England said, and (among others) Senator Lindsey Graham of South Carolina, a Republican, suggested, after he saw the Pentagon's full range of images on May 12. "Some of it has an elaborate nature to it that makes me very suspicious of whether or not others were directing or encouraging," Senator Graham said. Senator Bill Nelson, a Florida Democrat, said that viewing an uncropped version of one photo showing a stack of naked men in a hallway—a version that revealed how many other soldiers were at the scene, some not even paying attention—contradicted the Pentagon's assertion that only rogue soldiers were involved. "Somewhere along the line," Senator Nelson said of the torturers, "they were either told or winked at." An attorney for Specialist Charles Graner Jr., who is in the picture, has had his client identify the men in the uncropped version; according to the *Wall Street Journal*, Graner said that four of the men were military intelligence and one a civilian contractor working with military intelligence.

V.

But the distinction between photograph and reality—as between spin and policy—can easily evaporate. And that is what the administration wishes to

In this photograph, Specialist Charles Graner Jr., who identified men in another Abu Ghraib photo, poses over handcuffed detainees lying on the floor.

happen. "There are a lot more photographs and videos that exist," Rumsfeld acknowledged in his testimony. "If these are released to the public, obviously, it's going to make matters worse." Worse for the administration and its programs, presumably, not for those who are the actual—and potential?—victims of torture.

25   The media may self-censor but, as Rumsfeld acknowledged, it's hard to censor soldiers overseas, who don't write letters home, as in the old days, that can be opened by military censors who ink out unacceptable lines. Today's soldiers instead function like tourists, as Rumsfeld put it, "running around with digital cameras and taking these unbelievable photographs and then passing them off, against the law, to the media, to our surprise." The administration's effort to withhold pictures is proceeding along several fronts. Currently, the argument is taking a legalistic turn: now the photographs are classified as evidence in future criminal cases, whose outcome may be prejudiced if they are made public. The Republican chairman of the Senate Armed Services Committee, John Warner of Virginia, after the May 12 slide show of image after image of sexual humiliation and violence against Iraqi prisoners, said he felt "very strongly" that the newer photos "should not be made public. I feel that it could possibly endanger the men and women of the armed forces as they are serving and at great risk."

26   But the real push to limit the accessibility of the photographs will come from the continuing effort to protect the administration and cover up our misrule in Iraq—to identify "outrage" over the photographs with a campaign to undermine American military might and the purposes it currently serves. Just as it was regarded by many as an implicit criticism of the war to show on television photographs of American soldiers who have been killed in the course of the invasion and occupation of Iraq, it will increasingly be thought unpatriotic to disseminate the new photographs and further tarnish the image of America.

27   After all, we're at war. Endless war. And war is hell, more so than any of the people who got us into this rotten war seem to have expected. In our digital hall

of mirrors, the pictures aren't going to go away. Yes, it seems that one picture is worth a thousand words. And even if our leaders choose not to look at them, there will be thousands more snapshots and videos. Unstoppable.

COMPREHENSION

1. Summarize Sontag's harsh condemnation of the Bush administration's prosecution of the Iraq war.
2. Sontag writes that the photographs coming out of Abu Ghraib "are us" (paragraph 7). What does she mean? Would you agree or disagree with the implications of her statement? Why?
3. Explain what Sontag finds to be uniquely powerful about photography as an art form.

RHETORIC

1. Sontag structures her essay around the dual subjects of photography and the American involvement in Iraq. Explain what her purpose is and how she links these two subjects.
2. What is Sontag's claim and in what place(s) does she state it? Where does she make logical, ethical, and emotional appeals? Are you persuaded by her argument? Why or why not?
3. Sontag includes six illustrations in the essay similar to the four we have included here. What is her objective? Does she mention additional photographs? How do the photographs enhance the message?
4. Sontag divides her essay into five numbered sections. How does each section serve to advance her argument?
5. How does Sontag's use of connotation and definition—of *torture, enemy combatants, the erotic life,* and so forth—serve her purpose?
6. What conclusions does Sontag draw "regarding the torture of others"?

WRITING

1. Sontag alludes to the popular radio commentator Rush Limbaugh. Find out more about this personality, and in an expository essay explain why Limbaugh would disagree with Sontag's argument.
2. **Writing an Argument:** Conduct your own research on Abu Ghraib, and then stake out an argumentative position on it. Develop logical, ethical, and emotional appeals to support your position.

NETWORKING
Applying 21st-Century Literacies

Using Visuals and Hyperlinks to Enhance a Definition Essay: Write your own extended definition of torture, linking it to a specific situation like Abu Ghraib. Add visuals and hyperlinks to support your definition.

Saving the Life That Is Your Own:
The Importance of Models
in the Artist's Life

Alice Walker

*Alice Walker (b. 1941) was born in Eatonton, Georgia, and now lives in San Fran-
cisco and Mendocino County, California. She attended Spelman College and graduated
from Sarah Lawrence College. A celebrated and prolific novelist, short-story writer,
poet, and essayist, she has also been active in the civil rights movement. Walker often
draws on both her personal experience and historical records to reflect on the African
American experience. Her books include* The Color Purple *(1976), which won the
American Book Award and the Pulitzer prize;* You Can't Keep a Good Woman
Down *(1981);* Living in the World: Selected Essays, 1973–1987 *(1987);* The Temple of My Familiar *(1989);* By the Light of My Father's Smile *(1999);* The Way
Forward Is with a Broken Heart *(2001); and* Devil's My Enemy *(2008). The following essay, from* In Search of Our Mothers' Gardens *(1983), offers a highly personal-
ized and perceptive analysis of the importance of influence on both art and life.*

1   There is a letter Vincent van Gogh wrote to Emile Bernard that is very meaningful to me. A year before he wrote the letter, van Gogh had had a fight with his
domineering friend Gauguin, left his company, and cut off, in desperation and
anguish, his own ear. The letter was written in Saint-Remy, in the South of
France, from a mental institution to which van Gogh had voluntarily committed himself.

2   I imagine van Gogh sitting at a rough desk too small for him, looking out at
the lovely Southern light, and occasionally glancing critically next to him at his
own paintings of the landscape he loved so much. The date of the letter is December 1889. Van Gogh wrote:

> However hateful painting may be, and however cumbersome in the times we
> are living in, if anyone who has chosen this handicraft pursues it zealously, he
> is a man of duty, sound and faithful.
>   Society makes our existence wretchedly difficult at times, hence our impo-
> tence and the imperfection of our work.
>   . . . I myself am suffering under an absolute lack of models.
>   But on the other hand, there are beautiful spots here. I have just done five
> size 30 canvases, olive trees. And the reason I am staying on here is that my
> health is improving a great deal.
>   What I am doing is hard, dry, but that is because I am trying to gather new
> strength by doing some rough work, and I'm afraid abstractions would make
> me soft.

Six months later, van Gogh—whose health was "improving a great deal"— 3
committed suicide. He had sold one painting during his lifetime. Three times
was his work noticed in the press. But these are just details.

The real Vincent van Gogh is the man who has "just done five size 30 can- 4
vasses, olive trees." To me, in context, one of the most moving and revealing
descriptions of how a real artist thinks. And the knowledge that when he spoke
of "suffering under an absolute lack of models" he spoke of that lack in terms of
both the intensity of his commitment and the quality and singularity of his
work, which was frequently ridiculed in his day.

The absence of models, in literature as in life, to say nothing of painting, is 5
an occupational hazard for the artist, simply because models in art, in behavior, in growth of spirit and intellects—even if rejected—enrich and enlarge
one's view of existence. Deadlier still, to the artist who lacks models, is the
curse of ridicule, the bringing to bear on an artist's best work, especially his or
her most original, most strikingly deviant, only a fund of ignorance and the
presumption that, as an artist's critic, one's judgment is free of the restrictions
imposed by prejudice, and is well informed, indeed, about all the art in the
world that really matters.

What is always needed in the appreciation of art, or life, is the larger per- 6
spective. Connections made, or at least attempted, where none existed before,
the straining to encompass in one's glance at the varied world the common
thread, the unifying theme through immense diversity, a fearlessness of
growth, of search, of looking, that enlarges the private and the public world.
And yet, in our particular society, it is the narrowed and narrowing view of life
that often wins.

Recently, I read at a college and was asked by one of the audience what I 7
considered the major difference between the literature written by black and by
white Americans. I had not spent a lot of time considering this question, since it
is not the difference between them that interests me, but, rather, the way black
writers and white writers seem to me to be writing one immense story—the
same story, for the most part—with different parts of this immense story coming from a multitude of different perspectives. Until this is generally recognized, literature will always be broken into bits, black and white, and there will
always be questions, wanting neat answers, such as this.

Still, I answered that I thought, for the most part, white American writers 8
tended to end their books and their characters' lives as if there were no better
existence for which to struggle. The gloom of defeat is thick.

By comparison, black writers seem always involved in a moral and/or 9
physical struggle, the result of which is expected to be some kind of larger freedom. Perhaps this is because our literary tradition is based on the slave narratives, where escape for the body and freedom for the soul went together, or
perhaps this is because black people have never felt themselves guilty of global,
cosmic sins.

This comparison does not hold up in every case, of course, and perhaps 10
does not really hold up at all. I am not a gatherer of statistics, only a curious

reader, and this has been my impression from reading many books by black and white writers.

11   There are, however, two books by American women that illustrate what I am talking about: *The Awakening,* by Kate Chopin, and *Their Eyes Were Watching God,* by Zora Neale Hurston.

12   The plight of Mme Pontellier is quite similar to that of Janie Crawford. Each woman is married to a dull, society-conscious husband and living in a dull, propriety-conscious community. Each woman desires a life of her own and a man who loves her and makes her feel alive. Each woman finds such a man.

13   Mme Pontellier, overcome by the strictures of society and the existence of her children (along with the cowardice of her lover), kills herself rather than defy the one and abandon the other. Janie Crawford, on the other hand, refuses to allow society to dictate behavior to her, enjoys the love of a much younger, freedom-loving man, and lives to tell others of her experience.

14   When I mentioned these two books to my audience, I was not surprised to learn that only one person, a young black poet in the first row, had ever heard of *Their Eyes Were Watching God* (*The Awakening* they had fortunately read in their "Women in Literature" class), primarily because it was written by a black woman, whose experience—in love and life—was apparently assumed to be unimportant to the students (and the teachers) of a predominantly white school.

15   Certainly, as a student, I was not directed toward this book, which would have urged me more toward freedom and experience than toward comfort and security, but was directed instead toward a plethora of books by mainly white male writers who thought most women worthless if they didn't enjoy bullfighting or hadn't volunteered for the trenches in World War I.

16   Loving both these books, knowing each to be indispensable to my own growth, my own life, I choose the model, the example, of Janie Crawford. And yet this book, as necessary to me and to other women as air and water, is again out of print. But I have distilled as much as I could of its wisdom in this poem about its heroine, Janie Crawford:

> I love the way Janie Crawford
> left her husbands
> the one who wanted to change her
> into a mule
> and the other who tried to interest her
> in being a queen.
> A woman, unless she submits,
> is neither a mule
> nor a queen
> though like a mule she may suffer
> and like a queen pace the floor.

17   It has been said that someone asked Toni Morrison why she writes the kind of books she writes, and that she replied: Because they are the kind of books I want to read.

This remains my favorite reply to that kind of question. As if anyone read- 18
ing the magnificent, mysterious *Sula* or the grim, poetic *The Bluest Eye* would
require more of a reason for their existence than for the brooding, haunting
Wuthering Heights, for example, or the melancholy, triumphant *Jane Eyre.* (I am
not speaking here of the most famous short line of that book, "Reader, I married
him," as the triumph, but, rather, of the triumph of Jane Eyre's control over her
own sense of morality and her own stout will, which are but reflections of her
creator's, Charlotte Brontë, who no doubt wished to write the sort of books *she*
wished to read.)

Flannery O'Connor has written that more and more the serious novelist 19
will write, not what other people want, and certainly not what other people
expect, but whatever interests her or him. And that the direction taken, therefore, will be away from sociology, away from the "writing of explanation," of
statistics, and further into mystery, into poetry, and into prophecy. I believe
this is true, *fortunately true;* especially for "Third World Writers"; Morrison,
Marquez, Ahmadi, Camara Laye make good examples. And not only do I believe it is true for serious writers in general, but I believe, as firmly as did
O'Connor, that this is our only hope—in a culture so in love with flash, with
trendiness, with superficiality, as ours—of acquiring a sense of essence, of time-
lessness, and of vision. Therefore, to write the books one wants to read is both
to point in the direction of vision and, at the same time, to follow it.

When Toni Morrison said she writes the kind of books she wants to read, 20
she was acknowledging the fact that in a society in which "accepted literature"
is so often sexist and racist and otherwise irrelevant or offensive to so many
lives, she must do the work of two. She must be her own model as well as the
artist attending, creating, learning from, realizing the model, which is to say,
herself.

(It should be remembered that, as a black person, one cannot completely 21
identify with a Jane Eyre, or with her creator, no matter how much one admires
them. And certainly, if one allows history to impinge on one's reading pleasure,
one must cringe at the thought of how Heathcliff, in the New World far from
Wuthering Heights, amassed his Cathy-dazzling fortune.) I have often been
asked why, in my own life and work, I have felt such a desperate need to know
and assimilate the experiences of earlier black women writers, most of them
unheard of by you and by me, until quite recently; why I felt a need to study
them and to teach them.

I don't recall the exact moment I set out to explore the works of black 22
women, mainly those in the past, and certainly, in the beginning, I had no desire
to teach them. Teaching being for me, at that time, less rewarding than stargaz-
ing on a frigid night. My discovery of them—most of them out of print, abandoned, discredited, maligned, nearly lost—came about, as many things of value
do, almost by accident. As it turned out—and this should not have surprised
me—I found I was in need of something that only one of them could provide.

Mindful that throughout my four years at a prestigious black and then a 23
prestigious white college I had heard not one word about early black women

writers, one of my first tasks was simply to determine whether they had existed. After this, I could breathe easier, with more assurance about the profession I myself had chosen.

24   But the incident that started my search began several years ago: I sat down at my desk one day, in a room of my own, with key and lock, and began preparations for a story about voodoo, a subject that had always fascinated me. Many of the elements of this story I had gathered from a story my mother several times told me. She had gone, during the Depression, into town to apply for some government surplus food at the local commissary, and had been turned down, in a particularly humiliating way, by the white woman in charge.

25   My mother always told this story with a most curious expression on her face. She automatically raised her head higher than ever—it was always high— and there was a look of righteousness, a kind of holy *heat* coming from her eyes. She said she had lived to see this same white woman grow old and senile and so badly crippled she had to get about on *two* sticks.

26   To her, this was clearly the working of God, who, as in the old spiritual, ". . . may not come when you want him, but he's right on time!" To me, hearing the story for about the fiftieth time, something else was discernible: the possibilities of the story, for fiction.

27   What, I asked myself, would have happened if, after the crippled old lady died, it was discovered that someone, my mother perhaps (who would have been mortified at the thought, Christian that she is), had voodooed her?

28   Then, my thoughts sweeping me away into the world of hexes and conjurings of centuries past, I wondered how a larger story could be created out of my mother's story; one that would be true to the magnitude of her humiliation and grief, and to the white woman's lack of sensitivity and compassion.

29   My third quandary was: How could I find out all I needed to know in order to write a story that used *authentic* black witchcraft?

30   Which brings me back, almost, to the day I became really interested in black women writers. I say "almost" because one other thing, from my childhood, made the choice of black magic a logical and irresistible one for my story. Aside from my mother's several stories about root doctors she had heard of or known, there was the story I had often heard about my "crazy" Walker aunt.

31   Many years ago, when my aunt was a meek and obedient girl growing up in a strict, conventionally religious house in the rural South, she had suddenly thrown off her meekness and had run away from home, escorted by a rogue of a man permanently attached elsewhere.

32   When she was returned home by her father, she was declared quite mad. In the backwoods South at the turn of the century, "madness" of this sort was cured not by psychiatry but by powders and by spells. (One can see Scott Joplin's *Treemonisha* to understand the role voodoo played among black people of that period.) My aunt's madness was treated by the community conjurer, who promised, and delivered, the desired results. His treatment was a bag of white powder, bought for fifty cents, and sprinkled on the ground around her house, with some of it sewed, I believe, into the bodice of her nightgown.

So when I sat down to write my story about voodoo, my crazy Walker aunt ₃₃ was definitely on my mind.

But she had experienced her temporary craziness so long ago that her story ₃₄ had all the excitement of a might-have-been. I needed, instead of family memories, some hard facts about the *craft* of voodoo, as practiced by Southern blacks in the nineteenth century. (It never once, fortunately, occurred to me that voodoo was not worthy of the interest I had in it, or was too ridiculous to study seriously.)

I began reading all I could find on the subject of "The Negro and His Folk- ₃₅ ways and Superstitions." There were Botkin and Puckett and others, all white, most racist. How was I to believe anything they wrote, since at least one of them, Puckett, was capable of wondering, in his book, if "The Negro" had a large enough brain?

Well, I thought, where are the *black* collectors of folklore? Where is the *black* ₃₆ anthropologist? Where is the *black* person who took the time to travel the back roads of the South and collect the information I need: how to cure heat trouble, treat dropsy, hex somebody to death, lock bowels, cause joints to swell, eyes to fall out, and so on. Where was this black person?

And that is when I first saw, in a *footnote* to the white voices of authority, the ₃₇ name Zora Neale Hurston.

Folklorist, novelist, anthropologist, serious student of voodoo, also all- ₃₈ around black woman, with guts enough to take a slide rule and measure random black heads in Harlem; not to prove their inferiority, but to prove that whatever their size, shape, or present condition of servitude, those heads contained all the intelligence anyone could use to get through this world.

Zora Hurston, who went to Barnard to learn how to study what she really ₃₉ wanted to learn: the ways of her own people, and what ancient rituals, customs, and beliefs had made them unique.

Zora, of the sandy-colored hair and the daredevil eyes, a girl who escaped ₄₀ poverty and parental neglect by hard work and a sharp eye for the main chance.

Zora, who left the South only to return to look at it again. Who went to root ₄₁ doctors from Florida to Louisiana and said, "Here I am. I want to learn your trade."

Zora, who had collected all the black folklore I could ever use. ₄₂

That Zora. ₄₃

And having found *that Zora* (like a golden key to a storehouse of varied ₄₄ treasure), I was hooked.

What I had discovered, of course, was a model. A model, who, as it hap- ₄₅ pened, provided more than voodoo for my story, more than one of the greatest novels America had produced—though, being America, it did not realize this. She had provided, as if she knew someday I would come along wandering in the wilderness, a nearly complete record of her life. And though her life sprouted an occasional wart, I am eternally grateful for that life, warts and all.

It is not irrelevant, nor is it bragging (except perhaps to gloat a little on the ₄₆ happy relatedness of Zora, my mother and me), to mention here that the story I wrote, called "The Revenge of Hannah Kemhuff," based on my mother's experiences during the Depression, and on Zora Hurston's folklore collection of the 1920s, and on my own response to both out of a contemporary existence, was immediately published and was later selected, by a reputable collector of short stories, as one of the *Best Short Stories of 1974.*

47   I mention it because this story might never have been written, because the very bases of its structure, authentic black folklore, viewed from a black perspective, might have been lost.

48   Had it been lost, my mother's story would have had no historical underpinning, none I could trust, anyway. I would not have written the story, which I enjoyed writing as much as I've enjoyed writing anything in my life, had I not known that Zora had already done a thorough job of preparing the ground over which I was then moving.

49   In that story I gathered up the historical and psychological threads of the life my ancestors lived, and in the writing of it I felt joy and strength and my own continuity. I had that wonderful feeling writers get sometimes, not very often, of being *with* a great many people, ancient spirits, all very happy to see me consulting and acknowledging them, and eager to let me know, through the joy of their presence, that, indeed, I am not alone.

50   To take Toni Morrison's statement further, if that is possible, in my own work I write not only what I want to read—understanding fully and indelibly that if I don't do it no one else is so vitally interested, or capable of doing it to my satisfaction—I write all the things *I should have been able to read.* Consulting, as belatedly discovered models, those writers—most of whom, not surprisingly, are women—who understood that their experience as ordinary human beings was also valuable, and in danger of being misrepresented, distorted, or lost:

Zora Hurston—novelist, essayist, anthropologist, autobiographer;

Jean Toomer—novelist, poet, philosopher, visionary, a man who cared what women felt;

Colette—whose crinkly hair enhances her French, part-black face; novelist, playwright, dancer, essayist, newspaperwoman, lover of women, men, small dogs; fortunate not to have been born in America;

Anaïs Nin—recorder of everything, no matter how minute;

Tillie Olson—a writer of such generosity and honesty, she literally saves lives;

Virginia Woolf—who has saved so many of us.

51   It is, in the end, the saving of lives that we writers are about. Whether we are "minority" writers or "majority." It is simply in our power to do this.

52   We do it because we care. We care that Vincent van Gogh mutilated his ear. We care that behind a pile of manure in the yard he destroyed his life. We care that Scott Joplin's music *lives!* We care because we know this: *The life we save is our own.*

COMPREHENSION

1. Explain the significance of Walker's title. How does it serve her purpose and guide readers to her thesis? What is her thesis?
2. According to the author, what is the importance of models in art? What is the relationship of models to life? List the models in Walker's life. Which of them stand out?
3. Paraphrase Walker's remarks on the relationship between black American and white American writing.

RHETORIC

1. Walker uses many allusions in this essay. Identify as many as you can. What is the allusion in the title? Comment on the general effectiveness of her allusions.
2. Is the author's style and choice of diction suitable to her subject matter and to her audience? Why or why not?
3. Why does the author personalize her treatment of the topic? What does she gain? Is there anything lost?
4. Walker employs several unique structuring devices in this essay. Cite at least three, and analyze their utility.
5. Explain Walker's use of examples to reinforce her generalizations and to organize the essay.
6. Which paragraphs constitute Walker's conclusion? What is their effect?

WRITING

1. Write an essay expanding the meaning of Walker's remark "What is always needed in the appreciation of art, or life, is the larger perspective" (paragraph 6).
2. If you were planning on a career as a writer, artist, actor, or musician, who would your models be, and why?
3. **Writing an Argument:** Argue for or against Walker's proposition that the absence of models in art and life is an "occupational hazard" (paragraph 5).

NETWORKING
Applying 21st-Century Literacies

Keeping an "Importance of Models" Blog: Consider the importance of models in your life as a student (and as whatever else you hope to become: a dancer, basketball player, social worker, business executive, nurse). Maintain a blog in which you devote entries to individuals whom you've either studied or studied with, who inform your intellectual, artistic, athletic, professional, and/or personal growth. In each entry, describe this person and explain, with examples, what he or she has done or said that inspires you; record what you've learned and are continuing to learn from this person.

Synthesis: Connections for Critical Thinking

1. Write an essay comparing and contrasting literature and any other art form. What merits or limitations does each form have? Which do you find more satisfying? Which form is more accessible? Use at least three essays in this chapter to illustrate or support your thesis.
2. Write an essay exploring the importance of role models in art and literature. Refer to the essays by Walker, Welty, and Gates to address the issue.
3. Analyze the illustrations that appear in the essays by Updike, Gates, and Sontag. What do the images contribute to the text?
4. Welty, Alexie, Walker, and other writers in this chapter provide extended examples of art and artists. How do they develop these examples? What strategies do they use? Are their goals similar or not? Explain your response.
5. Use the essays by Welty, Updike, and Gates to explore the question of excellence in the arts. Answer this question: How do you know the work of art is good?
6. Examine the role of the artist in society and the artist's purpose in or duty to society. How would the writers in this chapter address this issue?

NETWORKING
Applying 21st-Century Literacies

Conduct an online search for articles that support or challenge the claim that the arts can influence behavior or beliefs. Connect your findings to essays by at least three writers in this chapter.

 CH 10   **www.mhhe.com/mhreaderbrief1e**

- *Image Gallery:* Chapter images in color
- *Literature and the Arts:* Information on the authors in this chapter
- *Ch. 10 Networking*

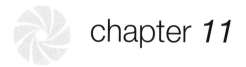

chapter *11*

Nature and the Environment

How Do We Relate to the Natural World?

We are at a point in the history of civilization where consciousness of our fragile relationship with nature and the environment is high. Even as you spend an hour reading a few of the essays in this chapter, it is estimated that we are losing 3,000 acres of rain forest around the world and four species of plants or animals. From pollution, to the population explosion, to the depletion of the ozone layer, to global climate change, we seem to be confronted with ecological catastrophe. Nevertheless, as Rachel Carson reminds us, we have "an obligation to endure," to survive potential natural catastrophes by understanding and managing our relationship with the natural world.

Ecology, or the study of nature and the environment, as many of the essayists in this chapter attest, involves us in the conservation of the earth. It moves us to suppress our rapacious destruction of the planet. Clearly, the biological stability of the planet is increasingly precarious. More plants, insects, birds, and animals became extinct in the 20th century than in any era since the Cretaceous catastrophe more than 65 million years ago that led to the extinction of the dinosaurs. Within this ecological context, writers like Carson become our literary conscience, reminding us of how easily natural processes can break down unless we insist on a degree of ecological economy.

Of course, any modification of human behavior in an effort to conserve nature is a complex matter. To save the spotted owl in the Pacific Northwest, we must sacrifice the jobs of people in the timber industry. To reduce pollution, we must forsake gas and oil for alternate energy sources that are costly to develop. To reduce the waste stream, we must shift from a consumption to a conservation ethos. The ecological debate is complicated, but it is clear that the preservation of the myriad life cycles on earth is crucial, for we, too, could become an endangered species.

The language of nature is as enigmatic as the sounds of dolphins and whales communicating with their respective species. Writers like Barry Lopez and Rachel Carson and the vision expressed in the letter of Chief Seattle help us decipher the language of our environment. These writers encourage us to converse with nature, learn from it, and even revere it. All of us are guests on this planet; the natural world is our host. If we do not protect the earth, how can we guarantee the survival of civilization?

PREVIEWING THE CHAPTER

As you read the essays in this chapter and respond to them in discussion and writing, consider the following questions:

- According to the author, what should our relationship to the natural world be?
- What claims or arguments does the author make about the importance of nature? Do you agree or disagree with these claims and arguments?
- What specific ecological problem does the author investigate?
- How does the author think that nature influences human behavior?
- What cultural factors are involved in our approach to the environment?
- Is the writer optimistic, pessimistic, or neutral in the assessment of our ability to conserve nature?
- Do you find that the author is too idealistic or sentimental in the depiction of nature? Why?
- Based on the author's essay, how does he or she qualify as a nature writer?
- How have you been challenged or changed by the essays in this chapter?

Classic and Contemporary Images
ARE WE DESTROYING OUR NATURAL WORLD?

Using a Critical Perspective   Imagine yourself to be part of each of the scenes depicted in these two illustrations. How do you feel, and why? Now examine the purpose of each image. What details do the artists emphasize to convey their feelings about our relationship to the natural world? What images does each artist create to capture your attention and direct your viewing and thinking toward a specific, dominant impression?

The painters of the Hudson River School such as John Frederick Kensett (1816–1872) celebrated American landscapes in their art, painting breathtaking scenes in meticulous detail. In *Along the Hudson* (1852), the beauty of the river is unspoiled.

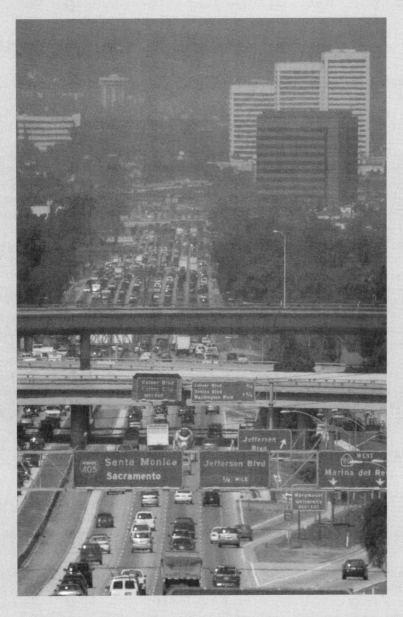

Vehicles travel on the 405 Freeway where it intersects with the 10 West
Freeway in Los Angeles. California could take the lead in the international
effort to reduce global warming after the state's Air Resources Board
gave approval to a package of regulations that would cut
vehicle emissions by as much as 25 percent.

Classic and Contemporary Essays

DO WE OWN NATURE?

The simple yet passionate reflections of Chief Seattle regarding the destruction of a worldview are complemented by the more scholarly and learned meditations, nearly a century and a half later, of the esteemed naturalist and writer Barry Lopez. Chief Seattle mourns the death of a way of life, a way of thinking, and a way of being as he accepts that the cultural world of his people is doomed to disappear with the encroachment of "civilization." The white man exploits nature, uses nature, and perhaps most radically of all, perceives himself as apart from nature. This is in profound contrast to the ways of Chief Seattle's people, who saw themselves as in harmony with nature or, more specifically, as inseparable from it—as inseparable perhaps as from a part of their own bodies. Chief Seattle's address is simple. And so perhaps is his message, although one should not confuse simplicity with lack of profundity. Barry Lopez has a similar message. Writing from the perspective of a 21st-century naturalist and teacher, Lopez speaks of "a sense of responsibility toward children." He urges adults to both teach and learn from children about the wonders of nature and how the natural world can inform us about our human condition. With a personal touch, Lopez recounts key encounters with children and nature, finding evidence of that union with nature that Chief Seattle spoke of so eloquently. Although Chief Seattle and Barry Lopez speak in different levels of discourse and from different perspectives, they share an awe of nature and a desire to inform their respective audiences of the sacredness of all life.

Letter to President Pierce, 1855

Chief Seattle

Chief Seattle (1786–1866) was the leader of the Duwamish and other Pacific Northwest tribes. The city of Seattle, Washington, bears his name. In 1854, Chief Seattle reluctantly agreed to sell tribal lands to the U.S. government and move to the government-established reservations. The authenticity of the following speech has been challenged by many scholars. However, most specialists agree that it contains the substance and perspective of Chief Seattle's attitude toward nature and the white race.

1   We know that the white man does not understand our ways. One portion of the land is the same to him as the next, for he is a stranger who comes in the night and takes from the land whatever he needs. The earth is not his brother, but his enemy, and when he has conquered it, he moves on. He leaves his fathers'

graves, and his children's birthright is forgotten. The sight of your cities pains the eyes of the red man. But perhaps it is because the red man is a savage and does not understand.

There is no quiet place in the white man's cities. No place to hear the leaves 2 of spring or the rustle of insect's wings. But perhaps because I am a savage and do not understand, the clatter only seems to insult the ears. The Indian prefers the soft sound of the wind darting over the face of the pond, the smell of the wind itself cleansed by a mid-day rain, or scented with the piñon pine. The air is precious to the red man. For all things share the same breath—the beasts, the trees, the man. Like a man dying for many days, he is numb to the stench.

What is man without the beasts? If all the beasts were gone, men would die 3 from great loneliness of spirit, for whatever happens to the beasts also happens to man. All things are connected. Whatever befalls the earth befalls the sons of the earth.

It matters little where we pass the rest of our days; they are not many. A few 4 more hours, a few more winters, and none of the children of the great tribes that once lived on this earth, or that roamed in small bands in the woods, will be left to mourn the graves of a people once as powerful and hopeful as yours.

The whites, too, shall pass—perhaps sooner than other tribes. Continue to 5 contaminate your bed, and you will one night suffocate in your own waste. When the buffalo are all slaughtered, the wild horses all tamed, the secret corners of the forest heavy with the scent of many men, and the view of the ripe hills blotted by talking wires, where is the thicket? Gone. Where is the eagle? Gone. And what is it to say goodbye to the swift and the hunt, the end of living and the beginning of survival? We might understand if we knew what it was that the white man dreams, what he describes to his children on the long winter nights, what visions he burns into their minds, so they will wish for tomorrow. But we are savages. The white man's dreams are hidden from us.

COMPREHENSION

1. What does Chief Seattle suggest is the major difference between the white man's relationship with nature and that of the red man?
2. Chief Seattle claims that perhaps the red man would understand the white man better if he understood better the "dreams" and "visions" of the white man. What does Chief Seattle suggest by these terms?
3. Chief Seattle refers to Native Americans as "savages." Why?

RHETORIC

1. The author uses a number of sensory details in describing both nature and the white man's crimes against nature. How does the eliciting of sensations help determine the relationship between writer, text, and reader?
2. The letter is written simply, with simply constructed paragraphs and sentences. What does this style suggest about the writer's voice?

3. There is a noted absence of transitional expressions in the writing, that is, such linking words as *in addition, furthermore, nevertheless,* and *moreover.* How does this absence contribute to the directness of the writing?

4. The author uses the convention of the series, as in the following examples: "For all things share the same breath—the beasts, the trees, the man" (paragraph 2) and "When the buffalo are all slaughtered, the wild horses all tamed, the secret corners of the forest heavy with the scent of many men, and the view of the ripe hills blotted by talking wires" (paragraph 5). What is the rhetorical effect of this device?

5. Note the opening and closing sentences of the letter. How do they frame the letter? What do they suggest about one of its major themes?

6. Some scholars dispute the authenticity of the letter, attributing it to a white man who was attempting to articulate the essence of Chief Seattle's oratory in an effort to champion Native American causes. What elements of the letter resemble the rhetorical elements of a speech?

WRITING

1. Write a 250-word summary in which you compare and contrast the major differences between the white man's and the red man's perception of and relationship to nature as conceived by Chief Seattle.

2. For a research project, trace the use of the word *savage* as it has been used to describe Native Americans.

3. **Writing an Argument:** Argue for or against the view that the charge by Chief Seattle that the white man is contemptuous of nature is still valid today. Use at least three points to support your thesis.

NETWORKING
Applying 21st-Century Literacies

Writing a Radio PSA: Public service announcements, or PSAs, which you've likely heard on your campus radio station or NPR, are advertisements designed to raise awareness about issues, not sell products or services. Draft a PSA that informs or educates the public about an environmental issue.

Children in the Woods

Barry Lopez

Barry Lopez (b. 1945) was born in New York City but grew up in southern California's San Fernando Valley, which at the time was still largely rural. He attended the University of Notre Dame (BA, 1966) and the University of Oregon (MA, 1968), and he pursued additional graduate work before starting a career as a full-time writer. Lopez's early essays in such periodicals as National Geographic, Wilderness, Science, *and* Harper's *established him as an authoritative voice in the environmental movement. His first major nonfiction work,* Of Wolves and Men *(1978), brought him national acclaim, an American Book Award nomination, and the John Burroughs medal for nature writing. His venture into fiction with* River Notes: The Dance of Herons *(1979) and* Winter Count *(1980) were also well received. Among Lopez's other books are* Arctic Dreams: Imagination and Desire in a Northern Landscape *(1986),* Crossing Open Ground *(1988),* The Rediscovery of North America *(1991),* Crow and Weasel *(1999), the autobiography* About This Life *(1999), and a short-story collection,* Resistance *(2004). Lopez sees himself as a storyteller, someone who has the responsibility to create an atmosphere in which the wisdom of the work can reveal itself and, as he has written, "make the reader feel part of something." In this essay from his collection* Crossing Open Ground, *Lopez sets himself and other children in the natural world in order to discover their own part of something.*

When I was a child growing up in the San Fernando Valley in California, a trip 1 into Los Angeles was special. The sensation of movement from a rural area into an urban one was sharp. On one of these charged occasions, walking down a sidewalk with my mother, I stopped suddenly, caught by a pattern of sunlight trapped in a spiraling imperfection in a windowpane. A stranger, an elderly woman in a cloth coat and a dark hat, spoke out spontaneously, saying how remarkable it is that children notice these things.

I have never forgotten the texture of this incident. Whenever I recall it I am 2 moved not so much by any sense of my young self but by a sense of responsibility toward children, knowing how acutely I was affected in that moment by that woman's words. The effect, for all I know, has lasted a lifetime.

Now, years later, I live in a rain forest in western Oregon, on the banks of a 3 mountain river in relatively undisturbed country, surrounded by 150-foot-tall Douglas firs, delicate deer-head orchids, and clearings where wild berries grow. White-footed mice and mule deer, mink and coyote move through here. My wife and I do not have children, but children we know, or children whose parents we are close to, are often here. They always want to go into the woods. And I wonder what to tell them.

In the beginning, years ago, I think I said too much. I spoke with an ency- 4 clopedic knowledge of the names of plants or the names of birds passing through in season. Gradually I came to say less. After a while the only words I spoke, beyond answering a question or calling attention quickly to the slight difference between a sprig of red cedar and a sprig of incense cedar, were to elucidate single objects.

I remember once finding a fragment of a raccoon's jaw in an alder thicket. I 5 sat down alongside the two children with me and encouraged them to find out who this was—with only the three teeth still intact in a piece of the animal's maxilla to guide them. The teeth told by their shape and placement what this animal ate. By a kind of visual extrapolation its size became clear. There were other clues, immediately present, which told, with what I could add of climate and terrain, how this animal lived, how its broken jaw came to be lying here. Raccoon, they surmised. And tiny tooth marks along the bone's broken edge told of a mouse's hunger for calcium.

6 We set the jaw back and went on.

7 If I had known more about raccoons, finer points of osteology, we might have guessed more: say, whether it was male or female. But what we deduced was all we needed. Hours later, the maxilla, lost behind us in the detritus of the forest floor, continued to effervesce. It was tied faintly to all else we spoke of that afternoon.

8 In speaking with children who might one day take a permanent interest in natural history—as writers, as scientists, as filmmakers, as anthropologists—I have sensed that an extrapolation from a single fragment of the whole is the most invigorating experience I can share with them. I think children know that nearly anyone can learn the names of things; the impression made on them at this level is fleeting. What takes a lifetime to learn, they comprehend, is the existence and substance of myriad relationships: It is these relationships, not the things themselves, that ultimately hold the human imagination.

9 The brightest children, it has often struck me, are fascinated by metaphor—with what is shown in the set of relationships bearing on the raccoon, for example, to lie quite beyond the raccoon. In the end, you are trying to make clear to them that everything found at the edge of one's senses—the high note of the winter wren, the thick perfume of propolis that drifts downwind from spring willows, the brightness of wood chips scattered by beaver—that all this fits together. The indestructibility of these associations conveys a sense of permanence that nurtures the heart, that cripples one of the most insidious of human anxieties, the one that says, you do not belong here, you are unnecessary.

10 Whenever I walk with a child, I think how much I have seen disappear in my own life. What will there be for this person when he is my age? If he senses something ineffable in the landscape, will I know enough to encourage it?—to somehow show him that, yes, when people talk about violent death, spiritual exhilaration, compassion, futility, final causes, they are drawing on forty thousand years of human meditation on *this*—as we embrace Douglas firs, or stand by a river across whose undulating back we skip stones, or dig out a camas bulb, biting down into a taste so much wilder than last night's potatoes.

11 The most moving look I ever saw from a child in the woods was on a mud bar by the footprints of a heron. We were on our knees, making handprints beside the footprints. You could feel the creek vibrating in the silt and sand. The sun beat down heavily on our hair. Our shoes were soaking wet. The look said: I did not know until now that I needed someone much older to confirm this, the feeling I have of life here. I can now grow older, knowing it need never be lost.

12 The quickest door to open in the woods for a child is the one that leads to the smallest room, by knowing the name each thing is called. The door that leads to the cathedral is marked by a hesitancy to speak at all, rather to encourage by

example a sharpness of the senses. If one speaks it should only be to say, as well as one can, how wonderfully all this fits together, to indicate what a long, fierce peace can derive from this knowledge.

COMPREHENSION

1. What is Lopez's primary purpose in this essay? How does the title relate to the purpose?
2. Does Lopez assume his audience has the same value position as he does? Why or why not?
3. What, ultimately, does Lopez want children to learn about the natural world? How does he teach them?

RHETORIC

1. Does Lopez state his thesis or imply it? Justify your response.
2. Why does Lopez use a personal tone or voice at the start of this essay? How does his opening paragraph connect to the body of the essay?
3. Cite instances where Lopez moves from vivid description to response and reflection.
4. Where does Lopez employ the comparative method, and toward what objective?
5. What extended metaphor does Lopez establish in the final paragraph? Is this an appropriate and effective metaphor to end the essay? Why or why not?

WRITING

1. Write a narrative and descriptive essay in which you recount a childhood experience that taught you something about the natural world.
2. How would you speak to children if you were taking them on a nature walk? Write a reflective essay addressing this question.
3. **Writing an Argument:** Argue for or against the proposition that you can learn profound truths about yourself and the world by immersing yourself in nature.

NETWORKING
Applying 21st-Century Literacies

Promoting the Natural World from the Virtual One: Create a blog or the home page of a Web site, the purpose of which is to get visitors excited about a natural space—a nearby national park, a reservoir, the Everglades—or an environmental issue—an endangered species, the effects of global climate change, ways to be more "green" around campus, etc. Think of creative ways to use text, visuals, videos, sound, and even music to appeal to your readers.

Synthesis: Classic and Contemporary Questions for Comparison

1. Chief Seattle and Barry Lopez ponder the destruction of nature as a physical and spiritual presence. In what ways are their stakes in this destruction the same? In what ways are they different? Does either writer have the power to effect a transformation in our attitude toward nature? Explain.

2. It has often been said that intellectual knowledge changes one's relationship with the world environment. In what ways has Lopez's "book learning" and erudition made him a different person from Chief Seattle? Base your response on the style and tone of each author.

3. Chief Seattle is literally the leader and spokesperson of a defeated nation. How does he preserve his dignity in the face of being conquered? How does he indicate to the white man that his "victory" is temporary? Lopez, on the other hand, is a successful member of his society: esteemed naturalist, award-winning writer, popular lecturer. What is his relationship to society and to America? Explain by referring to the text.

Why I Hunt

Rick Bass

Rick Bass (b. 1958) was born in Fort Worth, Texas, and grew up in the Texas hill country where his grandfather taught him how to hunt. His collection of essays, The Deer Pasture *(1985), recounts his Texas years, the ethos of hunting, and the allure of the outdoors. Bass studied at Utah State University (BS, 1979) and worked as an oil and gas geologist in Mississippi for eight years. His time working in the oil fields of the deep South is documented in* Oil Notes *(1979). Bass has written more than a dozen works of nonfiction and fiction, many of them reflecting environmental issues and people's search for balance in the natural world. An environmental advocate and land conservationist, Bass lives in the remote Yaak Valley on the Montana–Canada border, a region depicted in books such as* Winter: Notes from Montana *(1991),* Brown Dog of the Yaak: Essays on Art and Activism *(1999), and* The Roadless Yaak: Reflections and Observations about One of Our Last Great Wild Places *(2002). His most recent book of fiction is* Nashville Chrome *(2010). Bass wrote this vivid and provocative essay on the allure of the hunt for* Sierra *magazine in 2001.*

1   I was a hunter before I came far up into northwest Montana, but not to the degree I am now. It astounds me sometimes to step back particularly at the end of autumn, the end of the hunting season, and take both mental and physical inventory of all that was hunted and all that was gathered from this life in the mountains. The woodshed groaning tight, full of firewood. The fruits and herbs

and vegetables from the garden, canned or dried or frozen; the wild mushrooms, huckleberries, thimbleberries, and strawberries. And most precious of all, the flesh of the wild things that share with us these mountains and the plains to the east—the elk, the whitetail and mule deer; the ducks and geese, grouse and pheasant and Hungarian partridge and dove and chukar and wild turkey; the trout and whitefish. Each year the cumulative bounty seems unbelievable. What heaven is this into which we've fallen?

How my wife and I got to this valley—the Yaak—15 years ago is a mystery, 2 a move that I've only recently come to accept as having been inevitable. We got in the truck one day feeling strangely restless in Mississippi, and we drove. What did I know? Only that I missed the West's terrain of space. Young and healthy, and not coincidentally new-in-love, we hit that huge and rugged landscape in full stride. We drove north until we ran out of country—until the road ended, and we reached Canada's thick blue woods—and then we turned west and traveled until we ran almost out of mountains: the backside of the Rockies, to the wet, west-slope rainforest.

We came over a little mountain pass—it was August and winter was al- 3 ready fast approaching—and looked down on the soft hills, the dense purples of the spruce and fir forests, the ivory crests of the ice-capped peaks, and the slender ribbons of gray thread rising from the chimneys of the few cabins nudged close to the winding river below, and we fell in love with the Yaak Valley and the hard-logged Kootenai National Forest—the way people in movies fall with each other, star and starlet, as if a trap door has been pulled out from beneath them: tumbling through the air, arms windmilling furiously, and suddenly no other world but each other, no other world but this one and eyes for no one, or no place, else.

Right from the beginning, I could see that there was extraordinary bounty 4 in this low-elevation forest, resting as it does in a magical seam between the Pacific Northwest and the northern Rockies. Some landscapes these days have been reduced to nothing but dandelions and fire ants, knapweed and thistle, where the only remaining wildlife are sparrows, squirrels, and starlings. In the blessed Yaak, however, not a single mammal has gone extinct since the end of the Ice Age. This forest sustains more types of hunters—carnivores—than any valley in North America. It is a predator's showcase, home not just to wolves and grizzlies, but wolverines, lynx, bobcat, marten, fisher, black bear, mountain lion, golden eagle, bald eagle, coyote, fox, weasel. In the Yaak, everything is in motion, either seeking its quarry, or seeking to avoid becoming quarry.

The people who have chosen to live in this remote valley—few phones, 5 very little electricity, and long, dark winters—possess a hardness and a dreaminess both. They—we—can live a life of deprivation, and yet are willing to enter the comfort of daydreams and imagination. There is something mysterious happening here between the landscape and the people, a thing that stimulates our imagination, and causes many of us to set off deep into the woods in search of the unknown, and sustenance—not just metaphorical or spiritual sustenance, but the real thing.

6   Only about 5 percent of the nation and 15 to 20 percent of Montanans are hunters. But in this one valley, almost everyone is a hunter. It is not the peer pressure of the local culture that recruits us into hunting, nor even necessarily the economic boon of a few hundred pounds of meat in a cash-poor society. Rather, it is the terrain itself, and one's gradual integration into it, that summons the hunter. Nearly everyone who has lived here for any length of time has ended up—sometimes almost against one's conscious wishes—becoming a hunter. This wild and powerful landscape sculpts us like clay. I don't find such sculpting an affront to the human spirit, but instead, wonderful testimony to our pliability, our ability to adapt to a place.

7   I myself love to hunt the deer, the elk, and the grouse—to follow them into the mouth of the forest, to disappear in their pursuit—to get lost following their snowy tracks up one mountain and down the next. One sets out after one's quarry with senses fully engaged, wildly alert: entranced, nearly hypnotized. The tiniest of factors can possess the largest significance—the crack of a twig, the shift of a breeze, a single stray hair caught on a piece of bark, a fresh-bent blade of grass.

8   Each year during such pursuits, I am struck more and more by the conceit that people in a hunter-gatherer culture might have richer imaginations than those who dwell more fully in an agricultural or even post-agricultural environment. What else is the hunt but a stirring of the imagination, with the quarry, or goal, or treasure lying just around the corner or over the next rise? A hunter's imagination has no choice but to become deeply engaged, for it is never the hunter who is in control, but always the hunted, in that the prey directs the predator's movements.

9   The hunted shapes the hunter; the pursuit and evasion of predator and prey are but shadows of the same desire. The thrush wants to remain a thrush. The goshawk wants to consume the thrush and in doing so, partly become the thrush—to take its flesh into its flesh. They weave through the tangled branches of the forest, zigging and zagging, the goshawk right on the thrush's tail, like a

shadow. Or perhaps it is the thrush that is the shadow thrown by the light of the goshawk's fiery desire.

Either way, the escape maneuvers of the thrush help carve and shape and 10 direct the muscles of the goshawk. Even when you are walking through the woods seeing nothing but trees, you can feel the unseen passage of pursuits that might have occurred earlier that morning, precisely where you are standing— pursuits that will doubtless, after you are gone, sweep right back across that same spot again and again.

As does the goshawk, so too do human hunters imagine where their prey 11 might be, or where it might go. They follow tracks hinting at not only distance and direction traveled, but also pace and gait and the general state of mind of the animal that is evading them. They plead to the mountain to deliver to them a deer, an elk. They imagine and hope that they are moving toward their goal of obtaining game.

When you plant a row of corn, there is not so much unknown. You can be 12 fairly sure that, if the rains come, the corn is going to sprout. The corn is not seeking to elude you. But when you step into the woods, looking for a deer—well, there's nothing in your mind, or in your blood, or in the world, but imagination.

Most Americans neither hunt nor gather nor even grow their own food, 13 nor make, with their own hands, any of their other necessities. In this post-agricultural society, too often we confuse anticipation with imagination. When we wander down the aisle of the supermarket searching for a chunk of frozen chicken, or cruise into Dillard's department store looking for a sweater, we can be fairly confident that grayish wad of chicken or that sweater is going to be there, thanks to the vigor and efficiency of a supply-and-demand marketplace. The imagination never quite hits second gear. Does the imagination atrophy, from such chronic inactivity? I suspect that it does.

All I know is that hunting—beyond being a thing I like to do—helps keep 14 my imagination vital. I would hope never to be so blind as to offer it as prescription; I offer it only as testimony to my love of the landscape where I live—a place that is still, against all odds, its own place, quite unlike any other. I don't think I would be able to sustain myself as a dreamer in this strange landscape if I did not take off three months each year to wander the mountains in search of game; to hunt, stretching and exercising not just my imagination, but my spirit. And to wander the mountains, too, in all the other seasons. And to be nourished by the river of spirit that flows, shifting and winding, between me and the land.

COMPREHENSION

1. Why did Bass and his wife fall in love with the Yaak Valley? What does this fondness for wild places tell us about his character and interests?
2. Explain the relationship between the people residing in the Yaak Valley and their fondness for hunting.
3. Does Bass apologize for his fondness for hunting? Explain your response.

RHETORIC

1. Bass wrote this essay for the official magazine of the Sierra Club, of which he is an active member. Why would an organization whose goal is the preservation of wilderness and wildlife agree to publish an article expressing love for hunting? How does Bass anticipate objections to his argument?
2. What is Bass's claim and where does he state it? Does he rely on logical, ethical, or emotional appeal—or a combination—to advance his argument, and why?
3. What causal connection does Bass establish between landscape and human behavior? Where does he use comparison and contrast to distinguish this place and its people from other places and other Americans?
4. Cite examples of Bass's descriptive skills. How does description enhance the appeal of the writer's argument?
5. What is the dominant impression that Bass creates of the Yaak Valley region?
6. Evaluate Bass's conclusion. How does it serve as a writer's justification for hunting?

WRITING

1. Select a natural landscape that you know well and, including description as one rhetorical strategy, explain how this site affects the behavior of people and their ethical values.
2. **Writing an Argument:** What is the difference between killing the game that you consume and buying meat in a grocery store or supermarket? Is one act more ethical than the other? Compose an argumentative essay dealing with this issue.

NETWORKING
Applying 21st-Century Literacies

Interpreting an Organization's Web Site: Locate the Web site for the Sierra Club. Summarize the organization's goals, and then evaluate whether Bass's essay conforms to these objectives.

The Environmental Issue from Hell

Bill McKibben

Bill McKibben (b. 1960) was born in Palo Alto, California. After receiving a BA from Harvard University (1982), McKibben became a staff writer for the New Yorker. *McKibben's chief concern is the impact of humans on the environment and the ways in which consumerism affects the global ecosystem. A prominent writer for the environmental movement, he has published several books, among them* The End of Nature *(1989),* The Age of Missing Information *(1992),* Long Distance: A Year of Living

Strenuously *(2000),* Enough: Staying Human in an Engineered Age *(2003), and* The Bill McKibben Reader: Pieces from an Active Life *(2009). In the essay that follows, which was published in* These Times *in 2001, McKibben argues for a new approach to global warming.*

When global warming first emerged as a potential crisis in the late 1980s, one academic analyst called it "the public policy problem from hell." The years since have only proven him more astute: Fifteen years into our understanding of climate change, we have yet to figure out how we're going to tackle it. And environmentalists are just as clueless as anyone else: Do we need to work on lifestyle or on lobbying, on photovoltaics or on politics? And is there a difference? How well we handle global warming will determine what kind of century we inhabit—and indeed what kind of planet we leave behind. The issue cuts close to home and also floats off easily into the abstract. So far it has been the ultimate "can't get there from here" problem, but the time has come to draw a road map—one that may help us deal with the handful of other issues on the list of real, world-shattering problems.

Typically, when you're mounting a campaign, you look for self-interest, you scare people by saying what will happen to us if we don't do something: All the birds will die, the canyon will disappear beneath a reservoir, we will choke to death on smog. But in the case of global warming, that doesn't exactly do the trick, at least in the time frame we're discussing. In temperate latitudes, climate change will creep up on us. Severe storms already have grown more frequent and more damaging. The progression of seasons is less steady. Some agriculture is less reliable. But face it: Our economy is so enormous that it takes those changes in stride. Economists who work on this stuff talk about how it will shave a percentage or two off the GNP over the next few decades. And most of us live lives so divorced from the natural world that we hardly notice the changes anyway. Hotter? Turn up the air-conditioning. Stormier? Well, an enormous percentage of Americans commute from remote-controlled garage to office parking garage—it may have been some time since they got good and wet in a rainstorm. By the time the magnitude of the change is truly in our faces, it will be too late to do much about it: There's such a lag time to increased levels of carbon dioxide in the atmosphere that we need to be making the switch to solar and wind and hydrogen power right now to prevent disaster decades away. Yesterday, in fact.

So maybe we should think of global warming in a different way—as the great moral crisis of our time, the equivalent of the civil rights movement of the 1960s.

Why a moral question? In the first place, no one's ever figured out a more effective way to screw the marginalized and poor of this planet than climate change. Having taken their dignity, their resources, and their freedom under a variety of other schemes, we now are taking the very physical stability on which their already difficult lives depend.

Our economy can absorb these changes for a while, but consider Bangladesh for a moment. In 1998 the sea level in the Bay of Bengal was higher than normal, just the sort of thing we can expect to become more frequent and severe. The waters sweeping down the Ganges and the Brahmaputra rivers from the Himalayas could not drain easily into the ocean—they backed up across the country, forcing most of its inhabitants to spend three months in thigh-deep water. The fall rice crop didn't get planted. We've seen this same kind of disaster over the past few years in Mozambique and Honduras and Venezuela and other places.

6   And global warming is a moral crisis, too, if you place any value on the rest of creation. Coral reef researchers indicate that these spectacularly intricate eco-systems are also spectacularly vulnerable. Rising water temperatures are likely to bleach them to extinction by mid-century. In the Arctic, polar bears are 20 per-cent scrawnier than they were a decade ago: As pack ice melts, so does the op-portunity for hunting seals. All in all, the 21st century seems poised to see extinctions at a rate not observed since the last big asteroid slammed into the planet. But this time the asteroid is us.

7   It's a moral question, finally, if you think we owe any debt to the future. No one ever has figured out a more thoroughgoing way to strip-mine the present and degrade what comes after—all the people who will ever be related to you. Ever. No generation yet to come will ever forget us—we are the ones present at the moment when the temperature starts to spike, and so far we have not re-acted. If it had been done to us, we would loathe the generation that did it, precisely as we will one day be loathed.

8   But trying to launch a moral campaign is no easy task. In most moral crises, there is a villain—some person or class or institution that must be overcome. Once the villain is identified, the battle can commence. But you can't really get angry at carbon dioxide, and the people responsible for its production are, well, us. So perhaps we need some symbols to get us started, some places to sharpen the debate and rally ourselves to action. There are plenty to choose from: our taste for ever bigger houses and the heating and cooling bills that come with them, our penchant for jumping on airplanes at the drop of a hat. But if you wanted one glaring example of our lack of balance, you could do worse than point the finger at sport utility vehicles.

9   SUVs are more than mere symbols. They are a major part of the problem— we emit so much more carbon dioxide now than we did a decade ago in part because our fleet of cars and trucks actually has gotten steadily less fuel effi-cient for the past 10 years. If you switched today from the average American car to a big SUV, and drove it for just one year, the difference in carbon dioxide that you produced would be the equivalent of opening your refrigerator door and then forgetting to close it for six years. SUVs essentially are machines for burn-ing fossil fuel that just happen to also move you and your stuff around.

10   But what makes them such a perfect symbol is the brute fact that they are simply unnecessary. Go to the parking lot of the nearest suburban supermarket and look around: The only conclusion you can draw is that to reach the grocery, people must drive through three or four raging rivers and up the side of a can-yon. These are semi-military machines, armored trucks on a slight diet. While they do not keep their occupants appreciably safer, they do wreck whatever they plow into, making them the perfect metaphor for a heedless, supersized society.

11   That's why we need a much broader politics than the Washington lobby-ing that's occupied the big environmental groups for the past decade. We need

to take all the brilliant and energetic strategies of local grassroots groups fighting dumps and cleaning up rivers and apply those tactics in the national and international arenas. That's why some pastors are starting to talk with their congregations about what cars to buy, and why some college seniors are passing around petitions pledging to stay away from the Ford Explorers and Excursions, and why some auto dealers have begun to notice informational picketers outside their showrooms on Saturday mornings urging customers to think about gas mileage when they look at cars.

The point is not that such actions by themselves—any individual actions— 12 will make any real dent in the levels of carbon dioxide pouring into our atmosphere. Even if you got 10 percent of Americans really committed to changing their energy use, their solar homes wouldn't make much of a difference in our national totals. But 10 percent would be enough to change the politics around the issue, enough to pressure politicians to pass laws that would cause us all to shift our habits. And so we need to begin to take an issue that is now the province of technicians and turn it into a political issue, just as bus boycotts began to make public the issue of race, forcing the system to respond. That response is likely to be ugly—there are huge companies with a lot to lose, and many people so tied in to their current ways of life that advocating change smacks of subversion. But this has to become a political issue—and fast. The only way that may happen, short of a hideous drought or monster flood, is if it becomes a personal issue first.

COMPREHENSION

1. According to McKibben, what are the causes of global warming?
2. What instances of ecological disaster does the writer say will occur if we do not change our habits?
3. Why is a new approach to the problem of global warming needed? What approach does McKibben suggest?

RHETORIC

1. How does McKibben's title capture the tone of the essay? What is his purpose in writing the essay? Does he see his readers as hostile or sympathetic to his position? How do you know?
2. How does McKibben develop his introduction? Why does he pose questions? Where does he state his claim?
3. Does McKibben make his argument through appeals to reason, emotion, ethics—or a combination of these elements? Justify your response.
4. How does the writer contend with possible objections to his position on global warming?
5. Explain the pattern of cause and effect that McKibben uses to structure his essay.
6. What varieties of evidence does the writer present to support his claim? What extended illustration does he provide? How effective is it, and why?
7. In the concluding paragraph, McKibben issues a call to action. How does the body of the essay prepare the reader for this persuasive appeal?

WRITING

1. Write an essay in which you explain your own sense of the causes and effects of global warming.
2. Research your state's policy toward global warming. Present your findings in a summary essay.
3. **Writing an Argument:** McKibben argues that SUVs are a primary cause of wastefulness and global warming and that both moral persuasion and political activism are required to change consumers' habits. Do you agree or disagree with his assertions? Write an argumentative essay responding to this issue.

NETWORKING
Applying 21st-Century Literacies

Delivering an Oral Presentation: Reshape your response to any of the three assignments under Writing to function as an oral presentation; incorporate visual aids (digital or hard copy) and one carefully designed and written handout for your listeners.

The Obligation to Endure

Rachel Carson

Rachel Carson (1907–1964) was a seminal figure in the environmental movement. Born in Pennsylvania, she awakened public consciousness to environmental issues through her writing. Her style was both literary and scientific as she described nature's riches in such books as The Sea around Us *(1951) and* The Edge of the Sea *(1954). Her last book,* Silent Spring *(1962), aroused controversy and concern with its indictment of insecticides. In the following excerpt from that important book, Carson provides compelling evidence of the damage caused by indiscriminate use of insecticides and the danger of disturbing the earth's delicate balance.*

1   The history of life on earth has been a history of interaction between living things and their surroundings. To a large extent, the physical form and the habits of the earth's vegetation and its animal life have been molded by the environment. Considering the whole span of earthly time, the opposite effect, in which life actually modifies its surroundings, has been relatively slight. Only within the moment of time represented by the present century has one species—man—acquired significant power to alter the nature of his world.

2   During the past quarter century this power has not only increased to one of disturbing magnitude but it has changed in character. The most alarming of all

man's assaults upon the environment is the contamination of air, earth, rivers, and sea with dangerous and even lethal materials. This pollution is for the most part irrecoverable; the chain of evil it initiates not only in the world that must support life but in living tissues is for the most part irreversible. In this now universal contamination of the environment, chemicals are the sinister and little-recognized partners of radiation in changing the very nature of the world—the very nature of its life. Strontium 90, released through nuclear explosions into the air, comes to earth in rain or drifts down as fallout, lodges in soil, enters into the grass or corn or wheat grown there, and in time takes up its abode in the bones of a human being, there to remain until his death. Similarly, chemicals sprayed on croplands or forests or gardens lie long in soil, entering into living organisms, passing from one to another in a chain of poisoning and death. Or they pass mysteriously by underground streams until they emerge and, through the alchemy of air and sunlight, combine into new forms that kill vegetation, sicken cattle, and work unknown harm on those who drink from once pure wells. As Albert Schweitzer has said, "Man can hardly even recognize the devils of his own creation."

It took hundreds of millions of years to produce the life that now inhabits the earth—eons of time in which that developing and evolving and diversifying life reached a state of adjustment and balance with its surroundings. The environment, rigorously shaping and directing the life it supported, contained elements that were hostile as well as supporting. Certain rocks gave out dangerous radiation; even within the light of the sun, from which all life draws its energy, there were shortwave radiations with power to injure. Given time—time not in years but in millennia—life adjusts, and a balance has been reached. For time is the essential ingredient; but in the modern world there is no time.

The rapidity of change and the speed with which new situations are created follow the impetuous and heedless pace of man rather than the deliberate pace of nature. Radiation is no longer merely the background radiation of rocks, the bombardment of cosmic rays, the ultraviolet of the sun that have existed before there was any life on earth; radiation is now the unnatural creation of man's tampering with the atom. The chemicals to which life is asked to make its adjustment are no longer merely the calcium and silica and copper and all the rest of the minerals washed out of the rocks and carried in rivers to the sea; they are the synthetic creations of man's inventive mind, brewed in his laboratories, and having no counterparts in nature.

To adjust to these chemicals would require time on the scale that is nature's; it would require not merely the years of a man's life but the life of generations. And even this, were it by some miracle possible, would be futile, for the new chemicals come from our laboratories in an endless stream; almost five hundred annually find their way into actual use in the United States alone. The figure is staggering and its implications are not easily grasped—500 new chemicals to which the bodies of men and animals are required somehow to adapt each year, chemicals totally outside the limits of biologic experience.

6   Among them are many that are used in man's war against nature. Since the mid-1940s over 200 basic chemicals have been created for use in killing insects, weeds, rodents, and other organisms described in the modern vernacular as "pests"; and they are sold under several thousand different brand names.

7   These sprays, dusts, and aerosols are now applied almost universally to farms, gardens, forests, and homes—nonselective chemicals that have the power to kill every insect, the "good" and the "bad," to still the song of birds and the leaping of fish in the streams, to coat the leaves with a deadly film, and to linger on in soil—all this though the intended target may be only a few weeds or insects. Can anyone believe it is possible to lay down such a barrage of poisons on the surface of the earth without making it unfit for all life? They should not be called "insecticides," but "biocides."

8   The whole process of spraying seems caught up in an endless spiral. Since DDT was released for civilian use, a process of escalation has been going on in which ever more toxic materials must be found. This has happened because insects, in a triumphant vindication of Darwin's principle of the survival of the fittest, have evolved super races immune to the particular insecticide used, hence a deadlier one has always to be developed—and then a deadlier one than that. It has happened also because, for reasons to be described later, destructive insects often undergo a "flareback," or resurgence, after spraying in numbers greater than before. Thus the chemical war is never won, and all life is caught in its violent crossfire.

9   Along with the possibility of the extinction of mankind by nuclear war, the central problem of our age has therefore become the contamination of man's total environment with such substances of incredible potential for harm—substances that accumulate in the tissues of plants and animals and even penetrate the germ cells to shatter or alter the very material of heredity upon which the shape of the future depends.

10   Some would-be architects of our future look toward a time when it will be possible to alter the human germ plasm by design. But we may easily be doing so now by inadvertence, for many chemicals, like radiation, bring about gene mutations. It is ironic to think that man might determine his own future by something so seemingly trivial as the choice of an insect spray.

11   All this has been risked—for what? Future historians may well be amazed by our distorted sense of proportion. How could intelligent beings seek to control a few unwanted species by a method that contaminated the entire environment and brought the threat of disease and death even to their own kind? Yet this is precisely what we have done. We have done it, moreover, for reasons that collapse the moment we examine them. We are told that the enormous and expanding use of pesticides is necessary to maintain farm production. Yet is our real problem not one of *overproduction*? Our farms, despite measures to remove acreages from production and to pay farmers *not* to produce, have yielded such a staggering excess of crops that the American taxpayer in 1962 is paying out more than one billion dollars a year as the total carrying cost of the surplus-food storage program. And is the situation helped when one branch of

the Agriculture Department tries to reduce production while another states, as it did in 1958, "It is believed generally that reduction of crop acreages under provisions of the Soil Bank will stimulate interest in use of chemicals to obtain maximum production on the land retained in crops."

All this is not to say there is no insect problem and no need of control. I am saying, rather, that control must be geared to realities, not to mythical situations, and that the methods employed must be such that they do not destroy us along with the insects. 12

The problem whose attempted solution has brought such a train of disaster in its wake is an accompaniment of our modern way of life. Long before the age of man, insects inhabited the earth—a group of extraordinarily varied and adaptable beings. Over the course of time since man's advent, a small percentage of the more than half a million species of insects have come into conflict with human welfare in two principal ways: as competitors for the food supply and as carriers of human disease. 13

Disease-carrying insects become important where human beings are crowded together, especially under conditions where sanitation is poor, as in times of natural disaster or war or in situations of extreme poverty and deprivation. Then control of some sort becomes necessary. It is a sobering fact, however, as we shall presently see, that the method of massive chemical control has had only limited success, and also threatens to worsen the very conditions it is intended to curb. 14

Under primitive agricultural conditions the farmer had few insect problems. These arose with the intensification of agriculture—the devotion of immense acreages to a single crop. Such a system set the stage for explosive increases in specific insect populations. Single-crop farming does not take advantage of the principles by which nature works; it is agriculture as an engineer might conceive it to be. Nature has introduced great variety into the landscape, but man has displayed a passion for simplifying it. Thus he undoes the built-in checks and balances by which nature holds the species within bounds. One important natural check is a limit on the amount of suitable habitat for each species. Obviously then, an insect that lives on wheat can build up its population to much higher levels on a farm devoted to wheat than on one in which wheat is intermingled with other crops to which the insect is not adapted. 15

The same thing happens in other situations. A generation or more ago, the towns of large areas of the United States lined their streets with the noble elm tree. Now the beauty they hopefully created is threatened with complete destruction as disease sweeps through the elms, carried by a beetle that would have only limited chance to build up large populations and to spread from tree to tree if the elms were only occasional trees in a richly diversified planting. 16

Another factor in the modern insect problem is one that must be viewed against a background of geologic and human history: the spreading of thousands of different kinds of organisms from their native homes to invade new territories. This worldwide migration has been studied and graphically described by the 17

British ecologist Charles Elton in his recent book *The Ecology of Invasions*. During the Cretaceous Period, some hundred million years ago, flooding seas cut many land bridges between continents and living things found themselves confined in what Elton calls "colossal separate nature reserves." There, isolated from others of their kind, they developed many new species. When some of the land masses were joined again, about 15 million years ago, these species began to move out into new territories—a movement that is not only still in progress but is now receiving considerable assistance from man.

18   The importation of plants is the primary agent in the modern spread of species, for animals have almost invariably gone along with the plants, quarantine being a comparatively recent and not completely effective innovation. The United States Office of Plant Introduction alone has introduced almost 200,000 species and varieties of plants from all over the world. Nearly half of the 180 or so major insect enemies of plants in the United States are accidental imports from abroad, and most of them have come as hitchhikers on plants.

19   In new territory, out of reach of the restraining hand of the natural enemies that kept down its numbers in its native land, an invading plant or animal is able to become enormously abundant. Thus it is no accident that our most troublesome insects are introduced species.

20   These invasions, both the naturally occurring and those dependent on human assistance, are likely to continue indefinitely. Quarantine and massive chemical campaigns are only extremely expensive ways of buying time. We are faced, according to Dr. Elton, "with a life-and-death need not just to find new technological means of suppressing this plant or that animal"; instead we need the basic knowledge of animal populations and their relations to their surroundings that will "promote an even balance and damp down the explosive power of outbreaks and new invasions."

21   Much of the necessary knowledge is now available but we do not use it. We train ecologists in our universities and even employ them in our governmental agencies but we seldom take their advice. We allow the chemical death rain to fall as though there were no alternative, whereas in fact there are many, and our ingenuity could soon discover many more if given opportunity.

22   Have we fallen into a mesmerized state that makes us accept as inevitable that which is inferior or detrimental, as though having lost the will or the vision to demand that which is good? Such thinking, in the words of the ecologist Paul Shepard, "idealizes life with only its head out of water, inches above the limits of toleration of the corruption of its own environment. . . . Why should we tolerate a diet of weak poisons, a home in insipid surroundings, a circle of acquaintances who are not quite our enemies, the noise of motors with just enough relief to prevent insanity? Who would want to live in a world which is just not quite fatal?"

23   Yet such a world is pressed upon us. The crusade to create a chemically sterile, insect-free world seems to have engendered a fanatic zeal on the part of many specialists and most of the so-called control agencies. On every hand there is evidence that those engaged in spraying operations exercise a ruthless power. "The regulatory entomologists . . . function as prosecutor, judge and

jury, tax assessor and collector and sheriff to enforce their own orders," said Connecticut entomologist Neely Turner. The most flagrant abuses go unchecked in both state and federal agencies.

It is not my contention that chemical insecticides must never be used. I do 24 contend that we have put poisonous and biologically potent chemicals indiscriminately into the hands of persons largely or wholly ignorant of their potentials for harm. We have subjected enormous numbers of people to contact with these poisons, without their consent and often without their knowledge. If the Bill of Rights contains no guarantee that a citizen shall be secure against lethal poisons distributed either by private individuals or by public officials, it is surely only because our forefathers, despite their considerable wisdom and foresight, could conceive of no such problem.

I contend, furthermore, that we have allowed these chemicals to be used 25 with little or no advance investigation of their effect on soil, water, wildlife, and man himself. Future generations are unlikely to condone our lack of prudent concern for the integrity of the natural world that supports all life.

There is still very limited awareness of the nature of the threat. This is an era 26 of specialists, each of whom sees his own problem and is unaware of or intolerant of the larger frame into which it fits. It is also an era dominated by industry, in which the right to make a dollar at whatever cost is seldom challenged. When the public protests, confronted with some obvious evidence of damaging results of pesticide applications, it is fed little tranquilizing pills of half truth. We urgently need an end to these false assurances, to the sugar coating of unpalatable facts. It is the public that is being asked to assume the risks that the insect controllers calculate. The public must decide whether it wishes to continue on the present road, and it can do so only when in full possession of the facts. In the words of Jean Rostand, "The obligation to endure gives us the right to know."

COMPREHENSION

1. What does Carson mean by "the obligation to endure"?
2. What reasons does the author cite for the overpopulation of insects?
3. What remedies does Carson propose?

RHETORIC

1. What tone does Carson use in her essay? Does she seem to be a subjective or an objective writer? Give specific support for your response.
2. How does the use of words such as *dangerous, evil, irrevocable,* and *sinister* help shape the reader's reaction to the piece? What emotional and ethical appeals do such words indicate?
3. Examine the ordering of ideas in paragraph 4, and consider how such an order serves to reinforce Carson's argument.
4. Paragraph 9 consists of only one (long) sentence. What is its function in the essay's scheme?

5. Examine Carson's use of expert testimony. How does it help strengthen her thesis?
6. How effectively does the essay's conclusion help tie up Carson's points? What is the writer's intent in this final paragraph? How does she accomplish this aim?

WRITING

1. Write an essay in which you suggest solutions to the problems brought up in Carson's piece. You may want to suggest measures that the average citizen can take to eliminate the casual use of insecticides to control the insect population.
2. Write a biographical research paper on Carson that focuses on her involvement with nature and environmental issues.
3. **Writing an Argument:** Write an essay titled "Insects Are Not the Problem; Humanity Is." In this essay, argue that it is humanity's greed that has caused such an imbalance in nature as to threaten the planet's survival.

NETWORKING
Applying 21st-Century Literacies

Composing an Interactive Argument Essay: Create question 1 or 3 under Writing as an electronic document, one that readers can interact with by clicking on links that take them to other essays and articles that both support *and* refute your position. Post the essay on a Web site or blog and enable comments so your classmates (or other readers) can actively engage with your topic. Respond to at least two comments, being sure to keep dialogue civil and arguments well supported. Make your Works Cited page interactive as well, documenting all sources and linking to any that are available on the Web.

Am I Blue?

Alice Walker

Alice Walker (b. 1944) was born in Eatonton, Georgia; attended Spelman College; and graduated from Sarah Lawrence College. Besides being a prolific novelist, short-story writer, poet, and essayist, she has also been active in the civil rights movement. She often draws on both her own history and historical records to reflect on the African American experience. Some of her well-known books are The Color Purple *(1976),* You Can't Keep a Good Woman Down *(1981),* Living in the World: Selected Writings, 1973–1987 *(1987),* The Temple of My Familiar *(1989),* By the Light of My Father's Smile *(1999),* The Way Forward Is with a Broken Heart *(2001), and* Why War Is Never a Good Idea *(2007). In the following essay from* Living in the World, *Walker questions the distinctions commonly made between human and animal.*

For about three years my companion and I rented a small house in the country 1
that stood on the edge of a large meadow that appeared to run from the end of
our deck straight into the mountains. The mountains, however, were quite far
away, and between us and them there was, in fact, a town. It was one of the
many pleasant aspects of the house that you never really were aware of this.

It was a house of many windows, low, wide, nearly floor to ceiling in the 2
living room, which faced the meadow, and it was from one of these that I first
saw our closest neighbor, a large white horse, cropping grass, flipping its mane,
and ambling about—not over the entire meadow, which stretched well out of
sight of the house, but over the five or so fenced-in acres that were next to the
twenty-odd that we had rented. I soon learned that the horse, whose name was
Blue, belonged to a man who lived in another town, but was boarded by our
neighbors next door. Occasionally, one of the children, usually a stocky teenager, but sometimes a much younger girl or boy, could be seen riding Blue.
They would appear in the meadow, climb up on his back, ride furiously for ten
or fifteen minutes, then get off, slap Blue on the flanks, and not be seen again
for a month or more.

There were many apple trees in our yard, and one by the fence that Blue 3
could almost reach. We were soon in the habit of feeding him apples, which he
relished, especially because by the middle of summer the meadow grasses—so
green and succulent since January—had dried out from lack of rain, and Blue
stumbled about munching the dried stalks half-heartedly. Sometimes he would
stand very still just by the apple tree, and when one of us came out he would
whinny, snort loudly, or stamp the ground. This meant, of course: I want an apple.

It was quite wonderful to pick a few apples, or collect those that had fallen 4
to the ground overnight, and patiently hold them, one by one, up to his large,
toothy mouth. I remained as thrilled as a child by his flexible dark lips, huge,
cubelike teeth that crunched the apples, core and all, with such finality, and his
high, broad-breasted *enormity*; beside which, I felt small indeed. When I was a
child, I used to ride horses, and was especially friendly with one named Nan
until the day I was riding and my brother deliberately spooked her and I was
thrown, head first, against the trunk of a tree. When I came to, I was in bed and
my mother was bending worriedly over me; we silently agreed that perhaps
horseback riding was not the safest sport for me. Since then I have walked, and
prefer walking to horseback riding—but I had forgotten the depth of feeling
one could see in horses' eyes.

I was therefore unprepared for the expression in Blue's. Blue was lonely. 5
Blue was horribly lonely and bored. I was not shocked that this should be the
case; five acres to tramp by yourself, endlessly, even in the most beautiful of
meadows—and his was—cannot provide many interesting events, and once the
rainy season turned to dry that was about it. No, I was shocked that I had forgotten that human animals and nonhuman animals can communicate quite
well; if we are brought up around animals as children we take this for granted.
By the time we are adults we no longer remember. However, the animals have
not changed. They are in fact *completed* creations (at least they seem to be, so

much more than we) who are not likely *to* change; it is their nature to express themselves. What else are they going to express? And they do. And, generally speaking, they are ignored.

6   After giving Blue the apples, I would wander back to the house, aware that he was observing me. Were more apples not forthcoming then? Was that to be his sole entertainment for the day? My partner's small son had decided he wanted to learn how to piece a quilt; we worked in silence on our respective squares as I thought . . .

7   Well, about slavery: about white children, who were raised by black people, who knew their first all-accepting love from black women, and then, when they were twelve or so, were told they must "forget" the deep levels of communication between themselves and "mammy" that they knew. Later they would be able to relate quite calmly, "My old mammy was sold to another good family." "My old mammy was _____." Fill in the blank. Many more years later a white woman would say: "I can't understand these Negroes, these blacks. What do they want? They're so different from us."

8   And about the Indians, considered to be "like animals" by the "settlers" (a very benign euphemism for what they actually were), who did not understand their description as a compliment.

9   And about the thousands of American men who marry Japanese, Korean, Filipina, and other non-English-speaking women and of how happy they report they are, *"blissfully,"* until their brides learn to speak English, at which point the marriages tend to fall apart. What then did the men see, when they looked into the eyes of the women they married, before they could speak English? Apparently only their own reflections.

10   I thought of society's impatience with the young. "Why are they playing the music so loud?" Perhaps the children have listened to much of the music of oppressed people their parents danced to before they were born, with its passionate but soft cries for acceptance and love, and they have wondered why their parents failed to hear.

11   I do not know how long Blue had inhabited his five beautiful, boring acres before we moved into our house; a year after we had arrived—and had also traveled to other valleys, other cities, other worlds—he was still there.

12   But then, in our second year at the house, something happened in Blue's life. One morning, looking out the window at the fog that lay like a ribbon over the meadow, I saw another horse, a brown one, at the other end of Blue's field. Blue appeared to be afraid of it, and for several days made no attempt to go near. We went away for a week. When we returned, Blue had decided to make friends and the two horses ambled or galloped along together, and Blue did not come nearly as often to the fence underneath the apple tree.

13   When he did, bringing his new friend with him, there was a different look in his eyes. A look of independence, of self-possession, of inalienable *horse*ness. His friend eventually became pregnant. For months and months there was, it seemed to me, a mutual feeling between me and the horses of justice, of peace. I fed apples to them both. The look in Blue's eyes was one of unabashed "this is *it*ness."

It did not, however, last forever. One day, after a visit to the city, I went out 14
to give Blue some apples. He stood waiting, or so I thought, though not beneath
the tree. When I shook the tree and jumped back from the shower of apples, he
made no move. I carried some over to him. He managed to half-crunch one.
The rest he let fall to the ground. I dreaded looking into his eyes—because I had
of course noticed that Brown, his partner, had gone—but I did look. If I had
been born into slavery, and my partner had been sold or killed, my eyes would
have looked like that. The children next door explained that Blue's partner had
been "put with him" (the same expression that old people used, I had noticed,
when speaking of an ancestor during slavery who had been impregnated by
her owner) so that they could mate and she conceive. Since that was accomplished, she had been taken back by her owner, who lived somewhere else.

Will she be back? I asked.   15

They didn't know.   16

Blue was like a crazed person. Blue *was*, to me, a crazed person. He galloped 17
furiously, as if he were being ridden, around and around his five beautiful
acres. He whinnied until he couldn't. He tore at the ground with his hooves. He
butted himself against his single shade tree. He looked always and always toward the road down which his partner had gone. And then, occasionally, when
he came up for apples, or I took apples to him, he looked at me. It was a look so
piercing, so full of grief, a look so *human*, I almost laughed (I felt too sad to cry)
to think there are people who do not know that animals suffer. People like me
who have forgotten, and daily forget, all that animals try to tell us. "Everything
you do to us will happen to you; we are your teachers, as you are ours. We are
one lesson" is essentially it, I think. There are those who never once have even
considered animals' rights: those who have been taught that animals actually
want to be used and abused by us, as small children "love" to be frightened, or
women "love" to be mutilated and raped. . . . They are the great-grandchildren
of those who honestly thought, because someone taught them this: "Woman
can't think" and "niggers can't faint." But most disturbing of all, in Blue's
large brown eyes was a new look, more painful than the look of despair: the
look of disgust with human beings, with life; the look of hatred. And it was
odd what the look of hatred did. It gave him, for the first time, the look of a
beast. And what that meant was that he had put up a barrier within to protect
himself from further violence; all the apples in the world wouldn't change
that fact.

And so Blue remained, a beautiful part of our landscape, very peaceful to 18
look at from the window, white against the grass. Once a friend came to visit
and said, looking out on the soothing view: "And it *would* have to be a *white*
horse; the very image of freedom." And I thought, yes, the animals are forced to
become for us merely "images" of what they once so beautifully expressed.
And we are used to drinking milk from containers showing "contented" cows,
whose real lives we want to hear nothing about, eating eggs and drumsticks
from "happy" hens, and munching hamburgers advertised by bulls of integrity
who seem to command their fate.

19   As we talked of freedom and justice one day for all, we sat down to steaks. I am eating misery, I thought, as I took the first bite. And spit it out.

COMPREHENSION

1. What is the major thesis of the essay? Is it stated explicitly in the text, or does one have to infer it? Explain.
2. In paragraph 5, Walker states that animals are *"completed* creations (at least they seem to be, so much more than we) who are not likely *to* change." What does she mean by making this distinction between animals and humans?
3. What is the significance of the title of the essay? Does it have more than one meaning? Explain your answer.

RHETORIC

1. In paragraph 4, Walker creates a vivid description of Blue. How does she achieve this?
2. In paragraph 7, Walker makes a cognitive association between the relationship between humans and animals and the relationship between whites and blacks during slavery. Does this transition seem too abrupt, or is there a rhetorical reason for the immediate comparison? Explain.
3. Explore the other analogies Walker makes in paragraphs 8 and 9. Are they pertinent? What is the rhetorical effect of juxtaposing seemingly different realms to convey one central idea?
4. Walker often breaks the conventions of "college English." For example, paragraphs 8 and 9 both begin with the coordinating conjunction *and.* Paragraph 12 begins with the coordinating conjunction *but.* Paragraphs 15 and 16 are only one short sentence each. Explain the effect of each of these rhetorical devices. Find three other unusual rhetorical strategies—either on the paragraph or sentence level—and explain their effects.
5. In paragraphs 17 and 18, Walker speeds up the tempo of her writing by beginning many of the sentences with the conjunction *and.* What is the purpose and rhetorical effect of this strategy, and how does it mimic—in linguistic terms—Blue's altered emotional state?
6. Walker seems to have a profound empathy for animals, yet it is only at the end that she is repulsed by the thought of eating meat. What rhetorical strategy is she employing in the conclusion that helps bring closure to her meditation on Blue? Does it matter whether the culminating event actually occurred in her experience, or is it all right for an essayist to use poetic license for stylistic purposes?

WRITING

1. Write a personal essay in which you describe your relationship with a favorite pet. Include your observations of, responses to, and attitude toward your pet. Compare and contrast this relationship to those you have with humans.

2. Some writers have argued that it matters little if certain "nonessential" endangered species become extinct if they interfere with "human progress." Argue for or against this proposition.

3. **Writing an Argument:** Argue for or against one of the following practices: (**a**) hunting for the sake of the hunt, (**b**) eating meat, or (**c**) keeping animals in zoos.

NETWORKING
Applying 21st-Century Literacies

Exploring Multiple Sides to an Issue: Approach question 3 under Writing as an exploratory, rather than an argumentative, essay. Use online research to examine at least three different ways of approaching one of the possible issues, such as eating meat, and arrive at a thesis only in your conclusion.

The Greenest Campuses:
An Idiosyncratic Guide

Noel Perrin

Noel Perrin (1927–2004) was born in New York City and worked as an editor before starting a career as a college instructor at the University of North Carolina and then Dartmouth College, where he taught beginning in 1959. He was awarded two Guggenheim Fellowships, contributed to numerous periodicals, and authored more than 10 books. His subject matter ranges from the scholarly, such as Dr. Bowdler's Legacy *(1969)* and Giving Up the Gun: Japan's Reversion to the Sword, 1543–1879 *(1979), to his experiences as a part-time farmer. Among the latter are* First Person Plural *(1978),* Second Person Plural *(1980),* Third Person Plural *(1983),* Last Person Plural *(1991), and* A Child's Delight *(1998). His concerns about the environment made him a popular speaker on ecological issues. In the following essay, first published in the* Chronicle of Higher Education *in April 2001, Perrin creates his own "best" college guide by ranking institutions of higher learning according to their environmental awareness.*

About 1,100 American colleges and universities run at least a token environmental-studies program, and many hundreds of those programs offer well-designed and useful courses. But only a drastically smaller number practice even a portion of what they teach. The one exception is recycling. Nearly every institution that has so much as one lonely environmental-studies course also does a little halfhearted recycling. Paper and glass, usually.

2   There are some glorious exceptions to those rather churlish observations, I'm glad to say. How many? Nobody knows. No one has yet done the necessary research (though the National Wildlife Federation's Campus Ecology program is planning a survey).

3   Certainly *U.S. News & World Report* hasn't. Look at the rankings in their annual college issue. The magazine uses a complex formula something like this: Institution's reputation, 25 percent; student-retention rate, 20 percent; faculty resources, 20 percent; and so on, down to alumni giving, 5 percent. The lead criterion may help explain why Harvard, Yale, and Princeton Universities so frequently do a little dance at the top of the list.

4   But *U.S. News* has nothing at all to say about the degree to which a college or university attempts to behave sustainably—that is, to manage its campus and activities in ways that promote the long-term health of the planet. The magazine is equally mum about which of the institutions it is ranking can serve as models to society in a threatened world.

5   And, of course, the world is threatened. When the Royal Society in London and the National Academy of Sciences in Washington issued their first-ever joint statement, it ended like this: "The future of our planet is in the balance. Sustainable development can be achieved, but only if irreversible degradation of the environment can be halted in time. The next 30 years may be crucial." They said that in 1992. If all those top scientists are right, we have a little more than 20 years left in which to make major changes in how we live.

6 All this affects colleges. I have one environmentalist friend who loves to point out to the deans and trustees she meets that if we don't make such changes, and if the irreversible degradation of earth does occur, Harvard's huge endowment and Yale's lofty reputation will count for nothing.

7   But though *U.S. News* has nothing to say, fortunately there is a fairly good grapevine in the green world. I have spent considerable time in the past two years using it like an organic cell phone. By that means I have come up with a short, idiosyncratic list of green colleges, consisting of six that are a healthy green, two that are greener still, and three that I believe are the greenest in the United States.

8   Which approved surveying techniques have I used? None at all. Some of my evidence is anecdotal, and some of my conclusions are affected by my personal beliefs, such as that electric and hybrid cars are not just a good idea, but instruments of salvation.

9   Obviously I did not examine, even casually, all 1,100 institutions. I'm sure I have missed some outstanding performers. I hope I have missed a great many.

10   Now, here are the 11, starting with **Brown University.**

11   It is generally harder for a large urban university to move toward sustainable behavior than it is for a small-town college with maybe a thousand students. But it's not impossible. Both Brown, in the heart of Providence, R.I., and Yale University (by no means an environmental leader in other respects), in the

heart of New Haven, Conn., have found a country way of dealing with food waste. Pigs. Both rely on pigs.

For the past 10 years, Brown has been shipping nearly all of its food waste 12 to a Rhode Island piggery. Actually, not shipping it—just leaving it out at dawn each morning. The farmer comes to the campus and gets it. Not since Ralph Waldo Emerson took food scraps out to the family pig have these creatures enjoyed such a high intellectual connection.

But there is a big difference in scale. Where Emerson might have one pail of 13 slops now and then, Brown generates 700 tons of edible garbage each year. Haulage fee: $0. Tipping fee: $0. (That's the cost of dumping the garbage into huge cookers, where it is heated for the pigs.) Annual savings to Brown: about $50,000. Addition to the American food supply: many tons of ham and bacon each year.

Of course, Brown does far more than feed a balanced diet to a lot of pigs. 14 That's just the most exotic (for an urban institution) of its green actions. "Brown is Green" became the official motto of the university in August 1990. It was accurate then, and it remains accurate now.

Yale is the only other urban institution I'm aware of that supports a pig 15 population. Much of the credit goes to Cyril May, the university's environmental coordinator, just as much of the credit at Brown goes to its environmental coordinator, Kurt Teichert.

May has managed to locate two Connecticut piggeries. The one to which he 16 sends garbage presents problems. The farmer has demanded—and received—a collection fee. And he has developed an antagonistic relationship with some of Yale's food-service people. (There are a lot of them: The campus has 16 dining facilities.) May is working on an arrangement with the second piggery. But if it falls through, he says, "I may go back on semibended knee to the other."

Yale does not make the list as a green college, for reasons you will learn 17 later in this essay. But it might in a few more years.

Carleton College is an interesting example of an institution turning green 18 almost overnight. No pig slops here; the dining halls are catered by Marriott. But change is coming fast.

In the summer of 1999, Carleton appointed its first-ever environmental 19 coordinator, a brand-new graduate named Rachel Smit. The one-year appointment was an experiment, with a cobbled-together salary and the humble title of "fifth-year intern." The experiment worked beyond anyone's expectation.

Smit began publishing an environmental newsletter called *The Green Bean* 20 and organized a small committee of undergraduates to explore the feasibility of composting the college's food waste, an effort that will soon begin. A surprised Marriott has already found itself serving organic dinners on Earth Day.

Better yet, the college set up an environmental-advisory committee of three 21 administrators, three faculty members, and three students to review all campus projects from a green perspective. Naturally, many of those projects will be buildings, and to evaluate them, Carleton is using the *Minnesota Sustainable Design Guide,* itself cowritten by Richard Strong, director of facilities.

22   The position of fifth-year intern is now a permanent one-year position, and its salary is a regular part of the budget.

23   What's next? If Carleton gets a grant it has applied for, there will be a massive increase in environmental-studies courses and faculty seminars and, says the dean of budgets, "a whole range of green campus projects under the rubric of 'participatory learning.'"

24   And if Carleton doesn't get the grant? Same plans, slower pace.

25   Twenty years ago, **Dartmouth College** would have been a contender for the title of greenest college in America, had such a title existed. It's still fairly green. It has a large and distinguished group of faculty members who teach environmental studies, good recycling, an organic farm that was used last summer in six courses, years of experience with solar panels, and a fair number of midlevel administrators (including three in the purchasing office) who are ardent believers in sustainability.

26   But the college has lost ground. Most troubling is its new $50-million library, which has an actual anti-environmental twist: A portion of the roof requires steam from the power plant to melt snow off of it. The architect, Robert Venturi, may be famous, but he's no environmentalist.

27   Dartmouth is a striking example of what I shall modestly call Perrin's Law: No college or university can move far toward sustainability without the active support of at least two senior administrators. Dartmouth has no such committed senior administrators at all. It used to. James Hornig, a former dean of sciences, and Frank Smallwood, a former provost, were instrumental in creating the environmental-studies program, back in 1970. They are now emeriti. The current senior administrators are not in the least hostile to sustainability; they just give a very low priority to the college's practicing what it preaches.

28   **Emory University** is probably further into the use of nonpolluting and low-polluting motor vehicles than any other college in the country. According to Eric Gaither, senior associate vice president for business affairs, 60 percent of Emory's fleet is powered by alternative fuels. The facilities-management office has 40 electric carts, which maintenance workers use for getting around campus. The community-service office (security and parking) has its own electric carts and an electric patrol vehicle. There are five electric shuttle buses and 14 compressed–natural-gas buses on order, plus one natural-gas bus in service.

29   Bill Chace, Emory's president, has a battery-charging station for electric cars in his garage, and until recently an electric car to charge. Georgia Power, which lent the car, has recalled it, but Chace hopes to get it back. Meanwhile, he rides his bike to work most of the time.

30   How has Emory made such giant strides? "It's easy to do," says Gaither, "when your president wants you to."

31   If Carleton is a model of how a small college turns green, the **University of Michigan at Ann Arbor** is a model of how a big university does. Carleton is changing pretty much as an entity, while Michigan is more like the Electoral College—50 separate entities. The School of Natural Resources casts its 6 votes

for sustainability, the English department casts its 12 for humanistic studies, the recycling coordinator casts her 1, the electric-vehicle program casts its 2, and so on. An institution of Michigan's size changes in bits and pieces.

Some of the bits show true leadership. For example, the university is within 32 weeks of buying a modest amount of green power. It makes about half of its own electricity (at its heating plant) and buys the other half. Five percent of that other half soon will come from renewable sources: hydro (water power) and biomass (so-called fuel crops, which are grown specifically to be burned for power).

The supporters of sustainability at Michigan would like to see the university 33 adopt a version of what is known as the Kyoto Protocol. The agreement, which the United States so far has refused to sign, requires that by 2012 each nation reduce its emission of greenhouse gases to 7 percent below its 1990 figure. Michigan's version of the protocol, at present a pipe dream, would require the university to do what the government won't—accept that reduction as a goal.

The immediate goal of "sustainabilists" at Ann Arbor is the creation of a 34 universitywide environmental coordinator, who would work either in the president's or the provost's office.

Giants are slow, but they are also strong.   35

Tulane University has the usual programs, among green institutions, in 36 recycling, composting, and energy efficiency. But what sets it apart is the Tulane Environmental Law Clinic, which is staffed by third-year law students. The director is a faculty member, and there are three law "fellows," all lawyers, who work with the students. The clinic does legal work for environmental organizations across Louisiana and "most likely has had a greater environmental impact than all our other efforts combined," says Elizabeth Davey, Tulane's first-ever environmental coordinator.

At least two campuses of the **University of California** (Berkeley is not among 37 them) have taken a first and even a second step toward sustainable behavior. First step: symbolic action, like installing a few solar panels, to produce clean energy and to help educate students. With luck, one of those little solar arrays might produce as much as a 20th of a percent of the electricity the university uses. It's a start.

The two campuses are Davis and Santa Cruz, and I think Davis nudges 38 ahead of Santa Cruz. That is primarily because Davis the city and Davis the university have done something almost miraculous. They have brought car culture at least partially under control, greatly reducing air pollution as a result.

The city has a population of about 58,000, which includes 24,000 students. 39 According to reliable estimates, there are something over 50,000 bikes in town or on the campus, all but a few hundred owned by their riders. Most of the bikes are used regularly on the city's 45 miles of bike paths (closed to cars) and the 47 miles of bike lanes (cars permitted in the other lanes). The university maintains an additional 14 miles of bike paths on its large campus.

40   What happens on rainy days? "A surprising number continue to bike," says David Takemoto-Weerts, coordinator of Davis's bicycle program.

41   If every American college in a suitable climate were to behave like Davis, we could close a medium-sized oil refinery. Maybe we could even get rid of one coal-fired power plant, and thus seriously improve air quality.

42   The **University of New Hampshire** is trying to jump straight from symbolic gestures, like installing a handful of solar panels, to the hardest task of all for an institution trying to become green—establishing a completely new mindset among students, administrators, and faculty and staff members. It may well succeed.

43   Campuses that have managed to change attitudes are rare. Prescott College, in Prescott, Ariz., and Sterling College, in Craftsbury Common, Vt., are rumored to have done so, and there may be two or three others. They're not on my list—because they're so small, because their students tend to be bright green even before they arrive, and because I have limited space.

44   New Hampshire has several token green projects, including a tiny solar array, able to produce one kilowatt at noon on a good day. And last April it inaugurated the Yellow Bike Cooperative. It is much smaller than anything that happens at Davis, where a bike rack might be a hundred yards long. But it's also more original and more communitarian. Anyone in Durham—student, burger flipper, associate dean—can join the Yellow Bike program by paying a $5 fee.

45   What you get right away is a key that unlocks all 50 bikes owned by the cooperative. (They are repaired and painted by student volunteers.) Want to cross campus? Just go to the nearest bike rack, unlock a Yellow, and pedal off. The goal, says Julie Newman, of the Office of Sustainability Programs, is "to greatly decrease one-person car trips on campus."

46   But the main thrust at New Hampshire is consciousness-raising. When the subject of composting food waste came up, the university held a seminar for its food workers.

47   New Hampshire's striking vigor is partly the result of a special endowment—about $12.8 million—exclusively for the sustainability office. Tom Kelly, the director, refuses to equate sustainability with greenness. Being green, in the sense of avoiding pollution and promoting reuse, is just one aspect of living sustainably, which involves "the balancing of economic viability with ecological health and human well-being," he says.

48   **Oberlin College** is an exception to Perrin's Law. The college has gotten deeply into environmental behavior without the active support of two or, indeed, any senior administrators. As at Dartmouth, the top people are not hostile; they just have other priorities.

49   Apparently, until this year, Oberlin's environmental-studies program was housed in a dreary cellar. Now it's in the $8.2-million Adam Joseph Lewis Environmental Studies Center, which is one of the most environmentally benign college buildings in the world. The money for it was raised as a result of a deal that the department chairman, David Orr, made with the administration:

He could raise money for his own program, provided that he approached only people and foundations that had never shown the faintest interest in Oberlin.

It's too soon for a full report on the building. It is loaded with solar panels— 50 690 of them, covering the roof (for a diagram of the building, see www.oberlin .edu/newserv/esc/escabout.html). In about a year, data will be available on how much energy the panels have saved and whether, as Orr hopes, the center will not only make all its own power, but even export some.

Northland College, in Wisconsin, also goes way beyond tokenism. Its 51 McLean Environmental Living and Learning Center, a two-year-old residence hall for 114 students, is topped by a 120-foot wind tower that, with a good breeze coming off Lake Superior, can generate 20 kilowatts of electricity. The building also includes three arrays of solar panels. They are only token-size, generating a total of 3.2 kilowatts at most. But one array does heat most of the water for one wing of McLean, while the other three form a test project.

One test array is fixed in place—it can't be aimed. Another is like that 52 sunflower in Blake's poem—it countest the steps of the sun. Put more prosaically, it tracks the sun across the sky each day. The third array does that and can also be tilted to get the best angle for each season of the year.

Inside the dorm is a pair of composting toilets—an experiment, to see if 53 students will use them. Because no one is forced to try the new ones if they don't want to—plenty of conventional toilets are close by—it means something when James Miller, vice president and dean of student development and enrollment, reports, "Students almost always choose the composting bathrooms."

From the start, the college's goal has been to have McLean operate so effi- 54 ciently that it consumes 40 percent less outside energy than would a conventional dormitory of the same dimensions. The building didn't reach that goal in its first year; energy use dropped only 34.2 percent. But anyone dealing with a new system knows to expect bugs at the beginning. There were some at Northland, including the wind generator's being down for three months. (As I write, it's turning busily.) Dean Miller is confident that the building will meet or exceed the college's energy-efficiency goal.

There is no room here to talk about the octagonal classroom structure made 55 of bales of straw, built largely by students. Or about the fact that Northland's grounds are pesticide- and herbicide-free.

If Oberlin is a flagrant exception to Perrin's Law, **Middlebury College** is 56 a strong confirmation. Middlebury is unique, as far as I know, in having not only senior administrators who strongly back environmentalism, but one senior administrator right inside the program. What Michigan wants, Middlebury has.

Nan Jenks-Jay, director of environmental affairs, reports directly to the 57 provost. She is responsible for both the teaching side and the living-sustainably side of environmentalism. Under her are an environmental coordinator, Amy Self, and an academic-program coordinator, Janet Wiseman.

58   The program has powerful backers, including the president, John M. McCardell Jr.; the provost and executive vice president, Ronald D. Liebowitz; and the executive vice president for facilities planning, David W. Ginevan. But everyone I talked with at Middlebury, except for the occasional student who didn't want to trouble his mind with things like returnable bottles—to say nothing of acid rain—seemed at least somewhat committed to sustainable living.

59   Middlebury has what I think is the oldest environmental-studies program in the country; it began back in 1965. It has the best composting program I've ever seen. And, like Northland, it is pesticide- and herbicide-free.

60   Let me end as I began, with Harvard, Yale, and Princeton. And with *U.S. News*'s consistently ranking them in the top five, accompanied from time to time by the California Institute of Technology, Stanford University, and the Massachusetts Institute of Technology.

61   What if *U.S. News* did a green ranking? What if it based the listings on one of the few bits of hard data that can be widely compared: the percentage of waste that a college recycles?

62   Harvard would come out okay, though hardly at the top. The university recycled 24 percent of its waste last year, thanks in considerable part to the presence of Rob Gogan, the waste manager. He hopes to achieve 28 percent this year. That's feeble compared with Brown's 35 percent, and downright puny against Middlebury's 64 percent.

63   But compared with Yale and Princeton, it's magnificent. Most of the information I could get from Princeton is sadly dated. It comes from the 1995 report of the Princeton Environmental Reform Committee, whose primary recommendation was that the university hire a full-time waste manager. The university has not yet done so. And if any administrators on the campus know the current recycling percentage, they're not telling.

64   And Yale—poor Yale! It does have a figure. Among the performances of the 20 or so other colleges and universities whose percentages I'm aware of, only Carnegie Mellon's is worse. Yale: 19 percent. Carnegie Mellon: 11 percent.

65   What should universities—and society—be shooting for? How can you ask? One-hundred-percent retrieval of everything retrievable, of course.

COMPREHENSION

1. Why does Perrin call his essay an "idiosyncratic guide" when environmentalism has become a major issue in most municipalities, regions, and countries?
2. Is Perrin's purpose to inform, argue, or both? Does he have a clear-cut thesis, or does he leave it up to the reader to infer the thesis? Explain.
3. What information is Perrin's informal guide providing that is not offered in more conventional college rankings? Is he suggesting that parents and students consider "green rankings" in choosing which college to apply to? Explain.

RHETORIC

1. What purpose might Perrin have for choosing to create a "green guide" for colleges when there are so many other institutions or items he could have selected for review, such as corporations, towns, cities, automobiles, and numerous household products? What makes colleges and universities a particularly apt target?
2. Usually, Ivy League colleges are at the top of college guide lists as most desirable. Where do they rank on Perrin's list? What ironic statement is Perrin making by providing their rankings on the "green scale"? What is he implying about American values, particularly as they pertain to education?
3. Colleges and universities often pride themselves on the renown of their faculties. Who are the people Perrin cites as models of academic worth? Why has he chosen them?
4. What is the ironic purpose behind the author mentioning "Perrin's Law" (paragraph 27)? Is it a true "law," like the law of gravity? What body of knowledge is the author satirizing by invoking such a law?
5. Perrin is not didactic, since he does not recommend that other colleges adopt the environmental measures his model colleges have chosen. Would more direct advocacy on his part have strengthened his argument or weakened it, or not have had any effect? Explain.
6. In Perrin's conclusion, he changes his purpose from providing a purely informational assessment to offering a strong reprimand and recommendation. Why does he wait until the concluding paragraph to do so?

WRITING

1. Describe an environmentally friendly practice conducted at your college or university. Is it truly helpful for the environment, or is it largely symbolic?
2. Compare and contrast the academically oriented courses and programs offered at your school with what your institution actually does in the way of helping the environment. Discuss which of the two priorities is more prominent, and why.
3. **Writing an Argument:** Argue for or against the proposition that a magazine such as *U.S. News & World Report* should include environmental awareness and practice in its formula for assessing the rankings of colleges.

NETWORKING
Applying 21st-Century Literacies

Creating a Facebook Group for a Cause: With several of your classmates, create a Facebook group that calls for action or raises awareness about an environmental issue or natural space that is relevant to your campus or local community. Consider carefully what you'll call the group (names are important!), and in a mission statement, articulate what you hope to accomplish by organizing it.

The Last Americans: Environmental Collapse and the End of Civilization

Jared Diamond

Jared Diamond (b. 1937), who was born in Boston, is a physiologist, ecologist, and prolific writer who has published hundreds of popular and scientific articles. He has a BA from Harvard University (1958) and a PhD from Cambridge University (1961). Currently a professor of geography at UCLA and formerly professor of physiology at UCLA's School of Medicine, Diamond has conducted research in ecology and evolutionary biology in New Guinea and other southwest Pacific islands. As a field researcher and director of the World Wildlife Fund, Diamond helped to establish New Guinea's national park system. He received the Pulitzer prize for Guns, Germs, and Steel: The Fates of Human Societies *(1997). Another well-received book of Diamonds's is* Collapse: How Societies Choose to Fail or Succeed *(2004). In the following essay, which appeared in the June 2003 issue of* Harper's, *Diamond examines the environmental crises and failures of previous societies and civilizations, and how we might be able to learn lessons from these lost worlds.*

I met a traveler from an antique land
Who said: Two vast and trunkless legs of stone
Stand in the desert. . . . Near them, on the sand,
Half sunk, a shattered visage lies, whose frown,
And wrinkled lip, and sneer of cold command,
Tell that its sculptor well those passions read
Which yet survive, stamped on these lifeless things,
The hand that mocked them, and the heart that fed:
And on the pedestal these words appear:
"My name is Ozymandias, king of kings:
Look on my works, ye Mighty, and despair!"
Nothing beside remains. Round the decay
Of that colossal wreck, boundless and bare
The lone and level sands stretch far away.

—"Ozymandias," Percy Bysshe Shelley

1   One of the disturbing facts of history is that so many civilizations collapse. Few people, however, least of all our politicians, realize that a primary cause of the collapse of those societies has been the destruction of the environmental resources on which they depended. Fewer still appreciate that many of those civilizations share a sharp curve of decline. Indeed, a society's demise may begin only a decade or two after it reaches its peak population, wealth, and power.

Recent archaeological discoveries have revealed similar courses of collapse 2
in such otherwise dissimilar ancient societies as the Maya in the Yucatán, the
Anasazi in the American Southwest, the Cahokia mound builders outside
St. Louis, the Greenland Norse, the statue builders of Easter Island, ancient
Mesopotamia in the Fertile Crescent, Great Zimbabwe in Africa, and Angkor
Wat in Cambodia. These civilizations, and many others, succumbed to various
combinations of environmental degradation and climate change, aggression
from enemies taking advantage of their resulting weakness, and declining trade
with neighbors who faced their own environmental problems. Because peak
population, wealth, resource consumption, and waste production are accompanied by peak environmental impact—approaching the limit at which impact
outstrips resources—we can now understand why declines of societies tend to
follow swiftly on their peaks.

These combinations of undermining factors were compounded by cultural 3
attitudes preventing those in power from perceiving or resolving the crisis.
That's a familiar problem today. Some of us are inclined to dismiss the importance of a healthy environment, or at least to suggest that it's just one of many
problems facing us—an "issue." That dismissal is based on three dangerous
misconceptions.

Foremost among these misconceptions is that we must balance the environ- 4
ment against human needs. That reasoning is exactly upside-down. Human
needs and a healthy environment are not opposing claims that must be balanced; instead, they are inexorably linked by chains of cause and effect. We
need a healthy environment because we need clean water, clean air, wood, and
food from the ocean, plus soil and sunlight to grow crops. We need functioning
natural ecosystems, with their native species of earthworms, bees, plants, and
microbes, to generate and aerate our soils, pollinate our crops, decompose our
wastes, and produce our oxygen. We need to prevent toxic substances from ac-
cumulating in our water and air and soil. We need to prevent weeds, germs,
and other pest species from becoming established in places where they aren't
native and where they cause economic damage. Our strongest arguments for a
healthy environment are selfish: We want it for ourselves, not for threatened
species like snail darters, spotted owls, and Furbish louseworts.

5   Another popular misconception is that we can trust in technology to solve our problems. Whatever environmental problem you name, you can also name some hoped-for technological solution under discussion. Some of us have faith that we shall solve our dependence on fossil fuels by developing new technologies for hydrogen engines, wind energy, or solar energy. Some of us have faith that we shall solve our food problems with new or soon-to-be-developed genetically modified crops. Some of us have faith that new technologies will succeed in cleaning up the toxic materials in our air, water, soil, and foods without the horrendous cleanup expenses that we now incur.

6   Those with such faith assume that the new technologies will ultimately succeed, but in fact some of them may succeed and others may not. They assume that the new technologies will succeed quickly enough to make a big difference soon, but all of these major technological changes will actually take five to thirty years to develop and implement—if they catch on at all. Most of all, those with faith assume that new technology won't cause any new problems. In fact, technology merely constitutes increased power, which produces changes that can be either for the better or for the worse. All of our current environmental problems are unanticipated harmful consequences of our existing technology. There is no basis for believing that technology will miraculously stop causing new and unanticipated problems while it is solving the problems that it previously produced.

7   The final misconception holds that environmentalists are fear-mongering, overreacting extremists whose predictions of impending disaster have been proved wrong before and will be proved wrong again. Behold, say the optimists: Water still flows from our faucets, the grass is still green, and the supermarkets are full of food. We are more prosperous than ever before, and that's the final proof that our system works.

8   Well, for a few billion of the world's people who are causing us increasing trouble, there isn't any clean water, there is less and less green grass, and there are no supermarkets full of food. To appreciate what the environmental problems of those billions of people mean for us Americans, compare the following two lists of countries. First ask some ivory-tower academic ecologist who knows a lot about the environment but never reads a newspaper and has no interest in politics to list the overseas countries facing some of the worst problems of environmental stress, overpopulation, or both. The ecologist would answer, "That's a no-brainer, it's obvious. Your list of environmentally stressed or overpopulated countries should surely include Afghanistan, Bangladesh, Burundi, Haiti, Indonesia, Iraq, Nepal, Pakistan, the Philippines, Rwanda, the Solomon Islands, and Somalia, plus others." Then ask a First World politician who knows nothing, and cares less, about the environment and population problems to list the world's worst trouble spots: countries where state government has already been overwhelmed and has collapsed, or is now at risk of collapsing, or has been wracked by recent civil wars; and countries that, as a result of their problems, are also creating problems for us rich First World countries, which may be deluged by illegal immigrants, or have to provide foreign aid to those countries, or

may decide to provide them with military assistance to deal with rebellions and terrorists, or may even (God forbid) have to send in our own troops. The politician would answer, "That's a no-brainer, it's obvious. Your list of political trouble spots should surely include Afghanistan, Bangladesh, Burundi, Haiti, Indonesia, Iraq, Nepal, Pakistan, the Philippines, Rwanda, the Soloman Islands, and Somalia, plus others."

The connection between the two lists is transparent. Today, just as in the past, countries that are environmentally stressed, overpopulated or both are at risk of becoming politically stressed, and of seeing their governments collapse. When people are desperate and undernourished, they blame their government, which they see as responsible for failing to solve their problems. They try to emigrate at any cost. They start civil wars. They kill one another. They figure that they have nothing to lose, so they become terrorists, or they support or tolerate terrorism. The results are genocides such as the ones that already have exploded in Burundi, Indonesia, and Rwanda; civil wars, as in Afghanistan, Indonesia, Nepal, the Philippines, and the Solomon Islands; calls for the dispatch of First World troops, as to Afghanistan, Indonesia, Iraq, the Philippines, Rwanda, the Solomon Islands, and Somalia; the collapse of central government, as has already happened in Somalia; and overwhelming poverty, as in all of the countries on these lists.

But what about the United States? Some might argue that the environmental collapse of ancient societies is relevant to the modern decline of weak, far-off, overpopulated Rwanda and environmentally devastated Somalia, but isn't it ridiculous to suggest any possible relevance to the fate of our own society?

After all, we might reason, those ancients didn't enjoy the wonders of modern environment-friendly technologies. Those ancients had the misfortune to suffer from the effects of climate change. They behaved stupidly and ruined their own environment by doing obviously dumb things, like cutting down their forests, watching their topsoil erode, and building cities in dry areas likely to run short of water. They had foolish leaders who didn't have books and so couldn't learn from history, and who embroiled them in destabilizing wars and didn't pay attention to problems at home. They were overwhelmed by desperate immigrants, as one society after another collapsed, sending floods of economic refugees to tax the resources of the societies that weren't collapsing. In all those respects, we modern Americans are fundamentally different from those primitive ancients, and there is nothing that we could learn from them.

11   Or so the argument goes. It's an argument so ingrained both in our subconscious and in public discourse that it has assumed the status of objective reality. We think we are different. In fact, of course, all of those powerful societies of the past thought that they too were unique, right up to the moment of their collapse. It's sobering to consider the swift decline of the ancient Maya, who 1,200 years ago were themselves the most advanced society in the Western Hemisphere, and who, like us now, were then at the apex of their own power and numbers. Two excellent recent books, David Webster's *The Fall of the Ancient Maya* and Richardson Gill's *The Great Maya Droughts,* help bring the trajectory of Maya civilization back to life for us. Their studies illustrate how even sophisticated societies like that of the Maya (and ours) can be undermined by details of rainfall, farming methods, and motives of leaders.

12 By now, millions of modern Americans have visited Maya ruins. To do so, one need only take a direct flight from the United States to the Yucatán capital of Mérida, jump into a rental car or minibus, and drive an hour on a paved highway. Most Maya ruins, with their great temples and monuments, lie surrounded by jungles (seasonal tropical forests), far from current human settlement. They are "pure" archaeological sites. That is, their locations became depopulated, so they were not covered up by later buildings as were so many other ancient cities, like the Aztec capital of Tenochtitlán—now buried under modern Mexico City—and Rome.

13   One of the reasons few people live there now is that the Maya homeland poses serious environmental challenges to would-be farmers. Although it has a somewhat unpredictable rainy season from May to October, it also has a dry season from January through April. Indeed, if one focuses on the dry months, one could describe the Yucatán as a "seasonal desert."

14   Complicating things, from a farmer's perspective, is that the part of the Yucatán with the most rain, the south, is also the part at the highest elevation above the water table. Most of the Yucatán consists of karst—a porous, sponge-like, limestone terrain—and so rain runs straight into the ground, leaving little or no surface water. The Maya in the lower-elevation regions of the north were able to reach the water table by way of deep sinkholes called cenotes, and the

Maya in low coastal areas without sinkholes could reach it by digging wells up to 75 feet deep. Most Maya, however, lived in the south. How did they deal with their resulting water problem?

Technology provided an answer. The Maya plugged up leaks on karst 15 promontories by plastering the bottoms of depressions to create reservoirs, which collected rain and stored it for use in the dry season. The reservoirs at the Maya city of Tikal, for example, held enough water to meet the needs of about 10,000 people for eighteen months. If a drought lasted longer than that, though, the inhabitants of Tikal were in deep trouble.

Maya farmers grew mostly corn, which constituted the astonishingly high 16 proportion of about 70 percent of their diet, as deduced from isotope analyses of ancient Maya skeletons. They grew corn by means of a modified version of swidden slash-and-burn agriculture, in which forest is cleared, crops are grown in the resulting clearing for a few years until the soil is exhausted, and then the field is abandoned for fifteen to twenty years until regrowth of wild vegetation restores the soil's fertility. Because most of the land under a swidden agricultural system is fallow at any given time, it can support only modest population densities. Thus, it was a surprise for archaeologists to discover that ancient Maya population densities, judging from numbers of stone foundations of farmhouses, were often far higher than what unmodified swidden agriculture could support: often 250 to 750 people per square mile. The Maya probably achieved those high populations by such means as shortening the fallow period and tilling the soil to restore soil fertility, or omitting the fallow period entirely and growing crops every year, or, in especially moist areas, growing two crops per year.

Socially stratified societies, ours included, consist of farmers who produce 17 food, plus nonfarmers such as bureaucrats and soldiers who do not produce food and are in effect parasites on farmers. The farmers must grow enough food to meet not only their own needs but also those of everybody else. The number of nonproducing consumers who can be supported depends on the society's agricultural productivity. In the United States today, with its highly efficient agriculture, farmers make up only 2 percent of our population, and each farmer can feed, on the average, 129 other people. Ancient Egyptian agriculture was efficient enough for an Egyptian peasant to produce five times the food required for himself and his family. But a Maya peasant could produce only twice the needs of himself and his family.

18   Fully 80 percent of Maya society consisted of peasants. Their inability to support many nonfarmers resulted from several limitations of their agriculture. It produced little protein, because corn has much lower protein content than wheat, and because the few edible domestic animals kept by the Maya (turkeys, ducks, and dogs) included no large animals like our cows and sheep. There was little use of terracing or irrigation to increase production. In the Maya area's humid climate, stored corn would rot or become infested after a year, so the Maya couldn't get through a longer drought by eating surplus corn accumulated in good years. And unlike Old World peoples with their horses, oxen, donkeys, and camels, the Maya had no animal-powered transport. Indeed, the Maya lacked not only pack animals and animal-drawn plows but also metal tools, wheels, and boats with sails. All of those great Maya temples were built by stone and wooden tools and human muscle power alone, and all overland transport went on the backs of human porters.

19   Those limitations on food supply and food transport may in part explain why Maya society remained politically organized in small kingdoms that were perpetually at war with one another and that never became unified into large empires like the Aztec empire of the Valley of Mexico (fed by highly productive agriculture) or the Inca empire of the Andes (fed by diverse crops carried on llamas). Maya armies were small and unable to mount lengthy campaigns over long distances. The typical Maya kingdom held a population of only up to 50,000 people, within a radius of two or three days' walk from the king's palace. From the top of the temple of some Maya kingdoms, one could see the tops of the temples of other kingdoms.

20   Presiding over the temple was the king himself, who functioned both as head priest and as political leader. It was his responsibility to pray to the gods, to perform astronomical and calendrical rituals, to ensure the timely arrival of the rains on which agriculture depended, and thereby to bring prosperity. The king claimed to have the supernatural power to deliver those good things because of his asserted family relationship to the gods. Of course, that exposed him to the risk that his subjects would become disillusioned if he couldn't fulfill his boast of being able to deliver rains and prosperity.

21   Those are the basic outlines of Classic Maya society, which for all its limitations lasted more than 500 years. Indeed, the Maya themselves believed that it had lasted for much longer. Their remarkable Long Count calendar had its starting date (analogous to January 1, A.D. 1 of our calendar) backdated into the remote

preliterate past, at August 11, 3114 B.C. The first physical evidence of civilization within the Maya area, in the form of villagers and pottery, appeared around 1400 B.C., substantial buildings around 500 B.C., and writing around 400 B.C. The so-called Classic period of Maya history arose around A.D. 250, when evidence for the first kings and dynasties emerged. From then, the Maya population increased almost exponentially, to reach peak numbers in the eighth century A.D. The largest monuments were erected toward the end of that century. All the indicators of a complex society declined throughout the ninth century, until the last date on any monument was A.D. 909. This decline of Maya population and architecture constitutes what is known as the Classic Maya collapse.

What happened? Let's consider in more detail a city whose ruins now lie in   22 western Honduras at the world-famous site of Copán. The most fertile ground in the Copán area consists of five pockets of flat land along a river valley with a total area of only one square mile; the largest of those five pockets, known as the Copán pocket, has an area of half a square mile. Much of the land around Copán consists of steep hills with poor soil. Today, corn yields from valley-bottom fields are two or three times those of fields on hill slopes, which suffer rapid erosion and lose most of their productivity within a decade of farming.

To judge by the number of house sites, population growth in the Copán   23 valley rose steeply from the fifth century up to a peak estimated at around 27,000 people between A.D. 750 and 900. Construction of royal monuments glorifying kings became especially massive from A.D. 650 onward. After A.D. 700, nobles other than kings got into the act and began erecting their own palaces, increasing the burden that the king and his own court already imposed on the peasants. The last big buildings at Copán were put up around A.D. 800; the last date on an incomplete altar possibly bearing a king's name is A.D. 822.

Archaeological surveys of different types of habitats in the Copán valley   24 show that they were occupied in a regular sequence. The first area farmed was the large Copán pocket of bottomland, followed by occupation of the other four bottomland pockets. During that time the human population was growing, but the hills remained uninhabited. Hence that increased population must have been accommodated by intensifying production in the bottomland pockets: probably some combination of shorter fallow periods and double-cropping. By A.D. 500, people had started to settle the hill slopes, but those sites were occupied only briefly. The percentage of Copán's total population that was in the hills, rather than in the valleys, peaked in the year 575 and then declined, as the population again became concentrated in the pockets.

What caused that pullback of population from the hills? From excavation of   25 building foundations on the valley floor we know that they became covered with sediment during the eighth century, meaning that the hill slopes were becoming eroded and probably also leached of nutrients. The acidic hill soils being carried down into the valley would have reduced agricultural yields. The reason for that erosion of the hillsides is clear: the forests that formerly covered them and protected their soil were being cut down. Dated pollen samples show that the pine forests originally covering the hilltops were eventually all cleared, to be burned for fuel. Besides causing sediment accumulation in the valleys and depriving valley inhabitants of wood supplies, that deforestation may have begun to cause a "man-made drought" in the valley bottom, because forests play a major role in water cycling, such that massive deforestation tends to result in lowered rainfall.

26   Hundreds of skeletons recovered from Copán archaeological sites have been studied for signs of disease and poor nutrition, such as porous bones and stress lines in the teeth. Those skeletal signs show that the health of Copán's inhabitants deteriorated from A.D. 650 to 850, among both the elite and commoners, though the health of commoners was worse.

27   Recall that Copán's population was growing rapidly while the hills were being occupied. The subsequent abandonment of all of those hill fields meant that the burden of feeding the extra population formerly dependent on the hills now fell increasingly on the valley floor, and that more and more people were competing for the food grown on that one square mile of bottomland. That would have led to fighting among the farmers themselves for the best land, or for any land, just as in modern Rwanda. Because the king was failing to deliver on his promises of rain and prosperity, he would have been the scapegoat for this agricultural failure, which explains why the last that we hear of any king is A.D. 822, and why the royal palace was burned around A.D. 850.

28   Datable pieces of obsidian, the sharp rock from which the Maya made their stone tools, suggest that Copán's total population decreased more gradually than did its signs of kings and nobles. The estimated population in the year A.D. 950 was still around 15,000, or 55 percent of the peak population of 27,000. That population continued to dwindle, until there are few signs of anyone in the Copán valley after around A.D. 1235. The reappearance of pollen from forest trees thereafter provides independent evidence that the valley became virtually empty of people.

29 The Maya history that I have just related, and Copán's history in particular, illustrate why we talk about "the Maya collapse." But the story grows more complicated, for at least five reasons. There was not only that enormous Classic collapse but also at least two smaller pre-Classic collapses, around A.D. 150 and 600, as well as some post-Classic collapses. The Classic collapse was obviously not complete, because hundreds of thousands of Maya survived, in areas with stable water supplies, to meet and fight the Spaniards. The collapse of population (as gauged by numbers of house sites and of obsidian tools) was in some cases much slower than the decline in numbers of Long Count dates. Many apparent collapses of cities were nothing more than "power cycling"; i.e., particular cities becoming more powerful at the expense of neighboring cities, then declining or getting conquered by neighbors, without changes in the whole population. Finally, cities in different parts of the Maya area rose and fell on different trajectories.

30   Some archaeologists focus on these complications and don't want to recognize a Classic Maya collapse at all. But this overlooks the obvious fact that cries

out for explanation: the disappearance of between 90 and 99 percent of the Maya population after A.D. 800, and of the institution of the kingship, Long Count calendars, and other complex political and cultural institutions. Before we can understand those disappearances, however, we need first to understand the roles of warfare and of drought.

Archaeologists for a long time believed the ancient Maya to be gentle and 31 peaceful people. We now know that Maya warfare was intense, chronic, and unresolvable, because limitations of food supply and transportation made it impossible for any Maya principality to unite the whole region in an empire. The archaeological record shows that wars became more intense and frequent toward the time of the Classic collapse. That evidence comes from discoveries of several types since the Second World War: archaeological excavations of massive fortifications surrounding many Maya sites; vivid depictions of warfare and captives on stone monuments and on the famous painted murals discovered in 1946 at Bonampak; and the decipherment of Maya writing, much of which proved to consist of royal inscriptions boasting of conquests. Maya kings fought to capture and torture one another; an unfortunate loser was a Copán king with the to us unforgettable name of King 18 Rabbit.

Maya warfare involved well-documented types of violence: wars among 32 separate kingdoms; attempts of cities within a kingdom to secede by revolting against the capital; and civil wars resulting from frequent violent attempts by would-be kings to usurp the throne. All of these events were described or depicted on monuments, because they involved kings and nobles. Not considered worthy of description, but probably even more frequent, were fights between commoners over land, as overpopulation became excessive and land became scarce.

The other phenomenon important to understanding all of these collapses is 33 the repeated occurrence of droughts, as inferred by climatologists from evidence of lake evaporation preserved in lake sediments, and as summarized by Gill in *The Great Maya Droughts.* The rise of Maya civilization may have been facilitated by a rainy period beginning around 250 B.C., until a temporary drought after A.D. 125 was associated with a pre-Classic collapse at some sites. That collapse was followed by the resumption of rainy conditions and the buildup of Classic Maya cities, briefly interrupted by another drought around 600 corresponding to a decline at Tikal and some other sites. Finally, around A.D. 750 there began the worst drought in the past 7,000 years, peaking around the year A.D. 800, and suspiciously associated with the Classic collapse.

The area most affected by the Classic collapse was the southern highlands, 34 probably for the two reasons already mentioned: It was the area with the densest population, and it also had the most severe water problems because it lay too high above the water table for cenotes or wells to provide water. The southern highlands lost more than 99 percent of its population in the course of the Classic collapse. When Cortés and his Spanish army marched in 1524 and 1525 through an area formerly inhabited by millions of Maya, he nearly starved because he encountered so few villagers from whom to acquire corn. The Spaniards passed within only a few miles of the abandoned ruins of the great Classic cities of Tikal and Palenque, but still they heard or saw nothing of them.

35 We can identify increasingly familiar strands in the Classic Maya collapse. One consisted of population growth outstripping available resources: the dilemma foreseen by Thomas Malthus in 1798. As Webster succinctly puts it in *The Fall of the Ancient Maya*, "Too many farmers grew too many crops on too much of the landscape." While population was increasing, the area of usable farmland paradoxically was decreasing from the effects of deforestation and hillside erosion.

36   The next strand consisted of increased fighting as more and more people fought over fewer resources. Maya warfare, already endemic, peaked just before the collapse. That is not surprising when one reflects that at least 5 million people, most of them farmers, were crammed into an area smaller than the state of Colorado. That's a high population by the standards of ancient farming societies, even if it wouldn't strike modern Manhattan-dwellers as crowded.

37   Bringing matters to a head was a drought that, although not the first one the Maya had been through, was the most severe. At the time of previous droughts, there were still uninhabited parts of the Maya landscape, and people in a drought area or dust bowl could save themselves by moving to another site. By the time of the Classic collapse, however, there was no useful unoccupied land in the vicinity on which to begin anew, and the whole population could not be accommodated in the few areas that continued to have reliable water supplies.

38   The final strand is political. Why did the kings and nobles not recognize and solve these problems? A major reason was that their attention was evidently focused on the short-term concerns of enriching themselves, waging wars, erecting monuments, competing with one another, and extracting enough food from the peasants to support all those activities. Like most leaders

throughout human history, the Maya kings and nobles did not have the leisure to focus on long-term problems, insofar as they perceived them.

What about those same strands today? The United States is also at the peak of its power, and it is also suffering from many environmental problems. Most of us have become aware of more crowding and stress. Most of us living in large American cities are encountering increased commuting delays, because the number of people and hence of cars is increasing faster than the number of freeway lanes. I know plenty of people who in the abstract doubt that the world has a population problem, but almost all of those same people complain to me about crowding, space issues, and traffic experienced in their personal lives. 39

Many parts of the United States face locally severe problems of water restriction (especially southern California, Arizona, the Everglades, and, increasingly, the Northeast); forest fires resulting from logging and forest-management practices throughout the intermontane West; and losses of farmlands to salinization, drought, and climate change in the northern Great Plains. Many of us frequently experience problems of air quality, and some of us also experience problems of water quality and taste. We are losing economically valuable natural resources. We have already lost American chestnut trees, the Grand Banks cod fishery, and the Monterey sardine fishery; we are in the process of losing swordfish and tuna and Chesapeake Bay oysters and elm trees; and we are losing topsoil. 40

The list goes on: All of us are experiencing personal consequences of our national dependence on imported energy, which affects us not only through higher gas prices but also through the current contraction of the national economy, itself the partial result of political problems associated with our oil dependence. We are saddled with expensive toxic cleanups at many locations, most notoriously near Montana mines, on the Hudson River, and in the Chesapeake Bay. We also face expensive eradication problems resulting from hundreds of introduced pest species—including zebra mussels, Mediterranean fruit flies, Asian longhorn beetles, water hyacinth, and spotted knapweed—that now affect our agriculture, forests, waterways, and pastures. 41

These particular environmental problems, and many others, are enormously expensive in terms of resources lost, cleanup and restoration costs, and the cost of finding substitutes for lost resources: a billion dollars here, 10 billion there, in dozens and dozens of cases. Some of the problems, especially those of air quality and toxic substances, also exact health costs that are large, whether measured in dollars or in lost years or in quality of life. The cost of our homegrown environmental problems adds up to a large fraction of our gross national product, even without mentioning the costs that we incur from environmental problems overseas, such as the military operations that they inspire. Even the mildest of bad scenarios for our future include a gradual economic decline, as happened to the Roman and British empires. Actually, in case you didn't notice it, our economic decline is already well under way. Just check the numbers for 42 our national debt, yearly government budget deficit, unemployment statistics, and the value of your investment and pension funds.

43 The environmental problems of the United States are still modest compared with those of the rest of the world. But the problems of environmentally devastated, overpopulated, distant countries are now our problems as well. We are accustomed to thinking of globalization in terms of us rich, advanced First Worlders sending our good things, such as the Internet and Coca-Cola, to those poor backward Third Worlders. Globalization, however, means nothing more than improved worldwide communication and transportation, which can convey many things in either direction; it is not restricted to good things carried only from the First to the Third World. They in the Third World can now, intentionally or unintentionally, send us their bad things: terrorists; diseases such as AIDS, SARS, cholera, and West Nile fever, carried inadvertently by passengers on transcontinental airplanes; unstoppable numbers of immigrants, both legal and illegal, arriving by boat, truck, train, plane, and on foot; and other consequences of their Third World problems. We in the United States are no longer the isolated Fortress America to which some of us aspired in the 1930s; instead, we are tightly and irreversibly connected to overseas countries. The United States is the world's leading importer, and it is also the world's leading exporter. Our own society opted long ago to become interlocked with the rest of the world.

44   That's why political stability anywhere in the world now affects us, our trade routes, and our overseas markets and suppliers. We are so dependent on the rest of the world that if a decade ago you had asked a politician to name the

countries most geopolitically irrelevant to U.S. interests because of their being so remote, poor, and weak, the list would have begun with Afghanistan and Somalia, yet these countries were subsequently considered important enough to warrant our dispatching U.S. troops. The Maya were "globalized" only within the Yucatán: the southern Yucatán Maya affected the northern Yucatán Maya and may have had some effects on the Valley of Mexico, but they had no contact with Somalia. That's because Maya transportation was slow, short-distance, on foot or else in canoes, and had low cargo capacity. Our transport today is much more rapid and has much higher cargo capacity. The Maya lived in a globalized Yucatán; we live in a globalized world.

If all of this reasoning seems straightforward when expressed so bluntly, one 45
has to wonder: Why don't those in power today get the message? Why didn't the leaders of the Maya, Anasazi, and those other societies also recognize and solve their problems? What were the Maya thinking while they watched loggers clearing the last pine forests on the hills above Copán? Here, the past really is a useful guide to the present. It turns out that there are at least a dozen reasons why past societies failed to *anticipate* some problems before they developed, or failed to *perceive* problems that had already developed, or failed even to try to solve problems that they did perceive. All of those dozen reasons still can be seen operating today. Let me mention just three of them.

First, it's difficult to recognize a slow trend in some quantity that fluctuates 46
widely up and down anyway, such as seasonal temperature, annual rainfall, or economic indicators. That's surely why the Maya didn't recognize the oncoming drought until it was too late, given that rainfall in the Yucatán varies several-fold from year to year. Natural fluctuations also explain why it's only within the last few years that all climatologists have become convinced of the reality of climate change, and why our president still isn't convinced but thinks that we need more research to test for it.

Second, when a problem *is* recognized, those in power may not attempt to 47
solve it because of a clash between their short-term interests and the interests of the rest of us. Pumping that oil, cutting down those trees, and catching those fish may benefit the elite by bringing them money or prestige and yet be bad for society as a whole (including the children of the elite) in the long run. Maya kings were consumed by immediate concerns for their prestige (requiring more and bigger temples) and their success in the next war (requiring more followers), rather than for the happiness of commoners or of the next generation. Those people with the greatest power to make decisions in our own society today regularly make money from activities that may be bad for society as a whole and for their own children; those decision-makers include Enron executives, many land developers, and advocates of tax cuts for the rich.

Finally, it's difficult for us to acknowledge the wisdom of policies that clash 48
with strongly held values. For example, a belief in individual freedom and a distrust of big government are deeply ingrained in Americans, and they make sense under some circumstances and up to a certain point. But they also make

it hard for us to accept big government's legitimate role in ensuring that each individual's freedom to maximize the value of his or her land holdings doesn't decrease the value of the collective land of all Americans.

49 Not all societies make fatal mistakes. There are parts of the world where societies have unfolded for thousands of years without any collapse, such as Java, Tonga, and (until 1945) Japan. Today, Germany and Japan are successfully managing their forests, which are even expanding in area rather than shrinking. The Alaskan salmon fishery and the Australian lobster fishery are being managed sustainably. The Dominican Republic, hardly a rich country, nevertheless has set aside a comprehensive system of protected areas encompassing most of the country's natural habitats.

50   Is there any secret to explain why some societies acquire good environmental sense while others don't? Naturally, part of the answer depends on accidents of individual leaders' wisdom (or lack thereof). But part also depends upon whether a society is organized so as to minimize built-in clashes of interest between its decision-making elites and its masses. Given how our society is organized, the executives of Enron, Tyco, and Adelphi correctly calculated that their own interests would be best promoted by looting the company coffers, and that they would probably get away with most of their loot. A good example of a society that minimizes such clashes of interest is the Netherlands, whose citizens have perhaps the world's highest level of environmental awareness and of membership in environmental organizations. I never understood why, until on a recent trip to the Netherlands I posed the question to three of my Dutch friends while driving through their countryside.

51   Just look around you, they said. All of this farmland that you see lies below sea level. One fifth of the total area of the Netherlands is below sea level, as much as 22 feet below, because it used to be shallow bays, and we reclaimed it from the sea by surrounding the bays with dikes and then gradually pumping out the water. We call these reclaimed lands "polders." We began draining our polders nearly a thousand years ago. Today, we still have to keep pumping out the water that gradually seeps in. That's what our windmills used to be for, to drive the pumps to pump out the polders. Now we use steam, diesel, and electric pumps instead. In each polder there are lines of them, starting with those farthest from the sea, pumping the water in sequence until the last pump finally deposits it into a river or the ocean. And all of us, rich or poor, live down in the polders. It's not the case that rich people live safely up on top of the dikes while poor people live in the polder bottoms below sea level. If the dikes and pumps fail, we'll all drown together.

        Throughout human history, all peoples have been connected to some other
52 peoples, living together in virtual polders. For the ancient Maya, their polder consisted of most of the Yucatán and neighboring areas. When the Classic Maya cities collapsed in the southern Yucatán, refugees may have reached the northern Yucatán, but probably not the Valley of Mexico, and certainly not Florida. Today, our whole world has become one polder, such that events in even Afghanistan and Somalia affect Americans. We do indeed differ from the Maya, but not in

ways we might like: We have a much larger population, we have more potent destructive technology, and we face the risk of a worldwide rather than a local decline. Fortunately, we also differ from the Maya in that we know their fate, and they did not. Perhaps we can learn.

COMPREHENSION

1. Explain the significance of Shelley's poem "Ozymandias" for Diamond's essay.
2. What are the "three dangerous misconceptions" (paragraph 3) about the environment that Diamond discusses?
3. List all the civilizations that Diamond mentions in this essay. Which civilization does he emphasize? According to Diamond, why did previous civilizations fail, and how do these collapses provide guides to the state of contemporary American civilization?

RHETORIC

1. State Diamond's argument or major proposition. Where does his claim appear most clearly? What minor propositions does he develop? How does he deal with opposing viewpoints?
2. What types of evidence does the writer provide to support his claim?
3. Why does Diamond divide his essay into so many sections? What relationships do you detect between and among these sections?
4. Where does Diamond use comparison and contrast and causal analysis to organize parts of his essay?
5. How does classification operate as a rhetorical element in this article?
6. Assess the relative effectiveness of Diamond's conclusion. How does the ending serve as a coda for the entire essay?

WRITING

1. Write an essay focusing on a local environmental problem. Analyze the ways in which this environmental problem affects the lives of nearby residents.
2. Select one civilization that Diamond mentions. Conduct research on this civilization, and then write a report on the environmental factors that led to the decline of that society.
3. **Writing an Argument:** Write a persuasive essay in which you warn readers about three environmental dangers confronting the United States today.

NETWORKING
Applying 21st-Century Literacies

Analyzing the Use of Images: How do the illustrations in this essay interact with Diamond's written text? What is their rhetorical purpose, and how do they influence the text's tone?

Synthesis: Connections
for Critical Thinking

1. Using support from the works of Lopez, Carson, Chief Seattle, and others, write a causal-analysis essay tracing our relationship to the land. To what extent have history, greed, and fear helped shape our attitude? Can this attitude be changed? How?

2. Consider the empathy and sensitivity Walker has toward animals. How do her attitude and perceptions coincide with the views expressed by Bass and Chief Seattle concerning the natural world?

3. Write a letter to the op-ed page of a newspaper objecting to a governmental ruling harmful to the environment. State the nature of the policy, its possible dangers, and your reasons for opposing it. Use support from McKibben, Diamond, and any other writers in this chapter. Extra reading or research may be necessary.

4. Consider why we fear nature. Why do we consider it an enemy, an alien, something to be destroyed? How would Walker, Lopez, and Chief Seattle respond to this question? Do you agree or disagree with them?

5. Both Lopez and Diamond use narration and description to explore our relationship to the land. How do they approach their subject in terms of language, attitude, and style?

6. Choose an author in this chapter whose essay, in your opinion, romanticizes nature. Compare his or her attitude with that of a writer with a more pragmatic approach to the subject. Compare the two views, and specify the elements in their writing that contribute to the overall strength of their arguments.

7. Perrin uses enumeration and illustration to structure his essay. What are some of the strengths and weaknesses of employing traditional and orderly means of presenting one's thoughts?

8. Write an essay titled "Nature's Revenge" in which you examine the consequences of environmental abuse. Consider the short- as well as the long-term effects on the quality of life. Use support from any three writers in this chapter to defend your opinion.

9. Write specifically about our relationship to other living creatures on our planet. Is it one of exploitation, cooperation, or tyranny? How does this relationship influence how we treat each other? Explore the answers to these questions in an essay. Use the works of Lopez, Walker, and Chief Seattle to support your thesis.

NETWORKING
Applying 21st-Century Literacies

Join an online newsgroup devoted to addressing a specific environmental issue—for example, atomic waste, overdevelopment, or environmental regulations and deregulations. Follow the conversation of the newsgroup for one month. Write an essay describing what the chief concerns of the newsgroup members are, how they address issues regarding the environment, and what specific actions they recommend or take over the course of your membership.

CH 11   www.mhhe.com/**mhreaderbrief1e**

- *Image Gallery:* Chapter images in color
- *Nature and the Environment:* Information on the authors in this chapter
- *Ch. 11 Networking*

Credits

Photos and Illustrations

Text

Gitlin, Todd. Excerpt from "Supersaturation, or, The Media Torrent and Disposable Feeling" from *Media Unlimited: How the Torrent of Images and Sounds Overwhelms Our Lives* by Todd Gitlin. Copyright © 2001 by Todd Gitlin. Reprinted by arrangement with Henry Holt and Company, LLC.

Goodlad, Lauren M. E. "Why We Love 'Mad Men,'" *The Chronicle of Higher Education*, August 31, 2009. Reprinted by permission of the author.

Gregorian, Vartan, "America, Still on Top," *Newsweek*, August 20–27, 2007. Reprinted by permission of the author.

Hall, Edward T. "The Arab World," from *The Hidden Dimension* by Edward T. Hall, copyright 1966, 1982 by Edward T. Hall. Used by permission of Doubleday, a division of Random House, Inc.

Ivins, Molly. "Is Texas America?" *The Nation*, November 17, 2003. Copyright Estate of Molly Ivins. Reprinted by permission of Pom, Inc.

Jacoby, Susan. "When Bright Girls Decide That Math Is 'a Waste of Time'" by Susan Jacoby. Copyright © 1983 by Susan Jacoby. Originally appeared in *The New York Times* (1983). Reprinted by permission of Georges Borchardt, Inc. on behalf of the author.

King, Martin Luther Jr. "I Have a Dream." Reprinted by arrangement with The Heirs to the Estate of Martin Luther King Jr., c/o Writers House as agent for the proprietor New York, NY. Copyright 1963 Dr. Martin Luther King Jr; copyright renewed 1991 Coretta Scott King.

Kingsolver, Barbara. "Stone Soup" (pp. 135–45) from *High Tide in Tucson: Essays from Now or Never* by Barbara Kingsolver. Copyright © 1995 by Barbara Kingsolver. Reprinted by permission of HarperCollins Publishers.

Lopez, Barry. "Children in the Woods" from *Crossing Open Ground*. Scribner's, 1988. Reprinted by permission of SLL/Sterling Lord Literistic, Inc. Copyright by Barry Holstun Lopez.

McKibben, Bill. "The Environmental Issue from Hell," *In These Times*, April 30, 2001. This article is reprinted with permission from *In These Times* magazine (www.inthesetimes.com).

Murray, Donald M. "The Maker's Eye: Revising Your Own Manuscripts," *The Writer*, 1973. Copyright © 1973 by Donald M. Murray. Reprinted by permission of The Rosenberg Group on behalf of the author's estate.

Perrin, Noel. "The Greenest Campuses: An Idiosyncratic Guide," *Chronicle of Higher Education*, April 6, 2001. Used with permission of Elisabeth Perrin.

Priestley, J. B. "Wrong Ism." Extract by J. B. Priestley from *Essays of Five Decades* (© J. B. Priestley, 1968) is reproduced by permission of PFD (www.pfd.co.uk) on behalf of The Estate of J. B. Priestley.

Quindlen, Anna. "Sex Ed" from *Living Out Loud* by Anna Quindlen, copyright © 1987 by Anna Quindlen. Used by permission of Random House, Inc.

Rodriguez, Richard. From *Hunger of Memory: The Education of Richard Rodriguez* by Richard Rodriguez. Reprinted by permission of David R. Godine, Publisher, Inc. Copyright © 1982 by Richard Rodriguez.

Ross, Deborah. "Escape from Wonderland: Disney and the Female Imagination." Reprinted from *Marvels & Tales: Journal of Fairy-Tale Studies*, Vol. 18, No. 1 © 2004 Wayne State University Press, with the permission of Wayne State University Press.

Schlesinger, Arthur M. Jr. "The Cult of Ethnicity, Good and Bad," *Time*, July 8, 1991. Copyright © 1991 by Arthur M. Schlesinger Jr, reprinted with permission of The Wylie Agency LLC.

Index